Oxford Socio-Legal Studies

Law as Last Resort

CW00344747

OXFORD SOCIO-LEGAL STUDIES

General Editor: Keith Hawkins, Reader in Law and Society, and Fellow and Tutor in Law of Oriel College, Oxford.

Editorial Board: John Baldwin, Director of the Institute of Judicial Administration, University of Birmingham; William L. F. Felstiner, Professor, Law and Society Program, University of California-Santa Barbara; Denis Galligan, Professor of Socio-Legal Studies and Director of the Centre for Socio-Legal Studies, Oxford; Sally Lloyd-Bostock, Reader in Socio-Legal Studies, University of Birmingham; Doreen McBarnet, Senior Research Fellow, Centre for Socio-Legal Studies, Oxford; Simon Roberts, Professor of Law, London School of Economics and Political Science.

International Advisory Board: John Braithwaite (Australian National University); Robert Cooter (University of California-Berkeley); Bryant Garth (American Bar Foundation); Volkmar Gessner (University of Bremen); Vittorio Olgiati (University of Milan); Martin Partington (University of Bristol).

Oxford Socio-Legal Studies is a series of books exploring the role of law in society for both an academic and a wider readership. The series publishes theoretical and empirically informed work, from the United Kingdom and elsewhere, by social scientists and lawyers which advances understanding of the social reality of law and legal processes.

LAW AS LAST RESORT

Prosecution Decision-Making in a Regulatory Agency

KEITH HAWKINS

UNIVERSITY PRESS

Great Clarendon Street, Oxford OX2 6DP

Oxford University Press is a department of the University of Oxford.
It furthers the University's objective of excellence in research, scholarship,
and education by publishing worldwide in

Oxford New York

Auckland Bangkok Buenos Aires Cape Town Chennai
Dar es Salaam Delhi Hong Kong Istanbul Karachi Kolkata
Kuala Lumpur Madrid Melbourne Mexico City Mumbai Nairobi
São Paulo Shanghai Taipei Tokyo Toronto

Oxford is a registered trade mark of Oxford University Press
in the UK and in certain other countries

Published in the United States
by Oxford University Press Inc., New York

© Keith Hawkins 2002

The moral rights of the author have been asserted
Database right Oxford University Press (maker)

First published 2002

All rights reserved. No part of this publication may be reproduced,
stored in a retrieval system, or transmitted, in any form or by any means,
without the prior permission in writing of Oxford University Press,
or as expressly permitted by law, or under terms agreed with the appropriate
reprographics rights organization. Enquiries concerning reproduction
outside the scope of the above should be sent to the Rights Department,
Oxford University Press, at the address above

You must not circulate this book in any other binding or cover
and you must impose this same condition on any acquirer

British Library Cataloguing in Publication Data
Data available

Library of Congress Cataloging in Publication Data
Data available

ISBN 0-19-924388-3 (hbk.)
ISBN 0-19-924389-1 (pbk.)

1 3 5 7 9 10 8 6 4 2

Typeset by Kolam Information Services Pvt. Ltd, Pondicherry, India
Printed in Great Britain
on acid-free paper by
Biddles Ltd, Guildford and King's Lynn

For Alexander, Nicholas, and Edmund Hawkins,

who once were little men

Preface

> In the inspection of factories . . . we 'are not acting as policemen . . . We have endeavoured not to enforce the law . . . [W]e should simply be advisors of all classes . . . we should explain the law, and . . . we should do everything to induce them to observe the law. . . . A prosecution should be the last thing we should take up.'
>
> (Alexander Redgrave, Her Majesty's Chief Inspector of Factories, 1876)

> 'HSE inspectors do not approach their task with a view to seeking out legal violations and prosecuting error. They seek to promote reasonable compliance with good standards. . . . An essential part of the inspector's armoury is nevertheless the power to take enforcement action, either through the issuing of a statutory notice or, as a last resort, prosecution.'
>
> (Health and Safety Commission, 1990)

This is a book about the life of the legal system. Its object is to illustrate a way of thinking about legal decision-making in the context of prosecution cases in a regulatory agency. Through that, it tries to say something about decision-making behaviour in general. Though the setting is governmental regulation, the study focuses more on the processes of the law, rather than regulation per se, for the way in which prosecution is used in the enforcement of regulation reflects wider processes generally observable in the legal system. I hope what follows will be of interest to scholars of regulation, as well as those in socio-legal studies, criminal justice, and those concerned with the legal system in general. The work speaks to the creation and shaping of legal cases and their attrition, as well as to the processes involved in the use of prosecution, both in regulatory systems of control and in other more familiar arenas of social life in which criminal law is central. It develops and applies a theory of decision-making which connects broad features in the environment of a legal bureaucracy with the details of decisions in individual cases.

The focus of the book is an enquiry into the conditions under which legal officials, working in this case in occupational health and safety regulation, deal with a problem by electing the public and consequential course of prosecution. It centres, therefore, on the decision-making of legal officials, and on the regulatory bureaucracy as a legal organization, rather than on the victims or their accidents. (The appalling things that can happen in the workplace should be perfectly clear in the illustrative use of data throughout the book.) A detailed, multilevel analysis is made of the ways in which regulatory officials respond to a range of events arising from activities in the workplace that have resulted in death or injury to employees or members of the public, and the ways in which these officials handle occupational risks to people. Such matters are not often the stuff of criminal trial. Exploring them engages in important issues relating to the public face of law, and the meaning of the formalities of law in the arena of the courtroom, and their impact on pre-trial legal processes. *Law as last resort* seeks to understand how and why prosecution decisions are made (and I include here those equally important decisions *not* to prosecute) and how use of the formal processes of the criminal law connects with concerns to advance, preserve, and protect the health and safety of people in the workplace and members of the public. The book is a companion to an earlier work, *Environment and enforcement: regulation and the social definition of pollution* (1984), which showed that in the enforcement of regulation the moral status of violations is central, with the decision to prosecute heavily influenced by the environment of moral and political ambivalence within which regulatory agencies work. One of the arguments in *Environment and enforcement* is that it is precisely the ambivalence surrounding rule-breaking, as it acts on regulatory agencies and their inspectors, that leads to a particular level of prosecution and determines the kinds of cases that are selected for prosecution. The present book explores these and many other ideas in much greater detail and depth.

Like the earlier book, this is a study in the use of discretion by legal actors. It is written in the interpretive tradition. This means that law is treated, not as a formal structure of more or less unproblematic rules, but as a constantly shifting, negotiated, emergent matter, a system of meanings, constantly evolving, and constantly dependent on social context. The book documents and analyses the routine practices and decision-making of a set of legal actors. The reality portrayed is the reality experienced by decision-makers, particularly (but by no means exclusively) regulatory inspectors. What emerges is the reality they regard as relevant. Their silences may indicate that something was taken for granted. Equally they may indicate that something was ignored. The analysis questions the prevailing instrumental conception of law, and seeks to get beyond unitary ideas about the instrumentalism of law and the monolithic character of legal organizations, to present a finer-grained analysis of the details of ordinary legal life. It treats the law as central to social action, but not with the concreteness and inexorability that lawyers and policy-makers might imagine. However, in contrast with much of the socio-legal work in the interpretive tradition, the analysis does not play down the relevance or importance of formal law, but treats it as central to what officials in a legal bureaucracy actually do, or omit to do. For them, law exists in a variety of guises: as a statement of ideal to be attained, as a set of values, as rules that sometimes permit or constrain action, or as rules that can be recruited to justify action already taken. This book seeks to show how the ideals of the law are sometimes carried through into practice, but how formal requirements located in one part of the legal structure may conflict with the broader ideals which inform a bureaucracy's legal mandate, largely defeating its purpose.

Prosecution seems to be quite commonly used as a last resort not only in systems of regulatory control (Kagan & Lochner, 1998), but also in some more familiar areas of law enforcement. Indeed, attrition of cases is a constant feature generally in the legal system. This is true of ordinary criminal law enforcement, where the number of offenders convicted is a small proportion of those apprehended by the police. In fact, much of the criminal process is shaped by a need to avoid criminal trial. Thus in the early stages of handling a crime, discretion is exercised not to proceed, or decisions are made to caution a suspect, rather than to take further action. In later stages there is the widespread use of bargaining, and the practice of sentence discounting, processes employed in an effort to avoid trial by securing a guilty plea. Case attrition seems to be even more marked in some areas of the civil law, where trial is a means of concluding a dispute reserved for very few cases indeed, as the extensive and thorough survey of the experience of personal injury victims conducted by Donald Harris and his colleagues has shown (Harris *et al.*, 1984). In the civil process the thrust of extensive pre-trial negotiations (assuming a dispute even gets as far as to involve lawyers) is directed to searching for a solution to the problem that will avoid the costs, risks, and delays of going to court. It seems safe to conclude that one of the pervasive patterns in many, perhaps most, forms of legal disputing is the use of the courtroom as a place of last resort (Merry, 1990). In short, 'full blown adjudication is rare, expensive, and avoided assiduously' (Galanter, 1986: 182).

Though regulation and its enforcement are often bound up with intractable and frequently emotive questions of public policy, this book quite deliberately presents as dispassionate an analysis as possible. Except for the occasional aside, it does not take a position on important policy questions about the extent to which prosecution should be used, the kinds of case in which it should be used, or whether the criminal sanction is the most appropriate, efficient, or effective way of attaining regulatory objectives. Readers will find no arguments that prosecution is used too much or too little, or in the right or wrong sorts of case. The book does, however, draw conclusions about how legal officials actually make decisions that should assist those who are concerned with questions of policy in at least two ways. First, it can provide a way of thinking about the issues for those who wish to contribute to the debate about whether current enforcement practices are in need of modification, and in particular whether the present balance between persuasion and punishment is appropriate. Second, it can contribute to broader questions of regulatory strategy and throw light on the suitability of current techniques of command and control regulation, on the forms of regulatory control that are desirable, and on the place in a regulatory system, if any, prosecution should hold. Neither does the book attempt to evaluate the impact of prosecution on the behaviour of employers, or on rates of occupational illness or injury, except in so far as it is concerned with inspectors' own opinions and perceptions about the effectiveness of prosecution in controlling occupational illness and injury. The structure of the book is shaped by a concern to illustrate an argument about legal decision-making and the data are woven into the narrative. The work is written as a coherent whole, and an unfolding picture should gradually emerge into clearer focus. Each chapter should, however, be able to stand on its own, so readers with particular interests may skip chapters. Finally, though the analysis is lengthy, it does not claim to be exhaustive. Thus, for example, in discussing framing, I do not wish to suggest that the forms that I analyse are the only ones to be found: my purpose is to select leading examples of disparate forms of framing.

Adopting a position of scholarly detachment is not in any way to diminish the nature or scale of the problem that occupational health and safety inspectors confront every day. Human health and well-being, and ultimately human life, are constantly at stake in the regulation of workplace health and safety. 'Occupational fatalities usually occur in ones and twos,' the Health and Safety Executive (HSE) (1978: 5) has said. '[T]hey are unspectacular, and arouse fleeting local interest, yet each one is a personal tragedy for a family.' In the aggregate the figures of death and injury arising from occupational causes are striking. In 1999 the Health and Safety Commission (HSC) (1999: 93–7) reported clear downward trends both in the numbers and rates of fatal injury to workers over the last 10 years, and in the non-fatal major injury rates for employees and the self-employed. Even so, it estimated for 1998/9 that 257 workers would be fatally injured, that the major injury rate would be more than 120 per hundred thousand employees, and the rate of those injured for more than three days to be 561 per hundred thousand employees. The HSC (1999: 97) concluded that it was 'now getting to the difficult core and hitting the law of diminishing returns'. Indeed, the most recent figures indicate that the number of people killed at work in the year to March 2000 increased by more than a third (Clement, 2001).

The data for occupationally induced illness offer an even more vivid indication of the scale of the problem. In 1995 an estimated 2 million individuals in Great Britain were suffering from an illness which they believed was caused by their current or past work, at an annual cost of about £10 billion (Health and Safety Commission, 2002: 4). More than 720,000 of these people were no longer employed. Of the remaining 1.3 million, 624,000 lost an estimated total of 18 million working days because of work-related illness (Health and Safety Commission, 1998*b*: 99; 1999). Members of the public are also vulnerable to illness and injury, fatal or otherwise, arising from workplace activities. The HSC (1999: 57) estimated that 368 members of the public suffered a fatal injury as a result of work activity in 1998/9 (a number that includes railway suicides), with around 23,600 suffering non-fatal injuries (a substantial reduction compared with the previous figures). And while it is natural to focus on the human costs, the economic implications of occupational death, ill health, and injury are also enormous: the cost of accidents and ill health to the nation is believed to be between 2 and 3 per cent of gross domestic product (F. B. Wright, 1995: 7). At the same time, prosecution work absorbs a substantial part of the agency's resources. HSE's Field Operations Directorate spent, for example, a total of 112 inspector years on formal enforcement work in 1998/9 (Health and Safety Commission, 1999: 83).

It may not intrude on a regulatory inspector's everyday activities very often, but when it does, prosecution introduces problems of a special kind. Many inspectors claim that the decision to prosecute is one of the most difficult features of their work. It demands discriminating use since it is the final hold they have on those they regulate, and it makes the inspector especially accountable to the regulatory agency. Prosecution brings a problem or an incident into the public, and sometimes the political, arena, yet takes the risky step of ceding ultimate control over the disposal of the matter to the magistracy or the judge and jury, untutored third parties. To prosecute is visibly to be taking sides in the fundamental dilemma of regulatory control which centres on how, and how far, the law with its costs and constraints can justifiably intervene in the conduct of business and industry. In the nature of things, prosecution tends to be used in those cases which have something special about them.

Acknowledgements

This study originated as one part of a larger programme of research into occupational health and safety conducted at the Oxford Centre for Socio-Legal Studies in the mid-1980s. That research was funded partly by the Economic and Social Research Council (ESRC) through its core grant to the Centre, and partly by a supplementary grant from the Health and Safety Executive (HSE). The book reports the results of research carried out over a period of more than fifteen years, in which fieldwork was carried out in two phases. The first took place between 1986 and 1989, the second between 1996 and 1998. The opportunity to develop and bring the research up to date in the second phase was made possible by a grant from the USX Foundation of Pittsburgh, Pennsylvania, awarded jointly to the Oxford Centre for Socio-Legal Studies and the Center for Law, Policy and Social Science at The Ohio State University, which has been associated with the work through its partnership with the Oxford Centre.

I wish to thank the ESRC, the HSE, and the USX Foundation for their generosity in funding this research. At the same time I stress that the analyses, views, and interpretations presented in this book are my own, and are not necessarily those of the HSE, the ESRC, or the USX Foundation.

I am most grateful to the HSE for its assistance. In both phases of the work the agency gave me access to its staff, operations, and sites, and cooperated fully with requests for interviews, arrangements for fieldwork visits, access to internal data, and so on. I must emphasize, however, that while the staff of the HSE were extremely helpful in allowing me to learn about their policies and practices, in no sense did they seek to influence the planning or conduct of my research or to control the dissemination of the research findings. I had a free hand in designing and conducting the work, in employing the methods of data collection I thought suitable, and in publishing the findings in the ways that I alone thought appropriate. HSE is continually evolving as an organization, and I have tried to report the legal position and HSE's practices during the fieldwork periods as accurately as I can. Some will have since changed, while at the same time recent innovations (such as the impact of the Human Rights Act or the imminent arrival of HSE's new Enforcement Management Model) make it impossible to be absolutely up to date.

I am especially grateful to the many individuals within HSE who have been extremely generous with their time. I thank all of the officials who assisted in the various data-gathering exercises, who patiently listened to my questions and discussed their practices and their ideas with me. As research subjects almost all of them must remain anonymous. However, while it may appear invidious to single out individuals by name, I would like to acknowledge the considerable support in embarking on and conducting this research that I received from Mr John Rimington, the HSE's then Director General, and Mr Jim Hammer and Mr David Eves, both former Deputy Directors General, and before that Chief Inspectors of Factories. I owe a particular debt to Mr Rimington, who made both phases of the fieldwork possible. More recently Mr Mike Cosman, now head of HSE's Construction Sector, has been a valuable source of information and help. He has also read and commented on a complete draft of this book (without, of course, necessarily endorsing my findings or conclusions). All of these officials have been very supportive of my research, and have never wavered in their commitment to the idea that researchers based in a university and conducting independent enquiries driven by their own scholarly concerns could nevertheless produce work that might be of direct benefit to a legal bureaucracy.

I have also been very fortunate in the help I have received from my academic colleagues. I am extremely grateful to the Provost and Fellows of Oriel College for providing me with a peaceful and supportive environment for scholarly research and writing. I would also like to thank those former members of the Centre for Socio-Legal Studies at Oxford who collaborated in the original research programme with HSE, especially Bridget Hutter, Sally Lloyd-Bostock, Peter Manning, Matthew Weait, and Jenny Dix (who administered the programme). I have been fortunate in receiving valuable comments from two colleagues, Andrew Ashworth and Richard Young, who have generously read a complete set of drafts. Alexander Hawkins and Sally Lloyd-Bostock made helpful observations on a number of chapters, and Alexander carefully transcribed the tapes of several long interviews. Peter Manning, as ever, has been an important sounding board for ideas over the years. I have mostly (but not always) followed the advice of my readers, and they, of course, are not to blame for the book's shortcomings.

Finally, I thank Su again, for her help, support, and encouragement. This book is affectionately dedicated to our three sons, who have grown up with it, especially for tolerating without any complaint their father's preoccupation with data analysis and drafting during more than one family holiday. Alexander bet me that in a book about prosecution I could not mention Eric Dolphy's name (why Dolphy, rather than Art Tatum, I am not quite sure), but Nickie and Edu had no such concerns, probably because they knew he would lose.

K.O.H.

Oxford
June 2002

Contents

Abbreviations

The following is a list of those abbreviations and acronyms appearing in this study that are used routinely both in published writings and in officials' organizational records.

1B	the rank of a trained field inspector
AD	area director
AgI	Agricultural Inspectorate
ALARA	as low as reasonably achievable
ALARP	as low as reasonably practicable
CBI	Confederation of British Industries
Con (WP) Regs	Construction (Working Places) Regulations, 1966
CPS	Crown Prosecution Service
DOT, DoT	Department of Transport
DP, D/P	deceased person
DPP	Director of Public Prosecutions
EHO	environmental health officer
ESRC	Economic and Social Research Council
FI	Her Majesty's Factory Inspectorate
FLT	fork-lift truck
FOD	Field Operations Directorate (of HSE)
H & S	health and safety
HGV	heavy goods vehicle
HMFI	Her Majesty's Factory Inspectorate
HSC	Health and Safety Commission
HSE	Health and Safety Executive
HSW Act or HSWA	Health and Safety at Work Act, 1974
IAPI	Industrial Air Pollution Inspectorate
IP	injured person
IRR	Ionising Radiations Regulations, 1985
LPG	liquid propane gas
MD	Managing Director
MQI	Mines and Quarries Inspectorate

NFA	no further action
NIG	National Interest Group
NII	Nuclear Installations Inspectorate
OSHA	Occupational Safety and Health Administration (USA)
PACE	Police and Criminal Evidence Act, 1984
PI	principal inspector
PLC	programmable logic controller
PR	prosecution (sometimes Prosecution Report)
PTO shaft	power take-off shaft
PUWER	Provision and Use of Work Equipment Regulations, 1992
RIDDOR	Reporting of Injuries, Diseases and Dangerous Occurrences Regulations, 1985
Robens Report	*Report of the Committee on Safety at Work, 1970–1972*
RPA	Radiation Protection Adviser
SFAIRP	so far as is reasonably practicable
TUC	Trades Union Congress

PART I

Formalities

1 Themes, Perspectives, Questions

1. INSTRUMENTAL AND OTHER USES OF LAW

What are the conditions under which the formalities of law in the courtroom come into play? This book explores how decisions are made to use the formal processes of the law as a way of putting an end to a problem in preference to other means of sanctioning, solving difficulties, or settling differences.[1] Its focus is the decision to prosecute—or not to prosecute—individuals and business organizations believed to have broken legal rules regulating occupational health and safety.[2]

It is by no means a straightforward matter for inspectors, their supervisors, and regulatory organizations as a whole to conclude that prosecution is the most appropriate course of action to take in a particular case, for this seemingly simple decision conceals many complex issues. A decision to prosecute taken within a regulatory agency is the culmination of a series of other decisions made about the desirability of handling a problem by reference to the formal procedures of criminal trial.[3] Sometimes many individuals contribute to the ultimate decision. Sometimes the decision may be driven by concerns that reach beyond the present case. There are also important bureaucratic aspects to the decision, and significant risks to both organization and individual in choosing

[1] There is little in the literature that speaks specifically to this question, the most notable exception being the rather dated American book by Weaver (1977). There are, however, a number of valuable studies which analyse aspects of the decision to prosecute in ordinary criminal law enforcement, without necessarily concentrating on case attrition. For examples of work in Britain, see J. Baldwin & McConville (1977) and Moody & Tombs (1982). There is a large American literature on pre-trial processes, a good deal of which is concerned specifically with plea-bargaining. Much of the most interesting work was published some time ago. See e.g. Alschuler (1968; 1975); Ericson & Baranek (1982); Heumann (1978); Mather (1979); Maynard (1984); Rosett & Cressey (1976); and *Law and Society Review* (1979). A more recent study is by McCoy (1993).

[2] Perhaps because matters are handled by a specialized inspectorate, operating largely in a decentralized structure, decision-making about prosecution seems to take place rather independently of the rest of the criminal justice system. Inspectors do refer to the Code for Crown Prosecutors as a source of guidance, for example, but only occasionally, it seems.

[3] I use the term 'prosecution' to cover all cases in which an occupational health and safety violation is brought to the criminal courts, whether or not the matter arrives there for trial or has prompted a guilty plea.

to prosecute, rather than to take another course of action. To prosecute brings a problem to public and possibly political attention, while granting final control over the fate of the case to decision-makers (the magistrates or the judge and jury) who are not knowledgeable about the technicalities or the economics of occupational health and safety regulation. Prosecution decision-making constantly compels regulatory officials to grapple with conflicting sets of values.

Most people probably think of law in instrumental terms. From an instrumental conception comes faith in law as a device to remedy our problems. We rely on law in the belief that it will change behaviour in the ways we desire. Regulatory bodies exist thanks to an instrumental view of law and its capacity to change things for the better. Law is there and used in practice, we assume, to achieve some practical end, to make a difference: these are what Joseph Gusfield (1981: 9) calls 'beliefs about the alterability of phenomena'. Indeed, the legitimacy of the act of prosecution inheres in instrumental claims about action in the public interest.

Prosecution is an important tool in an instrumental conception of law, its use intended to reduce the prevalence of undesired behaviours, events, or states of affairs. To prosecute in the regulatory arena is to invoke the criminal process so that the rule-breaker is not minded to violate rules in the future, or so that others who might also be tempted to break rules choose to do otherwise, for fear of an unpleasant fate. Prosecution on this view is an indispensable device of public policy. This utilitarian or reductivist conception of prosecution in the occupational health and safety arena as a way of reducing the extent of death, injury, and disease in the workplace emerges clearly from official statements by the Health and Safety Commission (n.d.: 10–11):

> 'The Commission expects that enforcing authorities will consider prosecution when:
>
> - it is appropriate in the circumstances as a way to draw general attention to the need for compliance with the law and the maintenance of standards required by law, especially where there would be a normal expectation that a prosecution would be taken or where through the conviction of offenders, others may be deterred from similar failures to comply with the law;
> - or there is judged to have been potential for considerable harm arising from breach.'

The instrumental view of law is almost certainly the dominant conception, and less consideration is given to law as created and used for expressive purposes. In this latter conception, law exists and is employed not so much as a means of achieving some practical aim, but as a way of declaring and affirming social ideals and values (Gusfield, 1970). Two aspects of this expressive approach are particularly relevant for this book, since prosecution is central to both. One is the use of prosecution as a symbolic device: as a forceful and dramatic way of making a moral statement about an undesirable or offensive matter—a deliberate flouting of the law, a particularly nasty act, or perhaps a neglect of one's obligations. The symbolic decision-maker would think of prosecuting in such circumstances because that legal response is deserved, rather than needed. Prosecution used in this way is not simply a necessary prerequisite to inflicting just punishment upon one who has broken a rule. The act of prosecution itself becomes a means of expressing important values about right and wrong. Law, and the way in which it is used, can make powerful statements. Law can condone, but it can also condemn.

The other expressive use of law I analyse is as an organizational device that can be bent to serve the particular purposes of the organizations deployed to implement it.[4] Organizations can turn the law to display not the law's, but their own presence: their activity, their responsiveness to the concerns of the public, and their ability to make a difference. Those who work in an organization are also subject to imperatives arising from membership of it, quite apart from those originating in their legal mandate. Organizational demands are not necessarily congruent with the instrumental demands arising from a legal mandate. Prosecution, as a public and dramatic act, is well suited to serve organizational purposes.

If the instrumental decision-maker is concerned with the achievement of practical consequences as the *raison d'être* of a decision, the expressive decision-maker is ultimately concerned with justifying decisions by reference to a personal sense of right or wrong, or an organizational demand. One of the questions to be explored is under what conditions law is actually used instrumentally, and under what conditions and by whom it is employed to serve expressive interests of a symbolic or organizational kind.

[4] I employ the contrast between instrumental and expressive, and between symbolic and organizational, as analytical devices. Legal decisions can serve both instrumental and expressive purposes, or symbolic and organizational ones. These terms can also change their meanings over time. To distinguish between instrumental and expressive approaches is not to suggest that they coexist in such discrete and contrasting terms (decision-makers adhere to both, in differing degrees) so much as to emphasize that they give rise to different decision-making and result in different prosecution strategies. That said, the contrasts are helpful ways of thinking about what legal decision-makers do.

Inevitably, there is often a tension in practice between instrumental and expressive values. The conditions under which one set of values should dominate are never self-evident to the decision-maker, and instrumental and expressive values often collide with each other. The character of each set of values is different: for example, an instrumental strategy can always be evaluated for its effectiveness in attaining a particular end, but the same is not as true of an expressive approach. In many cases there are hard choices, for decision-makers may seek to serve both sets of values in handling an individual case. For instance, regulation is a politically contentious matter, and policy-making and enforcement may be carried on in a context of fierce public debate, as was shown in the aftermath of the train crash outside Paddington station on 5 October 1999, which prompted vigorous arguments about the balance between safety and cost. These exchanges tap into popular and academic debates about business responsibility and responsiveness which are frequently overdrawn, being shaped by ideologically informed imagery of business and also by the position taken in the politics of regulation about the extent to which it is desirable or justifiable to seek to restrict business behaviour by means of legal rules. A broadly laissez-faire approach sympathetic to business tends to paint a picture of commercial activity being suffocated by crippling and insensitively applied regulation, while the pro-regulation lobby tends to portray business responses to regulation as self-interested, cavalier, and inherently non-compliant.

In practical terms, the fundamental dilemma for both policy and implementation is 'where to strike the balance between legal forbearance and strict enforcement if public policy is to achieve some socially optimal result' (Yeager, 1991: 280). Prosecution is frequently taken to be an indicator of agency activity in pursuit (or not) of its legal mandate. This makes the agency vulnerable to public criticism, and to headlines like 'HSE prosecuted in just one rail accident last year' (*The Independent*, 16 October 1999) or 'Feeble safety watchdog under fire' (*Independent on Sunday*, 7 November 1999). The regulatory response, as expressed by one Director General of the Health and Safety Executive (HSE), is that 'Prosecutions and investigations are worthwhile to punish flagrant wrongdoing and to deter other failures. But resources for workplace health and safety will never be unlimited: more prosecution means fewer preventative inspections and follow-up of complaints. I have yet to see evidence that more prosecution improves health and safety' (J. Bacon, *Independent on Sunday*, 11 November 1999).

This clash of opposing values is embedded in regulatory systems which are suffused with moral and political ambivalence that can make it very difficult as a practical matter both to formulate and to implement clear enforcement policies. In occupational health and safety regulation, for instance, the safety versus cost dilemma is especially acute, and 'HSE often finds itself between a rock and a hard place, with criticism from some quarters of "over-zealous" behaviour by inspectors, and from other quarters of lack of "zeal", e.g. in pursuing individuals for health and safety offences' (HSE, 1993, p. xiv).

Another clash of values sometimes arises when officials have to balance the expressive interests of justice (such as a desire for the deserved punishment of an offender or for consistency of treatment in which like cases are treated alike) against an instrumental need to attend to the special characteristics or demands of a particular case. Expressive expectations in others pose practical problems for the regulatory decision-maker. For example, the view of a former Chief Inspector of the Mines and Quarries Inspectorate (MQI)[5] was that prosecution 'satisfies the public to some extent, but it [does not] solve the problem. And that's what we're concerned about.'[6] Such informal comments acknowledge that prosecution can provide symbolic satisfaction to the public while doing little instrumentally to gain compliance or repair problems. Public pronouncements by the HSE sometimes seek to reconcile such conflicting values:

> 'The role of HMFI [the former Factory Inspectorate] is to provide help and advice within the capacity of its resources and selective but powerfully effective enforcement of the law. Such enforcement is as important in equity in support of those who do devote effort and finance to getting things right as it is necessary to impress on those who whether knowingly or through incompetence fail to do so that such failures will be for them, disruptive and expensive.' (Health and Safety Executive, 1978*b*: 11)

The clash of values can cause difficulties nonetheless when policy has to be formulated and practical guidelines drawn up.

It is in the nature of the structure of legal bureaucracies like regulatory inspectorates that the tensions arising from competing values such as these tend to be worked out in the field in the everyday decisions of inspectors who, though they operate at the lowest organizational level,

[5] Quarries inspection has now been hived off from mines regulation.

[6] Research methods and sources of data are noted later in this chapter, and discussed at length in the Appendix.

make decisions, as state officials, that carry a special authority. It is here that decisions are least open to scrutiny and therefore least accountable. Whether the inspector is concerned with instrumental or expressive values, however, prosecution is the most decisive way in which a firm can be punished—a more telling and effective response from the inspector's point of view, in fact, than the penalty handed down upon conviction, which in the eyes of the law is actually the formal punishment. This is because for the inspector the act of prosecution is itself an act of punishment, one in which he or she is intimately involved: 'A prosecution is a sanction,' said an official. 'It's taking someone to court ... to see if they've committed a criminal offence.'

The dominance of the instrumental view of law is such that it is almost certainly the primary concern of policy-makers, legislators, and the senior staff of regulatory bureaucracies, as well as members of the public. But it is a conception of law that has its difficulties. In particular, it raises questions not only about how effective law is (and can be), but also of the ways in which its effectiveness can be discerned. Indeed, one of the major problems which regulatory organizations must constantly confront is how they can establish and display their success in combating the problems they were set up to control. It is very difficult for regulatory agencies to exhibit their effectiveness in terms of the numbers of injuries or deaths that did not occur (J. Q. Wilson, 1989: 159), thus HSE's primary outputs, in the form of improved occupational health and safety, pose problems of evaluation and measurement:

> 'In [some] cases we have no difficulty in quantifying and assessing our inputs, outputs and net income, very largely as a private company would. Over most of our activity however we face the difficulty of defining the value of what we do. For example, to assess the "benefit" of accidents that do not occur because of our activity is clearly not possible. It is also extremely difficult to trace and so improve the connection between what we actually "produce" by way of inspection, guidance, standards etc. and what we hope is our real output, that is to say improved safety and health at reasonable cost.' (Health and Safety Commission, 1988: 32)

Much of what HSE does has a qualitative component, not readily susceptible to transformation into unproblematic performance indicators. This is true even for quantitative indicators. 'All the health and safety statistics we have', said the HSE's former Director General, 'are enormously imperfect, so we can only peer into glasses darkly to see whether situations are improving or not; even if we could identify whether they were or not, how much credit do you give to proper regulation, proper firmness, proper inspections?' (Hawkins, 1992*a*: 171).

HSE regards itself as creating certain real outputs: an improvement in health and safety in industry; reassurance to the public that it is being properly protected against certain risks; and ensuring that the commercial interests of the UK are being properly safeguarded (Hawkins, 1992*a*). The intractable problem, however, is that the organization can never satisfactorily determine whether and to what degree it (or other forces) has produced these outputs, and at what cost:

> 'Many factors external to health and safety also have to be carefully considered and weighed—where this is possible—to see whether they are distorting a trend (for example, the switching of a hazardous process from one workplace to another might lead to false conclusions about the success of a programme at workplace level; the effects of growth in any particular industry may result in a new generation of machinery which transforms the requirements for operator training; or the effects of recession may result in complacency about safety and health problems which might be vanishing only to re-emerge after recovery).' (Health and Safety Commission, 1983: 17)

Reductions in occupational death, disease, and injury are hard to attribute to changes in law or its enforcement without having a clear sense of the extent to which other influences, such as technological or economic shifts, or changes in working practices occurring independently of the law, have contributed to any observed effects. 'How much credit can you give', said the former Director General, 'to things like, let's say, changing mortality rates, increasing efficiency of the medical profession, the activity of safety organizations . . . public awareness, or whatever? The answer is you can't' (Hawkins, 1992*a*: 171).

Then there is the question of whether the law is being implemented in a desirable way:

> 'We have to satisfy ourselves from time to time that the management control that is being exercised on our behalf, over our programmes for enforcement and assessment, is implementing our policies effectively. There are serious limitations in attempting to measure "output" from these programmes in a purely quantitative way, for example by counting the number of basic inspections or "inputs" performed in any one year, comparing these with previous years, and using the figures as a way of monitoring performance either of the inspectorates or of industry in terms of improvements to health and safety.' (Health and Safety Commission, 1983: 17)

More acute difficulties arise in trying to unravel cause and effect. Appraisal is particularly troublesome in cases of exposure to toxic substances,

'when a period of industrial activity may be generating a problem which is not recognisable for a number of years; even once it has been identified, the process causing the problem may have changed over that period with advances in technology and it may be difficult to be certain of making the right diagnosis of what went wrong in the first place and what should be done in future.' (Health and Safety Commission, 1983: 17)

Problems are exacerbated where events are rare, or where latency problems make comparative analysis especially hard:

'Trends have to be watched over a considerable period of time before success or failure is apparent: about a decade, in the case of a programme to reduce a certain class of accidents—e.g. at power presses—and often much longer, perhaps as much as 40 years, in the case of efforts to reduce or eradicate industrial diseases, such as asbestosis and mesothelioma.' (Health and Safety Commission, 1983: 17)

The result is that, as a former Director General of HSE acknowledged frankly, 'there is no way in which we can evaluate either how far our final outputs are being met . . . and . . . what contribution we make to their being met, [or] if they are being met' (Hawkins, 1992*a*). Since displaying fewer accidents or higher levels of occupational health to scientifically acceptable standards is notoriously difficult, HSE is sometimes reduced, as a result, simply to asserting its effectiveness: 'precautions do work. It is always difficult to demonstrate the accident which hasn't happened or the ill health prevented' (Health and Safety Executive, 1982*c*, p. vii).

An important consequence of these difficulties with the usual indicators of instrumental effectiveness is that prosecution becomes important evidence, if not of organizational effectiveness, then certainly of organizational activity, for it is a public act that is clear, conspicuous, and apparently decisive, and unambiguously displays that HSE is pursuing its mandate. Prosecutions are 'a visible measure of achievement', said an area director, 'but . . . they're few and far between, and they come at huge cost' (97–04).[7] Correspondingly, a lack of prosecution is often taken

[7] See the Appendix, nn. 6 and 7, and the text there for the meaning of the codes employed to identify sources of data.

as the equivalent of a lack of enforcement (e.g. Hopkins and Parnell, 1984).

Another problem with an instrumental approach where organizations are concerned is that organizations themselves introduce further complexities. This is most apparent, for instance, where an inspector who for some time has had few, if any, prosecutions becomes preoccupied with a display to the organization of enforcement activity to indicate his or her industry and commitment by deliberately searching out and pursuing a prosecutable case (see Chapter 10). Prosecution is a decision made by individuals who are organizational actors. We tend to assume, however, that the same instrumental purposes are shared by all organizational actors. But that is not invariably the case, because the point of view of the individual organizational actor depends crucially on where within the organization a person is located: junior officials on the frontline see the world in very different terms from senior staff in offices. To assume that there is a common sense of purpose within a regulatory bureaucracy is to overlook the complexity of these agencies and the difficulties those at the centre of the organization routinely experience in maintaining control over the activities of those at the periphery. The ideas of repair or prevention of regulatory problems accompanied by a corresponding commitment to the instrumental use of prosecution are quite strong among those at the centre of the organization, but are almost certainly less strong among inspectors at the periphery (Hawkins, 1984). They, after all, are the ones confronted by intransigent employers; more importantly, they are the ones faced with the blood, pain, and drama of a workplace accident. They may well adopt a more punitive—a more expressive—approach as a result. This suggests that different penal theories may operate at different levels within a law enforcement organization, a possibility which points to a potential source of strain in the implementation of enforcement policies designed at the centre for instrumental purposes to be acted on by those at the periphery.

Whether employed in the pursuit of instrumental or expressive values, however, prosecution is one of the most important acts of a regulatory bureaucracy. Prosecution is the visible expression of the authority of the state. It displays the implementation of the law's formal mandate, and reflects the peculiar power of law and legal processes to publicize, dramatize, and emphasize. To prosecute health and safety violations is to use the law formally and explicitly; it is to bring a problem or an event to public attention through the medium of the criminal process, with all its implications of fault and blame.[8] Prosecution brings with it stigmatizing consequences, quite apart from the threat of conviction for the defendant, for criminal law carries important symbolic weight that alternative methods of enforcement do not possess. Prosecution is at once the culmination of a process of the public enforcement of the criminal law and the means by which the occasion for legal punishment arises. Without prosecution there can be no punishment, and little prospect of the public identification of a problem, or an offender. The heavy focus on prosecution decision-making should not obscure the fact, however, that it is a decision made in the context of other enforcement measures, formal (improvement or prohibition notices) or informal (verbal or written advice, exhortation, and the like).

Yet prosecution is merely one of a series of enforcement moves, of greater or lesser formality, employed by regulatory inspectors. If prosecution is used relatively rarely (in relation to the number of theoretically prosecutable matters that exist), it is important to observe that a great deal of law enforcement work is carried on by HSE inspectors. It is, however, work of an informal rather than a formal kind. The conception of enforcement in HSE, at least as expressed in public statements, is a broad one which includes all forms of compliance-seeking and is not simply a narrow view of enforcement as occurring with a sanctioning strategy organized around prosecution. Regulatory officials (and others) often speak of 'enforcement' as a synonym for 'prosecution'. This, however, is to overlook the wide range of other informal measures more commonly employed by field inspectors—and others, like police officers—in the course of enforcing the law. The HSE has said about this: 'discussion, persuasion and cooperation, leading to mutually agreed solutions, are preferred to coercion. In consequence, the Inspectorate has made only limited use of the full enforcement powers' (Health and Safety Executive, 1982*b*: 17). The interaction between formal and informal means of enforcement is crucial to a proper understanding of legal rule-enforcement. The relationship between prosecution and alternative forms of enforcement is often in the forefront of an inspector's mind. Prosecution is a small part of HSE's total enforcement activity, but it is one which consumes a disproportionate amount of resources, and is

[8] Though about 95 per cent of HSE prosecutions are brought in the magistrates' courts, which are usually regarded as dealing with trivial matters (McBarnet, 1981: 144), the proceedings are regarded by inspectors as serious, their public character and consequential outcomes contrasting with the privacy and informality of negotiated enforcement practices. Some inspectors, indeed, speak of the 'theatre' of court proceedings.

generally reserved for serious or dramatic matters. Yet ironically one reason why prosecution is so important in regulation is that while it is the ultimate formal expression of the law—a sort of legal sanction in its own right, as the analysis will show—it is the device that makes all other law enforcement possible by granting credibility to more private and informal practices and thereby, in the great majority of cases, foreclosing the possibility of costly prosecution and trial.

Prosecution is, then, a profoundly significant enforcement move for regulatory bureaucracies and their inspectors. Prosecutable cases are not something HSE inspectors frequently encounter in their everyday activities (the mean number of prosecution cases per inspector per year is two or three, though some inspectors of construction sites may mount a dozen or more). Yet though prosecution coexists with other formal enforcement procedures, in the form of notices (see Chapter 5), it is treated as work of a substantively different and important kind for a number of reasons. Prosecuting demands a significant individual and organizational commitment of time and financial resources. It also has a capacity to set precedents within and for the enforcing organization. At the same time, use of the courts and loss of control over the case means that to prosecute is to take a risk. Failure to convict risks making an inspector organizationally accountable, and the regulatory bureaucracy seem incompetent or ineffectual. Such risks inherent in using the law, as Chapter 12 shows, decisively shape both whether the law is enforced and how it is enforced.

The ambiguities, tensions, and risks that afflict those who enforce regulation come into play when decisions about prosecuting or not have to be made. But added to them are the special features of the public audience and the loss of control over the fate of the case, both of which are absent when inspectors enforce the law in their normal way and negotiate privately for compliance.

2. THE DEBATE ABOUT COMMAND AND CONTROL REGULATION

Prosecution is the central apparatus of command and control regulation, a form of legal control employed where market-based solutions do not work. The nature of such regulation is social control through the imposition of standards backed by the criminal sanction. 'The force of law', says Robert Baldwin (1997: 66), 'is used to prohibit certain forms of conduct or to demand some positive actions . . .'. According to the formal law, HSE officials may bring criminal prosecutions against employers who breach health and safety laws and regulations with a view to the punishment of those who violate those standards. This may all be done in the public interest. Command and control regulation is generally justified in instrumental terms, though it can recognize the symbolic importance of legally declaring the acceptability or otherwise of some forms of behaviour (R. Baldwin, 1997).

Traditional command and control regulation has, however, been subjected to an increasing number of critical analyses. Most academic criticism had American origins (Bardach & Kagan, 1982; Breyer, 1982). The main complaint was that regulatory agencies established to preserve the interests of the public had been co-opted by the very private interests they had been set up to restrain. Among the early exponents of this view were Samuel Huntington (1952) and Marver Bernstein (1955). A critical momentum was created and then given a substantial push in the 1960s in America by the activities of Ralph Nader. In the 1990s more sophisticated criticisms of command and control regulation began to appear in a series of publications, many of them the work of scholars in Australia. Their analyses embody a variety of proposals either to rationalize command and control systems, or to develop other regulatory models (Ayres & Braithwaite, 1992; Gunningham & Grabosky, 1998; Gunningham & Johnstone, 1999).

The first criticisms to be made about the apparent frailties of command and control regulation, then, tended to be accusations that it allowed pursuit of the interests of business rather than the public (see generally R. Baldwin, 1997). There are differences of opinion as to why weakening of regulatory authority should occur. On some views it is because of the 'capture' of the regulators (Bernstein, 1955; Makkai & Braithwaite, 1995; Mitnick, 1980; J. Q. Wilson, 1980). This happened when the relationship between the regulators and those they regulated became too close, leading the former to lose their essential sense of independence and detachment. In so-called 'life cycle' accounts of regulation it is because the energy of the regulatory body is sapped (Bernstein, 1955; Huntington, 1952). Some argue that it happens as a result of the activities of various interest groups (see Posner, 1974; Stigler, 1971). Others say it is because regulatory agencies have never been given a sufficiently clear mandate (Friendly, 1962). Yet others accuse command and control regulation of being costly and inefficient, of discouraging innovation, and focusing on short-term solutions (Sinclair, 1997: 529–31). Finally, some claim that command and control has failed because regulatory agencies have not really been established to protect the public interest, but exist essentially for symbolic purposes or to protect the very business interests they were established to restrain (Edelman, 1964; Kolko, 1963; 1965).

A second set of criticisms has been concerned with the legalism of this form of regulation. Commentators have drawn attention to the complexity and rigidity of its rules and the unnecessary cost and delay which are caused as a result (Bardach & Kagan, 1982; Stewart, 1988). There are also questions about the difficulties that arise when standards are set in articulating regulatory policy in the form of workable rules. Critics have argued that rules fail to restrain conduct that should be controlled, and that they sometimes penalize conduct unnecessarily (see R. Baldwin, 1995, ch. 6; Diver, 1983). This is partly 'because the informational requirements are so severe. Thus, anti-competitive effects must be addressed; the appropriate type of standard selected (see Ogus, 1994, Ch. 8)...and the level of exposure to judicial review may be high' (R. Baldwin, 1997). Johnstone (1994) has drawn attention to three further aspects of regulatory legalism that arise from the grafting of criminal prosecution onto occupational health and safety regimes: 'the abstracted nature of the trial, the event focused nature of the criminal law, and the individualistic nature of criminal liability.'

Finally, various scholars have been critical of the actual practice of command and control regulation, and particularly of enforcement in such regimes. Extensive empirical research has shown that the usual response of regulatory officials to companies which have breached standards is to negotiate with them to secure their compliance with rules, rather than to prosecute and punish them (e.g. Hawkins, 1984; Hutter, 1997). There are some who protest that command and control regulation is not enforced vigorously enough (e.g. Pearce & Tombs, 1990; 1991; Slapper and Tombs, 2000; but see also Hawkins, 1990; 1991), and argue for a more robust approach, while others point out that it is extremely difficult to craft rules that can discourage enforcement by bargaining (e.g. R. Baldwin, 1997).

The remedies advanced for the pathologies of command and control regulation vary. Some have suggested deregulation; some have accorded greater respect to ideas of self-regulation (Gunningham & Rees, 1997). In the last few years another line of argument has been heard. This is one which proposes the more subtle and finely tuned redevelopment of existing regulatory systems to make them at once more responsive to the pluralistic settings in which they must operate and more rational in their approach so that more effective and more efficient regulatory impacts may be achieved (see Ayres & Braithwaite, 1992; Gunningham & Grabosky, 1998; Gunningham & Johnstone, 1999; Sinclair, 1997). Prosecution remains central to these designs, however, for these critics would not abandon the power to prosecute, but rather embed it in a more sensitive and systematically deployed enforcement structure.

3. PROSECUTION AS A LAST RESORT

Whatever their vision of the place of prosecution in a system of regulatory control, however, it is likely that all the critics would agree that it is a move rarely made by regulatory agencies. Indeed, the perceived reluctance to prosecute in agencies like HSE is often the occasion for public and academic criticism. The Health and Safety Commission (HSC) reported recently that in 2000/1 HSE took 1,618 prosecutions. Note that in the same period there were 192,693 'regulatory contacts', more than 40,000 incidents and complaints, and 10,641 improvement and prohibition notices issued (Health and Safety Executive, 2002: 17).[9] Slightly more than 83 per cent of offences prosecuted resulted in conviction (Health and Safety Commission, 1998*b*: 57; see also Health and Safety Commission, 1999).[10]

Regulatory rule-breaking is commonplace and routine. The number of events and problems which could in theory give rise to prosecution is very large (if actually unknowable), and one source of difficulty for

[9] Prosecution for regulatory offences is also, it seems, a matter of last resort in the United States, where only 2 per cent of cases of formal administrative orders, and only 0.2 per cent of citations for serious violations were prosecuted in 1991 (Kagan, 1993). In general, US regulatory agencies seem to have resorted slightly more frequently in recent years to criminal prosecution, though reliance on the criminal sanction for regulatory offending is still very low in the United States. (The attraction of civil penalties in America is connected with their lower standard of proof.) At the same time the criminal law seems to be increasingly used for offences involving negligence or recklessness. Whether such apparently small increases actually produce any instrumental effects—assuming that this is the purpose of prosecuting—depends on how such shifts in policy and practice are perceived and responded to by the regulated community (Kagan, 1993).

[10] The prosecution statistics of HSE are based on the informations laid before the courts in England and Wales, and on the charges preferred in Scottish courts. 'Each information laid or charge preferred relates to a breach of an individual legal requirement and a duty holder may be prosecuted for more than one of these breaches.... Conviction statistics are based on the number of informations laid which resulted in a conviction.... Some informations laid are "alternative informations" which are laid in combination with other informations to produce a higher chance of conviction. If, for example, several alternative informations are laid against a duty-holder who then pleads or is found guilty of one or more of the charges, then the other alternative informations may be withdrawn' (HSC, 1998*b*: 57).

inspectors is the sheer volume of potentially prosecutable violations which they encounter: 'I might go into a factory... and see 15 or 20 or 25 alleged offences during an inspection,' said one inspector (86–28).[11] 'Now it's important that the factory occupier realises that every single thing I'm pointing out to him is a criminal offence.'[12] The usual response to a theoretically prosecutable breach of the law is to inform, bargain, demand compliance, or to issue a notice. To set the number of prosecutions against the huge number of theoretically prosecutable matters[13] leads inexorably to the conclusion that for HSE prosecution is an enforcement measure of last resort.

Prosecution can be thought of as a last resort in two ways. It is a last resort either in the sense that it is demanded because no alternative course of action is realistically possible, or it is a last resort because all alternatives to prosecution have been exhausted (see generally Emerson, 1981). The former use (in what can be regarded as 'big cases') is found where a matter is exceptional for the gravity of the harm done or threatened, or for its capacity to create public, and possibly political, concern. Accordingly, we read in HSC's (n.d.: 11) *Enforcement policy statement*: 'Other approaches to enforcement can often promote health and safety more effectively but, where the circumstances warrant it, prosecution without prior warning and recourse to alternative sanctions may be appropriate.'

The latter practice (acting where all alternatives have been exhausted) is found in cases of what Robert Emerson (1981: 9) calls 'routine troubles'. The normal approach in what can be termed 'routine cases' of prosecution is that 'inspectors do not enter plants looking for "criminals" or... to identify trivial shortcomings. Usually the first step will be for them to discuss with the occupier of the premises what they find and how matters can be improved without recourse to formal enforcement action' (Health and Safety Commission, 1994: 4).

The use of prosecution as an enforcement move of last resort goes back to Victorian times. Various historical studies of the enforcement of

[11] See the Appendix, nn. 6 and 7, and the text there for an explanation of the codes used.

[12] Or, as a construction inspector put it, 'You turn down more than you take... I see something daily, or even on every site, for which a valid case could be put forward quite easily' (86–63).

[13] Theoretically prosecutable numbers are actually quantitatively unknowable since a legally defined violation is socially constructed and also depends upon its being recorded officially. Many violations are undiscovered or unreported. My statement is based on the many accounts by inspectors in interview of the large numbers of violations they encounter, but about which they take no formal action, nor (sometimes) even record.

factory legislation (e.g. Bartrip & Burman, 1983; Bartrip & Fenn, 1980*b*; Johnstone, 1994: 61 ff.) have indicated that nineteenth-century inspectors relied heavily, like their present-day counterparts, on persuasion and advice as the main means of achieving their ends. Interestingly, however, prosecution was quite often employed in the 1830s in enforcing the early Factory Acts (Bartrip & Fenn, 1980*b*), but by 1860 its use had become relatively rare.[14]

There are various explanations for Victorian practices which are relevant to an understanding of current approaches to prosecution. Bartrip and Fenn (1980*a*, *b*) have argued that low prosecution rates were a consequence of limited resources. They also suggest, however, that the rarity of prosecution reflected the concern of inspectors to have the regulatory legislation respected: legitimacy was thought more likely to be attained by use of a conciliatory rather than a punitive approach. Inspectors were also conscious of legal problems in prosecuting. Formal action had to take place quickly, and difficulties were often encountered in securing good witnesses. The legal rules were thought to be too vague and uncertain, and magistrates (many of whom were industrialists themselves) reluctant to impose significant fines. Johnstone's (1994) survey of historical analyses of nineteenth-century factory legislation and its enforcement in England and in the Australian state of Victoria show a number of other important common influences at work, all of which conspired to depress the level of prosecution for violations of factory legislation. These included a view that employees were often to blame for accidents, coupled with a corresponding unwillingness to recognize the culpability of employers, and a recognition that inspectors were heavily dependent upon the cooperation of employers simply to be able to do their job. The result was a strong desire to advise and encourage employers rather than to sanction them for misconduct. 'The partial resolution of these contradictions', writes Johnstone (1994: 65, footnotes omitted),

> 'and the low penalties imposed by magistrates, led to the inspectorate devising a number of strategies. One was for inspectors to prosecute only when satisfied that the offence stemmed from the concrete element of intention on the part of the occupier. Only "wilful and obstinate" offenders should be prosecuted, and only after the employer had been given an opportunity to offer an exculpating explan-

[14] Historically the early Factory Acts in Britain were more concerned with restricting hours of labour for women and children than with the direct promotion of occupational health and safety. Enforcement practice seems to have reflected this aim: in 1879–80, for instance, fewer than 5 per cent of prosecutions were for breaches of safety regulations (Bartrip, 1987).

ation. In short, the early inspectors incorporated the notion of mens rea into their routine decisions about prosecution.'[15]

Carson (1974; 1979) has argued that prosecution as a last resort in Victorian times can be seen as evidence of a process of 'conventionalization' of occupational health and safety offences. His contention is that such offences were suffused with a sense of ambiguity which led to matters formally enacted as criminal becoming regarded as merely quasi-criminal and not as 'real crime' at all. The institutionalization of ambiguity of factory crime, he argues, is revealed, for example, in the fact that offenders were not dealt with as part of the usual criminal justice system, but by regulatory bodies, encouraging a general view that such offences were not 'criminal' in the generally accepted sense. Carson (1979; 1980) suggests that such an approach to enforcement was important for its support of industrialized life and the creation of the conditions for vigorous laissez-faire capitalism.

To speak of prosecution as a last resort is to convey enforcers' sense of reluctance in most cases to prosecute immediately where rules are broken, that is, in all but egregious cases of death and injury, or clear or striking breaches of the law. Indeed, it is often the case, as later chapters will show, that deaths at work are not necessarily followed by any formal enforcement action. Prosecution stands at the punitive end of an array of approaches to enforcement employed by inspectors in the regulation of occupational health and safety matters and is commonly regarded as the most drastic of enforcement moves. Its use is not constant across all inspectorates: those who work in HSE's Field Operations Directorate (FOD), which is comprised of the former Agricultural Inspectorate (AgI) and Factory Inspectorate (FI), probably make more frequent use of the power than others. It used to be assumed that the larger numbers of prosecutions in the former FI was itself a good indication that this inspectorate adopted more of a sanctioning strategy in its enforcement than other inspectorates.[16]

In the 1980s, in an era of semi-autonomous inspectorates which had been thrown together to make up the HSE in 1974, following the publication of the Robens Report, there were markedly different cultures and traditions of enforcement within HSE. Prosecution numbers in any

[15] This continues to be the case: see Hawkins (1984) in relation to environmental pollution, and Ch. 11 of this book, as regards occupational health and safety regulation.

[16] Such an assumption is not, however, tenable since it would be necessary to calculate a rate of prosecution per instance of discovered rule-breaking, a highly problematic matter given its socially constructed character.

inspectorate may to an extent be a function of policy, but are likely also to be attributable to features in an inspector's environment, a reflection of the character, as well as the number, of regulated sites. There are obvious and significant contrasts in the nature of the activities regulated by different regulatory bodies (see Braithwaite *et al.*, 1987), and these contrasts—in the numbers of regulated sites, or the extent to which a regulated population is known to enforcers—tend to be associated with different enforcement behaviour. Inspectors of factory and agricultural premises regulate more numerous, visible, and varied sites with immediately hazardous activity than did, for example, members of the former Industrial Air Pollution Inspectorate (IAPI).[17] In the days of the combined Mines and Quarries Inspectorate there were usually no more than one or two prosecutions a year, and in the Nuclear Installations Inspectorate (NII), almost always none at all (prosecution being made virtually redundant by extensive licensing powers).[18] Factory and agricultural inspectors are more likely, in the nature of things, to encounter violations, hazards, and non-compliance. Construction inspectors, for example, are routinely confronted with risky activities and work with an industry which has historically high levels of accidents. Such an inspector is more likely to use prosecution as a response to an accident, or as a sanction for a transient population. In such circumstances, formal legal action may correspondingly more frequently appear to be a desirable and viable enforcement option.

Another sense, then, in which prosecution is a last resort is that it is, with relatively few exceptions, a rare event for inspectors themselves. In 'less than one in every 25 visits does the need for enforcement by prosecution or formal notice arise' (Health and Safety Executive, 1986: 8). According to a former Chief Inspector of FI:

[17] See Weait (1989). IAPI was transferred from HSE in 1986 to the newly formed Her Majesty's Inspectorate of Pollution, which in turn was absorbed into the Environment Agency in 1996.

[18] In the case of NII, the power to withdraw or withhold a licence is probably a more extreme measure than prosecution. The NII rarely prosecutes because its 'sanctions are so much more powerful and immediate under the licensing system than they possibly could be in a court of law', a former chief inspector said. A delay of 24 hours in NII issuing a licence was said to be worth in the mid-1980s £250,000 to a power-generating company. As a result, the then chief inspector said, 'because the sanctions under that approval [i.e. withholding a licence] are so powerful, because delays are so expensive, we *always* get our way' (his emphasis). One of the very few prosecutions in which NII was involved (at the time of Phase I of the fieldwork the only prosecution) was of the nuclear reprocessing plant at Sellafield for the discharge of radioactive waste into the Irish Sea, a matter which predictably prompted considerable publicity.

'We are often seen within the [HSE] organization as being the sort of macho prosecuting arm of the Executive... But at the same time... the individual head count... is pretty small compared with the number of visits that an individual inspector does, the number of contacts that he has, and of course the number of offences that he comes across.'

This suggests the rarity of prosecution, even among those inspectors regarded (in agency parlance) as 'macho men'. 'The average factory inspector takes only three prosecutions a year,' the former Chief Inspector continued, 'and yet the factory inspectorate is regarded as an obsessive, well not obsessive, quite a keen prosecuting inspectorate.'

There may also be a link between rarity of prosecution and the formal decision-making structure within an inspectorate. While in the smaller inspectorates final decisions about prosecution are made in a centralized way at the top of the organization at the level of chief inspector, in FOD decision-making about prosecution is decentralized,[19] and therefore simpler. Here, the decision is effectively made by the inspector concerned, in conjunction with, and with the approval of, the appropriate principal inspector (PI).[20] A particularly important further practice for present purposes is that field inspectors in FOD in most instances actually prepare their cases for prosecution and appear in court to conduct the prosecution proceedings themselves.[21] Whether inspectorates are organized to prosecute on a centralized or decentralized basis, however, the importance accorded to prosecution by all the HSE inspectorates is suggested by the care with which they make decisions relating to it, and by the resources devoted to it.

Despite an increase shown in the most recent annual statistics, the number of prosecution cases in HSE has declined over time (Health and Safety Commission, 1999). One important reason for this downward trend may be the more complex hazards encountered, allied with the greater legal complexities now involved in preparing prosecution cases. This was a recurrent theme in recent interviews with HSE staff. For example, a PI claimed that enforcement had

'become much more complicated.... When I joined, prosecutions would usually be fairly straightforward. You know, there would be a finger off in a power press, and you'd go along and you'd get two statements from witnesses, and

[19] This was the case before the creation of FOD in the former FI, but not in AgI.

[20] Or if the PI is proposing the prosecution, with the approval of the area director (AD).

[21] The other inspectorates recruit local solicitors for the purpose, as did the former AgI before the creation of FOD. This is discussed further in Ch. 3.

away you'd go. . . . These days we have to think about being fair to the company. If we invite them in for interview, or we ask them for comment about what they've done before and after the investigation, we have to seriously consider whether we do that with PACE [Police and Criminal Evidence Act, 1984]. So that all adds to the investigation time, so there is no such thing now, in my experience, as what I would call a simple case. In the old days, people used to fall off scaffolds because there were no guard-rails. They were quite easy cases to take. But the world's moved on. We're not at that level. We're into things which generally are much, much more complex.' (97–01)

Certainly the view in HSE is that the downward trend does not reflect a change of regulatory policy; as an AD argued: 'The figures that come out could suggest a lessening of effort on enforcement activity, but I'm convinced that isn't the case. The effort, the time that we're spending on enforcement activity, is increasing, well, I'm sure it is, year on year. . . . For some reason we just keep counting informations . . .' (97–02).

This discussion prompts a number of important questions. If very large numbers of violations are known to inspectors, what explains how the large number of potential cases is reduced by such a striking amount? Why are so few violations treated as warranting even the beginnings of the formal process? If matters that are prosecuted have something special about them, what marks them out for this most drastic of enforcement moves? The last question is the particular focus of this book.

4. SCOPE, METHODS, AND DATA

The research methods and data sources on which the analysis is based are described at length in the Appendix, and merely outlined here. The research was conducted over a 15-year span from 1983 to 1998, with data from the field collected in 1986–9 (Phase I) and 1996–8 (Phase II). The book not only presents a detailed analysis at the level of the individual case, but is also sensitive to the wider organizational and structural forces at play in legal decision-making and accordingly addresses the broader picture of legal processes at work. This demands thick description, a fine-grained analysis which proceeds at several levels, with an appropriately detailed exploration of the empirical data. Inevitably, by the standards of socio-legal research monographs, this means a large book.

Though emphasis is given to decision-making within what used to be known as the Factory Inspectorate, the analysis is in effect based on studies conducted in a number of regulatory groupings within HSE.[22] In the 1980s FI was the largest of a number of inspectorates within HSE charged with the task of protecting and advancing the health, safety, and welfare of people in the workplace or members of the public vulnerable to workplace activity. There were also inspectorates to protect the health and safety of people at work in agriculture, mines and quarries, industrial air pollution, nuclear installations, and railways, as well as a number of smaller inspectorates (which I did not research) to monitor and control matters connected with explosives and offshore oil installations. The Factory and Agricultural Inspectorates have since been combined into a generic Field Operations Directorate into which quarries inspectors have also been absorbed, created in an effort to make field operations more efficient and rationally based, while air pollution work is now carried out by the Environment Agency.[23] Inspection work is directed by HSE, which implements policy formulated by HSC. The HSC, to which HSE is responsible, represents the major interest groups.[24]

As noted above, some of the organizational structures which were the setting for the practices analysed in Phase I of the fieldwork have changed during the course of the research.[25] There have also been some changes in procedures and in personnel. However, nothing has occurred, as far as I am aware, to invalidate the accuracy of those parts of the analysis based on data gathered in Phase I. Readers will readily be able to see when the data were collected by reference to the code indicating the source of the data which follows quoted interview material.[26] All names appearing in the data are fictitious. It should be noted that organizational changes involving, in particular, fusion within HSE of various institutional arrangements for inspection along functional lines have resulted in some alterations in the official labelling of various staff positions. For convenience and for clarity, however, I shall continue to use the older terms and refer where necessary to factory inspectors, agricultural inspectors, and so on, where generic references

[22] Local authorities also have legal enforcement responsibilities in many respects akin to those of the former FI, but this research does not include them, nor does it address the use of prosecution for failure to comply with a notice.

[23] See n. 17.

[24] Formal arrangements are discussed in more detail in Ch. 5.

[25] In reporting on fieldwork I sometimes use the present tense for convenience, although it is quite possible that some of the practices described may have changed to some extent.

[26] Interviews involving the most senior HSE staff (i.e. those above the level of area director) were all carried out in the late 1980s. These staff are referred to by their office; accordingly, no coding is used.

are inappropriate. Similarly, to avoid confusion, rather than use the organization's own titles, which have in some cases been altered over the research period, I have elected to use generic job descriptions. I therefore speak of 'inspectors', 'principals' or 'supervisors', 'area directors', and 'chief inspectors', regardless of the particular research period under discussion, and regardless of the formal titles these individuals now hold or may have held. I use these labels not to identify their office, but to describe what people do (hence frequent use of the lower case). Sometimes my labels may accord with a current organizational title, sometimes not. Similarly, I use the term 'agency' to refer to both the Health and Safety Executive, and its constituent parts—the various inspectorates of the 1980s, or the various divisions of the 1990s.

A variety of data-collecting methods were employed in the fieldwork, but the guiding principle throughout was to study the activities of officials in as natural a setting as possible. What follows is drawn from six sources. First, library research of studies of legal decision-making and regulation was undertaken to clarify general theoretical issues, in particular about the nature of decisions made by legal actors. Second, I studied HSE's own extensive list of publications to learn about its operations and its official perspectives on enforcement policies, practices, and problems.

Third, a number of lengthy tape-recorded interviews were conducted in Phase I with the chief inspectors, and some former chief inspectors, of all the main HSE inspectorates. These addressed general issues concerned with decision-making about prosecution, especially as seen from the officials' vantage point in the centre of the organization. The discussions covered matters to do with the formulation of prosecution policy as well as practices involved in making decisions about specific cases. Informal, tape-recorded interviews, which covered much of the same ground, but which also dealt with more specialized topics, were also held at the same time with HSE lawyers and other headquarters officials. In total 16 individuals took part in this part of the research.

The fourth source of data is correspondence and memoranda surrounding the issuing of infraction letters in the former Industrial Air Pollution Inspectorate. A documentary analysis was carried out to explore decision-making in a centralized organization, where the decision to prosecute was ultimately made at the deputy chief or chief inspector level. I was given access to material relating to all infraction letters issued in the years 1983, 1984, and 1985.[27]

[27] An early analysis of this material was carried out by Matthew Weait (1989).

Fifth, a much more extensive study was made of decision-making in a large decentralized decision-making structure, the Factory Inspectorate (FI). In such a structure, the decision to prosecute is not something which routinely involves senior staff (the exception being the newsworthy or otherwise difficult case). Four FI areas were selected for research, to represent those apparently making rather more and those making rather less use of prosecution, so as to tap into a wide spectrum of opinion and experience. These areas also had contrasting levels of economic prosperity and industrial activity, different types of industry and sizes of firms. The particular inspectors within each area selected as subjects were chosen to represent various industry groups which presented contrasting types of enforcement problem. Thus inspectors were sampled who worked in construction (a high-risk activity, with relatively frequent use of prosecution), chemicals (where hazards may be great and problems are often long-term, but use of prosecution is low), general manufacturing (the traditional core of FI work), and the National Interest Group (to see if there was any characteristic approach).[28] Within each of these selected groups, the principal inspector (PI) was interviewed together with two field inspectors (in HSE terminology, inspectors of 1B rank).[29] Each area director (AD) was also interviewed. The interviews, like those with headquarters staff, focused on the policy and practice of prosecution decision-making, and centred upon the respondents' ideas, practices, and attitudes. Nearly all interviews were tape-recorded. In total 52 inspectors were interviewed, a number which represented almost 10 per cent of FI's complement of 538 field inspectors then in post.

Finally, having carried out a preliminary analysis of the materials on the first five sets of data collected and published some findings (Hawkins, 1989*a*, *b*; 1992*a*), I collected additional data in 1996–8 to explore certain issues further, and to update the research and expand the database. Phase II had two principal components. First, I conducted a content analysis of the files of all cases prosecuted in a six-month period (1 January 1996 to 30 June 1996) in the same four regional offices of the HSE in which the fieldwork for Phase I had been carried out. Second, I conducted in the same offices a content analysis of all files involving workplace fatalities occurring over the same six-month period. The purpose of analysing the sample of fatalities was to allow some means of studying decision-making about potentially prosecutable cases which

28 There is more about the National Interest Groups in Ch. 5.

29 Selecting inspectors in this way also ensured that the majority of the field staff in the area were involved in the study.

were ultimately deemed unsuitable for prosecution. There were 68 files relating to prosecutions (three of which were also cases involving fatalities), and 25 relating to fatalities (three of which were prosecuted). While collecting these data, I also tape-recorded lengthy conversations with three of the four current ADs, and with two experienced PIs in the other area. The object of these conversations was to check that the preliminary analyses were not out of date. I have drawn extensively from them for illustrative purposes, but do not generally treat them as data sources in their own right.

5. THE ARRANGEMENT OF THE BOOK

Decision-making studies have in the past usually concentrated on the behaviour of so-called 'front-line' or 'street-level' officials in implementing or enforcing law, in which such actors are researched as gatekeepers to the formal legal process (Lipsky, 1980).[30] Without question, what these junior officials actually decide is extremely significant in legal organizations, owing to structural features which grant an important screening function to those who possess or assume the power to define problems, and to decide which problems warrant some form of intervention, as well as what kind of intervention. The decision-making power of junior officials is also important because the public image of the organization is very dependent on the character of the cases fed into the system by them. One significant area of legal life so far largely unexplored in socio-legal research, however, involves the way in which senior officials in the centre of a legal bureaucracy create the policies and the controls that seek to guide or constrain the making of decisions at its periphery. Both forms of decision-making—by inspectors in particular cases and the formulation of policy in the higher reaches of legal bureaucracies—are explored in this analysis. This is because it is necessary to discuss decision-making about prosecution on a number of levels, not only features in individual cases, but also groups of cases. At the same time, the social, political, economic, and organizational contexts in which each decision has to be made must be addressed, so that connections may be made between the macro- and micro-level forces at work.

[30] There are many studies of field-level decision-making in the literature of policing, though probably fewer concerned with social workers, probation officers, and the like. Among the exceptions are Asquith (1982); Cicourel (1968); Dingwall *et al.* (1983); Emerson (1969); and Prottas (1979).

The book is organized to move from general to particular in its analysis of the conditions under which prosecution is employed. Succeeding chapters steadily tighten the focus to reflect the handling and decision-making involved in potentially prosecutable cases. The sort of analysis attempted demands a high level of detail; otherwise it will not do justice to the complexities of the processes actually involved: hence the size of the book. Making decisions about prosecution may seem to be a relatively simple matter, both to an observer and often to the decision-makers themselves, and may often be presented to others as a simple matter. However, the underlying reality, when exposed, is usually much more complex.

This book employs a naturalistic way of thinking about legal decision-making, an approach outlined in the context of a theoretical discussion of its important features in Chapter 2. The processes involved in creating and handling potential prosecution cases within HSE are analysed in Chapter 3, which also explores the pre-trial bargaining and tactical decisions that are made about charge and forum.

Part II of the book, Chapter 4, analyses the 'surround', that is, the social, political, and economic environments within which untoward events occur and within which prosecution decision-making is carried on. Part III deals with the 'field', or the defined setting in which decisions are made. It comprises three chapters. Formal arrangements and the legal powers possessed by HSE and its inspectorates are the subject of Chapter 5. Chapter 6 considers the making and meaning of policy about prosecution in HSE. The imagery and symbolism of prosecution are the subject of Chapter 7, in which prosecution is analysed as a public act conveying messages and appearances to audiences.

Part IV, the largest of the book, is devoted to analysis of the decision-making 'frames' employed by individual decision-makers to make sense of what they encounter. Chapter 8 explores their theories of compliance and punishment which organize their ideas about enforcement. The part played by instrumental concerns about the effectiveness of prosecution in assessing the prosecutability of a particular case is discussed in Chapter 9. In Chapter 10 attention turns to decisions about prosecution which are shaped by the organizational concerns of individual officials. In Chapter 11 there is a detailed exploration of conceptions of blame and the conditions under which prosecution is regarded as a deserved outcome. An analysis of the legal frame is presented in Chapter 12, which looks at the play between formal legal rules and informal organizational practices. This for practical purposes compels decision-makers to attend to the strength or weakness of any case in purely legal terms, whatever its merits on other grounds. Even the most compelling incident requires scrutiny from a legal point of view to see if it is watertight, even though from a policy point of view the matter is regarded as an 'obvious' prosecution case.

Chapter 13, the final Part, serves to summarize the analysis and present some reflections on the nature of prosecution, legal decision-making, and law. This last chapter is followed by an Appendix, in which the sources of data and the data-collecting methods are discussed in some detail, together with an account of how the research was conducted.

2 Organizing Ideas

The purpose of this chapter is to outline the theoretical perspective which informs the empirical analysis in the book. Before this, however, a brief treatment is needed of some other relevant organizing ideas and approaches: the naturalistic character of the enquiry, the view taken of the nature of decision-making in legal systems[1] (and legal bureaucracies in particular), and some current thinking about enforcement practices in regulatory systems. The discussion in this chapter is directed towards the behaviour of legal actors, but may also have broader relevance since what is presented here is a general way of thinking about decision-making.

1. NATURALISM

How are we to study something as elusive as decision-making? The approach adopted in this book can be characterized as one of naturalism.[2] Naturalistic research seeks to remain true to the nature of the social world studied. The perspective is derived from interpretive sociology and differs substantially from the positivistic analyses of decision-making in legal settings that have tended in the past to dominate the socio-legal and, in particular, the criminal justice literature (Hawkins, 1986). Among the problems of positivist analysis are a rather mechanistic view of legal decision-making, and a narrow field of vision. Too strong an element of positivism tends to produce an oversimplified and monochrome picture of legal decision processes. For example, to see legal decisions as guided and constrained solely by existing legal rules, whether they exist in the form of statutes, case law, or other influences discernible in the policy statements of legal bureaucracies, is to ignore the social, political, and

[1] I shall speak of 'the legal system' for convenience, though it is more realistically to be viewed as a loosely coupled set of subsystems.

[2] This is an integral part of a broader theoretical framework on decision-making that I have been developing with Peter K. Manning, whose contribution to these ideas I would like to acknowledge. A much more detailed analysis should ultimately appear in Hawkins & Manning (forthcoming), from which I have drawn. On the development of the naturalistic approach, see Hawkins (1986; 1992*b*); Manning (1986; 1992); Manning & Hawkins (1989); for a critique, see J. Black (1997).

economic contexts in which those decisions are made and the richness, subtlety, and complexity of all the processes involved. Again, the conception of the discrete case being decided by an informed legal actor thoughtfully and rationally weighing up the issues within a legal framework (a conception held both by lawyers and by those social scientists wedded to positivism) is, from the point of view of naturalistic analysis, unrealistic and distorted. Instead, what needs to be addressed is the various contexts in which decisions are made, and the conditions that lead to certain legally consequential outcomes (rather than others), which in turn need to be identified and explained. Legal decisions are often equated with specific, often formal, decision points at which visible individuals (such as regulatory inspectors) or groups make choices. These decisions are actually the formal culmination of many earlier decisions that are, in effect, glossed with a name or label such as 'a prosecution'. In reality matters are much more complex.

Although decisions are made at many points in the legal system, and by a variety of individuals, only some are recognized as legal decisions. It is not enough, however, to map out the personnel and the various institutional arrangements for making decisions and then to suggest what seems empirically to determine outcomes by correlating input data with decision outcome, since this does not address analytically the connection between the two. To understand the nature of this connection, the naturalistic perspective treats the link as forged by the sense-making activities of individual decision-makers. This is not by any means, however, to propose an individualistic view of legal decision-making. To focus on a single decision point, or on a single type of decision, risks excluding the social context that surrounds legal decision-making, the field in which the decision is set and viewed, as well as the interpretive and classificatory processes of individual decision-makers. For the purposes of the present analysis, it also needs emphasizing that in regulatory bureaucracies all legal decision-making takes place within an organizational context which imposes a set of particular objectives and introduces new constraints upon the decision-maker.

In this book decisions are analysed as far as possible in their natural settings, and unencumbered by the assumptions of positivism (in particular, of rational choice decision-making; Hawkins, 1992*b*). A naturalistic approach to decision processes allows decision-making to be described and analysed in its natural state, while respecting the complexities of ordinary behaviour. Assumptions are not made about the aims of the decision-maker or the task of decision-making. It is not assumed that decision outcomes are produced in a mechanical way when certain criteria are present. Indeed, the approach does not make the positivist assumption that decision-makers employ 'criteria' or 'factors' in their decision-making, nor that the use of certain criteria or factors leads inexorably to a particular outcome. Instead, decision-makers are regarded as ascribing meaning to salient features in a case. Decisions are treated as interpretive practices. Thus, although it is commonly said that decisions are made 'on their merits', a naturalistic approach takes the position that there is nothing self-evident or taken for granted about a decision, and that what is regarded as 'merited' is not only open to interpretation in each case, but only makes sense in the context of each decision. What does it mean to talk of looking at a case 'on its merits'? What are 'the merits' that so self-evidently determine outcomes? How are the 'merits' of a case determined? A positivist focus is much too narrow, for it omits the processes of sense-making and interpretation that lie behind a decision, and it excludes the role of non-legal rules and influences such as those exerted by the organization itself, or by the economy, or by the perceived political climate. Legal decisions, like other kinds of decision, are made not in a vacuum, but in a broader context of demands and expectations arising from the environment in which the decision-maker lives and works. An explanation of decision-making behaviour therefore requires attention to the social, political, and economic setting, including the general climate of opinion, as well as the organizational context in which decisions are taken. All of these create pressure for action or inaction or conspire to make a particular decision outcome seem more or less rational in a particular matter. In a naturalistic approach the perspective is the decision-maker's; the sense that is made and the rationality of a decision are the sense and rationality of that decision-maker.

The meaning, relevance, and salience of any feature are themselves shaped by a variety of forces in the decision-maker's environment. In other words, the variety of outcomes possible need to be located in the context of the social forces at play in the decision process. Similarly, legal rules, institutions, and procedures are merely one set of forces in a field of forces that act both on the individual legal official who exercises a power to decide and on that official's organization. Legal rules cohabit with others which also act on how decisions are made. Analysis must consider not only what is brought to any decision, but the constraints, both tacit and explicit, that act on decision-makers, not least the organizational context in which decisions are made.

2. A HOLISTIC PERSPECTIVE ON LEGAL DECISION-MAKING

Writing about legal decision-making has tended to take the individual case and the individual decision-maker as the primary unit of analysis when attempting to explain decision behaviour (Emerson, 1983).[3] One implication of a claim that a case is decided on its merits is that a case exists as a discrete entity, and decisions are made about its fate quite independently of wider forces and constraints. Thus it is often taken for granted that legal decisions are made by individuals, except where institutional arrangements demand that they be made collectively. The concern for the individual case is not surprising, since legal actors and bureaucracies (as well as socio-legal and criminological researchers) think about and typically assemble problems for decision into individual 'cases', each relating to a particular and concrete matter and existing in the form of a discrete unit by which each one may be recorded, worked on, referred to, stored, or passed on. It is important to revise this individualistic view, since it is partial, and fails to describe the reality of the processes. Legal decision-making has instead to be seen in a holistic or systemic perspective (Hawkins, 1992*b*), so that decisions are not treated as the work of individual legal actors behaving autonomously and independently of others. This means broadening the idea of the 'case' to recognize that a legal decision is often the product of different officials acting at different times making decisions serially. This results in cases being decided in the context of other decisions. These may be already made or about to be made, or decisions made about other actual or hypothesized cases (Emerson, 1983; Hawkins, 1992*b*), or in anticipation of what subsequent decision-makers might do (Emerson & Paley, 1992). These ideas need to be explored a little further.

1. Producing Decisions in Series and in Parallel

While an individual may readily be seen as responsible for making a particular decision, a very great deal of legal decision-making is a collective enterprise in which several people, either formally or informally, take part in deciding. In a formal sense many legal decisions are clearly required to be made collectively, as, for instance, when a jury retires. Where an outcome is the product of a number of decision-makers acting in concert in this way, we can think of decisions being made in parallel, since a number of people work simultaneously towards a collective

[3] Some of the ideas in this part of the chapter have appeared in Hawkins (1992*b*; 1997).

outcome. Where any differences of view about outcome occur between individual decision-makers, they have often to be negotiated into an outcome that can be presented as the group's decision (like a jury verdict), unless provision is made for dissenting views to be aired (as with judges hearing an appeal, or majority jury verdicts). What is presented as a collective view is sometimes further complicated by interpersonal features. In resolving differences about what a particular decision outcome should be, matters such as expertise, experience, status, and personal charisma frequently influence choices made, for they confer an interpersonal authority to have cases decided in particular ways at the behest, as it were, of particular individuals (Hawkins & Manning, forthcoming).

Most legal outcomes are not produced as a result of decision-making in parallel, however, though neither are they the work of a discrete individual. Different areas of the legal system are in general organized so as to require that decisions be made serially. If we think of case-creating and case-handling activity as involving matters that are handed on in the legal system from one point to the next for resolution, we can think of decision-making as a serial process. The creation of a legal case is itself often a problematic and chancy matter (Hawkins, 1984, ch. 5), but, once created, an individual case in the legal system is typically moved from one decision-maker to another until it is resolved, discarded, or otherwise disposed of (or in civil processes until one party exits). The sequence of decisions contributes in some way to the final outcome, whatever that outcome might be, whenever it arrives. Similarly, we can think of cases following careers within a decision-making system, of legal actors as part of a network of relationships existing within and between various segments of legal systems, and of the legal system as a serial referral system in which cases are handed on from one organizational actor or segment to another until the matter is disposed of in some conclusive way.

The implications of a serial conception of legal decision-making are very important for a number of reasons. First, the conception recognizes that power is dispersed across legal institutions and across individuals. It is not the case that people have an equal influence in shaping the decision outcome. In such circumstances a decision by an individual frequently does not settle matters (though a particular individual may set a case on a particular course which will lead, inexorably, to a particular destination), but merely makes a decision that leads to the case being handed on to another individual or organization. It should be noted that individual actors in a serial referral system often exercise a decisive, indeed, final authority: to drop the case. Power resides, *inter alia*, in the capacity of decision-makers to discard cases or not create them in the first place ('turning a blind eye'), or to redefine a matter. In the criminal process, for example, a matter may be redefined as a 'dispute' or 'problem' rather than an 'offence', thereby diverting the case, and putting it beyond the reach of the criminal law. Power resides in the structural position of the individual at the point at which choice is made. Second, a facet of this is that a decision made at one point in the system may close off or profoundly restrict the choices open to a later decision-maker. The diffusion of decision-making power means that serial procedures tend to concentrate greatest effective power in the hands of those, like regulatory inspectors, who act as gatekeepers at the periphery of their organization where it is generally less visible, thus less controllable. Third, it is often the case that effective power to decide is frequently assumed by actors other than the official allocated formal legal authority to exercise discretion. For example, real power is afforded by the legal system to those who create or assemble material relevant to a decision for those formally allocated authority to decide. Those supplying information may create a frame for the subsequent exercise of discretion by describing or presenting the case in a particular fashion, thereby setting cases off in a particular direction, and producing clear and specific expectations as to what the 'right' decision should be (in the context of police decision-making, see Sanders, 1987). Related to this, a fourth consequence of a serial decision-making system is that what is described as a 'decision' finally reached is sometimes nothing more than a ratification of an earlier decision or set of decisions made in the handling of a case. This may be so, even though that prior decision may appear—if it 'appears' in the records at all—in the guise of a recommendation or a mere expression of opinion (Hawkins, 1986). Indeed, some people who supply information or evaluation may have such an enormous influence on the subsequent handling of a case that it becomes difficult to conceive of the visible, formal point of decision as being the place at which real power to determine an outcome was exercised.

These points suggest that discontinuities may occur in the serial handling system, as conceptions of objectives, relevant values, and so on change depending on where in the system particular power to decide is located. Decision-makers acting at different points might be expected to have different priorities; indeed, there may not only be different sets of resource or other institutional constraints operating, but also quite different value systems (Manning & Hawkins, 1989). As cases move on in the sequence of handling decisions, the matters attended to by decision-makers and the nature of the constraints to which they feel subject may also shift with changes in time or organizational location. Decision-making about prosecution in regulatory agencies has a serial character, the length and complexity of the process increasing with 'big' (that is, serious or newsworthy) cases and structural features in the particular organization (see Chapter 3).

2. Rarity and Repetitiveness

The character of decision-making is heavily influenced by the frequency with which decisions are made. Some sorts of decision are rare events for some individuals, while there are others who make decisions of the same kind repeatedly and sometimes rapidly.[4] Organizational work often requires decisions to be made in repetitive ways (Emerson & Paley, 1992; Feldman, 1992; Manning, 1992). The experience of making the same sorts of decisions about the same sorts of people or problems contributes to the emergence of what Skolnick (1966) termed 'perceptual short-hand': a way of classifying and appraising each matter by focusing on the extent to which it presents features held to be typical of other such cases. This is possible because decision-makers develop understandings of what are 'normal cases' and 'normal ways' of deciding (Sudnow, 1965) which lead to the development of 'typifications'.[5]

Typification is one of a number of ordering processes in decision-making (as used in prosecution work: see Frohmann, 1997). Typification arises partly because familiarity with the broad features of routine cases gives decision-makers confidence in being able to see similarities in other cases, and partly for reasons of efficiency, saving the resources and sometimes the anxiety otherwise involved in addressing each new case afresh. It is not only a way of making decisions quickly and at little cost, but a process that becomes simpler and more routine as decision-makers gain experience, hardening with the passage of time (Rubinstein, 1973). Typification also provides a rational defence against criticism, since a

[4] This distinction between 'one-shot' and 'repeat-player' decision-makers is a familiar one in the socio-legal literature; Galanter (1974). For an example of a study involving highly repetitive legal decision-makers, see Gilboy (1991).

[5] These processes encourage resistance to change. Recent research shows that victim impact statements make little difference to the sentencing of criminal cases because, when they fall outside the normal expectations, they are dismissed as unreliable: Erez & Rogers (1999).

decision in a particular matter may be aligned with other typical cases, and therefore presented as routine and unexceptional practice. Routine decision-making stemming from repetitive behaviour is also more likely to be stable, consistent, and therefore predictable than the more individualistic decision-making behaviour reserved for those cases that seem unusual in some way, or those decisions not normally made in repetitive ways. Typification leads to a particular decision outcome in routine cases since a matter categorized in a particular way will be routinely dealt with in the way reserved for cases of that kind. The crucial decision here, therefore, is bound up in the typification itself: the allocation of matters to categories or fitting particular cases into a type of case (see, for illustration, Rosett & Cressey, 1976; Sudnow, 1965). A matter deemed to be 'normal', 'typical', or 'routine' will be dealt with in normal, typical, or routine ways.

Another consequence of repetitive decision-making is the development of precedent. English lawyers think of precedent in connection with judicial decision-making in common law systems, but it is also particularly instructive for administrative officials in bureaucracies where regular working practices crystallize into organizational precedents. Like typification, precedent serves important functions for decision-makers. It grants access to a repertoire of accustomed ways of handling problems, helping to make the task of decision-making quicker and easier. Precedent also helps to instruct other decision-makers. Not least, precedent acts as a refuge when judgement is questioned: an existing precedent can be pointed to as a persuasive device. Bureaucratic officials tend to develop their own sense of precedent for their decision-making, a practice which may culminate in suggesting to them in effect that, for all practical purposes, they possess little or no discretion in a particular matter. The practical consequence of this behaviour is that organizationally or subjectively created precedents can acquire the same binding force as legal or bureaucratic rules. Such subjectively created rules can be extraordinarily resilient and durable. Furthermore, the forces contributing to the creation of precedent are not necessarily the same as those that keep it in effect (Lempert, 1992).

Legal cases in a serial handling system also have a future as well as a past, and decisions may not just be backward-looking, reflective, or reactive, but may have a strong anticipatory or predictive character. An especially important function of precedent is the capacity of the past to clarify for decision-makers what is likely to happen in future. The degree to which knowledge about past practice is regarded as reliable and predictions about future events are made with confidence is derived in turn from the frequency with which decisions are made. Furthermore, the experience of having to make the same sorts of decisions over and over again builds up in the participants a stock of knowledge about the decision-making practices of others, allowing decision-makers to anticipate what others are likely to do in the future handling of a case. Repetitive decisions, routinely made, enable colleagues to learn how to understand coded communications which artfully convey 'the truth of the matter' involved in a past decision (Emerson, 1991). This knowledge makes it possible for decision-makers to penetrate or look behind earlier decisions to understand the 'real meaning' of those earlier decisions, much as people regularly 'read between the lines' to understand what is actually being said in a statement or report, and to get to grips with the real issue (Young, 1996). Looked at this way, it is hard to sustain the idea of the individual actor making decisions according to legal rules or standards alone, uninfluenced by the existing or anticipated decisions of others.

In general, it is decision-making of an anticipatory kind that makes possible the bargaining on which so much of the criminal and civil justice systems rely for their continued viability. In adversarial legal systems legal actors often decide in anticipation of what 'the other side' will do, for example, in opting to settle out of court (Ross, 1970), or in anticipation of what others, to whom cases will be handed on for further processing, will do (Emerson & Paley, 1992). Similarly, regulatory inspectors contemplating court action have to anticipate questions from their principals, or problems that might arise concerning the nature or sufficiency of available evidence and decide on their enforcement strategy accordingly. While prosecution decisions are not regarded as routine matters, and none are made repetitively, the decision-making of those who are more familiar with prosecution as an enforcement strategy (construction inspectors, for example) may lead them to adopt some of the traits of a repetitive, rather than a one-shot, decision-maker. This is more likely to be true also of principal inspectors who routinely review recommendations for prosecution made by several field inspectors.

Sometimes anticipatory behaviour may be used in an artful way by one decision-maker to attain a particular kind of preferred outcome in a decision to be made by another, as when listing clerks route certain criminal cases for trial by particular judges with known sentencing proclivities in particular kinds of case which are regarded as especially appropriate (Lovegrove, 1984; see also Emerson & Paley, 1992; Utz, 1978).

3. Individual and Organizational Decision-Making

Decision-making in law is in various ways not only an individual or collective but frequently an organizational matter. Prosecution decision-making is organizational activity, and to understand it from a naturalistic perspective demands a sensitivity to the character of organizational life and to the settings inhabited by organizations. Organizations are themselves caught up in a complex network of interorganizational relations that constrain individual options and discretion, and reflect political processes at work.

Many different types of decision have to be made within the organization. In occupational health and safety regulation, for instance, there are a variety of inspectorial and supervisory decisions (ostensibly individual decisions), administrative and policy decisions (collective decisions), as well as governmental decisions. The norm for making organizational decisions is deciding according to conventions and within background assumptions of a routine character. Indeed, routine is an especially salient feature of organizational life, and important in stabilizing and reproducing organizational decisions (Manning, 1992). Routine orders the process and sequence of decision-making. Routines used to shape and control the flow of work are embedded in beliefs or ideologies growing from the mandate of the organization, and represented publicly in organizational discourse (Manning, 1987*a*). Such routines are often a powerful force for conservatism or inertia, and are closely linked with values found in the occupational or organizational culture, such as 'Don't disagree with me and I won't disagree with you' (Hawkins, 1971), 'Don't stick your neck out', or 'Don't rock the boat' (Manning, 1992).

Decisions made by officials are affected in special ways by their organizational contexts. For example, organizations have rewards to give, including rewards for consistency in decisions, or the production of appropriate levels of desirable organizational activity (arrests by police officers were surely one of the first types of performance indicators to be recognized). Similarly, different effects occur as a result of personal interaction that takes place when groups of organizational decision-makers have to make decisions. Research has documented the influence of organizations upon individuals of 'pressures to produce' (Manning,

1980); of social typifications of sets or groups of cases (Cicourel, 1968; Sudnow, 1965; Waegel, 1981); and of moral typifications of other organizations by decision-makers that guide their actions towards such organizations (Hawkins, 1984). Organizational decisions are not usually made independently of each other, but in ways that take account of the implications of the handling of the present case in a particular way for the handling of other cases, and vice versa (Emerson, 1983; Emerson & Paley, 1992). Caseload effects may occur when a particular case is decided within the context of a set of cases (Emerson, 1983). Or there may be sequence effects which act on an individual decision, arising from the order in which cases are decided, in which previous decisions constrain present ones, or where the anticipation of a future decision shapes the outcome in the present case (Emerson, 1991). Organizational context serves powerfully to constrain and shape decisions.

4. Decisions about Cases and Decisions about Policy

It is important to distinguish between decisions made about particular cases and decisions about how to deal with classes of case. The former are case decisions, the latter policy decisions. The case decision is a discrete choice about the action to be taken on a specific matter. Decisions also have to be made, however, about groups of cases or problems, in which the formulation of general legal and organizational objectives and their attainment is a primary concern. A policy decision speaks to the handling of types of case or classes of acts or events in a coherent and generalized way. A good deal of decision-making in legal bureaucracies is concerned with matters of policy because broad legislative intent has to be interpreted and translated into organizational practice that is not only workable but capable of repetition. The policy process in a regulatory bureaucracy determines in effect what the precise reach of any law will be, what forms of enforcement are to be employed, and what burdens are to be imposed upon those who are subject to regulation. Bureaucratic policy is, as a result, an important part of an inspector's decision field (see Chapter 6).

The formulation of policy demands a different form of legal decision-making. A broad legal mandate, such as that typically granted to regulatory organizations like HSE, will give rise to huge areas of administrative discretion which needs to be given form and purpose. That form and purpose is expressed in legal bureaucracies in statements of organizational policy. An analysis of prosecution decision-making must address the question of how the discretion embedded in legislative structures granting administrative officials a legal mandate takes a specific form, and in particular how actors at the centre of their regulatory bureaucracies interpret their mandate, what informs its content, and how it is converted into a form intended to guide action relating to prosecution at the periphery. Constraints upon broad policy restricting what a legal bureaucracy can do may arise internally (the result of such matters as staffing, or the exercise of active choice among officials) or externally, where perceived social, political, or economic matters assume importance. Many aspects of policy decision-making are remote from decisions about cases. This is due partly to the fact that policy is the embodiment of a set of values and assumptions located at the centre of the organization which contrast with the forms of knowledge employed by those at the periphery. Policy at the periphery—to the extent that field inspectors are conscious of it at all—exists in a concrete, particularistic, here-and-now form, in which over-inclusive rules pose practical problems. The result is that at the periphery of the organization what is regarded as rational action is connected more with an inspector's capacity to solve a particular problem (recall James Q. Wilson's (1968) finding that among police officers, one of the qualities most prized is the ability to 'handle a situation'). So far as field inspectors are concerned, the requirements of policy often seem to be rather remote from the decisions that have to be made in response to the demands of the real world (Manning, 1987*b*). Often the rules themselves create difficulties (R. Baldwin, 1995; J. Black, 1997). Rules and policy guidance are poor at targeting specific problems or predicting particular kinds of event (hence the widespread resort to administrative discretion). If front-line decision-makers are in fact conscious of policies or rules, they may regard them as of variable status. Indeed, regulatory rules tend often to be deployed as reference points around which a legal actor may organize decision-making about cases in a rather unconstrained way. This is possible in legal bureaucracies since discretion tends to be squeezed out to, or assumed by, those at the periphery, where it may be exercised largely invisibly and immune from organizational control.

This is not to suggest, however, that at field level policy is irrelevant to decisions, for 'outcomes are typically effected in an acceptable fashion by actions that are describable . . . as in accordance with rules' (Zimmerman, 1971: 237). What is understood as organizational policy about prosecution may well be simplified at the periphery to a simple conception of what the core issues are or what the organization's broad aim is. Those who have actually to implement policy are concerned with the practical: with specific cases, and particular instances in which a policy may be relevant, and may indeed be applied. But equally there may be cases where practical demands—often of an expressive kind—may overtake policy. In such circumstances, the existence of policy makes an organizational actor accountable, and this may prompt resort to the use of formally acceptable justifications (or 'presentational rules'; McConville *et al.*, 1991; Smith & Gray, 1983), by way of explanation for an act or omission. An exercise which at least begins as collective, prescriptive, abstract, and general in character tends to be reshaped and attenuated by organizational decision-making in the course of its application to the problems of the real world.

3. ENFORCING REGULATION

The practice of prosecution must be located in a broader criminal justice context. Prosecution may be regarded as a method of 'formal' legal enforcement, in contrast with informal approaches like persuasion, education, and so on. A perspective is needed of its place as the culmination of a series of informal law enforcement processes that occur routinely in areas of regulatory control like occupational health and safety or environmental protection.[6] Earlier empirical research on the enforcement of regulation has shown that the idea of law enforcement tends to mean different things in formal and informal settings (Hawkins, 1984). Prosecution employs the law in an explicit fashion, and in accordance with certain standard and visible procedural formalities.[7] Formal enforcement is often reserved for weightier matters: the seriousness and visibility of the problem confronted, the harm done or threatened, or the persistent failure to comply of the regulated person or firm.

[6] There is now a substantial empirically informed literature on the enforcement of regulation. See esp. Bardach & Kagan (1982); Braithwaite (1985); Braithwaite, Walker, & Grabosky (1987); Carson (1970*a*, *b*; 1982); Grabosky & Braithwaite (1986); Gray & Scholz (1993); Hawkins (1983*b*; 1984; 1990; 1991); Hawkins & Thomas (1984); Hutter (1988; 1989; 1997); Kagan (1978; 1984; 1989; 1994); Kagan & Scholz (1984); Kelman (1981); Law Commission (1969); Manning (1987*a*); Pearce & Tombs (1990; 1991); Reiss (1983; 1984); Richardson, *et al.* (1982); Scholz (1984); Schuck (1972); Shover *et al.* (1984, 1986); Vogel (1986).

[7] Notices (discussed in Ch. 5) are also a form of formal enforcement standing between bargaining and prosecution. They have their own distinctive functions, but omitting them from this discussion does not affect the line of argument.

One of the most distinctive features of informal law enforcement, wherever it is carried on, is its negotiated character. A criminally enforceable rule violation is not simply a matter defined by law, but one that is socially constructed. A breach may not necessarily come to light at all, but if it does, it may not be attended to by a regulatory inspector. If attended to, it may well be dealt with by informal means. These informal measures are dependent for their impact and effectiveness upon the personal competence and negotiating skills of individual inspectors, as well as their experience. They range from conciliatory measures with the regulated subject, such as persuasion, advice, and education, through to more formal and punitive approaches such as the issuing of improvement or prohibition notices. What particular method is adopted depends generally on the seriousness of the violation or the hazard, or on the response of the regulated to earlier enforcement efforts, a failure to comply usually prompting a more punitive response (Hawkins, 1984; see also Rock, 1973). Sometimes the formalities of prosecution are reserved for those who fail to comply sufficiently.

If the formal conception sees enforcement as integral to punishing the breach of a legal rule, the informal conception treats it as the application of measures designed to attain the legal mandate. On this latter view, an inspector will be more interested in safer and healthier workplaces than in convictions. The law plays a different role in informal compliance-oriented processes of enforcement, as compared with the sanctioning processes of formal enforcement. In the latter, the law is employed explicitly to serve retributive or deterrent purposes by the use of trial and punishment. In informal approaches to enforcement, however, the law plays a subtler role. While prosecution may sometimes be used in an effort to punish or deter, its actual use is much more commonly suspended, with the threat of prosecution employed as a device to concentrate the mind of the regulated, in an effort to ameliorate a problem or condition or to prevent the recurrence of an act. Negotiation is relied on heavily in the enforcement of regulation (as well as in the legal system more generally), to foreclose use of the formal law. When negotiation fails, however, the formal law enters in a more explicit guise. Though it is not actually used much, prosecution is central to systems of negotiated compliance. It is constantly employed, but in the background, as a veiled threat to concentrate the rule-breaker's mind on the necessity of compliance.

The ideas of 'compliance' or persuasion and 'sanctioning' or punishment are useful as ways of thinking about law enforcement, and particularly about the idea of enforcement as an array of measures on a continuum between the formality and punitive power of prosecution at one end, and benign advice to secure compliance at the other. In reality, law enforcers use approaches at various points on this continuum in different circumstances. Indeed, a 'big' or 'bad' case may well prompt an immediate prosecution. Different emphases given these various strategies make prosecution more or less prominent in inspectorates, as the following contrasting comments by chief inspectors suggest: 'it is a very visible part of our enforcement activity' (Factory Inspectorate, FI); 'we never raise prosecutions as an issue [when training inspectors]. It's just not an issue with us. Just not an issue' (Mines and Quarries Inspectorate, MQI). The former MQI was an inspectorate which rarely prosecuted, not least because it largely dealt with one major employer, the National Coal Board.

The leading actor in any discussion of regulatory enforcement is the field inspector. Many regulatory bureaucracies depend heavily upon inspection as the means by which their demands are imposed upon those whom they regulate. HSE is no exception and inspection is the primary point of contact between it and those whose activities it seeks to regulate. Routine inspections are not simply an opportunity for inspectors to assess compliance, they also serve as a means of providing business with detailed knowledge and advice. Inspection work depends heavily on face-to-face interaction between the regulatory agent and individuals from the regulated firm, which tends in turn to encourage a preoccupation among inspectors with the solution of immediate and pressing problems. Inspectors employ a flexible approach to problem-solving, and decisions about compliance tend to have a private and negotiated character. Above all, inspectors are practical people. 'A number of inspectors, particularly those who had been in the field for a long time,' writes Johnstone (1994: 205), in his Australian study of occupational health and safety inspectors, 'were at pains to indicate that the measure of a good inspector was not the number of prosecutions brought, but rather the inspector's ability "to get things fixed"' (see also Braithwaite, 1985; Grabosky & Braithwaite, 1986).

A number of important features in the structure and processes of regulation give rise to the negotiated character of regulation. The character of enforcement work is problematic since regulation fundamentally implies some tolerance of the problems which prompt public concern. The prevalent informal enforcement technique is bargaining, which is fostered in a variety of circumstances (Hawkins, 1984, ch. 6; see also

Winter, 1985). First, enforcement policy and standard-setting are themselves the subject of administrative discretion (in contrast to much of public policing), and therefore subject to negotiation. The central legislation in occupational health and safety regulation, which relies on a concept of what is 'reasonably practicable', illustrates this well. Negotiation in the practice of law enforcement exploits high administrative discretion and the low visibility in which most regulatory (and other law enforcement) officials work and leads to practices such as turning a blind eye to a violation, or not reporting a problem to superiors, or to controversial outcomes, such as inconsistency in the standards enforced.

Second, the nature of the law enforcement relationship (as in much policing work: Manning, 1977) is symbiotic. The regulatory agency needs the cooperation of businesses simply to be able to do its job efficiently and effectively. For business this means a willingness to comply with regulatory requests, to share relevant information, or to warn if a problem arises on site so that remedy or precautions can be effected immediately. The inspector, in other words, is heavily dependent upon those regulated. Business, for its part, is equally dependent upon its regulators, since it needs the inspector's knowledge and free expertise so that it may comply with its obligations relatively cheaply. Most important of all, however, it needs the forbearance of the inspector so that present, theoretically prosecutable, non-compliance is not immediately sanctioned to the full extent permitted by law. The possibility of repair is bound up in this, since one reason for continuing non-compliance is the inability to make quick remedial responses.[8] On this view, therefore, prosecution is rarely warranted because it is morally—not instrumentally—inappropriate.

Third, the nature of the enforcement relationship which inspectors have with employers is central to any analysis of their prosecution behaviour because it crucially affects their decision-making. Equally, employers are often regarded as part of the problem, and HSE inspectors more explicitly act in legalistic fashion by using and referring to the law more frequently when they deal with employers they believe to be ill-intentioned and ill-informed. Inspectors engage in adaptive behaviour, responding to the precise nature of the relationship with each employer,

[8] For instance, a former Chief Inspector of MQI thought that compliance strategy was compelled for his inspectorate because 'Few things around the mines, and certainly nothing of great consequence . . . can be changed quickly,' leading to contravention of the law that is 'going to be tolerated . . . sometime until it's practicable . . . to bring [the plant] back into compliance.'

and the apparent character of each, with a willingness to negotiate a solution or compromise being greater where well-intentioned employers are concerned (R. Baldwin, 1987: 32). The way in which incidents are judged and enforcement moves selected is based upon characterizations of the individuals and the regulated businesses inspectors deal with. Characterization is a means by which inspectors can impose order and rationality on their exercise of discretion and facilitate action. If an individual is judged positively (to be trustworthy, for example, or cooperative, knowledgeable, or committed), an amicable and cooperative response is likely from the regulatory official. Cooperation from inspectors will manifest itself in terms of a greater willingness to dispense advice or guidance, with a strong tendency to aim for compliance with desired standards. The presence of the condition of trust, the presumed cooperativeness on the part of the regulated, and an absence of big or bad examples of rule-breaking, all lead to a strong presumption that informal enforcement techniques should be employed wherever possible. If, however, the individual is assessed negatively—to be uncooperative and unconcerned (a 'cowboy')—inspectors are much more readily disposed to adopt a sanctioning strategy. This is more likely to be an immediate response where the organization employing the individual is similarly regarded. For inspectors who wish to act instrumentally, the congruence of the imagery implies more deep-seated and persistent problems. In this case, formal legal action is required, especially if this is likely to draw the attention of higher management to the inaction or uncooperativeness of their employee. For those inspectors who act expressively, however, pejorative imagery indicates that punishment is deserved.

If a firm fails to respond to a regulatory official's enforcement efforts then, over time, more pejorative characterizations in the way the organization is regarded will begin to assert themselves. This in turn is likely to influence the way in which an event, accident, or state of affairs is regarded. For instance, an event may be perceived to be the result of negligent or deliberate rule-breaking behaviour if it is at the site of a 'cowboy' organization.

A fourth feature is the degree of stability or instability in the enforcement setting in which the inspector works. Regulatory legislation speaks to particular audiences defined by the conduct subject to regulation. This has implications for the capacity of enforcement agents to know, and therefore negotiate with, those whom they are regulating. A senior official in the Industrial Air Pollution Inspectorate (IAPI, an inspectorate with a very favourable ratio of inspectors to regulated sites) compared the work of his inspectors with those in the Factory Inspectorate, where the ratio was much less favourable:[9]

'They [factory inspectors] find the body on the floor or the man with his hand cut off, or something horrible. You know human life has been damaged or taken. We are not in that game... We are dealing with a relatively small number of works and [an] even smaller number of companies, most of whom we not only have contact with on an individual inspector/works basis, but many of them I meet nationally once a year to review the whole question of air pollution control for their business.'

Much regulatory rule-breaking in occupational health and safety occurs in stable settings, and in entirely predictable ways by virtue of fixed sites and its continuous, repetitive, or episodic character. Similarly, it usually involves a known or potentially knowable violator. Where the occurrence of rule-breaking is unpredictable, or where it is designed to evade discovery and detection, thereby leading to timing and location which are unpredictable, law enforcement has to occur after the event. In these circumstances, while they continue to be concerned with repair and remedy for preventive purposes, inspectors are more preoccupied with responding to the particular violation. Punishment is often regarded as appropriate in such circumstances, since the harm has already been done. Thus the more enforcement is directed towards strangers or a transient population, the more likely it is that sanctioning strategy will be employed.[10] Sanctioning is largely concerned with rule-breaking, where compliance strategy is focused on results.

[9] There is variation in the ratio of inspectors to sites in the work of different HSE inspectorates. For example, whereas the ratio of factory inspectors to regulated premises in the 1980s was 1:747, it was only 1:68 for the then IAPI inspectors (Hutter, 1989: 164). The latter were able to visit premises much more frequently and for longer than factory inspectors, the greater contact giving them a much more detailed knowledge of each workplace, its machinery, processes, and site, as well as its management, workforce, and systems of work. This in turn permitted them to negotiate for compliance to a much greater degree than was possible for factory inspectors, who had to monitor a population of employers and employees largely unknown to them. Where IAPI also policed a population of strangers, however, it too behaved more like FI. Its statistics show a number of prosecutions in the early 1980s for cable-burning offences (where defendants were typically itinerant and not, like others regulated by IAPI, on fixed sites), but very few prosecutions in other circumstances (see also Weait, 1989). There is variation within inspectorates as well: construction inspectors more frequently deal with strangers or transients than those in chemicals work (see, further, Ch. 4).

[10] Continuing relationships are much harder to establish where inspection resources are overstretched by the sheer number of regulated sites. The result is that, for all but the largest firms or those sites with a high proportion of risks, the frequency of visiting by inspectors is very low. Inspectors may also regard it as rational to prosecute where the lack of

Compliance strategy is regularly found, therefore, where a continuing or personal relationship exists between inspector and employer[11] because it is based on and creates the conditions for the growth of trust. Trust is central to the viability of informal law enforcement. As was said in another context, 'There are lower risks involved in dealing with known parties because the transaction is grounded in personal relationships. Recurrent exchanges reaffirm friendship. Trust and reliability are marvellously efficient lubricants to economic transactions' (Powell, 1985: 203). An important ingredient in the stability of the enforcement relationship and the growth of trust is past experience. A stable personal relationship between enforcer and the regulated allows a history of encounters and past performance to assume greater importance in the decisions made. The regulated firm's past will often exist in the personal knowledge of the inspector. Otherwise, the inspector will at least have ready access to an organizational record.

4. TOWARDS A THEORY OF LEGAL DECISION-MAKING

Although decision-making is frequently explained by reference to 'criteria' or 'factors' said to have been taken into account in making a particular choice, this book is based on a wider conception that decisions can only be understood by reference to their broad environment and particular context: their surround, fields, and frames (Hawkins & Manning, forthcoming). Decisions about regulatory prosecution are made in a rich and complex environment, which acts as the setting for the play of shifting currents of broad political and economic values and forces and in which untoward events occur. To understand the nature of decision-making fully, some connection needs to be forged between these forces in the decision-making environment, and the processes that individuals

enforcement resources leads to very low frequencies of inspection. This is especially the case where there are no continuing personal relationships that inspectors may wish to protect in the long term, which might make prosecution seem inappropriate. This was the strategy in the Agricultural Inspectorate in the 1980s, where large numbers of regulated sites, involving in many cases inherently risky activity, had to be inspected by a relatively small number of inspectors. The inspectorate believed that it was rational to engage in prosecution quite regularly, in the hope thereby of generating some deterrent effect.

[11] This has in fact long been the case. Bartrip's work (1987: 40–1) suggests that the small and relatively concentrated location of employers in the white lead trade in the 19th century made it possible for continuing relationships to be developed by the factory inspectorate. He argues that the absence of prosecution in the lead trades in the late 19th century was evidence of the existence of a strategy of compliance made possible by good working relationships.

engage in when deciding about a particular matter. The concepts of surround, field, and frame enable this connection to be made. Thus, for example, the surround of a political climate of regulation characterized crudely as pro-business, as favouring less regulation or greater emphasis upon self-regulation, helps to shape the particular field in which enforcement policies are formulated and decisions taken in particular cases by the application of the decision frames thereby deemed appropriate. Decisions about legal standards and their enforcement, like other legal decisions, are made, then, in a much broader setting (their 'surround') and within a context, or 'field', defined by the legal and organizational mandate. Decision 'frames', the interpretive and classificatory devices operating in particular instances, are influenced by both surround and field.

The term 'factor' is usually treated as an item of information used in reaching a decision. This is treated in positivistic research as important since it is assumed that a factor helps determine outcome. What is more important, however, is what that piece of information means to the person making the decision and what its relevance is to the decision made. Meanings themselves can shift as factors are framed differently. The key concept in understanding what is going on, therefore, is not the factor, but the frame. Framing is a means by which factors are selected and their meaning in decision-making organized. For example, if a special enforcement campaign is mounted in an effort to reduce the prevalence of a particular kind of rule-breaking, the way in which the inspector defines and views an instance of that activity and what it means will be affected by the existence of the special campaign.

1. Surround

The surround is the broad setting in which regulatory (or other) decision-making activity takes place. The importance of the surround is that it is the site for those unexpected and untoward events which regulatory agencies have been created to cope with, the problems of individual accidents or ill health in the workplace, or those less routine and frequent but egregious events that prompt public and political concern. Both workers and members of the public may be victims. The surround serves as an environment not only for individual decision-making, but also for the activities of the legal bureaucracies in which such decision-making takes place, for they, like other legal organizations, are actors in social, political, and economic space.

The surround is not, however, unchanging. Political and economic forces may shift, and in these circumstances the social surround of the organization changes. The altered condition now replaces the earlier surround, becoming part of a new organizational and decision-making environment for legal officials. However, it is important to bear in mind Peter Manning's (1992) observation that an event in the social surround is analytically distinct from the organizational response to that event. The event takes its meaning from the enactment process by which the organization responds to the interpreted environment (Weick, 1979). Changes that occur in the surround prompt changes in the particular setting for a decision, the field. Equally, a change in the surround may cause a change in the way certain events are interpreted and classified, the frame. The media are central to the transmission and interpretation of such events.

The position of HSE could be characterized as one of extreme vulnerability to various newsworthy disasters involving loss of life or extreme injury to people, whether employees or members of the public. Indeed, there were in the 1980s a number of major events that shook confidence in public safety, and caused great political concern: the fire at Bradford City Football Club (1985), the capsize of the *Herald of Free Enterprise* (1987), the fire at King's Cross underground station (1987), the explosion and fire at the *Piper Alpha* oil rig (1988), the railway accident at Clapham Junction (1988), the Hillsborough Stadium deaths (1989), and the sinking of the *Marchioness* pleasure boat (1989). In the more recent past there have been the train crashes at Southall, Ladbroke Grove, and Hatfield. The surround is unbounded, however, and regulatory agencies are not immune to events occurring beyond national boundaries. Major disasters involving occupational health and safety in other countries, such as those at Seveso, Chernobyl, or Bhopal, also enter the public and political consciousness easily, thereby creating expectations and imposing demands on the regulatory organization (see Manning, 1992), as well as those regulated. The disaster at Bhopal, for example, is said to have greatly affected chemical companies in the United Kingdom.

The decision-making surround is not open to control by the regulatory bureaucracy. All it can do is to react to events and problems as they pop up, or respond to gradual shifts in the surround that become apprehended differently. Law enforcement may adapt in two ways. There may be changes in enforcement policy which are then conveyed out from the centre of the regulatory organization to the periphery for action by inspectors. Equally, a change in the surround can prompt an immediate change in practice, as individual inspectors modify their own decision-making in light of what they perceive to be changed expectations among their interested publics.

2. Field

Within the social surround is the decision field. This term describes a defined setting in which decisions are made. 'A decision field is the social basis for labeling a situation of deciding: the seen-as-relevant-at-the-moment assemblage of facts and meanings within which a decision is located' (Manning, 1992: 261). While events in the surround are not open to control by the organization, the field, in contrast, is something defined by and acted on by the organization. The field for prosecution decisions is shaped by the decision-maker's legal and organizational mandate, and is defined by a variety of features. The law itself determines the contours and reach of the field of a legal bureaucracy like a regulatory agency, by awarding it a mandate. The field contains sets of ideas about how its ends are to be pursued. These may exist at a formal level in the form of policies, expectations, and the like about the organization's mandate and how it should be attained. But they also exist in an informal way in the expectations, notions, and aims held by staff at all levels in the organization. Organizational hierarchy is important here, as the conception of the decision field may well vary according to the nature of the job done, the level of seniority of the staff involved, and so on. For practical purposes legal and organizational aspects of the mandate come together to be defined by the decision-maker in occupational terms. For the HSE inspector, in particular, the decision field is delimited by mandated conceptions and routines connected with the task of monitoring the relevant environment of workplaces to assess risks and untoward events threatening the well-being of employees and members of the public. Fields constitute both the 'background' and 'foreground' for decision-making activity, with foreground matters being seen against a background of assumptions in the field. For instance, inspectors have routine conceptions of 'risks', 'accidents', 'problems', and so on, which assist them in making sense of the difficulties that come to light.

The contents of the field are, like those of the surround, not immutable but open to change. The decision field remains relatively stable in organizations, however, anchored by the fixed occupational roles and tasks sanctioned by the legal bureaucracy, and the routine ways in which people make sense of what they encounter (Manning, 1992), though the field varies according to organizational location (what risk means to regulators also varies at different points in the organization). Change within the organization to enable it to adapt to its shifting realities tends to come about slowly. This is partly a result of a lack of resources, partly a consequence of its being comprised of expert, professional people who need to be persuaded of the benefits of organizational change, and partly because there is only limited scope for the organization to adapt to pressures for change since so much of its work is reactively initiated, in which it must respond to events and public expectations of immediate action.

Salient features shape the content of the decision field and, in turn, framing behaviour. For example, the extent to which prosecution is actually used is, of course, a function of the resources available to inspectors' organizations, and inspectors are keenly aware that they have very limited personal resources in handling any particular problem. The more frequently they visit workplaces, the more opportunity there is for the development of a field of stable personal relationships. The perceived character and responsiveness of industry to regulation is another element in an inspector's field (the variety of employer encountered is enormous). A further feature in the field shaping the readiness to think about prosecution is the frequency with which inspectors encounter difficult problems and the nature of the risks they encounter. Inspectors have different levels of expectation, depending on the number and type of the hazards they face. The frequency with which inspectors encounter hazards can mean that prosecution becomes a more familiar enforcement response. Stability of relationships which arises from inspectors having worked for long periods in an area without moving elsewhere encourages complaints to be reported. However, for many inspectors relationships with many regulated firms may be non-existent, or at least marked with considerable instability which 'can be a problem in two ways', according to an inspector (86–40). 'One is if they keep changing the management [thereby hindering the progress towards compliance]. And the other is if we inspectors keep getting moved from group to group or area to area or from just one patch to another. If you've built up relationships, it's finished.' This can also pose a problem of adaptation and adjustment for firms since inspectors work in different ways and may impose different demands.

3. Frame

The conception of the decision frame is central to a naturalistic perspective on decision-making, since framing is the means by which the everyday world is linked with the legal world. Its properties therefore deserve somewhat more extended discussion.[12]

The decision frame exists within a field. If a decision field describes the legally and organizationally defined setting in which decision-makers work, the frame speaks to the interpretive behaviour involved in the decision-making about a specific matter. The frame describes how features in a particular problem or case are understood, placed, and accorded relevance (see further, Sanders & Young, 2000: 75).

Social surround, decision field, and decision frame are in mutual interaction. Surround and field influence which frames move from background to foreground and vice versa. Field affects frame, as when people recognize that background factors in decision-making, in the words of a chief inspector, 'condition their judgment', or otherwise shape the way that a particular event or problem is regarded. Similarly, features in the surround, such as the general state of the economy, may intrude into the frame used by inspectors in an individual case, as where it seems important that they have some sense of the worth of a company, since this may 'explain' a firm's non-compliance.[13]

A frame is a structure of knowledge, experience, values, and meanings that decision-makers employ in deciding. It addresses the question 'What is going on here?' (Goffman, 1974). Framing involves a variety of processes. Human beings always seek to impose meaning and order upon events they experience and it is the frame that provides the rules and principles that guide that understanding of what events experienced mean. A frame can be seen as a set of rules for guiding the performance of a task, or a set of ways of organizing the ascription of meaning to events, and the other raw material in the field deemed relevant. There can be framing by means of interpretation (making sense of what is presented), classification (what kind of a case is this?), or task, which is organizationally determined in settings of greater decision-making heterogeneity.

[12] Though I do not propose to go into the level of detail presented in Peter Manning's (1992) excellent analysis, or in Manning and Hawkins (1990), on both of which I have relied extensively. Frame analysis is elaborated at length in Goffman (1974).

[13] It is for this reason that prosecution files sometimes report operating profit, turnover, and other financial statistics of a company facing prosecution.

In practical terms, frames organize the content and meaning of cases, the conventional units by which the legal system knows its raw material, and which reduce unique human experience to ritualized formal accounts amenable to the application of legal and organizational understanding and handling. The frame is rather like a code that not only shapes the nature of the response, but also informs and even confirms it. The existence of a frame, however, does not in itself isolate the particular facts needed to make a decision. A frame must be applied to an event and its 'facts' selectively retrieved and organized by the application of the frame. Facts and frame are reflexive: facts narrow the potential frame while the frame provisionally applied may cause some facts to be discarded or disabled, others to be introduced, and yet others to be reinterpreted. Put another way, frames are reflexive in the sense that they both constitute 'reality' and selectively identify the facts that sustain a social reality.[14]

Frames are shaped by a variety of features: image and belief, views about good and bad, right and wrong, and so on. They instruct a decision-maker how to understand a case, a problem, or a person. Frames are influenced in part by occupational and professional ideology, varying according to the view of the world held by the decision-maker as a result of his or her professional training and socialization: psychiatrists may frame matters in terms of 'mental health'; judges may frame matters in terms of what is 'legal'. Another shaping feature can be the type of decision subject (for example, legal decision-makers do not generally regard adults in the same way as they do children). Frame can be influenced by status or office: frames coexist among field and principal inspectors (PIs), as well as their seniors, but are not so much identical as overlapping. The way in which an inspector makes sense of a problem might not necessarily coincide with the way a more senior official might. Conceptions of purpose also frame matters. The exercise of gathering, reporting, and assessing facts is itself a form of framing operation in which the frame determines what information is sought, seen as relevant and significant, and what that information conveys. The personal disposition of the decision-maker can also lead to the adoption of distinctive frames. 'Prosecution-mindedness' is a term some inspectors employ to describe the character of a particular decision frame which suggests a personal proclivity to prosecute. 'Prosecution comes naturally to some

[14] One example is in Grady's (2002) work on the way in which the police assumptions that victims of domestic violence are women feeds into the construction of statistics that reinforce that very assumption.

people,' said an experienced inspector. 'Some people find it very difficult. Some people enjoy taking cases. Some don't' (86–11). Differences in framing of this sort may well result in differences in decision outcome.

Framing in occupational health and safety regulation involves inspectors making sense of signals they receive from the surround and field. In HSE work the seriousness of the event and the seriousness of the risk of harm are two consistent features in the first stage of framing in the prosecution decision. How these are framed, however, may shift according to the field and surround in which the decision is to be made. These matters can later shed their relevance when the legal frame is applied, and a frame is authoritatively imposed. In their place come legal standards of proof and legal tests of relevance (see Chapter 12). In effect, the frames derived from the organizational mandate and personal conceptions of blame and desert are later overlaid with the legal frame to see if the problem being handled can satisfy values associated with success in formal legal proceedings—such matters as evidential sufficiency and relevance, persuasiveness, and so on. If it can, the matter is transformed from being a potential legal case into a prosecution case. If prosecution is a possibility, the legal frame has to be superimposed on the case (see Chapter 12). The prosecution case now becomes an assemblage of materials interpreting an event or a series of events in adversarial ways, and, in particular, in ways pointing to the legal guilt of the alleged rule-breaker. Moral guilt is usually an essential condition to transform a matter into a prosecution case (see Chapter 11). Notions of moral and legal blame may be both stated and implied.[15] Different framing behaviour exists at different organizational levels thanks to the complexity of organizations. Framing is therefore a layered phenomenon. Not all frames have equal capacity to coerce or change behaviour or meanings; the nature of legal authority is to impose consequential outcomes, the judgment of a court being the ultimate authoritative imposition of the legal frame.

The frame provides a guide to outcome and prompts decision and action rendered appropriate by it. For example, a frame provides an understanding of the cause of events and the motivation of human

[15] Establishing the moral guilt of a rule-breaker is unnecessary in a legal system employing strict liability, but in the files of potential prosecution cases it is used extensively by inspectors as a persuasive device (see Ch. 11). This practice is important because frames can be contentious and open to disagreement. This is particularly the case where the matter is mutually recognized as a legal one, for in the Anglo-American common law conflict is institutionalized.

behaviour. This, in turn, moulds the approach to enforcement adopted by inspectors, shaping for instance, the degree to which they see their job as a matter of negotiating for compliance rather than sanctioning to punish wrongdoing.

Frames are keyed, that is, they are indicated by cues or signs such as a word, act, or event. How such cues or signs are recognized and what they mean depends on the frame employed. What the particular frame is to be can be negotiable. For example, in a bargaining relationship there may be negotiations early on about the key and the frame that are to be adopted to govern the transaction or to mark out the territory on which matters are to be conducted. When keyed, however, the frame is provisional and what is keyed may be rekeyed or transformed so that a new frame is brought into play. Frames are always contingent, and there is always room for negotiation and redefinition within a frame. Once something is keyed, it can be transformed or rekeyed, and new meaning will appear. This occurs when a field is penetrated by events occurring in the social surround, leading to a questioning of the established relationship between a key and a frame. For instance, an apparent failure by an employer to maintain the safety of equipment, despite warnings by an inspector, may key a 'negligent employer' frame for that inspector when an accident occurs. The adoption of this frame, thus keyed, may culminate in a decision to prosecute. Similarly, a matter framed as 'non-serious' (and therefore set on a course for informal enforcement) may be rekeyed as 'serious' by a subsequent word, action, or event, such as a second accident on the premises.

In legal decision-making in general, one of the most important forms of rekeying occurs when a dispute, conflict, risk, or accident is redefined not as a matter to be resolved informally by the relevant parties, but, in the eyes of some participants, as a matter for the formalities of the courtroom (Mayhew & Reiss, 1969). This sort of rekeying has fundamental implications for the meaning of the outcome of the dispute, for a change in meaning means a change in locus, scope, and consequences, and quite possibly the degree of formality used to produce a decision. A change in the frame may lead to the reinterpretation of existing facts or the selection of different facts. This process may or may not prompt a different outcome, for when frames change, outcomes do not necessarily change. A change in frame provides, rather, an occasion for the development of a new basis for defining new material as relevant (and discarding other, previously relevant, material) as well as a new basis for interpreting the decision to make the outcome rational. Though frames may change, they do vary in the extent to which they are resistant to disruption that threatens the definition of the situation they have in part created. Certain frames can be said to be more resistant to negotiation or change than others. An event or matter framed by an inspector as 'a bad case' is resistant to reframing, and much less likely to be reframed by the PI whose task is to approve the recommendation for prosecution.

Framing is not only an interpretive act, a way of making sense for decision-making purposes; it is also a classificatory act, prompting particular forms of action. What information suppliers choose to present for decision, and how they choose to present it—what they focus on, emphasize, or omit, for example—frames reality for the ultimate decision-makers. Frames penetrate records, and given their durability, spread their effects across time, different hands, and even jurisdiction. This attribute of framing is especially important in organizations, where there is extensive reliance on the paper record, with its accounts, evaluations, and proposals. Within organizations, information suppliers such as inspectors are the important actors because they are at the heart of those decision-making processes that frame in certain facts potentially bearing on the composition of a case to be decided about, or frame out those other materials deemed irrelevant or otherwise unnecessary. Such processual framing is a powerful screening or persuasive device.

Differences in framing occur in a serial decision-making system, as information and evaluation move through an organization or between organizations. Changes may occur as a case moves to different parts of the organization. A matter framed in one way at the point where it crosses the organizational threshold and becomes a 'case', may be framed in a contrasting way by decision-makers who act later in the system. At different points in the process, different frames will be dominant, including one that characterizes the reason for the legal organization to take action, and another shaping the decision to seek prosecution. In each of these contexts, a frame is used, often retrospectively, to define the meaning of the events and to link facts and actions to outcomes and consequences. These changes occur as a result of movement of the case towards the application of the legal frame. The higher the level of decision-making in an organization, the more conscious of wider audiences and the outside world decision-makers become. This can create a tension because there is a sense in which they are receivers of already well-formed views on a particular matter and may become, rather than decision-makers, ratifiers of decisions made at lower levels by those less sensitive to the organization's environment. Frames may be used by people who are not necessarily aware of the differences in the perspectives by which they are assembling and interpreting the facts.[16] This means that outcomes will not necessarily indicate the degree to which different decision-makers are using complementary frames, since competing frames may result in similar outcomes.

Organizations frame events, as well as individuals. Or more precisely, organizationally located decision-makers frame events in organizationally intelligible ways. A frame in use in an organization, such as an 'avoidable accident' (as might be employed in an HSE field office), indicates that organizational actors have assembled the distinctive cues that key that frame. Organizations create bounded concerns within their mandates. In HSE regulation events called 'accidents' occur initially in the surround and produce a routine organizational response which, if an 'accident', will be a reactively initiated event. In contrast, a 'problem' will be a proactively initiated matter, discovered in the course of proactive monitoring. While framing in organizations creates patterns, it does not necessarily determine what information is sought, or seen as relevant and significant, and what such information conveys for organizational action.

Frames, then, control and organize the raw material for decision. They include facts, omit or discard them, or change their meaning. Extant facts can be framed in or out over the career of a case in a serial legal decision-making process. The field inspector's frame is likely to be contested by the rule-breaker in informal negotiations that precede a possible prosecution. Legal frames that define facts as legally relevant and have potential for authoritative consequences can overlap with organizational frames. Legal framing involves assembling the legally relevant facts and applying them; the frame constructs and selectively integrates knowledge and justifies its presence. The process creates a context for framing by others, shaping the way in which it is presented to colleagues for decision. This is the process of 'case construction' (Sanders, 1987; Sanders & Young, 2000), a process which determines the assembly of material that is selected and defined as relevant from the diversity of matter in the social world. Such a frame may be used, for example, by an inspector in assembling and organizing a prosecution case file, using the elements thought to be required to persuade the PI that this is 'a prosecution case'. There is often a tension in legal bureaucracies between organizational practices and the 'shadow' of the anticipated

[16] Frames vary in their clarity and the degree to which they complement or are consistent with other frames. The clarity of a frame refers to the extent to which it produces valid and reliable results when repeatedly applied.

legal frame. Organizational frames may be shaped by organizational decision-makers anticipating legal moves, just as legal frames may in some cases be shaped by organizationally dominant frames.

Within the legal institution, frames vary in number, kind, and salience. The salience of a frame has to do simply with the extent to which it is recognized and talked about as a feature of the field. In regulatory matters, inspectors may use salient interpretive frames in reaching conclusions about the moral character of an organization (see Chapter 11). Theories of corporate compliance and non-compliance form two important and salient frames that operate within regulatory bureaucracies (see Chapter 8). The workplace alleged to be in violation of the law will be considered in light of the severity of the rule-breaking (the damage, actual or potential, presented by the rule-breaking), the site's known past record of responsiveness or unresponsiveness to advice, and its compliance (or otherwise) with enforcement efforts. The result will be a 'compliant' or 'non-compliant employer' frame used in deciding about prosecution. Once settled upon, the frame then provides a clear way of thinking further about the event.

There are various types and hierarchies of frame. A master frame in legal terms is that which defines a matter as 'legal' in the first instance. Rule of law ideas, for instance, constitute a master frame that guides and instructs legal actors as to how conduct is to be understood (as subject, for instance, to due process values and assumptions: Packer, 1969). Frames may demand translating activity by legal actors to achieve a fit with the master frame in operation. For example, a prosecution action involves the application of the master legal frame and here an important task for the inspector is to translate the existing raw material of the case, including existing frames (which may be suspended for the time being), into a frame intelligible by the law (how this process works is the subject of Chapter 12). When the prosecution is approved and the inspector or lawyer prepares the case for prosecution, the process of reframing the matter in legally intelligible terms continues. It has already begun because a key concern of a supervising inspector in deciding whether or not to approve a prosecution case is how well the problem can be made to fit the legal frame. Inspectors therefore typically set—and are required to set—parts of their reports and recommendations within the legal frame. In this way, a supervisor is able to judge the strength—the legal strength—of the prosecution case (see Chapter 3).

Legal reframing involves aligning the facts of the case with existing legally meaningful principles or rules. This exercise uses legal facts to frame other legal facts, and to compare these arguments with previous legal authorities or arguments of similar sort. Some facts, and certainly the way in which the facts are to be understood, are normally contested in encounters governed by the law, almost by definition. In a contested trial in an adversarial system, the inspector's (the prosecution's) frame will be tested against a competing frame formally presented by the defendant to the court, which seeks to offer an alternative and much more benign set of meanings of the critical event or breach and is intended to exculpate the defendant. Thus, frames adopted by contesting lawyers may differ, and the interpretive frames employed may reframe some of the facts thereby excluding them from consideration. A lawyer for an employer will use alternative interpretations garnered from other sources (and probably some of the same sources, in some cases), and alternative interpretations of the same facts in an effort to persuade the court to come to a quite different conclusion from the prosecution's case (preferably a not guilty finding, or, failing that, at least a substantially reduced sentence). So much is inevitable in an adversarial legal system, for the adversarial structure of the Anglo-American common law encourages a contest between highly contrasting frames.

3 Pre-Trial Processes

1. DISORDERLY PATTERNS

The decision to prosecute is a screening decision (Hawkins & Manning, forthcoming). It is a decision about whether a particular organization or person, and whether a particular act or state of affairs can be—should be—characterized as criminal and gain access to the formal criminal justice process. Various pre-trial processes are set in motion when the staff of a regulatory agency decide that prosecution may be the appropriate way to respond to a breach of the law. The decision to prosecute is most helpfully seen as a culmination of a series of determinations made about the fate of a case in a decision-making system that is primarily (but not exclusively) serial in character, since the decision in a particular case is an outcome comprised of a prior series of often complex ancillary decisions. The sequence of enforcement decisions usually begins with the inspector, though the process is occasionally set in motion by a complainant. How extended and complex the series of decisions is depends on the structure of decision-making authority and the procedures employed to resolve the matter.

Pre-trial processes shape the outcomes of the decision about whether and how to prosecute, and can contribute substantially to the precise outcome of the prosecution in court. Legal issues pervade the decision-making, and become dominant when the legal frame is applied (Chapter 12). A provisional decision to prosecute may be taken early on in the process, and may serve to precipitate other decisions which need to be made before a final decision about legal action. In exploring the character of these processes, I shall focus on the activities of field inspectors in HSE's Field Operations Directorate (FOD), rather than those staff who work in other HSE inspectorates and employ different decision-making procedures.[1] I use material from prosecution files from FOD, collected in 1997–8, as the chief source of data, with some material from interviews with area directors (ADs) and principal inspectors (PIs)

[1] The same sorts of issues and processes are likely to be found in other inspectorates (if in more attenuated form).

added for illustrative purposes. This analysis will inevitably raise a number of issues that need to be explored in more detail later, particularly in Chapter 12, which returns to the pre-trial decision-making site as a way of illustrating the application of the legal frame.

While the key pre-trial decision is whether or not to prosecute, this question is less the focus of this chapter than the processes surrounding crucial supporting decisions that have to be made in the course of deciding about prosecution itself. They include what charge or charges to prosecute with (there is usually a variety of potential charges), how many informations to lay, whether or not to target an individual as defendant rather than, or in addition to, a corporate entity, and the choice of forum: whether to prosecute the matter in the magistrates' or the Crown Court. Once the decision to prosecute has provisionally been made, the occasion for pre-trial bargaining with the defendant frequently arises.

The first decision for an inspector is whether to treat a problem as a potential prosecution. This question is not something that can be considered by HSE staff in the abstract; it can only be considered in conjunction with a number of subsidiary, but nonetheless very important, matters which all have a bearing on the decision about the prosecution in principle. These pre-trial decisions do not take place in a clear and orderly sequence, for reality is messier than that. The issues need to be analysed separately, but to do so is to suggest a spurious orderliness in the process. Furthermore, organizational processes and the rough sequence of decisions impose various patterns on pre-trial practices, but the contingencies and disturbances that often occur lead to the irony of disorderly patterns of decision-making.

A decision to prosecute in principle for instrumental or expressive reasons may still founder when the legal frame begins to be applied (see Chapter 12). When calculations are made about the prospects of winning the case,[2] questions are asked about the strength of the evidence, especially the quality of possible witnesses, or the reaction of the defendant to the violation or the prospect of prosecution. However, once it has been determined in principle to prosecute a case, the character and extent of the prosecution have to be clarified because in most cases it is by no means obvious that a particular violation or series of violations commands a self-evident response.

[2] Weaver (1977: 81) says that most of the cases in the US anti-trust division are rejected because the case cannot possibly be won. But she goes on to note that some of the most interesting decisions that lawyers make occur when they decide not to prosecute even though the case might be won.

Enforcement work in regulation is a matter of continually adaptive decision-making about the appropriate tactics regulators should employ when faced with violations. Prosecution is merely one of these decisions. Not only is it a rather rare one, it is also special in the sense that it is not simply something to be sorted out on the spot, like most regulatory enforcement work in the field. A decision has to be made immediately that a matter is potentially a prosecution, however, so that evidence may be collected. But that is merely the initiation of the process. As matters are taken further and other officials are involved, these off-the-cuff, immediate responses tend to give way to more reflective and considered decisions, usually made in the office, sometimes following discussion with colleagues. Pre-trial prosecution processes are therefore comprised of a mixture of impromptu and studied decision-making. Clearly, the balance between the considered and the extempore varies according to the stage in the sequence of decisions the process has reached. The impression often conveyed by inspectors is that initial decisions about whether or not to proceed with a matter as a potential prosecution are swift and virtually spontaneous. The different surrounds and fields that inspectors occupy may present some of them with more occasions to discover violations and more opportunity to treat prosecution as a viable course of action (see Chapter 4). Some may have ample time to decide whether to take action, others very little. For example, an inspector dealing with an accident on a construction site may well have to decide on the spot whether prosecution is an appropriate course of action so as to collect evidence that might otherwise be lost. In a case of possible occupational ill health, by contrast, an inspector may be overtaken by all sorts of doubt about whether prosecution is the right approach, particularly in view of the legal difficulties such cases frequently encounter.

A decision to prosecute at the pre-trial stage is always provisional. The contingent character of the decision-making adds to the apparent complexity of the process. Inspectors may sometimes conclude that an act, event, or practice clearly warrants a prosecution (what some of them think of as a 'cut-and-dried' case). This does not mean, however, that the matter will actually culminate in a prosecution in court. Inspectors, as a practical matter, must start from the position that a prosecution will follow, if only because they will have to collect evidence that may otherwise be lost. The initial decision may subsequently be modified, and in some cases take a different course, or be abandoned, in light of developing features in the case and its handling which lead to a reframing of some of the issues. Yet when inspectors make a preliminary decision that a matter is prosecutable, they are aware that for a number of reasons the case may well founder later. First, when a prosecutable matter comes to light, inspectors know that they will have to share their discretion with colleagues who might take a different view about the merits of the case. Second, as the matter is given further reflection, and as more evidence emerges, the case for the prosecution may, in the inspector's view, become less compelling. In particular, the demands of the legal system itself for its own standards of proof may lead to a decision to handle the matter in a way that avoids the risk of failing to convict (see Chapter 12). Third, decisions about prosecution are, of course, subject to negotiation not simply among staff within the agency, but between the agency and the potential defendant and his or her legal advisers. The result is that inspectors can never start from the position that a matter is clearly and categorically one that will be prosecuted.

2. THE VISIBLE PROCESS: INSPECTOR AS LEADING ACTOR

The structural position of field inspectors in the organization makes them central figures in pre-trial decision-making. They have a high degree of autonomy: they control to a substantial extent which violations are attended to, which rule-breakers are drawn into the formal system of law enforcement, and how matters are to be handled. The high level of autonomy is found whether inspectors, like those in construction work, operate in an environment in which rule-breaking is normal, familiar, even expected behaviour, or whether it is something less frequently encountered, as is the case, for instance, with inspectors of chemicals plants (see Chapter 4). The field inspector is the official in closest contact with the real world of occupational health and safety problems, and therefore the person who decides in the first place whether a problem needs remedying or whether it might be ignored. An initial screening decision to take some sort of enforcement action in which the matter gains access to the enforcement process (whatever that might consist of) exerts in turn great influence over the outcomes of later decisions. The inspectors' role confers on them decision-making power in the organization as possessors of the most extensive knowledge of precipitating acts or events, and the key participants.[3] The inspector also enjoys special power

[3] Much of the inspector's background knowledge of the case arises from routine inspection, which is crucial to bringing potentially prosecutable cases to light where accidents are not involved, since this informs the inspector of the character of the workplace, its

as the controller of description and evaluation, on which the initial recommendation to the principal inspector is based.

Where the routine enforcement of regulation is concerned, decisions tend to have a private and bargained character, and to be aimed in general at repairing a problem by securing the compliance of regulated firms. In these circumstances, the thought of prosecution is not something that inspectors immediately entertain, unless the problem has an egregious character—a death or serious injury, or a newsworthy event. Where the problem lacks egregiousness, inspectors generally work their way more cautiously towards a decision to treat a matter as a potential prosecution. However, they have to act quickly since evidence decays, so they need a clear idea about their enforcement strategy early on. When inspectors have begun thinking seriously about prosecution, and have begun to engage in the preparatory work of collecting evidence, they almost always have a very good reason for doing so. As one of them said, 'You don't go into a case until in your own mind you're pretty certain it's worthwhile' (86–26).

The processes of prosecution begin to be shaped from the moment inspectors reach a provisional decision to prosecute in principle since it means that the matter is taken up by the organization as something to be given formal consideration. Inspectors' initial disposition to prosecute and their collection of evidence culminate in their production of prosecution process papers which typically describe the breach or event, list relevant witnesses, and present an argument as to why the case should be prosecuted. The papers also rehearse all possible charges that might be brought (if only to defeat some or all of them later), and seek to anticipate the defences that may be raised by the potential defendant. An inspector works towards the decision to prosecute as he or she discusses the matter with the supervising officer, the PI, and sometimes more senior staff. Later, as the sequence of decisions moves on, and the matter increasingly takes on the appearance of a legal case, an inspector may be involved in debate with lawyers, and in negotiations with the potential defendant. These processes are themselves shaped by and take place in the inspector's decision field, which serves as a context for the play of matters such as the regulatory culture of the inspectorate, the legal framework and ideological environment within which it operates, as well as the broader political and economic forces at work in the surround of the inspector and the agency.

management, and workforce, important resources in the framing process. Investigation following an accident is also an important source of such information.

3. PRE-TRIAL DECISION-MAKING STRUCTURES

More control over the ultimate outcome seems to be exerted by inspectors in the decision whether to prosecute in principle than over the question of how to prosecute, on which the prosecution files reveal more disagreement. This is probably because inspectors, given the demands on their time and the number of violations they routinely encounter, only bring in matters that conform to some organizationally sanctioned idea of a clearly prosecutable case. There is much more scope for a difference of view over the choice and number of charges, however, and the amount of debate evident in the case files is an indicator of the extent of theoretically prosecutable rule-breaking with which inspectors are regularly confronted.

1. Centralized Decision-Making

Decisions about prosecution in occupational health and safety regulation are made in both centralized and decentralized organizational structures within HSE. How crucial the field inspector's role is, however, depends on the organizational structure employed in making prosecution decisions: the way in which a regulatory body organizes itself to produce decisions about prosecution is significant for the numbers and types of case that are selected for the courts.

Centralized decision-making is found in those smaller HSE inspectorates which, compared with FOD, do not make relatively frequent use of prosecution.[4] Decisions about prosecution in these inspectorates consist of a series of recommendations to prosecute routinely referred upwards for final decision from the inspector to senior officials, often including the chief inspector. This makes for an extended referral system in which a matter deemed potentially prosecutable is handed on from the screening official through several pairs of hands until the matter is finally resolved.[5] If it is decided to prosecute a matter, solicitor agents are then instructed to conduct the prosecution on behalf of HSE.

[4] In the 1980s the Mines and Quarries (MQI) and Industrial Air Pollution Inspectorates were examples of organizations making prosecution decisions in a centralized way. The Nuclear Installations Inspectorate (NII) simply did not think in terms of prosecution when its inspectors encountered violations because it had power to suspend or withhold a licence to operate a nuclear power plant. In view of the potential financial cost to the generating company this seemed to NII to be a much weightier threat or sanction than prosecution.

[5] Data relating to such centralized decision-making were collected only in Phase I of the fieldwork.

Those inspectorates that instructed solicitor agents to prosecute their cases preferred, perhaps not surprisingly, to maintain this practice in the belief that there were disadvantages in having field inspectors actually appear in court, as is the practice in FOD. A former Chief Inspector of Mines and Quarries, for example, felt that to have his inspectors prosecute in person, rather than instructing a lawyer to do the work, would demean their status in being seen to have to do the job themselves. Much of the mines and quarries inspector's authority in negotiating for compliance was thought to be derived from his standing in local mining communities as a familiar and respected figure. Not prosecuting in person, the former Chief Inspector said, 'puts us that bit above, and that's where people like to see us'.

2. Decentralized Decision-Making: Inspectors as Advocates (or Not)

The decentralized form of decision-making employed in the 1980s and before in the factory inspectorate has now been adopted for inspectors in FOD. A variety of staff may take part in pre-trial decision-making in FOD, including the field inspector, the PI, sometimes the AD, specialist inspectors, and very occasionally an HSE solicitor or a barrister. In routine cases, however, the matter normally only involves the inspector and his or her immediate superior, the PI. Between them they make the decision whether or not to prosecute, together with the supporting decisions about charge, forum, and defendant. Unless the case is being proposed by the PI, it is only the exceptional matter, by virtue of its legal difficulty or its actual or potential notoriety, that may attract the attention of the AD or headquarters officials.[6] Control from the centre is less direct in this form of organization.[7]

The effective power of field inspectors in the decentralized organization of FOD is even greater than their counterparts in the smaller inspectorates. The decentralized character of the organization grants these inspectors wide control because it is they who initially determine that a matter may be prosecutable, and make the initial proposal to prosecute in routine cases, subject only to approval by their PI. While a decentralized structure gives scope to field and principal inspectors to deal with problems short of using the formal legal system, this is true even

[6] The detailed analysis in this chapter, and all data collected in 1997–8, in Phase II of the fieldwork, involve decision-making by inspectors working in this decentralized structure.

[7] In Scotland prosecution is the responsibility of the Procurator Fiscal; see Jamieson (1985).

in a centralized organization: 'I've no idea how many cases are actually discussed [by the field inspector and his superior] and don't go any further,' said a former Chief Inspector of Agriculture.

'There must be a large number, but I just wouldn't know. In the nature of things, we really only hear about the [prosecutions] that take place.... [Y]ou rely very much on the training and expertise of the inspectors, and whether you've brought them along right to recognize situations where perhaps they should be doing enforcement before anything else.... I'm not sure you can dictate centrally about large numbers of prosecutions.'

An important source of control over the case for FOD inspectors is the fact that, in contrast with many other law enforcement officials, they are intimately involved in the preparation and prosecution of their cases in the magistrates' courts. While prosecutions in the smaller centralized inspectorates are conducted by solicitor agents instructed by HSE, inspectors in FOD employ the practice of earlier factory inspectors in routine cases and act as advocates in court, personally conducting proceedings against the defendant.[8]

There are some exceptions to this general rule, however. In cases where the inspector who was investigating, and who would normally prosecute, is likely to be called as a witness, HSE uses an agency solicitor. In some cases, pressures on inspectors' time may be a reason for instructing a solicitor agent. One of the prosecution files, for instance, contained a letter in which a PI explained to her AD that 'The prime reason for handing this case over [to an outside solicitor] was that... it came at a time when the pressure was on to generate visit numbers [i.e. increase inspections] and [the former AD] agreed we should not undertake the case ourselves' (P97–38). The burden on resources remains a potent reason. It was said by another AD that the use of solicitor agents was

'becoming more routine, generally because we have been under pressure to deliver other outputs such as more inspections. And it's partly a time saving measure, particularly when cases are likely to be defended or, you know, particularly difficult with legal arguments... [Inspectors taking their own cases] is now generally regarded as an across-the-board policy in our part of HSE. But, on the other hand, we've all been having these sort of extra pressures to deliver other

[8] The formal position is that the power to prosecute is restricted to duly authorized inspectors and the Director of Public Prosecutions (DPP). Others can only institute proceedings with the consent of the DPP. HSE inspectors may therefore conduct proceedings in a magistrates' court, even though they may have no legal qualifications (F. B. Wright, 1995: 105).

aspects of the work programme so there has been more of a tendency to bring in solicitor agents.' (97–02)

Other circumstances in which an inspector would not conduct proceedings were pointed out by another AD:

'We have changed [the] culture [so] that new inspectors into agriculture have to do their own prosecutions. But we've still got the fifty-five year olds. It would be silly trying to train someone of that age to take their own prosecutions—quite a nerve-racking thing—so we still use solicitor-agents. And having found that they have their uses, we now have, in this region, regional criteria for the use of solicitor-agents. In other words, if you get somebody who was personally aggrieved at being told that they were going to be prosecuted, and there's a bit of, almost, not physical aggravation, but very violent reaction, and that could translate itself into a courtroom repetition, then we distance ourselves by using a solicitor.' (97–05)

Then there are other cases

'where we anticipate a not guilty plea, where the law may be called into question, and in a procedural sort of sense—you know, we're pretty good on the factual case law—but procedural stuff can throw us a bit. If we know that there's a solicitor going to be appointed by the other side, who's one of these eager so-and-sos who's going to earn their corn, why should we get our knickers in a twist? So we are now much more used to using solicitor-agents. Once you do that, or once you go to the Crown Court and you have a barrister, you learn that they [have legal representation] all the time, and so why don't we do it?' (97–05)

The practice of inspectors acting as advocates in their own cases is regarded within FOD as valuable, as another AD observed:

'There is . . . a great sense of satisfaction, I think, for some of the inspectors as individuals, because we are quite rare in being an organization which both investigates and prosecutes in the same person, and it's an opportunity for an inspector to, if you like, complete a piece of work, and indeed to go beyond the prosecution, to go back to the company and say "OK, you've been prosecuted, you know, you've had your fine, let's now see how we can stop it happening again, learn the lessons and take it forward." And that's a very important part of closing the circle, because we tend to have longer term relationships with organizations—we don't just come in and prosecute and never see them again; so that's important. I think taking a case to court also sharpens inspectors' legal and forensic skills—there's a danger of becoming somewhat complacent if your skills are never tested, and, you know, it's a useful reminder that they are law enforcement officers, they have to work within a framework of accountabilities.' (97–04)

There has been some debate in HSE, however, about the desirability of having inspectors act as advocates in some of the more difficult cases. According to a PI:

'There's been a lot of argument one way and another about whether we use agency solicitors for difficult defended cases. On the other hand, the old school, like my boss, they think it's a test of your manhood taking defended cases. But, you know, operationally, it's very time-consuming. There are arguments for saying it's right that you should have a go at defended cases because it makes you think very hard about evidence.'[9] (97–01)

The decision as to whether a case is handled by HSE or farmed out is usually the local PI's, in conjunction with the AD: 'It's a decision made on a variety of factors, the ongoing workload on an inspector's time and, again, if the inspector who would normally conduct the case is required to give evidence then it's seen as often simpler to get the solicitor in rather than drag another inspector who's up to their ears in . . . some major investigation' (97–02). One AD estimated the proportion of cases handled by solicitors to be

'Definitely a minority. I'd say perhaps about 15 per cent, something like that. And some cases, of course, do stand more of a chance of perhaps getting to Crown Court, and the decision is taken at an early stage. . . . [S]o we like to involve a solicitor agent from the outset rather than land a case on them when they can't have any influence . . .' (97–02)

In such a personalized system of prosecution, control of the case and its ultimate fate assumes especial importance for the field inspector. Inspectors who act as advocates tend to develop a certain possessiveness in the handling of a matter, for a potential prosecution case becomes a piece of their personal property, something to which they may develop a high level of commitment. Indeed, as an AD put it, 'The fact that the inspector is involved right throughout the process gives them a sense of ownership but also accountability, which perhaps other regulators don't have when you simply put up a file and lose track of it thereafter' (97–04). This proprietorial sense is stiffened by other demands on an inspector's resources. In HSE the time an inspector spends on a prosecution has to compete with other jobs, and has to be budgeted for. Since the same individual manages the prosecution case from beginning to end, not only

[9] The argument that appearing before an independent tribunal will encourage careful preparation of the case was also found in relation to social security adjudication and appeals officers (J. Baldwin *et al.*, 1992).

may legal risks loom larger for the inspector concerned, but the outcome of the case may be seen by senior colleagues as a mark of competence or otherwise. The inspector who prosecutes a case in person is open to be subjected, formally or informally, to a higher degree of organizational accountability (see Chapter 10).[10] Hence, in the preliminary decisions in a decentralized inspectorate about whether or not to prosecute, a predominant preoccupation is not so much the substantive issue of whether a prosecution is deserved or needed, but rather a pragmatic assessment of whether the prosecution will be successful (see Chapter 12).

4. CONTROL OF DECISION-MAKING IN A DECENTRALIZED INSPECTORATE

Bureaucratic control over the outcomes of decisions about prosecution is important for the furtherance of policy, especially the attainment of greater consistency in decision-making about individual cases. Control may be easier when decision-making is centrally organized because cases are routed through the same channels and usually result in the same senior official deciding the ultimate fate of the case. This can impose a measure of consistency of approach. To the extent that consistency is an important value in such decision-making, there will be more of a problem in decentralized decision structures, where many different individuals will be deciding broadly similar cases. Control by those at the centre over the decision-making process at the periphery becomes especially important in a decentralized organization.

Given their autonomy and significant screening role, the field inspectors in FOD are the targets of efforts to control decision-making, and the PIs the chief means by which the organization exerts control and transmits regulatory policy and values. In routine cases, the inspector is required to make a recommendation about the appropriateness of prosecution to the relevant PI, and if so with what charge or charges.[11] Sometimes the AD will be involved:

'For example, if things are going on indictment, then yes, they do come to me for approval, or approval of the approval. Or if cases have either been put up by the principal inspectors or, you know, where the principal inspectors have been

[10] It used to be the practice in the 1980s that reports of prosecutions in which the Factory Inspectorate had been involved went to HSE headquarters.

[11] It is not possible to discern from analysis of prosecution files how many matters originally treated by field inspectors as potentially prosecutable are dropped on the decision of the PI, though the degree of control exerted by PIs in most cases is clear.

heavily involved themselves in evidence collecting then it's a safeguard to put it to me for an objective viewpoint and consideration.' (97–02)

In difficult cases an AD can in turn ask the advice of senior colleagues and HSE lawyers. According to a former Chief Inspector of Factories, 'Very few decisions are taken at the Executive level but those which are, are of great public interest, have significant political overtones which affect the whole image and credibility of the Executive [and] will be considered at that level. Very few. Not more than one or two a year.'

In general, the AD (and occasionally headquarters officials) tend to be more important in exerting control over matters of prosecution policy than in deciding about individual cases, as the following example suggests. It involved a self-employed person charged with a breach of RIDDOR (Reporting of Injury, Diseases or Dangerous Occurrences Regulations, 1985). A farm worker had walked into an 11,000-volt power cable carrying an aluminium ladder, and the AD mused in a memo to her field inspector:

'Personally, I would have been inclined to prosecute [the defendant] as well under the Electricity at Work Regulations. He had been made well aware of the risks from overhead lines on his farm and could have done far more to prevent a very foreseeable serious incident, e.g. by not having aluminium ladders in the first place or putting some warning on the ladder itself! She concluded '... I rather doubt whether you would have achieved any more in terms of total penalty. The main thing is, you have taken him to Court and have achieved a result which should have certainly made an impact upon him and others in the farming community. Well done.' Someone else had observed, in a hand-written note to the memo, that '[The AD] makes a pertinent observation. I did think about this [presumably using the Electricity at Work Regulations], but the fact that the [injured person] decided, off his own bat, to carry out the work mitigated against it in my view. Worth keeping in mind though.'[12] (P97–25)

By reflecting on the record in this way, the AD is setting out some general conditions for and against prosecution for the benefit of the inspector concerned, and possibly others.

Inspectors make recommendations about formal legal action accompanied by a rationale. In one typical case,

an injured person had had an arm trapped in a machine, having followed an unsafe system of working. 'It will be explained to the Court that savings made by this system of work were insignificant when compared to the cost in terms of injury to the IP [injured person]', said the inspector in a report to his PI. 'It will

[12] The defendant was fined £750 plus nearly £400 in costs.

also be explained that the risks involved were so high that the system of work was totally unacceptable.'[13] (P97–15)

Inspectors not only justify to their superiors the reasons for a proposed prosecution, but also put forward what, precisely, they suggest by way of charge, forum, or defendant. This is usually done in a rather detailed way by written reports, as well as oral communication. The formal approval by a PI recorded in the case file usually obscures the degree of informal contact and debate with the field inspector, though an indication of it does surface in some files.

Examples of both direct and subtler forms of control were evident in the prosecution files. In a case in which an excavator had fouled overhead power lines,

> a sceptical inspector who had doubts about the strength of the evidence was talked into a prosecution by his PI. He originally did not recommend any prosecution of anyone, because of the strength of the defence case, as he saw it. He thought the firm was clearly to blame, but felt it 'may have a good defence in that they do otherwise have safeguards for overhead power lines, are fully aware of the dangers and precautions, and would be entitled to expect instructions . . . to be properly followed. It is also possible that rural magistrates would not look favourably on the behaviour of the [crane] driver who had been instructed of the dangers and was fully aware of the position of the power lines.' The inspector was over-ruled because 'It was considered that [the defendant] had failed to exercise the necessary control to prevent the incident.' In the event, the case was lost, the magistrates dismissing the two counts. (P97–18)

For relatively inexperienced inspectors, the control exercised by PIs serves to educate and socialize them into the decision-making conventions and procedures of the organization. This is a process which will grant them some sense of the conditions under which prosecution is normally expected within the organization. Sometimes the decision is marked as a matter for negotiation, as when queries about additional or alternative charges conclude with remarks like 'The approving officer may wish to discuss this option' (P97–50). This is one way in which the officials settle on what is the 'best' or most easily won charge.

The extent to which a field inspector or PI exerts real control also varies. In general, however, the prosecution files suggest a fair degree of congruence in their views on the question of prosecution in principle, but to what extent the paper record masks earlier differences of view, it is

[13] No fine was recorded.

hard to say. Congruence may be expected for a variety of reasons. It may reflect the degree of control wielded over the field inspector by the PI. Or there may be a tendency, given their common experience, for field and principal inspectors to see problems in much the same way, and thus to come to the same general conclusions. Equally, it may reflect the practice of some first-level decision-makers to design their recommendations to accord with the known decision-making proclivities of those who have to receive and approve them (Emerson & Paley, 1992). Again, the PI may sometimes be reluctant, in recognition of the organizational need to support a junior colleague, to question the field inspector's judgement.

The structural position of field inspectors as initial screeners of problems for access to the system of law enforcement grants them considerable power. The PI is dependent on the field inspector for the initial decisions made, and for information: 'I think the quality of the decision-making they are engaging in out there is little subject to my control,' said one PI (86–51). The PI is not regularly involved in collecting evidence in addition to the inspector and has therefore to rely on the field inspector's descriptions, accounts, and judgement, whether presented orally or in writing. The inspector not only has direct and immediate contact with the problem, but also develops a commitment to having the case handled in a certain way: 'If I see a good case that's worth a prosecution, I will do my damnedest to persuade my PI,' said a chemicals inspector (86–55). As the official screening events for access to the system of regulatory control, the inspector is able to construct a particular view of the reality of the case for the PI: 'But then I think we've been the ones who've been dealing with the company face to face. And I think perhaps we're in the best position to make that decision, rather than somebody looking at a collection of paperwork' (86–34). This conviction is transmitted in inspectors' reports to PIs. It may happen innocently, but may also be done consciously: 'If [inspectors] want to prosecute they will present it towards the hard end of the range [of words and expressions]. If they don't, they'll present it towards the soft end' (86–26). A number of inspectors acknowledged that their control was such that 'assuming there's a breach, you can always get a case' (86–63). In effect, the inspector frames the way in which the issues are regarded by the PI: 'I've done that. I've consciously done that,' said one, talking of the choice of particular words or the ordering of ideas. 'I think it would be perfectly possible to slant things in one particular direction or another. I'm sure it must be'... (86–24). Others spoke in blunter terms: 'We can... prejudice any future decisions in the way that we write something' (86–34).[14] 'Obviously, if you think a case is serious then the report is so slanted as to present the case as being serious.' said another. '[Y]ou try to present as balanced a picture as possible, but inevitably that picture is biased by the attitude you received on site' (86–29). The PIs are alert to the practice, having been field inspectors themselves. And the practice is not necessarily confined solely to the writing of prosecution reports. One PI suggested of his inspectors that their written weekly reports 'will convey what they want you to know' (86–39).

Field inspectors are thus well placed to be persuasive: the events described, the characters involved, and so on, are presented as the inspector has seen them and wants the PI to see them. Inspectors are positioned to ensure, deliberately or unwittingly, that matters in a case tend to point in the direction of a particular outcome (see Sanders, 1987). By engaging in such case construction behaviour, inspectors can frame matters for prosecution persuasively. After all, the PI 'can only go by what you put on paper' (86–25). Inspectors frequently employ institutionalized categories as justification and reason by means of them. These categories amount to recipe phrasing—a kind of 'boilerplate' justification that makes it harder to disagree with, since conventional reasoning presumes a conventional response.

But sometimes the PI is no mere ratifier of a decision made by the field inspector. The PI need not accept the inspector's recommendation to prosecute. And where the inspector brings a problem to the attention of the PI but is reluctant to prosecute, the PI can advise or instruct the inspector to proceed. In fact there appeared to be few instances of disagreement between inspectors and PIs. This may be because some PIs may be unwilling to intrude excessively upon the autonomy of their inspectors, but it may also reflect the inspector's ability to frame the reality of the problem for the PI, so that a particular decision seems appropriate to the person asked to approve it.

Where there is little or no disagreement over the prosecution in principle, PIs may well want to exert control over ancillary decisions, or over matters of presentation. A number of prosecution files carried lists by PIs of points where the field inspector's prosecution report needed improvement. Sometimes PIs would add handwritten memos asking

[14] Lynxwiler *et al.* (1983: 430) found that their inspectors 'confidently asserted' that they could influence the size of a fine by the using in their reports certain words or phrases to which courts were sensitive. See also Duff (1997).

their field inspectors to attend to certain points in the recommendation, clearly giving guidance to less experienced junior colleagues. Sometimes control by the PI can be very direct, as in the following case in which a nursing home had failed to comply with an improvement notice. A two-page handwritten note from the PI to the field inspector was critical of the way in which he had proposed the prosecution and his handling of the case so far:

> 'It [the report] is very wordy—I prefer a style where your leading memo points me at things I need to read rather than your lengthy exposition which includes everything... Evidence collection was good but your weak link is date. Don't overlook the obvious, everything on an information has to be proved. It would have been relatively easy to get the Nurses to say "Everything I am describing on this statement was true on [a particular day]", even if they couldn't remember exact event dates.... The report describes good work but do talk more with me as I have not found it terribly easy to read or absorb. With a large amount of evidence you need to develop a very positive, succinct, economical style...' (P97–39)

The most direct example of control appeared in another case in a memo from a PI making no fewer than eight separate points of instruction on the inspector's proposed prosecution. The latter had argued for a prosecution under the Health and Safety at Work Act, 1974 (HSW Act), s. 2 (1), but the PI said it could not be taken. The inspector's first effort at completing the prosecution report and input form was marked 'NOT approved' (*sic*) by the PI. A second effort under Regulation 13 (1) Woodworking Regulations was also not approved by the PI, who suggested she use PUWER (Provision and Use of Work Equipment Regulations, 1992) instead (P97–46).

Specialist inspectors are frequently called upon in pre-trial deliberations for their expertise in dealing with particular problems, and they may also introduce some control since they regularly take a position on the merits of prosecution. In one of the cases sampled, for instance, a report by a specialist inspector supported legal proceedings. In a letter to the PI the inspector offered two pieces of technical preventive advice, concluding: 'I am willing to support legal proceedings based on the failure to maintain the safety device and an improvement notice for recommendations 17 and 18 [the technical advice]' (P97–29). The expertise of such inspectors accords their advice a special legitimacy. If followed, backing from respected colleagues such as these may also be useful to inspectors after the event as a justification for any decisions taken.

5. PRE-TRIAL CHOICES

The most important pre-trial choice to be made by the inspector is the decision to prosecute in principle. I do not propose, however, to devote much attention to this decision in this chapter. This may seem perverse, but this question is the subject of most of the remaining analysis, and the supporting processes need to be described and examined first. The issue of whether prosecution is the right course of action cannot be divorced from ancillary decisions, particularly those about possible charges. The issues involved in pre-trial choices tend to unfold in the handling of the case. They are complicated by the reflexive nature of the decision-making. For instance, an inspector concerned to achieve a certain level of penalty in a particular case will have to think about the number and type of charges, and about the forum for the prosecution.

Calculations by inspectors involve both the past reconstruction of a case and the future construction of the risks of losing in court posed by the case (see also Reiss, 1989). Much of the decision-making involved at the pre-trial stage is of an anticipatory kind, in which a particular decision is based on expectations about how subsequent decision-makers will behave. Later decisions to be anticipated include, most prominently, the result of the case, and (in a successful prosecution) the level of any penalty likely to be imposed by the court. The undesired outcomes to be avoided are losing the case, or winning but suffering a derisory penalty. The level of penalty they can anticipate has been a constant concern for some HSE staff in recent years and HSE has publicly condemned some penalties imposed by the courts as inadequate and counter-productive.[15] Yet very large fines still represent a tiny proportion of a large company's profits (Wells, 2001: 33). It is a matter which inspectors sometimes debate in deciding whether prosecution is the appropriate course of action, or whether some other form of enforcement is preferable. What inspectors interpret as the unsympathetic attitude of the courts to regulatory cases is

[15] Concern about the sanctioning practices of magistrates in regulatory offences in general (not simply occupational health and safety violations) has frequently been expressed. For instance, the then Minister responsible, Mr Michael Howard, complained in a letter to the Chairman of the Magistrates' Association (5 Feb. 1990) that 'Fines of a few hundred pounds, for example, against large building contractors for serious breaches of health and safety legislation are unlikely to have the required deterrent effect.' These firmly instrumentalist views were endorsed by the then Chairman of the Health and Safety Commission (HSC) (Press Release by Dr John Cullen, 5 Feb. 1990). The Code for Crown Prosecutors notes that a prosecution 'is less likely to be needed' if the court is likely to impose a nominal penalty.

sometimes enough to deter them from prosecuting (Hutter, 1997: 224–5).

The prospect of prosecution introduces an element of uncertainty into inspectors' work, given that they are concerned with the future and various anticipated outcomes to a range of possible decisions. This gives much of the decision-making a speculative, even hesitant, quality.[16] The note of doubt and ambivalence emerges clearly in the following case in which officials weigh up various options in trying to fit 'the facts' of the case to possibly relevant legal definitions as they anticipate potential responses from the defendant:

An employee lost two fingers of his right hand while cleaning powder out of an unguarded screw elevator. The file recorded that prosecution was proposed 'as company was prosecuted last year over similar incident.' The file contained hand-written jottings by the PI to the field inspector in the form of questions about the evidence to be adduced, with a further note asking '... can we discuss? 6 pack Prosecutions—lots of Brownie points but I am not sure about PUWER Reg. 11. Reg. 22 would be ideal but I doubt if this is "maintenance".' A formal note from the PI following discussions with the inspector and a colleague then recorded a change of heart, noting that it had been decided that prosecution under the regulations suggested was inappropriate. Instead, the PI observed: 'I am inclined to the view that a prosecution for a breach of Section 2 of the HSW Act is probably the best way forward... The offence boils down to inadequate guarding/lack of a safe system of work for the powder recovery operation. I think the firm will be able to throw in all sorts of issues in mitigation e.g. the activities of the supervisor and the apparent verbal acknowledgement by the supplier that it was common practice to empty the screw elevator in the way that they were doing. However none of this is a defence and I think prosecution is justified.'

Another hand-written note discussed the legal issues at some length, debating whether other Regulations could be used. The PI's response to this was that the [company's risk] assessment was clearly defective: 'I would be tempted to lay several charges mixing hardware/software aspects and do some plea bargaining—if I was sure the magistrates wouldn't recommend indictment.... I agree that the system for clearing residue was inherently unsafe *whoever did it,* [others were] just as endangered as IP [injured person], so claims about everyone being trained to do it means they were trained to use an unsafe system. Rely on expert witness here to stress misunderstandings and mistaken start up are foreseeable, and that severity of injury demands high guarding standard.... Overall I would go for Section 2 HSW.... I would not approve *yet* but I think there's a case there.' [emphases original]

[16] This is despite the fact that inspectors are given official guidance in the form of the Code for Crown Prosecutors and HSC's (now revised) *Enforcement policy statement* (Health and Safety Commission, n.d.), which is discussed further in Chs. 6 and 7.

The inspectors finally decided to prosecute, concluding that the HSW Act was more appropriate in this case than any Regulations.[17] (P97–64)

Of the several sources of uncertainty in pre-trial processes, the most important involves the possible outcome. The many contributory decisions in the pre-trial process mean that inspectors have to work towards a decision about prosecution in principle, because the matter is always open to be changed or discarded up to the point of the trial. Once inspectors are clear that a matter is one that ought to be treated as a potential prosecution, they then have to approach all cases pre-trial as if they are destined for prosecution. The other choices to be made pre-trial must be seen as an exercise in reducing uncertainty. Once the uncertainty suffusing the pre-trial process is resolved, and the inspector can begin to treat the matter as a potential prosecution with some confidence, the case is locked into a particular trajectory.

If the decision is not to prosecute an otherwise suitable case, inspectors can often turn this to their advantage with a firm, for the appearance of relenting creates an opportunity for effective remedial work with a suitably chastened employer. A decision not to pursue a matter to court is sometimes made where inspectors anticipate that a prosecution, even if successful, would be categorized by magistrates as one involving a 'technical' matter, not warranting much of a sanction. Such an outcome is regarded by inspectors as counter-productive. For example, in a case in which a dragline excavator had fouled power lines, the third such incident in a four-year period, the inspector observed that her

'overall impression is that the firm have quite a good health and safety culture and are trying very hard to manage health and safety effectively. I feel that this affair could be used to good effect to exert more pressure on [the company] to sort out their overhead power line problems on this site . . . rather than pursue them on a breach which may be viewed as "technical" by Magistrates. I would therefore not recommend prosecution of [the company] or any other party in this matter.'[18] (P97–18)

To decide by reference to anticipated outcomes of decisions made by others compels attention to a number of subsidiary issues. Inspectors aim

[17] The company pleaded guilty to a charge under s. 2 of the HSW Act, 1974, and was fined £5,000 plus £290 costs.

[18] This was the inspector's initial view, which she subsequently reversed (presumably after discussions with her PI and possibly other colleagues). The defendant, an individual, pleaded not guilty to two counts under the Electricity at Work Regulations, 1989, and the Quarry Vehicle Regulations, 1970. The magistrates found the defendant not guilty on both counts.

in pre-trial decision-making to maximize the chance of success while trying to ensure that the case is penalized appropriately with a commensurate sanction. This means a careful evaluation of the strengths and weaknesses of the case, framed in legal terms (see Chapter 12). For instance, inspectors' decisions about the informations to be laid may be determined by how well the matter can be made to fit with decided cases, or by the existence of supporting guidance in the form of a relevant Advisory Code of Practice. Similarly, it is important for them to assess the competence of possible witnesses, but trying to gauge the quality of witnesses can be tricky. An observation which noted 'IP a bit vague at times and doesn't remember much about the accident. Director... likely to come across clearly' (P97–57) is a clear indication that other parts of the case need to be strong for HSE to be confident of a conviction on the particular charge mooted. In another case the inspector proposed to prosecute three partners for only the second of two offences: 'Although an earlier offence was committed on 10 June,' he wrote, '...I do not intend pursuing the matter as Harris[19] would not make a reliable witness.' The witness' peace of mind was also evidently an issue, as the inspector stated that he felt 'his well-being will be further harmed should he be requested to give evidence' (P97–62).

Once a provisional decision to prosecute has been made, questions then arise as to what to prosecute for, a matter of the number and type of charge, of the forum for the prosecution (magistrates' court or Crown Court), and whether to prosecute a company or an individual. There are a number of objectives that inform these decisions, but prominent among them is a concern for the expected level of penalty. This is a matter of commensurability, of ensuring a good fit between the offence and the penalty. Both instrumental and expressive values are at stake here. In other words, HSE staff have a general sense of what each case ought to be worth and make their pre-trial decisions accordingly. The care with which they deal with pre-trial decisions also reflects a preoccupation with the management of appearances.

1. Number and Choice of Charges

Senior staff concerned about the public image of the agency and the instrumental impact that a conviction may have sometimes observe that the quality of the prosecution is sometimes more important than the

[19] All names are fictitious throughout.

quantity of charges in a conviction. Inspectors routinely rehearse a number of possible charges with their PIs and move to a greater or lesser extent in conjunction with their superiors to decide on charges using working rules that amount to principles of selection. These I shall call the principles of parsimony, precision, and simplicity.

(a) Parsimony. The inspector's first requirement is parsimony in the number of charges brought. The aim is not simply to win the case, but to win it clearly and decisively, securing an appropriate penalty, and not attenuating the force of the conviction by throwing in too many issues. Inspectors can often afford to be very selective about which matters to prosecute and to choose the most egregious from a wide array of violations. This concern lay behind an inspector's decision to abandon two other possible grounds of prosecution which he had originally proposed in a case in which two workers had fallen through a roof. In explaining this decision, he commented that he did 'not want to dilute the fragile roofing case' (P97–05).

The principle of parsimony is a powerful one, underpinned by not only an expressive desire for commensurability but also a concern for organizational resources. In a case of serious violation of the asbestos regulations, the inspector wrote: 'As the manner in which Mr Dixon set up and conducted the demolition contract could be seen to have broken almost every health and safety rule I can think of, there is obviously a wide range of potential charges which he could be asked to answer. However, it is quite obvious that there is little point in presenting a vast number of charges against him . . .' Because of the scale of the defendant's derelictions and the risk presented both to his employees and to the public, the inspector recommended two charges relating to the disregard of his duties involving to the control of asbestos (P97–30). Too many charges, even in a big case, would appear to be heavy-handed.

One particular public impression that must be avoided is vindictiveness, a matter deeply implicated in the value of commensurability, hence HSE's adoption in its *Enforcement policy statement* (Health and Safety Commission, n.d.) of the principles of proportionality, consistency, transparency, and targeting. Although HSE is often in the position of being able to gain convictions on a number and variety of charges should it elect to do so, inspectors often choose otherwise. There may be good reason to avoid an unnecessary expenditure of resources. '[P]art of my principle would be "Don't go for many charges anyway", unless it's particularly necessary to do so,' said an AD, 'because we are making a point, and we can make it once, and in a more efficient way. I mean, I think we are driven much more by efficiency than we used to [be], and therefore, it's efficiency and effectiveness that we evaluate' (97–05).

Another reason for parsimony is the need to maintain good relationships with regulated firms. This is a recognition of the fact that the inspector has to keep visiting their premises and prefers to sustain the cooperation of those regulated. There is also an important expressive constraint against appearing to be heavy-handed where there seem to be mitigating circumstances. Where there are mitigating factors, one charge is often regarded as sufficient. 'There were obviously lots of other law that could have been used—HSW Act S. 2, Management of Health and Safety Regulations Reg. 3 and 4,' wrote an inspector in one case, 'but I choose to use only one as it was a small business, who until then had not been brought to our attention' (P97–38). To pursue too many charges risks appearing heartless. Inspectors are probably more concerned with avoiding the appearance of vindictiveness to the court than the public. To be sparing in the number of charges suggests to the court that the defendant is not being persecuted. Otherwise, the level of penalty imposed may be threatened if the defendant is able to engage the sympathy of the magistrates. If inspectors have a working conception of what a conviction is worth, many of them believe that so, too, do magistrates. 'It's better to get £2,000 on one count, rather than £400 on five,' said one inspector (86–63), though another was unconcerned: 'it doesn't matter how many charges you finally get them convicted on. The magistrates have a fixed figure in mind, and they just divide it by the number of penalties, so just one guilty plea is divided by one, and if there's three, they divide it by three' (97–03). This is because the penalty imposed carries a strong symbolic message; the lower the penalty on each count, the more the violation is belittled. This is another reason for inspectors to focus on only one or two of an array of possible charges. It was not always this way. 'When I first joined the department,' said an inspector, 'when one was prosecuting a firm it was thought to be a good thing, say, to throw in make-weights like sort of administrative matters, such as not having the right forms posted, or not having the general registers available, and so on . . . I suspect that sort of prosecution nowadays would have scant sympathy from within the courts or wider' (86–38).

There is also a very important tactical reason to avoid the appearance of heavy-handedness. Inspectors believe that multiple charges are more likely to encourage a not guilty plea and a defence, and this in turn opens up the possibility of HSE losing part or all of the case. Parsimony in the number of informations laid, on the other hand, is thought more likely to encourage a guilty plea, possibly via a bargain. This is clear from the following prosecution report from an inspector to his PI about the defendant company, in a case in which an employee had been killed in the collapse of a trench: 'Attitude. Total co-operation, and from conversations at the Inquest, their solicitor indicated that they would plead guilty so long as the charges were not "over the top". This means that I have presented only one charge here out of the several that are possible.' The report also recommended summary trial (P97–34). This case suggests that there might also be a connection between a defendant's 'attitude' and the inspector's charging behaviour. 'Attitude', an institutionalized category, is often very important in terms of the number of charges selected. The implication of the inspector's remarks is that a less cooperative employer might well face more than one charge, thereby becoming vulnerable to a higher total penalty.[20]

The case also, however, points to an important countervailing principle. The growing practice of pre-trial bargaining means that sometimes inspectors may feel they need to proceed on more charges than are necessary, so as to have something to surrender in the bargaining process. An AD noted that

> 'People will ring me up and say "We have been given this opportunity [to secure a guilty plea by dropping a charge], what do you think?" And my answer's "Fine." Because as far as I am concerned, in the generality—I can envisage some circumstances . . . a fatal accident, perhaps, or a major incident, where one would have to look very carefully . . . But in the generality, if one has decided . . . that enforcement by way of prosecution is the important thing, it is the actual doing that, and whether we have three charges or one, generally speaking, I'm not too fussed about it. . . . There can be high profile ones . . . where I think I would have to be a bit more careful. So what I'm saying is, it is going on, and basically I think that will be taken by principal inspectors as a decision, and there is no head office sort of nervousness, that I'm aware of . . .' (97–05)

(b) Precision. A second principle in the selection of charges is precision. If parsimony speaks to self-imposed constraints on the number of charges, precision addresses the type of charge. Some inspectors believe that it is essential to hit the target with the most appropriate charge to increase the chances of conviction. 'I tend to omit side issues, to get the evidence for

[20] The defendant was conditionally discharged for 12 months. Costs of £400 were awarded to HSE.

the one case I want. You may discuss issues with the firm, but in terms of proceedings I go for one particular case' (86–63). There has to be a concentration on the core issue, and the charge selected must avoid in any way distracting the magistrates, who might otherwise end up returning not guilty verdicts, or failing to sanction as heavily on the various counts as they might. In choosing the charge, therefore, it is important that it reflects the gravity of the alleged offence.

Precision is allied with a concern for clarity of purpose, which derives from an instrumental view of prosecution. While inspectors do not always have an instrumental end in view in opting for prosecution in the first place, there are some cases, as the analysis will show, in which they do want criminal proceedings to produce change for the better. In such circumstances, a charge that will have a broad impact on the future attitudes and behaviour of management is especially attractive. The generality of the HSW Act, 1974, often has a strong appeal in this respect, whether or not it is used in conjunction with other legislation or regulations. This was clear in a case in which the inspector justified a decision to prosecute under the HSW Act where an employee who had been trapped in a machine and badly burned suffered the amputation of the middle fingers of both hands. A prosecution was desirable, the inspector said, 'since this could be used to draw in training in safe systems of work . . . The breach of the PUWE [Provision and Use of Work Equipment] Regulations is also straightforward. The guard was missing, access was possible to the dangerous heat sealing head—the accident occurred.' The 'initial attitude [of the company] was one of almost "not our fault" . . . The union rep . . . complained . . . management showed little interest in site health and safety. . . . If these cases are *not* pursued it may well "damage" management "attitude" to health and safety' (P97–36).[21]

Precision means that messages can be conveyed more reliably and accurately to their audiences, assisting in the avoidance of any possible criticism by the industry or the public. It is important, for example, to indicate by the charge, if at all possible, precisely who is to blame, and who was at risk. This is another way in which the charge can be aligned with the desert of the case. This was clear in a major case in which an employee had been killed in an explosion and fire in a dock. The records show that it was believed that the company, in pre-trial skirmishing, had tried to place blame on the employee concerned, in an effort to avoid

[21] The defendant was fined £11,000 for breach of s. 2 of the HSW Act, and £3,500 for breach of PUWER. Costs were nearly £1,500.

senior-level responsibility. There was a long memo from the AD to the inspector involved:

'As you know, I am concerned that cases under both s. 2 and s. 3 [HSW Act] could be seen as victimisation, and in preparation for any complaint (or TV appearance if the case is unsuccessful) I wanted to be clear about [the QC representing HSE's] view.' The AD went on to say that she had talked to an HSE solicitor who believed 'the essential features' to be that: 'The possible consequences could have been very great; the widespread public concern in a sensitive area needs to be taken into account'; the Court should be informed of 'the dangers beyond those to employees, and this is more properly done by bringing the s. 3 case'; the fire-fighters were actually exposed to additional risk since the integrity of the plant was prejudiced and they had to approach closely to cool adjacent tanks off; 'the firm involved was a substantial one' and, 'should an offer be made by the firm's legal advisers, with two cases available we can take a pragmatic view.

On this basis I agree with the advice that we should go ahead with both s. 2 and s. 3 cases.'[22] (P97–28)

It is interesting to see in this case the rationale that the firm was 'substantial' (that is, they could afford any fine, they were a big and 'responsible' firm), and it was partly because they were big that a prosecution was indicated. It is also noteworthy that the AD observed that HSE could afford to be 'pragmatic', that is, HSE could afford to bargain, if necessary.

(c) Simplicity. A third requirement is that the available evidence allows the selection of charges which are simple and intelligible. Many of the matters HSE inspectors routinely deal with are extremely complex and require engineering, mechanical, medical, and other forms of technical knowledge. Simplicity is especially important given that the defendant's guilt will be determined by untutored people—either lay magistrates, or (less often) the members of the public in the jury room. It is essential, therefore, that charges are easily comprehended not only by the magistrates and any lawyers involved, but also by the defendant. In these circumstances simplicity is believed to be a great virtue, making life easier for the inspector and increasing the chances that the case gets what it deserves, in terms of both verdict and penalty. This happened in a big case involving five charges under the Asbestos Regulations and the

[22] The company pleaded guilty to both, and was fined £75,000 on each, plus £20,000 costs.

Asbestos (Licensing) Regulations, where the PI noted firmly to his inspector:

'I think we will be able to defend ourselves—are there others in the frame who may be in a less strong position? I am sure you're right in believing he may try to show a lack of understanding of issues put to him and it is this aspect which makes it essential that the charges brought are few and easy to comprehend and those you propose fit that bill.'[23] (P97–30)

Prosecution is usually easier under a charge for breach of regulation (rather than the HSW Act) but this has to be set against the lower sanctions available for such a breach.[24] The evidence required to prove guilt under the HSW Act may also cause inspectors problems in this respect, and possibly lead to an HSW Act prosecution being dropped in favour of a more manageable charge:

'...I think...you'll find that there are a lot more systems cases, management cases, and even if, on occasions, we end up taking a specific regulation, it may well be because the evidence to prove the management case may be rather intractable. But having taken the decision that on our professional assessment the management system is defective, and therefore we want to bring that to the attention of the magistrates and indeed to emphasize it to the company, we may take a straightforward case to prove our point, but be very clear in saying to the company that this is just a sample case, and then the underlying issues are this, this, and this.' (97–04)

But if the HSW Act has to be used, the need for simplicity still obtains:

In a possible prosecution of an employee at work, it was thought s. 7 HSW Act was appropriate, but the question was which subsection to use, as the note by the inspector suggests: '[T]here is no offence by the company for which he was responsible, only his own.' S. 7 (a) 'is a simpler charge than 7 (b) and so seems more appropriate. A section 7 (b) charge would require further evidence about the company policy Mr Knight was failing to comply with, which may not exist! I think 7 (a), read broadly, allows us to say he was putting other people at risk by his bad example.' (P97–31)

2. Choice of Forum

The decision about which forum is to be selected for trial raises a number of issues. The working assumption among HSE inspectors is that cases

[23] The defendant in this case was convicted and sentenced to three months' imprisonment.

[24] These questions all demand more detailed analysis, presented in Ch. 12.

are taken to the magistrates' court, with the Crown Court employed only in special circumstances.[25] As the following examples from prosecution files show, justifications for proposing summary trial in the magistrates' court or trial on indictment in the Crown Court often run together, though it is easier to discuss them separately.

(a) Commensurability. The first concern, one which may have expressive as well as instrumental dimensions, is once again for the general level of the possible penalty achievable in a particular forum.[26] The task, as HSE staff see it, is to maximize the conditions under which the most appropriate penalty can be achieved, though they recognize that the question of the precise penalty is out of their hands. Inspectors normally anticipate the penalty that may be imposed on conviction in a particular case and align it with their own sense of what the case is worth in retributive or deterrent terms. They do not have a clear idea of what a case is worth since they probably do not prosecute frequently enough to develop the exact sense that a highly repetitive decision-maker gains (see e.g. Sudnow, 1965). They seem instead to acquire a general impression that a case is, or is not, worth a certain level of penalty:

'Another change which has had an effect, consciously or unconsciously, has been the differing levels of fines between the main sections of the Health and Safety at Work Act, where the maximum, in a magistrates' court, is £20,000, and all the regulations offences, where the maximum is £5,000. And again, I think there has been an element of tactical use of those charges in order to try and get what is perceived as a reasonable fine available to the magistrates sufficient for them to impose a reasonable penalty without having to take the case up to the . . . Crown Court.' (97–04)

[25] The Crown Court is reserved for cases in a rather narrowly defined set of conditions. In the sample of cases from the prosecution files, only three were actually prosecuted in the Crown Court. However, it is notable that in several other cases serious consideration had been given to trial on indictment, but at some point HSE opted for summary trial. Some of these decisions seem to have been reached as a result of pre-trial bargaining (see below).

[26] This concern to reflect the gravity of the violation comports with Factory Inspectorate policy in the early days of HSE. A former Chief Inspector of Factories reported that he 'was . . . sometimes asked why HMFI [Her Majesty's Factory Inspectorate] has not made more use of the power given under the HSE Act to take proceedings on indictment with the consequence of an unlimited fine. Once again, in their approach to this new power, inspectors have been guided by the broad criteria set out by the HSC—the gravity of the offence, the adequacy of the powers of sentence of the summary court, the record of the offender and his previous response to advice. It is, of course, the gravity of the offence and not the severity of the injury or the injuries that must primarily be considered' (HSE, 1977: 8). This is a view about wrongdoing that may sometimes be difficult for those caught up in the incident to apprehend (quite apart from the general public).

The magistrates' court has the advantage for inspectors of offering a good chance of a conviction. Summary trial is also useful, even so far as commensurability is concerned, because the lesser penalties may fit an inspector's conception of the desert of the case better. This is clear from the reasoning in a case in which the inspector concerned had rehearsed the rationale for summary trial in his notes for his speech to the magistrates. The offence was being tried summarily at HSE's request, he wrote, because a small company was involved, the penalty in the magistrates' court was appropriate, the matter was relatively straightforward, there was no wider public involvement, and it was an appropriate case to be heard by the Bench (P97–44). Summary trial may be more attractive with individual (rather than corporate) defendants. Inspectors must weigh these considerations against the advantages of Crown Court trial, such as the greater publicity and the unlimited fine. The penalty has a profoundly important expressive dimension to it, for it is a symbolic indicator of the worth of victims involved in an accident. This was amply demonstrated by the outrage expressed in 1999 by families of the victims over the fine of £1.5 million imposed on Great Western Trains for its part in the railway accident at Southall in which there were a number of fatalities.

Besides, the power of the magistrates to refer a matter to the Crown Court for sentencing can encourage inspectors to opt for summary trial, even where the case has some serious features. In a case in which the victim had been crushed to death in machinery, and evidence had been given at the inquest that safety checks had not been carried out, the PI reminded his AD in a memo that 'In the Magistrates' Court the case can be referred upwards for sentencing and it is thought that this is likely, but not guaranteed, once the previous conviction is cited' (P97–40).[27]

Though the Crown Court carries with it the capacity to impose a heavier penalty than the magistrates' court, the decision for the inspector is not simply one of choosing one forum or the other. The choice must still be aligned with the decisions about the number and kind of charges selected, because of their implications for the level of penalty exacted. It is conceivable that, given the right charges, some cases tried summarily may be sanctioned more heavily by magistrates than others tried on indictment. If an offence is regarded as serious and thus deserving of a substantial penalty, an inspector may well be tempted to use s. 2 or other

[27] The matter was not referred, and the magistrates imposed a fine of £17,500 and nearly £1,000 costs.

sections of the HSW Act in a summary trial rather than a breach of a regulation, because breach of the former carries a £20,000 maximum fine, compared with a £5,000 maximum for breach of the latter:[28]

'I don't think you would find it written down anywhere, but I think subconsciously people are saying, "Well, if I take one case under the Management Regulations, with a maximum of £5,000, are the magistrates going to consider that they've got adequate scope to impose a penalty, bearing in mind all of the discounts that magistrates apply for, you know, a first offence, and for an early plea of guilty, and all the rest of it?" You could find that their maximum that they could impose could be £2,000 in reality, and yes, I think to an extent there is a decision as to whether that is adequate, and of course at the end of the day, it has always been part of our policy to consider whether we should ask for cases to go up on indictment, and part of that is considering whether the courts have got adequate penalties.' (97–04)

In a big case in which an employee had suffered high doses of radiation, a solicitor for HSE argued that trial on indictment was not necessary:

'All cases we take arise from serious circumstances, but this case did not to my understanding have that extra degree of seriousness and complexity which would require that we propose prosecution on indictment. The HSW Act s. 2 charge would of course attract the £20,000 maximum fine. No doubt this is in part a medical matter—how serious were the actual or potential ill health effects associated with circumstances and charges that we are proposing? My understanding was that the record of the firm was not all bad, and that the over-exposures... were not evidence of serious threats to health and life.' The inspector in this case also 'fundamentally disagreed' with a proposal for trial on indictment put forward by a specialist inspector, citing the absence of 'either flagrant or reckless breaches', and evidence to suggest gross neglect or a serious lack of concern by the employer for the wellbeing of his employees. (P97–53)

These remarks suggest the use of additional tests, not of a legal kind so much as social cues which suggest when the weightier sanctioning of the Crown Court is or is not appropriate.

There is a corresponding desire to reflect the gravity of the violation and to try cases on indictment if the violation is a 'bad' or 'flagrant' one, though inspectors are more selective about this. Sometimes the push for the Crown Court may come from the centre of the HSE organization, propelled for reasons of regulatory policy and organizational self-interest. In the big asbestos case referred to earlier, the file reported that

[28] Though the magistrates can now fine up to £20,000 per count in some cases, even though they may not be so bad as to warrant committal to the Crown Court for sentence.

'For various reasons (the gravity of the circumstances, the unrepentant nature of the contractor and the current asbestos campaign) [the HSE's Solicitor's Office] has persuaded us to ask for a Crown Court hearing' (P97–30).[29]

Some inspectors take the view that the real penalty to the employer is to be measured in terms of fine and costs together. They believe that many magistrates tend to think in terms of an appropriate total penalty, and to conflate costs and penalties in calculating that total. Accordingly, when considering whether or not to prosecute and with what charges, they adapt by estimating possible costs and penalties together, for fear that if HSE asks for a large amount in costs, the magistrates may decide that the costs are sufficient punishment and impose a lesser penalty, such as a conditional discharge without a fine. Alternatively, HSE may have a suitable fine imposed by the court but then find that the court awards no costs, or only a part of their costs. One experienced PI claimed that awareness of costs was becoming increasingly important in inspectors' pre-trial decision-making, observing that the press and the public tended to focus much more on the level of the fine as the indicator of the degree of the defendant's culpability rather than the fine and costs (97–03).

(b) Publicity. A second reason to try the matter on indictment is that a successful prosecution in the Crown Court is likely to generate more publicity favourable to HSE and its interests than would follow a conviction in the local magistrates' court.[30] This policy reflects HSE's position as a public body with public responsibilities. A major advantage of trial in the Crown Court for HSE is that it provides a firmer platform for the display of its activity in responding to any violation which was not

[29] Others may occasionally seek to influence decisions about choice of forum. In the case of the big explosion and fire, a relative of the victim actually wrote to the defendant company's solicitors to say that the victim's family regretted that the case was being heard in the Crown Court: 'We do not agree with this view and have told the HSE so.' Whether this position was taken because the family wanted to feel more confident that the defendant company would be convicted, or for some other reason, is not clear from the prosecution file (P97–28).

[30] Following publicity about the low fine imposed on the BBC after an outbreak of legionnaires' disease at its Portland Place headquarters some years ago, HSE was criticized for taking the case to the magistrates' court. The House of Commons Select Committee on Employment took the view that such cases should be taken on indictment. HSE's response to this was that it was very costly and time-consuming to do this, that the decision was a matter for the magistrates to make, that the public impact of a case was a matter taken into account by the HSE, and in this case speed of conviction was thought to be more important. Nonetheless, HSE did announce that it would take all future cases involving legionnaires' disease to the Crown Court (F. B. Wright, 1995: 108).

only an important breach of the rules, but also had serious consequences. The Crown Court is accordingly regarded as the appropriate forum in high-profile cases, since it confers a special visibility upon the particular occupational health and safety problem, and upon the defendant, as well as fostering the appearance of HSE as an active, effective, regulator. At the same time the interests of general deterrence and the public display of the power and responsiveness of the regulatory agency can both be advanced (see Chapter 7).

An event, therefore, that seems clearly at the pre-trial stage to be serious and newsworthy is much more likely to culminate in a Crown Court trial, as is evident in the remarks of the inspector in the big case involving an explosion and fire at an oil storage terminal, in which a worker was killed and £100,000 of damage was done:

According to one of the five press cuttings in the file, the victim was engulfed in flames which were so intense it took fire fighters eight hours to reach his body. It was another ten hours before the fire was put out. Apart from the employee's death, the inspector reported that the '... fire and explosion ... put a great many more at risk including fire-fighters and employees of other firms. Prosecution is recommended in the Crown Court,' he concluded, adding in mitigation: 'This firm have attempted to control health and safety issues and have taken steps to reduce risk on site. Unfortunately their control over the activities involving the death of [the victim] were insufficient.' The indicators of seriousness in this case were identified as '... massive fire, the death of an employee and the substantial risks the emergency services were put to. On top of this were risks to persons off-site since, had the whole installation caught fire (and there was a real danger of this at one stage), then other employees within the dock complex would have faced real threats to their lives.' This list culminated in a proposal to prosecute on indictment: 'I feel that an offence as serious as this with the consequences it did have (and those that could have followed) warrants such a prosecution....' The inspector raised the issue of publicity, arguing that a failure to prosecute in Crown Court would itself be conspicuous: 'As you know a great deal of public concern over the integrity of major hazard sites has been generated as the result of this major fire. If HSE then fails to bring proceedings then public concern over major hazards sites will be increased. It is important to show that the law has been breached in order for a serious fire like this to occur.' (P97–28)

HSE is concerned to display its presence and effectiveness not only to the public, but also to regulated firms, as the inspector's report in the same case indicates (see Chapter 7). The value of the Crown Court and its sanctioning power for this special audience is clear: prosecution here shows that HSE is in charge:

'It is important that we send a clear message to the industry. One impression that did come over to me during the investigation was of complacency. I suspect that the industry sees itself as the experts in the field and may be less than receptive to ideas from HSE. This incident shows that their confidence in their own ability may be misplaced.... However I am recommending that the proceedings be taken in the Crown Court where the fines in respect of [the company] would be unlimited.' The instructions from the HSE Solicitor to counsel in relation to the two charges under the HSW Act, 1974 proposed in this case observed that 'likely costs to the company of accepting our findings are likely to be very high indeed. Similarly, this prosecution will be of interest and importance throughout the whole industry. In the view of [HSE], [the company] appear likely to fight this case very strongly.' (P97–28)

(c) Administrative Values. Management interests are also relevant to the question of forum. First among a number of powerful administrative preoccupations at work is the question of the time and trouble involved for an inspector in investigating, preparing for, and actually prosecuting a case. Inspectors have to balance the demands of preparing the case and appearing in person to prosecute it in the magistrates' court against the different demands of instructing a solicitor and preparing to give evidence in the Crown Court where those involved have to make a much greater commitment of time. This has the effect of deflecting limited regulatory resources from preventive work. The inevitable delay in bringing proceedings is a second disincentive to trial on indictment. The delay can be very substantial (it may well be a year or more after the offence before a health and safety case is heard) because a busy Crown Court understandably gives priority to cases where a defendant is in custody. Third, the idea of trial as a troublesome matter is frequently run together with a consciousness of the extra monetary cost of going to Crown Court. A final concern is that these various costs might be amplified by the defendant who enters a not guilty plea in response to the prospect of appearing in the Crown Court.

These matters often act together as strong disincentives to taking a prosecution on indictment. Some of the remarks by inspectors in their reports suggest that their normal practice is in general to avoid the extra time and trouble that would be involved. 'It is recommended that the case is suitable for summary trial and that the penalties on summary conviction would suffice,' one inspector observed to his PI. 'Trials on indictment are both time consuming and expensive' (P97–10). 'Having taken account of... the workload on this [group],' wrote the PI in a case involving a fatality, 'I have reluctantly come to the conclusion that

I should recommend the case be taken summarily and, I hope, disposed of quickly' (P97–40). In the major asbestos case, comments by the PI to his field inspector suggest a clear inclination to use the magistrates' court, rather than the Crown Court:

'I accept that the situation was a serious one which may have engendered public alarm had it been more widely known; both factors which would suggest that Crown Court might be more appropriate. However, as there appears to have been no previous advice or enforcement (the Waste Regulation Authority prosecution notwithstanding) and as the actual risk would be very difficult to quantify, I consider that the Magistrates Court can and should deal with the case. The possible time and costs involved in Crown Court proceedings against a sole trader whom we have had no previous contact with is unlikely to be justified. You may also remind the bench that they can refer cases for sentencing if they feel their powers are inadequate! If [the individual] decides to plead "not guilty" it would also provide an ideal opportunity for you to take such a case. If you still feel very strongly that Crown Court is warranted, please let me know and I will discuss with the AD as our success record in this area is not high.' (P97–30)

(d) Control. Inspectors are constantly preoccupied with the possible outcome of the proceedings. It is important for them to feel that they retain some control over the handling and outcome of a case. To take a case on indictment means a sense of a greater loss of control over the case by inspectors who can no longer prepare and prosecute the matter themselves, as they would choose, and where witnesses are more vulnerable to skilful cross-examination. These are added incentives for some inspectors to view magistrates' courts as the preferred site of prosecution. As an AD put it, 'Once you get involved in the Crown Court, once it's taken out of our hands as inspectors, we often lose control and we often lose the case . . . which we would otherwise have won [in the magistrates' court].' The adversarial nature of trial and the difficulties it can cause for production of evidence tend to be magnified with trial on indictment. In one fatal case, a lengthy handwritten note from the AD on the bottom of a memo to her from the PI makes this very clear. On choice of forum, she said:

'We are anxious that the outcome of the inevitable proceedings should best reflect the seriousness of the management shortcomings and I believe you and I both now incline towards a Magistrates' Court hearing. We could envisage some scope for clouding of the issues and unpredictability in a jury trial. The point about the need for the matter to be brought to a conclusion quickly is also important.

Besides, [there is] the inevitable distress faced by the relatives of the [dead person] the longer this goes on (as well as a strain for [the field inspector] and yourself). The passage of time would not help witness' credibility in the face of cross-examination before a jury, where even small gaps in recall can be exploited. The fact that no inquest has yet taken place does not make things any easier since there has been no opportunity to air the evidence. Therefore, please proceed on basis of summary trial.' (P97–40)

For inspectors the chief threat to the conviction of the case in the Crown Court comes with the vagaries of jury decision-making, where magistrates, in contrast, are regarded as producing more predictable outcomes. The advantages of Crown Court trial have to be set against the waywardness of juries. Part of the problem is that juries may sometimes fail to understand some of the nuances in the evidence. However, equally significant in some cases is that juries may be thought to have sympathies with the defendant. In a case involving a 'badly executed piece of gas-fitting work,' in which a pregnant mother and her 2-year-old child were badly affected by carbon monoxide poisoning, the AD said, in a memo to the PI concerned,

'the seriousness of the incident, and the fact that the evidence is good, mean that we should still proceed. . . . You have recommended summary trial. We have been under some pressure to ensure the seriousness of these contraventions is brought out by taking cases on indictment. However, our most recent attempt was unsuccessful partly due, our Counsel thinks, to the Jury having artisan tendencies, and this was a first offence, I agree.' The earlier lost case referred to was detailed with a letter from the barrister concerned to the solicitors, giving four reasons for failure to convict. First, there was no direct evidence that accused fitted the fire. Second, the case was somewhat stale. 'This is always a handicap to the prosecution.' Third, the jury were ignorant of the defendant's previous conviction and its full circumstances, and this 'left them with a *relatively* trivial regulatory offence.' The HSE inspectors commented that without the earlier conviction there would have been no prosecution. 'In these circumstances [the jury] are left wondering why the full majesty of the Crown Court trial with wigs and gowns is necessary.' Finally, the customer departed from her initial statement, and 'the artisan jury sided with the unpaid workman rather than the high-handed customer who departed from her "police" statement.' The PI eventually recommended summary trial, though the matter was heard in the Crown Court at the defendant's election.[31] (P97–32: his emphasis)

[31] The defendant was convicted on two counts and fined £1,000 on each, with nearly £200 in costs and a compensation order of £845.

3. The Target: Individual or Company?

A troublesome decision often to be made pre-trial is concerned with the target of any charges. Inspectors often have the choice of targeting the company, an individual, or both, but the working rule is 'We would expect the company to fulfil its legal obligations to its employees in the first place' (86–05). The enforcement of conventional crime schools us to think readily of prosecution as something mounted by an organization against an individual defendant. In the occupational health and safety arena, however, as in some other areas of regulation, prosecution of individuals—as opposed to companies—is less common, whether the individual is a director or manager, on the one hand, or an employee, on the other.[32] The general practice is that regulatory prosecution is normally a proceeding conducted by representatives of one organization against representatives of another.

Only when an inspector is completely satisfied that the company has fulfilled its obligations will the prosecution of an individual be considered.[33] This is because the duty imposed upon employers by s. 2 (1) of the HSW Act to ensure, so far as is reasonably practicable, the health, safety, and welfare at work of all employees tells inspectors that employers should be capable of controlling risks. The thrust of the legislation is reinforced by inspectors' moral stance that companies should bear the burden of responsibility since it is they who are in a position to control the activities of their employees, and they who impose the pressures of production upon individuals. Besides, companies often connive at the rule-breaking of their employees, and rule-breaking usually occurs at the behest of the company, for its benefit, to meet its production schedule, or as a result of inadequate provision for training. Individuals were thought to be wholly at fault only rarely.

There are also practical problems in prosecuting individuals. It is generally a simpler matter to collect evidence when the employer is likely to be charged. Inspectors often feel that the individual concerned, in contrast, will not wish to say anything which may incriminate themselves, neither will their fellow workers. The person has often been punished already in suffering an accident, and this tends to make prosecution appear otiose. Since individuals who are prosecuted suffer the consequences—the possible injury, the penalty and stigma of prosecu-

[32] There were 16 prosecutions of individuals in the sample of prosecution files.

[33] There is similar reluctance to prosecute directors and managers in Australia, such action only being taken in narrowly defined circumstances (Streets, 1998).

tion—it is also possible that magistrates may be more sympathetic to them. The result is that inspectors adopt stricter standards in their decision-making practices, for 'You've got to be very careful that [the individual is] not being scapegoated in some way, and the company can then feel it's done all it needs to do' (86–54). It is not surprising, therefore, that some inspectors had never prosecuted an individual employee, and many of those that had had done so rarely. The practical test would seem to be that prosecution is not to be seriously considered unless there is 'some element of flagrant disregard or wilful disregard . . . on the part of an individual' (86–27). Inspectors are acutely aware that prosecution stains an individual's reputation and identity: 'I don't think any of us likes prosecuting individuals, because of leaving a person with a criminal record' (86–29). Furthermore, it is morally difficult for inspectors to prosecute an employee without prior notice.

Inspectors probably find it easier to prosecute directors and managers. In general, only clear and wilful breaches by individuals are likely to be proceeded against by HSE (F. B. Wright, 1995: 136), for two reasons. First, in keeping with the spirit of the HSW Act, HSE regards the company—the employer—as responsible for the systems of work, the provision of protective equipment and the like, and the general environment of the workplace. HSE's rationale was explained by an AD:

> 'Directors we have done, as well as the company, if they had a particular control over the incident; but they're quite difficult cases to prove. Employees—because generally the philosophy has been that the employee doesn't create his own environment (it should be planned for him by the employer, who is in control of everything), and therefore there are only a few circumstances where somebody's been given all the training, all the kit, all the knowledge, has been monitored, to make sure that they've absorbed all that, and can do it properly, and then goes off and does something . . . And unless you can show all those things, we've always said, "Well, the control, and the remedy, in putting the thing right in terms of what caused it really should be on the employer." And it's pretty unusual to say "No".' (97–05)

HSE's concern to ensure that the workforce is properly trained by the management in health and safety matters contributes to the general disinclination to prosecute an individual if it is believed that a violation was due to some failing on the part of the management. In one big case,

> radiation dosemeters worn by employees showed high readings which were regarded by specialist inspectors as incompatible with compliance with the requirements of the Ionising Radiations Regulations, 1985. It was not clear

how such high exposures could have occurred, but investigation did reveal inadequacies in supervision and monitoring. The field inspector reported that '... at a visit by inspectors in Dec 1994 it was found that [the individual concerned] had bypassed an interlock on an alarm on a radiography enclosure.' There was debate as to whether to prosecute the individual on a HSW Act, 1974 s. 8 charge in addition to a prosecution of the employer. This was the original intention because, as the PI wrote to the AD, 'we caught him "red handed" with a disabled gamma alarm in a radiography enclosure during our investigation.' But the AD replied that a simultaneous prosecution of the employee under HSW Act s. 8 'might adversely affect the prosecution of the company.' Prosecution of the employer in this case was originally strongly urged by FOD, a memo in the file observing: 'We are doubtful of the wisdom of taking the HSWA [HSW Act] section 8 case against [the individual] on the grounds that this may deflect from the emphasis of the whole proceedings, that is, the poor management system operated by [the company], the lack of supervision and the failure to reduce exposures as low as reasonably practicable. Rather, [the individual's] alleged tampering with a safety device should be presented as further evidence against the employer. We recommend that the s. 8 case be dropped while recognising that the Area will have the final say on this.' HSE subsequently withdrew the prosecution. (P97–53)

The second reason for HSE's reluctance is that the prosecution of an individual is thought to present a greater risk of losing the case. 'Probably we agonize more where individuals are concerned', said an AD, 'because our experience is that ... courts seem to require higher levels of proof to convict an individual rather than a company' (97–02). The courts are perceived to be unsympathetic to the prosecution of individuals, and many inspectors voiced the suspicion that they were much more likely to succeed if they targeted the organization: 'Inspectors felt that the courts did not tend to understand or deal sufficiently harshly with health and safety or environmental cases,' writes Hutter (1997: 225), 'and were especially sensitive to the likelihood of the magistrate or jurors being sympathetic to particular types of cases. The most frequently cited example was the prosecution of individuals.' The increased risk of losing is a deterrent to legal action of which inspectors are very conscious, as is evident in an inspector's note in a prosecution file: 'Overall, all parties seem to have considerable mitigation, if not defence, in this matter and therefore legal proceedings, whether against the firm or [the individual] personally, would by no means have a certain outcome. Also, even if there were a guilty plea, the level of mitigation may result in an insignificant fine which would not be satisfactory from HSE's point of view' (P97–18).

There is an expressive as well as an instrumental aspect to this risk of losing which stems from the fact that criminal liability for individuals personalizes responsibility and the penalty in a particularly telling way. This is particularly the case where the non-compliance of an individual is clear and conspicuous:

'I think there are occasions when an individual has so clearly done something wrong, outside his terms of reference, that there is no excuse for it, that you have got to take him to court and say "Look, this person was charged with ensuring that these machines were properly guarded and there's no argument about whether or not it was or was not guarded, it didn't have any guarding on it at all! It was completely missing! Guards were taken off the machine . . . He'd just made a total, utter, horrible, mistake." The management do rely on him getting it right.' (97–03)

However, in the absence of what seems to be clear fault, inspectors fear that prosecuting individuals risks the appearance of vindictiveness:

In a case in which a worker died after falling through a roof, the PI observed: '[The company] is a small firm and Mr Terry is a working foreman rather than a manager and for this reason, I do not feel it appropriate to prosecute him personally, even though he was in charge of the worker.' It was also noted that the firm had not been prosecuted before, nor had been issued with improvement or prohibition notices.[34] (P97–11)

The individual seems here almost to be more of an object of understanding (if not sympathy) because he is 'a working foreman', and not a white-collar company manager. In another fatal case, in which the victim fell from a home-made work platform supported, but unsecured, on the forks of a fork-lift truck being driven by a director of the company, the inspector noted, 'Although [the individual] could be prosecuted under the HSW Act, Section 37, being a director, due to personal circumstances this may well be excessive and I recommend that he is not prosecuted as an individual' (P97–26). This again suggests that in the inspector's view the director simply did not deserve prosecution.[35]

[34] The defendant pleaded guilty to two charges. There was a fine of £3,000 under the Construction Regulations, and £10,000 under s. 2 of the HSW Act.

[35] Desert was prominent also in the views of a former Chief Inspector of MQI about the framing of mines and quarries legislation. He recognized a reluctance to prosecute, because it 'is not sport for us because of the way in which the duties are set out in the Mines and Quarries Act. They're set out in person. Now even FI are reluctant to prosecute persons, the individual.' In FI, however, proposals to prosecute individuals would, in the 1980s, usually go to headquarters since it was a more serious matter than prosecuting a company. Similarly, in the Agricultural Inspectorate in the mid-1980s, 'There are', said an inspector,

Where it judges the circumstances warrant it, however, HSE will consider prosecution of senior members of a company's management, even though it is generally held to be more difficult to collect evidence to prosecute an individual than a company. HSE has stated its belief in the importance of any such prosecution having the capacity to be widely recognized as deserved, if the confidence of management as a whole is to be retained (Health and Safety Commission, 1993: 3). Accusations of vindictiveness can be defeated if the defendant can be presented in a less sympathetic light. This is possible if, for example, the penalty will not seem harsh, because the defendant has ample means to pay a fine. In the major asbestos case, the inspector referred to the defendant's being 'adequately resourced', a point raised by the PI, who wanted to know what the evidence for this was. The inspector replied that he wanted to

'make the point that although he is a small contractor he owns a number of valuable assets, such as his farm, and therefore would have the financial resources from which any fine imposed by either Court could be extracted from him. I would not wish to be seen to be recommending Crown Court action against a contractor whom I knew could not possibly afford to meet the fines levied against him ... [I]t appears to be the case that the farm is, in fact, his property along with a fairly significant number of items of construction plant which form the basis of his plant hire business.' The inspector went on to accede to the PI's suggestion that trial should take place in the magistrates' court, rather than Crown Court ('our record in the Crown Court has not been particularly good to-date and [I] accept that it may be wise to bring Mr Dixon before the magistrates who I hope will have the good judgment to refer him to the Crown Court for sentencing should he be found guilty'). (P97–30)

The following case, in which an excavator had fouled overhead power lines, is typical of the ways in which such cases are formally justified by inspectors:

'The circumstances of this incident show a serious lack of overall control by Mr Bentley [the manager] which could have resulted in serious injury or fatality. The instructions of his manager to provide supervision were not followed.' In mitigation, it was said, 'Mr Bentley appears to have been "thrown in at the deep end" by the firm. He will claim he misunderstood the instruction to supervise at all times. Neither the firm nor the [crane] driver are blameless in this matter.

'two inhibitions, I think. One is that the inspector knows it's the bloke's own money that you are talking about. And invariably the confrontation is in his own home, and that's an inhibition if you think about it. ... I can see ... where you translate from going along advising and making some progress to saying "It's not enough. I need more from you," is a difficult step to take.'

However, Mr Bentley was in the best position to prevent the incident and should have been aware of GS6 precautions.' A hand-written set of reasons for prosecuting was then added by the field inspector: 'Very serious matter. Potential for fatal accident. Lot of overhead powerlines and dragline excavator with a long jib needs highest precautions. Potential [for] accident very high. Direct supervision required for s. 98 to organise and not done.[36] Manager instructed to provide supervision—none provided. Inadequate instructions to driver. Manager in control, aware of risks and G86 breach . . . [Prosecution] of Manager proposed, although firm and driver not blameless.' HSE lost this case, having failed to show that the defendant was a manager under s. 98 of the Mines and Quarries Act. (P97–18)

The decision to prosecute here may well have been influenced by the fact that the company had been prosecuted once before and also served with a prohibition notice, both in connection with the dangers of overhead power lines.

Prosecution of the employer is often claimed to be much more in keeping with the instrumental aim of producing change in contrast with the prosecution of an individual, which is regarded as punitive (though sometimes justifiable also as a general deterrent). As critics have pointed out, the law might carry more of an instrumental threat to those contemplating non-compliance if managers and directors thought that there was a risk that, if convicted, they might personally be stigmatized and punished—even imprisoned—for a criminal violation of a regulatory offence (Johnstone, 1994; Wells, 2001; cf. Geis & DiMento, 1995).

6. PRE-TRIAL BARGAINING

Various pre-trial practices involving negotiations between prosecution and defence are found in the administration of criminal justice (Darbyshire, 2000; Sanders & Young, 2000). The term 'plea-bargaining', which is often employed to refer to such negotiations, is an imprecise one and often used imprecisely in the literature, since there are various forms of explicit and tacit bargaining. There are bargains over a possible reduction in the number or the severity of charges to be laid, in return for a guilty plea. There may also be negotiations about the defence offering a guilty plea in return for the possibility of a reduction in sentence, the result of the practice of sentence discounting, the courts' routine reward for a plea of guilty. A similar effect may be achieved by a defendant who

[36] Four other reasons were also given at this point but the handwriting in the file was too poor to be readable.

successfully bargains with the prosecution to have the case tried summarily by the magistrates, rather than on indictment in the Crown Court. The purpose of such bargaining from the prosecution's point of view is to achieve a conviction and penalty while at the same time avoiding the possibility that the case would be lost if the defendant were to plead not guilty and go to trial, creating the opportunity to challenge possibly weak evidence. The point of plea-bargaining from the defendant's perspective is to narrow the discretion of any subsequent decision-maker (in this case, the sentencing court) such that the penalty to be imposed upon conviction will be less than might otherwise be expected. Pre-trial bargaining inevitably constrains the extent of the court's powers; that is its purpose.[37]

However, there is a difference of view in the socio-legal literature about what underlies pre-trial negotiations. One school of thought suggests that such bargaining is a way of serving management and crime control values in the criminal process (Packer, 1969) as efficiently as possible by maximizing the number of convictions at the lowest cost in terms of money and time. This claim is contested, however (Darbyshire, 2000; Schulhofer, 1984), though in the context of HSE practices, it was supported by an experienced PI who, when asked the main purpose of plea-bargaining, said: 'It is to speed it up. Everybody wants a guilty plea. Courts don't want defended cases, nor does society, so we're after a quick resolution . . . and if the defendant is going to plead guilty [so much the better] . . . ' (97–03). An AD took the view that if plea-bargaining will secure a conviction, then that was reason enough:

> 'It certainly applies in some cases. I mean if a defendant is perhaps exhibiting all the right signals of having learnt from the exercise, and they're perhaps—you know, the message to the general world at large is perhaps not a great factor, and the seriousness of the offence is not so very great, then, yes, I mean, the resources question would certainly play a part in the decision-making, because there's no point in, you know, in tying-up inspector time unnecessarily. Because, I mean they are very resource-intensive, defended cases. So yes, it does figure, but on important ones there's a limit beyond which we won't go.' (P97–02)

The alternative theory about the purpose of pre-trial bargaining gives less emphasis to the values of economy and efficiency and more to the expressive value of justice. On this view, pre-trial bargaining is engaged in by the participants because it offers an attractive and effective way of

[37] There may also be implications for any civil action; see below.

ensuring that a case receives fitting punishment (e.g. Heumann, 1978; Rosett & Cressey, 1976).

Tacit forms of bargaining are also to be found in the pre-trial regulatory process. For example, a type of implicit bargaining is observable in the conspicuous efforts sometimes made by a firm facing prosecution to display compliance and 'the right attitude'. Some firms seem to be well aware that evidence of mitigation, as displayed in their subsequent efforts to comply, can diminish the apparent seriousness of an act or event. The response of the violator to the possibility of prosecution is sometimes important for HSE, and efforts to repair the source of the problem or the damage may mitigate to the extent of ensuring that the case is tried summarily. Thus in a case in which employees suffered a form of occupational asthma as a result of exposure to glues that they had been spraying, the inspector wrote:

> 'I have explained to the company that they will have to suffer the pain of the proceedings referred to above, and this present proposed action, before we hopefully can draw a line and move forward. As a result of the more positive approach, I would recommend summary proceedings with an explanation of the above as reasons for not going for indictment.' (P97–13)

The files revealed no case, however, in which efforts at repair were sufficient to persuade HSE to drop the proceedings.

How much pre-trial bargaining went on in the past in HSE is not clear. Some inspectors claimed it was not permitted in FI during the 1980s.[38] However, it is clear from the records of prosecution files and from conversations with officials that the practice certainly goes on now. A PI acknowledged that bargaining in terms of a reduction in the number or severity of charges that may be laid sometimes takes place between HSE inspectors and defendants, or their legal representatives:

> 'I mean, the instructions [in the past] were, "You do not do it. If you decide you were taking two cases, you will take those two cases."... And then that became slightly absurd, when you *were* faced with situations where you went

[38] Though Hutter found that it went on: 'In some cases securing a conviction was so highly valued that "horse trading" or "plea-bargaining", as it is more formally known, was entered into. In all of these cases the reputational damage which could be incurred by a prosecution was clearly intended as a specific deterrent. Similarly, prosecution as a reminder of obligations and responsibilities was intended as a specific deterrent, although the cause of general deterrence could also be met. The evidence of other studies suggests that these inspectors were correct in their assumption that companies are concerned to create and maintain good reputations and are hence susceptible to adverse publicity being used as a form of social control' (Hutter, 1997: 222, references omitted).

through a defended case, when they would have said "Well, if you dropped one of those, we would have pleaded guilty." So a practice started to grow of doing the odd deal . . .'

Q: 'When would this have been, roughly, would you say?'

A: 'Ooh. I . . . ten-ish years ago I would say—I wouldn't rely on that—but you always had to justify it to head office. Head office saw cases and would ask questions. I mean, I think that over the last ten years, we've become much less sensitive about that, and what I'm aware of is the odd time that people will ring me up and say "We've been given this opportunity, what do you think?" And my answer's "Fine!" ' (97–05)

One reason for the greater use of bargaining was said to be that it has spilled over into regulatory prosecution from solicitors more accustomed to the practice in conventional criminal work: 'Solicitors seem to think that it's normal practice, as the police do it, the CPS [Crown Prosecution Service] do it, so I think why do we make rods for our backs, make it harder putting one information in, which they defend like mad and argue, when others put in three, and drop two off, and get one, and everybody's happy. Well, justice is done' (97–03).

Study of prosecution files will not always reveal when pre-trial bargaining about plea, charge, or forum has taken place. In some files there was evidence that charges originally proposed had been dropped or changed without any recorded explanation. For example, a woman in one case had had a finger trapped as a result of an uncovenanted stroke of a power press she was operating. She was taken to hospital and needed four stitches in the wound, though no work time was lost. There were originally two charges proposed: one under s. 14 (1) of the Factories Act, 1961, and the other under Reg. 4 (23) of the Electricity at Work Regulations, 1989. This latter charge was later withdrawn, though no reason was given in the file for this. It is not possible to say, therefore, whether the guilty plea to s. 14 (1) of the Factories Act, 1961, was entered in return for HSE's dropping the charge under Regulation 4, though it may be significant that the firm had originally entered a not guilty plea. This was subsequently changed to guilty, and the firm fined £300 (P97–07).

Conceptions of desert can mean not bargaining at all in some cases. Sometimes the inspector's view of the just outcome and penalty for the case is such as to foreclose the possibility of bargaining. It is again important for inspectors that a good fit is attained between their conception of the deserts of the case and the likely outcome, in terms both of verdict and of penalty:

'There are quite a number of cases where we don't—you know, where we feel that we've pared down the charges, which is often the case, to the minimum that adequately represents the circumstances. And, you know, if it is a serious case, and we feel that every charge has a key part of the story to tell, then there have been cases where we haven't conceded at all. There's one ongoing now where I think we've let them have one [i.e. been willing to drop one charge], but they wanted two, and we said "No". So they're defending—which is a large international company. And so be it.' (P97–02)

There were a number of cases in the files, however, where the willingness of either side to bargain emerged clearly. In one, for example,

A 35 year-old employee of a roofing company fell through a rooflight when doing maintenance work. No precautions had been taken. The man fell ten metres while holding a gas cylinder, fracturing his pelvis and skull. He had to spend four weeks in hospital, and had suffered long term neurological effects. His employer was prosecuted under Regulation 36 (1) of the Construction (Working Places) Regulations, 1966 for allowing the injured person to pass across fragile material where a fall of more than two metres was possible, without taking any of the prescribed precautions. A second charge under s. 3 HSW Act was entered as an alternative. This, said the inspector in a letter to a solicitor acting for HSE, 'was not proposed initially, as there was good evidence regarding employment. However, *when the defendant indicated that a plea of not guilty was to be entered, it was felt sensible to "cover the bases."* . . . There are obviously lots of other law that could have been used', the letter continued, '—HSW Act s. 2—Management of Health and Safety Regulations Reg. 3 and 4, but I chose to use only one as it was a small business, who until then had not been brought to our attention.' The addition of the HSW Act charge prompted a complaint from the solicitor for the defendant that the firm had done a great deal of work in preparing for trial on the original charge: 'It was readily apparent that no enquiries had been made to ascertain [the injured person's] status. He is and was self-employed and consequently the original charge was misconceived.' The letter went on to complain that the solicitor had not received full disclosure as a result of the introduction of the new charge. 'Because of the manner in which this matter was investigated and has been dealt with to date, we would have no alternative but to apply for a Wasted Costs Order against the prosecution. This will involve several thousand pounds. . . . Entirely without prejudice as to plea and without making any admissions of fact or evidence for or on behalf of our client, we would be prepared to take instructions from him on the basis that he could be formally cautioned for the latter allegation. This would require the prosecution to offer no evidence in respect of the Construction (Working Places) Regulations case. We would not apply for a Wasted Costs Order. He could be allowed to withdraw his plea in respect of the new matter and thereafter the Summons be withdrawn and again we would make no application for costs against the HSE.'

For HSE's part, a letter from an HSE solicitor to the defendant's solicitor stated: 'In the event of your client electing Summary Trial and pleading guilty to the [second] summons... the first summons will be withdrawn. If not, the Prosecution will proceed with both matters on the basis indicated.' The original plea was of not guilty to both charges. Eventually HSE dropped the charge under HSW Act, 1974 s. 3. The defendant later changed his plea to one of guilty to one charge under the Construction (Working Places) Regulations, 1966.[39] (P97–33; my emphasis)

Bargaining about the number of charges or about the possibility of lesser charges requires that one or more charges be added so that they may later be surrendered, as part of the bargain. Overcharging for bargaining purposes is an attractive way of producing results: 'The thing is, that if you put in just for the guarding case, then they may defend that; there's nothing to bargain on.... Others may disagree, but I actually find that psychologically this business works, and they come out saying "Thank you very much for dropping those two off."... [A]nd whether you've pleaded to one or two, it's still a conviction, and as far as we're concerned, it's still got convicted for the incident' (97–03). The speaker, an experienced PI, was in no doubt about the value of the practice, but acknowledged that it was not yet

'common practice... although it is something which is obviously creeping in, is actually putting in charges for a bargaining purpose. And it's a useful tool—very good psychological weapon. You put in five informations and they'll plead guilty to none. You drop three and they'll plead guilty to two and they'll think they've won something, but you've still got two convicted on. You put two in, they'll defend the two. I would use it—we use it quite a lot.' (97–03)

It is important, however, if an inspector embarks on pre-trial bargaining, that the charges that are laid 'follow the usual rules; that is, they've got to be sustainable, because... you can't just throw them in as confetti' (97–03). The following case is typical of this approach, and the debate that sometimes goes on between field inspectors and PIs:

A gas fitter was accused of installing defective flueing and ventilation which had resulted in a couple and their baby receiving hospital treatment. Four counts under the Gas Safety (Installation and Use) Regulations, 1984 were proposed originally and notified to the defendant. In a report to the PI, the inspector considered some strategic pre-trial questions: 'We might be prepared to bargain away charge number 1 for a plea to charge number 2,' which he had already decided went 'to the heart of the matter.... We have all the evidence we would

[39] He was fined £1,500 plus £1,500 costs.

normally need for such a case. The occupiers will make good witnesses and have given consistent statements.... The question remaining for us is whether we would accept a plea to either Reg. 25 (5) or 25 (1) (b) charge, thereby accepting his [defendant's] version of events, and a possible lower fine (he could mitigate that it is a "technical" breach) or hold out for a conviction to a Reg. 27 (1) on the basis of the prosecution's version of events.' Eventually only two charges were used.[40] (P97–16)

Offering to drop a charge can be especially useful to the prosecution if it may be one that could turn out to be difficult to prove:

In a case in which a worker had fallen from a platform, fracturing his skull, the defendant had been charged under s. 29 (1) HSW, 1974 and PUWE Regulations 1992 Reg. 5(1) for failing to provide an item of work equipment. A note from the inspector to the PI said: 'If they plead to the S2 [*sic*] we offer no evidence on the Regs; if they contest both we pursue both. The regs. are both down to a battle between the specialists' views and who to believe.' The PI replied: '...I agree with your proposal. I feel the Regs case may be weak and doesn't really contribute to the accident. The report...is interesting and I doubt if some of his legal conclusions are sound but it gives the mitigation to us. Your prosecution answers it all.' In the event, the defendant did not agree to plead guilty, and HSE prosecuted both charges. As the inspectors had envisaged, the case under the Regulations was difficult to prove and the defendant succeeded with a not guilty plea to the charge under the PUWE Regulations, but was found guilty under the HSW Act and fined £3,500 plus £500 costs. (P97–23)

A variant in the pre-trial manoeuvring over number and type of charges is for HSE to put up alternative charges. This tactic may be deployed if there is a likelihood that the defendant may plead not guilty to one of a pair of charges. There is a tendency to keep both going if HSE is faced with a not guilty plea. One example of this approach appears in the case cited above of the 35-year-old employee of a roofing company who fell though a roof light, where the inspector concerned wrote of the need, when the defendant indicated that a plea of not guilty was to be entered, to 'cover the bases'. This may be an effective way of securing a conviction while avoiding costly preparatory work, such as that typically involved in clarifying the sometimes complicated enquiries into the employment status of a worker:

'[I]f...a proposition comes forward from the defence, and they say, "Well, we'll plead guilty to this if you do that", then we will consider that on its merits. If we

[40] The defendant was convicted on both, receiving two fines of £700 each plus nearly £600 in costs, and a £500 compensation order.

could still put the facts of the case in front of the magistrates without being unduly constrained, then, you know, that may be a cost-effective option; and sometimes, indeed, we will deliberately put up alternatives. So if it's not clear as to the employment status of an individual—that there could be an argument as to whether they were employed or self employed—then rather than involving ourselves in that argument, which ultimately will be a question for the court to decide, we might put up an alternative HSW section 2, section 3 charge, and say to the firm "You can choose which one you plead to, and we'll drop the other."' (97–04)

As these remarks suggest, the initiative to bargain is sometimes taken by the defendants, as in the following case in which the victim had fallen through a window of a nursing home, sustaining fatal injuries. The defendant's solicitors had written to HSE setting out points in his favour, concluding:

'We therefore would submit to you that there was more than adequate assessment of risk carried out, and confirmed. We would indicate an intention to enter a guilty plea in the Magistrates' Court to the charge of failing to restrict the window openings, which we see as an absolute offence, and on which basis we would invite you to withdraw the second charge of assessment of the risk.' In an effort to secure HSE's consent to the bargain, the solicitors portrayed the defence as having made a substantial concession: 'In that event the defence would not make any application for costs against the Prosecution for the withdrawal of that second matter, notwithstanding the substantial costs that have been incurred in the investigations and the instructions to the Expert. The matter could proceed on the basis of this guilty plea at the next hearing . . . ' The inspector replied that HSE agreed on the basis outlined, adding: 'I trust that we can proceed on the basis of a guilty plea at the next hearing.'[41] (P97–68)

Another form of pre-trial negotiation involves bargaining about forum, the purpose of which is, so far as the defendant is concerned, to achieve the quicker court appearance, lower penalty, and lesser publicity of the summary trial.[42] In the case involving employees who contracted

[41] To cement the bargain, the defendant's solicitors wrote in response to the inspector's request that they confirm the arrangements: 'We confirm that upon the Health and Safety Executive withdrawing the charge of failing to adequately assess the risk, a guilty plea will be entered by our Clients in relation to the other charge. No application for costs will be made against the Prosecution for the withdrawal of the first charge. We confirm therefore that the case can proceed by way of plea in mitigation at Court on the next occasion.' The guilty plea was to a breach of the Workplace (Health, Safety and Welfare) Regulations, 1992, which received a fine of £2,000 and nearly £1,000 costs.

[42] Changes in court rules now mean that magistrates have to consider plea before venue. Therefore, the opportunity to make formal representations on mode of trial has been lost.

occupational asthma as a result of spraying glues, the PI said in a letter to solicitors for HSE:

'Most unusually, I have been contacted by [a] . . . barrister to discuss alternatives that may enable the company to change their plea to one of guilty.' The expectation was also that they would revert to trial in the magistrates' court. 'Since our initial discussions, there have been a number of developments, not least of which is that counsel acting for the defendant has indicated that they *may* change their plea and the mode of trial, subject to modifications to the charges. After consideration, we have decided to accept this proposal.'

However, it is not always the case that the pressures on one side or the other are so compelling that a bargain is inevitable. 'After discussion with [the AD]', the PI continued, 'we have concluded that this new package is not quite robust enough to enable this course of action to proceed, although further developments may modify this view' (P97–13: emphasis original).[43]

Defendants are by no means powerless in pre-trial negotiations. After all, the defendant in any criminal matter has the power to plead not guilty and compel the prosecution to prove its case beyond reasonable doubt in open court. Other tactics are also possible. Defendants can issue threats in an attempt to raise the prosecution's anxieties about the prospects of success, or the costs of the case. In a case in which a woman was badly injured operating a power press on which the safety switch had been defeated, the defendant's solicitor wrote to HSE asking for 'your formal confirmation that no previous breach of these regulations is recorded against our client company and your confirmation that a prosecution has followed every breach of the Power Presses Regulations that have been found by Health and Safety Inspectors'. This disingenuous request is presumably a device to imply that the defence may be able to claim that it has been the victim of discriminatory practice if it is admitted by HSE that it has not always prosecuted for such a breach (in his reply, the field inspector ducked the point) (P97–63).[44]

The interdependence of relationships in regulatory enforcement revealed here is analogous to the bargaining about compliance and enforcement that occurs in the field between inspector and firm. Defendants have things to give (their cooperation in the proceedings, their future compliance with the regulatory agency's requests, and, most importantly,

[43] The firm pleaded guilty to three charges under the Control of Substances Hazardous to Health Regulations, 1994, and was fined £1,500 on each, with £2,500 costs.

[44] See also the bargaining about a Wasted Costs Order in the case of the roofing company employee who fell through a roof light.

a guilty plea), just as regulated firms give implied compliance, information, and cooperation to regulatory officials in their routine enforcement of the law. The fact that negotiations about the prosecution of occupational health and safety violations go on might suggest that arguments about pre-trial bargaining providing for more appropriate levels of punishment (e.g. Rosett & Cressey, 1976) are misplaced, since occupational health and safety penalties are low compared with those for conventional crimes. However, it is clear that the protagonists are not simply preoccupied with a concern to speed up the proceedings and to save resources, as conventional explanations would claim. While many of the bargains struck reveal a strong desire to expedite the matter, they also reveal a desire to achieve a commensurate penalty. In this sense, both theories of pre-trial bargaining in criminal justice are relevant to understanding what goes on pre-trial in occupational health and safety regulation.

7. CIVIL ACTION

In addition to any prosecution HSE might pursue, the aftermath of an accident often involves a civil claim by the victim or the victim's family. The criminal law system of state prosecution and punishment coexists here with the civil law system of personal claim and compensation. The character of tort compensation tends to be particularistic with a focus on winning monetary redress for an individual. Little is known about the degree to which the tort system has an impact on the prevalence of occupational health and safety problems or about the interrelationship of criminal and civil law systems of legal control in this area of regulation. One exception is work conducted by Freedman (1989), in which it was discovered that, ironically, factory inspectors were criticized by trade union officials for being too preoccupied with the faults of individuals and not sufficiently concerned with general systems of working, or with general hazards in the workplace. However, it is interesting to note that similar complaints were made by inspectors about trade union officials, who were said to be too concerned with winning compensation for injuries suffered by their members and too little involved in a more broadly activist approach to prevention (Hawkins, 1992*a*: 145–6).

Assistance in the pursuit of a civil claim may be provided by inspectors who sometimes give advice to injured persons, but only in the most general terms. Typical was a letter from an inspector to an injured person which instructed him that 'Any claim you wish to make for compensation will need to be made in the civil court. You should take legal advice if you wish to pursue this course of action' (P97–41). No record of civil action is normally kept in HSE prosecution files, except to the extent that it relates directly to HSE (usually in the form of requests from solicitors for photographic and other forms of evidence). HSE can assist civil litigants in material ways, as inspectors often point out. This help consists of the supply of factual statements by inspectors, together with photographs, for a standard fee. HSE is prepared to disclose relevant documents, but only after proceedings have commenced and pleadings have closed. This assistance is limited to relevant factual sections of investigation reports, any drawings or sketches, results of tests or sampling, photographs, advice sent before or after the accident, and witness statements, where the witness consents to disclosure.

While criminal and civil proceedings are separate matters, HSE inspectors are conscious that their decisions about prosecution may have implications for the pursuit of a civil claim.[45] The few inspectors who did discuss the relationship of a possible civil claim to any strategic decision about prosecution were divided over whether they were prepared to take the matter into account in the prosecution decision. Those who did seemed more concerned not to take a case that might be lost (and therefore damage a civil claim) than to take one which would probably win. 'It may be that if we prosecute a company that will significantly aid an injured person's civil action against the company,' said one. 'I don't think that should be an exclusive reason for prosecuting, but . . . it is a factor that does get taken into account.' Speaking of this problem, an AD referred to the example of the aggrieved individual: 'where they're pursuing a civil claim and they would like there to be an HSE prosecution to help speed and ease the path of their civil claim, then they will try and badger us to take action that we perhaps otherwise wouldn't have taken' (97–04). The problem for the inspector, however, is that 'If you've got a dodgy one [prosecution] you could muck up their civil claim by losing it' (86–51). Equally, the implications for a tort claim may mean that solicitors for the defendant in a criminal case can have a particularly strong incentive to achieve an acquittal, or, if acquittal seems unlikely, to bargain to reduce the number of charges. 'The motivation [for pre-trial bargaining], I would think,' said an AD, ' . . . is mainly the

[45] There is an automatic civil liability for breach of statutory duty under the HSW Act. This gives solicitors an incentive to encourage HSE to prosecute, since their clients' claims will often succeed because of HSE's action.

civil litigation; you know, that's what perhaps is concentrating their minds most of all . . . if they can get their clients off a charge which might have serious repercussions for a civil case, then that's often, I think, the angle that they come from' (97–02).

The parallel civil jurisdiction may also bring some benefits for the regulatory agency, by alerting HSE to previously unknown events, or to matters that may have been more serious than at first appreciated, as the following snatch of conversation indicates:

Q: 'I wanted to ask what part, if any, the . . . civil jurisdiction played in your decision-making about prosecution, because frequently you find letters in the files from solicitors for the injured party saying they've been instructed to bring a civil action. Is there any connection between the two things?'

A: 'Not in terms of the decision-making. What the effect can be is perhaps additional information, because there have been cases where perhaps an accident as reported by an employer is represented as being fairly minor and trivial, and it doesn't get selected because of that for investigation, and therefore nothing else of the process happens. And then maybe sometime later, we may get a letter from a solicitor acting for the injured person that puts quite a different perspective on it. Or sometimes we get solicitors' letters [referring to] accidents which have never been reported and should have been.' (97–02)

8. CONCLUSION

Pre-trial processes are a form of serial decision-making in which the handling of particular occupational health and safety problems has tactical concerns of a legal kind superimposed on them. In a legal bureaucracy decision-making is influenced not only by organizational options open to officials, but also by legal options that are realistically available. These legal questions demand that processes be directed towards screening out those cases that present features suggesting that prosecution may not be the appropriate response, as well as those potential prosecution cases that seem to have some element of legal weakness. Occasionally other cases may be screened out for failing to meet certain standards of gravity. Note, however, that inspectors are not just concerned with amassing sufficient evidence to gain a conviction, but are interested also in the penalty the case will attract from the court, a matter also inextricably tangled up with conceptions of the gravity of the violation. The small number of prosecution cases lost in the courts attests to the care given to this screening of risky cases by field and supervising inspectors.

One of the most important features in pre-trial decision-making about prosecution is the high degree of control which the regulatory agency, and in particular the inspector, exercises over the handling of the matter. The decision-maker at the point of entry to the organization is the key figure in a serial decision-making system by virtue of possessing the gatekeeper's intimate knowledge of the nature of the precipitating problem. The inspector remains central, whether the formal structure or procedures of the organization are such that the usual practice is for the field inspector to decide about prosecution, subject to approval by the PI (as in FOD), or whether the decision-making is centralized, ultimately resting in the hands of the most senior officials. But until a case finds its way into court, the regulatory organization maintains control over its fate. Inspectors determine whether to take action, that is, whether to create a case, and if so what sort of action to take. It is the inspector who initially determines whether prosecution is the right course of action, collects the evidence, questions possible witnesses, suggests what charges would be appropriate, and takes part in pre-trial bargaining. In a legal bureaucracy in which there is a strong desire not to lose cases, control of the process is an extremely important matter. But when the matter goes to the magistrates or Crown Court, control is lost to the court.

Pre-trial decision-making has an unfolding character. Inspectors are rarely, if ever, in the position of 'knowing' at the outset that a particular violation will be prosecuted. The decision about prosecution demands thought and reflection, and attention has to be given to the advice of colleagues, especially the PI. It is at this point in particular that broader issues of policy defined by the organization and especially its own concerns about how it manages appearances have to be clarified, together with the legal implications raised by the case. This means that any decision made pre-trial has a markedly provisional quality. The process can be seen accordingly as a series of supporting decisions by which inspectors seek to reduce the uncertainty surrounding the decision to prosecute.

It is important to keep analytically separate the policy questions for inspectors about whether a prosecution case is one about the right sort of matters and serving the right kind of purpose, from the technical question about whether the available evidence and the way in which it is presented will support a prosecution. Ironically, while the latter may seem to be a question of a lesser order, it is more likely to be the one which is more at issue in the discussions between field and principal inspectors, and more likely to require the advice of senior colleagues. Issues of broader policy, bound up with what sorts of case to prosecute at all, tend to be decided at field level by the most junior members of the regulatory organization.

Part II

Surround

4 Decision-Making Environments

1. THE SURROUND IN GENERAL

The surround is where both the predictable and the unexpected happen—the accidents that are the perennial concern of the inspector and the occasional disasters that become the special preoccupation of the regulatory agency. The surround is the setting not only for the individual drama and personal tragedy of a factory accident, but also the widespread public alarm prompted by a major incident such as a factory explosion or a train crash. The surround in which both the regulatory agency and its regulated firms sit has political, economic, and social facets.

As regulators conceive it, the surround may have an immediate and local character, or it may be remote. The surround is not, however, simply the setting for what might be termed naturally occurring undesired events. In its response to disaster, to changing public or political attitudes, or to shifts in the economic climate, government and media themselves becomes features in a regulatory agency's surround. If, for example, the political climate is interventionist, government may be inclined to devote more resources to permit an increase in the level of regulatory activity (see Hutter & Manning, 1990). Similarly, in times of economic prosperity there should in theory be more public money to enable allocation of more resources to regulatory agencies, while in the private sector there should be more money available to meet the more stringent requirements of occupational health and safety regulation. Prosperity and recession are conditions that themselves prompt untoward events, though their character or number may differ. Prosperity leading to increased levels of production is, for example, likely to increase risks and accidents to workers. Similarly, the media can also become a part of an agency's surround in the way they respond to events, especially to specific events 'which are used to characterize regulation and bring it vividly to public awareness' (Hutter & Manning, 1990: 108).

The general political, economic, and social facets of the surround in which regulation is carried out are an important presence in the individual decisions about prosecution that are actually made, though they act in subtle ways. The surround both shapes the formulation of agency policy and affects the making of decisions by inspectors in specific cases. What inspectors treat as possible and reasonable demands to make of an employer is a construction arrived at in light of the prevailing economic climate. The surround not only fashions part of the decision field in decision-making in discrete cases, it is important also for its ability to bring a particular decision frame into play. The result of this is that 'many of the more immediate and observable outcomes of regulatory activity, such as notices, prosecutions, fines and other indicia, are patterned by broad structural changes in a society as well as organizationally based decisions and discretion' (Hutter & Manning, 1990: 103).

From the political, economic, and social segments of the surround, then, spring the undesired events and problems that are ostensibly the raw material for regulatory control. Among the important features in HSE's surround in the course of this research were dramatic shifts in economic prosperity and activity, the advent of a government with pronounced ideological views about the value of regulation, and the occurrence of a number of disasters, both local and remote, that prompted public concern. The effect of all of these features is subtly to alter the expectations of employers, employees, and the public (as well as regulators) about the desirability and character of regulatory action. Matters have a greater or lesser propensity to burst out of the regulatory agency's surround, depending in part on how public positions are construed, their salience shifting with the political, economic, and social facets that exist as part of the surround. Disasters quickly bring with them changed expectations of a public or political kind about the necessity and appropriateness of responses, whether of repair or punishment. The more dramatic, the more damaging or widespread the disaster, the more matters are likely to erupt in a way that compels a regulatory response, since organizations like HSE are extremely sensitive to events occurring in their surround and to possible repercussions for the agency. The susceptibility of HSC and HSE to big events, in particular, is evident from their public utterances. 'Perhaps the most significant safety event of the year', said HSE in 1987, 'was one which happened outside our jurisdiction, the Chernobyl disaster. This had immediate and long-lasting physical and psychological effects' (Health and Safety Commission/Executive, 1987)... Such major incidents are 'high profile events, and HSE has to respond appropriately and be seen by the public to be responding. Major investigations and incidents requiring immediate attention demand a considerable amount of our time and effort' (Health and Safety Commission, 1999: 42).

A rich variety of important features are found in the surround. How events are interpreted and what are construed as appropriate responses by the agency are themselves intimately dependent upon interrelated social and political views, as well as on other features in the surround, such as the economic climate. Surveying major shifts in occupational health and safety, HSC commented wistfully that at the end of the 1980s developments

'that nowadays shape so much of our work had begun to outline themselves—increased activity in the industrial safety area by the European Community; the rise in public concern over industrial harms; and changes in industrial structure reducing the importance of the heavier industries. But we knew nothing then of the transnational implication of Bhopal or Chernobyl, or the global consequences of pollution, or of the Single European Act and the impact of qualified majority voting in the European Community.' (Health and Safety Commission, 1990*b*, p. viii)

1. Politics

The political environment within which HSE has operated over the last twenty years has changed markedly. The election to office of successive Conservative governments in Britain was seen by HSE inspectors in the 1980s as creating a context for their work that was generally opposed to regulatory activism. This sentiment intruded into the agency and was reflected at the time in the approach of many inspectors in their decision-making. The perceived hostility of government to regulation and the way in which it directly affected decision-making in individual cases was made clear by an inspector who commented in the mid-1980s: 'I think there's a political climate that suggests that the Civil Service ought to be seen as assisting industry, and not acting as a purely prosecution-minded policeman . . .' (86–38).

One aspect of the perceived governmental hostility was a sense of vulnerability in the agency, since it was an organization engaged in regulatory restraint in ways that had powerful implications for the conduct of business, operating as it did in a world suffused with high levels of ideological commitment to laissez-faire values. Another shift in the surround that occurred in parallel with developments in the economy was a reduction in the influence of trade unions and safety representatives, particularly at shop-floor level. Increasingly, trade unions and their officials had to take into account the very survival of companies and jobs (Health and Safety Executive, 1984: 1). As one analysis had it: 'economic recession, political individualism or modern neo-conservatism, and the media influence (which varies with events) tend to make agencies more visible and accountable for their actions and policies, especially when these policies are seen as potentially "interventionist" in character' (Hutter & Manning, 1990: 107).

HSE's vulnerability to the political climate became real in the early 1980s, before the beginning of the first phase of this research, when it suffered cuts in its resources, resulting in recruitment of new staff being suspended between 1980 and early 1983. These cuts were not quite as damaging as they might otherwise have been since, as the agency observed, the demise of hazardous heavy industries in the early 1980s had 'also provided some relief and to an extent disguised the consequences of the reduction in the number particularly of Factory Inspectors which [had] taken place' (Health and Safety Commission/Executive, 1987: 2).

The change in stance which HSE staff felt constrained to make in the 1980s—a subtle form of policy change—was not something formally articulated in writing, but was something to which they were sensitive, in the form of a shift in the political context of inspectors' work: 'The government of the day provides a feel as to what is appropriate . . . and this, I'm sure, will filter down. But there's no specifics I can put my finger on' (86–37). An area director (AD) suggested that this change in the political climate had a far-reaching impact on the general approach to enforcement in HSE:

> 'there has been a culture in HSE, perhaps picking up on the de-regulation movement. You know, some inspectors when they come into the job . . . they come in perhaps [with] more of a social worker mentality and see their role as being to advise and guide and counsel, rather than enforce. That sort of approach can gather momentum. . . . Given a wider perspective on HSE's position and work and role, you know, maybe the de-regulation and political aspects do get blown up a little bit, so that inspectors feel that it's not probably regarded as the right thing to do, to prosecute.' (97–02)

In the deregulatory climate of the late 1980s, in which government wished to reduce regulatory burdens ('cutting red tape'), HSE inspectors were, by ministerial diktat, not allowed to issue a notice without warning, nor without giving the employer the opportunity to make representations. Such warning had to come in the form of a letter saying the inspector was 'minded' to issue a notice. In this way, the surround intrudes into the decision fields and frames of the decision-maker.

Similarly, an opposite political shift in the surround, one towards greater intervention, will also spill over into enforcement behaviour in the field. The character of HSE's political surround changed during the 1990s, and especially following the election of the Labour government in 1997. This produced an immediate feeling within the agency that the political environment was more propitious for occupational health and safety regulation, and that, in some respects, the government would be sympathetic to the principle of more stringent regulation of industrial and business activity. 'Well, clearly there has been a change in the political climate since [the general election of 1997],' said an AD later that year,

> 'and there are some very supportive messages coming from the current administration about wanting a tougher enforcement line, about being willing to write to the Lord Chancellor, where they feel that fines are not adequate, about possibly looking at new offences, including causing death as a result of breaching health and safety legislation—I know they're looking at a recommendation from the Law Commission. We know that there are a number of health issues which are not currently particularly high priorities that the new government would like us to make higher priorities—stress is a good example.... The attitude towards de-regulation has changed—the most obvious manifestation is that what was called the Deregulation Unit is now called the Better Regulation Unit, but it does mean that they're looking at making regulations easy to understand and effective, rather than looking to actually do away with regulation. So, you know, there is a subtle undercurrent coming from ministers, *which conditions our outlook*.' (97–04; my emphasis)

The change of government, however, was not necessarily assumed to have significant implications for the level of resources awarded HSE, 'but, you know, it's still early days as far as that is concerned' (97–04).

2. Economics

Regulatory officials at all levels in HSE are conscious of the fact that occupational health and safety regulation is regarded, rightly or wrongly, as an economic burden on regulated industry, and that both the economic and the political climates are features influencing not only the degree of corporate compliance that might reasonably be expected in everyday enforcement work by inspectors but also the amount of support HSE might expect for its activities from the workforce. For instance, speaking in the mid-1980s, a former Chief Inspector of Factories observed:

'Through the economic pressures and so on . . . a number of the unions with whom we deal are very aware of the risk that over-active enforcement by an inspector might actively put such pressure on a firm that they have to close down part of their operation. . . . We're not in the business of putting firms out of business. Occasionally, perhaps, we might accept that our prosecution action might be the last straw in a dicey business, but on the whole, we're in the business of keeping people on the right side of the law within business . . . . One of our difficulties at the moment is that we are perceived in various quarters at some times and in Government as well, as being a burden that industry has to carry at a particularly difficult time of recession.'

The precise role of prosecution in a difficult economic climate is a particularly troublesome question for an organization like HSE. The enforcement problems for occupational health and safety inspectors change according to whether the economy is buoyant or in recession, with the state of the local economy, in particular, serving to change the emphasis of inspection work and the way in which the nature of risks and the occurrence of accidents are interpreted. In an economic recession, for example, the implications for industry are 'a critical review of costs in every field, a desire to eliminate wasteful or unnecessary expenditure and consequently . . . a much more overt questioning of the costs and benefits of health and safety legislation and of the practical precautions and procedures which that legislation requires' (Health and Safety Executive, 1980, p. v). There may well be more rule-breaking under such conditions, but there will also be a corresponding desire not to make life even more difficult for business by imposing stringent and costly demands by way of enforcement. On the other hand, there is also a need to reflect the legal mandate and concentrate management's mind on the importance of compliance. As a former Chief Inspector of Factories said, 'The economic factors [are] of very great importance in that most of the firms are devoting most of their attention, most of the time, just to staying in business. This can mean that safety can sometimes take a bit of a back seat. Therefore, the need to prosecute has to be much more borne in mind as an encouragement.'

In the Britain of the early 1980s there was a deep recession which not only ravaged many of the traditional and inherently dangerous industries but also created 'within industry, commerce and public authorities an almost unprecedented awareness of economic pressures' (Health and

Safety Executive, 1980, p. v). This created a poignant enforcement dilemma for an occupational health and safety inspectorate:

'Although there has been a declining trend in the numbers employed in manufacturing industry and construction, our field forces report that there has been no reduction in the problems faced. They consider that economic pressures have adversely affected standards in many premises and that an increase in the number of small firms and sub-contracting businesses, some of which have standards of safety and health which fall well below what is acceptable, has added to the problems of oversight.' (Health and Safety Commission, 1985: 19)

The *Report by HM Chief Inspector of Factories 1985* vividly portrayed the impact of a recession in the economy:

'Economic pressures have adversely affected working conditions in many premises and an increase in the numbers of small firms and subcontracting businesses, some of which have standards of safety and health which fall well below what is acceptable, has added to the Inspectorate's problems of resource deployment. The recession has led many employers to economise on safety. Some firms have made safety officers redundant and passed responsibility for safety to personnel officers, line management or security officers with little or no expertise in safety matters. Many firms are critically short of the necessary safety expertise to run their plants safely and in such circumstances the need for inspection and practical advice from inspectors is crucial. Inspectors do not seek, nor can they ever provide all the necessary safety input for a firm—that is not their role—but their intervention can and often does prevent a dangerous situation from turning into a manifest disaster.' (Health and Safety Executive, 1986: 8)

Indeed, there is a sense of desperation in some of the official HSE pronouncements about economic conditions in the early 1980s and their implications for occupational health and safety:

'New small enterprises are hard put to it to keep their financial and commercial heads above water. Whether they are the sort that make no concessions to new technology, efficiency or even old fashioned good housekeeping or whether they are highly competent in instrument, computer or laser technology, the majority are not alert to the hazards to which their employees are exposed, and are not well briefed on health and safety legislation and practice. Furthermore, few small employers belong to the employer federations many of which have done so much good work informing their members. In any case, there is an inevitable temptation to do only what shows a commercial and tangible benefit in the short term and the guarding of a machine or the provision of local exhaust ventilation to remove dust or fume may be regarded as unwarranted expenditure.' (Health and Safety Executive, 1984: 1)

HSE reported that there was evidence that the recession had resulted in drastically reduced expenditure by employers on training and on maintenance. 'Whilst of course it is right for employers to keep under review the scale and appropriateness of training, it remains a key requirement of Section 2 of the HSW Act which must be complied with' (Health and Safety Executive, 1982*c*, p. vii). Furthermore, 'Many companies under financial pressure had cut their maintenance activities to the bone and slimmed or dispensed with the services of safety specialists' (Health and Safety Executive, 1984: 1).

HSE also acknowledged the impact of recession on inspectors' decision-making: 'As the recession deepened . . . industrial and commercial management became increasingly preoccupied with economic survival and thus among other strategies inevitably reviewed the financial impact of occupational health and safety requirements. Inspectors too were compelled to consider their requirements and recommendations in the same light' (Health and Safety Executive, 1982*c*, p. v). HSE's view was not one of total pessimism, however, and it was able to claim that progress had continued to be possible, thanks to the flexibility inherent in the occupational health and safety legislation. It argued that it was too simplistic to regard the interplay of economic forces on social concerns, and more particularly the greater preoccupation with costs and benefits of occupational health and safety, as heralding a return to the uncaring society of the industrial revolution:

'Parliament and the Inspectorate have always necessarily been aware of economic reality. It is perhaps the very success of Parliament in drafting legislation which was sufficiently flexible to allow progressive improvement and the persuasiveness and pragmatism of the Inspectorate in working with progressive employers, trade organisations and the trade unions over the years that have resulted in enhanced standards of occupational health and safety without the cost or pace of such progressive improvement hitherto being seriously questioned. Indeed it is the continuing willingness of industry, working with the Inspectorate and trade unions in continuing to raise standards in particular fields . . . which justifies one in rejecting the suggestion that we are witnessing a creeping return to laissez faire.' (Health and Safety Executive, 1982*c*, p. v)

If economic recession poses problems for inspectors in terms of the correspondingly greater incentives for employers to cut corners, and for the degree of compliance inspectors feel they may reasonably expect from firms, economic recovery poses a different set of problems, not least the fact that increased economic activity generally increases the number and possibly the range of hazards faced by workers:

'From 1985 onwards the effects of industrial recovery in terms of safety demanded increased activity and vigilance by our inspectors, not least in identifying new industrial premises with hazard potential. The upward trend for serious injuries to workers from conventional causes, which had become unmistakable in 1985/86 took further hold. Coming as it does against a background of rapid industrial change, with the emergence of numerous small companies and sub-contractors often carrying out hazardous activities formerly undertaken by larger companies with well established safety traditions, it is a matter of serious concern.' (Health and Safety Commission/Executive, 1987: 2)

In such circumstances, greater readiness to take formal action seems defensible and desirable to a regulatory agency.

The economic environment within which HSE has worked over the last twenty years has altered even more dramatically than the political. While in periods of prosperity industry has 'less "economic excuse" for failure to comply... in recession... industries have fewer resources with which to demonstrate compliance and may begin to redefine regulation not as a "necessary evil" but as an "unbearable evil"' (Hutter & Manning, 1990: 107). There tends to be more approval and regulation of new plants where the local economy is prosperous; in times or areas of recession, however, more work is done by inspectors in simply maintaining existing standards (Hutter, 1997). Inspectors have reported consistently that they hold companies they think are prosperous to stricter standards in the belief that such firms can afford more in the way of compliance costs.

Following the upturn in the economy, HSE surveyed an industrial landscape that had been substantially transformed. There had been a major shift from agriculture, mining, and heavy manufacturing to service industries, many of which relied on significant technological innovation (F. B. Wright, 1995: 66). The old and inherently dangerous heavy industries founded in the nineteenth and early twentieth centuries had largely disappeared, making way for new businesses often reliant upon vastly different working methods and manufacturing processes. These new industries were often modest in size and relied extensively on subcontracting, different patterns of work, and the growth of self-employment. Instead of a highly unionized workforce and strong trades unions, there was a comparative lack of union representation.

These trends have continued in recent years. Instead of the concentration of large numbers of workers in major sites, there are now many more workplaces, but they are smaller and their sheer numbers cause particular problems for HSE:

'The increasing fragmentation of industry is probably the most worrying development we face. For HSC, which makes considerable efforts to consult widely—this fragmentation, along with the lack of union representation of many workers, means that the number and range of those we are consulting is reducing. Who else is there for instance, with the knowledge, representative nature and commitment of the TUC?' (Health and Safety Commission, 1999, p. ix)

Fragmentation of industrial activity also made inspection and control especially difficult, HSC reporting that the ever increasing number of small businesses made it impossible for inspectors to achieve direct contact with them (Health and Safety Commission, 1999, p. ix).

Recently changes in technology employed in the new industries have combined with the increased public awareness of risks to safety and, perhaps more importantly, anxieties about threats to health in extending the demands upon the HSE and its inspectorates. These changes, as a result, have given rise in turn to different problems of policy-making and enforcement for an organization which has had to adapt to new realities.

2. PROPERTIES OF THE LOCAL SURROUND: CONSTRUCTION AND CHEMICALS INDUSTRIES

The local surround harbours the particular risks that may be realized in the form of accidents and the occasional calamity. This is where the surround is most likely to intrude into the inspector's decision-making field and frame. It is a more immediate environment for inspectors, comprised of the local economy, local industries, and their workplaces. How inspectors conceive of their surround suggests to them not only the nature and extent of risks they confront, but also what degree of compliance may be expected from their attempts to implement the legislation, with correspondingly profound implications for the particular enforcement tactics they adopt. The character of the surround and its regulated population also serves as a context for the development of framing since it is the setting for the definition of an untoward matter as something warranting official attention (or not). This may, in turn, shape whether and how enforcement discretion is exercised. The surround is, therefore, intimately connected with the ways in which inspectors go about their work, and what sorts of decisions they make about enforcement when they encounter violations.

Inspectors monitor health and safety risks in widely contrasting settings. Risk, so far as they are concerned, has a composite character incorporating both the likelihood that something untoward may happen and the gravity of any undesired event. This dual conception varies according to an inspector's precise job and the characteristics of regulated firms. Since each inspector is allocated to groups in the HSE organization according to the nature of the particular industries which they handle (with inspectors dealing exclusively with the construction industry, for example, or monitoring chemicals plants), each one tends to have a more homogeneous conception of risk and the nature of the problems to be encountered than might otherwise be expected from the hugely varied nature of work in health and safety regulation.[1] Inspectors frequently drew attention to contrasts in prosecution decision-making among colleagues in different industry groups and in their own behaviour on moving between groups. There is more scope for prosecution, for example, in heavy industries because inspectors find the breaches and the risks more serious and more obvious. Following the demise of the coal industry, problems of occupational ill health are increasingly associated with light or high tech industry, though it was said that 'maybe they only come to the fore because you don't have the glaring safety problems' (86–43).

The inspectors' local surrounds, as opposed to the remote, but no less real, surround in which accidents like Chernobyl occur, differed in the four Factory Inspectorate (F1) areas researched.[2] One area was heavily populated by old, declining, heavy industries. Another was one of mixed industry, with a certain amount of traditional manufacturing work. The third area had a representative cross-section of industry, with employers and unions described as traditional, not very progressive, and rather insular. The fourth had never had any significant heavy industry, and, even in the mid-1980s, boasted modern, high tech industries.

Two major industries, construction and chemicals, can be contrasted to illustrate how the surround shapes and provides a context for the making of decisions in individual cases. Both industries were commonly cited by inspectors as prototypical examples of those with distinctive characteristics—in many respects inspectors treated them as if they were polar opposites—which in turn prompt particular kinds of enforcement response. Some of the typical features of these industries serve as examples of significant properties in the inspector's surround, which are extremely important influences in enforcement decision-making. They suggest that decisions to prosecute (or not) cannot simply be seen as the

[1] Inspectors do have their experience broadened, however, by their occasional transfer between industry groups, or between different administrative areas.

[2] FI in Phase I; HSE Field Operations Directorate in Phase II.

product of the exercise of discretion by an official about a discrete matter, guided to an extent by organizational policy, but otherwise largely immune from wider political, economic, and social forces.

1. Prosperity

The chemicals industry is in general less immediately vulnerable to the vagaries of the economy than construction work, owing to a relatively high proportion of large and prosperous companies. In contrast, the vicissitudes of the economy have had a marked effect on the building industry over the last twenty years, creating stress reflected in the degree of regulatory compliance encountered by inspectors. The recession of the early 1980s led to ruthless competition, and many firms were put under extreme pressure. Costs had to be kept to the bare minimum, profit margins were small, clients constantly demanded speedy completion of work, and legally required safety measures often seemed costly and time-consuming to effect. Construction inspectors suggested that the cost of scaffolding for safety purposes, for example, could be equivalent to the total profit on a building job. Compelled by economic self-interest, safety precautions were often reduced or abandoned. Consequently, many construction firms came to be regarded by inspectors as having a substantial incentive to save on safety. The position was tersely summed up by a construction principal inspector (PI): 'It's cut-throat with the pricing. They just cut corners' (86–39).

If the recession of the early 1980s brought with it forces which gave construction employers a real incentive not to comply with regulation, in the greater prosperity which arrived later in the decade different problems presented themselves. The risk of fatal or major injury in construction continued to be over twice the average for all industries and construction also accounted for nearly 70 per cent of injuries to self-employed people. But this was now the result of other forces: 'the very substantial increase in construction output, labour turnover and overtime working' (Health and Safety Commission, 1990*a*: 80).

2. Visibility

Visibility of violation is a prerequisite to effective law enforcement. The risks in what construction firms do, or fail to do, may be directly visible to inspectors and others, but sometimes hazards may be physically remote or even invisible to scrutiny, as is often the case in the chemicals industry. The higher visibility associated with activities means a greater likelihood of violations of the law being discovered and becoming an event in an inspector's surround. Illegal working practices are not concealed behind factory walls in construction, but are exposed for all to see, not simply inspectors who happen to be passing a building site, or competitors in the building industry who feel they are being undercut by unfair practices, but also members of the public.[3] Indeed, one construction PI claimed that 'The majority of complaints we get on construction come from members of the public who are walking past the site' (86–39). Construction work is also readily accessible, posing more hazards to the public than many other industrial activities. Sites exercise a peculiar fascination for the public, many of whom are also aware that they present especial risks to children.

Where violations and hazards are largely invisible, there are significant barriers to inspection and enforcement. This is the position with most chemicals plants. Manufacturing processes go on within enclosed buildings and equipment, and any hazards which are likely to arise do so as the result of internal reactions. Speaking of nuclear power plants, which are in many respects comparable with large chemicals plants, a former Chief Inspector of the Nuclear Installations Inspectorate (NII) observed that 'It's very difficult, visually, to go round and see anything wrong, whereas the factory inspector going to a construction site, or to a factory, may see machines unguarded or scaffolding incorrectly built. Unless you're very experienced, you can't just look at a nuclear plant and tell whether it's being operated badly or not.'

The problems of invisibility must be overcome by reliance on the goodwill, cooperation, and trust of site managers to be able to gain any sense of what is actually going on in the workplace. 'We need to be on close terms with [people in nuclear power plants] because we need so much information,' said the former Chief Inspector of NII. 'And I think we so need their trust, as they need ours . . . There is a great deal of information flowing between our inspectors and the people on site.' Trust is enhanced where inspectors have relatively few sites to oversee

[3] The big asbestos case (P97–30) only came to HSE's attention with a phone call from an employee of a competitor firm. In this case inspectors found a demolition site littered with asbestos and strewn with broken asbestos roofing sheets, some of which had been thrown onto bonfires. There were no welfare facilities or protective equipment, and seemingly no plan of work. It was reported that employees were ignorant of the risks and were tearing down the building without any thought for a safe system of work or the possible presence of asbestos. The case was regarded as so serious that it was the subject of two Parliamentary Questions, and the defendant received what was believed to be the first immediate prison sentence imposed for a Health and Safety offence.

and can remain in close contact with those they regulate. 'We have two dozen or so nuclear sites to see to,' the former Chief Inspector went on. 'FI have something like, I guess, half a million factories... We visit our sites every two or three weeks for several days at a time... The most frequent they ever visit a place is once a year and then perhaps for an hour or two.' Because of this, NII staff get to know staff on the site 'extremely well'. This familiarity provides an opportunity to negotiate for compliance in a setting in which the prospect of prosecution is remote. A further implication of a personal enforcement relationship, according to a former Chief Inspector of Factories, is that 'It's quite clear that if you're in a place every fortnight, the whole relationship between yourself and the occupier [directors and managers] is different. You become associated with current practice by implication.' In this way, personal relationships become central in determining the character of any enforcement action. Such a situation of mutual dependence and trust is a barrier to the use of prosecution, since formal action is readily regarded by those regulated as a hostile act, one deeply disruptive to good relationships.[4] All of these points could apply equally well to the regulation of chemicals plants.

3. Instability

Different industries have different working practices whose control is more easily attained where they are stable and predictable. A variety of conditions creates instability. There are 'the constantly changing circumstances of the site, the presence of a multiplicity of contractors, the frequently high turnover of labour and the... exposure of the construction site worker to adverse weather' (Health and Safety Executive, 1979: 10). The safety organization of a large factory deals with a single workforce in a fixed place of work, but much of the work in the construction industry lacks this stability.

The size of a company is frequently taken by inspectors as an indicator of both willingness and ability to comply (see Chapter 8). The larger the company, inspectors believe, the easier in general the enforcement task. Large firms have a fixed headquarters and staff, and inspectors can become acquainted with their safety officers, gaining an opportunity to negotiate for compliance which is denied small firms. 'The larger [construction] companies do set up an organization for safety... the smaller

[4] For those who argue for more vigorous use of prosecution such good personal relationships are a source of concern.

ones do not,' said a construction PI (86–59). Large construction companies tend to resemble other kinds of industrial enterprise in their responsiveness to regulatory control, but most firms are small and given to instability and volatility. In a special report on the construction industry, HSE observed that almost 80 per cent of fatal accidents appeared to have occurred in medium-size and smaller firms, involving few companies with household names. Problems were caused by a vast number of small firms in all sections of the industry which were thought to show little or no positive interest in safety initiatives. HSE thought these were precisely the firms which lacked 'the specialist safety input which their managements and men desperately need if there is to be any real impact on the hard core of fatal and reported accidents due, for example, to falls of persons, which accounted for 56% of all fatal accidents' (Health and Safety Executive, 1979: 7).

Many chemicals firms are large, and many of them are household names. Chemicals plants—perhaps most places of work—are marked for the HSE inspector by predictable and stable working practices. The works often represent a major investment for the company concerned and have large-scale manufacturing processes. Small companies, frequently expected by inspectors to have fewer resources to devote to health and safety, are in general not expected by them to adhere to the same standards as larger, especially multinational, companies. The latter, in contrast, are believed to have both the resources and the specialist knowledge to enable them to comply (Hutter, 1997), and can be held, inspectors claim, to stricter regulatory standards. This practice contrasts with a widely held scholarly view which claims that large companies are often held to less stringent standards or are less burdened by regulation than smaller ones (e.g. Grabosky & Braithwaite, 1986; Shover *et al.*, 1984; Yeager, 1991). Part of the implication of disreputability attaching to small firms is connected with the greater difficulties of 'communicating with and influencing individuals and small firms, many without any semblance of safety organisation and training facilities' (Health and Safety Executive, 1986: 1).

It is said that one reason for the high level of deaths and serious injuries in construction has been a failure of management control. Effective control on site is often hard to achieve: 'Even large firms in the construction industry have a workforce at least part of which is divided into small gangs in distant and transient places of work' (Health and Safety Executive, 1979: 10). Furthermore, 'The work is repetitive and, consequently, there is little supervision; indeed, supervisors are often actively engaged in the work' (Health and Safety Executive, 1981: 1). There is usually a strong financial incentive to work quickly and only to attend to the more obvious safety measures: 'Those concerned with site safety must not only interest themselves in the big job on the big site and in technical complexity but also in the mundane problems of fragile roofs, site transport, bosun's chairs and tower scaffolds' (Health and Safety Executive, 1979: 10).

Problems of control are exacerbated by substantial, possibly increasing, dependence upon subcontracting in the building industry, which tends at once to create fragmentation in working practices and to enfeeble effective safety management on the site. Inspectors often have difficulties in understanding the nature of the relationship between the client, the contractor, and the subcontractor when it is necessary to establish questions of responsibility. Both the main contractor and client are usually reluctant to become too involved in how the work is actually performed. Furthermore, the 'speed at which the job is done may be affected by the nature of the contract and by systems of payment. Contractors and sub-contractors work at different speeds towards different targets. Darkness and weekend working make supervision difficult, and scaffolds are frequently plundered by the unscrupulous. [These are all] factors which make the construction industry so dangerous and difficult to control . . .' (Health and Safety Executive, 1978*b*: 11). It is not possible to say what part subcontracting has played in accidents in the construction industry, but 'the bald fact is that it remains over twice as dangerous as manufacturing' (Health and Safety Commission/Executive, 1987: 3; see also C. Wright, 1986).

The quality of management and workforce in the building industry has prompted criticism from many inspectors. Management in construction is generally regarded as ill-informed about safety matters, as often disorganized, and as sometimes disreputable. The site manager is a key figure but often acts rather independently of the company. There is often failure to plan adequately. Indeed, the lack of effective management and planning increases the probability of an inspector opting for prosecution since it is thought more likely to obstruct the chance of negotiating a remedy to a problem. 'The growth of management contracting, with a departure from traditional relationships between the contractor and those who work on the site and not necessarily even in direct contractual relationship with him makes the proper planning of the job of even greater importance . . .' (Health and Safety Executive, 1986: 1). No premises are needed, and no one needs to be qualified to set up a construction company. Since clients generally demand the quickest and cheapest job, much of the building industry is organized to satisfy this demand. HSE (1986: 1) has 'contrasted the performance of safety conscious construction firms . . . with those whose sorry performance reflects their lack of interest, skill, and knowledge. The changing face of the industry in which a significant growth in the number of individual firms has coincided with a work force which has remained static or declined compounds the problems.'

The impermanence of building work probably allows a large amount of unregulated construction to go on. Indeed, construction inspectors sometimes encounter firms previously unknown to them only when they have an accident. And even when contact is made, 'a lot of the contractors we may not see again', said a PI, 'because they may not do another job again in this area' (86–39). The smaller construction companies tend to be engaged in much more ephemeral work, which poses particular problems of control. A small contractor will not need to report to HSE that construction work is being undertaken, unless it is for six weeks or more. Otherwise, as a PI put it, 'The only time we'll know of it is if we pass it in the street' (86–08). Many inspectors think that in such circumstances a non-punitive enforcement measure, such as a letter, may not be taken seriously because it is known that the chances of a return visit by an inspector while work is still under way is very remote.

Construction work is characterized by greater instability of personal relationships, and a management and workforce readily regarded in pejorative terms as 'out for a quick buck' (86–55), as ill-informed, and unconcerned about health and safety matters: 'The quality of the management is far poorer than in a factory, far poorer. For every [household name] there are thousands of Joe Soaps Ltd.' (86–63). 'Eighteen of the 35 accidents happened to men whom the construction industry would refer to as "cowboys",' said HSE (1981: 7), in a special report on fatalities in the construction industry:

> 'This particular sector of the industry is likely to remain an enigma so far as conventional accident prevention techniques are concerned. There will never be enough factory inspectors to enforce the law on every tiny site nor can the established part of the industry bring sufficient pressure to bear on those whose chief source of income depends on private individuals and the owners of small businesses who will frequently seek the cheapest price without regard for safety. Improved social awareness of the problem might help, but not until construction safety attracts a wider audience through the national media and the community at large recognises the avoidable risks which attend most simple building operations.'

As inspectors see it, 'the quality of the particular individual [in construction work] . . . is so variable' (86–35). The building trade is 'so peripatetic, it's so badly-organized. It's wide open to the cowboys and the fly-by-night characters' (86–63). The pervasive implications of disreputability in the construction industry were accompanied by suggestions that some individuals were 'feckless' (Snashall, 1990), 'vigorous', and 'aggressive' in their responses to inspectors, which also encouraged a greater willingness among inspectors to prosecute. One construction inspector of many years' experience summed up the industry as one which required 'hard-speaking, tough policies' (86–03) because of the kind of people he typically encountered (he had prosecuted nearly 200 cases). In contrast with construction work, employers in the chemicals industry were described by a chemicals PI as 'fairly literate and knowledgeable' (86–38). In his opinion, if an inspector could establish a need for compliance, the employer would typically comply without much question. Presumably in keeping with this conception of the greater responsibility of the chemicals industry, the PI suggested that violations of the law which did occur tended to be accidental, rather than deliberate.

4. Transience

Transience in the nature of work creates risks which in turn are more difficult to manage. Transience, consequently, is closely related to the prevalence of death and injury in the workplace. Construction and chemicals industries tend, however, to be associated with different kinds of risk which confront their workforces. Chemicals plants present distinctive risks. The scale of damage that might be done in a catastrophe could be much larger than in construction.[5] Risks here extend beyond individuals, to a greater extent than in construction. They can involve major hazards arising from events such as leaks or explosions which threaten an entire plant, all who work in it, and possibly members of the public. These risks demand that inspectors concentrate more on preventive work, on the identification and assessment of large-scale hazard, to foreclose the possibility—however remote—of a catastrophe. In chemicals plants there is a constant risk of some serious untoward event occurring, and firms have, as a result, a considerable incentive to work safely as a matter of commercial self-interest (Genn, 1993), a constraint that operates quite independently of the law. Self-interest is

[5] The names Bhopal, Flixborough, and Seveso carry self-evident meaning with them in a health and safety organization like HSE.

seen as a powerful motivating force in the chemicals industry, not only in reducing the risk of catastrophe but also in avoiding the loss of skilled workers through injury. Such firms are regarded by inspectors as very cooperative and very willing to spend money in the cause of safety.[6] In general, such companies are seen as well-organized concerns, possessed of a responsible attitude (one chemicals inspector remarked that 'many of them genuinely care for their workforce, they really do'), and very aware of their public image (86–33).[7] As a result, it seems generally to be believed that there is little likelihood of a major untoward event in the chemicals industry.

Construction work, in contrast, is largely transient and fugitive. The dynamism of the construction workplace presents a large number of immediate and obvious risks to individual workers, compared with the chemicals industry. The constantly changing character of construction work means also that its risks change: 'The risks move on as the job moves on. You dig a hole and you've got the risks of a hole. You build a scaffold and you've the risks of falling . . . You have a whole series of risks', said a construction PI (86–22). Indeed, on 'virtually every building site there are situations that could kill, and that's not true of every factory' (86–63). Building is an ephemeral activity involving inherently dangerous working methods. Building sites have no permanence about them, moving rapidly, and often rather unpredictably, through a series of phases (excavation, foundations and groundwork, construction, roofing), which present different, constantly changing risks. Changing tasks mean changing workforces and different working methods. Since the site and work on it have no permanence, there is no opportunity to install any but the most temporary of safety features. While a factory is a stable place whose work processes and labour force may change little over the years, a large construction site is very different. '[E]very day it's different. It's not like a factory where you go back next week, and it'll be the same next year' (86–22). The principal hazards in most construction work cannot be eliminated by the once and for all provision of physical protection, but need effective planning, which is very difficult to manage owing to the magnitude of the risks, the complexity of organizational relationships,

[6] Whether this attitude signals a cultural difference is hard to say, though British regulatory officials do seem to be less cynical about the motivation of regulated industry than their American counterparts; see Vogel (1986).

[7] Any disposition to compliance among chemicals firms may be further encouraged by other regulatory bodies. The pharmaceuticals industry, for example, is also regulated by the Medicines Inspectorate, which, in laying down standards for good practice, may help contribute towards improved health and safety.

and the uniqueness of each site (Health and Safety Executive, 1983: 26). The practices of the construction industry combine to create a volatile working environment. 'This industry is characterised by a diversity of activities, employee skills, and employer size and systems and there is a high degree of mobility in both projects and personnel' (Health and Safety Commission/Executive, 1987: 3). While a person in a factory 'tends to be confined to one place of work, a site worker has in general a great deal more freedom of movement and a degree of choice as to how he sets about a job; he must accept that he therefore has a corresponding degree of responsibility for the safety of himself and his fellow workers' (Health and Safety Executive, 1979: 9). The lack of a stable and coordinated social organization in construction work leads to mistakes, and mistakes lead to accidents (Reimer, 1976). The result is more dramatic accidents to people in construction than in other industries: the construction industry is said to have the highest rate of reported fatal and major accidents in all the main employment sectors.[8]

Many of the deaths and injuries in construction arise from a curious amalgam of the effects of routine working practices: 'Construction accidents mostly happen to men going about their daily business' (Health and Safety Executive, 1979: 10). Mundane workforce activities tend to obscure the hazards they frequently harbour. HSE (1981: 7) has drawn attention to 'the failures often by experienced and sensible men and managements to see the element of danger in a commonplace, repetitive activity'. The inherent danger, according to HSE, seems to attract 'men who find the element of danger stimulating. These issues are especially difficult to resolve, because they are concerned with individual and group behaviour rather than with the provision of physical safeguards' (Health and Safety Executive, 1981: 1).

Such complex and dynamic patterns pose serious problems of control. Preventive efforts demand a high degree of coordination and a

> 'commitment to safety and health of many other people: architects, who design buildings which can be erected in safety, which will not be liable to collapse at intermediate stages of construction and which can be maintained safely; clients,

[8] 'Spate of building trade deaths goes on as two more killed', read a headline in the *Independent* (24 July 2000), the article continuing: 'The number of deaths on construction sites has risen by 20 per cent in a year... the news is expected to lead to severe criticism of construction companies for putting profits above safety.' The risks of the construction industry have been a constant concern for HSE, and the news will be unwelcome to HSC, which reported, with evident relief, a reduction in worker fatalities from 90 to 76 in 1997, 'the lowest figure recorded in the last two decades' (Health and Safety Commission, 1998*a*, p. xi).

who can often influence the contractor's attitude by considering safety as well as production and who can sometimes be an extra pair of experienced eyes on the site; and of safety advisers who can help line management to recognise the patterns of activity which can be systematically made safe and look for the unregarded dangers in the commonplace repetitive activities whose power to kill and maim is [an] unfortunate theme'. (Health and Safety Executive, 1981: 8)

Problems arising from transience lead to an acceptance in HSE that the risks to the individual employee routinely encountered by construction inspectors are more numerous and more serious than in most other types of industry. This in turn leads to an expectation that these inspectors will be much more frequently involved in prosecuting violations of the law. Indeed, much of the construction inspector's decision-making is shaped by the high frequency of accidents. Law enforcement on construction sites often occurs reactively, once an accident has happened. Where an accident has already occurred, an inspector is confronted with an existing event which increases the demand for a response. The event will usually be one which is much less given to the repair or remedy which is possible with pre-emptive enforcement where inspectors monitor their environment for risks. A risk presented offers more enforcement options than a risk realized: 'In the construction group, it tends . . . to be firefighting—going out and investigating incidents. So . . . often I'm presented with a situation where . . . I see something wrong, when an incident has occurred. . . . Once I've got a fatal accident I've narrowed down the range of options open to me' (86–35).

3. CONCLUSION

Features in the inspectors' surround are associated with the conditions under which untoward events happen. These same features have profoundly important implications for the way in which regulations are written: 'Regulations which try to establish a safe place of work in the construction industry, with its almost infinitely variable activities, cannot possibly meet the needs of every trade nor the access problems presented by every part of every structure' (Health and Safety Executive, 1979: 10). Yet while there were occasional complaints that some regulations were 'vague and nebulous' (86–05), a more general view was that most construction cases were relatively simple to prepare for prosecution. Many of the relevant regulations are well established and have changed relatively little. Compared with other areas of occupational health and safety regulation, there is often a series of violations, and the nature of the rule-breaking is usually such that matters are seen as being clear-cut and less likely to prompt indecision by inspectors as to appropriate action. 'With a company that never sends you any notices, never does a job which lasts more than six weeks, and has still got somebody with a broken leg or a fractured pelvis because he fell off a roof and he didn't have any equipment, you haven't got a lot of choice' (86–59).

Readiness to prosecute is intimately connected with the character of the surrounds and fields in which inspectors operate. The nature of the construction inspector's local surround is such that it gives rise to many more undesired events than is the case for other types of inspector, creating many violations and many corresponding opportunities for law enforcement. The distinctive features of construction work outlined above—its sensitivity to economic pressures, its visibility, the instability of its working practices, and the transience in the work itself—'often demand [the] justice [of prosecution] to get things done' (86–08). Construction inspectors typically portrayed themselves as routinely confronted by a substantial number of prosecutable matters which encouraged a greater willingness to go to court. However, the sheer number of possible cases meant that many of them had to be dealt with in ways short of prosecution. 'If you wanted to go ahead on a construction site,' said one inspector, 'you could come home every day with a case full of prosecutions' (86–35). Furthermore, the inspector has to decide about action immediately: 'Everything you do has to be done there and then' (86–32). This is because, so far as the inspector is concerned, the transience of construction activity means that decisions about what action to take have to be made on the spur of the moment, since the chances of a quick return to the site for a follow-up visit to check on progress, to propose remedial measures, or to continue negotiating for compliance are remote, given the other typical demands on an inspector's time.

This encourages two tendencies. One is to err on the side of severity in enforcement, with the more serious and immediate risk being more likely to invite sanctioning, rather than negotiating for compliance. This would be regarded as instrumentally rational, given HSE's view that 'The construction worker, however simple his job, usually exercises a high degree of personal choice which effectively determines whether he has an accident or not' (Health and Safety Executive, 1978*b*: 12).[9] The other

[9] 'This inevitably means', HSE (1978*b*: 12) has concluded, 'that a certain number of serious accidents will always happen.'

tendency among construction inspectors is to act quickly. The unstable and transient character of building work mean that time is a luxury:

'If you have a factory, you have a stable situation. You can go to a factory, see a problem, say an unguarded machine. That machine will be there in three months time, twelve months time. You can go to a building site, you're seeing a dynamic situation. It'll be totally different tomorrow, and the day after. Therefore, if you say "Do this, and I'll come back tomorrow to make sure it's been done," that particular job could be over by tomorrow. You can't do the basic visit, as with a factory, followed by a check visit in three months. . . . With construction, you may never see the company again, so you've really got to decide when you see the situation "Well, do I serve a notice and stop the job? Do I prosecute? Or do I merely advise?" But you have to decide there and then. And if you're going to prosecute you get the evidence there and then. There is far more prosecution without prior warning because prior warning is impracticable, because if you've never seen the firm before, you may never see them again.' (86–63)

The significance of this for enforcement decisions is not only that 'You've got to make the instant decision in construction' (86–22), but that decision should be one to 'Hit 'em hard and quickly, otherwise they've disappeared.' (86–20). In contrast, one chemicals group inspector, conscious of his own and his colleagues' willingness to negotiate for compliance, thought that other industry groups saw him and his colleagues 'as a bunch of softies'.

Most places of work, however, have predictable locations and stable working practices, providing inspectors with the opportunity to negotiate for compliance. As a construction PI put it: 'you can get at management and you've got some reasonable chance of there being a continuity in the workforce . . . You can keep the pressure on 'til they get it right' (86–59). Similarly, the stability and privacy of chemical plants provide far fewer opportunities for inspectors to prosecute. On most construction sites, however, the inspector is policing not a known population, but a population of strangers.[10] Transience means, therefore, that there is not only little possibility of working with smaller companies to improve standards of compliance in future, there is also likely to be no history of prior relationships with the firm, removing the possibility of deciding on the basis of a firm's prior record. The available tools of enforcement provide a simple choice for the inspector, one of taking formal action

[10] The more frequent use of prosecution for itinerant cable-burners by the Industrial Air Pollution Inspectorate in the mid-1980s (in contrast with its usual strategy of negotiated compliance) is a good example of this tendency.

(issuing a prohibition notice or deciding to prosecute), or taking no action. Inspectors sometimes take no action because the available legal devices may be unsuitable for the nature of the problem they are ostensibly intended to remedy. While some inspectors do use improvement or prohibition notices, others believe they have 'almost no place in construction work' (86–22) since they are ill-suited to the regulation of transient sites and workforces. Informal techniques of enforcement are even less satisfactory: 'Unless you're in there taking some fairly positive action, letters and that type of action aren't as effective because the site changes . . . ' (86–35). In these circumstances, construction inspectors could, in general, justify a relatively high level of prosecution as a means of keeping the construction industry aware of the dangers of its work and the risks of non-compliance.

The regulatory surround shades here both into the inspector's field and into the decision-making frame. The risks associated with construction leads inspectors to frame the nature of the problems they encounter in a particular way. They develop a routine expectation that they will regularly have to contend with rule-breaking which is serious enough to warrant prosecution, as several of them made clear: 'Every building site you go on to there is a breach of the law, probably several breaches of the law' (86–29); 'Cases are virtually thrust upon you—they're there' (86–02); 'I'm sure I could find a dozen cases in a day' (86–53); 'Factories, you can go months without seeing anything of major importance,' whereas 'on every single construction site you can see situations where a man can kill himself' (86–63). The result is that construction inspectors are readily regarded as more prosecution-minded than the rest of their colleagues.[11]

A very different picture emerges from the enforcement of chemicals regulation, where the problems tend, in comparison with construction, not to be simple matters. The complexity of the processes and their general lack of visibility mean that it is difficult for an inspector to decide quickly whether or not to prosecute. The level of personal contact between inspector and regulated firm also encourages a greater willingness to negotiate for a solution to a problem, while the resource implications of a possibly complicated prosecution also persuade inspectors to give serious consideration to other methods of enforcement. The pre-

[11] Some inspectors no longer in construction enforcement work observed how their previous experience had affected their attitudes and the way in which they would frame cases.

occupation of the chemicals inspector, who may be involved in only one or two prosecutions a year—if any—becomes 'Are we able to allocate the time it's going to take?' (86–33), even though, ironically, some construction inspectors may be involved in a dozen or more prosecutions annually.

PART III

Field

5 Formal Structure and Practice

The decision field marks out the boundaries of a legal decision-maker's mandate, creating the setting within which decisions are made. The field is defined by the law, the legal institution, and the legal bureaucracy in its formulations of policy. It is further delineated in the ways in which the organization communicates other aspects of its legal mandate to its audiences. These issues are the subject of this and the next two chapters.

1. THE ROBENS COMMITTEE AND THE HSW ACT, 1974

Two competing views speak to the attainment of safe and healthy working conditions by means of legal regulation. One is that it is largely a matter of the responsibility and choice of those at work. The other is that desirable standards of occupational health and safety demand the provision in the workplace of appropriate conditions and systems of work. The first embodies an individualistic conception of act or omission and compels attention to the behaviour of each employed person. The second shifts the focus from individual employees towards employers, who are regarded as responsible for providing healthy conditions and safe work systems for their employees (Johnstone, 1994). The latter view forms the organizing assumption of the Health and Safety at Work Act, 1974 (HSW Act).[1]

This legislation is the cornerstone of the present system of occupational health and safety regulation in Britain and has its origins in the *Report of the Committee on Safety at Work*, chaired by Lord Robens and published in 1972 (Robens, 1972). This is not the place for any detailed discussion of the Robens Report, about which there is a large and often critical literature (James, 1992; R. C. Simpson, 1973; Woolf, 1973), except to make three points relevant to the matter of law enforcement. First, Robens's main concern was to attain greater coordination and efficiency of effort in the pursuit of improved occupational health and

[1] The nature and early effects of the HSW Act are analysed by Dawson *et al.* (1988).

safety, and this was thought most likely to be achieved by adopting a unified health and safety inspectorate (Robens, 1972: 63; F. B. Wright, 1995: 44).

Second, the Robens Committee adopted a rather benign conception of the problem of enforcing occupational health and safety regulation. Its stance was shaped by an assumption that not only the workforce but also management had an identity of interest in the maintenance of high standards of occupational health and safety. This led them to be sympathetic to the idea of self-regulation, a notion whose viability in the context of occupational health and safety regulation is less than clear. Indeed, the idea that there is an assumed identity of interest has been criticized many times, not least by HSE (1980, p. v) itself:

> 'it is too simplistic to assume that there will always be an identity of approach between management and trade unions to health and safety. Whilst it is of course in the interests of both sides of industry to reduce the suffering and cost of accidents and ill health, there will be quite legitimate differences of view on the amount of financial or personnel resources to be devoted specifically to health and safety or on the allocation of priorities to particular jobs. The severity or extent of a potential hazard, the costs and benefits of particular, perhaps alternative, preventive measures and the allocation of priorities are all matters of legitimate discussion between managers, safety representatives and inspectors.'

One implication of Robens's temperance was an argument for a more discriminating approach to enforcement (Robens, 1972: 146). On the role of prosecution, in particular, the Report was very circumspect, and adopted a highly constrained and selective view of the conditions under which it ought to be used:

> 'Criminal proceedings are inappropriate for the generality of offences that arise under safety and health at work legislation. We recommend that criminal proceedings should, as a matter of policy, be instituted only for infringements of a type that the imposition of exemplary punishment would be favourably expected and supported by the public. We mean by this offences of a flagrant, wilful or reckless nature which either have or could have resulted in serious injury. A corollary of this is that the maximum fines should be considerably increased.' (Robens, 1972, para. 263)

Third, though the idea of self-regulation was given currency, and the Act, following Robens, introduced changes, such as the creation of a comprehensive and integrated legal edifice, that were in many respects far-reaching, it did not alter the fundamental assumption of the viability of a command and control structural model of regulation.

The HSW Act significantly broadened the scope of occupational health and safety regulation. It incorporated two principles already well established in the law: that a duty of care is owed to other persons who may be affected by any work being carried out, and that those who control premises in which work is being undertaken are under a duty of care to those at work (Health and Safety Executive, 1983: 23–7). Perhaps the central assumption of the Act is that most accidents arise through the failure of management, rather than through failures of hardware (equipment and the like). This is expressed in the specific duty the HSW Act s. 2 places upon employers to ensure the health, safety, and welfare at work of all of their employees. The Act is not, however, legislation that is simply concerned with employers and their employees. It recognizes the public's interest, as potential victims of misfortune arising from events occurring in workplaces, in the attainment of high standards of occupational health and safety.

These general principles are typical of the character of much of the legislation, which is broad and unspecific, and relies heavily on a notion of informed administrative discretion. The Health and Safety Commission (n.d.: 5) later described the HSW Act as

> 'goal setting—setting out what must be achieved, but not how it must be done. Guidance on how to achieve the goals is often set out in Codes and there is also a wide variety of advisory material describing good practice. Neither Codes nor guidance material are in terms which necessarily fit every case. In considering whether good practice has been adopted, Inspectors will need to take relevant Codes and guidance into account, using sensible judgement about the extent of the risks and the effort that has been applied to counter them...'

Sometimes, however, the law is more prescriptive and stipulates in detail what has to be done. 'For example, all mines must have more than one exit; contacts with live electrical wires must be avoided. Prescriptive law limits the discretion of the duty holder and the enforcer' (Health and Safety Commission, n.d.: 5).

One of the main purposes of the HSW Act is to ensure that safety is a pervasive value in any work activity, which requires consideration be given to safe methods even before work begins. Section 2 of the Act casts its major obligations in terms of the provision and maintenance of systems of work that are safe 'so far as is reasonably practicable', specifically requiring a weighing of cost and trouble against the severity or extent of the hazard and likely benefit. The interpretation of 'reasonably practicable' which qualifies the duty of care introduced by the HSW Act must be made 'at a point of time anterior to the accident'.

The principle of reasonable practicability demands much of health and safety inspectors and how they exercise their discretion. It must be said, commented the HSE (1980, p. v) in a later report,

> 'that in the view of inspectors this is . . . a high standard because, where there is a significant hazard, inspectors and indeed the Courts, are likely to take a good deal of persuading in a particular instance that the cost of precautions, or the trouble of setting up a safe system of work is disproportionately high. Even if legal obligations are not qualified by reasonable practicability the inspector still has to be aware of costs in discussing with management, and indeed all concerned, the time scale within which it is realistic to expect modifications or improvements to be carried out. Inspectors live in a real world where design, manufacture, supply and fitting take time and where finance has to be programmed. Work people equally are realists and though the proposed time scale may be argued over and modified, they accept that this is generally the right way to proceed.'

Section 3 of the Act obliges an employer or self-employed person to conduct 'his undertaking' in such a way as to ensure so far as is reasonably practicable that persons not in his employment (such as members of the public) are not exposed to risk. Section 4 places duties on persons who have, to any extent, control of premises: those with power to control a particular risk should exercise that power.

In pursuit of the goal of a coordinated and efficient occupational health and safety regime, the legislation merged the existing inspectorates for factories, mines, agriculture, explosives, nuclear installations, and alkali works to operate under the control of two newly created bodies, the Health and Safety Commission (HSC) and the Health and Safety Executive (HSE) (F. B. Wright, 1995: 45). When HSE was set up in 1974, some 3,500 posts were transferred to it from a variety of government departments previously carrying health and safety responsibilities. The HSW Act also gave to inspectors new powers of enforcement, but the distinct identity and the practices of each inspectorate were maintained (leading to the survival of their local cultures), and it has only been in recent years that they have been eroded to a considerable extent with the creation of a generic field inspectorate.

One impact of the 1974 Act, then, was a significant enlargement of the reach of workplace regulation, bringing several million people within the scope of occupational health and safety legislation for the first time. The extension of the protective legislation to cover the public against risks from 'work activities' changed the balance of the work of the Factory Inspectorate (FI).[2] Whereas traditional areas of responsibility for FI were factories, construction sites, docks, shipyards, some offices, and the like, the HSW Act brought statute law to bear on a broader range of sites and problems: the medical service, schools, further education institutions, as well as transient activities associated with fairgrounds and exhibitions. '[R]ightly or wrongly,' HSE (1980: 15) reported, 'risks to the general public create more concern than most risks to workers, and the change has led to a disproportionate increase in our workload. We have also taken responsibility for some six million workers not previously covered by protective legislation.' FI adapted to its extra responsibilities throughout this period by cutting out work of low priority in order to meet the new demands (Health and Safety Executive, 1980: 15).

The most substantial of the enforcement bodies under the Act—in terms of resources and breadth of responsibilities—was HSE itself. When HSE was first established, therefore, expansion of the organization was the order of the day, and by mid-1979 the number of HSE staff had risen by about one-fifth to 4,200. By far the largest part of the increase, about 450 of the extra 700 posts, was allocated to the FI and its support staff, though the increase in staff was felt to be significantly smaller than the increase in demand arising from the new workload.

2. HSC AND HSE

Among the most salient of the innovations of the HSW Act was the creation of a new institutional framework for the management of occupational health and safety, with the formation of the HSC and the HSE. HSC is a governing body which comprises a chairman and nine members appointed on a fixed term basis, with no automatic right of reappointment. Members are appointed by the Secretary of State after consultation with organizations representing employers, employees, local authorities, and other relevant bodies. The primary tasks of the Commission are to formulate occupational health and safety policy, and to oversee the work of the Executive and local authorities.

[2] '[T]his new field [suffers from] . . . problems encountered in the numerous occupations which are now covered by the law and also those arising from the other new obligation on employers and the self employed to have regard to the health and safety of the public who may be affected by their activities' (Health and Safety Executive, 1977: 5).

The corporatist reorganization of the Executive and Commission reflects their position centred between industry and the unions, on the one hand, and government, on the other. Their basic constitutional position and the division of authority were described by a former member of the Executive as follows:

> '[F]undamentally the nature of the relationship between ministers and the HSC is one of hands-off and, on the whole, let the Commission get on with the job and do what it decides it ought to do, intervening only on exceptional occasions, and only in rather minor ways. The Executive, on the other hand, is the clear controlling body and is in the lead when it comes to changing these policies, the individual policies of the divisions and inspectorates . . . The tendency has been for the Executive's influence on inspectorial work activities, divisional resources, and sometimes individual decisions, to get stronger and more pervasive.' (Hawkins, 1992*a*: 150–1)

The Health and Safety Executive is comprised of a Director General and two other members, one of whom serves as Deputy Director General. They are appointed by the Commission with the approval of the Secretary of State (the other two members also being appointed after consultation with the Director General). The functions of the Commission and the Executive are specified in the HSW Act, HSE being primarily responsible for operational matters. 'Each of the Boards [Commission and Executive] meet [*sic*] regularly to discuss strategic direction and plans, formulate policy on key issues etc in order to maintain full and effective control over all significant policy, regulation and guidance, compliance, organisational and financial issues' (Health and Safety Commission, 1999: 119).

The management of HSE involves the discharge of three main types of work. The formal position has been summed up by HSC (1993: 67) thus:

> '*Policy* The policy branches advise the Health and Safety Commission on the need for changes in legislation or standards. Their work includes negotiations on European Community proposals and liaison with a wide range of national and international organisations. They depend for their expertise on advice from and close liaison with staff carrying out the other types of work.
>
> *Operations* Operational staff inspect industrial activity, give advice, investigate accidents and enforce compliance with legal requirements and reasonable standards. The great majority of such staff are in the Field Operations Directorate which brings together the Factory, Agriculture and Quarries Inspectorates, the doctors and nurses of the Employment Medical Advisory Service, and specialist inspectors and scientists in Field Consultancy Groups. The remainder are in

separate divisions covering Railways, Mines, Nuclear Installations and Offshore Safety. The latter two divisions deal with policy as well as operational issues for their respective industries.

Technological, scientific and medical These staff supply technological, scientific and medical back-up to other parts of HSE and to Government on industrial health and safety matters, including the extent and nature of risks, the effects of hazards on individuals or the environment, and appropriate standards. They play a vital part in operational activity, in the making of safety standards, often in international negotiation, and the assessment of safety cases for nuclear and major hazards installations.'

The HSC and HSE structure is a model of a corporatist approach to governance (see generally G. K. Wilson, 1985). Put another way, the Commission embodies a theory of assent in the formulation of regulation. The notion is that the assent of the bodies representing employers and employees to policies to be implemented is sought and obtained as part of the process of creating those policies. Once gained, the theory runs, it will be correspondingly easier to introduce policy to an otherwise reluctant industry since employers will know that their representatives have participated in the policy-making process. Given the inherent ambiguities in the concept of social regulation, the notion of assent is important in that in theory it should, so far as employers are concerned, establish the legitimacy of regulatory enforcement.

There are, however, flaws in the theory. While the notion of assenting interested parties may be an attractive and useful device to foster a certain legitimacy and to encourage the commitment to regulation of both sides of industry (as represented by the Confederation of British Industry and the Trades Union Congress), it does suggest an inherent conservatism in seeking change. This effect may act in a variety of ways. For instance, it is acknowledged that the interaction of criminal and civil law, the latter with its implications for compensation for harm suffered, produces a reluctance to change from both sides of industry (Health and Safety Executive, 1987*a*: 20). Another problem is that the Confederation of British Industries (CBI) and the Trades Union Congress (TUC) are unable to acquire knowledge about and represent in the policy-making process the views of the very large number of small and medium-sized firms subjected to occupational health and safety regulation. The CBI, in contrast with the TUC, does have a large number of advisory bodies which are able to give proposals quite detailed scrutiny. It is not clear, however, to what extent they are in contact with smaller firms. There is evidence that, to the extent that they know anything about it, such firms tend not to feel part of the process (Genn, 1993). While the structure of the Commission may afford an important, if unrepresentative, part of industry direct access to policy-making, there remain significant implications for the degree of legitimacy accorded the whole regulatory process by numerous smaller employers. A related problem with the notion of assent is that it rests on the assumption that once a policy has been formulated, the CBI and TUC have the influence to make it work among all employers, not simply the larger ones.

3. THE EUROPEAN DIMENSION

The international aspects of occupational health and safety at work have substantially occupied the Executive's attentions, consuming an expanding proportion of HSE's resources in the last 15 years or so. The growing engagement of international bodies, particularly the European Union, in determining mandatory health and safety standards has increasingly shaped the priorities and policies of the Commission and HSE as a whole. This applies particularly as regards the Commission's role in developing proposals for legislative reform, and HSE's duty to provide for adequate enforcement of European statutory requirements (Health and Safety Commission, 1990*a*: 16). The Single European Act, ratified in 1987, is regarded within HSC and HSE as a watershed, particularly in its introduction of qualified majority voting in the Council of Ministers in areas in which much of the work in the health and safety field is based. This Act in effect paved the way for a shift from national to European primacy in policy-making in occupational health and safety regulation.[3]

HSC and HSE take part in negotiations in various international bodies over regulations, conventions, technical standards, or other protocols which will then in some sense bind signatory countries. HSE officials participate in preparing the UK negotiating position on Directives, in consultation with the Commission, UK government departments, Parliament, and industry. HSC (1990*a*: 17) has reported that 'HSE officials are also involved in taking the agreed line forward in discussions and negotiations in the EC institutions and increasingly . . . in bilateral talks with other Member States. Equally of importance is HSE's participation

[3] This was reflected in the broad scope of the Third Action Programme on Safety, Hygiene and Health at Work, adopted in Oct. 1987, which included substantial new elements concerning the safety of workers at the workplace (Health and Safety Commission 1990*a*: 17).

in UK and EC-level committees developing technical standards for "new approach" directives.' HSE officials generally contribute in this way on behalf of the UK government, as well as the Commission.[4]

In the late 1980s the HSC and HSE made considerable efforts to align European thinking on health and safety matters with domestic policy and practice. Important advantages were to be gained from this, as a former Director General explained:

'In most of the areas which Europe wants to regulate, we have already got perfectly satisfactory regulations and the only question is whether we are going to be forced through the business of structural change in order to accommodate to anything new that would come out. *But* they are also in a sense an opportunity, because it does become possible to get European law on the statute book sometimes more quickly than it might appear naturally here. So the Commission's present policy, I think, is one of doing less and less work of a purely domestic kind, and allowing the European work to be the main engine, but at the same time to do domestic work from the point of view of establishing a UK line that is likely then to prevail in future European discussion.' (Hawkins, 1992*a*: 162: emphasis original.)

The closer the alignment with domestic policy and practices achieved, the lower the costs upon employers, while 'Failure in . . . negotiations can have significant adverse effect on our trading interests' (Health and Safety Executive, 1987*b*: 4). In this way, health and safety policy-making is bound up with important issues affecting the national economy.

However, the consequential processes of domestic negotiation and implementation lead to the further expenditure of resources, a problem sometimes exacerbated by the procedures for review. An area director said on this:

'An increasing amount of our legislative programme has been taken up in meeting EC directives; so, since the Robens Report in 1974, we had an internal programme of legislative reform, which was designed to do away with the old industry or topic-specific regulations, and bring in its place the more goal-setting cross-cutting regulations of the type like the Management Regulations, and so on. But in fact our ability to do that has been somewhat constrained by European Directives, the most significant batch of which was the six-pack that came in in 1992, which was implementing the Framework Directive which resulted in the Management Regulations, Manual Handling, Provision and Use of Work Equipment, Workplace Health, Safety Regulations, and so on. And that was really a very major shift in emphasis; I don't think it changed the legal standards

[4] HSE also shares information and expertise with other countries or international bodies without formal commitment.

significantly, but it did mean that in some areas we've actually gone away from what we were seeking to do with these goal-setting, general regulations to perhaps rather more prescriptive and topic-specific regulations. (And I think I'd quote Display Screen Equipment Regulations as an example of that; something that wasn't seen to be a high priority issue for regulation internally, but where we were driven to identify it as a separate topic with its own set of regulations in order to meet a European imperative.) Also, a number of the regulations . . . have taken up a huge amount of policy time, and probably had a big impact on industry, things like packaging and labelling, and transport of dangerous goods, which are horrendously complicated. And those regulations have been revised probably half a dozen times in almost as many years, and are incredibly complicated.' (97–04)

There are difficulties with health and safety initiatives inspired in Europe, and there seems to be little doubt that the European dimension has made the regulatory task more complex for those at the centre of the organization, not least because of the different legal or regulatory conceptions in play. For example, European Directives focus on the nature of risks posed rather than on the nature of the workplace or work process (F. B. Wright, 1995: 200). And although it emerges following a process of discussion and consultation, European health and safety legislation is sometimes cast in terms which cause problems for HSE; in particular, it may be too detailed, or too prescriptive. Indeed, one of the interesting general problems which crops up in regulation with a European dimension stems from differences between English and continental legal systems. These differences between systems in the common law and civil law traditions bear on the place of administrative discretion. The HSC itself explained it this way:

'UK health and safety legislation recognises that it is impossible to eliminate all risks arising from work activities, and imposes absolute duties only where these are appropriate and can be fulfilled. Otherwise duties are usually qualified by "so far as is reasonably practicable" (SFAIRP). Other EC Member States recognise that it is impossible to guarantee absolute safety, but it is understood that under Continental legal systems there is no need of a qualification like SFAIRP because their courts exercise flexibility in how they interpret seemingly absolute legal duties; and that, in general, those on whom the duties lie are expected to approximate towards the stated legal objective. In the common law countries (UK and Ireland) however legal requirements are generally interpreted literally. The Framework Directive sought to address this by including a provision allowing Member States to exclude or limit the responsibility of employers in certain circumstances. The UK did not find the solution fully satisfactory, but believes that UK law achieves the objectives of the Directive at least as well as other Member States, and that no fundamental change is required to the UK system of health and safety law.' (Health and Safety Commission, 1990*a*: 17)

The impetus behind this growing internationalization of the work is not simply a desire for harmonization of occupational health and safety regulation practice. The question of public safety has in recent years become a particular matter of international concern, partly owing either to the enormity or the transnational character of a number of catastrophes (such as Chernobyl, the Basle pollution incident on the Rhine, Seveso, and Bhopal). Quite apart from their intrinsic magnitude, such events can threaten the credibility of an entire industry.

4. STRUCTURES AND RELATIONSHIPS

The HSE has a complicated structure of directorates and inspectorates, together with other supporting branches. For present purposes, the Field Operations Directorate (FOD), which presides over inspection, is the most important. The existing operational teams are managed by seven regional directors of field operations, drawn from various disciplines, who have responsibility for planning, budgeting, and performance monitoring within their regions.

Within FOD, inspection work is organized geographically over the seven regions, each of which has its own director of operations (whom I shall refer to as an area director (AD) throughout).[5] ADs are assisted by a number of principal inspectors (PIs), each of whom supervises the work of a group of field inspectors. There are also a number of specialist inspectors.[6] The PIs in turn manage the work of a distinctive 'National Interest Group' (NIG),[7] comprising of two or three field inspectors and possibly one or more trainee inspectors. Each NIG is responsible for formulating and coordinating national policy on the regulation of particular types of industries which share common problems, such as construction, chemicals, and general manufacturing.

[5] The present organizational arrangements are simpler now than in the 1980s. At the time of Phase I of the research each inspectorate was organized in distinctive ways, the Factory Inspectorate being divided into 20 administrative areas.

[6] 'Specialist inspectors, of whatever discipline, provide advice to the general inspectorate on technical problems. They do not normally carry out primary inspection, except as the "agents" of the principal inspector concerned with the employer, and in closely defined circumstances. Their work in the main, consists of responses to requests for help from within HSE' (Health and Safety Executive, 1982*a*: 8).

[7] Sometimes also known as a 'National Industry Group'. In 1997 the NIGs became 'sectors'.

The NIG is the means by which new problems in occupational health and safety regulation are brought to light and new rulings established and transmitted back to the field. Under the direction of the AD, it is responsible for ensuring, as far as possible, consistency of enforcement standards, coordination of enforcement initiatives, priorities, the dissemination of technical information, and the development of relationships with employers and trade union organizations. Of particular relevance is the objective of maintaining consistency of enforcement practice in relation to that industry (Health and Safety Executive, 1978*a*: 25). The NIGs are intended to act as catalysts, stimulating interest by employers' and employees' organizations in systematic approaches to and initiatives in health and safety, and the production of publications and training aids (Health and Safety Commission/Executive, 1987: 21). It is noteworthy that the NIG also allows for direct access to the organization by industrialists who wish to discover or criticize the attitude or practice of an inspectorate. This machinery is an important means of addressing matters of equity which inevitably arise where inspectors are placing their own ad hoc interpretations of rules upon real problems. In this way, the HSE hopes to be able both to channel and to absorb pressure from employers and unions, while endeavouring to maintain the confidence of both.[8]

The operational aims of HSE's various inspectorates reflect the instrumental commitment to prevention and repair embodied in the HSW Act. Their organizational structure reflects the primacy accorded various forms of monitoring: a large proportion of HSE's staff is employed at field level conducting inspections and liaising directly with regulated employers. HSC and HSE officially take a broad view of enforcement by their inspectorates:

'The term "enforcement" does not only mean taking punitive action, but covers the whole range of procedures adopted by inspectorates to ensure employers are aware of and comply with their responsibilities under health and safety

[8] Other NIG functions include the identification of problems peculiar to the industry concerned, assessing the need for development of technical standards and practical guidance, in close consultation with both sides of the industry, and promoting self-regulation. The objectives of each NIG are to provide 'a centre for the collection of data about practices, precautions and standards, and to provide guidance; to develop contacts with bodies representing interests in that industry; management, unions, suppliers of equipment and professional organizations; to pinpoint health and safety problems in the industry, whether general or specific; to develop ideas about ways of improving health and safety performance in the industry; and to stimulate thinking and promote constructive and planned initiatives by the industry itself' (Health and Safety Executive, 1978*a*: 25).

legislation. The inspectors' main concern is not to identify particular breaches of health and safety legislation so that they can prosecute the offender, but to ensure that management recognises its responsibilities for the control of hazards, to provide an effective policy for health and safety, proper organisation to carry it out and arrangements to ensure safe systems of work and to check the results regularly. Since the emphasis is very often on the provision of advice and relevant information, numbers of prosecutions and enforcement notices should not be used as a measure of our enforcement activities.' (Health and Safety Commission, 1978: 21)

As well as any abstract skills the job might demand, the level of personal liaison required depends on the persuasiveness of inspectors and their interpersonal competence. Compliance with occupational health and safety regulation is about the provision of hardware on the one hand and the adoption of systems of work on the other (some HSE groups deal more with the former rather than the latter). Indeed, one of the problems of occupational health and safety regulation is balancing control by physical hardware and absolute requirements against systems of work, operatives, and a general duty of care. These latter lack the clarity and comfortable certitudes of the former:

'A safe system of work, in its broadest sense, is the way a task is organised so that risks to health and safety are eliminated or at least reduced to their lowest reasonably practicable level. It may be simple, informal and involve only two or three distinct steps or conditions or it may be a complex and lengthy written statement covering many actions made under a variety of constraints and using numerous different protection techniques.' (Health and Safety Executive, 1983: 26)

The nature of the inspector's job is such that individuals are accorded a high level of discretion and each one handles problems on a case-by-case basis.

The combined HSC and HSE is a regulatory body of prodigious complexity and size.[9] The scale of HSE's operations is correspondingly vast, as was made clear in a recent annual report:

[9] There were 1,497 inspectors in post at the beginning of Apr. 1999, including those on non-inspection duties (such as line management, or contributing to policy or technical standards). These included 1,415 FOD members, 271 in the Chemicals and Hazardous Installations Division, 97 in the Railway Inspectorate, 35 in the Inspectorate of Mines, 237 in the Offshore Safety Division, and 224 in the Nuclear Safety Directorate (Health and Safety Commission, 1999: 61). With a commitment of well over 2,000 staff years, what is described generally as 'law enforcement' claimed the lion's share of staff resources in 1998/9 (Health and Safety Commission, 1999: 59–60).

'We have responsibility for securing compliance in over 540,000 establishments and numerous transitory work sites (for example, construction sites and fairgrounds)—around 13.2 million people. Local authorities enforce the Act under the direction of HSC in around 1,250,000 establishments, mainly in the lower risk sectors—involving some 8.5 million people. In a typical year we make over 170,000 face-to-face contacts including preventive inspections and investigate some 33,000 accidents or complaints. Others with important roles in the safety system include employees and safety representatives, trade associations, professional and voluntary organisations, insurance companies, and health and safety practitioners.' (Health and Safety Commission, 1997: 7)

The wide range of premises and hazards HSE covers, and its specialized forensic and other support capacities, make HSE 'unique among enforcement authorities in the UK—and probably in the world' (Health and Safety Commission, 1990*a*: 3). The huge array of responsibilities in such a large organization results in considerable complexity, but perhaps more important than their sheer number is their changing character, since there have been enormous shifts in economic, political, and technological life in the last quarter of a century.

Complexity in HSC and HSE is inevitable because the combined organization, as an expression of Robens's attempt to impose a conception of unified objectives and institutions on occupational health and safety regulation, has to address a richly diverse world of problems. This task, moreover, is one that has always had to be accomplished with what many claim to be modest resources. The complexity of the organization is also a consequence of HSE's birth as the progeny of several shotgun marriages. Nearly all the inspectorates with occupational health and safety responsibilities were brought together (some originally as unwilling partners) under the umbrella organization of HSE. Each of them was characterized by disparate institutional arrangements and mandates, contrasting traditions, practices, and occupational cultures, and different levels of resource. Similarly, they worked in environments suffused with different expectations and problems.

Throughout the 1970s and 1980s HSE remained essentially a federal structure. One implication of this for HSE (as well as for the fieldwork for Phase I of this research) was that the constituent inspectorates had different structures and personnel, and had to be dealt with on different footings. Accordingly, a crucial part of the Executive's work in earlier years was concerned with the management and coordination of the activities of its diverse inspectorates. This was something of a challenge, given that before the creation of HSE each inspectorate had acted quite autonomously. Coordination often proved difficult. A former member of the Executive put it this way: 'each inspectorate did its own thing and had been doing its own thing for a *very* long time. The degree to which there was any central control of these policies was absolutely minimal at that time, and so bringing the inspectorates together within the HSE and erecting above the inspectorates layers of control and command was something which was quite new to the inspectorates' (Hawkins, 1992*a*: 165–6: emphasis original).

Complexity arises also in the relationships which HSC, HSE, and the members of the Executive must maintain with a wide variety of groups and interests. These include not simply members of HSE's immediate audience—people in the workplace, employers, and their representative groups—but also ministers, the media, and the public. HSE's relations with the Health and Safety Commission are of prime importance. The Executive's task here is to advise the Commission on its policies, functions, and standards, and manage various functions on its behalf (Health and Safety Executive, 1987*b*: 7). The HSC (1985: 1) made clear the breadth of its relationships some years ago:

> 'While for general purposes answering to the Secretary of State for Employment, we are responsible in varying degrees to seven other Secretaries of State. Our actions reach out to affect every industrial activity, so that the commercial implications of what we do can be considerable. Even if the HSW Act did not put the main onus on those who create the risks to find the solutions, such a scope would imply a massive range of contact between the central authorities and industry, commerce and the government services concerned and a need to verify proposals through extensive consultation.'

Almost inevitably, HSE finds itself at the centre of an intricate web of political relationships with industry, characterized by a former Director General as 'industrial politics', the number and variety of which inculcate a broad sense of accountability to different groups and interests. These relationships stem from not only the structure and procedures of the Commission but also the underlying tasks and obligations of occupational health and safety regulation. Connections need to be maintained with a large number of industry associations and trade unions. While HSE is regarded as in large part looking after the basic health and safety of trade union members through a system of criminal liability, the unions are particularly interested in assisting their members with civil claims. They also have a strong interest in maintaining employment levels, though senior HSE officials believe that there may be occasions when this may actually run counter to good safety practice. Another aspect of 'industrial politics' is connected with industry's own approach to the public and the public's anxieties about certain kinds of hazard: the chemical and nuclear industries, for instance, are regarded as particularly conscious now of the need to reassure the public. The result of all of this, it has been said, is that the 'Executive's most typical activity and skill is . . . negotiation' (Health and Safety Executive, 1987*b*: 5).

HSE is often involved in the relationship between industry and the public, since its policies impose obligations upon industry in its conduct towards the public, such as openness and the need to inform the public about risks. Much of the pressure which is applied to it from outside arises from concern with the standards which HSE is to apply in interpreting the words 'reasonably practicable' in the HSW Act. The Commission, as the most important policy-making body, has devised ways of organizing and controlling pressures upon it, maintaining a large number of advisory committees dealing with different industries, and several major subject committees which handle matters such as toxic substances, nuclear installations, hazardous or dangerous substances, pathogens, and so on. These bodies have representation from both sides of industry with, in the case of the subject committees, the addition of experts (Hawkins, 1992*a*).

A particularly important set of political relationships must be maintained by Commission and Executive with the government of the day. The broad stance of successive governments has been one of sensitivity to the growing concern among the public about health and safety issues, and the public's instinctive sympathies with various forms of policing and controlling activity. The Executive is, however, very conscious of operating in a social and political environment which has changed considerably over recent years. In the 1980s successive Conservative governments were generally regarded as wishing to give the maximum degree of freedom to industry while presiding over the minimum of activity by the state (Chapter 4). One shift in governmental attitudes, described by a former Deputy Director General, was that

> 'the thing that causes attention now [late 1980s], which did not cause attention . . . perhaps, when we started . . . is the fact that on the whole occupational health and safety legislation does have a cost, that its benefits are actually difficult to demonstrate, particularly if they are . . . prevention of ill-health in the long and distant future. . . . [In the past], in the wake of the Health and Safety at Work Act, in reasonably prosperous times, we were the white knights with . . . substantial political support, and indeed employers' support . . . There

was . . . a very forward-looking atmosphere at that time in the wake of the Act, in the wake of Robens. . . . The atmosphere is very different [these days], a "looking at everybody" now. That's probably a right discipline.' (Hawkins, 1992*a*: 156)

The speaker pursued this theme by explaining that political changes had 'put a discipline on us, and of course actually what you find is that sometimes you can actually make a pretty good case and so . . . perhaps it's made for better legislation . . . and better and sharper policies . . . So it hasn't been all bad, but it's been all uncomfortable' (Hawkins, 1992*a*: 156).

By the late 1980s, however, political attitudes became more complicated, the government's position not being one of simple opposition to the idea of social regulation in principle, as was often assumed. The need for regulation was then thought to be less a concern of the government than the mode of regulation adopted: 'There clearly are things that need tackling,' said the former Director General at that time, 'and people would be astonished and angry if they thought they were not being tackled' (Hawkins, 1992*a*: 156).

The government of the day is always a force to be reckoned with since it can exert considerable control over what the HSE does. First, it controls HSE's resources. Second, it scrutinizes the Executive's plan of work. As a former member of the Executive put it, it considers 'all the policies and enforcement, the whole panoply of things which we do, looks at those periodically, and decides whether or not the balance is right . . . whether there are particular omissions that they would like to see filled, or whether there are particular things which they think are being overdone. But I think the government does have rather rough and ready priorities . . . ' (Hawkins, 1992*a*: 158). This description possibly implies a false degree of structure and initiative to the process, as the speaker went on to suggest. Rather,

'The Commission sends in a draft plan of work to the departments [which] look at that plan of work from the point of view of their own sectoral interests in it, and make comments on it. These come back to us, we make such adjustments as seem sensible, the plan of work goes back to ministers; if we fail to respond to some particular and major interest in the department they are likely to tell us. If we fail to direct resources to a sufficient degree to some particular thing . . . they are likely to tell us . . . So it's not, as it were, a coherent and integrated sort of reaction on the part of the government, it's really a whole series of quite . . . specific suggestions about changes which might be made. Any differences which remain are settled by some form of compromise.' (Hawkins, 1992*a*: 158)

A third source of governmental control arises from HSC's responsibility to ministers for all it does. 'It is a curious relationship, of course,' said a former member of the Executive,

> 'because it is supposed to be . . . at arms length, it's not meant to be a relationship in which the government is telling the Commission what to do, it's leaving it to the Commission to decide what to do, and . . . it reacts to the Commission's suggestion . . . Now from time to time the government will take a slightly different view . . . in a particular area . . . and will suggest to the Commission that it should change [its approach]. The Commission considers this and will react to the government as it sees fit in all the circumstances . . . [Q]uite clearly, no-one's interests are served . . . by there being any overt conflict between the two . . . bodies.' (Hawkins, 1992*a*: 158–9)

Governmental interest in and control of the work of the Commission and the Executive must be distinguished, of course, from interest from particular politicians, which may sometimes appear in the organization to arise randomly, and to play only a minor part in the general scale of priorities of the Commission, the Executive, or, indeed, the government. Such political interest of an individual kind becomes visible when, for example, a certain minister concentrates on a particular policy or proposal, possibly prompted by a specific incident or by a constituency matter (Hawkins, 1992*a*: 159–60).

Fourth, Secretaries of State can, in principle, direct the Commission or Executive to act in particular ways. Though this has never been done, the existence of such a power must inevitably have implications for the attention which members of the Commission or the Executive pay to less formal communication from ministers, especially given the high level of contact between the Executive and ministers and their officials. 'Nevertheless,' said a former Director General,

> 'the independence that we have is real, because it would always be possible for us to make a public matter of intervention by ministers in anything that really was significant. The Commission, after all, is a public body. It's not obliged to be polite to Ministers of the Crown. . . . [A]nd, of course, the Opposition takes a very considerable interest and watches very carefully to see that we are not unduly interfered with, and it does its best to remind the government of the need for us to have an adequate level of resources.' (Hawkins, 1992*a*: 159)

Finally, the political complexion of the party in power may have recondite implications for control of the regulatory process of a very different sort. Bargaining strengths within the Commission may be subtly influenced, giving one side or the other a greater degree of confidence and determination in arguing for its position in negotiations. Thus 'Although the Commission operates by consensus,' said a senior official,

> 'the fact that the ultimate arbiter is now [in the late 1980s], a Conservative minister, rather than a Labour minister, means inevitably that the CBI is likely to take a harder negotiating line.... [There have been] examples in the recent past...where ministers knew that the Commission was incapable of coming to a decision, where they have taken the initiative themselves...and have simply ruled, and they have legislated.'

These effects may be more widely observable, affecting the willingness (or otherwise) of employers to accept the advice of HSE officials on certain matters at the implementation as well as at the consultative stage. Certainly, in the late 1980s there seemed to senior HSE officials to be a greater confidence displayed in general by employers in the conduct of industrial relations.

Political concerns of a broader character tend to suffuse the whole process of health and safety regulation in the higher reaches of the organization, for policy innovation or change here is as much a product of political debate as of the dispassionate analysis of scientific evidence allied with expert advice. Though a matter may be discussed and argued in scientific terms, 'At the end of the day...,' said a former Director General,

> 'a political judgment will be reached... It will be such questions as whether such and such an industry can adapt quickly enough to a new limit, whether it needs a transition period or not.... Or it may be the simple allegation that it costs too much to deal with it, so at the end of the day you reach something... by political means, at least as much as by expert means.' (Hawkins, 1992*a*: 156)

5. SUBSEQUENT CHANGES

Quite apart from HSE's much increased international commitment, evident in its focus on Europe, the HSE organization of the 1980s found itself in a social and political environment of a very different character from that of the 1970s. During the 1980s HSC (1993, p. x) reported that there had been a number of important trends affecting occupational health and safety regulation. A gradual shift of resources and greater interest in occupational health and hygiene had occurred,[10]

[10] Exemplified by the introduction of the Control of Substances Hazardous to Health Regulations.

together with a better appreciation of the consequences of occupational ill health, in terms of time off work and premature retirement. Another shift was in the balance of regulatory activities towards major hazards and the protection of the public from industrial harms, and, connected with this, a marked increase was noticeable in public concern for the environmental aspects of the work of HSC and HSE, especially hazards involving nuclear or large chemical installations, and newly perceived threats posed by advances in areas such as biotechnology (Health and Safety Commission, 1993, p. x). Finally, there was a steady acquisition of new responsibilities, including those for supervision of the Advisory Committee on Genetic Modification (1983), major new obligations for the control of major hazards under the Seveso Directive (1984), safety regulation of gas transmission (1985), much enlarged responsibilities under the Food and Environmental Protection Act for control of pesticides (1986), and responsibilities as customer for nuclear safety research on established systems (1990), railway passenger safety (1990), and offshore safety (1991).

The environment of recent years has again altered, with the organization becoming preoccupied with questions of accountability. Given the complexity of HSE's operations, it is not surprising to discover that the agency has a correspondingly complicated sense of accountability which sometimes surfaces in decisions to be made about the prosecution of a particular violation. A former Deputy Director General summed up the position in a personal way with words which also serve well to define a working conception of the HSE's mandate:

> 'I really see myself as accountable very much to the trade unions and employed persons... in terms of being accountable for providing a proper measure of anticipatory protection and oversight of standards. I think we're accountable to workpeople. I think we are accountable to employers in terms of giving them sensible advice, providing equitable enforcement (I think equity is an important component of enforcement, so that in fact... those who don't comply don't get an unfair advantage). I think we're clearly accountable to the public in terms of the protection of the public from work activities, very much the major hazard field and things like fairgrounds, school children, health service. And we're clearly accountable to politicians to provide them with good advice and to provide them with a service, or to provide an Executive service which doesn't leave them politically vulnerable—via the Commission, of course.' (Hawkins, 1992*a*: 163–4)

This question of accountability has in turn been connected with the constant concern for resources, since HSE must continue to conduct its traditional functions while accumulating the new responsibilities that have arisen. All of these add to the burden on the organization's resources.

Change is a recurrent theme in the life of the agency and the political, economic, and technological changes in the last quarter of a century have led to substantial changes in its structure. An outside observer might be forgiven for thinking that the agency reinvents itself every few years, since organizational arrangements or practices rarely seem to be left untouched for long. Two major reorganizations were carried out within HSE during the conduct of this research, mainly in an effort to ensure a consistent approach to health and safety problems across a wide range of industries. In the reorganization which took place in the period 1986–7 (during Phase I of this research) the Factory Inspectorate (FI) and the Agricultural Inspectorate were linked within the same HSE division. The Agricultural Inspectorate's field force was realigned from an eight-region structure to fit into HSE's area framework for the FI.[11] This resulted in area directors (ADs) exercising a line management function for the thirty agricultural inspection groups under the general management of the Chief Agricultural Inspector and his headquarters.

The second reorganization, which came into effect in April 1990, reached further. Its purpose was to achieve an integration of HSE's field operations. The reorganization followed a major review of HSE's fieldwork, which had recommended that a new Field Operations Directorate (FOD) be created to include the various inspectors in the field and the technical, scientific, and medical teams who previously worked in separate divisions.[12] HSE created, in effect, a generic field force placed for the first time under unified management (Health and Safety Commission, 1990*b*, p. x). The reorganization brought together the Agricultural, Factory, and Quarries Inspectorates, HSE's field consultant groups, field scientific support units, and staff from the Employment

[11] On 1 Apr. 1985 it was planned to have around 160 agricultural inspectors, of whom about 150 would be employed in the field, and among whom would be a number of new assistant inspectors recruited during 1984. Some 80 support staff were allocated to the inspectorate, most of whom were also intended to be in the field. Further support was provided by staff allocated to the FI for management purposes, in shared area offices. The FI was at the time responsible for about 320,000 workplaces (Health and Safety Commission, 1985: 21).

[12] At the end of Phase I of fieldwork, in 1988–9, HSE's then inspectorates—for Factories, Agriculture, Mines and Quarries, Nuclear Installations, and Explosives—had enforcement responsibility for over 700,000 fixed premises in total, with an additional, unquantifiable number of transient sites (Health and Safety Commission, 1990*a*).

Medical Advisory Service. They came together into the FOD, said an AD,

'within a new regional structure, and the aim of that was to make FOD much more multi-disciplinary, to integrate the planning, so that it involved the medical people and the specialists much more in planning, and to give a greater regional identity to plans. And by bringing, in most cases three and in one case four, of the old areas together, it meant that there was an opportunity to compare and contrast and get greater consistency in the organization compared with the previous, largely independent, 20 areas.' (97–04)

This second reorganization was in pursuit of greater uniformity of policy and practice in the operation of HSE at all levels, and one of its explicit aims was to achieve more consistency in prosecution work. The benefits of an integrated approach to field activities were said to be closer coordination between inspectors, specialists, and medical staff, including more systematic sharing of information.

The two reorganizations brought about significant changes in the nature of occupational health and safety regulatory practice. One consequence has been an increase in managerialism. Principal inspectors (PIs), for example, now spend less time actually working in the field, and more supervising the activities of their field inspectors.[13] Similarly, the nature of the inspector's job has also become more office-bound since field staff have increasingly been expected to write their own notes on personal computers (and have been given keyboard skills for the purpose) at the expense of secretarial staff. Predictably, the amount of paperwork inspectors are confronted with has increased, largely the result of the introduction of new legal formalities following the passage of the Magistrates' Courts (Advance Information) Rules, 1985 (which entitle an accused person to be furnished with advance information about the evidence upon which the prosecutor proposes to rely in criminal proceedings), the requirements for advanced disclosure in connection with the provisions of the Police and Criminal Evidence Act, 1984 (PACE), and the Criminal Procedure and Investigations Act, 1996 (Sanders & Young, 2000).

There have also been a number of other developments over the last ten years:

'different inspectorates have come into HSE. So the Offshore Safety Directorate was created after Piper Alpha, and we took over that responsibility from the

[13] This may have been partly the result of several retirements of experienced inspectors which took place in the early 1990s. They were replaced by less experienced people.

Department of Energy; the Railway Inspectorate came over from the Department of Transport. We've also in that time had changes in policy so that the policy divisions have been reorganized and streamlined; and the most recent major change was the senior management review, which restructured the senior management of the organization, and took out a number of layers of management.' (97–04)

These innovations have demanded a greater degree of legalistic behaviour by inspectors. The result of the Magistrates' Courts' Advanced Information Rules, according to an AD, was that

'where we have to disclose the evidence we're intending to rely on at a very early stage. . . . I think that has been potentially beneficial, because we generally apply a high degree of rigour to our approvals process, and we believe that in a majority of cases, the evidence is pretty incontrovertible. And therefore by disclosing it at an early stage, you do, I think, encourage a guilty plea, because the evidence is all set out, without having to wait to come to court to hear what we've got to say.' (97–04)

PACE was also thought to have been beneficial from the point of view of HSE's interest in securing guilty pleas. This was because the additional formality of tape-recording interviews

'perhaps has an effect on individuals in getting them to recognize the seriousness of what's involved. They very often have solicitors present, which means that, providing the statements are subsequently admissible because we've followed the procedure correctly, it's much harder for them to subsequently defend the case. So that can be a benefit, but it's been a new skill, and we've had to put a lot of training effort into it.' (97–04)

Life has changed significantly for inspectors in other ways over the last 20 years, as a result of the institutional restructuring. One AD suggested that

'suddenly they are inspecting industries which they hadn't any previous experience in. Just one example is agricultural inspectors. The agricultural industry is now linked in organizational terms with the woodworking industry. So inspectors who've previously inspected in agriculture are now required to inspect woodworking factories as well, which is quite a profound change for them, because the issues, and indeed some of the older legislation, are very different. So, yes, there are a number of inspectors, quite a high proportion, who have suddenly had to do very different types of inspection. . . . The other change is that for the major hazard work and the chemical industry, that has now been hived off to become a completely different part of HSE . . . But the impact has not been even. In some parts, indeed in the region as well as the country, the individual inspectors are doing much the same things as they were before—reporting to and working with much the same people as they were before. But in other parts there has been a very profound upheaval.' (97–02)

Other tasks are growing more complex. There are an increasing number of small and dispersed businesses to deal with. Many of the new regulations which have been introduced, often of European origin, are more complicated than earlier provisions. Some of these developments have impinged on enforcement, as an AD made clear:

'Something which was not an organizational change but which was an attitudinal change was a rebalancing of our effort from being predominantly safety to now being, I would guess, 50/50 safety and health. And therefore one thing I'm sure you would notice in looking at our enforcement—perhaps not so much prosecution as enforcement notices—is that we have put a lot more effort into health matters. And there's a long term programme called "Good health is good business" which is a five or more year programme of tackling a succession of occupational health issues, and each of those programmes has a broad enforcement strategy linked to it. And other issues, like asbestos, you would find, I think, are still very much to the fore in all of our activities.' (97–04)

The changes in attitude referred to have imprinted themselves on the general practices of inspectors.[14] In particular, they are now said more frequently to be considering companies' arrangements for the management of health and safety, backed up by enforcement action in appropriate circumstances, to tackle root causes rather than just the symptoms of undesirable conditions (Health and Safety Commission, 1993: 3). Area autonomy continues to be large but various forms of information and advice come from headquarters. There is also written guidance. However, 'The bedrock of our activity remains the work of our field forces,' HSC (1999, p. xiii) has said:

'Their contacts with employers and workers—to give advice and where necessary to take formal action—are a powerful impetus to improved standards of health and safety. During the year, we made 183,000 regulatory contacts, exceeding our target; 78% of inspector time was spent in direct contact with clients and related activities; and 79% of planned inspections were to small firms. But we are victims of our own success in raising the profile of health and safety. We receive more complaints about working conditions each year (29,500 this year, 7,000 more

[14] A corresponding impact of the HSW Act is said to have been a change in the attitudes of employers, making them more aware of occupational health and safety issues. Inspectors thought this was reflected in changes in their use of notices and in organizational ideology. One summed it up simply as 'a swing away from the enforcing side to the advising side' (86–10).

than we had forecast) so this year we could investigate only 80% of them. The challenge is a perennial one: how should we best use our resources—information, advice, guidance, inspection, investigation of accidents and complaints, enforcement action etc. to make the most effective interventions—in today's diverse, complex and distributed labour market and in the context of today's societal expectations?'

These measures reflect the proportion of time spent by operational inspectors producing outputs, such as inspections, investigations, and prosecutions; they include the associated office time devoted to managing and processing such work (Health and Safety Commission, 1999: 44). Inspection remains the dominant activity of HSE's field force. According to HSE (1980, pp. vi–vii), the frequency with which inspections are undertaken in any premises depends on need—the standards of safety, health, and welfare found at the premises at the last visit, the potential inherent hazard to employees or members of the public, and the quality of the management and its ability to maintain standards and adapt to change. 'Thus premises with a high inherent risk, or poor standards of health and safety or management, will be visited more frequently than those which have a low potential hazard, are well equipped and competently run.'[15]

Despite the huge political, economic, and technological changes of the last quarter of a century, and HSE's own restructurings, the fundamental character of enforcement work in HSE seems not to have changed significantly, and certainly not between the first and second phases of the research fieldwork, as a PI made clear:

'The problem is that industry and the activities that we enforce have moved on a lot since [the mid- to late 1980s], as has the legislation. So there's probably not a great deal of change in the decision-making process, but there has been a lot more effort . . . put into trying to make it consistent, I think. The difficulty we've got is that we've moved away in ten years from prescriptive, the older prescriptive legislation, through the generality of the Health and Safety at Work Act, and in a way, we're back now to some prescription, but on a much more general level. Because in the early days, the prescription was in relation to specific industries

[15] Risk assessment is now one of the central regulatory themes in occupational health and safety. It is carried out by a 'competent person' or group who identify hazards, evaluate risks, and control measures, record the assessment, and regularly review the position. Hazards are graded as major (causing death or serious injury); serious (causing injury or disease capable of keeping an individual off work for three days or more); minor (causing minor injury, but without stopping the normal flow of work; or nil (no risk of injury or disease). Major and serious categories are both reportable under RIDDOR (Reporting of Injuries, Diseases and Dangerous Occurrences Regulations, 1985).

and specific activities under the Factories Acts and the other Acts that we enforced . . . We had the umbrella Health and Safety at Work Act, but very often we would be enforcing the Factories Act (fencing of machinery). We've moved now where under the Health and Safety at Work Act new legislation has been made—what we call the six-pack of regulations, the Management Regulations, etc. etc. which in their own way are specific, but they're specific to a much wider range of industry. So instead of just looking at factories . . . my remit extends to things like landfill sites. Well, there's a big doubt as to whether the Factories Act would have applied to landfill sites in the old days, so we would've had to have used the general [HSW] Act. Now we've got the option of using the new regulations.'[16] (97–01)

The final possible change to consider is the direct impact of reorganization within HSE on prosecution behaviour in particular. The general view of HSE staff consulted in 1997–8 was that decision-making about prosecution had not been affected by these formal restructurings in any significant way. Judging broadly from the contents of the prosecution files, it seems that inspectors' aims and the ways in which they conduct their work remain largely unaltered. Any changes that have occurred seem to have been of a procedural rather than a substantive kind. In terms of case types, most of those prosecutions sampled in 1997 were for violations involving incidents that could also have happened 50 years ago, such as accidents with power presses, crushes in machinery, problems with gas fires, falls, the collapse of unsupported trenches, and the other 'traditional' problems routinely encountered by factory inspectors.[17] It is often the case that changes in legal procedures seem not to have much of an impact on the substantive decision-making of the officials concerned (McConville *et al.*, 1991), and occupational health and safety regulation seems to be no exception:

'I don't think that any of those changes in procedure have affected the number or type of cases. They're about "how" rather than "whether". Obviously it does mean that when we decide to embark on a prosecution, we may expect that the whole process will take longer, and that inevitably is the case, but I think it's sharpened us up, in terms of how we gather evidence.' (97–04)

When asked whether the place or the conduct of prosecution had changed since the mid-1980s, one AD replied:

[16] See Ch. 12 for an analysis of how this option is exercised.

[17] Of the 68 cases in the sample of prosecutions, three involved matters of occupational ill health, and three carbon monoxide poisoning arising from faulty gas installations. Two more were welfare cases, and one was a prosecution for failure to comply with a notice. In other words, 59 prosecutions were for a variety of accidents.

'Well, the nature of it has changed quite a bit, in that cases are much more complex now. I mean, I think part of this is changing patterns of employment. There's much more contracting out in industry and that necessarily brings with it complications as to who is responsible. I think also that companies are much less willing to put their hands up and say, you know, "Sorry, it's a fair cop," partly because industry generally has been encouraged to see itself in a different light rather than to regard itself as having a divine right to exist without impediment from bureaucrats, and partly because the legislation has become less black and white. You know, more cases are potentially defendable, or arguable, anyway.' (97–02)

It seems reasonable to conclude that the character of prosecution decision behaviour itself seems to be largely unchanged, as between the first and second phases of the research. However far-reaching the administrative reorganization, it seems not to have affected inspectors' fundamental practices.

6. LEGAL POWERS

The legal powers of an HSE inspector are neatly summed up in HSC's brochure (1998*c*, n.p.) *What to expect when a health and safety inspector calls*:

'Where the breach of the law is relatively minor, the inspector may tell the dutyholder, for example the employer or contractor, what to do to comply with the law, and explain why. The inspector will, if asked, write to confirm any advice, and to distinguish legal requirements from best practice advice.

Improvement notice

'Where the breach of the law is more serious, the inspector may issue an improvement notice to tell the dutyholder to do something to comply with the law. The inspector will discuss the improvement notice and, if possible, resolve points of difference before serving it. The notice will say what needs to be done, why, and by when. The time period within which to take the remedial action will be at least 21 days, to allow the dutyholder time to appeal to an Industrial Tribunal if they so wish . . . The inspector can take further legal action if the notice is not complied with within the specified time period.'

Such a notice would be served on the person 'who is deemed to be contravening the legal provision, or it can be served on any person on whom responsibilities are placed, whether he is an employer, an employed person, or a supplier of equipment or materials' (Health and Safety Commission, 1979: 9).

'*Prohibition notice*
Where an activity involves, or will involve, a risk of serious personal injury, the inspector may serve a prohibition notice prohibiting the activity immediately or after a specified time period, and not allowing it to be resumed until remedial action has been taken. The notice will explain why the action is necessary. The dutyholder will be told in writing about the right of appeal to an Industrial Tribunal . . .' (Health and Safety Commission, 1998*c*, n.p.)

The purpose of this notice is 'to stop the activity giving rise to this risk, until the remedial action specified in the notice has been taken. It can be served on the person undertaking the activity, or on a person in control of it at the time the notice was served' (Health and Safety Commission, 1979: 9).[18]

'*Prosecution*
In some cases the inspector may consider that it is also necessary to initiate a prosecution. Decisions on whether to prosecute are informed by the principles in HSC's *Enforcement Policy Statement.* Health and safety law gives the courts considerable scope for punishing offenders and deterring others. For example, a failure to comply with an improvement or prohibition notice, or a court remedy order carries a fine of up to £20,000, or six months' imprisonment, or both. Unlimited fines and in some cases imprisonment may be imposed by higher courts.' (Health and Safety Commission, 1998*c*, n.p.)

The focus of the analysis on prosecution in this book should not obscure the importance to HSE inspectors of improvement or prohibition notices as a means of promoting compliance (though it should be noted that prosecution may also be employed as the sanction for failure to comply with improvement or prohibition notices).[19] Inspectors do not lightly embark upon either form of enforcement: a notice requires careful drafting to deal precisely with future methods of working, use of the plant

[18] HSE has become increasingly reliant on notices. Provisional figures for 1998–9 indicate that 10,844 enforcement notices were issued, an increase of 22 per cent compared with the number issued in the previous year. The 8,911 notices issued in 1997–8 represented an increase, in turn, of 20 per cent, compared with 1996/7, when 7,444 notices were issued (the lowest number in recent years). Based on provisional figures in 1998/9, 6,328 improvement notices were issued (an increase of 43 per cent compared with the number issued in the previous year) and these represented 58 per cent of the total number of notices issued, compared with 50 per cent in 1997/98 and 51 per cent in 1996/97. There were also 198 deferred prohibition notices (2 per cent of the total number of notices issued), which was the same proportion as in the previous two years. Of the improvement notices issued, 96 per cent were immediate, the same proportion as in the previous year (Health and Safety Commission, 1998*b*: 55).

[19] Failure to comply with notices is rare. In research carried out in the 1980s HSE (1985*b*) discovered that well over 90 per cent of its notices were complied with.

or substances, and so on, whereas a prosecution has to be managed extremely carefully not only to avoid wasting a great deal of past work or failing to convict, but also to avoid jeopardizing future efforts at securing compliance. The formal position, according to the HSC (1999: 39), is that in most cases,

> 'information, guidance and advice are sufficient to ensure that health and safety requirements are complied with. Where formal action is appropriate, the issue of an improvement or a prohibition notice normally provides a quick and effective means of securing the necessary improvements. The HSC expects, through its Enforcement Policy Statement, that enforcing authorities will consider prosecution when, for example, there is judged to have been the potential for serious harm arising from a breach, or when the gravity of a breach taken together with the general record and approach of the offender warrants it.'

The notice procedure has, in the opinion of many inspectors, altered the role of prosecution. Notices are sometimes used instead of prosecution. A notice allows inspectors to escape any problems likely to be created by prosecuting. It can also achieve a show of activity, one that avoids possible problems that may arise with a particular case.

But in general inspectors believe that notices and prosecution serve essentially different, if related, functions and are appropriate to different enforcement goals (Lloyd-Bostock, 1987: 23). To prosecute is to make a decision of a different order from one to issue a notice. Prosecution tends to be conceived of in broader terms and to be treated as general in purpose, where notices are seen to be much more specific and precise, and to have a problem-solving character. A notice essentially represents a private enforcement transaction between the inspector and the employer, but prosecution is a public matter with a correspondingly wider potential impact. While a notice tends to act in a practical way at shop-floor level, a prosecution is believed to have more of an impact on the boardroom, thanks to its public character. For this reason, inspectors with instrumental objectives hope that it may prompt a broad organizational solution to a general problem, rather than a specific remedy for a particular difficulty. Notices are not regarded as a sanction by inspectors in the way that prosecution is. Instead they are thought to offer a better chance of attaining a remedy without a risk of encouraging management to fight the issue. Nonetheless, notice powers are viewed by inspectors as effective enforcement devices: 'You don't need to prosecute, because you've got power' (86–19). Notices, like prosecution, offer an opportunity to bargain and they also have the great virtue, from the viewpoint of an inspector, of being an enforcement technique remaining within the inspector's control. This contrasts strongly with the decision to prosecute which sees the ultimate control of the case pass into the hands of the courts, losing much of the problem-solving character of a notice. Factory inspectors in the mid-1980s believed notices were not appropriate enforcement methods following accidents because in such circumstances immediate action was necessary. The improvement notice allows time for compliance, and the more stringent criteria required for the use of a prohibition notice may not be present (Lloyd-Bostock, 1987: 23).[20] In short, notices are employed in a strongly instrumental way to get things done, whereas prosecution is often seen expressively as a deserved sanction for some act or omission.

Licences are another formal, if much less used, technique of enforcement. They are crucial to the regulation of occupational health and safety in nuclear installations. Licensing has an impact on the licensee through the use by the Nuclear Installations Inspectorate (NII) of its system of consents and approvals. A consent is a formal permission given by NII to a licensee to permit the conduct of a particular operation, such as restarting a reactor:

> 'The consent to proceed is a powerful device for ensuring that all the necessary information has been accumulated and assessed before the work proceeds. If action is needed between two holding points, each requiring a consent, the action is achieved either by discussion or, in rare cases, by the issue of an extra licence condition. The use of consents has the advantage of allowing the Inspectorate to impose their requirements on the operator's programme but, at the same time, it tends to make the inspector more of a participant and less of an intervener in the licensee's operations.' (Health and Safety Executive, 1978*b*: 25–6)

The penalties available to the courts to sanction breaches of occupational health and safety provisions, and in particular the way in which the courts have made use of them, have been contentious issues over the years. HSC has repeatedly expressed concern that the general level of penalties imposed by the courts does not reflect the seriousness of the cases before them,

> 'given that lives can be put at risk and unscrupulous companies can profit from flouting health and safety law. We have been working with other Government

[20] But of course there are always circumstances where the hazard is so great, or the risk of serious bodily injury so immediate, that inspectors feel that it would not be right to allow any time for compliance (Health and Safety Executive, 1980, p. v).

departments to consider what more can be done to deter those who flout the law. We welcome the Lord Chancellor's recent comments in a speech to magistrates in which he emphasised the importance of the sentences which judges and magistrates hand down for health and safety (and environmental) offences, and that they should reflect the seriousness with which society views failings in these areas. The Lord Chancellor urged magistrates not to refrain from using the maximum penalties if they are deserved.'[21] (Health and Safety Commission, 1998*a*: 30)

Over the years penalties have been increased and the courts have shown willingness to use their greater powers. In the magistrates' courts fines imposed have increased as the maximum fines permitted have increased. It seems extraordinary to report that in 1976 the maximum fine was £400, and the average fine imposed was £89. Penalties were increased subsequently, and the maximum level of fines was again raised in 1992, leading HSC (1993, pp. xiv–xv) to state briefly in its annual report for that year its prosecution policy, while at the same time expressing the hope that the courts would take advantage of the greater room for manoeuvre:

'HSE does not prosecute unless we are satisfied that a serious breakdown of reasonable precaution has taken or is taking place. When we are so satisfied, we will bring before the courts either the firm or if the breakdown is clearly in our view attributable to her or him, any individual, director or worker who can properly and reasonably be accused. We have a statutory responsibility to enforce the law, and can only follow our policy of moderation and restraint on the basis that when we do act, the courts will register the full extent of the dereliction.'

The penalties currently available upon conviction for occupational health and safety violations are fines (up to £20,000 in the magistrates' courts, unlimited in the Crown Court) and imprisonment (up to two years, following trial on indictment). Provisional figures for 1998–9 show that the average fine for convictions following health and safety legislation prosecuted by HSE was £5,038, an increase of 7 per cent compared

[21] The report did not mince words: 'In the light of these results we have set tough targets in 1997/98 for getting HSE inspectors out and about to see firms and for other enforcement activities. We will also be reviewing our activity on the issue of enforcement notices and working closely with the Government to try to get penalties applied properly by the courts where companies or individuals flout health and safety law: some today are ridiculously low. We need to be seen to be acting and enforcement action must have bite. But the main duty is with people in industry—they have a legal obligation to manage safety and operate safely and they need to do better' (Health and Safety Commission, 1998*a*, p. xi).

with the average of £4,694 in 1997–8.[22] Readers can come to their own conclusions about the adequacy of these penalties from the illustrative cases appearing later in this book.

HSC seems to be concerned more with the fines imposed by the courts than with the level of fines made available by the legislature. One reason for the reluctance of the courts to sanction as heavily as HSC or HSE would wish was said to be that

> 'some magistrates courts (sheriff summary courts in Scotland) which may see health and safety cases relatively infrequently do not sufficiently distinguish them—in terms of their potentially more serious consequences, of death, injury, loss of livelihood—from the day-to-day round of petty crimes. Some examples of cases where, in HSC/E's view, the courts took an unduly lenient view were set out in a paper presented to the Select Committee on Employment . . .' (Health and Safety Commission, 1990*a*: 3)

HSC's concern for adequate levels of sanction seems to be driven less by instrumental interests than expressive ones. For instance, in 1978 it observed that 'where serious offences often resulting in death or serious injury are punished with a paltry fine, this devalues the work of all those who are making real efforts to reduce occupational hazards' (Health and Safety Commission, 1978: 22). Twenty years on HSC (1999: 40) expressed anxiety 'that the general level of penalties imposed by the Courts does not match the real seriousness of health and safety offences, which can and do sometimes lead to terrible injury, ill health and death'.[23]

[22] Both figures, however, are lower than the average fine in 1996–7, which at £6,274 was the highest average so far attained. Note that these figures are distorted by large fines. If fines of £100,000 or more are excluded, the average fine per conviction would have been £3,442 in 1998–9, compared with £3,805 in 1997/8, and £3,113 in 1996/7 (Health and Safety Commission, 1998*b*: 57).

[23] It went on to approve the judgment in the Court of Appeal (*R. v. F. Howe and Son (Engineers) Ltd* [1999] 2 All ER 249) which said that health and safety fines were too low. The Court said that a fine must be large enough to bring home to those who manage a company, and their shareholders, the need for a safe environment for workers and the public; also that generally where death is the consequence of a criminal act it is regarded as an aggravating feature of the offence. The penalty should reflect public disquiet at the unnecessary loss of life. The Court also identified a number of aggravating features which would be relevant when considering the gravity of future cases and matters which should underpin future sentencing. This decision has resulted in a greater number of cases being committed to the Crown Court for sentence. 'The case provided the first clarification of the correct approach to sentencing for health and safety offences and a basis for inspectors drawing sentencing matters to the Court's attention. . . . A continued trend towards markedly higher penalties would be invaluable in bringing home the importance of complying with health and safety law, and deterring the minority whose cavalier attitude gives rise to special concern. We also

This neatly makes apparent the centrality of desert and the symbolism of the penalty which, as this book shows, are crucial features in the prosecution decision-making of HSE inspectors.

welcome the message sent by the Courts, following a nine-month jail sentence for putting employees and public at risk from illegal work with asbestos. Failure to control properly such risks is a serious offence, sometimes made all the more repugnant when corners are cut for profit' (Health and Safety Commission, 1999: 40–1).

6 Prosecution Policy

1. CLEARING THE GROUND

Enforcement policy is that which inspectors apprehend as official guidance on how to do their regulatory work. Policy in regulatory bureaucracies is an important part of the formal definition of their decision-making field. Yet the nature of policy is such that it rarely reaches field staff in a form they find clear or helpful in guiding the particular decisions about enforcement, and especially prosecution, that they have to make. This chapter discusses, *inter alia*, why this is so, concentrating on bureaucratic policy about prosecution and the extent to which it constrains case decision-making. Doing this requires attention to questions such as how to think about policy, its origins, and why it may not be transmitted through the regulatory organization and into action at the periphery in a pristine form. The argument is that the attenuation of regulatory policy arises as a result of the vague or general formulation of policy, the vagaries of its transmission to the field, and the competing demands on inspectors' decision-making arising from the practical character of their work.

In the abstract, policy may appear to be the embodiment of an instrumental expression of law. In practice, however, various opportunities are opened up for the making of expressive decisions in the actual processes of decision-making, since policy is not impervious to the wide variety of extraneous forces which come to be superimposed upon inspectors' decision-making. The problem for bureaucratic policy is not simply the extent to which it can effectively be communicated within the organization, so much as whether it is able to overcome the practical imperatives that determine what inspectors do.

The law constitutes the most significant part of the regulatory agency's field. It outlines what Peter Manning describes as 'grand policy', which gives concrete expression to the occupational health and safety values to be advanced, preserved, and protected by the regulatory agency.[1] The

[1] I have benefited substantially in writing this chapter from Manning's (1987*b*) unpublished analysis of the Nuclear Installations Inspectorate (NII).

agency's understanding of its legal mission and powers is in turn articulated in its statements of policy. 'Grand policy' exists in the form of general declarations about agency work and beliefs and centres upon questions connected with what to regulate and how to regulate. In a formal conception of policy its meaning and objectives are intended to remain relatively invariable over time, its implementation to be consistent, and its substance open to systematic review and revision. This is an 'iterative' conception of policy, emphasizing its invariant, known, and clearly understood character (Manning, 1987*b*).

Policy is the means by which a link is forged between legislative intention and practical action. Various forces prompt policy initiatives in occupational health and safety regulation: new hazards, low standards, a new public concern, a stimulus from Europe, or feedback from policy or field staff, from industry or trades unions. Within the broad framework given by the law, it is the task of the regulatory agency first to interpret and crystallize its own conceptions of what the thrust and meaning of the legal framework is, and then to reinterpret it in terms that are organizationally intelligible and capable of transmission within the organization to guide the work of those within it, especially those occupying the periphery. Formal policy is actually defined and declared by senior officials at the centre of the regulatory organization and embodies their conception of the law's purpose and the organization's mandate.

The conventional view of policy is most relevant and useful when considering how policy-makers at senior levels in a regulatory bureaucracy regard their task. General prosecution policy exists in the form of statements of principle about the broad conditions under which there would be a presumption or expectation that prosecution would follow a violation of the law. Both the substance of prosecution policy and the form in which it is expressed are important, and may, in their different ways, have an impact on routine enforcement decision-making in individual cases, affecting both the numbers and kinds of problem eventually selected for prosecution by inspectors. Policy not only represents the formal, official conception of the inspector's decision field, it is also intended to shape the way in which individual cases are framed.

Prosecution policy in HSE is itself part of a broader set of bureaucratic stipulations relating generally to the advancement of occupational health and safety. Policy exists in different forms: apart from the law, there are bureaucratic rules or statements, as well as forms of practice which are often unarticulated. These are aimed at shaping what the decision-maker attends to, how a problem should be addressed and dealt with, and what outcomes are most appropriate. Written formulations include formal statements, guidelines, and codes of practice. When a bureaucracy like HSE thinks of policy, it has in mind the making of substantive regulatory policy about the problems out in the world that need its guidance and control. Such questions are in a state of constant flux. In the occupational health and safety arena, for example, the concern for hazards has shifted from the simple question whether or not legislation ought to be employed, or which risks should be regulated, to focus on how legal rules are to be enforced: with what degree of stringency or accommodation (Kagan, 1978), or with what balance between sanctioning and compliance strategies (Hawkins, 1984).

HSE may well devote less time and effort to the making and refinement of enforcement policy in comparison with its other forms of policy work. Nonetheless, formal bureaucratic policy about the conditions under which prosecution is officially regarded as desirable is intended to be an important presence for inspectors, forming and constraining their decision field and acting in turn upon the framing processes involved in deciding the fate of each case. However, three sorts of impediment tend to frustrate enforcement policy. First, such are the practical pressures to which inspectors are subject in handling cases that official assumptions about the extent to which formal policy provides effective guidance may be misplaced. If it is to make a difference, policy has to be superimposed over whatever external forces, arising from political, economic, or organizational sources, act on inspectors. Policy has, secondly, to transcend internal constraints, such as beliefs about compliance and punishment, or the desire to blame, to which inspectors are subject when they make law enforcement decisions. A third impediment is the structure through which enforcement is carried out, the inspectorate. Discontinuities occur in the transmission of policy from the centre for implementation by inspectors at the organizational periphery. The policy that is declared as part of the organizational mandate has a tortuous course to run before it reaches the inspector. Since inspectors are officials with high levels of legal discretion, who work largely autonomously in low-visibility settings, making policy real and effective in its guidance at field level represents a considerable challenge to agency managers. When policy reaches the field for implementation, it may still be subject to all sorts of modification, even assuming that inspectors are clear about what policy requires.

Given the special character of prosecution—its visibility, its gravity, its potential for inconsistent application, and its costly implications for the regulated and for the agency—it is inevitable that those at the centre of the organization should seek a high degree of control over how enforcement decisions are made at the organizational periphery.[2] Though enforcement policy is designed with the specific intention of shaping the inspector's decision frame when particular cases are being considered, in reality other forces may lead an inspector to decide otherwise, as subsequent chapters will show. The primary reasons for the attenuation or distortion of enforcement policy in a regulatory bureaucracy are to be found in the nature of policy itself and in the structure of the organizations through which it is to be implemented.

2. ENFORCEMENT POLICY AS A FORMAL CONCEPTION

In Manning's (1987*b*) view, policy has no accepted definition; furthermore, he argues that the orthodox conception of policy in the political science literature is too simple. Instead, there are various ways of thinking about the nature of policy and policy-making. The first and dominant conception of policy-making is firmly instrumental in character. This is a view of policy as an abstract declaration intended to have practical consequences. Thus the conventional conception sees policy as 'a formalized, often written, and systematically disseminated set of guidelines, rules, objectives, and in particular, goals' (Manning, 1987*b*) which are the product of careful thought, judgement, and planning. In the context of regulatory enforcement, this means a formal statement intended to guide decisions and enforcement action by regulatory inspectors. On this view, regulatory policy is directed towards the future and the anticipation of possible conditions and events; it typically has long-term aims, and it often makes explicit the expected consequences of action or intervention. Its character is not only proactive and preventive, but also generic, for it seeks to provide a blueprint for coherent and consistent action within a regulatory organization in keeping with its legal mandate. To operate effectively in instrumental terms, enforcement policy needs to be stable and known, both by those who are supposed to implement it and by those whose ultimate compliance is sought, for it is intended to have an impact both on regulatory officials and on those who are subject to regulation.

[2] How such control may be exerted more effectively is beyond the scope of this book.

A second way of thinking about policy is as an official declaration to a public audience of what the regulatory organization is for and how it would officially like to be understood to be doing its work. Here policy serves as an expression of how the agency interprets its legal mandate and how it intends to respond to the harms and hazards which it is expected to combat. This view of policy exists as a statement of the problems a regulatory agency anticipates will arise in its surround and which are worth acting on. The sensitivity of HSE to its surround and its audiences is evident in comments made by a former Director General, who observed in her foreword to a recent annual report that following the change of government after the 1997 general election there would inevitably be changes in HSC/E's policy environment, with new challenges and pressures (Health and Safety Commission, 1998*a*). The audiences for this formal statement were presumably not only inspectors and principal inspectors (PIs), but also regulated industries, the media, and the public.

A third way of thinking about policy in HSE is as a layered and variably focused phenomenon, as sets of guidance coexisting in different forms and with possible differences in substance. This view also recognizes that policy has to operate in different places: at headquarters, area, National Interest Group (NIG), and field levels, and at varying levels of generality. It exists simultaneously enshrined in the law, in the senior bureaucracy of the agency and its interpretations of the legal mandate, as well as in temporary local initiatives. This view of policy is sensitive to its various origins—Commission and Executive, chief inspector, area director (AD), PI, or NIG—and field inspectors recognize that they are subject to various types of enforcement policy emanating from these different quarters. Some policy prescriptions have a generic character and are intended to apply to the activities of all relevant staff throughout the agency. Others planned to address particular problems have an ad hoc or local focus. This form of prosecution policy is much more specific in relevance and application and is designed to speak to activity at a particular time or within a geographical area, or within a particular sector of regulatory activity. Enforcement initiatives are sometimes not intended to be long-lasting but rather to be local and ephemeral, such as a crackdown on a current problem in a certain area. The significance of a specific policy such as a crackdown is that it provides for the individual inspector a clear example of a new element in the decision field that may well alter the decision frame, its local and temporary character having an impact on the inspector's decision field 'here' and 'for now'. This is the most explicit form of policy-making about enforcement, but by definition, while coexisting with grand enforcement policy, it addresses only comparatively narrow areas of regulatory control, such as construction sites, gas safety, or asbestos. It is sometimes associated with innovations, such as new regulations that constitute a new jurisdiction for enforcement.

A major characteristic of local or focused initiatives is that they are essentially short term. Indeed, even national initiatives on specific matters also tend to be short-term answers for particular problems. The control of asbestos was cited as an example by one PI, who spoke of something that 'comes in with a rush and then it recedes, [although] it's no less important'. But soon some other matter has taken its place as an organizational preoccupation (86–51). A former Chief Inspector of the Factory Inspectorate (FI) explained the approach, noting that prosecution policy had to adapt to specific circumstances, and that a policy to prosecute can equally imply a policy not to prosecute: 'We sit down with [people in policy branches] and decide that we will have a . . . very high profile enforcement action initiative for a year or two when regulations are brought in. Or we might decide quite the reverse.' He continued with the example of the complex packaging and labelling regulations, a subject which, he said,

> 'does not . . . lend itself to an instant high profile enforcement action involving prosecution . . . I think we have to find a period of calm and education before we start getting very heavy with prosecutions . . . I see that as a different kettle of fish from, say, the asbestos hazard, which is well known, has been well publicized, where we know that people are prepared to take quite serious risks with people's health just to . . . save a lot of money quickly . . . That, I think, we have to hit hard.'

Policies about prosecution in the 1980s varied in the degree to which they were explicit or tacit, and in the extent to which they were general and lasting in application, or specific and ad hoc. With the possible exception of broad statements by the Commission and the guidelines issued by FI (but applicable in theory, if not so much in practice, across the other inspectorates) most policy ideas about prosecution were—and probably still are—regarded by inspectors as tacit and as rather unspecific. The following remarks by former chief inspectors capture some of this: 'This isn't something that's laid down on paper anywhere, I don't think' (Agricultural Inspectorate, AgI); 'If you look at our stated instructions to inspectors, I'm afraid you won't find much of a statement about prosecution policy there. Not one that I would regard as helpful anyway'

(FI); 'It's run on a "reasonably practicable" basis, which is not defined in any way' (Mines and Quarries Inspectorate). These comments also indicate the autonomy enjoyed by the former inspectorates before the Field Operations Directorate (FOD) and suggest the degree to which prosecution policy was regarded in the past as largely a matter to be decided upon and interpreted by each inspectorate.

That said, identifiable policy about prosecution did exist in the mid-1980s in various forms in the inspectorates. Each inspectorate treated itself then as autonomous in the matter, whereas the reorganization into FOD was intended to lead to some standardization in the substance of policy and integration of practice. What the inspectorates in the 1980s did seem to share in common, so far as any enforcement policy was concerned, was a recognition that their inspectors were less subject to policy directives about prosecution than they were to certain broad assumptions about how they should work. There was also an acknowledgement that formal enforcement involved the exercise of substantial discretion at field level by individual inspectors. Some of this is suggested in the following comments of a former Deputy Director General of HSE: 'there are guidelines for prosecution, but basically the inspector is required and expected to get results over time. The prosecution isn't just "I came in on Wednesday and it was wrong, so I'll prosecute on Thursday." . . . We expect people to act in a strategic manner, rather than reacting in a parking warden manner.'

3. ENFORCEMENT POLICY AS A PRACTICAL CONCEPTION

If the formal view of policy emphasizes statements of sacred values and broad approaches to problems, another view is concerned instead with policy as a practical matter. It treats a formal conception of policy as inadequate, if the aim is to understand its practice and complexities, since it does not do justice to reality. A practical conception of policy focuses on what policy actually means to those in the regulatory organization whose behaviour is ostensibly subject to its guidance and constraint. On this view, a useful way of understanding the nature of enforcement policy is to learn how inspectors make sense of rules or guidance. This perspective on policy emphasizes its organizational character, and attends to its complex, fluid, and protean nature. It discourages a simple or static view of policy, or treatment of it as relatively immutable unless changed by subsequent policy deliberation (Manning, 1987*b*).

The formal conception of policy is flawed in various ways. First, its ostensible instrumentalism is misleading. In the formal conception, policy is a dispassionate, objective, and rational statement of objectives, but in practice it frequently has a powerful expressive content. Manning (1987*b*: 3) has argued that regulatory policy embodies social, particularly moral, values: action is moral here in the sense of trying 'to achieve some valued state of affairs'. He holds that all governmental action has a strong moral component, despite the apparently neutral and objective language of most policy analysis. To the extent that it does serve to display some moral attitude or stance, enforcement policy is therefore deeply implicated in a value position.

The moral character of policy shows through in a number of ways. For example, the instrumental conception would have it that policy is dependent upon the existence of information, but an important ingredient in policy is the beliefs of the policy-makers. Besides, information is not necessarily neutral, but frequently has an expressive character, since it serves 'to display a moral attitude or position' (Manning, 1987*b*: 7). Manning argues that the relationship between policy and information is not self-evident, nor is the essential character of information itself a simple or obvious matter. Often there is imperfect information about a problem and information does not of itself suggest a policy option. There may indeed be several possible policy options available for any particular problem. The policy choice that prosecution is to be generally a matter of last resort is partly the consequence of a moral position. This is true also in the case of enforcement practice. The pervasive reliance by inspectors upon negotiated compliance as the fundamental enforcement strategy rests ultimately on moral foundations. While the possibility of prosecution and legal punishment remains as a threat, as a resource to be drawn on ultimately by inspectors if necessary, the compliance of the regulated is primarily sought through an enforcement strategy which fundamentally exploits a sense of moral obligation about standing by our word and living up to our side of a bargain. Furthermore, the extent to which such moral persuasion is effective in occupational health and safety regulation 'hinges on the acceptance of the value-laden term safety' (Manning, 1987*b*: 6).

As well as the intrusion of values, definitions of problems by policy-makers are an amalgam of their prior assumptions about the nature of the problem they are addressing and what they anticipate to be the responses of others to possible courses of action which may be taken. In practice, it can be difficult to distinguish how much of a policy has been based on fact and how much on the broad framework of assumptions held by policy-makers. Such assumptions are integral to the general business of regulation on both sides: in the organization in its policy-making and inspection work, and in regulated companies in arriving at strategies of response to enforcement efforts. Though policy may appear to provide a clear-cut instrumental definition of the decision field and may be intended by policy-makers to do so, it may in practice be comprised of many different aims, values, and assumptions which add to the complexity encountered in efforts to understand the nature of policy.

A second flaw in the formal conception is that the conventional 'top-down' view of policy is too simple (Barrett & Fudge, 1981; Ham & Hill, 1993). Prosecution policy is to be seen not merely as a clearly articulated set of statements intended to guide action, but rather as comprising various kinds of influence emerging from diverse sources. In the context of regulatory organizations the origins of policy are in reality extraordinarily complex, as Peter Manning's (1987*b*) research with NII or Paul Rock's (1986) analysis in the criminal justice field have suggested. Manning found that policies in NII were developed in different ways, and carried on in different settings and with different degrees of formality. In practice policy was shaped and constrained by many forces, and was sometimes driven by the timetables of others, such as licensees, or the work of international bodies. Policies varied in scope, generality, and long-term impact, and addressed both routine work as well as responses to extraordinary events like accidents (Manning, 1987*b*). Rock's extensive empirical work led him to stress the importance of the accidental and the haphazard in the making of policy. However else it may be regarded, he argues, policy is to be seen as a product of local histories and personalities, and of particular people, their own pasts and careers (Rock, 1986).

A third problem is that policy in practice in an organization is often characterized more by flux and uncertainty than would be expected from a formal account of the nature of bureaucratic policy-making. The anticipatory character of policy often contributes to uncertainty since the consequences of possible policies may not be fully knowable in advance, either because the precise kind of response required is apparent only after certain action has already been taken and further information gathered, or because it is unclear what those regulated may be prepared to agree to or actually do (Manning, 1987*b*: 7). Where the response of the regulated cannot be predicted, the uncertainty may be resolved or at least clarified by trying out a particular policy option in order to elicit a response.

There can also be an ironic lack of clarity in enforcement policy. This emerges in the following rather hesitant remarks of an AD who, when asked whether there had been any changes in HSE's prosecution policy, as opposed to practice, over the last 10 years, said:

> 'Not overt policy, no. Practice, I think yes, with—but it's difficult to say where the division is between the two, because, you know, policy can sort of come—doesn't always have to be stated as "This is a change of prosecution policy"—it's more that people can assume that something is policy by the general sort of messages that they receive over a number of years, and just as the sort of talk that is around the organization about how we work.' (97–02)

Another way of thinking about policy as a practical matter is to see it as existing in the aggregated doings of officials within the organization. Arguably, any patterned action by field staff amounts to a form of practical policy. Repetitive decision-making producing roughly similar outcomes in roughly similar cases amounts to the crystallized expression of a form of policy.[3] The patterned nature of the aggregated acts of inspectors adds up, in effect, to an enforcement policy since they possess three of the major characteristics of policy: they are stable, predictable, and lasting. Furthermore, these practices may be regarded by those subject to regulation as, in effect, the implementation of policy. Indeed, practice imposes its own restraints, for inspectors are very conscious of 'the way in which we normally decide this kind of case' (cf. Sudnow, 1965). Such action may be prompted by a common set of constraints to which inspectors are subject, in the form of an awareness of common practice and an appreciation of the value of precedent or a set of values which they hold in common.

Patterned decisions by inspectors may also be made as a result of matters entering the organization directly from the surround, and it is possible to think of policy as patterned responses to perceived changes in the organization's surround which come to affect the decisions of officials independently of bureaucratic policy. These changes may be in political events, attitudes, or values, in the economic climate, or in social expectations. Specific events may produce a similar effect: an egregious case, a public panic, or a major disaster may enter from the surround and

[3] I make no apology for the clumsy qualifications here: discussions about disparity in the sentencing literature frequently fail to address the question of how we recognize similarity or difference, consistency or inconsistency. Daly (1994) is an exception.

change an individual inspector's decision-making in a direct way, quite independently of any official policy response from the centre of the organization. Here, changes in the surround change the field and directly affect the way in which particular matters are framed by individual decision-makers.

4. SOURCES OF ENFORCEMENT POLICY

There is a formal declaration of broad principles in HSC's *Enforcement policy statement*, but rather than specify the conditions under which particular decisions should be made, HSE's principles of enforcement are procedural. They indicate a particular concern for the consistency with which enforcement decisions are made, reading, in part:

'PRINCIPLES OF ENFORCEMENT
The enforcement of health and safety law should be informed by the principles of *proportionality* in applying the law and securing compliance; *consistency of approach*, targeting of enforcement action and *transparency* about how the regulator operates and what those regulated may expect. . . .

Consistency
Consistency of approach does not mean uniformity. It means taking a similar approach in similar circumstances to achieve similar ends. . . .

Transparency
Transparency means helping duty holders to understand what is expected of them and what they should expect from the enforcing authorities. It also means making clear to duty holders not only what they have to do but, where this is relevant, what they don't. That means distinguishing between statutory requirements and advice or guidance about what is desirable but not compulsory.' (Health and Safety Commission, n.d.: 7–8)

It is fair to say that prosecution has not been regarded as a matter for extensive policy formulation in any of the HSE inspectorates. The approach instead has been pragmatic. Though a former chief inspector spoke of a 'general prosecution policy' in FI, he went on to articulate it in vague and practical terms, suggesting that 'if. . . an inspector is dealing with an employer who quite clearly is wilfully and flagrantly in breach of the [Health and Safety at work, HSW] Act [1974] on many occasions, sooner or later he's got to be brought to task. . . [Inspectors] are not allowed, really, to let somebody get away with something for ever.' Inspectors also tend to think of enforcement policy in practical terms which emphasize those understood ways of acting when confronted by certain kinds of problem. It is in these circumstances that policy is most capable of being expressed in a clear and precise way to impinge upon an inspector's discretion, changing, quite explicitly, the field within which the inspector operates. Thus, for example, 'There used to be an instruction to prosecute if you found a locked fire exit... You had to get permission... if you found one and didn't want to prosecute' (86–26). Such guidance is not regarded in general as very helpful, hence the comments of a former Chief Inspector of AgI who explained in the mid-1980s why there was no guidance to agricultural inspectors which

'will say, for instance, that you should go out and when you meet this you should prosecute. We virtually never go down that road... I think the actual decisions about prosecution are really made in accordance with the exact circumstances that face an inspector. And you can't tell him that he must prosecute in particular cases, in my view.' (86–39)

There are various sources of practical enforcement policy to which field inspectors are subject. The primary source of policy for them is the initiative taken at headquarters, in the centre of the HSC/E organization, of which the most general and far-reaching is HSC's *Enforcement policy statement* (n.d.).[4] Lines of communication exist for the ready transmission of this sort of general policy out to more distant parts of the organization, as an AD made clear:

'I mean there are lots of management systems for communication, so there are rigid communication systems in that the Director of Field Operations Division will have monthly meetings with his regional directors... and then the regional director will have monthly meetings with me and people like me. So there's no difficulty in edicts on high coming down... whether the edicts... cover this particular area or not.' (97–05)

Formal guidelines intended to assist in the making of decisions about prosecution were available for factory inspectors in the 1980s, but did not appear to be a major influence on case decision-making.[5] They were believed not to be particularly helpful, except for inexperienced inspectors. People tend to remember ideas rather than words, and to the extent

[4] It is not necessary to rehearse the substance of this *Statement* here. It is discussed in other chapters where it is substantively more relevant to the analysis, and especially in Ch. 7.

[5] Only a quarter of the inspectors said that they learned which cases to prosecute from following FI guidelines and decided cases, and most of those acknowledged that use of the guidelines had occurred early on in their careers.

that inspectors claimed to know or use the guidelines, it was, with few exceptions, as a series of linked ideas, rather than of specific instructions. One complained that they were 'extremely general' (86–24), that they essentially articulated common sense, and as a result were not helpful. The guidelines did not really impinge on the inspectors' almost intuitive and palpable sense of what was 'a prosecution case'. A PI said: 'I seldom refer to the guidance... because I have a clear idea whether a case should be prosecuted or not... You learn it as you go' (86–51). Another PI did not use the guidelines, for a more banal, but nonetheless important, reason: 'There's no way we can follow all our instructions, they're now so massive' (86–42). There was also a recognition of the crucial point that, ironically, guidelines themselves need interpretation and adaptation: 'Relative to construction... there are so many serious situations which, clearly, if you use the HSE guidelines fully, you'd never do anything but take prosecutions... You tend to [raise] your threshold of what you consider serious matters, and obviously reduce the numbers to a manageable amount on that basis' (86–07).[6]

Some inspectors thought that some of the guidelines were inappropriate in certain circumstances and ignored them. For instance, some acknowledged that they succumbed to the strong pressures upon them to prosecute after an accident, in the face of formal policy:

> 'the FI guideline not to prosecute after accidents; now I've always ignored that... for several reasons. It's important to be seen to be doing something after an accident, because that's when the average man wants to know what the Factory Inspectorate's been doing. Secondly, you get better evidence after an accident, because people have seen their colleague lying crumpled in a heap on the floor. I think you get better fines after an accident. So I've always totally ignored that guideline. And I think other people have, too... It's always very easy for people in Headquarters... to sit there and work out what's best for the guys at the sharp end. But the guys at the sharp end are the ones who have to do all the work, therefore it's their judgment that counts... I ignore what they say and follow my own instincts.' (86–63)

Guidelines are useful for inspectors, as an AD pointed out, 'to refer to when you've got a problem' (86–19). They tend to be used more as a means of reassurance or ratification, by checking whether a particular case is, as a matter of agency policy, one which should be prosecuted when the inspector has already decided to prosecute. When used in this

[6] The difficulty of trying to guide decision-making by policy statements in conventional prosecutions is clear from work by Hoyano *et al.* (1997).

fashion, the guidelines serve as a means of justifying the legitimacy of a decision already taken.

Then there are various individual officials, of varying levels of seniority, who act as key figures in the creation of practical policy in the inspector's world, the chief inspector, AD, PI. There is also the NIG. These are not only a means for the transmission of formal policy from the centre to the periphery of the organization, but also sources of practical policy. The chief inspector is significant in producing policy with general applicability within an inspectorate which may have a marked impact on prosecution practice at field inspector level. Change is most noticeable when a new appointee introduces a new policy, or causes a shift in settled practice by appearing to endorse particular values or types of approach. The practical effect may amount to a change in policy, even though no new prosecution policy initiative may be formally articulated. Change occurs here simply as a consequence of inspectors' adaptation to shifts in the decision field and in the consequential framing of individual cases. Thus a former Chief Inspector of AgI said of the impact of his own appointment: 'I think there is a marked change in enforcement on the punitive side. But I can't honestly say that that's the result of any particular policy of mine. It may be that by placing emphasis on particular aspects of enforcement that the response from the field force has been to look harder at whether they should be prosecuting or placing notices . . .'

There is in practice within HSE a conception of local or area as well as national policy. Indeed, it was at area level in the former FI that policy tended to be seen by inspectors in much more practical terms. In an organization with decentralized decision-making about prosecution, like the former FI and the present FOD (and possibly in some more centralized inspectorates), the AD is a crucial source of policy in an inspector's decision field, both serving as a channel for the transmission to the field of policy originating at headquarters and conveying a closer and more direct sense of policy than that which emerges from a remote organizational centre. The AD is also an important source of policy initiative at the local level. Indeed, some inspectors found it possible to talk of an area policy which, though influenced by national policy, had its own character. The AD is in a strong position to colour general practice in prosecution decision-making within a particular area, leading to a distinctive approach in the ways in which inspectors frame cases. So much is implied in the words of an inspector who worked in an area presided over by an AD well known for his decided views about the need to use prosecution very selectively: 'Our area policy is an interpretation of overall FI policy' (86–34). In context, this implied a divergence from a general enforcement policy towards a locally less punitive approach.

There seem, however, to be different conceptions among ADs about the extent to which they do, or should, impose their own preferences on the work of inspectors. One, for instance, expressed interest in the types of cases that were being prosecuted in the area, but not in their number, while another simply preferred not to be directive: 'It's up to the AD to set the line for the area and let the PIs get on with it' (86–14). A third, who was regarded by a number of the field force as having a marked impact on the approach to prosecution in his area, acknowledged, 'I can steer them a little bit in talking about the case they're thinking of taking' (86–27). Though this 'steering' was general and diffuse, by influencing the broad climate of opinion in the local office it served to shape the culture of the area and thereby the inspectors' decision fields and framing.

Inspectors also responded to expectations held by their PI. The PI is a significant figure who acts in a very direct way on an inspector's decision-making. The PI may pass on new programmes of inspection work originating from the centre, may create a conscious focus on particular regulatory problems, or may issue clear guidance. A PI reported, of the beginning of his career, 'My District Inspector in those days was a very keen prosecutor. The AD was again a very keen prosecuting man . . . We were basically instructed to do about twelve prosecutions a year each' (86–22). The PI is most important in FOD as the official who exerts a direct influence over field inspectors in the process of evaluating cases proposed by them for legal action. This allows them not only to superintend preparation of cases for prosecution, but also to guide the inspectors' decision-making quite explicitly (see Chapter 3). The particular influence exerted here relates to the number and kind of case the PI will support, as well as the number and kinds of charge deemed appropriate. These forms of influence help inspectors to develop a clear sense of their PI's decision-making proclivities, and from them to develop a set of expectations about the PI's probable stance on any particular matter which may seem to inspectors to be suitable for prosecution. Sometimes a PI is quite explicit about an approach to be adopted. A construction inspector observed that 'What [the PI] would say is "Don't look for anything unreasonable, but where that particular incident is serious enough to justify [prosecution] then I would wish you to think very carefully before you turn it down" ' (86–30). Influence may also come from the PI in a tacit form with changed expectations among inspectors arising from a new appointee's provenance. This is often to be seen in the formulation of local enforcement initiatives where action is taken to combat particular problems which may be peculiar to a local industry within the area.

A further source of enforcement policy for HSE inspectors is the National Interest Group. The NIGs are important in contributing to the formulation of local initiatives and as the source of countrywide prosecution policy about specific matters, such as, for instance, demolition work in the construction industry. The NIGs were described by an AD as 'taking a more proactive line in terms of standard-setting, and perhaps with campaigns that might be running at a particular time'. The implication for enforcement practice is that the NIGs exert

> 'influence in the decision to prosecute . . . if HSE has got a particular campaign in progress, or just having happened, where a sort of holistic approach is taken, you know, with publicity, with advertising, with a general policy of raising a certain topic at preventive inspections, and, you know, a campaign of investigating accidents on that . . . particular topic. And yes, I think prosecution is part of that whole approach.' (97–02)

Prosecution behaviour at inspector level, however, can be altered by policy changes which do not necessarily speak directly to formal enforcement, but rather subtly alter the field within which the inspector works. Thus the preoccupation of NIGs with particular regulatory problems and the design of a programme of inspection to attain express objectives tends inevitably to draw attention to specific areas of concern and thereby to concentrate enforcement activity upon them. An example was given by a former Chief Inspector of AgI:

> 'The last couple of years we have done a fair amount of work on guarding of power take-off shafts . . . Now because that's been going on and because inspectors have been having information, they have probably spent more time looking at PTO shafts than they might have done two or three years ago. And because they've found what we expected them to find—that things are not well—there has been, I should think, a detectable increase in the number of prosecutions relating to that aspect of machinery.'

Enforcement policy, as inspectors receive it, exists then not only in the form of direct attempts to guide the decision-making at field level but also in less direct forms of guidance. The views of senior staff are often not so much conveyed to inspectors as apprehended by them: after all, meetings and documents 'give you a feel for the HQ views on enforcement policy' (86–19).

Policy also resides in the culture of the inspectorate, or the area office, as an AD suggested:

'I think it can come from a number of directions, and within the organization the influence down—you talk about the influence down the organization—it's probably more in terms of the sort of phrases, attitudes, and way of speaking that perhaps filters down through our policy and headquarters sections. A lot of them are not inspectors by background, and so they tend to think that the way ministers speak reflects what inspectors are doing. And it starts to become sort of part of a—not necessarily an ingrained culture—but sort of part of the environment that, you know, "We only prosecute under certain circumstances."' (97–02)

Indeed, much of what reaches inspectors appears to exist in the form of unarticulated expectations or presumptions, sometimes of a local character, of which they are broadly aware. For example, speaking of enforcement policy following a fatal accident, one AD observed: 'generally speaking, our policy on prosecution following fatal accidents is fairly firm, but certainly in this region, we take the view that there is a presumption in favour of prosecution following a fatal accident, and that very careful consideration has to be given to not prosecuting in those circumstances' (97–04).

Different sources of pressure act systematically on inspectors and channel their activities. While policy may be transmitted out through the organization from the centre in orthodox and intended ways, individual inspectors are not immune from broader political and economic forces which may serve to constrain their enforcement in various ways independently of organizational policy. Broad constraints which arise externally from other inspectorates, from regulated industries, and significant features in the regulatory organization's surround, such as the state of the economy, come into play to shape practical policy. Financial and other constraints directly impinging on particular policy concerns spring from general government policy about industry and the economy, as well as its ideological cast. Equally, broader conceptions of political and economic policy articulated by the government of the day act as important influences on inspectors' conception of prosecution policy. The perceived conviction of a government about the need to reduce the burdens on industry or to improve standards of occupational health and safety may generally encourage either a greater reluctance or a greater willingness among inspectors to prosecute. At the same time, the organizational preoccupation within an inspectorate to be seen to be doing something about a particular problem may operate independently of this sensitivity to the political or economic climate. However, it is essential when analysing legal decision-making always to distinguish between specific cases, where precise pressures and constraints act on prosecution decision-making, and those general forces shaping the use of prosecution located in the general climate of opinion about classes of case or general matters of enforcement policy.

Any change in enforcement decision-making can be produced both by guidance or direction from the centre of the organization, and by inspectors' own perceptions and beliefs about appropriate enforcement action that is congruent with changes in the regulatory agency's surround. General or local enforcement policy directives may seek more discriminating use of prosecution. Inspectors are conscious that the economic and political climate seems to make prosecution generally more or less appropriate; they are also practical people, aware of the ways in which those forces act directly on their decision-making on a particular matter. Thus one inspector reported: 'We've all been told not to prosecute the small businessman, make life harder for him. And I bear this in mind' (86–40). Similarly, a construction group inspector remarked: 'We're asked regularly to use our discretion on very small builders' (86–17). Sometimes inspectors are sufficiently sensitive to the political climate in which they work that they respond to it directly in their decision-making, in the absence of any formal statement of a change in policy. One said bluntly, 'I think it would be unwise for the factory inspectorate to go out at this time and clobber the small firm' (86–37). An AD explained how settled policy and practice could be subtly altered:

'. . . I think undoubtedly the position of the previous [Conservative] government had an influence in terms of—perhaps making people very conscious that they needed to be able to justify prosecution. . . . [T]en, no, perhaps, say, fifteen years ago there would be some offences which might seem alright—you know, perhaps paper offences, or could be interpreted as such—which, because we'd have a zero tolerance policy . . . on some subjects, for instance, power press safety, around [a particular city], I mean, again, I suppose this was the influence of the then superintending inspector—we're probably going back about 20 years now. But it was clearly established that there was a zero tolerance level with regard to infringements of the Power Press Regulations. And that policy, combined with the advent of the regulations, has made a dramatic effect on accident rates—they absolutely plummeted. So, yes, you can get shifts in policy in this way, and in those days, I think, there was more done on the precautionary level. You know, you didn't necessarily wait for an accident to happen, as much as the case is now, or latterly.' (97–02)

The result, the AD went on, was that it became

'difficult to say, you know, when policy becomes practice, or what is the difference between the two. But nowadays... most prosecutions that are taken are the result of accidents rather than perhaps what was found during a routine inspection. And that has been a very significant change, and I think it's probably largely driven by, you know, by the sort of political mores of the time, and feeling, "Well, if somebody's lost an arm..." Not only is there more public expectation of revenge—you know, this is sort of part of the culture of our time, so there's that pressure, but also, of course, it's much more instantly obvious to any third party as to why prosecution is being taken.' (97–02)

These remarks place the political and economic climate as perceived by HSE staff as part of the contemporary culture, and matters to be acted on. They show how changes in the broad political and economic climate comprising the regulatory surround can affect the type, as well as the numbers of prosecutions taken.

More precise governmental policy about regulation and public expenditure feeds through as a further source of policy guidance of an indirect sort. This arises with decisions made by the organization about the allocation and use of resources at field level which, in turn, affect staffing and recruitment within the inspectorate. Shifts in the allocation of resources within the organization may create tensions in the practical application of policy which are hard to control and which may prompt adaptive behaviour by inspectors:

'We're given central guidelines which we're expected to meet, particularly with the amount of time spent on inspection and the number of inspections done. Now that is a little bit difficult because, with some of these other categories like investigation we are very much driven by what comes in, and if we have a larger number of fatal accidents one year, or a lot of complaints about dangerous gas fittings, then we have to respond to those. So a lot of that is very difficult for us to control and is largely outside our control. So it does make it difficult to meet obligations or expectations from the centre to deliver a set number of inspections and it generally is met by inspectors working more hours than are called for.' (97–02)

Some changes in prosecution behaviour are, however, less of an incidental consequence of other changes in enforcement strategy than they might seem. Since prosecution is a central part of the appearance of legal enforcement, where the inspectorate acquires new responsibilities, as FI did in the 1980s with gas safety, 'It will look a little odd', said an AD, 'if we are doing the inspections and the investigations in the field, and we don't produce a rather similar number of cases [as before]' (86–19). Such policy initiatives reach the inspector in a precise form, changing the decision field in a decisive way. The features in the field become clear and categorical, creating a virtual imperative to decide in accordance with the new policy, hence the comments of one inspector who said: 'People get hurt installing gas appliances. In these circumstances there's no discussion. It's an automatic prosecution.' Indeed, there are various breaches, the inspector continued, 'for which prosecution is virtually automatic. These are . . . for example, working without a licence, working without medical examinations, flagrant flouting of asbestos control legislation. [These] are automatic prosecution offences' (86–07).

Inspectors are, then, the recipients of constant policy initiatives from different quarters, and since the form and source of these initiatives may vary widely and they have limited resources, they sometimes find that the policy they are required to attend to is confusing. An experienced PI, with a predictably pragmatic approach to such matters, was only too conscious of the complexity of present policy imperatives and the difficulties they can cause for field inspectors:

> '[W]e are driven in lots of different directions . . . since we've had the Citizen's Charter requirement. Since HSE's raised its public profile . . . we get a continuous stream of complaints. Now we have to react to those complaints. . . . We're dragged in one direction by them, we're dragged in another direction by our planning system, and our commitment to doing so much in the way of basic inspection, and then we're told on the other hand that legal action is a priority. Now, you don't have to be a wizard to work out that something's got to give.' (97–01)

It is difficult to escape the conclusion that what shapes the kinds and numbers of cases prosecuted in broad terms (that is, excluding those cases that are the result of specific initiatives) is derived more from the culture of the inspectorate or subcultures within it, from inspectors' personal values and their own conception of their organization's interests, and from constructions of the broad political and economic climate, than from directions laid down by senior staff in formulating bureaucratic policy.

5. THE STRUCTURE OF INSPECTORATES

Regulatory control relies heavily on inspectorates established to monitor states of affairs and to repress infrequent and undesired events such as accidents. The fate of formal policy depends on the extent to which it can be transmitted effectively from the centre to the periphery of the regulatory inspectorate. Substantial resources are allocated to the periphery in inspectorates, leading to an organizational structure that is bottom-heavy. This sort of structure is also responsible for the creation and maintenance of large amounts of administrative discretion at the periphery of the organization where inspection and enforcement work is marked by a pervasive reliance on case-by-case decision-making.

The flow of policy is not necessarily a matter of simple transmission from centre to periphery (or from top down). Policy is not generally transmitted out to the periphery from the centre in an unblemished form; it does not remain pristine and undistorted in the way in which it is received and applied by field staff.[7] This is because policy is often altered in its transmission as a consequence of the structure of inspectorates, and the contrasting tasks of policy-maker and policy-applier, who are located in different organizational spaces. The way in which inspectorates are structured means that those in the centre can never be sure how those at the periphery will receive and respond to a particular policy. In relatively decentralized organizational structures like regulatory inspectorates and the police (perhaps the classic example of an inspectorate enjoying high autonomy at the periphery), field-level enforcers are subjected to constraints and pressures peculiar to their tasks and position in the organization. Organizational structure becomes a particularly important feature shaping the extent to which official policy can become a feature in an inspector's decision field.

What policy means within an organization is not a problem where people work on the basis of a shared set of beliefs in response to external problems to which an agency must react in proper and accountable

[7] Another form of policy transmission is horizontal in character. This occurs when data or ideas move across sections of an inspectorate, from one segment of the organization to another. Policy initiatives originating in an NIG would be of this type. Occasionally, however, Manning (1987*b*) found that transmission from the field inwards to the centre may also occur as inspectors would feed important matter suggesting a change in policy to those at senior levels in the organization. A further kind of policy transmission could also take place with a flow of information occurring as a result of the close relationships which an inspectorate maintains between itself and many of its regulated firms. This is a form of inter-organizational transformation and is also important in shaping what is seen as policy and determining substantially the volume of the work of an inspectorate.

fashion. However, shared beliefs and common strategies are not always to be found. Ideas about prosecution expressed by HSE staff are more frequently associated with discrete events or incidents than with organized, abstract approaches to enforcement strategy, or classes of case or problem. This may partly be in recognition of the fact that, as a former Chief Inspector of FI put it, 'It's all very well for us to think thoughts about strategic objectives at headquarters, but converting them to action on the shop floor level is much more difficult.' Indeed, there is a clear view that a matter as rare and special as the decision to prosecute must essentially be left to the individual judgement of the inspector, subject to screening and control by senior staff. This allows disparate views to emerge. If the essential characteristics of the formal view of policy are its abstract quality and its generality of application, the focus of an inspector's work is on achieving and maintaining compliance on a pragmatic and particular case-by-case basis.

Inspectors occupy very different worlds from policy-makers and senior officials, the structure of inspectorates leading to a significant difference of perspective between those who make policy and those who implement it.[8] It is also a source of tension. The organizational distance between the centre and the periphery creates difference in the working conceptions of what the job of regulation is about. The different worlds inhabited by senior officials and inspectors are important because they profoundly shape what inspectors regard as policy, and what may actually be received at the periphery of a regulatory inspectorate as policy. Inspectors are vulnerable to pressures which may not affect policy-makers at all, or in the same way, or to the same degree. For instance, field staff feel they should use their power to prosecute in certain ways to respond to particular expectations in the local community, which results in a kind of prosecution policy existing independently of area or headquarters management. In these circumstances inspectors' sensitivity to matters which may directly affect their exercise of discretion does not emerge from formal policy on law enforcement as transmitted out from the centre of the organization. Policy dictates do not always address what inspectors regard as real problems:

[8] Herbert Kaufman (1960: 70) observes that organizational actors who may originally possess similar attitudes and values will often develop divergent points of view according to their place and the functional specialities with which they are associated. Kaufman cites an example given by Herbert Simon (1957: 214) in which an official serving as acting departmental head for his absent superior rejected a number of proposals he himself had initiated with the memorable remark that 'from up here, things don't look the same as they do from down there'.

'We might end up prosecuting a fitter who's put in a gas appliance with, you know, the most minor of leaks because that is what the [HSE] organization wants. Whereas a Works Engineer might have done something fairly dramatic which hasn't actually hurt anybody, and we'll give him a good lecturing and write to the company.' (86–51)

The differences in perspective are a constant source of tension. Problems are viewed according to organizational standpoint and give rise to different priorities. Senior officials at the centre of an organization think more readily in policy terms. 'There is evidence', writes Weaver (1977: 107), for example, 'that . . . the higher officials were located in an organizational hierarchy the more likely it was that a potential legal case would be decided on policy grounds.' Inspectors, in contrast, think in practical terms. They are employed at field level to survey their environment of work sites for unacceptable levels of non-compliance, to reduce hazards and to pre-empt the possibility of accidents. Because of the number and complexity of regulated sites, carrying out these tasks results in individuals working with high degrees of autonomy, and inevitably making low-visibility, often unaccountable, decisions. The nature of the work is characterized by a constant preoccupation with practical solutions to immediate and concrete problems. Inspectors are involved in face-to-face encounters with those whom they regulate; they have to deal with particular problems and precise issues, and compliance itself (or at least what an inspector may define as an acceptable degree and kind of compliance) usually demands the expenditure of time and money. This leads to compliance acquiring a negotiated character. While policy-makers are conscious of having to work within constraints which are not immediately apparent to enforcers, the latter, on the other hand, think that policy-makers give insufficient regard to the practicalities of enforcement. They want intelligible and easily enforceable regulations which permit ready prosecution when necessary and which do not have major implications for the resources of the inspectorate and its day-to-day operations (R. Baldwin, 1987: 20). The inspector's instinct is to focus on individual problems, or particular incidents or cases. Any matter causing especial concern is assessed in the context of other current problems to be dealt with, while long-term plans or policies remain in the background (Manning, 1987*b*). Those in the centre of the regulatory organization are more concerned with the abstract, the future, and the general. Those at the periphery prefer the practical, and are as much concerned with the past as the future. Their concern is with the uncertainties of the real world while the world seen from the centre is seemingly more rational, orderly, and predictable. Problems crowd in at the periphery—matters have to be dealt with here and now, while the centre thinks in terms of the long term, the standardized, and the generic. The world here is also real (though inspectors may sometimes doubt it), but the nature of that reality is very different from that experienced in the field. In the centre, law enforcement policy is a matter of strategic decision-making about classes of case. Here officials engage with the hypothetical, the imagined reality, in which decisions are general, prospective, and proactive in character, and preventive and pre-emptive in intent. Such decisions are made in reflective, considered, calculated ways, and ostensibly more in keeping with rational choice ideas. At the periphery, decisions are made reactively, by an individual dealing with actual cases and real problems, deciding here and now, off the cuff, particularistically, and possibly in ways inconsistent with ideas of rational choice. This is because problems to be dealt with at the regulatory periphery are not generally defined as related to policy but are treated simply as decisions that have to be made each day (Manning, 1987*b*).

There may also be important differences in the institutionalized beliefs at the centre and at the periphery of regulatory inspectorates. Conceptions of risk differ. They penetrate the centre of the regulatory organization where preventive or remedial policies must be devised for classes of problem, and are viewed through the lens of natural scientific rationality in the abstract, as concepts, or as aggregated statistics of actual or potential numbers of corpses, cancers, and catastrophes. In the centre of the organization a particular risk is not an immediate and precise problem demanding action, as it often is in the field. It is an exemplar of a general threat compelling a strategic response in the form of modification of or innovation in policy. Risk here is in a sense speculative, general, and concerned with trends, patterns, and large forces. In the field risk is immediate, concrete, and particular. In the centre there tends to be a view of regulatory rule-breaking as largely calculated and therefore as deterrable. At the periphery the behaviour may more readily be seen as morally bad or wilfully persistent and therefore as deserving of retributive punishment. Thus strategies of social control may vary according to the decision-maker's organizational location, emphasizing instrumental views in the centre but expressive views at the periphery. It follows from this that the reasons why inspectors initiate an enforcement move may by no means be the same as the reasons why their seniors continue or discard the matter.

Tension between centre and periphery gives rise to a particular problem in terms of the forms by which grand policy is expressed and transmitted in regulatory inspectorates. This has important implications for the degree and kind of guidance that may be exerted by those at the centre over the activities of those at the periphery. A formal conception of policy stresses the importance of rules. Policy-makers in occupational health and safety tend to see no hindrance to the successful application of policy because it has emerged from consensual tripartite negotiations (R. Baldwin, 1987).[9] The approach is to use standard rules and hope that these will be applied in a consistent and dispassionate way. At the same time, policy-makers rely on the adaptive capacity of inspectors to employ their discretion in choosing whether and how to apply the rules in any particular setting that gives special difficulty. A major source of uncertainty stems from trying to guide discretion using words, for rules are pliable in their application to real and precise problems. It should not be surprising, therefore, that there are also differences in the way rules are perceived at various levels within the HSE organization. Rules have an impact on behaviour in different ways, depending on how they are actually written. Policy-makers tend to think in broad and generic terms while enforcers feel compelled to adapt a general rule to a particular situation in order to solve a problem. Policy-makers' concern for the generic is partly to avoid problems of under-inclusiveness, partly to achieve consistency of standards. Robert Baldwin (1987) has argued that a rule is not necessarily 'good' for all purposes, however, and that it is not possible for policy-makers to design rules effectively in the absence of a clear model of enforcement. The fact that policy-makers tend to assume that good packages of rules are good for all purposes exacerbates the contrast in perspective between policy-makers and enforcers. The strong preference among enforcers for precise rules which are easier for them to handle contrasts with the tendency of policy-makers to opt for broad rules tending to over-inclusiveness. Ironically, the tendency towards generic forms of rule which was given a substantial impetus in the concepts and drafting of the HSW Act has been accompanied by a mass of regulatory detail which has prompted complaints from many employers that occupational health and safety law is both too complex and often suited only to the interests of big

[9] Indeed, the dominant characteristic of regulatory policy-making in occupational health and safety regulation is consultation with industry, an approach which originated in 19th-century practice (Bartrip, 1987).

companies which have the resources to learn precisely what is demanded of them (R. Baldwin, 1987).

The form in which a broad policy is expressed (whether by legal rule, bureaucratic guidance, or lesser statement) can be very influential in terms of how and whether law is enforced (see Chapter 12). Baldwin identified one school of thought within HSE on the form policy should take as favouring specific rules and absolute duties. This is a position typically held by those at the periphery. This approach is wary of the enforceability of general rules and principles which call on employers to take such action as is 'reasonably practicable' (R. Baldwin, 1987; 1995). The pervasiveness of discretion at field level means that concepts such as 'reasonableness' have a very variable quality in practice. While such terms may be useful descriptions of an aspiration or an underlying stance, there are no rules describing what amounts to 'reasonable' behaviour, nor the prospect, were they to exist, that they would mean the same thing and would be interpreted consistently by different inspectors. Moreover, rules may not simply be amenable to different interpretations within an organization horizontally (across, for instance, inspectors) but open to differences of interpretation vertically (between different levels in the organizational hierarchy). Similarly, different interpretations may be found in different segments of an organization. The exercise of legal discretion is ultimately a human process.

In general, it is assumed that the broader the rule, the greater the interpretive latitude given to those who must enforce that rule, but in fact those who have to apply policy have a preference for precise rules (which ostensibly confer less discretion upon them), a preference that is very evident in inspectors' precise decision-making about the legal strength of a prosecution case (see Chapter 12). Precise rules may be narrower in application, however, thus less attractive to policy-makers with their generic concerns. While inspectors may regard precise rules as more easily enforceable, they are not *ipso facto* necessarily thought to have a greater impact on hazards or problems, and may in fact have the opposite effect. According to Baldwin, there are others in HSE who tend to dislike precise rules, a position typical of those at the centre. The aversion to precise rules is the result partly of the impossibility of anticipating all possible contingencies, and partly of the difficulties of designing suitably detailed rules, which leads to a huge and unwieldy mass of law and regulation. It is noteworthy in this connection that some inspectors feel themselves overburdened with a vast array of rules to enforce, though they do not apparently feel hampered in doing their enforcement work by any lack of a detailed knowledge of the law (R. Baldwin, 1987: 28). Inspectors are practical people and are simply concerned with knowing the core of the relevant rules and regulations.

The character of the work in an inspectorate tends to subvert the application of centralized policy. This leads in turn to considerable organizational distance between centre and periphery, posing serious problems of organizational control. The result is an organization with a heavily decentralized and potentially fragmented character, one with strong 'centrifugal tendencies' (Kaufman, 1960). These tendencies threaten the stability of the inspectors' decision field and make it imperative from the point of view of management of the organization that action is coordinated to foreclose the possibility of fragmentation and inconsistency, for it is important for those at the centre to have policy transmitted to the periphery in as pristine and undistorted a form as possible (see Kaufman, 1960; Lipsky, 1980). In such a setting, action must be coordinated through generalized rules and procedures and cemented by organizationally recognized practices (Manning, 1987*b*: 8–10). Coordination within an inspectorate comes about both by informal means, by the emergence of shared and agreed ways of acting and making decisions which constitute the culture of regulatory enforcement, and by more formal policy means whereby inspectors are subjected to various general rules, policies, and procedures for acting and deciding. The control of front-line discretion, one of the general problems in legal bureaucracies, is especially important in the contexts of regulation and policing, given the consequential character of prosecution decision-making.

6. CONCLUSION

The formal view of policy is of a blueprint intended to coordinate action across time, place, and person. As part of the formal definition of the decision field, it is usually cast in general terms. The decision field is given broad shape by the *Enforcement policy statement* (Health and Safety Commission, n.d.), but its terms are sufficiently wide as not to give any specific guidance. In practice, however, enforcement policy changes as the surround changes, creating new decision fields for those who decide about prosecution in particular cases. Much is left to the discretion of inspectors to make decisions as they see fit. What is taken to be policy also changes over time and is thoroughly permeated with value positions, even where it might appear to be the embodiment of neutrality or objectivity. What goes into the making of, and is treated as, policy may be a product of people's conceptions of fact, of values, or of expectations. What also ends up as policy of a kind are various sorts of organizational traditions, or mutually recognized ways of understanding and acting upon matters. To this extent, policy is very much more than formally articulated statements of rule or principle. This means that for those organizational actors who work at the periphery, what the centre regards as 'policy' can never be clearly known. Policy is not therefore the clear and settled matter that it is generally assumed to be, since in practice its meaning and content are always unclear and uncertain. Formal policy, as it lives in the mind of the inspector, exists in a refracted form.

It is the inspectorates that substantially determine the reality of regulatory policy by shaping in a practical sense what becomes policy. It is in the field that the purposes of the law are expressed. There policy has to be applied on a particularistic, case-by-case basis, being adapted through an individual inspector's use of discretion to address specific problems. The use of discretion here may be informed by a general instrumental concern to advance health and safety, and may indeed result in a more sensitive, finely tuned application of discretion in particular cases. Enforcement policy in a regulatory organization is a changing and flexible thing, in considerable part owing to the way in which discretion is employed in the field. Enforcement practices deviate from formal stipulations because of the pressures and demands acting upon the regulatory inspector, which sometimes present opportunities to turn a blind eye or otherwise to act in ways not contemplated by formal policy. The need of inspectors to attend to the demands of practical problems therefore risks blunting the broad regulatory purpose.

Decision-making power varies according to organizational structure and the location of the actor, and one of the defining characteristics of inspectorate structures is that those at the centre are heavily dependent upon decisions made by those at the periphery who have the power to choose whether and how to communicate with the centre about rule-breaking and other problems. In such ways lower-level officials exert power over their organizational superiors, who are left to legitimate field-level practices and decisions. The broader and more abstract conceptions of grand policy find it difficult to penetrate the inspector's daily work, dominated as it is by intensely practical concerns. The high levels of administrative discretion flowing from the structure and character of inspectorates is very important in allowing inspectors considerable autonomy. High discretion is demanded as a practical matter owing to the sheer number of violations of the law and the degree of variation in the gravity of discovered violations. Inspectors feel compelled, as a result, to reserve formal legal action primarily for the more serious, deliberate, or persistent violations and withhold it when the harm done or risks created do not seem serious, or when the costs of remedial action appear excessive in relation to the risk created, or when the violator responds cooperatively to regulatory demands. These priorities demand in turn that regulatory inspectors expedite decision-making by employing working categories and forms of perceptual shorthand. Case-by-case decision-making and the constraints of handling a problem tend as a result to insulate the inspector from the designs of grand policy, creating a particular problem for policy-makers of ensuring that so far as is possible inspectors make decisions consistently. Yet policy can be valuable for field-level decision-makers in a way not contemplated in the formal conception. Even though formal policy does not necessarily act directly upon inspectors' decision-making to the extent that policy-makers might wish, policy is valuable for inspectors, since a statement of policy may sometimes become a way for inspectors to justify enforcement decisions possibly made for officially unacceptable reasons. Here it acts as a form of 'presentational rule' (Smith & Gray, 1983).

Ideally enforcement policy should be capable of implementation in the same way in different places and at different times, and different inspectors use prosecution in response to similar problems under similar conditions. One of the main objectives of broad regulatory policy is that it not only state important aims and values, but also underline the desirability of consistency in decision-making. The fragmentation of discretion, however, raises the threat of inconsistency. Since inspectors see their task as to handle situations, and respond to the immediate problem, it becomes difficult for those at the centre of the bureaucracy to penetrate the inspector's decision field to ensure that policy is adopted and acted on. It is difficult to escape the conclusion that so far as prosecution is concerned, the symbolic and organizational imperatives to which inspectors are routinely subjected serve to attenuate or even to smother the force of formal enforcement policy in shaping the inspector's decision field.

It is unfortunate that relatively few socio-legal studies of regulation (or, indeed, of anything else) seem to have addressed the nature, making, and transmission of policy in legal bureaucracies. While lawyers (e.g. Davis, 1969) have been concerned with the control of field-level discretion, the emphasis so far given to socio-legal studies of the strategies and practices of field-level regulatory enforcement risks creating an imbalance in our understanding of the character of regulatory control, for it is also important to understand how decisions are made about what to regulate, how to regulate, and what standards to impose. It is equally important to appreciate how these decisions actually connect with regulatory action. Any thorough understanding of the nature of bureaucratic policy implies an empirical understanding of its practice.

7 Symbols and Images

1. PROSECUTION AS A PUBLIC ACT

Prosecution makes a statement. It is the occasion when the regulatory agency turns its face to various audiences, and gives special notice to people of its activities. It is at once a public and a dramatic act, one carrying with it various meanings. It is a formal and newsworthy means of announcing the enforcement of the law and the defence of public interests, and the most important way in which an agency announces it is taking sides in the business of regulation. It is also a declaration in which various forms of symbolism and imagery are implicated. The symbolic statement conveys a moral message that has a substantive content; employing imagery is concerned with the creation of a particular appearance or impression. Regulatory officials do not simply decide whether or not to prosecute on the basis of features inherent in a particular event or problem, but also look to what the act of enforcement will mean to various interested audiences. This is an organizationally shaped part of the decision field, a means of buttressing the agency's legal mandate.

Prosecution, as a form of communication, takes analysis of its use into the realm of the expressive,[1] for here conveying messages or manufacturing appearances is more important than effecting some practical and desirable change in the world.[2] This use of prosecution is most significant in the distinctive environment of moral and political ambivalence which suffuses regulation in general. The use of symbolism and imagery is important for an agency subject to the various forms of ambivalence surrounding its regulatory activities, which create conflicting expectations

[1] The use of prosecution by individual officials has also to be seen as a form of expressive behaviour within an organizational context since it is a means of displaying their activism and serious intent. Ch. 10 focuses on the use of prosecution by officials for explicitly organizational purposes.

[2] To use prosecution expressively may also support an instrumental function. But while attempts to portray the organization as a credible legal actor may, for example, contribute to a deterrent effect, the instrumental end is not necessarily, if ever, the primary concern of the decision-maker in such cases.

in its environment. This expressive use of prosecution arises from HSE's place as an official body operating in an area of public, commercial, and political concern whose decisions about law enforcement have powerful implications for the conduct of business. Given the uncertainties and differences of opinion in HSE's environment about the kind and degree of regulatory restraint deemed desirable, the appearances the agency creates and the fundamental values it seems to embody are particularly important.

Central to this ambivalence is a tension between activist, pro-regulatory values of restraint and laissez-faire values that are more resistant to regulation. As a law enforcement authority the regulatory agency is in an especially difficult and exposed position, caught between publics with competing interests regarding the degree and kind of legal regulation necessary to control the undesirable consequences of industrialized life (Hawkins, 1984). By the use or conspicuous non-use of prosecution following events receiving widespread publicity, a regulatory agency makes powerful statements about its position on political issues and can contain conflicting ideological positions. The competing pressures from HSE's opposing interested publics can be handled with the occasional, carefully selected prosecution to manufacture the appearance of activity, for there is often a need for the regulatory agency to be seen to be taking decisive action, especially if matters of human health and safety are clearly at stake. The tension between conflicting values as it surfaces in occupational health and safety regulation is often expressed popularly as one between safety and profit.[3] When expressed in such simple terms, the political vulnerability of the agency is clearly exposed, not least because health and safety for workers and members of the public is generally regarded as a sacred value, one whose attainment is believed, at least rhetorically, to be beyond virtually any price. On this view, prosecution is the formal and public condemnation of a morally (as well as legally) culpable employer for failing in basic duties owed to employees to safeguard their health and safety. And where HSE responds to complaints about non-compliant companies taking unfair competitive advantage, it is presented with an opportunity both to punish for the moral breach and to show that it is even-handed in its enforcement and sanctioning practices.

Yet reliance on regulation by the threat or application of criminal penalties places the regulatory body in a position of curious vulnerability,

[3] As it was, for example, in the aftermath of the Ladbroke Grove train crash.

which it manages with the kinds and numbers of cases that it chooses to prosecute. It is not simply that there is a compelling need to be seen to be taking action, especially given the importance of the values at stake, but which cases are selected for prosecution is of crucial significance. By its choice of cases for prosecution, or its decisions to rule out prosecution, as well as in its general level of prosecution activity, a regulatory agency seeks to balance the competing demands for enforcement activity from those who expect it, while at the same time it tries to avoid the appearance, to those who adopt laissez-faire values, of being oppressive, or a burden on productive industry. HSE's position is one both of power and vulnerability, making for considerable sensitivity within the agency to matters which have the capacity to create public concern. As a result, prosecutions may sometimes be undertaken in cases where instrumental effectiveness is not the primary preoccupation.

That instrumental concerns are not always even the dominant official prosecutorial purpose is evident from HSC's *Enforcement policy statement*, where it is said: 'Enforcing authorities must use discretion in deciding whether to initiate a prosecution. *Other approaches to enforcement can often promote health and safety more effectively* but, where the circumstances warrant it, prosecution without prior warning and recourse to alternative sanctions may be appropriate' (Health and Safety Commission, n.d.: 11; my emphasis).

Compared with the enforcement tactics routinely deployed by inspectors which are characterized by incrementalism, informality, and low visibility, prosecution is abrupt, formal, and public. Prosecution, indeed, is the most visible and decisive act of any undertaken by regulatory bodies. The courts and the formalities of the legal process in effect present the regulatory agency with a public platform, as was acknowledged by a former Chief Inspector of the Nuclear Installations Inspectorate (NII): 'I don't have a public image. The courts do, you see. Courts have a public image which people are prepared to accept. The government regulator, certainly one like me, doesn't.' The public stage is essential because some wrongs or events in the occupational health and safety world are felt to be so big or so bad that the official response has to extend beyond the particular cast of characters in any particular local drama to become more widely known:

> 'Sometimes, because [prosecution] is an expression of concern, I think really a public expression of concern, then it shows members of the public who have an interest or are concerned, that we are taking action, and are using our powers, where just talking to firms and getting their agreement to do something would seem an inadequate response from a regulatory authority.' (97–02)

A discussion of prosecution as a public act, however, must avoid simplifying a complex set of processes. The broadly political pressures and expectations to which HSE is subject come and go. They comprise a mix of both general and more specific interests, since the messages of prosecution speak to classes of case as well as to individual events. Conflicting messages from different sources act on and within the organization: some demand a reduction in the burdens of regulation, others demand that something be done about specific problems such as asbestos, or rail safety, or gas safety, or whatever else might be a matter of current public concern. Some demand formal action in a particular case, while others are indifferent or occasionally even obstructive. The effect of such conflicting currents of expectation and opinion is to add to the difficulty of HSE's position and to open the agency to the possibility of criticism from some quarter or other. These features in HSE's surround come to constitute part of an inspector's decision field. That inspectors were conscious of, and looked to, the broader social and political context in which they worked seems clear from the remarks of a principal inspector (PI) that 'A civil servant has to be fairly well-attuned to the way the wind blows and the climate of the times' (86–38), or the words of an air pollution inspector, who said, 'Most prosecutions are for incidents or series of incidents that may well have led to complaint, but it has been our view of the management's attitude to things over a lengthy period that it has now got us to the point of saying "We've got to make a public example of this."' In short, prosecution 'is a way of... reinforcing our identity and role and function, because very often at the end of the day it is these sorts of activities which get HSE most noticed in the public eye' (97–02). Expressive action is important as it maintains the legitimacy of the organization and quietens opposition (Edelman, 1964). Legitimacy is an imperative for public organizations, hence regulatory agencies' practices help to secure them their place in the moral order (Rees, 1997; Selznick, 1992).

2. AUDIENCES

The regulatory bureaucracy is an actor on a public stage whose audiences constantly scrutinize its activities and accomplishments, thereby placing demands on it to display various signs of its impact and effectiveness. Prosecution is an important device with which HSE conducts its relations with its interested audiences, among whom are the public, the media, employers, business competitors, or industry in general. The important messages to be conveyed by prosecution are not simply statements about harm done or hazard threatened, or about the wilfulness or persistent non-compliance of a rule-breaker. There are also things to say about the fundamental values of the legal process, and about the regulatory agency itself.

Prosecution lets audiences know that justice has been done. It is a powerful form of declaration showing, for instance, that an inspector or the regulatory agency are serious and not to be trifled with. Or prosecution may address a particular individual or group as a way of showing who is in charge. And like all of those who play to audiences, regulatory bodies are concerned with how well they are received. In the case of occupational health and safety regulation, the agency is most concerned to gain and retain the trust of the public, employers, and employees, and to appear to them to be a credible authority. Prosecution as a form of communication is an important means of establishing the organization's credentials in these various ways.

As a public act, prosecution is a clear and visible indicator, one capable of making unequivocal statements to the regulatory agency's audiences:

> 'it is easier to demonstrate what we've achieved where there is a visible output, and a prosecution, an enforcement notice, an accident investigation, they're all visible outputs; whereas those less tangible things like compliance are harder to demonstrate, harder to measure. But yes . . . we do use prosecution as a way of demonstrating our seriousness about a particular issue. And where we have prosecuted, we try and gain maximum impact from that by the use of publicity, so we get a gearing effect from the prosecution. It is important to demonstrate that we are prepared to take things that far, we are prepared to put the resources into taking a case to court. We're even prepared to lose some, on occasions, you know, in order to try and get clear understandings as to what the boundaries are.' (97–04)

1. General Audiences

The idea of 'the public' as an audience for prosecution is an adaptable concept. It may sometimes refer to other employers in the same industry or in the same locality, sometimes to a localized public of interested citizens in the vicinity of a particular site, and sometimes to a wider, larger, and more amorphous audience. Among these general audiences for HSE's activities are the media, regulated firms, a particular industry, trade unions, ministers, and politicians, in addition to the public. The case that is capable of stirring the interest or anxiety of the public usually attracts the interest of the media as well, and augments the potential for critical reactions:

> 'The public and the media loom quite large, because [prosecution] is the only way they'll know what work we do . . . All they hear about us is where there's an incident and something is expected to occur as a result of our investigation. I think the public and the media see us very much like the police in that respect . . . We do respond to the public expectation and we do take some action.' (86–02)

The public dimension is regarded by some inspectors as especially important because they view themselves essentially as legal representatives of the public: 'I think any organization, any individual with the organization, would like to feel that the way they're acting fits in with what the public would expect. After all we're employed by the public' (86–02). It follows from this that inspectors should display particular concern for threats to the public. Thus it is the case that 'Things that go over the fence from . . . factories have a far greater significance [for HSE] than the people inside [them]' (86–51). This comment was made by a PI reflecting on the fact that HSE had over the years become more aware of a wider public beyond the factory gates, a public which itself was now better informed about and sensitive to occupational health and safety matters.

The public often announces itself to HSE by voicing its anxieties in the form of complaints to the agency. In such circumstances prosecution is an important means by which the public can be reassured that action is being taken on its behalf. The temptation for HSE to try to restore public confidence by prosecution will be stronger where members of the public have themselves fallen victim to a workplace incident. This is the case even in those inspectorates which make little use of prosecution. For instance, speaking of a particular event that was prosecuted in the mid-1980s, an air pollution inspector observed: 'A large number of people reported sickness and streaming eyes and things, and we felt that there was in that situation . . . no way that we could not make a formal declaration and [generate] publicity that there was something gone wrong that shouldn't have gone wrong.'

Inspectors have a conception of the public as interested in occupational health and safety, perhaps concerned about it, but perhaps not very knowledgeable or discriminating in understanding its problems. Their view is that workplace hazards and the actual failures of employers seem to be broadly homogeneous in the public mind. The public is not believed to differentiate between, for instance, a failure to guard machinery, on the one hand, and the ways in which workers handle toxic substances, on the other. If the public is not regarded as having an informed perception of occupational risks, however, that does not diminish the importance of its complaints, nor make them less real:

> 'There certainly is a much greater public concern [these days], and that manifests itself in the increasing number of complaints that we receive; but it's very skewed. The public are concerned about some things, but not about others; so they're concerned about public safety—we probably get far more complaints about fencing of construction sites to stop children getting in, or tiles being dropped in the street, than we do about the safety of construction workers themselves. Equally, we get complaints about gas safety, about fairgrounds, about schools, about leisure centres and all of those sorts of things in far greater numbers than complaints from employees about their own working conditions.' (97–04)

The public can be especially vocal in its complaints and criticisms where there has been a major incident, or when a fatality has occurred. In keeping with this, the public is viewed by inspectors generally as rather punitive, and given to assuming that whenever there is an accident, somebody should be punished. This is especially so where sections of the public have a particular interest in the handling of a case, perhaps owing to their connection with the victim. Occasionally MPs may be involved, a matter which sometimes provokes debate among inspectors about the proper course of action in light of their particular influence. Interest from politicians can bring about a change of course in the handling of a case, as happened during a fieldwork visit to one of the area offices, provoking the inspector concerned to complain: 'In my own mind I believe if we hadn't had this letter from this MP we should have dealt with this case in our normal way' (86–10). The significance of such specific political interest is suggested by the fact that prosecution files show that it is sometimes explicitly mentioned by field staff in discussion with PIs as a matter to take into account when finally deciding about prosecution.

The media form a very different sort of audience. Prosecution is a legal act often likely to attract the attention of the local and occasionally the national media, therefore making HSE's enforcement action or inaction readily communicable on a wider scale. The media are the means by which the agency is able to transmit important messages to other audiences. '[O]ften the media do pick up on our cases, and, you know, we do have quite a lot of free, no-hassle publicity as a result of our enforcement action' (97–02). Put simply, prosecution is 'One of the few ways in which we get our name in the newspapers' (86–40). There is added significance in the fact that, as a former HSE Director General explained, 'The media are . . . important . . . elements in all the [relevant] politics . . .' (Hawkins, 1992*a*: 155).

The major media vehicle both for transmitting public concern to the agency, and by which the agency informs its audiences of its activities, is the press. Many of the prosecution files carried cuttings of newspaper accounts of the court proceedings relating to the particular case. HSE is also able to use the press to publicize enforcement crackdowns which it runs from time to time to highlight official concern about certain occupational health and safety problem areas (construction work, gas safety, and asbestos are three past examples). This is another means of displaying HSE's initiative and energy to the public, in addition to whatever deterrent effect may reside in the publicity.[4] The use of advertising by HSE to draw attention to a particular problem, whose impact might then be enhanced if the campaign is actually taken up by the media themselves (as in the noise campaign run in the 1980s), is also dependent, of course, on the skilful use of the press.[5] Such efforts help to place and keep the regulatory organization on the map. However, there is also a possible difficulty, for while the media can be particularly useful in assisting enforcement where an inspectorate must deal with a numerous and scattered population of regulated sites (which makes conventional and comprehensive inspection impossible, as in the agricultural industry), the risk for an agency which cultivates a higher profile may well be that more demand is placed upon those inspectors who work in an organization many of whose activities are already substantially constrained by limited resources.

However, the media are not only an audience for the agency's enforcement activities, and a means by which HSE can inform and educate; they are also the source of occasional criticism and accusations of inactivity which demand careful defence by the agency:

[4] In a crackdown it is possible that a relatively small increase in absolute numbers being prosecuted could, with effective publicity, be perceived by the targeted industry as greatly increasing the risks of being caught and prosecuted.

[5] The value of any message sent in the act of prosecuting obviously depends on the extent to which it is communicated to those at whom it is aimed, on the extent to which it is appropriately perceived by the regulated community, and the extent to which the regulated audience is able to act on it (its 'regulatory space', as Fiona Haines (1997) puts it).

'[Y]ou've to have a good reason for your actions, that has justified why you're prosecuting to the court but equally justifies to the media, if necessary, why you're not. And you've got to have a good story, and something extremely credible. And if you haven't got a good story, and there's somebody lying dead on the deck . . . I want it to be shown that we're actually, professionally, we're doing what the public want, what people would've expected.' (97–03)

HSE staff recognize that relationships with the media are tricky because the character of much publicity is beyond the regulatory agency's guidance or restraint. In the first place, beyond drawing matters to their attention, it is hard to exert any form of control over the media: their interest is regarded as fickle, as easily created 'only at time of crisis or drama' (Health and Safety Executive, 1987*a*: 69). Besides, it is difficult to handle and plan for. According to a former Director General,

'We have got to be very careful in the way we . . . approach or use the media because . . . the name of their game is drama, and drama means taking sides and archetypally we are not taking sides, we are above the battle. Although we live in a world where there can be a lot of drama, like a chemical plant going up . . . we are not for creating it, we are on the whole for damping it down.' (Hawkins, 1992*a*: 155)

Another important audience for prosecution activity comprises employers in general, as was made clear in a memo by the area director (AD) in a big case in which a worker died in an explosion and fire at an oil terminal: 'This was a very serious incident,' he wrote, 'indicating a lack of proper management control and for which there is considerable local concern. Other employers are awaiting our action with interest. We know the firm (albeit not the same limited company) had committed similar breaches' (P97–28). This was a major case, and it is likely that one of the AD's aims in approving the prosecution was to project messages not simply beyond the local area but also beyond the particular industry.[6]

2. Special Audiences

Among a number of special audiences for HSE's enforcement activities are the local public, firms in the area, other firms in the particular industry, or other industries in which similar working practices or hazards may be found. Pressure for prosecution is often exerted by victims and their families, who expect action in cases affecting them, and in such circumstances the individual inspector and sometimes the

[6] For further details of this case see text accompanying n. 22 of Ch. 3 and p. 90.

regulatory organization feels especially constrained to display responsiveness.

To amplify the force of the message to these audiences, it is common practice for the HSE Press Office in London to issue an 'operational note' carrying notification of an impending prosecution to local and specialist press.

In one case, the engineering manager of a large factory had been seen ascending 20 feet to inspect a roof on an unsecured pallet resting on the forks of a fork lift truck. He had then stepped from the pallet onto the roof. He was prosecuted as he was at the time the person in charge of the factory. The inspector concerned wanted to draw attention to the manager's behaviour, complaining to his PI [principal inspector] of his 'appalling example'. He dismissed the idea of warning him, opting for prosecution because it 'would bring home more clearly how bad we [at HSE] think this action was to that company and with luck to a wider audience via local press.' The inspector sent a note to other colleagues in his area office to the effect that the prosecution had been cleared by the Press Office at headquarters and a notice put out to the trade specialist press, adding 'I suspect it might be of interest also to the local press in [two local towns], so I'd be grateful if you would pass it on at the right moment.'[7] (P97–31)

The local management of a regulated firm which is the subject of prosecution, its workforce, and key individuals within it constitute another important special audience. The use of prosecution here may often be allied with an instrumental purpose, especially as the prosecution of a particular site frequently comes to the notice of the company's headquarters management. 'Often a prosecution is the only way of being able to make an impression on a firm... [Senior management] start dealing out the kicks down the line and begin to affect the people we're interested in' (86–56). These comments suggest the extent to which HSE is dependent upon the effectiveness of a company's internal control and sanctioning system in enhancing any instrumental impact that may be produced by legal action. Sometimes a company's management is itself the particular target of legal action. In a case in which a woman had had her hands trapped in a machine, suffering severe burns and the amputation of the middle fingers of both hands, the inspector recorded:

'The co are a large multinational with well developed health and safety staff and procedures. The basic cause of the accident is due to poor management/

[7] The defendant was fined £500, with almost £320 in costs, having pleaded guilty to a charge under s. 7 (a) of the HSW Act (failing 'to take reasonable care for the safety of himself').

supervision. PR [prosecution] is proposed since this is a very clear way of demonstrating to Company management... health and safety needs to be competent—it was not at this site or at this machine.' Among the 'Special reasons' for prosecution, it was said: 'This is a big co, who should and can do better than this re health and safety. The accident causes are basic but have resulted in a very serious and disfiguring injury to both the IP's [injured person's] hands. The guard may have been missing for up to 4 weeks previously, possibly longer.' The inspector concluded that there was nothing in the facts of the case that could serve by way of mitigation.[8] (P97–36)

A primary justification for the use of prosecution in this particular instance seems to be to make a clear statement to the management of a big company about the importance of constant compliance with occupational health and safety requirements, and the costs of failure.

The regulated industry of which the defendant company is merely a part is another special audience for prosecution. A typical example of this concern arose in a Process Paper in a case in which an elderly woman had drowned in a hospital bath. The inspector observed, by way of supporting a recommendation to prosecute: 'We should make it clear that the duty in Section 3 HSW Act includes a duty of care towards patients and that it extends to acting reasonably for their protection if they are confused, mentally ill or suicidal. A prosecution will now send a strong signal to the industry' (P97–24).[9]

The government of the day and its relevant ministers constitute a special political audience for HSE's prosecution activity. The message to be conveyed by a prosecution here may help the minister concerned deflect potential criticism of governmental torpor. Or the message may be the more general one to its political masters that HSE is resolutely fulfilling its legal mandate. Both these concerns are evident in the following snatch of conversation with an AD:

Q: 'And presumably [senior] people... are able to use your... input, and your colleagues' input as a way of displaying to government that HSE is doing a job?'

A: 'Is doing a necessary job, yes. Yes.'

Q: 'So "Please don't cut our budget", or whatever message you wish to convey?'

[8] The company pleaded guilty to two counts, and was fined £11,000 under HSW Act s. 2 (1), and £3,500 under Provision and Use of Work Equipment Regulations, 1992 (PUWER), Reg. 11 (1) (failing to take effective measures to prevent access to dangerous parts of a machine). Costs were nearly £1,500.

[9] The defendant company pleaded guilty to a charge under s. 3 of the HSW Act, and was fined £7,500. There was no reference in the file to costs.

A: 'Yes, that's true, and, I mean . . . very much with the last [Conservative] government . . . individual ministers were, you know, very quick to realize, I think, themselves the importance of being able to say "HSE is prosecuting" where some incident has occurred which, you know, there would be absolute uproar about if action hadn't been taken.' (97–02)

The need to attract the attention of a particular target audience encourages inspectors to think seriously about the merits of prosecuting a particular matter. This is especially the case with offences that intrinsically might not otherwise be regarded as sufficiently serious to warrant prosecution, such as violations of welfare provisions. In one case a construction firm was accused of having failed to provide a supply of hot water and a trained first-aider on a building site. The inspector's rationale emphasizes the importance attached to securing and maintaining compliance, especially if an inspector is in the offing:

'Apart from the general standards at the site in respect of welfare and first aid being nothing short of abysmal, the cases have been brought to show construction companies that if they are expecting a visit from an inspector then they should do everything in their power to ensure compliance. It is patently obvious that this company did not. Hopefully the publicity which may be generated from a successful prosecution may stimulate other companies into coming to terms with the fact that the 20th century is now upon us and that such basic facilities (such as hot water) as described are the right of every human being wherever he or she has to work.'[10] (P97–61)

3. EXPECTATIONS

The awareness that there is an audience for enforcement creates in inspectors a set of expectations that they and HSE need to be seen to be taking action in propitious circumstances. From the organization's point of view, responsiveness to the demands of various audiences is the most effective way of blunting possibly adverse criticism: 'I mean, I'm not being defensive, I hope. Publicity after the event wouldn't drive us, but the knowledge of public interest is one of our criteria. I mean, there's no doubt about that; and that comes from whether it's a protest group, an individual family, an MP; all these things . . . ' (97–05). Such vulnerability tends to make the regulatory agency more sensitive and responsive to

[10] The company pleaded guilty to two counts under the Regulations for Health and Safety (First Aid) and Construction (Health and Welfare), and was fined £1,000 and £750, respectively, with an order for nearly £300 in costs.

specific pressures upon the organization and its actors, and these drive towards prosecution in certain cases, or certain classes of case, that crop up from time to time. For example,

> 'There are pressures to be seen to be enforcing against asbestos. That's the "in" thing at the moment.... There are *political pressures which perhaps push you into a case you might not otherwise have been prepared to take on board* that might not necessarily even be that important. But because it's asbestos, you feel you've got to have a go. They are unspoken pressures.' (86–63; my emphasis)

Inspectors were most frequently aware of pressures upon the organization to prosecute which arose as a result of egregious individual incidents. The nature of these forces can be sufficiently powerful that inspectors feel compelled to justify a decision not to prosecute. Such cases can arise in any number of ways: 'Where there's a serious incident you have to be able to justify not prosecuting. Where there's public interest, you have to justify not prosecuting' (86–29). One of the more familiar of these serious incidents is 'If you've got a multiple fatality... there's so much political pressure put on the HSE to do something... If there has been a breach of the law... then the pressure to take the case will be almost overwhelming' (86–11). Or, as another inspector put it, 'When there's a fatality in a factory... I've a feeling we tend to lean over backwards to see if there's a prosecution' (86–10). What these sorts of remarks suggest is that vulnerability leads to the normal rules of stringency with which cases are assessed being redefined and relaxed in the face of a newsworthy case which brings with it a public expectation that action will be taken. In such circumstances 'good' companies may sometimes be prosecuted, even though there may be some sympathy for them among inspectorates in light of their past compliance. The external pressures may be irresistible in such exceptional circumstances as 'if it's a high profile incident in the town centre or near to a school, or something of that nature. You might be placed in the situation then, where perhaps although you thought on [the] previous record of the company it wouldn't be one that you'd put forward as the same case for prosecution, that you had to take it' (86–53). In such circumstances, the demand for public action may assume greater importance than any moral concern the inspector might entertain about whether the company really deserved to be prosecuted. The pressure to take action can be quite considerable and will also cause greater difficulty if the quality of the evidence available seems inadequate for prosecution purposes, even though it may also be the case that more evidence may be yielded by a dramatic incident. The pressure upon inspectors to act following a major incident is probably different only in degree from the pressure aroused when a fatality occurs in more routine circumstances. In both, the threshold at which the inspector prosecutes is lowered as a result of the weight of expectation, as one made clear: 'If something goes "Bang" there is an expectation that somebody will be brought to justice as a result. A scapegoat is required' (86–37). Here, both field and frame are altered by the event occurring in the surround.

These general pressures will often coincide with those from more specific sources. Certain forms of harm which arouse special public anxiety, such as that suffered by victims of radiation following a breach of the law, may prompt a greater concern for action. Victims usually have an interest in seeing a prosecution take place, if only to satisfy themselves that their suffering as victims has been formally acknowledged and declared in a court of law, and their innocence vindicated. Victims often have a further direct interest as claimants in a civil action, and sometimes they or their solicitors let inspectors know of their status:

> 'In some cases people have their own claims to make about compensation, and they realize that it can't do them any harm if there's also been a successful prosecution against the firm concerned. And some of the—I don't get pressure—but some of the hints I get from people who've been injured at work, they say they're going to make a claim and they're very keen to hear of any action that may be taken by us against the firm.' (86–40)

Trade unions, perhaps surprisingly, were not often referred to by inspectors as displaying much interest in the prosecution of employers. If unions were described as interested in legal proceedings at all, it was in connection with a civil claim for compensation rather than a criminal prosecution. Sometimes more interest in HSE's activities was reported to come from other industrialists, especially those concerned that a competitor's failure to comply would give it a commercial advantage. Those who have complied 'often say', reported a construction inspector, '"Well, what are you doing about the cowboys in the industry? I tender for a job and I put up scaffolding . . . and you'll take me to task if I don't do it. Yet there's other people who are getting away with it . . . and risking lives." So we've got pressures . . . from industry to take action' (86–17).

4. MESSAGES

HSE occupies a difficult public position as regulator of occupational health and safety in an ambivalent environment, in which there are powerful expectations about enforcement action. The agency manages relationships and expectations by the use of symbolism and imagery. Broad appearances can be conveyed through the creation and deployment of imagery, while the use of formal legal proceedings can also be employed to broadcast a particular symbolic message. For HSE, the act of prosecution can make at least three important sorts of symbolic statements. These messages endorse the principles of commensurability, consistency, and accountability. All three express familiar and deeply held moral sentiments and all can be made in ways that are to their audiences both clear and unmistakable. They gain their special force and relevance from the moral and political ambivalence suffusing the regulatory process.

However, to be too ready to use prosecution seems to some to convey messages of a different kind—of harassment, of persecution, of vindictiveness—that stem from the grafting of legal rules regulating safety, health, and welfare at work onto an existing structure of criminal law normally associated with the sanctioning of common criminals. The traditional law is heavily laden with the moral taints of culpability and disreputability and its capacity to stigmatize causes problems where the conduct complained of does not seem to violate long-standing, familiar, or sacred rules of conduct. Accordingly, from the regulator's perspective, the criminal law is to be used with great care; indeed, the pervasive search for evidence of the employer's blameworthiness as a prerequisite for prosecution in routine cases (see Chapter 11) may well reflect an implicit recognition by inspectors that to prosecute the blameworthy is to align the misconduct with other more familiar forms of criminal behaviour. It is to acknowledge and employ norms which are readily and mutually recognizable by all those with an interest in the enforcement behaviour of regulatory bodies. If, however, a regulatory agency decides to punish a seemingly 'blameless' violator, it risks appearing 'heartless' or 'spiteful'.

1. Commensurability

One important symbolic declaration, therefore, speaks to the appropriateness of prosecution. Those who are to be formally blamed and punished are those who are morally at fault. However, this is not enough, for the organization must show that its response to those who break rules is proportionate. Thus there are two elements to commensurability. One embodies the idea that the decision to prosecute is made to seem the fitting response to a particular act or event; the other that there is proportion in the extent to which a defendant is prosecuted (see Chapter 3), quite apart from the degree of the courts' response when sentencing for a breach of occupational health and safety law. Of these, the former—prosecution as the morally right response to a violation—is perhaps the more important. This is because, from the organization's point of view, it is essential not to be regarded as vindictive, for a prosecution deemed to be unfair causes resentment (cf. Kelman, 1981: 205–14).[11] However, the expectations of the general public in prosecution matters are generally interpreted as punitive, and some interested groups and individuals (not least the victim) want to see the criminal law in action. Yet, for the organization, balance demands an offsetting concern not to appear to business to be spiteful in seeming to harass employers in criminal court by prosecuting gratuitously. This concern demands careful choice of cases for prosecution, especially in view of the multiple audiences for HSE action. From the organization's point of view, it is important to get the context right to make the prosecution seem morally fitting and thereby more understandable to interested onlookers. If an inspector were to take a seemingly trivial case, a technical breach, for example, said an agricultural inspector,

> 'You would not get the sympathy of the court and you would not get a penalty that would appear to be penalizing the individual, and you would be unlikely to get the sympathy of the local press . . . A press report of a successful prosecution where the reporter himself identifies it as justified results in a much more advantageous to us press report.'

The importance of the principle of commensurability, expressed as a matter of proportionality, is not only recognized but given prominence by HSC in its *Enforcement policy statement* (n.d.: 6) which observes that:

> 'The enforcement of health and safety law should be informed by the principles of proportionality in applying the law and securing compliance . . . Proportionality means relating enforcement action to the risks. Those whom the law protects and those on whom it places duties (duty holders) expect that action taken by

[11] There is strong evidence of a backlash against the Occupational Safety and Health Administration (OSHA) in the United States in the early 1980s, following its initial, rather stringent, approach to enforcement. President Reagan's appointee as head of OSHA announced that the agency would no longer aim at 'punishing' industry, but at seeking its cooperation instead (Szasz, 1984: 113). Another consequence was a substantial reduction in the number of OSHA inspectors, and the closure of more than a third of the agency's field offices (Bardach & Kagan, 1982; Calavita, 1983; Noble, 1986; Szasz, 1984).

enforcing authorities to achieve compliance should be proportionate to any risks to health and safety and to the seriousness of any breach.'

One way of furthering the principle of commensurability is by ensuring that inspection activity is directed where it will seem most appropriate: 'Targeting means making sure that inspection is targeted primarily on those whose activities give rise to the most serious risks or where the hazards are least well controlled; and that action is focused on the duty holders who are responsible for the risk and who are best placed to control it—whether employers, manufacturers, suppliers, or others' (Health and Safety Commission, n.d.: 9). These instrumental concerns are buttressed by recourse to the symbolic. After all, it is more difficult to complain of prosecution as the act of overbearing public organizations when those whose deliberate or reckless violation of a rule has resulted in harm to another. Prosecution is a way of assigning certain employers to membership of a group deserving of censure or blame. To prosecute too frequently, however, or to prosecute the 'wrong' matters, may involve cases being taken to court which are less readily regarded as clearly deserving of such treatment. Such behaviour is easily characterized as excessively and undeservedly stringent action ('nit-picking'). Here, the underlying principle of commensurability is threatened, and risks accusations that the regulatory agency and its inspectors are officious and vindictive.

There is also a more pragmatic justification, as a PI suggested: 'I don't think it would do us any good for furthering our ends if we were seen by the public at large as being an organization that had poor judgment' (86–38). As a former Chief Agricultural Inspector put it: 'There's certainly no mileage if we take somebody for something simple and the local press reporter says "Bureaucratic officials" as his headline.' Some inspectors were willing to recognize that their exercise of discretion about whether to prosecute was shaped by a broad concern for the image of their inspectorate, and a desire to avoid what one AD was prepared to refer to as 'an abuse of state power' (86–31). They thought that to use prosecution too readily threatens to bring the law into disrespect and risks losing the goodwill of industry. In their view, the proper use of the power to prosecute demands restraint and balance. When confronted by cases whose moral deserts are debatable, inspectors may feel that the principle of commensurability is at stake, that it would be wrong to be too heavy-handed. Views about desert help people understand whether a 'good' or 'right' decision to prosecute has been made.

The particular meaning of commensurability is dependent upon the character of the regulatory surround, and especially the political and economic climate of the day (see Chapter 4). In the mid-1980s, for example, in an era of government that was regarded by regulators as fundamentally unsympathetic to the regulatory enterprise, an inspector could say: 'I don't see that [prosecution] is a very sensible policy, particularly given the political climate. I don't really see too much mileage in prosecuting somebody for a marginal offence if they're new to the game, trying to set up in business . . . ' (86–13). The addition of the qualifications by the inspector serve to excuse, and they implicitly suggest that to prosecute in such circumstances would appear vindictive, not only to the firm in question, but also to others. Excessive enthusiasm for prosecution would send the wrong message.[12] Some inspectors may be conscious of a personal constraint against being too ready to prosecute since to do so may suggest to colleagues in the organization a lack of competence in a regulatory inspector whose enforcement work is assumed to be based primarily on negotiation: 'You can take [prosecution] too far. People will start asking "'Can't this guy persuade people to do things?"' (86–63). The more powerful sentiment, however, is a moral one. Inspectors wish to avoid some employers feeling that they are being singled out for this punitive treatment, that they are being victimized, or 'got at'. From an instrumental point of view, prosecution is believed to be positively damaging if it does not seem fair to the defendant, as a PI suggested:

> 'Some people can take it as a very personal matter, a very vindictive approach, and it can have a very detrimental effect. But that's . . . one of the judgments you've got to make—whether you're going to achieve an improvement in management's awareness of health and safety across the board. And it may well be that prosecution may not achieve that and you may well achieve it by other means. That doesn't mean to say you have to be quiescent about a lot of things. You've got to be positive about it. But there are other ways of being positive, without going to court.' (86–36)

Thus another important aspect of the symbolic use of prosecution is that the employer's conception of commensurability fits the inspector's. When the understanding that an inspector has of the justice of his or her actions does not accord with the sense of justice of the regulated,

[12] As another inspector said: 'You don't want to produce the impression that it doesn't matter what you do, you're going to get hammered for it' (86–63).

the systems of meaning involved do not fit together and in these circumstances a prosecution will seem to the regulated to be vindictive. While there may be an imperative for an inspector to prosecute the clearly morally deserving, more caution is demanded where the degree of desert is more problematic. 'As long as you pitch it [the level of prosecution] at the point where you are prosecuting what are manifestly serious matters, then you will get . . . the understanding of the companies and the sympathy of the magistrates, which is very important' (86–56). The practical implication of this is believed to be that a higher rate of prosecution not only threatens the continued cooperation of employers but might also encourage increased numbers of defended cases.

The principle of commensurability also requires that there is a good fit between the violation and the punishment imposed, given that the court's sanction also carries significant messages.[13] HSE's efforts to make public statements about important values may be aided by magistrates or (more likely, given their greater sanctioning powers) Crown Court judges when sentencing. Since they determine the type and degree of criminal penalty imposed, the courts become another audience for and amplifier of the message the inspector wants to convey.[14] For example, the summary of the major case involving two violations of the Asbestos Regulations which had obtained extensive television and press coverage, noted that the defendant 'had pleaded guilty at the last minute but the judge said he intended to send a "message" to the industry'. That message was carried in an award of £4,000 costs and, more significantly, a sentence of three months' imprisonment (P97–30). Again, the inspector involved in the fatality arising from the major explosion and fire commented that 'the fine reflected the gravity of the case . . . This case clearly gives an indication to the petrochemicals industry about standards necessary' (P97–28). Apart from costs to reputation, the practical penalty for a defendant company may be more than the criminal fine plus costs, since in many cases injured employees pursue civil claims.

[13] Hence the remarks of one AD that 'One area where [public concern] does manifest itself as well is in demands from the public for retribution after death, and there has been a lot of concern over a number of prosecutions that the penalties are not severe enough under health and safety legislation, that the courts don't take breaches of health and safety legislation seriously enough' (97–04). This effect is particularly noticeable in the public debate about corporate criminal liability which surfaces whenever there is a major accident.

[14] The type and extent of the penalty selected is, of course, a matter not entirely outside the control of HSE, to the extent that HSE may determine the forum and does decide on the number and choice of charge (see Ch. 3).

The courts' penalties may not only endorse the agency's efforts to condemn the offender with a severe sanction but may sometimes undermine messages that HSE sends by enfeebling them with a lenient one. Sentencers' capacity to muffle the clarity of a statement embodied in a prosecution encourages inspectors to be conscious of the importance of careful selection of cases for prosecution. They fear that, as one put it, 'If you start taking trivial cases, you tend to trivialize even the serious case in [the magistrates'] eyes' (86–56). 'You would want to know at the end of the day that the fine was going to be worthy of the publicity,' said an AD. 'If it came out that he was given a conditional discharge, then the message that would come out of that [would be] "Not much point of worrying about your duties under the [HSW] Act as individuals, because the court only gives you a conditional discharge anyway"' (86–19). Expressions of disgust are sometimes to be heard when a fatality or serious injury is sanctioned with what seems to be a trivial fine.[15] People align punishment and crime, and an apparent lack of proportion mounts an important symbolic assault on the value of the injured or dead person, since it seems to place a derisory value on their worth as human beings. For this reason HSE inspectors sometimes write to family members explaining that a magistrates' court fine is no reflection on the worth of the member of their family who may have been killed or injured. Another significant form of symbolic action is any attempt at repair or remedy of the cause, following the injury or death of an individual. This is especially important for relatives. In the case of a schoolboy who died in an accident in a school corridor, the victim's father was reported in the local paper after the inquest as expressing dismay that six months after the accident there were still no warnings or signs in the corridor where his son's death had occurred (F97–09).

Some inspectors suggested that failure to win cases, or to gain a significant penalty following a conviction, might actually deter them from prosecuting. In a case in which a schoolgirl had been injured on a farm, and the convicted farmer had been given a conditional discharge, the AD concerned thought the slight penalty was probably evidence of rural magistrates showing sympathy to a defendant who, when the accident happened, had been engaged in what are regarded on farms as normal practices. The AD's particular fear was that the conditional

[15] Note in this connection the reaction of victims' families to the fine imposed on the train company after the fatal crash at Southall.

discharge in this case might encourage the inspector and PI concerned to think of their prosecution as a 'failure' (P97–35).

2. Consistency

A second important message to be transmitted in the number and kind of prosecutions mounted by HSE is that as a regulatory organization it is consistent in its response to the violations its inspectors encounter. Consistency of response symbolizes the even-handed, dispassionate, and predictable character of justice. Consistent enforcement means, ideally, that individual officials decide the outcomes of apparently similar cases in similar ways, that administrative areas decide in similar ways, and that such decisions are made consistently over time, as far as possible. The importance of the value of consistency is officially recognized in HSC's *Enforcement policy statement* (n.d.: 6) which speaks of the significance of 'consistency of approach, targeting of enforcement action'. The *Statement* (HSC, n.d.: 7) goes on, however, to emphasize that 'Consistency of approach does not mean uniformity. It means taking a similar approach in similar circumstances to achieve similar ends.'

Yet the appearance of consistency is extraordinarily difficult to achieve among any legal decision-makers and it remains an elusive ideal in regulation, given the amount of discretion exercised largely invisibly by highly autonomous officials. Nonetheless, consistency is a fundamental value of the legal process, not only one that officials seek to attain as a good in itself, but also one that provides a readily recognizable justification for a decision already made.

3. Accountability

The responsiveness of HSE to occupational health and safety problems tends to be gauged by others by reference to its activities in the courts. A third important symbolic message the regulatory agency must convey to its audiences therefore is that it is acting in the public interest to protect important social values. This compels HSE to show that it is accountable and responsive both to the concerns of people in the workplace, and to its other interested audiences: 'the other side of accountability', said an AD, 'is being accountable to the public and to ministers, and so on, because there is a public expectation that in certain cases, certain actions will result, and whilst we're not driven by that, we are aware of it, and we seek to demonstrate it in that way' (97–04). Some inspectors regarded prosecution as a fulfilment of the inspectorate's public duty: 'It reminds the public at large that we're doing our job' (86–53), and, said a former Chief Agricultural Inspector, 'apart from prosecution there is no sort of public [display of enforcement]'.

One of the cases in the sample of prosecution files illustrates this well. It involved an accident in a theme park, in which a small novelty passenger train had flipped over, injuring nine people, and in particular a 5-year-old boy. This sort of case immediately becomes a matter of some sensitivity within HSE since it involves injury not simply to members of the public, but to a child. In such circumstances, responsiveness to perceived public concern is important, and if it is swift, so much the better:

A Press Notice was prepared by HSE about the incident. The inspector noted to his PI: 'Ready to issue if and when you want. Could go [prosecute] anytime. The more days that elapse between accident the less likely "[Theme Park] Dangerous" headlines are to appear.' The inspector's notes observed that the 'ride exceeded safe limits. No attempt by employer to establish safe limits and operate to them. Brakes not maintained.' Many press cuttings, some from national papers, were in the prosecution file. All made the point that another accident involving the same ride in the same theme park had occurred 17 years earlier. A press officer for HSE issued another press release indicating that HSE was to prosecute on two charges, announcing the date, time and place of hearing (this information being underlined).[16] (P97–04)

5. APPEARANCES

Because prosecution confers a public character upon law enforcement, it can be turned opportunistically to HSE's advantage. Exploiting this advantage demands the manufacture and management of certain appearances to HSE's significant audiences. Such appearances do not convey a precise message about symbolically important values, so much as present an outward impression of the general character of the regulatory organization. Three of the most important appearances to be displayed are fairness, activity, and credibility.

1. Fairness

Given its public position, it is important for HSE to create the appearance of a state authority which responds to violations of the law in a

[16] The company pleaded guilty to two charges under the HSW Act ss. 3 (1) and 33 (1). It received fines of £12,500 and £3,000, with £6,000 in costs.

fair and just fashion. The regulatory organization must show that from time to time it is prepared to act decisively against those who break rules, in part because it is right to do so, in part because it is essential to protect the interests of those who do comply. This latter is justifiable on two moral grounds: that it is right that the deserving are punished, and the compliant are not; and that one does not profit from breaking the law. In the words of one inspector: 'It's unfair to expect all the good guys to notify us because it's a legal requirement, and to suffer the consequences of . . . the commercial disadvantage as the good guys . . . So it seemed perfectly reasonable to me, when I found the guy who wasn't playing the game, to clobber him for that' (86–26). To prosecute such offenders, it is believed, creates confidence in the regulatory process and reassures others that justice is being done.

To display the use of prosecution as fair, it has to be seen to fall on the clearly deserving, to avoid the appearance of arbitrariness. Though inspectors may be conscious of the dangers of appearing to be too conciliatory in their prosecution practices, they are also aware that when they do embark on the unusual step of prosecution, it is again essential that the selection of the very small proportion of violations to receive the sanction of prosecution should be made extremely carefully. 'Because we achieve the vast majority of what we achieve through co-operation with employers,' said a PI,

> 'it's very important that we don't become . . . seen as a nit-picking organization who at random decides to fall heavily on some poor unwitting occupier. I mean they virtually all accept that we could prosecute them every time we go into their factories. I've never come across an occupier who's said "I'm completely in the clear here." They all accept they're failing to comply with some legislation or other . . . but the vast majority are trying to provide a safe workplace, and they don't accept that they are bad enough to be prosecuted.' (86–01)

The appearance of fairness has, in addition to a substantive dimension, a procedural aspect, for it is regarded as important that all aspects of HSE's conduct of a prosecution seem fair to all concerned. For example, in one case in which a defendant landlady was charged with having failed to maintain a gas appliance, resulting in the death of a tenant, it was noted in the prosecution file that 'she appeared to be deeply upset to receive a caution before being interviewed'. The interview was postponed as a result to avoid 'any suggestions of heavy handedness on the part of HSE' (P97–37).[17]

Cases which present clear evidence of blameworthy conduct by an employer demand prosecution, not least because they possess properties that display both to employers and to members of the public clear moral failings. Thus HSC's *Enforcement policy statement* (n.d.: 11) speaks of prosecution as warranted by 'the gravity of the offence, taken together with the general record and approach of the offender... e.g. apparent reckless disregard for standards, repeated breaches, persistent poor standards'. A question put to an AD about what sorts of case would typically compel a prosecution produced a list of types. The capacity of each example to create a public appearance of a fair response to an egregious wrong, which itself creates public expectations, is clear from the following:

'if there's been a fatal accident then, I mean my view has always been that if there is a reasonable prosecution there in the circumstances, that we should look to take one because the public expects action to be taken if someone has lost their life. Also, if members of the public have been put at significant risk, and by that I mean perhaps tenants in rented accommodation who have been put at risk from dangerous gas fittings, or children on fairground rides who may have been put in danger, or innocent members of the public who might be walking underneath scaffolding and something falls off... are factors which are within our enforcement remit. I mean, I think that [with that] sort of individual there is a significant public expectation that we are there to look after their interests in health and safety. Again, if somebody has ended up maimed, or severely disabled for life, you know, I think we have to look very carefully to see if there is a prosecution in it. Now all of that is subject to there being sufficient evidence and a breach of the law, and that the employer or the duty holder has fallen down and has been, you know, negligent...' (97–02)

These are all instances where the use of prosecution is regarded as 'reasonable' and fair.

2. Activity

Another important appearance the regulatory agency must cultivate is that of activity. It must show itself to be energetic in the fulfilment of its

[17] The defendant was fined £3,500, with more than £1,300 costs, having pleaded guilty to a breach of the Gas Safety (Installation and Use) Regulations, 1994.

legal mandate, and not appear to be passive in the face of threats to the well-being of workers and the public. Prosecution is perhaps the most important way by which the organization is able to remind its publics of its continued presence and activity. A former Chief Inspector of Factories said in this connection: 'it is a very visible part of our enforcement activity. Far more visible than the many, many more instances where we have applied pressure successfully without recourse to prosecution ... It's a very partial indicator of our effectiveness, but sometimes it is useful to demonstrate that in a particular field of our work we have taken so many prosecutions ...' A degree of activity is important, since, as inspectors often say, 'There are some things where politically the public wants some action' (86–02). This action of publicly subjecting an offender to the criminal process partly offers public reassurance but also taps into instrumental demands by displaying that action is being taken to make workplaces healthier and safer for both employees and the public.

The comments of inspectors showed themselves to be particularly concerned with the appearance of activity, hence a PI's remark that 'If things go wrong you must be seen to do something' (86–11). Thus, for example, in a major case involving the exposure of employees to radiation, a specialist inspector justified a proposal to prosecute by arguing that 'this would be very useful for the wider interests of HSE' (P97–53). Such reasoning was often described as a 'political' pressure, perhaps in recognition of inspectors' feeling that matters not properly or normally part of the decision about prosecution had intruded into their decision field:

> 'If you have a particular case which is attracting a lot of media attention, you are under pressure—not internally—you feel you are under a lot of pressure, political pressure ... because if you don't it will look to those outside the inspectorate as if the inspectorate is not prepared to act when it should do ... You could be *under pressure to find a case, even if it wasn't there*, and you have to resist that.' (86–26; my emphasis)

The Executive in the 1980s was very conscious of the need to display appropriate activity and deliberately set out to raise its public image and secure a higher profile for HSE. '[O]ne of [our] purposes', said a former Director General, 'is to exhibit ourselves as people in whom the public can have confidence as controlling the particular risk, and when we are doing that we are probably addressing everybody.' Within the present agency, prosecution remains a particularly apt indicator of activity. HSC's *Enforcement policy statement* (n.d.: 11) observes of prosecution:

'it is appropriate in the circumstances as a way to draw general attention to the need for compliance with the law and the maintenance of standards required by law, especially where there would be a normal expectation that a prosecution would be taken or where through the conviction of offenders, others may be deterred from similar failures to comply with the law'.

The problem for the agency is to achieve what it deems to be the right balance between restraint and zeal, as a former Chief Inspector of Factories indicated: 'We don't want "No prosecutions." On the other hand, I don't want to be accused of being maniacally obsessed with prosecution to the risk of all else that we do. [The ADs] have to strike some sort of balance.' His comments suggest that the matter is negotiable in the organization and that the number of prosecutions actually taken is simply a matter of organizational choice. There are very few cases whose properties virtually compel prosecution.

Balance is demanded because this public enforcement move can create dangers for regulatory agency and inspector alike. A decision not to prosecute risks creating the appearance of inactivity in the face of harm or hazard and an impression that the regulatory organization is officially condoning a reprehensible act or omission. The appearance of quiescence is an affront to a public which expects an offender to be found and punished. More critical comment is likely to be prompted by a failure to act than from prosecuting the 'wrong' sort of case, simply because there is a general expectation that prosecution is—or should be—the normal response to a violation of the law resulting in injury or death. Complaints from the local public are an indicator of a demand for activity. In one case, for example,

a crane had collapsed in a built-up area. The inspector reported: 'There is a lot of local concern and we would like to pursue . . . a case.' Listed as a 'Special reason' for prosecuting was 'Potential fatal event which could have had off-site consequences.' In the inspector's Process Paper, the need for HSE to be seen to be taking action emerges clearly: 'Although the [matter] of the crane is a single straightforward and essentially a factual issue it does not tell the whole story surrounding the circumstances of the collapse. There is a political (local neighbours) and a lack of maintenance background to this issue. The scrap yard is in virtually a rural area and we have had complaints (this incident arose from a complaint) in times past about cranes operating on this site. As this collapse was about the most spectacular thing that could have happened we could come in for some criticism if action was not taken. A case for failure to examine under the Factories Act is the most straightforward case.'[18] (P97–02).

This is a prosecution in which there is explicit concern for HSE to act to avoid public criticism for failing to respond to a 'spectacular' event, one whose dangers were easily visible to the most untutored eye, and one that could have had grave consequences for members of the public unconnected with the site.

3. Credibility

A third preoccupation of the regulatory organization is with its presentation of itself to its audiences as a credible law enforcement agency. Use of legal powers helps to portray an agency as convincing and worthy of respect, attributes that fulfil the function of offering reassurance to workers and the public. It follows from this that public knowledge of the agency's powers and its enforcement practices is extremely important for inspectors, hence their frequent remarks such as, 'We've got to be seen as an inspectorate to be enforcing the law'[19] (86–22). The impression must be created of an agency's inexorable legal power. Prosecution is a key move in giving strength to the organization's appearance as convincing and decisive:

'We are there to perform a job and enforcement activity is something which we are uniquely given the powers to carry out. Other prosecutor organizations can inspect, advise, and give guidance and give lectures, but enforcement is something that has uniquely been given as a power to us. And if we don't use it then it calls into question the reason for our existence.' (97–02)

Similarly, an agricultural inspector observed that

'You have to be credible as an inspectorate, really. And one aspect of that is a visible prosecution policy that shows itself by numbers... and by a spread of what's done so that you can respond to people who ask questions about the industry and so on by pointing out that there are problems and in those cases we did prosecute.'

This stance is particularly crucial in a law enforcement organization which implements its legal mandate primarily in a conciliatory fashion,

[18] The defendant pleaded guilty to one charge under s. 27 (1) of the Factories Act, 1961, and was fined £500, plus costs amounting to nearly £140.

[19] Almost three-quarters of the inspectors discussing this point said they prosecuted partly out of concern to make themselves and their inspectorate credible.

for, to the extent that a strategy of compliance works, it does so as a result of the threat of prosecution occasionally made real (Hawkins, 1984).

Even though the actual use of prosecution is rare, it is nevertheless regarded as an integral part of inspectors' general enforcement strategy, and as such, it demands to be used from time to time. Negotiated outcomes are possible to an important degree only because enforcement is conducted by a public agency with a legal mandate, one clarified and underlined by the occasional public prosecution. As one inspector put it, 'Industry's got a lot of respect for the inspectorate, partly because we prosecute and we win' (86–28). Another said, 'We're an enforcing authority and I feel that if we didn't have these powers of prosecution then there are many firms who wouldn't take a blind bit of notice of our advice' (86–17). The appearance of credibility is important not only when inspectors deal with single events, such as an accident, but also when they have to handle the employer who persistently fails to comply. To prosecute here is to prosecute for failure of their usual strategy of compliance. It needs to be done sparingly 'because if you use it too often and it doesn't work, what the heck do you do after that?' (86–55). Both types of case demand that the agency make a public example of the violator, since not to act will risk questions being asked about the agency's energy, its public responsibilities, or its commitment to its mandate.

In the big case in which employees had suffered excessive doses of radiation, the inspector recommended prosecution, even though, as he recorded in the file, he had taken 'into account [the firm's] apparently genuine efforts to improve the health and safety of their employees.' Among the reasons for proceeding were the following:

'1. HSE needs to be seen to be acting decisively where employees are receiving high dose rates for site radiographers due to inadequate compliance with the regulations. Ionising radiation receives a high profile in terms of public perception of risk and HSE's response to persistent "high" dose rates needs to be appropriate and consistent. . . .

5. The industrial radiography industry appears to be a fairly close-knit industry in terms of communication. I believe therefore that it is most probable that other contractors in the area will be aware of [the firm's] problems and will be looking closely at how HSE responds to them.'

Among the 'Special Reasons' for prosecution in the summary were: 'Failure to prosecute may expose HSE to criticism', and 'High public profile of ionising radiation.' The inspector was prepared to acknowledge that the firm had strong mitigation on its side in the form of efforts it had already made to protect its workforce, but felt that decisive action was especially important in this case because of its high profile.[20] (P97–53)

Credibility is a significant matter for an individual inspector as well as for the agency, and is a preoccupation in routine inspection and enforcement practice:

Q: 'The credibility of the inspector is presumably also bound up with the credibility of the organization?'—'Yes'—'Now, do you as a manager feel, as it were . . . under a greater obligation to back up your inspectors second time around, to help them maintain their own credibility in order to help maintain the organization's credibility?'

A: 'Yes. I mean, at the end of the day, we have to, I mean, we can't sort of go away from a workplace where conditions are clearly unsatisfactory or dangerous, or there's a sort of blatant disregard for the legal requirements, and the place of health and safety legislation. I mean, we just can't do it. So, an inspector has to persist or hang in with a company until a position is reached where the company is acknowledging its duties and making progress towards rectifying them, or giving undertakings that they accept their obligations, and setting out what they're proposing to do. Now, as I say, if they don't do that, then there is nothing else that an inspector could do, because it's absolutely unacceptable, in my view, for an inspector to say "Oh well, this is[a difficult, obdurate, truculent employer, you know, I give up." You know, you can't do that, you can't walk away and leave people in obvious danger.' (97–02)

The use of prosecution as a valuable expressive device for an individual inspector grants a personal sense of credibility and a public identity as an enforcement official.

Not to prosecute when prosecution has been threatened impugns an inspector's credibility with, from an instrumental point of view, possibly unfortunate consequences: 'If you don't [prosecute], then I think your future dealings with that company will be very difficult because you've already missed the potential sanction you've threatened all along. It's no good to threaten something if at the end of the day you don't do it' (86–34). 'Unless we are prepared to enforce,' said an AD, 'then the advice that we give, and most of our dealings with duty-holders is advice, but it has no teeth, unless we're seen that we're prepared to get stuck in and follow it through at times' (97–02). This aspect of credibility is closely tied to another characteristic element of compliance strategy, namely the notion of reasonableness. For inspectors, enforcement practices that are

[20] The company pleaded not guilty to two charges, and HSE lost the case.

mutually regarded as 'reasonable' gain the respect of the regulated and assist the organization in doing its work efficiently and effectively. Ideally, the inspector acts reasonably to achieve respect and principled compliance, while reverting to prosecution occasionally to encourage the laggards and deter the unprincipled. In so doing, the inspector is also protecting the interests of the generally compliant company against its less principled competitors.

Credibility is a matter that transcends the particular cause for concern. It is important where the inspector is trying to put an end to a career of misconduct, or is responding to a big or dramatic incident or to public expectations that action will be taken. But credibility is important also with the less salient incidents which may not attract any publicity or public concern. The inspector will want to take some sort of action, possibly to prosecute in certain circumstances, if only to lay to rest the risk that if certain kinds of violation are not prosecuted, companies may go on to indulge in more serious breaches. But balance is again required. Nearly every inspector interviewed thought that it was possible to have too much prosecution, either because the rituals involved in laying an information were too much of a burden on the inspectorate's resources or because any beneficial impact would be diluted or destroyed from overuse, hence the comment: 'Generally speaking, the organization wants to be seen to be prosecuting. Not over-prosecuting, but at least to show its teeth occasionally' (86–25). While this argues for some sort of balance, it also implies at least a minimum level of enforcement activity. This might also enhance any general deterrent effect: 'What I . . . advocate is a scattering of prosecutions throughout the Area to let people know we still have teeth and we can bite when necessary' (86–21). Thus the inspector faced with an uncooperative firm is prepared to display a greater willingness to prosecute for subsequent violations. Indeed, several of the prosecution files recorded previous prosecutions of the same firm. An AD explained the rationale:

Q: '[I]f you reserve prosecution for the big and the bad cases, then . . .'

A [interrupting]: 'Or the severe provocation. You see, that's another element to it, I suppose, the credibility of the inspector. And this is probably why once a firm has been prosecuted, they perhaps tend to be prosecuted again within the next year or so. You know, part of the answer is because often they're poor performers anyway, with poor management attitudes. But also, the inspector is back against the wall in a way in terms of their own credibility. And, as I say, you can advise a company, you can take other measures against them, but if they still don't respond, then you have to prosecute really, to show you actually mean business. And once you've reached that position, you tend to go in a much shorter circuit.' (97–02)

A concern for credibility assists also in creating salient cases. A conception of the practical worth of the case in this respect is sometimes very evident in inspectors' written remarks. To prosecute cases which involve important points of policy may have value for an inspectorate as a whole by virtue of their capacity to establish a favourable precedent, though the possibility of losing does introduce risks. Or a case may be usefully pursued with a salient employer because to do so helps cement the credibility of the inspector and the agency as legally mandated enforcers exercising a powerful and legitimate authority.

The maintenance of enforcement credibility demands that both inspector and agency cannot afford to lose too many cases, for that threatens the public image of a supremely powerful body which the agency needs to foster. Failing to convict hints at vulnerability and weakness, and may damage any desired instrumental effects, as regulated firms are less likely to be deterred in future, at least in theory. Weaver (1977: 112) found that staff lawyers in the Antitrust Division of the Justice Department in Washington feared 'the effect of too many acquittals on the number of cases the division will be able to bring successfully in the future, as well as on the business behavior that they think the division's reputation affects'. Losing may not only damage the agency's efforts to secure compliance, and raise questions about its competence, it threatens its appearance as potent, unless the case can be portrayed as unusual or exceptional in some respect, as an AD argued:

'Am I upset when we lose a case? Well, yes.... But a lot of it depends on if the circumstances of the loss are going to create a general principle that might give others the impression that they... don't have to take some course of action which we've long been pushing or advocating, to do with the standards of guarding of a particular machine, or something like that.' (97–02)

The interests of preserving credibility are yet another demand for a measure of restraint in the use of prosecution, so as not to publicize any weakness in the agency. Rigorous screening of cases is needed so that when the agency goes into court it almost always wins, and is seen to win. The only exception to this rule occurs with the 'big case'—a matter that is so grave or newsworthy that the public and media appear to demand legal action, even though the case may be weak in law.[21]

[21] The radiation case (P97–53), discussed in the previous section, is an example.

The credibility created by a willingness to take formal action is also essential for an agency which routinely prosecutes in the magistrates' courts, the modesty of whose available penalties have long been a matter of concern for HSE. Prosecution is a way of ensuring that appearances transcend numerous, very small, and often highly fragmented sites that inspectors encounter in industries such as agriculture, construction, or light manufacturing. Where inspectors are unable to visit as many employers as they might like, the occasional prosecution may help maintain the impression of an agency with teeth effectively and responsibly fulfilling its legal obligations. This concern may be especially true where farmers and small industrialists are concerned, since for them a magistrates' court fine can be a quite significant sanction, rather than a tiny financial loss absorbed painlessly by a wealthy company.

6. THE BIG CASE

The regulatory agency's concern for the symbolism and imagery implicated in prosecution gains most prominence where egregious events are concerned. Such events are both a risk and an opportunity. While public attention tends to be captured more by the use of prosecution rather than a decision not to prosecute (which is much less visible and therefore knowable), problems can be caused for the agency by big, newsworthy cases—the major accidents or incidents that generate the unremitting attention of the media and the concern of the public.[22] Such events are by definition those likely to have great propensity for creating anxiety, in turn generating strong public and media demand that the agency 'do something'. But equally, a regulatory agency can exploit this demand to drive home the various declarations it needs to make. The sensitivity of HSE to its position as a public agency and the risks that big cases pose were clearly conveyed in the case of the prosecution of the nuclear reprocessing plant at Sellafield in the mid-1980s. This case involved a deliberate discharge of radioactive material well within the authorized amounts, but in the opinion of the jury the defendant company was not doing everything that was reasonably practicable to keep the radioactivity of the discharge as low as possible. Responding to a suggestion that without the publicity likely to arise from the prosecution NII would not have proceeded, a former Chief of the NII said:

[22] Among the prosecution cases this would include the death of a worker in the oil terminal explosion and fire (P97–28, discussed in Ch. 3), the asbestos case (P97–30, discussed in Chs. 3, 7, and 11), and the radiation case (P97–53).

'Yes, I think I'd have to agree with that. I mean, I could certainly see... that there are great difficulties involved in prosecuting... We might easily have lost in this case. I don't know what the outcome would then be. It's very time and resource consuming. I'm not certain at all whether safety is served in the long run... but clearly this is what the law is all about.... [I]t's there to satisfy the public that justice is being done... We might easily have lost... I was convinced [we had] actually, when we heard the judge's summing up, and so were my staff...'

This sort of case is an opportunity to dramatize the upholding of the law.

In some big cases the imperative to preserve credibility becomes so powerful that the agency feels compelled to take action even though it has reason to believe it may actually lose: 'Well, there is no point in taking cases to court if there is not a reasonable prospect of winning, unless there is some overwhelming public desire that we must take the case to court' (97–03). Particular characters emerge from the background in such cases to occupy centre stage. Routine decision practices may be suspended (Manning, 1992). The preoccupations within the regulatory agency these shifts create are evident from the report of the AD concerned in the big asbestos case. The matter was regarded as sufficiently serious to have become the subject of two Parliamentary Questions. The AD involved reported:

'I have... met the local MP and local councillor, and especially at this time leading up to local elections, this case is highly sensitive.' Elsewhere the AD observed that the local councillor was facing re-election and may have wanted to make his intervention in the matter an election issue. At a meeting with the AD, the councillor 'said he didn't think his constituents would be reassured by [HSE's] explanation [about the handling of the asbestos] and he may use his intervention as an election issue.' A letter to the inspector from a Senior Environmental Health Officer stated: '... this site continues to be at the forefront of local people's and the media's attention and I trust you will therefore ensure that the works on site are properly regulated.' The Senior EHO went on to say later that 'This Directorate is, of course, concerned that all necessary measures are taken to prevent risk to the local community and your comments would be welcomed with regard to these points so that all necessary assurances can be given to local people and elected members.' (P97–30)

In the big case, prosecution is one of the first matters an inspector thinks about, but it remains a 'last resort' in Emerson's (1981) first sense: it is demanded because no other course of action is realistically possible (see Chapter 1).

7. VULNERABILITY AND AMPLIFICATION

An important aspect of HSE's presentation of itself to its audiences is a sense of vulnerability. This arises from a variety of sources. It comes partly from the fact that members of the public may themselves be victims of untoward events and therefore have a particular interest in the prosecution of the matter. It comes partly from the sense of accountability regulatory officials feel to the public. It comes partly from the sense that there is an unpredictability in public behaviour and reactions where occupational health and safety problems are concerned, and partly from the variety, strength, and character of the conflicting expectations to which HSE is subject. Finally, the uncertainties of the legal process add to the sense of vulnerability. As a result, HSE's sensitivity to events in its surround makes it constantly alert to the kinds of problems that prompt public concern: 'A prosecution taken earlier this year', said an inspector, 'followed an accident to a 17-year-old boy on a Government training scheme. Had the accident involved an experienced, skilled adult, I think we might not have prosecuted. One of the considerations was that there had been a lot of public concern about accidents to people in Government training schemes, and that was one consideration in making the decision' (86–56).

Given the intrinsic ambivalence that suffuses regulatory work, HSE is frequently exposed to criticism and complaint. As a law enforcement body, the political vulnerability of a regulatory agency differs from the position of the police, for example, who tend not to be held accountable or made the target of public criticism when an egregious crime is committed, or when rates of crime in official statistics go up. The police work with a mandate secured in a high level of public and political consensus about the necessity of vigorous law enforcement in response to common crime. It is only recently that they have been accused of failing in their job of crime control.[23] Indeed, a growing crime problem can become the occasion for complaints by the police about lack of resources or the imposition by the law of unnecessary restraints on their behaviour. A regulatory agency, on the other hand, may be implicated, rightly or wrongly, in the occurrence of a major accident or in an increase in the prevalence of undesired events. These may set the agency in a poor light, and open it to criticism from the media and the public.

[23] This is perhaps as a result of the Stephen Lawrence affair. The *Evening Standard* (17 Apr. 2002) recently criticized the Metropolitan Police strongly for the 'rise in the capital's crime figures' and the 'appalling clear up rate'.

This exposure, and the nature of the public response, are tied to the degree to which a law enforcement agency's mandate is secure or not in the public consciousness. Critical comment can come from any of its audiences, but protecting the image and credibility of the organization occasionally demands that such criticism be muted, or the agency protected. Pressures may be created

> 'where people perceive a problem and they may complain to their local MP or go to their shop steward or their branch or whatever and say "Look, they have breached section whatever, why aren't you prosecuting them?" And there is a difficulty sometimes, I think we've all experienced it, of trying to explain our position... There are on occasion those pressures.' (86–61)

Vulnerability to criticism and complaint is associated with particular public expectations. When HSE acquires new responsibilities, therefore, it feels a need to display its presence, competence, and success as an enforcing agency with its new duties. The regulation of gas safety was sometimes mentioned as an example in this connection where, as one inspector put it, 'We're supposed to be doing as well or better than the Department of Energy [which used to have the responsibility]' (86–51), or, to quote another, the policy was 'to maintain the same level of activity' as before HSE took over responsibility for enforcement. Unless a case is intrinsically 'big', however, it is important for the agency to combat its sense of vulnerability by communicating effectively with its audiences. The messages of prosecution can be amplified and the force of the public statement enhanced by artful use of the media. Publicity is a way of conveying a sense of the risks of the workplace and of the way in which society seeks to control those risks. It is also useful where there may be no memory of actual accidents in a particular workplace. Prominent coverage is often given by newspapers to successful prosecutions, and reports of court proceedings frequently find their way into the local press carrying headlines like: 'Father-of-four "pleased" as company is punished' (P97–08). Publicity serves to protect the regulatory organization itself. If the way to display credibility and responsiveness is formal enforcement action and the delivery of punishment by the courts, the effective use of publicity allows an amplified message of HSE's power to be brought to both its regulated audience and its audience of onlookers. Such publicity is treated as an important tool within HSE since it helps underline both its credibility and its presence. The prosecution files sampled often contained cuttings from the local press of articles reporting the prosecution of an employer.

'I think it gives the impression, you know, which I would say is for the general good, that HSE is a, perhaps a stronger body of people, and a lot more ubiquitous than we actually are. And it perhaps gives the impression that we do get around, and I think that is all for the good. It . . . gives teeth to the advice that we give. In other words, it gives the impression that (which I hope is right) . . . we very often do leave our dealings with duty-holders as advice, but if they don't take any notice of it, if they just ignore it, then, you know, it may well be different next time.' (97–02)

Thus in the transmission of messages, or the manufacture of appearances, the clearer the statement implied by the prosecution and the more forcefully it can be made, the better. 'Perhaps more than we used to, we do try to generate publicity for cases that come to court. . . . So there certainly is that element. There's a lot of interest—the media take up prosecutions far more than they did years ago' (97–02).

Publicity is often used artfully by inspectors. If they are sufficiently concerned to achieve the wider dissemination of news about a prosecution, they will arrange publicity by sending notes to the local media inviting them to attend the hearing.

In a case in which a worker had had his hand crushed in a milling machine, losing all four fingers of his right hand when a safety bar failed to operate properly, the inspector had prepared a 'draft operational note' which she had sent to the Press Office of HSE in London. This contained the full postal address of the local magistrates' court, and the date and time of the hearing. There was also a two-page press release and a letter from the Rubber NIG circulated to 'Nominated Liaison Inspectors' about 'Publicity for prosecutions', reporting the desire of the editor of *Plastics and Rubber Weekly* to report prosecutions taken in the industry. Someone had hand-written a note to the inspector saying 'Definitely worth a go! (But check release with Press Office first).'[24] (P97–29)

The result of such use of publicity, inspectors believe, is that 'The message gets around. It gets around within industry, and it makes the advice that we give . . . advice with some teeth behind it rather than just pure advice, to be ignored if people want to' (97–02). In doing their best to generate as much publicity as they can in appropriate cases, inspectors will try to align a case with an HSE regulatory initiative to add extra weight to the message. This was evident in a note to an inspector from his PI: 'If handled with the help of the media the case should attract good publicity at the right time—Oct/Nov for the . . . HQ initiative due then!

[24] The firm pleaded guilty to one charge under s. 14 (1) of the Factories Act, 1961, and was fined £4,000, with more than £450 in costs.

Pl [please] discuss publicity—we will contact [the local HSE office]...' (P97–01).

In the case in which the injured person had had her hands trapped in a machine, suffering serious burns and the loss of both her middle fingers, the inspector made sure that the defendant's court appearance was brought to the attention of the local public via the press. The employer was a well-known company, and perhaps because of this HSE issued a press release before the prosecution. A short report of the successful prosecution was also faxed to the local BBC Radio station. In a memo to the AD, copied to the senior PI of the relevant NIG, the inspector reported that 'Local press were "primed" to the case via a press release I organised... the press appreciated this as some of the journalists who covered the story would not have known about it in advance and so would not have attended the court. Overall, a good result with a good level of publicity.' This prompted a reply from the AD: 'Congratulations on such a good result; pursuing what are often difficult cases involving training and supervision and targeting this as a clear priority objective like the food industry. It is pleasing that the Magistrates have understood the seriousness of the circumstances—no doubt due to your clear explanations.'[25] (P97–36)

A sense of vulnerability within the agency to the critical gaze of its various audiences is palpable, for while criticism may occasionally be heard following an act of prosecution, it is much more likely with decisions not to prosecute. 'I am very conscious of the fact', said an AD, 'that we sometimes do have to answer for usually what we haven't done, more than what we have done' (97–02). Publicity about HSE prosecution activities is useful as a means of foreclosing criticism of enforcement inactivity. Prosecution here is a kind of insurance policy—a means of avoiding or mitigating a risk to a regulator in cases where others expect serious enforcement action. Such expectations imply a view of prosecution as the norm, as a response that is routinely assumed. HSE's remit as a public body charged with important legal responsibilities renders it especially vulnerable to criticism about any perceived inaction on its part, and this makes it more difficult for the agency to explain why it has not prosecuted, rather than why it has. 'If you want to give an inspector a difficult job,' said an AD, 'give them the job of justifying why they're not taking action, as opposed to taking action—you can't lose taking action. Again—don't take me wrongly—we do not leap into taking cases. But

[25] The remark about the magistrates is presumably an expression of satisfaction with the level of fine imposed. The firm was convicted of one count under s. 2 (1) of HSW and one under PUWER and fined £11,000 and £3,500, respectively. Costs amounted to almost £1,500.

what I'm saying is, if we go through our criteria, and believe we are justified in taking a case, if we lose, we lose.' (97–05)

8. CONCLUSION

Any prosecution serves as a general statement by a regulatory bureaucracy indicating its presence and power as a law enforcer. 'In analyzing law as symbolic we are oriented less to behavioral consequences as a means to a fixed end,' wrote Gusfield (1970: 65) 'more to meaning as an act, a decision, a gesture important in itself.' And because 'organizations are sensitive to law's cultural components, they will often react to legal mandates through culturally meaningful signals and gestures' (Suchman & Edelman, 1997: 20). As a public act prosecution not only crystallizes and expresses the official response of an enforcement agency to lawbreaking, the act of prosecution also carries with it statements of profound symbolic importance, for it dramatizes notions about right and wrong. The power to prosecute is a power to condemn. Not to prosecute is to risk appearing to condone. Prosecution censures individual acts or omissions, and symbolizes the right response to wrongful behaviour. It declares the moral status of the violator, while endorsing the worth of the victim. In making these powerful statements in the realm of occupational health and safety, prosecution buttresses the moral standing of the regulatory authority and positions it in the broad political environment. At the same time, prosecution is a way of emphasizing and endorsing the authority and legitimacy of inspectors confronted with non-compliant firms: '[I]nspectors exploited the fact that prosecution was a public event which might bring the full weight of the criminal justice system to bear on offenders. The severity of this sanction was arguably heightened by the sparing use of prosecution by these inspectorates' (Hutter, 1997: 222). The practice of prosecution also confers authority on the body pursuing it, so long as the cause of the prosecution is itself regarded as legitimate. Where regulatory officials feel no moral ambivalence about their deserts—the 'bad' cases—there will be a punitive and public response. Prosecution thus displays and underlines various moral values to the public: in enforcing law within a familiar moral framework, regulators are cementing public beliefs, values, and attitudes about lawbreaking, and about what is right and proper. At the same time, the practice of enforcement in its most public form helps shape public perceptions of what health and safety violators and violations are really like (Carson, 1974: 80).

The use of prosecution creates impressions, then, especially that most public and dramatic picture of law being enforced. What this means in practical terms for the decision-making of inspectors is that they frequently address the issue of whether the prosecution of any matter would carry with it the potential for an important message that will serve the agency's broader interests. The need to dramatize a measure—but a carefully controlled measure—of activity becomes the more acute the more there is a lack of substantial moral and political consensus about the agency's mandate. By prosecuting the morally blameworthy, regulators place wrongful behaviour in a framework of values which is familiar and comprehensible to all, even the most zealous advocate of laissez-faire, anti-regulation ideas. What is punishable is not so much rule-breaking per se, as deliberation or negligence in rule-breaking, or uncooperativeness that amounts to a symbolic assault upon the inspector's and the agency's authority and legitimacy (Hawkins, 1984).

Prosecution is a way in which private trouble is transformed into public ordering. The formalities of the law are important here, given how deeply implicated prosecution is in appearances and their management. Prosecution is a way of publicizing and dramatizing the aims of the law, and particularly the undesired consequences of failure to comply with legal requirements. From the standpoint of the organization itself, prosecution is a salient means of presenting the public face of a regulatory bureaucracy. It shows to the public and other interested observers, especially in an era of constrained resources, that the regulatory organization is alive and doing its job. As a public agency, however, HSE is also subject to various constraints imposed by lack of resources, which compel a measure of restraint. What may be determined as appropriate action by the regulatory body may be dictated by organizational priorities. For example, one AD, when discussing a fall in the number of prosecutions in the period from January to April 1996, suggested that the numbers of cases prosecuted may have been somewhat reduced because '[organizational] attention was deflected into internal issues during that period'. That is, an internal reorganization going on within HSE then may have depressed the level of prosecutions.

The symbolic use of prosecution sustains moral cohesion in the social world, and reflects the fact that people are bound together by a common moral vision which dictates an appropriate response to wrongful behaviour. Ambivalence about right and wrong constitutes a symbolic threat.

Prosecution symbolically underlines the authority and legitimacy of regulatory inspectors and their organization when faced with deliberate, blatant, or persistent non-compliance. Selective symbolic action maintains the legitimacy of the regulatory organization while placating its opposition.

Part IV

Frame

8 Enforcers' Theories of Compliance and Punishment

1. ON COMPLIANCE

Earlier chapters have placed the prosecution decision in its surround and fields as a public, regulatory, and organizational mechanism. The scene is now set to explore how decision-makers make sense of features in the particular incidents and states of affairs they encounter in their occupational world, what they define as relevant, and how they reason about them. These are all questions about how they frame acts and events. Framing is a prerequisite to deciding whether they should act, how they should act, and for what purpose. An important frame guiding the decisions of all enforcement officials is theorizing about why people comply with the law (or not). The 'theories' of rule-breaking held by inspectors 'explain' non-compliance and suggest the enforcement strategy to be followed. Working theories of compliance and punishment also dictate what form of enforcement or sanction, if any, are appropriate for non-compliance.

Working theories of compliance and punishment also play a large part in agency policy-making, as well as agency enforcement practices at all levels. If this perspective on enforcement is important as a way of understanding the actual decisions made by a regulatory inspector about particular problems, these beliefs are significant also in the broader policy sense in determining the costs imposed on, and the benefits gained by business, and the corresponding levels of protection offered to those at risk.

Definitions of compliance are variable. The practical objective of inspectors is in general to attain an acceptable level of compliance with regulatory demands (see Hutter, 1997). Compliance exists in the working practices, evaluations, and decisions of enforcement agents. Compliance has a plastic quality, which is evident in variations in its definition that occur over time. Notions of conformity or otherwise can be bent, for example, in light of the general economic context in which judgements about compliance have to be made. The implication of this is that greater tolerance is shown during times of economic recession, where a further burden on an already hard-pressed firm may have consequences for levels of employment. What inspectors think of as compliant or non-compliant behaviour is, in practice, further complicated because they have to work both with employers and with the workforce who are the potential victims of any failure by management to allocate sufficient resources to the attainment of compliance.[1]

The task of a regulatory bureaucracy is to induce a potentially unwilling business organization to bear costs which for commercial reasons it would not wish to assume. It is possible, however, to overstate the economic disincentives to compliance, for business may also have from time to time a strong interest in the advancement of certain forms of social regulation. HSC (1988: 4) makes this point very strongly to business:

> 'The cost to industry of a major accident can run into millions, sometimes hundreds of millions, of pounds in direct and consequential losses. The overall impact—in terms of trauma to survivors and families, and of money and reputation—due to error and lack of precaution, will be sufficient to daunt the largest of companies. And the accumulated cost of smaller incidents represents an enormous inefficiency factor, often not yet measured by industry with anything like the precision it does other controllable sources of commercial loss. Such minor incidents, including disregarded near misses, are symptomatic of inadequate management controls, and a warning of major accidents to come. And for a very small company the cost of injury to a key employee can be greater even than this, for it may mean extinction.'

Whether or not compliance with regulation actually has a pay-off to business, its attainment is nonetheless clearly regarded as costly and time-consuming by many employers. Employers may well have a commercial incentive to resist regulatory enforcement or to seek to minimize its costs, and have an interest in the substance and scope of regulation as those matters are realized in the processes of policy-making and enforcement.

Though it is tempting to regard compliance in undifferentiated terms, the notion is complex and to be regarded as a process, as much as a state or condition. It is often remarked within HSE that health and safety

[1] Veljanovski (1987) found that greater tolerance (less stringency) is shown to struggling firms in times of recession. He discovered that there was less likelihood of action by inspectors following visits in areas where unemployment was high and where industries were experiencing declining levels of employment. This suggests that inspectors are conscious of the costs of compliance in using their discretion and of the implications of regulatory enforcement for levels of employment.

compliance is part of management, and that a well-managed, profitable company is likely to have well-managed and effective health and safety provisions. Some inspectors observed that even here compliance was not an unvarying condition or company response. Compliance is sometimes seen as a characteristic, self-interested response by certain types of industry (large chemicals firms, or new high-technology industries, for example). Sometimes it is regarded as a product of 'the attitude of management' (86–02). Where beliefs about compliance are tied partly to certain management figures, a change in company and workforce behaviour may occur when they move elsewhere. And even in a large company which is regarded as 'compliant', there may still be pockets of non-compliance, especially where certain hazardous practices go on, sanctioned by time, in the absence of a realistic appreciation by the people concerned of the risks involved, until someone is hurt. Regulatory inspectors often find that initial compliance is one thing, continuing compliance quite another. No inspector interviewed suggested that a condition of perfect or pure compliance was to be found anywhere, or even attainable: 'I don't think I've been to anywhere since I joined [HSE] that has complied', said one from a general manufacturing group (86–42), a sentiment echoed even more strongly by others, especially construction inspectors. In practice, the implication of this is that non-compliance is a familiar condition, a natural state of affairs, leading inspectors routinely to expect to find violations during site visits. Yet this idea of pervasive non-compliance coexists with the notion, widely believed by inspectors, that 'The vast majority of employers don't want to injure the health and safety of their employees' (86–11).

The assumption that employers have little incentive to comply with health and safety regulation and are unwilling, as a result, to comply with the requests of inspectors, except perhaps temporarily, is also one which does not reflect the complexity of actual experience. The assumption embodies a limited view of employers' incentives and disincentives to comply, and overlooks the fact that some have a strong economic interest in complying as a means of maintaining the well-being of their employees, quite apart from any moral compulsion to which they feel subject. It assumes in turn that regulated companies respond to the requirements of regulation in similar ways. But a 'good' (or 'bad') company is not necessarily good (or bad) for all purposes, which may well have policy implications for the targeting of inspections, and thereby a company's vulnerability to discovery as a rule-breaker. It is clear from research into employers' responses to regulation that some have a powerful material reason to comply and even to comply not only with the letter but also with the spirit of the law, attaining stricter standards than actually demanded by the law or the inspector. This often arises from a strong sense of risk to the safety of the enterprise should appropriate standards of care not be maintained. Employers also wish to avoid adverse publicity, to keep insurance costs down, to avoid loss of output arising from accidents, and to avoid trouble with trade unions (Genn, 1993). These incentives all operate largely or wholly independently of the law. Equally, inspectors' experience suggests that reasons for non-compliance vary. Some firms calculate the costs and benefits of compliance and non-compliance and opt for the latter as rational economic behaviour ('amoral calculators' in the typology devised by Kagan & Scholz, 1984).

Firms, like regulatory agencies, have policies about compliance. Whether compliance actually occurs as a result, however, depends on the effectiveness of their internal communication and sanctioning systems. Policy decisions by regulated organizations about compliance in principle may be compared with the practice of compliance or non-compliance in the actual workplace. For example, a company may, as a matter of policy, have a public position of 'We comply with the law, come what may'. But individuals within the organization may (for whatever reason) be less than compliant, or the company's system of internal control too weak to operate effectively—failing, for example, to identify or to restrain the worker who defeats a safety device in order to work more quickly, conveniently, or comfortably. Here much depends on the effectiveness of the sanctions and rewards which comprise the organization's own internal control system. One of the essential questions for socio-legal research in this area is to isolate the sorts of compliant behaviour that are specifically produced by the existence or enforcement of legal rules, and to specify under what conditions compliance occurs, in what parts of regulated organizations.

2. ENFORCERS' THEORIES OF COMPLIANCE

The making of regulatory policy is based on a system of beliefs held by officials both about the nature of regulated industry in general, and about specific firms and how they react to legal requirements. In the same way, how regulation is actually enforced is based on beliefs about regulated industries held by inspectors, including their conceptions of the needs of business and its incentives and disincentives to compliance. These beliefs comprise an enforcement frame, a means of making sense of the behaviour of business in response to regulation, and are derived from a number of sources. There are structural characteristics connected with such attributes as the size or wealth of business which are taken as indicators of the capacity of business to comply. Then there are characterizations, taken as indicators of the willingness of business to comply, about the nature of the business, the particular company, or the precise individuals routinely encountered within a company. Finally, there is inspectors' experience of responses by firms to regulatory efforts. Whether or not these are accurate or reliable sources of knowledge, inspectors' enforcement strategies and tactics are premissed upon them.

Factory inspectors were systematically asked why they thought companies complied or failed to comply with health and safety regulation. This topic was introduced into interviews on the assumption that since strategies of law enforcement, and specifically prosecution, are not random processes, they must to an extent be informed by enforcement agents' personal theories of compliance. Whether or not inspectors wish to enforce and to prosecute for instrumental or for expressive motives, they need to know why compliance occurs or fails, just as they must have some expectations as to what the effects of a prosecution in any case are likely to be. Inspectors' responses suggest that compliance cannot be regarded as a unitary concept, but is to be seen as variable and relative. To the extent that it is attained, inspectors believe that compliance is the product of a variety of forces. Their working theories fall into four broad categories, clustering around the central ideas of principled compliance, the legal threat, self-interest, and custom. Note that these inspectors' 'theories' of compliance are not necessarily exclusive but more than one may sometimes be held concurrently for the same firm, according to which regulation or sets of regulations they are thinking about, which parts of the firm, or which sites or individuals are involved. The theories are interesting for a number of reasons, not least that they are not excessively law-centred. That is, they draw attention to sources of compliance that may exist partly or wholly independently of the formal mechanisms of law and regulation.

1. Principled Compliance

First, inspectors believe that some employers comply on principle.[2] This is an expressive, rather than an instrumental, theory. Indeed, the most

[2] A clear majority of the inspectors said companies complied either because it was right to, or out of concern for their employees.

pervasive explanation put forward by inspectors as to why businesses complied was a moral one: 'In general, most companies want to do as much as they're able to do. [Because it's right?] Because it's right, yes' (86–34). 'I think there are very few who don't want to comply; very few,' said an AD. 'Most people . . . either have been trained that they should wish to comply . . . or are just decent, honest citizens who don't set out to harm individuals' (97–05). This behaviour may be regarded as principled compliance.

People often act in response to normative constraints, on the basis of moral dictates, on some conception of what they think is right: 'Even when opportunity, social sanctions, and legal sanctions are controlled for', writes Scholz (1984: 18), 'personal norms have been found consistently to be significant predictors of compliance.' In occupational health and safety regulation this is for one of two reasons. First, people feel they should comply as a matter of moral principle, namely that it is right that you do not threaten your employees' health or safety, in recognition of the moral duty not to subject others to hazard or damage. This idea is present in the comments of a PI, who said, 'I think the vast majority of modern management really do have a conscience' (86–22). This tenet produces a form of compliance occurring independently of the law. The second idea is that it is right to comply because there is a law requiring compliance and it is right to observe the law. People, in other words, comply in recognition of the legitimacy of the law (it is wrong to violate a law which requires you not to hazard the health or safety of your employees, whether or not you agree with that law). Thus inspectors would observe, for instance, that 'most companies want to comply with the law. They care about their employees and they want to abide by the law' (86–28). It is also recognized that individuals are the object of the law: 'People comply with the law. And fundamentally . . . [the law's principles] are generally accepted principles that people would wish to adhere to' (86–41).

Principled compliance was thought to be a strongly held sentiment among many employers. One PI said: 'People [in this country] are inclined to go along with rules and regulations' (86–01). This was not a theory of completely benign behaviour, however. It was recognized that sometimes what regulated business might say in principle and what it actually does in practice differ. It was said, for example, that if a piece of equipment arrived which had to be installed and was lacking guards, some employers would go ahead and install it and operate it in this condition. 'I think that people don't want to injure people. They may not want to pay tax; maybe they want to avoid it. People don't want to injure people, so they start from that point of view. I mean, wanting to, of course, and achieving are totally different things...' (97–05). Yet at the same time it was thought that those who actively do not comply were relatively few but what was more frequently found was a form of apathetic or negligent non-compliance. Presumably one of the most important practical acts of the regulatory inspector is to transform fundamentally good intentions of employers into practice, to produce a conception of business virtue (Haines, 1997).

2. Instrumental Compliance

A second theory is that some employers comply for instrumental reasons. Since a breach of the law may be visited with prosecution and legal punishment, they would wish, according to an economic model of behaviour, to avoid being caught and punished. This theory recognizes necessity (you comply because you have an economic interest in complying), or compulsion and calculation (you comply because there is a law which will penalize you if you do not and you are caught). A substantial number of inspectors believed compliance often occurred as the result of this instrumental response to the legal threat.[3] Here compliance takes place because there is a law which is enforced. Compliance occurring because a law exists which establishes duties or proscribes conduct upon pain of criminal conviction has to be distinguished from compliance in principle. In the latter, compliance is the product of an inner conviction that it is right; in the former it is the result of an external compulsion, dependent upon the extent of the penalty of prosecution and sanction, in conjunction with the subjective calculation of the risk of being caught. On this view, therefore, non-compliance will occur when the costs of compliance are outweighed by the benefits of non-compliance: 'There's a breach of the law and the people who are breaking that law probably have a good idea that they are breaking it, and that by breaking it they are saving themselves a bit of time or a bit of money.' In these circumstances, prosecution 'is a little bit extra to add to the cost of a job' (86–08; a construction PI). Except possibly for small, badly off companies, the deterrent effect of the law is believed, however, to reside more in the act of prosecution itself, rather than in the legal sanction, as one inspector

[3] Slightly more than half suggested the existence of sanctions, fear of prosecution, desire to avoid interference from the inspectorate, or wish to avoid damage to reputation (which would accompany the legal sanction) as reasons for compliance.

explained: companies are 'afraid of prosecution. I don't think they're bothered about the fine' (86–08). What companies also generally wish to avoid, it is thought, is the 'shame of being dragged into court' (86–08). Or, as another PI put it, 'We are a law-abiding nation, so people don't want to get their name in court' (86–11).

Avoidance of the costs of occupational accidents and ill health brings insurance into play, and this social institution may well assist compliance with legal requirements. Being subjected to formal legal action, whether by notice or prosecution, has to be reported to insurers, and inspectors sometimes draw employers' attention to the possibility that a civil action will force insurers to bear the cost of a possibly substantial damages claim, which will in turn work through into increased premiums. Pointing to the implications of insurance is another means by which inspectors can concentrate the corporate mind on the benefits of compliance:

'I think the attitude of insurers has changed, possibly more on the health side than on the safety side. You know, ultimately, insurers want to know what risk they're exposing themselves to, and I think on the safety side, you know, there's 150 years of experience of how often boilers explode, or cranes fail, or whatever, and, to an extent, and provided they get the right premium income in, they're not unduly worried about the nature of the risk. (In general terms, that may be being a little unfair.) When it comes to health issues, I think they do get seriously worried, because they could be walking into a long-term situation involving a lot of people, which it's very difficult for them to quantify; and I've noticed a shift in attitude of insurance companies much more towards prevention as part of their role than just simply, you know, maximizing their premium income. And so in relation to things like industrial deafness, or exposure to solvents, or whatever, insurance companies do tend to be more proactive. And they haven't as yet very often got to the stage of refusing to insure, or levying astronomical premiums, but certainly they will offer very attractive risk management services to companies, as an adjunct to their insurance business—often, you know, selling them, but nevertheless, doing so in a competitive way, so that there can be mutual benefit. [It] reduces the risk from the insurers' point of view, and reduces the premium from the insured point of view. And certainly in a number of areas, we work quite closely with insurers to make sure that we're promoting similar messages.' (97–04)

3. Self-Interest

A related idea held by inspectors is that certain types of companies comply as a matter of self-interest. This happens when it is necessary for employers to exercise special care to preserve their business from harm to itself or its employees, and looking after its employees' health and safety is an integral part of this. Occasionally, it was suggested, certain large companies (in the food industry, for example) are able to persuade other firms of the importance of complying, the incentive being the need for them to maintain commercial relationships. Self-interest was most commonly claimed to be an incentive for compliance in the chemicals industry. The remote risk of a drastic accident which could destroy a capital investment of enormous value encourages a view among regulators and regulated of the interests of production and safety as complementary. There is thought to be widespread ignorance among employers of the costs of ill health and accidents. In research it conducted into the actual costs of accidents to firms, HSE reported:

> 'all the firms engaged in the study were surprised at the extent of these costs, most of which were uninsured, did not appear in balance sheets, and represented a gross drag on their performance and profits. Much progress has also been made during the year in ascertaining and publicising the true (and considerable) extent of industrial ill health. . . . [T]he majority of employers attach more importance than they are often given Credit [*sic*] for to the human side of safety precaution; it may be right now to give as much attention to the financial side.' (Health and Safety Commission, 1993, p. xiv)

This idea frequently appears in HSE's prosecution files, which sometimes contain copies of printed figures indicating the costs of accidents to employers, suggesting that compliance might well be cheaper than continued non-compliance for the great majority. Inspectors often indicate incentives to compliance in correspondence with businesses with observations such as: 'Such accidents can result in high costs to your business e.g. from long periods of sickness absence, employment of temporary staff and civil claims for compensation' (P97–39). Calculation of the costs of occupational ill health and accidents covers a wide range of matters: material and product damage; plant, building, and equipment damage; legal costs, fines, and prosecution costs; expenditure on emergency supplies; the costs of production delays, overtime working, and temporary labour; investigation time; clerical effort; and the loss of experience and expertise in sick or injured employees. Internal company memoranda and reports on health and safety matters are routinely included in such cases. In one, an HSE document was quoted:

'where the paper suggested . . . that the costs of accidents can be as high as:—

* 37% of profit
* 5% of operating costs
* 36 times the insured costs

[This] must surely underline the view that we cannot afford not to invest in a positive safety culture, which does not depend solely on the provision of finance, more often it relies on the commitment of those within the organisation.' (P97–36)

Firms are sometimes given other incentives: 'Some of them have actually realized . . . that improving general safety at work does have other advantages. You can increase your efficiency productionwise and [in] other ways and generally make people happier' (86–40). Furthermore,

'The . . . reasons some firms have a better compliance rate than others, is not that they are "nice". It's that under some structural conditions, there are many factors other than regulatory fines that might impel a firm, for good profit-maximizing reasons, to comply—either initially, or to respond cooperatively when the inspector comes. The firm might be subject to expensive lawsuits for hazards that are also violations, or to costly accidents that would destroy their assets and their ability to sell their products and services. It is not primarily regulation that makes most established airlines service [their] planes, or factories maintain boilers and remove fire hazards, or an architect and contractor follow sound building practices that will keep the building from falling down, or an auto manufacturer install brakes that don't fail.'[4]

It should also be borne in mind that self-interest may not only drive business to violate legal regulations, but in some circumstances (when, for example, a plant is a major hazard) it can compel not only compliance, but a level of compliant behaviour in excess of the strict requirements of the regulations (Genn, 1993).

4. Custom

Custom is a final source of compliance. Employers, inspectors believe, sometimes comply because health and safety legislation is well established and familiar, and compliance is now regarded as the normal response to a series of well-known demands in the law. Compliance with legal requirements takes place simply because the law is there and is known, and is not therefore regarded as some sort of authoritarian upstart imposing new and unexpected demands upon employers: 'In this

[4] Robert A. Kagan, letter to the author, 2 Mar. 1990.

country, because we've had health and safety legislation since 1833... we've grown up with it. It's part and parcel of our lives, our running of business. It's not something new. So in the main, the larger companies take that on board' (86–10).

3. ENFORCERS' THEORIES OF NON-COMPLIANCE

Inspectors also hold a corresponding set of working theories about why employers do not comply. The emphasis given to principled compliance as a major source of conformity with the law suggests that compliance is seen substantially in moral and personal terms. There is, however, no precise symmetry in inspectors' theories about why companies fail to comply. Non-compliance tends to be regarded more in instrumental and organizational terms, as a consequence of lack of resources or a desire to avoid compliance costs, as a lack of organizational control, or a lack of knowledge and information (which themselves are closely connected with inadequate resources).

Since inspectors do not share a common theory of corporate compliance or non-compliance and most do not hold a unitary theory of compliance, but see different reasons for compliance or non-compliance for different types of firm in different circumstances, it follows that prosecution decision-making reflects these shifting views. Some indication of the coexistence of efforts at compliant behaviour with non-compliance appears in a memo from an inspector to his PI complaining about the shortcomings at a particular site:

> 'Despite attempts [by the company's safety officer] to change attitudes, ensure risk assessments were completed, he either didn't have time to deal with all the issues or if he did they were "swept aside" by the site management. The health and safety advisers at all levels can be criticized for the lack of effective actions... HSE I feel could also have monitored the site more closely and given the level of accidents occurring we should have shaken them up many years ago.' (P97–36)

Because regulation is articulated by means of legal rules, there is a tendency for enforcement agents to maintain a primary focus on compliance with rules, not on the impact of regulatory activity on the prevalence of undesired events or hazards. Explanations for non-compliance vary according to different types of industry groups. Employers are heterogeneous, with different levels of knowledge and access to information about their obligations under the law, different degrees of wealth and technical capacity to comply, and different kinds and levels of incentive to comply. This makes generalization hazardous, though inspectors engage in typification to make their decision-making more orderly. Among the construction inspectors, economic rationality is a dominant model of behaviour and the construction industry is also subject to comparatively simple, well-established regulations, such that inspectors presume that people 'must have known' they were violating the law. On the other hand, in general manufacturing, explanations may centre upon a general malaise or a simple failure of hardware as reasons for non-compliance. Different theories may well dictate different responses. And where a legal response is settled upon, it may demand different charges for different problems (for example, HSW Act s. 2 is thought more suited to a general malaise in a company). This again suggests the need for caution in seizing on a unitary explanation for regulatory rule-breaking.

1. Self-Interested Calculation

The self-interested calculator is the business that is motivated entirely by profit, a concept which equates with the 'amoral calculator' of Kagan and Scholz (1984). Such firms 'carefully and competently assess opportunities and risks', disobeying the law when the yields from non-compliance are higher. 'Non-compliance stems from economic calculation' (Kagan & Scholz, 1984: 67). In the model of Kagan and Scholz (1984), 'good' firms are described as 'political citizens',[5] while 'bad' firms are either 'organizationally incompetent' or 'amoral calculators'.[6] Some firms violate the law in a purposive or 'malicious' way, that is to say, they are regarded by inspectors as calculating the odds and deliberately choosing not to comply. This is the counterpart to instrumental compliance, but the theory explains that some employers choose to violate the law instrumentally because they wish to avoid the costs of compliance involved. The motivation to avoid compliance does not simply arise from lack of money. Sometimes firms 'just don't want to spend it, even though

[5] Who are, to quote Bardach & Kagan (1982: 64), 'guided by some conception of long-term self-interest. They are concerned about their reputations in the market-place, maintaining smooth labor relations, preventing lawsuits, and avoiding the stigma of being labelled a socially irresponsible lawbreaker. They would not necessarily act in a socially responsible manner if there were *no* realistic threat of regulatory enforcement . . .'. [Emphasis in original.]

[6] Kagan & Scholz (1984: 68) say that the three folk 'theories' of why violations occur 'are not mutually exclusive', that the same firm can act like either an amoral calculator, a rebel, or a blunderer vis-à-vis different regulations.

they have got it, and that is . . . significant,' as a former Deputy Director General of HSE put it. These firms

'contain people who understand there is a social need for control . . . but there are other priorities. . . . A lot of safety, of course, doesn't cost any money, it costs management effort and management time. Now that costs money indirectly, but it also costs managerial competence, it costs managerial imagination, it costs managerial effort. So they don't do it, because there are other things that they want to do with their time and effort.'

Inspectors believe them to be highly competitive and concentrated in particular industries, though not numerous. 'You meet very few people who deliberately couldn't care a damn, who aren't particularly concerned whether they injure their employees or cause long term health effects' (86–34). Non-compliance as a consequence of the failure of the legal threat is thought to occur most frequently in the building trade, where economic pressures act in a particularly direct fashion to produce extreme competitiveness among employers and where the widespread practice of subcontracting blurs lines of communication and responsibility, posing particular problems of control.[7] Some construction firms are believed to calculate the costs of compliance quite purposively and, where appropriate, to opt for non-compliance. In general, however, most HSE staff believe that non-compliance as a result of self-interested calculation is not widespread.

The idea of the calculating non-compliant firm is prominent in the academic literature and is widely accepted as an explanation for corporate misconduct ((Pearce & Tombs, 1990; Staw & Szwajkowski, 1975; Vaughan, 1983). What is needed, however, is a better understanding of the conditions under which firms choose not to comply. It is frequently assumed that industrial organizations are rational actors, yet little is known about the dynamics of decision-making within business organizations in relation to compliance with legal requirements, and whether (or to what extent) illegality is a result of rational calculation. It may well be that decision-making about compliance within firms is much more variable in relation to the conditions under which it occurs, or in relation to the legal demands involved. How much and what kinds of regulatory rule-breaking by business can be explained by reference to calculation? Is calculation good as an explanation across all forms of business organization, in all degrees of complexity and function, in all circumstances?

[7] All 11 specialist construction inspectors interviewed cited economic pressures as a cause of non-compliance.

The model of organizational actor as continuously rational is threatened by examples where people apparently do not calculate. Grabosky (1989), in research on illegality in the public sector, found evidence of careful assessment and weighing of risks and benefits by organizational actors in possibly two only of 17 cases.

The extent to which business calculates is an empirical question, and not something that we can know a priori. It is tempting to assume that businesses are unitary organizations whose behaviour is centrally determined as a result of calculation based on their shorter- or longer-term self-interest, and that the policies derived from such calculation are then transmissible down through the organization to guide the practices of its members. As a result, this makes it difficult to see that violations arising from mismanagement, inexperience, and ignorance are explicable in terms of calculation, though it is clear that 'even better organised companies will continue to be prone to error, omission and violation' (Pearce & Tombs, 1990: 35). Furthermore, 'good' firms do not always comply as a matter of principle, according to Bardach and Kagan (1982: 64); they are also concerned about costs and are not always willing to subordinate short-run cost considerations. Sometimes, therefore, they too may calculatedly violate the law.

2. Mismanagement

Inspectors sometimes encounter firms which are poorly organized and badly managed, or simply apathetic about the need for health and safety measures. 'There are some which are just incompetent,' said a former Deputy Director General. 'You know, you wonder how they actually make a profit. They just couldn't run, they're just disorganized.'[8] That such employers exist was recognized some years ago by HSE (1978*b*: 12): 'A code of regulations provides a system of safe work, but whatever emphasis is put on "self-regulation" there will always be employers who are so stubborn, so literal-minded, so unimaginative and so ill-organised that they will only act if specific requirements are enforced

[8] To work successfully, self-regulation, which is central to much occupational health and safety regulatory control, depends heavily on the competence of employers, as well as on their motivation. There is evidence, for example, which calls into question the willingness and ability of employers to conduct assessments required under the lead regulations about the nature and degree of their employees' exposure to lead. Smaller companies lack competent personnel and rely on inspectors to conduct assessments, a matter which is expensive in terms of the use of regulatory resources (R. Baldwin, 1987: 18–19).

upon them. For them the only answers are the well-filled notebook and the prohibition notice.' Non-compliance here occurs because employers lack the resources to enable them to do so, or because they lack a sufficient degree of organizational control to attain or maintain compliance.[9] Sometimes they lack the necessary knowledge, a particular problem where rules have been recently introduced. Non-compliance arising as a result of ignorance is usually dealt with in routine cases by information, education, and negotiation to achieve appropriate remedial measures. Ignorance tends, however, to be a condition found more frequently among small companies. This is because

'They don't have somebody who can sit all day scanning through health and safety magazines, that is aware that maybe a control limit for a substance has been halved. They haven't got the resources to be as aware of what's going on in the health and safety field as some of the larger companies.' The latter possess 'ways and means of finding out what their duties are and complying with them . . . They are able to do it, and they should do it.' (86–40)

3. Culture

A third theory is cultural in character, and suggests that some employers simply do not recognize the necessity or legitimacy of compliance with regulation:

'There's the sort of black economy. When I was a lad, it was always the railway arches, and it's still, to some extent, the "railway arch" culture. . . . I think we come across people now who want to work in that sort of environment and don't want to follow the law—in any circumstance. I mean, they just want to work in scruffy places and just [have] nothing to do with anything and just have money in their back pocket.' (97–05)

It is also believed that some firms fail to comply because they are wilfully neglectful or ignorant in not acting to conform. The problem is not simply a disdain for occupational health and safety regulation, but a rejection of legal authority in general. As a former Deputy Director General of HSE put it: 'There are . . . firms which simply reject the authority or legitimacy of the inspectorate . . . people who say "What the hell are you doing here?"' There is, he continued,

[9] These firms resemble Kagan and Scholz's (1984: 68) conception of the 'organizational incompetent', a business in which managers fail to manage properly, 'to calculate risks intelligently, to establish organizational mechanisms that keep all operatives abreast of and attentive to the growing dictates of the law'.

'a wide spectrum of people who don't comply with anything. You know, the wide-boy-back-street-end-of-the-trade. Not all back street employers are like that, but [some] don't have a road fund licence, they don't pay the rates as long as possible.... One is simply an irrelevance.... [T]raditional paternalistic companies [are] at the other extreme.... [They] do operate from [a] certain ethical [position] which does inform the style of the company.... The majority of places obviously fall between the two and I think they don't actually want to be bothered with health and safety.... [T]hey can see it's a potential source of cost, irritation, conflict.... [B]asically... they don't want to spend more than absolutely necessary, but they have a good idea that if they don't do... certain things like guard certain machines, at least see that certain chemical processes are properly done, the first inspector walking through the door is going to make a hell of a row.'

This theory incorporates a notion of non-compliance as a deliberate, symbolic rejection of regulation, and of the legitimacy of the agencies charged with its enforcement. The inspector is 'just somebody else coming along who's telling them how to run some aspect of their business', said a former Director General. 'There's a bit of a flexible attitude to law enforcement.' This sentiment is believed to be typical of a number of disreputable employers, particularly some in the construction industry. But in the experience of many inspectors there is little evidence that it is widespread; indeed, those employers who did not actively comply were said to be 'few and far between' (86–14).

4. THE SOCIAL CONSTRUCTION OF BUSINESS CHARACTER

To understand what 'explains' the compliance or non-compliance of any regulated business, enforcers try to extend their knowledge in various ways, or to make the knowledge they possess more manageable. They do this by using an amalgam of factual knowledge about a firm (its size, its wealth, and so on) and knowledge and beliefs derived from their own or their colleagues' experiences in dealing with a firm and its employees. Organizations are characterizable for inspectors by features such as their size, their patterns of behaviour, their responses to enforcement efforts, and the acts, omissions, and personal characters of those individuals representing the firm with whom they have to deal. An organization's reputation may derive not only from inspectors' dealings with a particular firm but from more widespread stereotypes associated with types of business or industry. These pieces of information are integrated into the social construction of business character, a form of knowledge which helps 'explain' why firms behave in the way that they do.[10]

For such 'explanation' to be possible demands a form of ordering. This is especially the case with business organizations, since they are not simple entities, but may be quite complex. The complexity of regulated organizations poses real problems of enforcement for the regulatory inspector. Multiple values, aims, and goals may reside at different points in the business organization; different pressures and constraints may act on different parts of the organization and on actors in different organizational positions. Some senior members of a firm may be 'principled compliers', but the existence of good formal organizational policies, rules, and procedures is not in itself sufficient for inspectors, who are more concerned with how effectively they are likely to be enforced in practice. Problems may be caused on the shop floor, where organizational control may be attenuated, especially if employees have incentives which lead them to cut corners and defeat safety mechanisms to meet production targets. And even though a firm's ostensible policy may be to comply with the requirements of the law or a regulatory agency, it must rely on individuals within the enterprise not only to act in compliant fashion themselves, but also to ensure the compliance of others. Many individuals within a firm may not, however, share its general policy on regulatory requirements. The more complex the organization, the more an inspector must rely upon the firm's internal control system as a means of securing compliance. The internal sanctioning system is often regarded as a more important vehicle of change than the legal penalty: 'I mean, if you take a big Multinational, you can get £20,000—but really, they're not really worried about the £20,000—the individual manager doesn't like having to explain to his director, and that director doesn't like explaining to the main board etc. etc. that it was their bit of the organization that was found with their pants down....' (97–05)

In short, it is perfectly possible for a firm to have a policy which supports compliance with regulation in principle, yet a workforce that is to some degree ignorant of its obligations or unwilling to recognize them, or a firm in which an apparently good response at the policy level is offset by weak organizational control, owing to poor internal communication or sanctioning systems. 'You know, these [policy statements] are

[10] Thus an inspector's knowledge of a firm is an important factor in deciding whether or not to investigate an accident: certain employers were usually thought of as 'good' on safety (Hutter, 1997: 17; Lloyd-Bostock, 1987).

often written from the point of view of everything working perfectly, the whole workforce always being present and available for work, and able to function perfectly, and the real world isn't like that' (97–02). As a result it is not always clear to inspectors what a firm's 'response' is, or even whether the firm is one to be regarded as fundamentally compliant, or an object of some suspicion. Some non-compliant individuals may not even be employees of the firm concerned, thereby making control over their activities more difficult. For this reason extensive subcontracting in the construction industry in Britain poses major enforcement problems for inspectors.

Decision-making about occupational health and safety compliance and other forms of regulation varies substantially within an organization according to the actor's place in the organizational hierarchy. The tasks and responsibilities in a firm of those at director or manager level are very different from those at supervisory or shop-floor levels. For instance, directors and managers make policy decisions about the degree to which the firm will comply with regulatory requirements, and provide the necessary resources. They also decide on the nature and extent of any non-compliance. The workforce, on the other hand, can also decide whether and to what extent to comply with the demands of management or enforcement officials.

Regulatory officials attribute to the organizations they deal with a complicated set of characteristics. They treat them as essentially unitary, and possessing a corporate identity and character, but they also view them as comprising a collection of diverse individuals. It is not only the reputation and cooperativeness of the company that is relevant to regulatory officials, but also their experience of subsidiary sites, particular individuals, or sets of individuals, within that organization and their experience of salient acts, events, accidents, and incidents. Inspectors also differentiate between large, multinational companies and their constituent work sites. The former are regarded as wealthy, possessing not only the financial but also the technical means to comply with regulation. This may not be true of the latter, which may well be regarded as unreceptive or even obstructive to enforcement in contrast with the parent company.

Inspectors adapt their enforcement decision-making in the light of responses they receive from particular firms. Small firms' responses to regulation differ from those of larger firms, where more frequent visits allow stable relationships to grow up between regulator and regulated.

Where a site is large, complex, risky, or otherwise likely to yield large numbers of potential sources of violation, inspections may be relatively frequent. Under these conditions the firm itself becomes familiar with regulatory expectations and responses. Where sites are small and simple, however, visits from inspectors are rare (sometimes occurring once every several years) and the firm's behaviour reflects the unfamiliarity of the 'one-shotter', rather than the 'repeat player' (Galanter, 1974): they are largely uninformed about the law and ignorant of the activities and expectations of the regulatory agency. Nonetheless, inspectors are able to build up a series of composite pictures of small firms from their various experiences in dealing with them which are continually drawn upon in enforcement decision-making.

The emergence and use of characterizations is a pervasive feature of decision-making behaviour in general. There is a common practice among inspectors to use simple imagery as a basis on which to exercise discretion. Their enforcement moves are based on an amalgam of particular knowledge and experience set against a more general perspective of the reputation of particular industries and occupations, all within a view of the politics and economics in the surround. Assumptions and various forms of imagery about the regulated order inspectors' decision-making. Their approach to prosecution work is premissed on a fundamental view of company behaviour, expressed in terms of 'No one likes being taken to court' (86–41). They tend to think of firms as 'good' or 'bad', 'prosperous' or 'struggling', and so on. Note that these are evaluative categories, not descriptions. Inspectors may find that a crude category may suffice for practical enforcement purposes ('good' or 'bad', 'cooperative' or 'cowboy'), but this simple dichotomy often conceals a more complex reality.

Inspectors' characterizations speak to the moral qualities attributable to an employer. The implications of such characterizations for enforcement behaviour can be enormous. These images and the categorization processes with which they are associated are very important because they serve to create different expectations in an inspector's mind about not only the willingness but also the capacity of a firm to comply, which leads in turn to the application of different standards of enforcement in practice. Large or wealthy firms are often said to be held to stricter standards of compliance on the grounds that they have more resources to enable them to comply and consequently there is less reason for their failing to comply. A simple categorization of employers as 'good' or 'bad' is frequently derived from the ways in which they have responded to enforcement, as judged by their general levels of compliance and their apparent cooperativeness. A violation located in a firm framed as 'bad' sets up expectations in the inspector's mind that it has been brought about deliberately or negligently. If a victim has also suffered harm, the inspector will be much more inclined to adopt a sanctioning rather than a compliance strategy of enforcement, possibly even contemplating prosecution. This is not to suggest that 'good' firms do not in fact have problems complying with occupational health and safety regulations. They do. However, a violation on the premises of a 'good' company is more likely to be framed as an 'accident' or an 'oversight', and may not even be thought of as a 'violation'. It follows (and the data in Chapter 11 also suggest this) that untoward events such as accidents may be regarded by inspectors differently, as more understandable or more excusable, when they occur in 'good' firms as opposed to 'bad' firms. They end up being treated correspondingly differently. The use of such terms leads to the adoption of particular decision frames, which in turn tend to prompt routine action. The crux of the matter is that seemingly 'accidental' behaviour is less likely to be prosecuted.

The following are among the most prominent sources of characterization.

1. Size

The distinction between large and small companies was one regularly observed by inspectors when discussing compliance. Size is important as a surrogate indicator for a number of other attributes held to be connected with an employer's willingness or ability to comply. In the case of small businesses especially, individual and organizational identities will be inextricably intertwined. The 'small' firm is assumed to lack resources and capacity to comply:

> 'A very small company is in it for money. Very few people know they're there . . . So they don't have a public conscience, particularly. They're there for the money. And it's in the smaller companies where there's perhaps a tendency to cut corners, perhaps even knowingly cut corners, simply because the money's very tight . . . The large companies are much more image conscious.' (86–55)

'Small' firms are regarded as more likely to have incompetent managers, to be more sensitive to the costs of compliance, and less able to buy health and safety expertise.[11] Many may not know of their precise legal obligations, a reflection of the infrequency of inspectors' visits, the length and complexity of much of the information disseminated by the organization, and the pressures under which many people work. 'Ignorance of the law is no defence,' said one inspector, 'but in practice, in the reality of the situation as I see it, these people often don't know where to go for advice, don't know what they should be doing, and of course have the much more immediate short term pressure of paying off the bank manager's loan, or getting orders.' While a good public image is regarded by a large firm as of enormous value, it is thought that there is less intrinsic value for the small firm in creating and preserving a good image. Small firms are also more likely to involve a population of strangers, so far as inspectors are concerned, or a group of transients (as in the construction industry) leading to a tendency to label disreputably ('cowboys'). The firms regarded as 'bad' are frequently small and struggling. They are sometimes ephemeral, appearing on the industrial landscape for a time but then disappearing. They are often viewed as having little or no interest in safety matters (Lloyd-Bostock, 1987: 17).

The description of a firm as 'large' was often taken to be virtually synonymous with 'prosperous', with implications for a company's ability and willingness to comply. In general, inspectors believe that big employers know the ropes, often have a competent safety officer, have the means to conform, and as a result are treated as more compliant, with possibly significant consequences for the way in which subsequent decisions are made about enforcement.[12] With large firms, securing compliance seems to be regarded as a relatively straightforward matter: '. . . where you're dealing with big, wealthy, responsible employers, you can get a lot done simply [by requesting changes]' (86–63). Large companies are also seen as less likely to be the victim of the incompetent management which

[11] Most industrial activity takes place in small and medium-sized places of work, whose number and dispersed character occupy a substantial amount of regulatory resources (for example, 58 per cent of factory inspectorate visits in 1988/9 were to premises with fewer than 25 employees (Health and Safety Commission, 1990*a*: 4) thereby posing the problem of what enforcement strategy to employ, especially given resource constraints. Most construction firms are small enterprises, and construction is one of the most hazardous of industries.

[12] The stereotype of the large, prosperous, and essentially compliant company was challenged only very occasionally: 'There are some multinationals whose philosophy is to make as much money as we can and to put little back,' said one inspector. '. . . I don't think they are particularly interested in health and safety.' These were not, however, widely expressed ideas.

afflicts small firms. 'In the good companies, the well-run companies, where they're financially profitable, you can see that in the main they manage health and safety quite well. They've got good management that can run the total package... In the poorer companies, the ones that aren't so financially viable, they tend to struggle when it comes to health and safety' (86–10).

One important implication of the working distinction drawn by inspectors between large and small, rich and poor, is that different expectations as to a firm's economic capacity to comply often lead to different standards being required. There seems to be a greater stringency in the demands placed upon the wealthier firms: 'One looks for better standards from bigger companies' (86–37). In striking contrast to the assertions of some academic commentators that powerful and wealthy companies enjoy a degree of immunity from the application of regulatory controls (e.g. Pearce & Tombs, 1990; Shover *et al.*, 1984; Snider, 1987), it would seem on the basis of this evidence that the contrary is more usual. An AD explained the rationale:

> 'We expect higher standards of those who ought to be well able to comply, and certainly we're not wholly consistent in the application of the law as a whole... If you've got a struggling company, you don't expect them to achieve the same level of performance and provision of benefit for their employees as you would expect [from] a rich company... And you might end up prosecuting the rich company for an activity which somehow is out of the reach of the small one anyway.' (86–19)

Inspectors reported in general on their greater willingness to be more tolerant in their prosecution decision-making where struggling firms were concerned, particularly where less serious matters were at stake, though 'If it's a safety issue and it's important, then they will have to comply' (86–63).[13] The following comment was typical: 'There are many marginal areas—cleanliness of welfare facilities, maybe—where you're going to give the smaller firm or the struggling firm more time to do it than the firm who are obviously prosperous' (86–11). Inspectors were in general clearer than more senior staff in HSE that less prosperous firms may be less stringently regulated. The note of hesitancy, even of indecision, is clear in the following remarks by an AD, when asked 'Do you go easier on struggling firms?'

[13] Only a small minority said they would not be more tolerant. A more substantial minority noted that they would behave in the normal way in clear-cut prosecution cases, but would be more tolerant in marginal cases.

'Financially struggling? [Long pause] I would think, as an overall statement, when decisions are taken—whether it's a prosecution or not—we have to take into account the circumstances, and, you know, what efforts people have made in the circumstances... But no, whether it's an individual or a company, if their behaviour has clearly been of a nature that we expect prosecution would be taken, then we prosecute, and it's up to the courts to decide about the penalty.... It's our job to bring it all to court.' (97–02)

Such an approach is supported both by an expressive rationale (it is unfair to punish the firm which may have fewer resources to permit it to comply) and an instrumental one (if a firm is struggling, prosecution will achieve little, if anything). Indeed, if the impact of prosecution is thought by the inspector concerned to be slight, that in itself may encourage a choice of a different enforcement move: 'If I thought it would have a marginal effect on the company, and I was achieving things there, I would exercise considerable caution in terms of prosecution' (86–01).

This variation in expectations of and treatment of firms according to their capacity to comply may be regarded as a form of principled inconsistency. Its implications may be far-reaching in view of the fact that the prosperity of companies and the location of industries are not distributed evenly over the country as a whole. Where there is less prosperity, there may also be other features which help confirm the patterns of compliance and enforcement. An inspector who had had experience in both the north and south of England referred to the different kinds of industry found in these areas. In the 1980s there were 'lower levels of employment up North and therefore people are not willing to vote with their feet because they know they've not got another job, and employers know they can get away with more' (86–42).

2. Type of Business

Closely related to characterizations about the size of firms is another set of views connected with type of business behaviour. Typifications of business also contribute to the embellishment of characterizations about whether a firm is 'good' or 'bad'. Some industries may be highly dependent upon safe systems of work for the very survival of their plants. The chemical and oil industries are prime examples here, because if a great deal of attention is not paid to the hazards involved in such undertakings, the consequences could conceivably lead to the destruction of the installation.[14] This is the sort of feature which encourages inspectors to adopt a benign decision frame organized around a conception of high standards and willing compliance. There are other occupations, however, about which there hangs an aura of disreputability, inviting the suspicion of inspectors. Prominent among them are some construction or demolition companies (Cranston, 1979: 34; Hutter, 1988: 64). For instance, a specialist inspector in one case noted that '*The accident is typical of those that occur on a demolition site* because of the lack of attention, by a demolition contractor, to the basics of implementing a safe system of work, that is structured, coordinated and managed correctly' (P97–59; my emphasis). Some types of industry, such as farming or construction work, are regarded as having a greater degree of antipathy towards legal regulation of their activities, partly because the costs of compliance are proportionately greater. The second-hand car and scrap metal businesses are also regarded with suspicion (indeed, their disreputable characterizations are shared more widely). Transience in an employer (as in the construction industry) may well affect the social construction of intention, since it is assumed that employees in the building trade will be 'here today and gone tomorrow', and as a result more likely to comply reluctantly, if at all. Small and transient businesses, such as small building firms, are usually held in low esteem and frequently referred to pejoratively as 'cowboy' firms or 'fly-by-night' operators.

3. History

The history of past enforcement efforts and business responses, as it resides in the regulatory bureaucracy's institutional memory or an officer's personal experience, also says something about the kind of firm being dealt with. The agency's experience of the business, and in particular the degree of readiness that has been displayed in complying with previous requests, together with its accident or incident record provide further evidence about the type of firm the inspector is dealing with. Regulatory organizations have memories of their own which can provide continuity in enforcement work where individual inspectors may be more transient. Knowledge lodges in the organizational memory about the kinds of employers, the kinds of problems dealt with. The past can provide an especially powerful way of understanding present behaviour.

[14] The disaster at Flixborough in the 1970s, in which a chemicals plant was destroyed in a huge explosion killing several people, remains firmly etched in the collective consciousness of HSE.

4. Business Contact

Whatever the size of the organizations they encounter, inspectors will only normally come into contact with certain designated individuals representing the enterprise in matters of occupational health and safety regulation. The perceived attitudes and actions of these contacts will become highly significant in determining enforcement moves. How an inspector assesses the character of individuals and especially those with whom they liaise directly is a further ingredient in assembling a picture of the moral character of the firm. In the inspectors' process of characterization, their contacts within a firm come to stand as representatives of the organization of which they are a part, helping to endow it with various human characteristics. In forming opinions about individuals, inspectors take a number of matters into consideration, in addition to any existing knowledge of them and their past. The contact person is judged in the context of the total organization and, more importantly, the organization is judged in the context of the individual. If an individual represents a type of enterprise which is generally poorly regarded by the regulatory agency, officials will not have high expectations of that organization's representative. Similarly, inspectors are more likely to start out with a benign frame of the firm and its employees if they deal with a contact with whom they have good relations.

5. ENFORCERS' THEORIES OF PUNISHMENT

Decision-making about prosecution may focus upon sanctioning an existing violation, in which case it will tend to be reactive, moral, and punitive, or it may centre upon correcting a condition or hazardous state of affairs, in which case its deployment will tend to be more instrumental, proactive, and remedial in character. Even here, a conception of blame will probably be a precipitating factor in such an approach, since in lay theorizing somebody is likely to be held responsible for allowing the existence of the hazardous condition in the first place. Factory inspectors, PIs, and ADs were asked systematically about their views on the purposes of prosecution. Almost all respondents discussed its purposes in terms recognizable as a conventional penal philosophy. Most, however, did not adhere to a single theory of criminal justice and punishment, but would volunteer a number of ideas. This is not surprising. Few people seem to hold exclusively to a simple theory of punishment. Furthermore, since most inspectors do not maintain a single view of the causes of non-compliance, it is to be expected that their penal theories would correspondingly contain a mixture of elements. There does seem to be one penal theory held in common, however, which underpins any others. Few inspectors actually used the word 'retribution' in discussing the matter, though a substantial minority did say the purpose of prosecution was to punish the lawbreaker.

Their responses suggest clearly that whatever else it may be intended to achieve, prosecution is regarded by inspectors as punitive action. Most responses to questions on the topic were couched in the moral language of blame and desert, suggesting a retributive, not an instrumental, purpose in prosecution. Many officials are not given to introspection on these matters, as is evident from the halting quality in the remarks of an AD on prosecution as retributive punishment:

> 'I think... undoubtedly that is a reason for prosecuting, and one that I would endorse, you know—I—moral justification—yes. But I suppose that probably the strongest prosecutions are where all three elements of punishment apply. You know, you have justifiable retribution, plus a deterrent effect, both on the individual company and the wider world, and hope that you've reformed the company as well, or reformed others' behaviour. So yes, I would say that the ideal prosecution would have all those three elements clearly evident.' (97–02)

The comments of a general manufacturing PI indicate a certain antipathy to an instrumental conception: 'If someone's stepped over the line... [prosecution is appropriate] even though it may not do any good in the sense of achieving change' (86–54). Of the three inspectorates examined in Hutter's (1997: 221) research in the mid-1980s, the Factory Inspectorate was most likely to mention retribution as the purpose of legal action: 'A much-quoted phrase about prosecution was "a punishment of wrongdoing".'

Inspectors were asked in Phase I of the research whether they had ever prosecuted a company that they thought was blameless. Almost all of them said quite simply that they had not done so (two said they had done so 'very rarely'). As a construction PI put it, 'I wouldn't go to court if I thought they were blameless' (86–59). Inspectors acknowledged, almost without exception, that one important reason they prosecuted was because it was a deserved response to the breaking of a rule or a bad act.[15] 'If there was a breach which I thought was serious, other things being equal,' said a construction group inspector, 'I would have a go. For pure punishment purposes' (86–63). It would seem, therefore, that

15 How they decide what is a bad act, and what is deserved, is discussed in Ch. 11.

whatever else inspectors may be seeking to achieve when they decide to prosecute, the punishing of blameworthy behaviour is a fundamental value. These views suggest strongly that law is treated in this area of social regulation as an essentially moral enterprise (see also Chapter 11).

This is not to claim, however, that inspectors did not sometimes adhere also to a general instrumental purpose of trying to change attitudes by means of prosecution. Indeed, this objective was cited as important, but how the change in attitude was to be achieved was often left unstated. Most of the statements of instrumental purpose by inspectors could be interpreted as part of a deterrent philosophy, and it may be that the importance of prosecution as a means of bringing about a 'change of attitude' resided in its capacity for deterrence.[16] The effectiveness of deterrence in corporate or white-collar offending is disputed (see Chapter 9).

Discussions of deterrence are usually organized in terms of individual (or 'specific') deterrence (the purpose of punishment is to persuade the lawbreaker, by making life unpleasant, to choose to do otherwise next time for fear of further punishment), or general deterrence (the purpose of punishment is, by the exemplary unpleasantness meted out to an offender, to persuade others, who might be similarly tempted, to restrain themselves).[17] It is clear that the threat of general deterrent punishment is an important value for many inspectors, as an AD suggested: 'By taking a case occasionally, one reminds all the others that something similar can happen to them'[18] (86–53). The message needs to be brought home as forcibly as possible, hence inspectors' practice of tipping off the local

[16] However, how much of a part ideas about deterrence played in actually shaping a decision to prosecute, and how much a deterrent rationale is used by inspectors after the event to justify a decision taken on other grounds, it is impossible to say.

[17] Closely allied with deterrence, of course, is a concern also for the credibility of the regulatory organization, which is widely seen as a desirable consequence of the use of prosecution (see Ch. 7).

[18] Inspectors generally laid emphasis on general deterrence as either an aim of or a justification for prosecution, though they acknowledged that this was in the absence of any knowledge of its effectiveness. Measuring the general deterrent effect of any criminal sanction is extremely difficult, of course, a matter which for many years was partly responsible for the high degree of scepticism among academic criminologists about the extent to which legal penalties have a general deterrent impact. Such scepticism needs to be treated with special caution where the concern switches from individual activity to organizational or corporate activity, because a great deal of what is done in these areas is more likely to be informed, calculated, and purposive. Corporate behaviour is often shaped by a general knowledge of the broad requirements of the law (even if detailed knowledge is lacking), and compliance (which almost always involves some sort of expenditure and demands some sort of positive activity by way of attaining compliance) can be the result of calculated behaviour.

press about an impending court case, and briefing them to achieve as full and accurate a report as possible (see Chapter 7). General deterrence might also be augmented by the efficient communication of reports of prosecutions through the tight network of relationships maintained in particular industries, or where an industry is clustered geographically. Similarly, there may be a greater pay-off with the selective prosecution of large, wealthy companies whose products and brands are household names, and correspondingly less with small and unknown companies. Companies usually want to protect their reputation, inspectors believe, independently of any impact a prosecution might have on their profitability, though in certain industries (construction was cited as an example) the potential loss of future work is an important further deterrent from misconduct.

Inspectors, however, often seem to employ a more complex deterrent philosophy. First, in addition to conventional ideas, it is also clear that deterrence means different things to HSE inspectors in different contexts. For instance, a conception of 'local deterrence' seems to operate. Hutter (1997: 221) found that instrumental reasons for prosecution became more prominent for inspectors if they were concerned about a high incidence of a particular type of accident in an industry. The decision might then be taken to prosecute the next major accident falling into this category.[19] Second, given that penalties for violation of occupational health and safety provisions are widely regarded as low, both in law and in practice, many inspectors in HSE treat the threat inherent in law enforcement, rather than punishment, as a more realistic deterrent for many firms. This thinking rests behind the emphasis HSE gives to its programmes of preventive inspection, which, it says, 'can be likened to the highly visible presence of the police patrol car on the motorway. Fear of detection of law breaking is for most a deterrent and spur to better performance. The expectation of inspection should not be underestimated as a spur to compliance with health and safety legislation.' Even here there is a moral dimension: 'Those who have chosen to comply must also be satisfied that law breakers will attract more attention' (Health and Safety Commission, 1988: 45). A third kind of deterrence exists in the internal sanctioning system which operates in many medium-sized and large companies in particular. The sanctioning of an aberrant individual by the company management may prove an effective

[19] The Railway Inspectorate apparently pursued such a strategy following a spate of accidents involving overturned cranes.

deterrent to others, even though no prosecution is actually mounted by HSE. The same process may operate on a large scale also. A prosecution may serve to take enforcement action out of the local sphere of an inspector negotiating with a manager or group of people in a local and private fashion, and instead bring the company's failings to the notice of those in senior positions in that and similar companies who ultimately control the purse strings and formulate broad corporate policy on health and safety matters.

6. CONCLUSION

Organizations are very human entities and subject to human frailties, not least lapses of conduct. Problems of organizational control therefore assume considerable importance. Such problems mount as organizations become larger and more complex, since their structure can impede ready knowledge and understanding of what is going on (Vaughan's (1996) concept of 'organizational secrecy' is relevant here). Organizational life and activities are controlled by using other organizations. The more complex the organization, the more complex the problem of control. Vaughan (1996; 1998) has drawn attention to the importance of institutionalized belief systems that operate in organizations. Various conceptions and assumptions of risk held by inspectors exercise an important influence over their working theories of compliance and non-compliance, and in turn over their monitoring and enforcement behaviour. These are examples of institutionalized beliefs about organizations and why they behave as they do. To categorize an employer as 'remorseful', 'cooperative', 'having a bad attitude', and so on reflects a recognized organizational practice, one whose meaning can be transmitted, once it is an item recorded in the files, across decision-makers and over time. Such beliefs then prescribe appropriate control measures.

To control organizational activities effectively and efficiently, a regulatory body needs to exert authority at the top of the company where policy decisions about the allocation of resources for occupational health, safety, and welfare, environmental control, and the like are made, and where internal communication and sanctioning systems are devised and operated. It is less efficient for inspectors to try to attack the problem on the shop floor, though this will vary depending on the particular nature of the industry. This may mean prosecuting for deterrent purposes, justified by the belief that organizations are rational actors making rational choices. Such beliefs, together with characterizations of offence and offender, in turn provide for inspectors an understanding of why companies comply or fail to comply. Even firms with a strong self-interest in compliance due to the remote possibility of catastrophe associated with inherently hazardous manufacturing processes will nevertheless attract close attention from inspectors. If, on the other hand, the risk of catastrophe to plant and self-preservation is low, it will be assumed that the company has correspondingly less incentive to comply, leading to a greater tendency to ascribe to the regulated firm a potentially less compliant character in general. This imagery is important not only because it serves as the basis on which an agency organizes its monitoring systems, but also because it leads to differences in the way in which inspectors make their enforcement decisions: the 'compliant' and the 'cooperative' are likely to have their rule-breaking framed more benignly than those who are not viewed so favourably. Accidents may well be more likely to be defined as 'excusable' when they take place on the premises of compliant or cooperative companies. The irony of all of this from a policy point of view, as Genn's (1993) findings suggest, is that the possibilities for self-regulation are likely to be greater in precisely those risky enterprises which in fact attract more formal monitoring by the regulatory agency but actually need less.[20]

One of the important features of characterization is the power it creates for generalization. Thus a large number of inspectors spoke of the pervasiveness of non-compliance. The problem was not one peculiar to the enforcement of occupational health and safety regulation, but was regarded as transcending other areas of social control. Inspectors claimed they would not be surprised to discover that a firm which was displaying reluctance to comply with their requirements was in difficulties with the Inland Revenue and other authorities, whether as a result of self-interested calculation that non-compliance was the cheaper course of action, or of sloppy management, or simply of a general malaise afflicting the company. The following comments by a chemicals inspector may be regarded as typical. Such firms, he said,

'have a different view of the law of the land, and I'm not just on about health and safety, now, I'm on about tax law and other laws. They have a certain view of the law of the land that's fairly flexible ... It's a sort of culture of ... "You get away

[20] However, to the outsider who might assume that workers have every incentive to avoid injury or ill health at work, it comes as a surprise to learn that inspectors view the workforce as equally varied in its attitudes and behaviour in response to regulation. To the extent that this is true, it ironically suggests that the idea of an 'identity of interest' which was a central tenet of the Robens Report between workforce and employers was ill founded.

with what you get away with," without there being any evil or malicious intent—the last thing they want is somebody hurt.' (86–33)

Characterization is potentially capricious as a great deal of law enforcement work is bound up with the manufacture of appearances. In the personal interaction between an inspector and a representative of a regulated firm, the artful and mutually recognized use of impression management threatens any trust that may develop. Inspectors' need to create an impression of willingness to enforce stringently by taking rigorous action at field level where necessary coexists with the desire of employers to give an impression of, for the most part, willing compliance. The position may be further complicated by the fact that a very large number of employers are in principle sympathetic to the aims of the regulatory system, but find those principles overtaken by commercial and organizational pressures towards rule-breaking. They all assent to the principle of safety, in the opinion of a former HSE Deputy Director General: 'They think it's a good thing and they are always very sad when somebody gets killed, or seriously injured, but . . . it's pressed out of their consciousness.' Here again the seeming contradiction between the understandings of inspectors about compliance and the reality, as expressed by employers, becomes apparent. Thus the reality, as a former Deputy Director General put it, echoing the findings of Genn's (1993) research, is that 'the majority are going to do as little as they can be pushed into'. Yet, in principle, as most inspectors believe, people want to comply:

'No employer . . . actually, actively wishes to contemplate any of his people being harmed. I think it's actually true. So you get a lot of lip service paid, and you get a fair amount of genuine engagement, and many employers of course have to have employees harmed and have taken matters far more seriously afterwards. *But*, there is an awful lot of back-sliding, and there are an awful lot of people who would sooner not know, and there are a still greater number of people who are ignorant [as] to the precautions that should be taken. So my attitude is far from benign.' [Original emphasis.]

He went on to describe the practical task for HSE inspectors as one that recognized that 'it is necessary to have sensible standards and it is also necessary for the impression to be abroad that those standards have got to be adopted'.

The paradox of regulatory control is that business is ultimately subject to the application of the criminal sanction if it fails to comply with regulatory demands. Yet regulatory agencies depend upon business for its cooperation in the enforcement of regulation. In a symbiotic relationship, bargaining between two sides with competing interests becomes central to the enforcement of regulation (Hawkins, 1984). Business in general wants to minimize the degree of regulatory intrusion and incur the minimum of costs, yet (with the possible exception of big business) it has an interest in benefiting from the expert knowledge and advice of the regulatory official. The inspector wants to secure the compliance of a generally reluctant business, yet is conscious of having often to depend upon the cooperation of that business for information or warnings of difficulties. The industrial air pollution inspectors employed by HSE in the 1980s, for instance, were reliant upon industry to let them know immediately there had been a breakdown in pollution control, since an early warning enabled them to deal with any subsequent complaints more adequately. A failure to inform the inspectorate was taken as a sign of 'bad faith'. Both sides may often share an interest, therefore, in manufacturing the impression that things are not what they seem. The metaphor of the game is helpful here in understanding the character of this enforcement relationship. New moves in the game may be made by either side as time passes, as one tries to achieve some tolerable notion of compliance while the other delays, or tries to get away with doing as little as possible, or in some cases continues to avoid complying. Furthermore, just as law may be made or enforced for instrumental or expressive reasons, so regulated firms may comply with it (or not) for instrumental or expressive reasons.

Inspectors frequently work with a complex idea of compliance. The tension between organizational policy and individual practice may be partly the reason why they can think of a company as fundamentally 'compliant' at the same time that it is in violation of a legal rule. The important implication, however, is that the framing process ensures the designation 'compliant' will affect whether a 'violation' is identified, and whether and how it is acted upon. For some, decision-making about the enforcement of regulation and prosecution can be seen as an all-pervasive moral enterprise. Equally, compliant behaviour is frequently explained in moral terms. In contrast, an instrumental explanation is often put forward for non-compliant behaviour, while at the same time there is also a moral response which is to punish the culpable and the deserving. Johnstone's (1994) study of prosecution decision-making in occupational health and safety regulation in Australia found that the inspectorate there tended to base its enforcement decisions on the moral blameworthiness of employers and occupiers. This is in keeping with

Carson's (1970*a,b*) earlier research in Britain, as well as with research in other areas of regulatory control. '[T]he principal indicia of... blameworthiness', writes Johnstone (1994: 198), 'was [*sic*] the employers' and occupiers' safety records and the general standard of machinery guarding. Also important were factors such as the co-operation of the employer, or the speed with which she or he responded to the inspectorate's recommendations.' The decision to prosecute or not hinges substantially on blame, so it is essential to see what blame actually means to decision-makers. This is the subject of Chapter 11.

9 The Instrumental Frame: Will Prosecution Have an Impact?

1. ON REGULATORY EFFECTIVENESS

It is usually assumed that prosecution is employed instrumentally to achieve a reduction in certain untoward events, undesired activities, or states of affairs. 'I think the overwhelming view is that health and safety legislation is there for a purpose', is a typical comment. 'We don't tend to prosecute for bureaucratic reasons, or for purely technical breaches, minor breaches' (97–04). For prosecution to be justified under an instrumentalist conception, a demonstrable connection between it and behavioural change must exist (Stenning *et al.*, 1990: 108). Thus the decision-maker who seeks to achieve instrumental effects frames problems, when contemplating formal action, in terms of the expected likelihood of correction, repair, or other indicators of reductive effectiveness. This is partly because the experience of many inspectors suggests that excessive optimism about the effectiveness of prosecution is misplaced: about half the factory inspectors interviewed did not think that prosecution necessarily has an impact on the behaviour of employers.[1] And where it might work, it was believed that its effectiveness is often marred because the legal process works too slowly. If it were clear to inspectors that prosecution had a discernible impact on levels of occupational health and safety, or even on levels of compliance, it might be expected, other things being equal, that inspectors would make rather more use of it than they do. But inspectors do not necessarily believe prosecution to be the obvious way to produce some desired practical impact.

That said, it is important to understand the conditions under which the beliefs held by law enforcers about the possible impact of prosecution upon a rule-breaker's future behaviour do enter prosecution decision-making. Such an instrumental calculation does intrude into pre-trial decision-making about whether to prosecute, to issue a notice, or to

[1] Johnstone (1994: 26) found a similarly low use of prosecution for occupational health and safety violations in Victoria partly due to inspectors' scepticism about the usefulness of prosecution.

take some less weighty enforcement action even if it is later dismissed in the process.

How regulatory effectiveness is to be discerned is not straightforward. Prosecution may sometimes be used instrumentally, in the hope of producing reductions in undesired behaviour by encouraging higher levels of compliance among those regulated through the deterrent force of the criminal process. Yet the impact of a regulatory system upon the prevalence of undesired events is very difficult to calculate, as is the impact of enforcement activity upon compliance (except where notices are concerned). Furthermore, compliance may itself sometimes be unpredictable and occasionally only tenuously connected with impact.

When addressing the ability of regulation to change the behaviour of people or business, it is important to distinguish impact from the question of compliance, concepts that are frequently conflated. Both are important from a policy point of view, but compliance is a useful measure of effectiveness only to the extent that it is strictly the cause of changes in behaviour or alterations of plant or environment which are themselves directly responsible for a reduction in the prevalence of occupational ill health or accidents. Excessive reliance on attaining compliance at the expense of a concern for its consequences may be misguided.[2]

Deterrence is the central form of instrumental theory in regulatory enforcement. Prosecution here creates the occasion for the application of punishment to effect a change in behaviour. On this view, prosecution works through the threat embodied in the legal process. It is either a rap across the knuckles for a rule-breaker to prevent a specific recurrence, or a solemn warning of an unpleasant fate for others who might be similarly tempted. General deterrence fits well with agency concerns for efficiency because from its point of view prevention is preferable to retrospective action; responding after a victim has suffered harm is also more costly than pre-emptive action to prevent misfortune. Preventive regulation can be conducted in a number of ways. Inspection should itself carry some deterrent threat with it, even if ultimately it is prosecution leading to punishment that is most likely to concentrate the corporate mind. The inspector who seeks to attain a beneficial impact upon the behaviour of employers has a tactical choice to make about the best sort of case to

[2] It may partly be for this reason that evidence from the United States suggested that the early activities of the Occupational Safety and Health Administration did not markedly improve occupational safety, while at the same time they appeared to add to the burden of costs on industry (Veljanovski, 1980; Viscusi, 1979; 1986).

prosecute: those selected for prosecution for instrumental purposes are determined partly by inspectors' anticipation of achieving something.[3] The precise firm selected should be unimportant in seeking a general deterrent effect, some inspectors would say, while recognizing that the prosecution of a major international company would attract more attention than the prosecution of some lesser-known business.

As well as employing a deterrent rationale, some inspectors may be concerned with a form of boundary maintenance in the denunciatory use of prosecution: by publicly condemning the disapproved behaviour, they believe that others may be encouraged to comply by conveying the feeling that evading the rules for reasons of economic advantage will not succeed. By denouncing we may maintain compliance in others, which is not quite the same thing as saying by punishing some we stop others who might be similarly tempted to violate the rules. The value of any message sent in the act of prosecuting depends, of course, on the extent to which it is communicated to those at whom it is aimed, on the extent to which it is appropriately perceived by the regulated community, and on the extent to which the recipient is able to act on it. These conditions are not always satisfied.

In view of inspectors' general pessimism about the instrumental effectiveness of prosecution, it is not surprising to discover that it is often not their primary concern when deciding whether or not to take legal action. Inspectors will prosecute, but this is frequently because they want to satisfy expressive purposes: they feel it essential to communicate with their regulated publics or their organization, or believe prosecution to be morally the right response. They will sometimes prosecute, furthermore, even when they do not imagine that the action will have any impact on an employer's behaviour, and they will often continue with a prosecution when an employer has already complied.

2. THE IMPACT OF PROSECUTION

1. Assessing Impact

The effects of a prosecution are uncertain at best, and inspectors find it difficult to gain any real sense of its potential effectiveness in any case. In general, where prosecution seemed to have had some effect, inspectors were less than sanguine about what it actually achieved, since its impact

[3] This was also true, Lloyd-Bostock (1987: 26) found, of the way in which accidents were to be selected for investigation.

varied in its intensity and duration. Where prosecution was thought to be effective, inspectors were rather unspecific as to the nature of the impact that was produced. This may partly reflect the fact that the notion is itself more complex than it might at first appear. While questions of impact and effectiveness in regulation are considered in respect of their consequences for the harms sought to be reduced, there are differences of perspective as to what these terms might mean. From a social policy point of view an effective prosecution would be one that promised to effect a reduction in the prevalence of threats to workplace health and safety. So far as the regulatory body itself is concerned, an effective prosecution may be one that assuaged the concern of the workforce and the public, or helped persuade external audiences, such as the media, of the effectiveness of the agency itself, possibly leading to an enhancement of its standing. For these reasons, HSE (1987*b*: 5–6) points to increased public reassurance, a reduction in industrial relations difficulties, and the protection of UK commercial interests as further important kinds of desirable impact. From the employer's point of view, however, an effective prosecution might be one that reduced the problem of occupational health and safety, consistent with a desire to minimize costs and further regulatory intrusion.

It is increasingly important in these managerialist times for regulatory agencies to present some persuasive indication of their effectiveness. Yet it is an extremely difficult matter to estimate the benefits produced by such agencies with any degree of confidence. If prosecution does have an impact on the behaviour of employers, it is important that inspectors can be clear when it occurs, since an instrumental decision-maker needs feedback in order to continue to make rational decisions; without it a decision to prosecute based on instrumental considerations becomes an act of faith: 'it's the same as power take-off shafts being missing in agriculture. Endless prosecution will not stop power take-offs not having guards on. But what else can we do? We can't give up . . .' (97–03).

While prosecution coexists with other forms of regulatory control, there will be problems in evaluating its impact:

'Do you measure inputs (from our point of view, numbers of visits, numbers of accidents investigated), or do you measure the softer things, like compliance? . . . We've done a lot of work on looking at that in order to try and help us to get the balance right between our different activities, so we can increasingly make a judgment as to whether it's more cost-effective with a particular risk or a particular group of employers to do a mail shot, to hold a seminar, to do an inspection blitz, to do an enforcement-led initiative, to produce publicity.

Whatever it may be, we're constantly trying to get more analysis of what works where, to enable us to target our resources more effectively.' (97–04)

Prosecution is viewed, therefore, as merely one device in a range of possible enforcement techniques which might produce the effects inspectors seek. For instance, advice is the appropriate strategy 'in the bigger, better companies' (86–35), which are sometimes regarded as complying beyond the requirements enshrined in the law. It should also be observed that assessments of impact depend on a clear understanding of the purpose of the legislation, which is arguably by no means self-evident, thereby making acceptance of the simple reductivist aim problematic (Snider, 1987).

Establishing the impact of a legal proceeding upon some aspect of behaviour is a difficult matter at the best of times. Tracing causal relationships between prosecution and some alteration in behaviour is difficult, and links may often be confused. For example, if an accident has occurred and has prompted a prosecution, it is difficult to be clear whether any subsequent change for the better in the behaviour of the defendant company that can be recognized is a result of the trauma of the accident, the drama of the prosecution, the pain of the penalty, or some other feature operating independently. Inspectors themselves find it hard to judge impact, either because stretched resources mean they have little opportunity to gain accurate feedback, or because any immediate and discernible impact simply does not last. An important task for evaluative research, then, is to establish the precise nature of any links between the enforcement efforts of an inspectorate and a rate of accidents or the prevalence of occupationally induced ill health. Any observed changes in the desired direction of apparently reduced levels of occupational accidents and ill health must also be shown to be a direct consequence of HSE activity. Inspectors do this in a common-sense way, forming their own views, which are drawn from their practical experience. However, to make some sort of connection between enforcement and the prevalence of problems is complicated, partly because a variety of other forces, many of which occur quite independently of enforcement activities, may also contribute to changes in such rates. These include shifts in the level of economic activity or developments of a technological kind. Difficulties in establishing cause and effect are exacerbated in the case of occupational ill health. Epidemiological evidence of the toxicity and carcinogenic effects of particular substances is often imprecise, and even where such evidence does exist, effects may be long term and unpredictable, since people do not react in the same way when exposed to a hazard. Furthermore, workers and employers often behave differently in response to hazards presented. It is possible, also, that some effects may be masked. For example, regulation may be effective in improving safety in some areas, but employers may compensate in the interests of cutting costs by relaxing regulatory requirements in other areas; or workers may relax their own standards in response to apparent improvements in workplace safety or occupational health provision produced by regulation. Inspectors may—possibly—be able to gain some idea of the extent to which prosecution can affect behaviour because they routinely record preventive measures taken before an accident and those taken afterwards. But any discernible change is likely to be prompted by the accident, or the possible use of temporary compliance as tactical behaviour by an employer in the hope of preventing a prosecution, rather than by legal action itself.

A system of regulation may produce various types of impact. The process of enforcement can have unintended effects among the regulated population as well as among regulatory officials themselves. It may help to think about HSE's general regulatory activity as an array of different sorts of prompts to action and compliance which vary in their form, character, and intensity, but not in their underlying purpose. This line of thinking is in keeping with the broad strategy of the Health and Safety at Work (HSW) Act, 1974, but it does not assist the problem of evaluating HSE's impact since qualitative differences are extremely important and their effects not easily assessed (Health and Safety Executive, 1987*b*: 17). Many of these prompts are intended to act in subtle ways; assessing their impact is correspondingly difficult. The impact of other aims, such as increased public reassurance, are inherently immeasurable in any scientifically acceptable way. The nature and structure of businesses also makes assessment of impact difficult.

Business organizations comprise individuals who may respond to prosecution, if at all, in varied and unpredictable ways. Each person has different degrees of commitment to compliance, and differential access to opportunities for rule-breaking. The structure of business organizations can also impede knowledge of what is going on. The result is that the internal dynamics of business organizations vis-à-vis compliance with legal rules are not yet well understood. There is a tendency in some of the literature to impute a high level of rationality to their decision-making, suggesting that many firms make a conscious decision whether or not to comply with regulation according to a calculation of whether the economic advantage rests with compliance or non-compliance. Such calculating behaviour implies a high level of knowledge and information (or at least beliefs) about the law, compliance costs, and enforcement strategies, as well as (in the medium-sized and larger firms), a high degree of internal control over the behaviour of employees.

Similarly, what prosecution means to a defendant—what sort of punishment it represents—is equally very variable. It is not surprising that inspectors varied in their responses about effectiveness, from the pessimism of remarks like 'very little, very little impact' (86–18), or 'I suspect we think it has more impact than it really does' (86–13), to the optimism of a construction inspector who said, 'Even with a defended, and a lost case, you can win an awful lot of battles [with the company] when you've gone to court' (86–63). 'In some cases, the fear of it is worse than the reality,' said an area director (AD),

> 'particularly where the magistrates perhaps don't award a very significant fine, it can have a demotivating effect. We've built something up, and said "This is very serious," devoted all this resource to gathering the evidence and preparing a case, and then the magistrates award a couple of hundred pound fine, which is pretty nugatory. But I think in the majority of cases, it's recognized all round that this is a serious matter, that there is an expectation that we will prosecute in many cases. We try and discuss it with the firm so it doesn't come as a surprise to them, and we try and put it into context and try and explain to them our reasons for doing so. Now clearly, there will be individuals who will be very anti-HSE following prosecution, think it's grossly unfair, and so on, but I think they are in the minority.' (97–04)

Firms are often ignorant of their precise legal obligations, a matter which is not helped by the infrequency of inspectors' visits, the volume and complexity of the relevant laws, or the pressures under which many people work. The ideological views about regulation held by senior management may be an important feature in shaping the responses of firms to regulatory enforcement efforts, but regulatory rule-breaking occurs at all levels within a regulated firm. Assessments of effectiveness are therefore complicated by the fact that compliance may mean different things and produce different kinds of behaviour at different locations in a firm: 'it depends who you ask, and if you actually get . . . to their safety professionals, they would feel very nervous if we stopped enforcing, because they, in the big companies, use that to get their directors playing what they believe is the safety game, which is beneficial to the company' (97–05). On the other hand,

'There is the category of people who we've given friendly advice over a few years, and they've just never taken it. Perhaps it *will* influence *them* if we take a prosecution. There are circumstances—yes, I can think of roofers where we've issued a few prohibition notices to roofing companies if they haven't had scaffold to stop them falling off, and then we've come across them again carrying on in exactly the same way, so you really do think there "Well, what else can I do if we're trying to influence them? We've issued prohibition notices, and they've put scaffolds up, but they're continuing to do that. Well, we'll have to see whether the penalty makes any difference to them." It will with some, it won't with others.' (97–05)

2. Perceived Impact

Since the ultimate effectiveness of legislation to promote occupational health and safety resides in its actual impact, rather than in the level of compliance attained, inspectors were asked in Phase I of the research what impact prosecution had, in their experience. This was in an attempt to obtain from those with substantial decision-making responsibility some estimate of how effective prosecution was in changing employers' behaviour in desirable ways. The question produced two striking, if contrasting, sets of answers. First, inspectors judge the instrumental effects of prosecution in terms of impact on compliance, rather than on reductions in hazards or accidents (other than in the particular company concerned). This is because assessments of the latter sorts of impact demand a level of information that inspectors cannot acquire, short of conducting systematic research. Second, it is an interesting reflection of the pressures field inspectors are under and their preoccupation with the efficient use of their time that the commonest response to the question was not one directed to the impact of prosecution on the behaviour of actual or potential rule-breakers, but to its impact upon their own time and workload. This finding again underlines the degree to which prosecution is an expressive and punitive ritual or a response to external pressures and expectations rather than an instrumental concern.

There was little consistency of view on the issue of the impact of prosecution upon the behaviour of employers. Few inspectors were willing to state without qualification that prosecution had a beneficial effect in reducing the prevalence of undesired behaviour. Despite the routine post-prosecution check visit (which in many cases should itself contribute to any impact), most inspectors were hesitant to claim the existence of a clear and beneficial effect, and often gave the impression of suffering from inadequate information and feedback. In general, responses to the question were mixed and sometimes rather uncertain. Some believed the impact of prosecution varied according to company. Name is more precious to some, money more precious to others, which may point to a distinction between large and small defendants. Similarly, impact depends on the character of the business: a 'good' company will be expected to produce a more far-reaching effect. A 'bad' company will be expected to be little affected by a prosecution, if at all. In other words, one of the signs of a 'good' company, so far as inspectors are concerned, is that prosecution has an impact on it, while prosecution has little or no impact on a 'bad' company. Some inspectors thought that any immediate and positive impact they might detect was not necessarily likely to last. A lasting impact on an employer's behaviour is the inspector's ideal, but many of them doubted how often this was attainable. Continuing compliance is likely to be more difficult to attain where it is a matter of working practices or safe systems of work, rather than the installation of hardware. A decrease in occupational safety problems was also thought more difficult to achieve through prosecution where enforcement was targeted against highly mobile and transient employers:

> 'in construction—people falling through roofs—you knew that it didn't matter how many prosecutions you took, you're still going to have people dying, falling through the roof... We in this group deal with gas-fitting work. It doesn't matter how many prosecutions we take.... It will not stop people who do unregistered work, but we take the prosecutions, not because we're going to—in the short term—stop people doing it, but it is telling everyone that if you do it, you may be prosecuted for it, you may be fined.' (97–03)

As one experienced inspector, who appreciated the methodological difficulties involved in establishing cause and effect, put it: 'We're not making much of an impact out there anyway... because we see such a small proportion' (86–43).

To the extent that prosecution does produce a beneficial impact upon future conduct, its coercive force would appear to be derived not simply from the legal process and its sanction, but also from its collateral consequences, such as the damage to the employer's reputation arising from the stigma of an appearance in criminal court associated with media reporting of the event, and the threat or reality of adverse consequences for individuals within the firm held to be responsible for the rule-breaking which brought it to court. In addition, a prosecution may serve to crystallize the feelings of shock within a firm in the aftermath of an accident to persuade it that it really needs to change its ways. Indeed, so powerful can the impact of an accident be, a prosecution may not be necessary to effect change:

'If you've had a fatal accident, most companies will do a hell of a lot, just by asking them. If you'd asked them the week before they wouldn't.... [But] if you go after the incident... people will do enormous things, without you. I mean, we had a quarry fatality recently, where in fact we just said, "Well, what are you proposing to do?" And they came forward with a huge long [list] of things. [They] probably [went] even further than we would have asked them or required them to do.' (97–05)

One important question about the impact of prosecution is whether there is any relationship between the nature of the precise legal charge employed and the behaviour of the firm after prosecution (see also Chapter 12). A prosecution brought for failure to observe some absolute and specific requirement may not produce as substantial an impact as a successful prosecution for a breach of a general, if vaguer, duty. A minority of inspectors believed that a prosecution for a breach of a general duty under s. 2 of the HSW Act would have a more far-reaching impact than a prosecution for breach of a specific duty, either because as a result 'they think more widely about the problem' (86–19; an AD), or because, as a principal inspector (PI) put it, employers find it easier to understand that such a prosecution requires a fundamental and broad remedy, rather than something small and specific (86–01). Others, however, believed that 'It doesn't matter what section [of the law] you take, the impact is pretty much the same' (86–52). This is because it is more important simply that a case was taken to court (or as one inspector (86–61) bluntly put it, 'the fact they got run in'), rather than what kind of case was prosecuted. Put another way, the experience of perhaps most inspectors is that where prosecution has a beneficial impact, that impact can be attained by prosecuting a narrow, focused, specific breach of the law as much as by using a section of broad applicability. In some circumstances, a PI explained, prosecution 'does shake an organization. Some organizations do effectively raise two fingers and change things very little. But most people, they don't just put a guard on the machine, they look around and do other things as well' (86–51).

In certain circumstances inspectors believe prosecuting may actually have damaging consequences. The damage that prosecution can do is in the harm it can cause to the personal relationships which inspectors cultivate with employers, for employers' attitudes are precisely what inspectors wish to change for the better. The prevailing view of the relative ineffectiveness of prosecution fits with a conception of regulatory enforcement as being primarily directed towards compliance-seeking, as a means of attaining the broad regulatory mandate. But most importantly it emphasizes again that prosecution is more significant in HSE (and quite probably other regulatory agencies) as an expressive rather than an instrumental measure. The following remarks were typical:

> 'I've absolutely no—I mean there've been times when I've felt it's had some impact for the good, and there've been times when I'm certain it's had some impact for the worse, in terms of my relationship with the firm. And there've been times when I've felt it's been . . . "OK. Well I'm turning up in court and pleading guilty, then I'm going back to my factory, then so what!" ' (86–25)

Other comments emphasized the mutual dependence that exists between regulatory agency and regulated firm suggesting that in some cases the various costs of prosecution could outweigh any benefits it produced. Compliance strategy relies heavily on the maintenance of secure personal relationships and trust, and these are believed to be damaged by prosecution, which is regarded by most employers as a declaration of hostilities. In these circumstances inspectors were dubious about the value of going to court: 'You have to feel there's a benefit at the end of it' (86–35). 'Co-operation ceases and you don't get advancement. Too much prosecution and they shut up shop' (86–41). Such comments again underline inspectors' preoccupation with achieving a good fit between their conception of the desert of the prosecution and the employer's.

When the use and effectiveness of prosecution were discussed with factory inspectors, many were unsure about whether to treat resort to the courts as a sign of success or failure. The answer generally depended on their preferred enforcement strategy. If it was an instrumental one of compliance-seeking by negotiation, backed up by the deterrent threat of prosecution (a strategy of remedy or prevention rather than an expressive one of sanctioning a wrongful act or omission), to prosecute after an accident was regarded as a sign of failure. Not all of them agreed, however: 'I've had it put to me over the years that people who prosecute have failed in their job because they have not got people to do what they wanted to do. I've always thought that was a cop-out' (86–02). There were inspectors who believed that prosecution could have a beneficial impact upon the behaviour of employers, if used in the proper circumstances. One inspector who, in contrast with many of his colleagues, was persuaded that prosecution often produced clear and favourable effects was convinced of the advantages that followed from prosecuting the right case: 'Prosecution is a great opportunity—if it's a well-taken case—to get in there and really turn them over' (86–61). Most inspectors, however, were more cautious. While they recognized that the worth of a prosecution was evaluated in largely moral terms, as to its appropriateness for a particular wrong done, they did not believe that it was a response which should be made virtually automatically, in response to a serious accident, event, or state of affairs.

The lack of conviction about the instrumental effect of prosecution is not surprising. Such impact as is discernible seems to vary from industry to industry. There was some sentiment that the impact of prosecution increased with larger and better-organized companies, in general, because of the greater stigma costs. It was also thought that enforcement campaigns associated with certain industries and particular hazards, such as asbestos, could produce a considerable impact. It is ironic that inspectors were more pessimistic about the impact prosecution had upon the construction industry, given that prosecution is much more heavily used in that particular sector. 'I can think of construction firms', said a construction inspector, 'which are a shambles, have been prosecuted, and remain shambolic' (86–63). 'I think in construction the impact is marginal,' he continued. 'Even the good firms are bad in construction... [because of] the quality of management and the quality of labour. They work unsupervised for so much of the time.' There are structural reasons for this. There is very little in construction work in the way of permanent safety hardware which can be installed, in contrast with factory machines which are easily guarded once and for all. In the construction industry compliance or non-compliance are to be found in the behaviour of site managers and workers, who, when work on a new site begins, are likely to be particularly vulnerable to pressures that make non-compliance tempting. Such features usually overpower any impact the law may seek to produce.

3. THE RATIONALE OF DETERRENCE

Although a substantial minority of inspectors held that general deterrence was one of the major purposes to be served by prosecuting an employer, few of them responded to the question about impact by referring to any general effect upon other companies which, in the absence of formal enforcement, might be similarly tempted to break the law. Some were pessimistic: one AD concluded that 'If you were to look at it in the very narrow sense, there are very few clients who are specifically affected by prosecution' (97–05). The focus of inspectors' concern tends to be the future conduct of the defendant company, not the future conduct of others. Indeed, deterrence is justified as an aim of prosecution mostly at senior levels in the agency.

Inspectors' uncertainty about general deterrence is not surprising, partly because assessing the general deterrent impact of the criminal sanction is an extremely difficult and complex matter (von Hirsch *et al.*, 1999; Zimring & Hawkins, 1973), and the individual inspector lacks the resources for any systematic appraisal of the problem. That said, inspectors did appear to use a deterrent rationale in particular circumstances. In a number of prosecution files comments would be made such as the following about an accident in which a roofer, working without scaffolding, fell 7 metres, fracturing his skull: 'A prosecution such as this will hopefully discourage other roofworkers from adopting such dangerous working practices' (P97–67). (The word 'hopefully' is surely significant.) Prosecution is sometimes used, for instance, in the hope that it will shock people into action: 'The number and type of prosecutions that one takes are influenced by the type of occupier that you're dealing with, the type of area [you're] in, whether there's a particular widespread problem that a few prosecutions will set an example—will they be seen by a wider audience, to encourage the others, so to speak?' (86–38). Similarly, encouraging constant vigilance also demands a deterrent emphasis. One PI reported of a case that it was

> 'An accident waiting to happen. Potentially unsafe system of work, absence of instruction and supervision and precarious place of work. This good company have clearly "slipped up" and the fact that it is a routine job does reveal a worrying loophole in the company's assessment/monitoring procedures... We should publicise this case as it emphasises problems that occur at routine maintenance type activities.' (P97–03)

This suggests that there may be deterrent value in prosecuting cases which present features that are familiar and commonplace. A quite different objective appeared in another case in which HSE was notified of a lorry discovered by a Department of Transport [DOT] examiner carrying six 19 kilogram liquid propane gas cylinders without a fire extinguisher. The inspector noted as 'Special reasons' [to prosecute]:

> 'Well known risk. Company failed to take proper precautions when using a hired vehicle. Defect noted by traffic examiner and worth pursuing to prosecution to encourage DOT inspectors.' In a handwritten memo to the PI, the inspector said the proposed prosecution was also 'for publicity—LPG [liquid propane gas] carried by a lot of people—lack of extinguishers a common problem.' In 'Special

mitigation' it was reported: 'Co made a mistake. Other vehicles adequately equipped.' The PI wrote: 'One case approved in order to gain publicity for the requirements (and our willingness to take action) and to encourage DOT inspectors to continue to inform HSE of deficiencies. The penalty may, however, be limited by the potential mitigation.' The inspector prepared a draft operational note a week before the prosecution, asking for it to be distributed as a News Release. It included a 'Note to editors' saying, *inter alia*: 'You are advised to check the date and time of the hearing with the Court nearer the time to ensure that the hearing has not been put back.' After the prosecution the inspector noted 'One reason for taking case was publicity—unfortunately no press attended.' (P97–27)

From a policy point of view, one of the problems with publicity is that press are only likely to want to attend newsworthy prosecutions, while the real need for deterrent impact may be in more mundane cases like that above.[4] This case is an interesting example of the use of the power to prosecute being aimed less at the deterrence of rule-breakers, but more at positively encouraging the vigilance and cooperation of other officials by signalling clear approval of their assistance.

A more significant deterrent threat is believed to occur with the adverse publicity associated with trial in criminal court: 'Two thousand pounds is peanuts for a big firm ... It's simply the fact that a big firm has got its name in the paper as having been prosecuted by the ... inspectorate. That's the punishment' (86–63). Bad publicity is one of the special effects of prosecution, something which other enforcement measures lack, implemented, as they are, in essentially private settings: 'They don't like going to court. They don't like having their names in the paper. You don't get that with a notice' (86–59). The effectiveness of stigma as penalty is thought to increase with the size and wealth of companies: 'Chemicals firms are very acutely conscious of the adverse effect of bad publicity. Acutely conscious ... It lowers their standing in the community' (86–38). Thus legal action is often justified by inspectors as a way of 'waking up the employer's ideas', 'showing teeth', or as a means of concentrating the minds of other employers through publicity.[5] It may be assumed that there will be a greater impact arising from

[4] The company pleaded guilty to a breach of Reg. 10 (1) of the Road Traffic (Carriage of Dangerous Substances in Packages etc.) Regulations, 1992, and was fined £1,000 with just over £400 costs.

[5] Given the moral character of the act of prosecution, and the general view that its instrumental effectiveness was rather weak and unpredictable, it is no surprise to discover that it is used much more heavily following accident investigations than other forms of visit. Lloyd-Bostock (1987) calculated that prosecution was 10 times more likely to follow an accident than a basic inspection.

adverse publicity in small or compact industries with highly coordinated information networks, though deterrence retains an appeal for inspectors as a way of transcending some of the enforcement problems posed by fragmented, dispersed, and ill-informed industries.

The impact of prosecution upon a company can also, of course, be an impact upon individuals within that company. Workers may feel a sense of commitment to a firm which itself encourages compliance: 'The more prestige people have and the more they think highly of their organization and their reputation, the more they're concerned to avoid it [prosecution]. The more it concerns them if they are prosecuted.' On the other hand, individuals may be held responsible by senior management for the failings which led to the corporate distress of a prosecution and this may itself act as a spur for individuals to comply with regulatory demands. In big companies, it is believed that the news of prosecution by HSE will reach board level, with corresponding implications for the individuals concerned, and similar embarrassment may be felt by subsidiaries of large international firms if there is a requirement that news of a prosecution be reported to head office. In small companies there may also be an impact since any deterrent effect in a prosecution may be greater the more the employer is part of the local community and vulnerable to the stigmatizing effects of criminal trial. In this way farmers or small industrialists may be affected as much as larger businesses.

Increased vulnerability to enforcement—the deterrence inherent in the risk of being caught breaking legal rules—was a more plausible deterrent to inspectors than the sanction that would follow conviction. With enforcement crackdowns the problem is in targeting the kind of behaviour which causes concern. In the Factory Inspectorate crackdowns were often concentrated on the construction industry, and the aim was to produce a local deterrent effect by saturating an area with enforcement activity. The same approach was adopted to combat the hazard of the power take-off shaft in the Agricultural Inspectorate.[6]

A related instrumental justification is the use of prosecution as a learning device, another aspect of its public character. The reasons for prosecuting in one case were given as: 'Highlights the use of PLCs [programmable logic controllers] for safety related systems, what can

[6] An agricultural inspector spoke of one test of deterrence he employed, remarking that 'We certainly used to get a feedback when we took a prosecution for an unguarded power take-off in a particular court that the sales of guards locally would increase. Local dealers would say to us "Yes, we knew you had a prosecution even though we didn't read it in the papers, because sales went up."'

go wrong and why guidance requires safety systems to be either hardwired or to have similar integrity as if they were hardwired. No mitigating circumstances' (P97–06). In another case in which a demolition worker had fallen 40 feet through a roof and had been paralysed from the chest down, the reasons for prosecuting were said to be that:

'Hudsons are a fairly large concern. They believe they have discharged their responsibilities to [the subcontractor] and that [the injured person] was an independent contractor in his own right to whom they had only minimal responsibility, they need to be strongly dissuaded from that point of view and must realise that they have responsibilities to people who are working on a site under their control.' The inspector recommended prosecuting under Reg. 6 (1) of the Construction (Working Places) Regulations 1996 for failing to ensure safe access and egress from the roof, and s. 3 HSW Act, 1974 for failing to ensure the health and safety of persons not in their employment.[7] (P97–59)

While a deterrent effect (in penal theory, if not in practice: von Hirsch *et al.*, 1999) resides in the threat of a legal penalty, the extent of the sanctions permitted by law often provoked criticism by inspectors, and the level of fines actually imposed by courts was generally regarded by inspectors as derisory. Visible variations in sentencing practice also concerned a number of them.[8] 'It's a fairly disheartening experience to take the case,' said one, 'put in the work, and then see the magistrates fine the company £20 or £25, which has happened' (86–56). One of the problems of financial sanctions, of course, is that they penalize defendants differently depending on their ability to pay. Some inspectors believed that for a small or struggling business a modest fine may have a considerable impact, while a fine at or near the statutory maximum is, for a medium-sized or large firm, painless.[9] This may encourage the view that the real threat of the legal process resides not in the application of the criminal sanction but in publicizing the company's lawbreaking by the act of prosecuting itself.[10]

[7] The firm was fined £2,500, with £1,430 costs.

[8] There are sufficiently few occupational safety and health prosecutions that each one is a rather rare event for most magistrates, given the size of most city benches. This means that magistrates have little prior experience to rely on both in trying and in sentencing such cases.

[9] To tailor fines more closely to the wealth of defendants unfortunately creates the appearance of even greater inconsistency of punishment, a problem which critics in the media of the Unit Fines scheme introduced in the Criminal Justice Act, 1991, and then hastily abandoned in the Criminal Justice Act of 1993, seem not to have appreciated.

[10] Notices were thought to be more effective at achieving compliance in a specific instance, a belief vindicated in research conducted by HSE (1985*a*) itself.

There is no clear view about the deterrent effectiveness of the criminal sanction in the regulatory arena. Some argue that white-collar offenders are more likely to be deterred than others (Jesilow *et al.*, 1993: 95 ff.), though observable effects are more complicated than might be expected (Gray & Scholz, 1991). Gray and Scholz (1993: 197) found that inspections with penalties often had effects on the severity and frequency of injury rates, the imposition of a legal penalty apparently concentrating the corporate mind to attend more closely to occupational safety. Others argue that corporations and managers are less amenable to deterrence strategies than we might imagine (Braithwaite & Makkai, 1991; Simpson, 1990; Yeager, 1986; 1991), and in a number of annual reports HSC/E have argued that low penalties do not carry much deterrent weight. 'For some authors,' writes Hutter (1997: 226), 'the arguments are ideological, with one view being that those involved in the enforcement process should be "reasonable" in their use of sanctions (Bardach and Kagan, 1982) and the opposing view being that the concepts of "reasonable" and "unreasonable" are always socially negotiated in favour of private capital (Pearce and Tombs, 1990; Yeager, 1991).' The nature of the sanction itself, DiMento (1986: 73) concludes, 'is less important than other factors in compliance. No enforcement strategy, when considered alone, universally motivates the corporation to behave.'

Another quite different deterrent effect of prosecution, one which operates in an anticipatory form, is the threat to inspectors themselves of failing to convict. The impact on inspectors of losing is substantial: it is 'a very big constraint' against prosecuting too readily (86–63). Such impact is on an inspector's standing within the agency and his or her reputation for competence. One inspector, interviewed in the mid-1980s, remarked: 'HSE goes potty about lost cases ... Were you to have a string of lost cases against your name, they'd be looking very carefully at you ... We are scared stiff of losing cases. Reports have to fly to headquarters within minutes of the case going down' (86–63).[11] A further implication of losing is that it is a drain on resources, threatening to add to an inspector's paperwork:

'I think there's quite a lot of methodology in the department about prosecution and historically... there are powerful disincentives against losing a case. You don't want to lose cases. The reason that you don't want to lose cases is that you've already done a helluva lot of paper work... yet when you lose it... someone has to make a decision quickly. "Is it something so important that the

[11] There now seems to be rather less concern within HSE about losing a case; see Ch. 12.

inspectorate ought to appeal?" . . . [S]o when you lose cases, there's paperwork involved, ostensibly to deal with this business of whether we ought to appeal or not.' (86–13)

4. THE PARADOX OF CONTROL

The most important impact of prosecution, it seems, arises ironically from its being threatened, rather than actually used. It stands in the background when inspectors bargain for the compliance of employers: 'It does have some influence at the negotiating table' (86–22).[12]

This is an aspect of the paradox of control: under certain conditions the suspension of formal legal action may serve to produce compliant behaviour more effectively than actual enforcement. This is partly because 'You get more out of a company by letting them off sometimes . . . They feel they've been given a fair deal. They feel they've been treated reasonably well and they will make an effort' (86–17).[13] Attempts are frequently made with this implied form of deterrence to persuade or coerce employers to compliance while pre-empting the need for court action. The threat of prosecution used in this way, inspectors believe, can open the way to a possibly constructive relationship with the defendant. Some of this emerges in correspondence which passes routinely between inspectors and employers which is often an occasion for the issuance of a discreet threat: 'I remind you that the maximum fine for failure to comply with an Improvement Notice is now £20,000'; or 'Failure to take action to control the risk of handling injuries can be very costly to your business as apart from loss of revenue due to sickness absence from work, the cost of replacement staff and possible prosecution fines, I am aware of civil claims for manual handling injuries which have resulted in awards as high as £345,000' (P97–39).

Some inspectors, however, were conscious of a risk that unveiling the legal penalty upon conviction might sometimes even be counterproductive if it did not appear as awful as it had been portrayed by them in prior negotiations with the company. The convicted company 'may

[12] Thus in the infraction letter, employed by the Industrial Air Pollution Inspectorate (IAPI) as the first stage in the formal enforcement process, it used to be stated that prosecution was being actively considered, though in practice this was often not the case; see Weait (1989).

[13] This is reminiscent of the more cooperative attitude of industrialists believed by water pollution inspectors to follow from the 'let-off' of pouring away a formal sample (Hawkins, 1984, ch. 8).

...realize that it's not as painful as they thought it was going to be. If they've come out of court with a £700 fine, they may well realize it's not as much a deterrent as the threats were' (86–34). The implications of this may enter into inspectors' tactical decision-making when weighing up the pros and cons of prosecuting, or selecting some less formal enforcement measure, in response to a violation. '...I think this is something that's actually got to be taken into account when doing the prosecution—that threats are sometimes more effective than the actual prosecution. [The] maximum fine ... to some firms is peanuts.' One important working rule in this connection is 'You've got to look at the response you're going to get from the company' (86–34). Speculating about this sort of impact may further encourage the tendency to prosecute the transient, for they are unlikely to be encountered a second time.

One of the most consistent findings about the impact of prosecution was that it is conceived of by inspectors substantially in terms of personal relationships, rather than of the employer's behaviour: 'The important thing...is the way you handle and deal with and relate to people. Because if you can't communicate you can't do anything' (86–32). The formalities of the law in general are believed to be potentially very damaging to the personal relationships of those caught up in the legal action. Inspectors frequently expressed concern that the managers of a firm alienated by a prosecution mounted against them could become indifferent to or even hostile towards the prospect of taking further remedial measures to improve their occupational health and safety standards. Furthermore, prosecution also posed a threat to relationships between the firm and HSE as a whole: 'It generally makes us less liked, of course, but it may in fact bring about the improvement we think is necessary. But there are plenty of recalcitrant people who if you're not careful, you can run them in every year...There are people who take things extremely badly' (86–21). Though some thought that 'It's not often that our cases end up with a significant worsening of relations between the inspector and the firm he has to go back and deal with... afterwards' (86–19; an AD), this was the view of a minority. Inspectors' preoccupation with the impact of prosecution upon relationships does suggest their importance in a regulatory agency which relies heavily upon compliance strategy, and its use of information, advice, bargaining, and informal persuasion or coercion as preferred means of enforcing the law. Where inspectors have established continuing relationships with key individuals in certain companies, avoiding any threat or disruption to those relationships becomes particularly important; hence the remarks of an inspector to a Deputy Chief Inspector of IAPI: 'In view of the decision to go ahead with the prosecution of this company, I considered that in the interests of our past and future working relationship I should inform [the General Manager] of our decision rather than wait until he received the information via the summons.'

Some firms, said a PI, 'take it very badly' (86–34). This happens particularly where the employer disagrees with the inspector about the necessity or appropriateness of prosecution. 'The problem arises with the feeling of total lack of any real justification for what the inspector did to the company [by prosecuting]. They say: "We don't accept that we should've been prosecuted." They have no feeling of guilt. So all you've done by that is to make our future relationship more difficult' (86–01). A PI portrayed the resentment of an imagined employer in the following terms:

> '"We're not going to know where we stand now. You're going to come in tomorrow and pick some nitpicking thing just to jump on us for." The feeling of grievance may be enhanced where the company... has thought that they've been so hard done by the decision to prosecute being taken that they've defended the action at all costs to themselves, perhaps at far greater costs to themselves than they would have incurred had they pleaded guilty and remedied the matters on site. And then if they've successfully defended... it can [also] have an adverse reaction.' (86–53)

If prosecution is to be less damaging and more effective, it was claimed, renewed personal contact with the convicted management before or immediately after the prosecution is important.

How real are the claims that prosecution damages personal relationships and makes the enforcement task more difficult, or to what extent such claims are apocryphal or part of office culture, is hard to know. When interviewed, inspectors rarely reported personal experience of damaged relationships but rather referred to the experiences of others.

5. CONCLUSION

HSE inspectors frequently use decision frames other than the instrumental one to guide what they do. Indeed, a central theme of this book is that the use of prosecution is based heavily on common-sense reasoning which has a moral basis. Prosecution is associated by most inspectors with retributive punishment, whose organizing idea demands the award of deserved punishment to a blameworthy individual or organization.

This demand generally takes precedence over other aims of a more utilitarian character. The retributive character of prosecution is particularly apparent where it is used following an accident or incident. Most inspectors acknowledged that they proceeded reactively, on the basis that prosecution was deserved by a blameworthy employer and that this approach was fundamental to any other aims in prosecuting a case (see Chapter 11). In these circumstances instrumental talk of prosecution as success or failure is inappropriate, since to prosecute to achieve maximum impact is not necessarily to prosecute those who are morally at fault. Prosecution used for symbolic purposes is a matter of being the right thing to do and a commensurate response to wrongdoing. Inspectors will prosecute even when they do not think such action will be effective in altering the behaviour of the firm in question or the behaviour of others who might be tempted. When used in these circumstances, the need for a good fit between the employer's and that inspector's sense of the desert of a prosecution is again crucial. The employer's conception of the legitimacy of the regulatory process rests on it, for they also think in retributive terms. Punitive treatment which is regarded as undeserved invites condemnation as vindictiveness, both by the employer and by the public. The worse the fit between breach and prosecution, the more an employer will resent being taken to court. Where there is a lack of fit, there may also be less impact: 'In some cases [prosecution] does have a considerable impact.... It really does, but in lots of others it doesn't. You know, they can't see that they've done anything wrong...' (97–02). This is a particular problem where an employer has conspicuously taken steps to remedy the cause for concern: 'there are many instances where the change will have occurred by the time the prosecution takes place. It *will* have an effect on people in the sense that as long as we follow the principle... that... it's justifiable, [then] we won't have a negative reaction to it, in most cases' (97–05: original emphasis). The formal law and any instrumental conception of its purposes are again substantially overlaid by each inspector's personal conceptions of desert.

There are important ironies in the use of prosecution. Sometimes its perceived ineffectiveness or counter-productiveness has acted to persuade inspectors to employ other enforcement methods. On the other hand, prosecution may well be used in cases where, from an instrumental point of view, employers may not need to be prosecuted. Furthermore, if prosecution is capable of producing a beneficial impact on employers in certain cases, inspectors were asked, 'Why not prosecute more frequently?' While it is true that inspectors would have to devote more time to the preparation of more cases, and would therefore be able to devote less time to other tasks, it is arguable that the gains might outweigh the losses. But there was no support for this idea. Instead, there was a consistent if implicit notion that inspectors are in general (perhaps predictably) prosecuting roughly the right number of cases. Many of them were concerned about neglecting other important areas of their work: 'If you're doing prosecutions you're getting an instant—probably—impact somewhere at that particular place. While you're writing it all up and doing your hard work, you're not inspecting five other places' (86–51). More prosecution also risked increasing the animosity of firms on whose cooperation the inspector ultimately depends. There was also, it was thought, a risk of trivializing the ultimate sanction, for fear that a higher rate of prosecution might lead to lesser fines, as magistrates' courts expressed their disapproval of increased activism by HSE and the prosecution of possibly less deserving cases. On this view, there is a rarity value in prosecution. All of this suggests that there is a sense among HSE inspectors that a certain equilibrium exists between the number of prosecutions taken and the impact they achieve, and that it may be disturbed if the level of prosecution is increased (or, presumably, decreased).

One of the inspectors' major preoccupations was with the attitudes of employers. Because HSE has limited resources and cannot monitor compliance as extensively as it would wish, inspectors have an interest in encouraging people to comply voluntarily, to regulate themselves consistent with Robens's philosophy. Their compliance strategy in general has to emphasize changing attitudes. Otherwise, rule-breaking 'cowboys' may be prosecuted primarily for individual deterrent purposes, and 'good' companies primarily to serve general deterrent ends. This might be a rational strategy for an enforcement agency with limited resources to adopt.[14] Yet, ironically, it is attitudes that are most likely to be adversely affected by a prosecution adjudged by a firm to be unjustified, while it is arguable that prosecution may fail to have an impact where it is most needed: on those who calculate that it is worth breaking the law.

[14] Inspectors find that some companies comply after an accident. Rationally, it could be argued that prosecuting them and taking up resources is unnecessary. But there is pressure to make symbolic statements and to be seen to be credible by others; the inspectors have also to be seen to be doing their job. However, a more rational policy might be to target those who are unwilling to comply under most circumstances, since they are the ones who need to be coerced into action.

One of the most important sorts of impact resides in prosecution as a general statement of a regulatory presence. Ultimately, an AD said,

> 'I think we would be naive if we expected prosecution to have a reformatory effect on the actual defendants in all cases. Sometimes it does, but there are plenty who you know perhaps feel aggrieved, sore about being prosecuted, or, you know, for whom it's water off a duck's back. But there are important messages to get to the wider world, and... if we can get some publicity for the cases that we take, and generally that is the case (you know, we do try to alert the local media), then I think the effect on other potential offenders—in other words the deterrent effect—is quite considerable. And it does illustrate what we regard as unacceptable behaviour, it does show that we've got a presence.' (97–02)

The denunciatory character of these remarks was endorsed by a PI:

> '[Prosecution] was done for punishment purposes; also... to show society, these people have been morally reprehensible in the way they've cavalierly conducted their undertakings, and we're going to show you that we're going to find the full rigours of the law for what's happened... And a clear message to the industry: "If you are going out to do incompetent work, watch out, you might end up in the same [position]." And hopefully raise the standards in the industry.' (97–03)

Ideally, as a general manufacturing inspector put it, '[Prosecution] should have some element of social change or social engineering in it.' His conclusion, however, was telling: 'I'm not convinced that it does' (86–41).

10 The Organizational Frame: Prosecuting as Advertising

1. IMAGERY IN ORGANIZATIONAL LIFE

Prosecution is very important as a special display of organizational activity. It announces the behaviour not simply of organizations themselves, but of individuals within organizations. While the public act of prosecution symbolically affirms fundamental values to important regulatory audiences, it also gives scope for individuals to make certain statements and create certain images within a specifically organizational context. This is because officials have audiences within the organization to whom they need to display their activity and competence. The internal organizational audience often acts as a powerful source of influence on inspectors' decision-making. Organizational life confers a distinctive character to their use of imagery, however, for these prosecution messages are dictated by organizational interests and the expectations of others within the agency. Regulatory organizations have mandates, objectives, and interests peculiar to them which serve to create a conception of the organizational interest. The influence of organizational values in decision-making is particularly noticeable where decisions about prosecution are involved because it is not only such a public and drastic act of enforcement, it is at the same time a very costly one. The regulatory agency has an interest in fostering a certain level of enforcement activity to reassure the public that action is being taken. Such action may also be justified instrumentally as maintaining or increasing the compliance of employers. This organizational interest reaches the inspector in terms of a need to produce the occasional prosecution for the organization's benefit.[1]

Just as prosecution can be employed by the regulatory organization itself as an indicator of its activity, credibility, and decisiveness (see Chapter 7), prosecution can be used by individuals within regulatory

[1] Though two of the areas had been selected for research because it was believed that they had the lowest rate of prosecution, inspectors in all four areas expressed anxieties about whether they were being active enough in prosecuting sufficient numbers of cases.

organizations as a sign of their industry, judgement, and competence. This is clear from the following piece of conversation:

Q: 'It is a way that the inspector can show you, as a manager, that he or she is doing their job, or is good at their job . . . ?'

A: 'Yes, yes it does. And I think also perhaps more widely within the organization. . . . I think a prosecution is an activity which inspectors uniquely have the powers to institute, and that some of them are conscious that, unless they show that those powers are being used, that there may be some who would perhaps see the dilution of the inspectorial job. So I think it's important.' (97–02)

Similarly, a principal inspector (PI) recognized that prosecution 'does no harm in relation to your career' (86–38) in view of its visibility within the organization as an indicator of activity. The implication of this, as this chapter will show, is that some prosecutions are taken by inspectors not because of any compelling intrinsic merit in the particular case, but in satisfaction of expectations within the organization.

In serving as a very important means by which individual organizational actors can convey signs of activity or competence to senior colleagues, prosecution is equally a method by which senior staff can evaluate the accomplishments of junior staff. Thus one inspector could report that he had deliberately prosecuted more cases in his early years because 'I wanted to impress my PI that I was a go-getter' (86–63). Allied with this incentive to activism is a view of prosecution within the culture of the organization as a 'virility symbol' or as 'a macho, sort of pints-in-the-bar' type of activity. I mean—it's an awful thing to say,' remarked an inspector, 'but whenever a group of inspectors get together . . . the talk sooner or later gets round to prosecution' (86–25). Another, reminiscing about the prosecution-mindedness of colleagues in a former area, observed that 'Some of them are out to get a big tally. They'd say "I've done a dozen so far this year"' (86–40). Prosecution's significance as a performance indicator providing a concrete index of activity and output is that it is much more salient than advice, education, bargaining, and the other moves of compliance strategy routinely employed in applying the law. Prosecution used in this way is employed by inspectors as an advertisement.

Inspectors have various audiences within the organization which will attend to their use of prosecution. The internal audience is comprised most immediately of the PI (who is the source of reports on and evaluations of the inspector's work), and the area director (AD). Ultimately there is an audience in headquarters: 'there's a whole raft of administrators in headquarters, and I mean, indeed, the Director General' (97–02). Inspectors are not alone in being conscious of an audience for their work. Awareness of an audience for specifically organizational activity leads inspectors to be sensitive to a need to prosecute certain kinds of case or certain numbers of case. The effect of these expectations may be reflected in terms of decisions about prosecution that are made in individual cases, and in terms of aggregate levels of prosecution, since organizational managers are concerned both with the prosecution of particular events or classes of problem, as well as with a broad number or rate of prosecution. Inspectors in turn respond in particular ways to these expectations.

Agency staff are encouraged to work in organizationally desired ways, and individual inspectors often find their decision-making shaped by the need to make various organizationally relevant statements, or, as an organizational actor, to create or avoid certain appearances. To prosecute or not is to make a declaration about an inspector's action or inaction, possible decisiveness or weakness, and so on. To avoid prosecution, or to decide against it too frequently, risks suggesting to their seniors quiescence, indolence, or even powerlessness. There are fears among some inspectors that they may be regarded as lazy if they are not seen to be enforcing the law by being in court from time to time. 'If you're doing nothing on enforcement—particularly on construction—people would look at your work carefully... because you are almost turning down opportunities to enforce rather than picking them up' (86–63). Pressure is sometimes exerted upon inspectors from within the organization by headquarters, by the AD, or by the PI: 'If you take no prosecutions, then you can't be doing the job properly because you've not been taking "appropriate enforcement action".' Apparent inertia will eventually come to the attention of senior staff. 'If an inspector never takes a prosecution,' said a former Chief Agricultural Inspector, 'one is a little bit suspicious about what his approach is to his work.'

A regulatory agency like HSE relies heavily upon the enforcement practices of its front-line staff both for the actual kind and level of regulatory activity that is carried out, and for the impressions of the agency and its policies that are conveyed to its regulated audiences. This demands a certain level of control of inspectors' activities so that the various declarations it needs to make—the symbols and images discussed in Chapter 7—are delivered effectively. One important figure in the control of inspectors' decision-making is the chief inspector. However, the personal attitudes and approach of the AD seems to be especially influential as the most senior person in direct contact with inspectors: 'If I've got perhaps four of my inspectorate... who aren't playing a part in the enforcement side of it, the impression which the public has out there of the law being enforced is all the harder for the other members to manage' (86–19).

There is a distinction to be observed between those pressures that remain in the surround of the organization but which, on being taken up by the regulatory organization, serve to redefine the decision-making field, and those that shift the way in which cases are framed to act directly upon an inspector's decision-making in a particular case. The inspector is also by no means immune to the broader political and economic pressures and constraints affecting regulatory agencies, even though they may not be taken up as a matter of agency policy. The former forces exist in a consciousness of broad climates of opinion about regulation and punishment or public expectations about occupational health and safety. Some of them may be quite specific, such as changed public views about the dangers of asbestos, while others remain rather broad and vague, such as a shift in political opinion about the necessity of activism or restraint in the more direct forms of regulatory control. A general consciousness of various publics with expectations about prosecution in the environment of the organization reaches inspectors by two routes. Inspectors are themselves directly aware of issues which prompt public concern from the ways in which the media report matters. But they are also made aware by their senior colleagues that they need to be seen to act in certain circumstances.

2. ORGANIZATIONAL EXPECTATIONS

One way in which seniors exert direct control over field-level decision-making about the number or kind of cases to be prosecuted is to create certain expectations sanctioned by the organization about the conditions under which inspectors should recommend prosecution. Inspectors, for their part, have clear expectations about the number of prosecution cases deemed organizationally desirable, as is evident from the comments of senior staff. The need to have inspectors display enforcement activity in the courts from time to time was clear from the remarks of ADs and PIs in varying degrees in all four areas researched, as was the sensitivity of inspectors to the concern. One PI put the force of expressive rather than instrumental demands very clearly: 'Sometimes I think it's more to please this organization that one prosecutes than to have an impact out there . . . There's a lot of organizational expectation in relation to prosecution' (86–51). This 'expectation' is usually one of greater prosecution activity, but sometimes one of greater restraint. One AD commented:

'Sometimes with . . . some of the older inspectors, there's been, it has been necessary to . . . exert some influence to increase some prosecution activity, because it is an interruption [to their normal work]. If you don't prosecute, you know, life is sweetness and light. You don't end up having very exacting work to do. You maintain a cordial relationship with the employers you're inspecting. You know, it's an easier option in some ways. But then when other people who have perhaps been injured are seeking redress or asking questions why action hasn't been taken then it's for us to answer the questions and find the excuses [laughs]. So I see it from that point of view as well.' (97–02)

How much inspectors feel a need to be seen to be prosecuting varies according to the nature of their work. In inspectorates where prosecution is not an unusual matter, it is regarded as virtually a routine part of the job, in a sense which is unlikely to hold good for those other inspectorates which rely much more heavily upon an enforcement strategy of compliance and employ prosecution only rarely. The same is true of groups within the Field Operations Directorate (FOD). One PI had reduced the numbers of informations laid by his construction group, but still declared unequivocal concern if his inspectors took no cases to court: 'We need the prosecutions. Got to have them' (86–22). In contrast, another PI asserted that restraint can be an equally important organizational value:

'In theory we can do as many prosecutions as we like. And I think inspectors themselves are making this judgment all the way along the line. They know that every accident that comes in, they could prosecute. But they know the organization will not value a huge level of prosecutions. They know that I'd rather see them inspecting our massive and totally unmanageable list of premises. And they also know that someone who prosecutes a lot will start to raise their profile . . .' (86–51)

Senior officials' expectations reach inspectors in the form of a set of pressures to take action in specified circumstances, coupled with a vaguer concern not to be excessively activist. 'There's times I feel I've prosecuted', said an inspector, 'because it's expected of me by the department' (86–17). Those senior staff who hold particular views about the value and desirability of prosecution may try to school their inspectors into adopting a more explicitly sanctioning or more conciliatory approach. As evaluators of organizational performance they are well placed to do this.

Inspectors may respond to bureaucratic expectations by producing higher levels of activity, such as more numerous (if more rapid) inspections. Alternatively, they produce more prosecutions as especially salient organizational indicators of activity if they fear that they are not meeting some actual or notional target number of prosecutions annually. Prosecution is especially apt in this connection, leading some inspectors actively to search out cases with features warranting a prosecution if they have not yet reached some actual or imagined organizationally desired number. One source of pressure for prosecution mentioned by a few inspectors which is passed on by their seniors arises when HSE acquires new responsibilities and needs to display its presence, competence, and success as an enforcing agency with new duties.

An important source of influence or direction here on both the number and the kind of prosecutions taken is the AD, whose views about the desirability of prosecution as an enforcement move, in either general or specific cases, may be transmitted directly to inspectors, or through regular meetings held with the PIs. It is easy for the AD to convey views about prosecution to junior colleagues. It was said of one AD, for example, that 'Anyone coming into the area soon learns when a case goes up to the area director by the questions he asks and the answers he gives that he's not in favour of prosecution. And it's a fairly strong-minded individual that will put himself out on a limb' (86–43). One direct source of control for ADs is to indicate clearly their precise expectations about the level of prosecution activity. One was asked, 'How do you encourage the gentler ones to be a little more fierce?' and replied:

> '[I]f someone goes a year or longer without having taken a case, then it raises certain questions because it's fairly unusual for an inspector doing a normal inspector's job not to come across some situation which would be worthy of prosecution. So it's handled usually through the principal inspector, who's line manager, and the principal inspector will perhaps look particularly at the investigation reports that the inspector returns. And if he felt there was a situation which on the face of it would be effectively worth prosecuting then, then we would send the inspector back with that remit.' (97–02)

Similarly, another AD exerted pressure via the area's industry groups, explaining what he did to ensure prosecution activity: 'If a group doesn't produce any prosecutions over a long period, I would talk to the principal inspector and say to him "It's odd that we haven't had any cases out of your group . . . Is it that things haven't been happening, or is it about your approach, or are you achieving results in some other way . . . ?"' (86–19).

One AD had adopted a highly directive approach. In a conversation about the use of prosecution as an organizational indicator, he was asked whether his policy was to take a few more cases, or to take cases of a particular kind:

'I think it means changes in both ways. It certainly means taking a few more cases. I am getting grumbles at the moment because I issued an edict a few weeks ago to the extent that every inspector, I *expect*, takes two prosecutions a year. Now my word 'expect' meant they don't *have* to take them in this year, but that has caused a fuss because people are taking a much more rigid—[Pauses] What I'm saying is that if I look over five years and they haven't taken ten, then I think that that is unacceptable. But I am not saying that they *have* to take two this year because it is clear that they may take footling cases and that's not what I want. In terms of the type of cases, I would be keen to see that we knew some of the modern legislation—the Management Regs.—but there is no doubt that that is difficult. Therefore I would not push that too hard. What I *would* say is that we ought to be doing prosecutions in a number of different ways. One is the easy way out of an incident. But [there are] also cases where people have ignored us, and have not, over a period of time, done what they have been asked to do. Or where we've come across things for the first time and conditions are so poor that as well as using notice procedures we also prosecute at that initial visit.' (97–05: original emphasis)

ADs' views about the merits of prosecution are also transmitted relatively easily in the routine processes in FOD which require that proposals for prosecution be submitted by inspectors for approval to their PI or AD.[2] The inspectors and PIs learn from experience which cases will or will not be approved. The AD's stance can act quite directly on the decision behaviour of field inspectors, as was suggested by one inspector, who described his current AD as 'not enamoured of prosecution':

'cases which get referred up get turned down by the area director. This spin off comes down to us at the grass roots that the area director does not prosecute. And therefore it's only natural for one to try and go along with his wishes to some extent. And if there are two courses open to you, prosecution or non-prosecution, you're likely to go along the non-prosecution route.' (86–43)

These remarks suggest the extent to which inspectors may make decisions in anticipation of what their organizational superiors may later decide. This inspector's view was corroborated in the remarks of a

[2] Where the PI is the primary inspector dealing with a potential prosecution, the approval of the AD must be secured directly. The AD will also see cases proposed by inspectors involving high-profile or otherwise difficult matters. See generally Ch. 3.

colleague in the same area office who had moved from another area where greater use was made of prosecution: 'From what I've heard since I've been here . . . the area director isn't interested in taking any prosecution that isn't absolutely watertight . . . I've been told that it's not very likely that one gets prosecutions approved if they have to go to him for approval' (86–40). Similarly, at PI level, there is concern if an individual inspector has had a blank period of prosecution activity:

> 'I would be looking at it, yes, and asking why. Because I know from my own experience that if people were to go for two years and never take a prosecution in a manufacturing group, you're certainly closing your eyes to something. . . . If people take no cases at all I can't believe they're doing their job . . . There is no alternative to prosecution [in certain cases] because the damage is done. There is no alternative. The case has got to be taken.' (86–11)

The AD's influence may operate more subtly in shaping the culture of the area office to create a generally recognized conception of 'typical' prosecution cases. Inspectors are readily socialized into the working norms and expectations of their group and their colleagues in the office. 'When I came here,' said an inspector who had spent some years in another area which he thought had a higher prosecution rate, '. . . I had to curb my feel for prosecution. I felt unhappy if I didn't have a couple on my desk at any one time' (86–43). Recently, however, he said, he had 'mellowed . . . because of the general climate, you're perhaps a bit more sympathetic'.

As well as expectation about numbers of cases to be prosecuted, senior staff have clear views about desirable types of case that should be taken to court. All prosecutions are not the same. A conception of the worth of the particular matter, or whether or not it is a 'good' case, is very important. Some have better attributes: some are 'quality' prosecutions. There is a need for 'good' cases, and a 'good' or 'quality' prosecution is prized much more than one which is routine and predictable. Senior staff are conscious that a prosecution has to be conducted well and has to be of a visibly deserving offender. Such a case responds decisively and effectively to public and possibly industry expectations, and should succeed in delivering a dramatic and unequivocal condemnation of especially blameworthy behaviour. HSE is seen with such cases to be offering reassurance while protecting workers and members of the public from occupational hazards by achieving the punishment of an offender and the possible deterrence of others. Activity may be rewarded by the organization, but only up to a point. Justifiable restraint is taken as a sign of an inspector's competence since it can suggest discernment and good judgement. As one inspector put it, it is not simply important to be taking action 'for the numbers, necessarily, but for the quality. If you get a reputation as not being crazy about it, but prosecuting adequate numbers, prosecuting good cases, and getting good results, then you get a good reputation' (86–56). Agency managers seek to achieve these aims by using prosecution as a form of performance indicator.

3. INDICATORS

Where individuals make a decision about prosecution with a special organizational audience in mind, prosecution becomes a sign of inspectors' activity and an indicator by which their industry and competence may be evaluated by senior staff. Prosecution is an important form of organizational communication, since it is one of the few ways in which an inspector's work will come directly to the AD's attention. As a salient, decisive, and organizationally desirable sign of activity, prosecution makes a very good performance indicator within a regulatory bureaucracy. 'Prosecution does tend to stand out because it means that there are papers floating around when the case is heard. . . . A copy of the . . . summary goes up to headquarters . . . so . . . one is seen by others to be doing something' (86–43).

That prosecution is an important evaluative tool for organizational managers is reflected in the concern some of them expressed about the necessity to encourage some of the more reluctant inspectors to prosecute more readily. The work of inspectors is now formally evaluated as a routine part of HSE's internal management:

Q: 'You review their performance with your principals regularly?'
A: 'Yes. Yes. Because every member of staff has an end of year performance review. So there is meant to be, and there is, discussion between the reporting officer, usually the field inspector's principal inspector, and myself . . . as to where the individuals should fit in the marking scheme because [with] performance related pay we have to mark individual performances—on a fairly simple scale—but nevertheless we do. So, yes, that necessitates a discussion with each individual.' (97–02)

'Getting numbers' and 'building a case' were the two most significant organizational constraints upon California Occupational Safety and Health Administration inspectors. In his detailed empirical study Joseph Rees quotes an inspector as saying:

'"Today we're issuing a lot of chickenshit citations... because you go out there and you feel you have to hammer on the guy to up your own quota, so to speak, and write a lot of other stuff that is really kind of meaningless." This is not to say that all or most citations are "chickenshit", he stresses, but only that many are. "If you don't write enough of this stuff you look bad yourself... So you're out there writing a whole bunch of chickenshit stuff because somebody is looking for numbers."' (Rees, 1988: 191–2)

Prosecution is an indicator that can be turned to personal advantage by an inspector. As an indicator of law enforcement work, it provides a concrete index of activity and output which is more visible and significant than advice, education, and the other moves of enforcement by compliance strategy. As a PI said, 'It's a sign I'm doing my job, I suppose, to my immediate boss' (86–01). The inspector is open to evaluation by senior officials not simply in terms of the number of cases prosecuted, but also by reference to his or her competence, evident in the ability to select 'good' cases and in the display of various skills in prosecuting. Senior staff regard a prosecution as a good indicator of some of the most important qualities required in the inspector's job. 'I certainly use it as a management tool,' said an AD:

'I, for example, see all completed prosecution reports, and I also see reports on fatal accidents where we're not prosecuting, to ensure that our enforcement policy is being followed, because we don't always write lengthy and detailed reports on all of our activities. And therefore it's an opportunity to look at the inspectors' powers of reasoning, their legal judgment, their skills, in terms of taking statements, of applying PACE [Police and Criminal Evidence Act, 1984] and all the other things... [Prosecution is] an opportunity to demonstrate their forensic skills, and how we use external experts, and draw them in. So yes, it has benefits from that point of view.' (97–04)

Another AD added a further set of indicators:

'I mean it is part of my policy of encouraging people to do things. What it also enables me to do in a simple way is to see what work they do because [there] will be previous inspection reports. I will see the way they write up things, I will see how they investigate accidents, I will see how they deal with lawyers. So in fact it's almost the best snapshot I can think of which automatically has to come to me without me having to say "Well, dig out all the work you did three weeks ago," which would be an enormous task for them, and would be horrendous for me, and would not be particularly focused. So... within these documents is much more than prosecution, there are a lot of elements in there, that I can see. And it does give me also an idea of the events, of the decision-making processes, and since I'm saying that enforcement is important and that consistency is important this is writing with a view to getting a handle on the quality bits of consistency, as well as numerical bits that I should be able to get off the computer.' (97–05)

Similarly, the conduct of a prosecution case offers good comparative clues for the PI or AD, marking out the more competent inspectors: 'The way an inspector carries out a prosecution can demonstrate abilities over somebody else. If it's a hard case to take, and he takes it and acquits himself well, this indicates quite a lot of things: his ability to prepare [and] to think on his feet in court [in] a very public area' (86–41). There are fewer hazards for the inspector who tries, wherever possible, to implement HSE's broad legal mandate of advancing occupational health and safety by bargaining in private, though the cost of this is the general lower visibility of success within the organization, as one AD made clear:

'The operational inspectors know that a bit of work of theirs will reach me, and no other work of theirs will reach me in terms of paperwork, unless I delve into the computer system to look at what people do, so *my* view is this is a spur to them . . . If they want to be noticed and if they want to get some work to me, this is one of the ways this happens. I always write a little note back thanking them for their work or spotting certain things that I thought were rather unusual which I'll take up with their boss. So that is something which I am getting around to do in terms of my part of monitoring of staff.' (97–05: original emphasis)

However, important though prosecution is for managers as a sign of activity, inspectors are more ambivalent about it. First, it impedes other inspection work, given the amount of time and effort each case demands, though in spite of these costs, inspectors are very conscious of the fact that 'It's something which they can measure. It's something which, frankly, gets you a good reputation' (86–56). One important advantage of prosecution over many other forms of inspection work is its capacity to create a paper record, which confers a concreteness and permanence upon the activity. Second, the parameters employed in evaluation are linked with organizational reward systems, inducing junior officials to present appropriate indicators of activity and effectiveness. In the nature of things, however, the parameters employed are those which are given to ready measurement rather than those which inspectors believe may give a truer indication of the most organizationally desirable qualities. One of the ADs interviewed had settled on indicators of his own:

'Each group has to plan all its work for the year in phenomenal detail, and one of the details that they are required to do is to plan how many enforcement notices they will issue and how many prosecutions they will take. It was looking at that in the round that got me the figure of two [prosecutions per year]. So, yes, I guess

I'm asking for a 70 per cent increase, and I don't expect to get that in the first year but it's a reasonable target to make. It moves us slightly back up the slope. So, yes, each inspector will have a target, and each group will have a target, each region will have a target, and I will be able to monitor that as we progress. One of the things I've now started to do is . . . I require every prosecution that has been taken, for me to have the file after it's been taken because I don't authorize it normally, unless it was a principal inspector who's actually a front line inspector doing it for us. It's all part of the management of it by letting people know that I see this.' (97–05)

A third reason for inspectors' ambivalence is that an indicator like prosecution is not an unqualified benefit for them, because the organization usually demands more than activity: it expects success as well. While the importance attached to prosecution within the agency ensures that an inspector's work is noticed, its use is also risky for the same reason, since there is always a chance of losing the case. A conviction tends to be routinely expected, while failure to convict is noteworthy. 'If you lose a case because you've not prepared it properly,' said one, 'that has to be a black mark' (86–42). A lost case is not only conspicuous within the organization, but inspectors in the mid-1980s feared that it risked being interpreted as failure, especially at headquarters: 'Nobody likes to lose a case, and our system here is that if you do you have to have a report in London the next day [which] is a big encouragement not to lose' (86–59). As another officer said, '. . . I don't want perhaps something I've made a bit of a balls-up [about] being seen by all and sundry in HQ: "How the hell did young [so-and-so] lose this case? It's open and shut!"' (86–13). 'I'm certain it's a black mark,' said another (86–63). The paper record within the organization is readily transmissible.[3] To lose a case risks impugning the inspector's competence and credibility within the organization, and possibly among some segments of the regulated population, a sentiment enhanced by the tendency of inspectors, inevitably, to see a prosecution as 'their case', as a piece of personal property, since most of them prepare and conduct the matter in court (see Chapter 3):

'If you're an inspector you're going to spend a considerable amount of time on your own, making decisions on your own out there in the field on your own, with nobody looking over your shoulder. And one has to be conscious, I think, of how your superiors see you because they have no real way of assessing . . . the effectiveness of the work that you do. Nobody can see it, the accidents you've

[3] As was the case in Factory Inspectorate in the 1980s, where a report would go to headquarters after every prosecution.

prevented or how successful you've been to persuade these guys to put up a noise-enclosing booth on a saw mill... So just now and again to demonstrate the full range of skills [an] inspector needs, [prosecution] is no bad thing.'

The final comment hints at the use of prosecution not simply as a sign of organizational activity, but as a studied, artful practice.

It is tempting for organizations to treat prosecution as a performance indicator. It is activity that can be counted in the aggregate, either by area or by individual inspector. This can give rise to the idea of prosecution quotas. There are two sorts of quota: one is what inspectors have lodged in their heads, the second is what ADs actually expect from their inspectors. These may not be the same thing:

'What we're very conscious not to do [in this area] though, is to set targets, and say, you know, "You must each take x number of prosecutions a year." We do have numbers in a plan, which are there as indicative numbers, as to what we expect may result, and we do globally look at individuals, to make sure that they are willing to use their full range of regulatory powers. And that means that we would be, if you like, as critical of those who overuse them as those who underuse them. But that will vary in the extent to which they're used according to the industry which they're regulating, their experience, and, to some extent, serendipity as to what actually happens in their patch during that period. But yes, you know, it's the coming together of a lot of different things which, you know, makes it an easy target for managers to see how people have performed.' (97–04)

However, though there may be no formal quota in many areas for a number of prosecutions to be taken, there is a strong sense among inspectors in general that a quota, for practical purposes, does exist. A construction PI said: 'I know that people tell us there's no league tables, but at the same time, I'm sure that every area director is looking at how many have been done in what area, and he doesn't want to be lowest' (86–59). One of the problems for inspectors of this 'virtual quota' is that it provides a basis for comparisons between areas and between individuals, and for the drawing of conclusions by superiors, whether or not they are warranted. The belief in the existence of such a quota is an encouragement to avoid extremes. 'There's one thing the ADs like, to be in the middle of the pack,' said a PI. 'They don't want to be the top prosecutor. They don't want to be the bottom prosecutor' (86–51).

Performance indicators and quotas are examples of how managerial approaches to have people produce in organizationally desirable ways can create perverse effects. Some inspectors were very concerned to let it be known that they were not preoccupied with annual numbers of prosecutions, perhaps feeling that such a consideration should not enter into their decision-making. Enter it did, however, for while they claimed that the sense of an annual quota of prosecutions was something from the past, as they did so, they would often go on to say they would feel uncomfortable if they went for some time without a case: 'If I do go a long period without a prosecution on my desk . . . I start to feel uneasy. I start to wonder whether I'm doing my job properly' (86–43). A chemicals group inspector admitted to being 'slightly bothered that I have not yet taken any prosecutions this year' (86–20). This leads in general to a feeling that organizational expectations created a particular pressure under which inspectors had to work. The existence of a quota, real or imagined, becomes another source of pressure on inspectors when they decide. There are varying expectations within the organization as to how much prosecution activity a particular inspector should be involved in, according to the type of work they do. This is particularly the case for those who work in sectors that tend to involve risky activities where there is an expectation of a correspondingly higher rate of prosecution. Construction inspection is, for instance, likely to yield many more theoretically prosecutable events than most other work sites (Chapter 4). Construction inspectors are accordingly expected to be busier in the courts than others: 'You don't so much go round looking for cases, so much as getting hit by cases as they appear,' said one (86–29), while his PI suggested that 'About half a dozen cases a year is about right' as a level of activity (86–22). 'There's certainly unspoken pressure. I'm quite certain of that,' said another (86–63). An AD acknowledged that 'if, you know, you were in a situation where somebody had not prosecuted, say, for two years, and they had a case which was 50/50, then I think yes, one would . . . err on the side of at least preparing it as a prosecution report; ultimately, if it doesn't meet the criteria, and the evidence isn't there, it's not going to get approved.' (97–04) The significance of a sense of a quota is that inspectors feel that their behaviour is evaluated by reference to, and they in turn make decisions in accordance with, a sense of the emerging pattern of decisions about prosecution over time.

4. CONSTRAINTS

1. Resources

If organizational expectations profoundly influence the number and kind of prosecutions taken by inspectors, organizational resources are a second important force. Resource constraints mean different things at different levels in the organization. At managerial levels the concern is a general one. Managers are preoccupied with reconciling conflicting calls upon the regulatory agency itself, which demand that it publicly sanction egregious violations while at the same time fulfilling a wide range of other commitments. How frequently prosecution is employed is an important question of agency policy. Speaking of the demands on organizational resources posed by prosecution, an official at headquarters observed that

> 'We found in the efficiency scrutiny that the very simplest case where there was to all intents and purposes an open and shut case, where we had a guilty plea in a magistrates' court, then the resource input from HSE to that case was at least five times greater than if one had simply written a notice. And that's the simplest circumstances. In other circumstances, the factor rises to 20-plus times. So there is a very big resource constraint on people doing prosecutions.'

An agency can prosecute more, but at the cost of doing fewer inspections, investigations, negotiations, report-writing, public relations, and so on. A general lack of resources within HSE means that only a small proportion of matters involving serious injuries can be investigated. Constraints are now imposed in principle by HSE's plan of work, which sets out the number of annual inspector hours to be spent on various tasks. This is an imperfect form of organizational control upon the activities of field staff, however, not least because the burden of prosecution upon an inspector's time is such that a small variation in the level of formal enforcement activity can have quite marked effects upon other areas of inspectors' work, as an AD explained:

> 'As far as possible [inspectors] are expected to conform to that plan [relating to the allocation of resources governing their activities] to manage things so that the end result comes to that. But we do have a particular priority with inspecting... So they were expected to increase the amount of time on that, but you will see that enforcement [prosecution] came out at twice what we had planned. Now the actual products of enforcement in terms of... informations heard [is] a meaningless figure, but notices—we did a hundred more than we had planned. So what the upshot of these figures is [is] really that for perhaps a little more enforcement activity in terms of the end product of a prosecution or a notice served... we needed quite a lot more time, almost double the time than we had thought at the beginning of the year.' (97–02)

At inspector level, expectations about the use of prosecution as an indicator of organizational activity are usually conceived of as a force pushing them into more prosecutions, rather than fewer. Resource constraints, however, tend to operate in the opposite way, restraining inspectors from prosecuting too frequently. This is because while prosecution is only a small part of the typical inspector's total enforcement activity, it consumes a disproportionate share of the organization's and the inspector's resources. This means that there is a limit to how responsive inspectors can be to pressures to prosecute, as organizational resources impose their own restraints upon certain forms of their activities. When a matter goes to court, these restraints take on an added significance, since prosecution is generally accepted within HSE as involving a special and heavy use of resources.[4] This discourages too ready a resort to prosecution. The greater demands of a court case on already stretched resources affects the rate of prosecution:

'[W]e haven't increased in numbers—I mean, we struggle in this office to keep staff together. I mean, we're always understaffed, and the problem with most understaffed offices is the huge workload. We're always understaffed on it, so I'm under pressure. We've got to get some prosecutions, keep that up, which means other work has to suffer. But even if I had twice as many staff, we might take a few more cases; that would be true; but, I don't think we'd take double.... What I'm happy to do is to say "Look, really, you know, we haven't got time to take this case—give me a couple more staff, we'll take it."' (97–03)

The conception of resource constraints held by senior staff is reflected in a concern for the general cost-effectiveness with which inspecting resources are deployed. What is needed from an organizational manager's point of view is a measure of balance because managers are acutely conscious of the need to maintain the appearance of activity. 'Part of my job at the moment...', said a PI, 'is to educate my junior inspectors into a sort of more cost-conscious approach to their work. I have a horrible feeling that they're still at the ticking-off-the-list stage. They have got 200 places to inspect in the course of the year, or whatever it is, and as long as they're ticking those off, they feel virtuous' (97–03).

Consciousness of resource implications among staff creates constraints against the too ready use of prosecution, for as a significant demand upon organizational resources, the use of prosecution is especially vulnerable to reduction. 'When staffing gets below a certain critical level... you have to

[4] HSE is unable to record the costs of prosecution itself, except in the narrowest way. Thus, expenditure on lawyers, witnesses, etc. amounted to £1.95 m. in 2001–2. Many of the costs of prosecuting are caught up in inspection and investigation activities. Perhaps a better indicator of the costs of prosecution is in the proportion of its 'activity' time on enforcement spent by FOD in 2001/2. This amounted to 16.2 per cent (HSE, private communication).

take . . . radical decisions about how you cope with the workload, that perhaps time-consuming activities, such as prosecution, have to be limited to very extreme cases' (97–02). This not only imposes severe restraints on what inspectors can do, but at the same time creates tricky problems when choosing which particular cases to prosecute. A PI explained:

> 'you can't have all prosecution, because you've got investigations to do, and you can't say "Well, I've got nobody to look at this"—that would be unacceptable, even more unacceptable than saying "Well, I'm not prosecuting for this." . . . But certainly, if somebody is lying dead on the deck from a gas explosion because the gas has bled from an uncapped gas supply, there would be a prosecution. If uncapped gas supply had resulted in just a gas leak but nobody dead (we have prosecuted this—I mean, it's a serious matter—but it doesn't mean we'd take them all) we might have to say "Look, sorry, you weren't injured, you know, we aren't taking this case." . . . [S]o it's a balancing act on the availability of staff time to take cases, [and] ensure that you do take what I call the "hardcore" cases—the really serious ones, where there's public expectation [of prosecution].' (97–03)

Inspectors have wide discretion in determining how they spend their time but are concerned with the efficient deployment of their personal resources of time and energy. One theme emerges more consistently and strongly than any other when inspectors think of the constraints which operate to depress the numbers of cases they may otherwise wish to prosecute. One observed plaintively, 'It's hard work, prosecuting' (86–25). This is a preoccupation especially in those inspectors who make infrequent use of prosecution since preparing a court case makes demands of time and careful attention which will have to be weighed up in the context of other demands upon their time and energy, as can be gauged from the following comments by the PI of a general manufacturing group: 'While you're not prosecuting you're visiting more premises and perhaps achieving more of an impact by use of less punitive methods, than if you were out there taking all those flaming statements and coming back to the office and spending days preparing a prosecution and worrying yourself sick why they're defending it when it looked to you straightforward' (86–51). A former Chief Agricultural Inspector suggested that a common reaction among agricultural inspectors contemplating the use of prosecution was one of 'Oh hell . . . if I go down this route I've got fifty reports I've yet to write . . .'. 'If I had more resources I would take more', said an inspector. 'I would take twice as many, maybe three times as many' (86–28). These words suggest vividly how resource constraints affect the decision to prosecute, for they demand that inspectors sacrifice other important activities.

A decision to mount a prosecution calls for considerable care and trouble being taken over the collection of evidence and the other preparatory work involved before trial. This is especially true of inspectors in FOD, who have to prepare to prosecute most cases in person, but it is true also of those who work in centralized organizations and who have to prepare cases for prosecution by solicitors. Some inspectors express distaste for prosecution because of the demands for such care and attention to detail in collecting evidence and preparing the case for court. The amount of time needed to work on a case varies widely. Some inspectors thought that construction cases were among the simplest to prepare, and of these the most straightforward would take at least an hour on site and another hour in the office afterwards. Other estimates, however, were considerably longer. One construction inspector calculated in the 1980s that even a straightforward case could involve a week's work, and spoke of one prosecution in which he had been involved which needed a month's work (86–17).[5] Defended cases are even more of a burden: 'You can spend three or four days preparing a defended case,' said a general manufacturing inspector, '[and] I've been in court three days on a defended case' (86–10). Recent increases in legal complexity mean that prosecution cases are now taking even longer to prepare.

Lack of time can be a major impediment to prosecution, since there is the constant fear among inspectors that rushing the preparation of the case will increase the chances of losing it. The site of an accident and its witnesses may be distant, and inspectors will have to weigh up the time and trouble involved in travelling to collect evidence in deciding whether or not to go ahead. A location remote from the area office encourages the use of alternatives to prosecution: 'The fact that you have to go down there [a very long way from the Area Office] . . . you must weigh up the time and trouble . . . and the fact that you might not get the evidence you want . . . Against that you have to judge whether it'll be easier to pick the phone up and rollock somebody' (86–08; a construction PI). This banal fact may serve to skew enforcement practices, leading to the distribution of prosecutions being distorted in favour of those scheduled for court

[5] The accident report in one case caused concern within the office involved, because the actual amount of time spent by three field officials amounted to 20 hours. 'However, due to the work recording required . . . this will only show that there were 7.5 hours contact. This would give the impression that this fairly complex investigation can be done in such a short time.' When this was raised by the AD concerned, she received a note that the matter was to be taken up 'because increasingly it is our "manufactured" outputs by which we are judged not what really occurs' (P97–17).

locations that are not too remote. The result is that 'If something happens down there,' said an inspector, pointing on the wall map to a town a considerable distance from the area office, 'it would receive less attention than something happening [where the area office is located]' (86–29). The prospect of devoting a great deal of time to a particular prosecution case raises serious misgivings in the minds of some inspectors: 'There comes a time when you ask yourself "Well, is this worth it?" and you wish you weren't involved' (86–09). A growing consciousness among inspectors of the importance of husbanding resources seemed evident as they attempted to meet various annual targets. This more structured work environment led them to be even more concerned with the demands upon their time presented by a decision to prosecute and the added intrusions that that would bring upon an already overburdened workload. Where the inspector is deterred by lack of time from prosecuting, the time and trouble involved may therefore simply persuade the inspector to abandon prosecution altogether, with all that that implies about collection of evidence, preparation of the case, court appearance, and so on, and encourage the use of other lesser, and less time-consuming, forms of enforcement such as a notice.

Prosecution is most likely to be regarded as a prominent and integral part of enforcement work by construction inspectors; for those who work in other sectors it tends to be treated as an unwelcome addition to routine inspection. In the construction groups especially, the general feeling is that resource constraints are such that they can only take notably serious cases to court. As one inspector put it: 'The problem at the moment is actually keeping down the number of prosecutions because . . . in this [construction] group, you have so many serious situations, it's "Which ones have I not got to undertake?"' (86–07). There is an irony here, however, in the fact that serious incidents not only compel inspectors to consider prosecution very carefully indeed and to think of not proceeding only when there is very good reason, they also demand in general more in the way of preparation: 'The amount of time gathering evidence—now that's an important consideration—there's a lot more time goes into serious incidents' (86–37). Resources are not an inexorable force in enforcement practice, however. In inspectorates making less use of prosecution as an enforcement move, resource constraints recede into the background in framing decisions. A former Chief Inspector of the Mines and Quarries Inspectorate, an agency which prosecuted no more than once or twice a year, could say, for example, 'We would not change our ways even if we had more resources . . . Had we more inspectors than we have, we wouldn't be seeking to have more prosecutions. It may well be we'd uncover more cases... but it wouldn't be a thought on my part that we're going to have more prosecutions now, because I've got more inspectors.'

Part of inspectors' concern with demands on resources stems from the uncertainty surrounding the prosecution process as well as its outcome. Incidents which on the surface present features which are associated with prosecution have to be treated at the outset as if they will be prosecuted, for the purposes of taking statements and collecting other potential evidence.[6] Once a decision has been made that the evidence is sufficient and that a prosecution will actually be pursued, the case then has to be prepared on the assumption that it will be defended, even though few are. Furthermore, as a PI said, 'You have to prepare sufficiently in case the case goes to Crown Court' (86–41), though again few do. Nevertheless, the uncertainty means the contingency must be guarded against: 'There are days when we go to the magistrates' court we may not know whether the case is going to stay in the magistrates' court, or is going to end up in the Crown Court. So that could bring another dimension of work. Considerable work' (86–41).

Consciousness of resource constraints has an impact on the way in which inspectors frame cases, evident in the blunt comment of one who said: 'If you've got too much work on at the time, then obviously you'll say "Do I prosecute or don't I prosecute? I haven't got time to prosecute. I haven't got time to take the statements." And therefore prosecution falls by the wayside' (86–29). Resource constraints may make some inspectors pay more attention to collateral sanctions, the availability of which can affect the propensity to prosecute, since they may appear to offer the possibility of attaining the ends of the legislation without the time, trouble, expense, and risks of prosecuting. So far as inspectors and their managers are concerned, time spent preparing a prosecution (whether or not the inspector prosecutes in person) is time that cannot be spent on their other important work. Inspectors respond to the tension between activism and limited resources with a greater commitment to the prosecution of the egregious act or event at the expense of matters defined as 'normal' or 'routine':

[6] For this reason, guidelines in the old Industrial Air Pollution Inspectorate stipulated that an infraction letter, the first stage in any prosecution in that agency, should not be written unless the evidence upon which it was based was itself secure enough to support a prosecution.

'The availability of staff time to do the prosecution—there is no point in starting down the line if you haven't got the troops to do it—and we can't spend all our time doing prosecutions and not the time doing different things. But there has to be a balance that we've got ten per cent of time for prosecution or even less, which means something else has to suffer—and we've got to justify that. And when it comes to what we should prosecute for . . . we follow the Guide for Crown Prosecutors; I mean, that's who we look at. . . . And we do that quite often to justify "Is there is an overwhelming public interest for me to take this case?" You know, "Is there a public expectation?"' (97–03)

The question of whether or not to prosecute is not simply one of deciding that the matter is a serious one, but whether prosecution is desirable, in relation to other demands upon an inspector's time. Sometimes this means that one possible case must be assessed in relation to other possible cases. Changes in the resources available to inspectors to do their work will change the ways in which they categorize and deal with potential matters (Emerson, 1983: 437). Fewer resources allow inspectors less time to devote to potential prosecution matters. Put in Lipsky's (1980: 36) terms, a problem may not be regarded as suitable for prosecution for reasons that have little to do with intrinsic features in the case, but a lot to do with the pressures upon an inspector.

2. Organizational Custom

Bureaucracies have memories, and past practice and experience may also serve as a constraint on prosecution decision-making. A way of deciding particular cases which becomes routine within a group or area tends to create a series of precedents which coalesce into an organizational custom. Some inspectors in the mid-1980s, for instance, displayed a tendency to explain current approaches by reference to past Factory Inspectorate history and practice. The existence of a 'tradition' defining events which conventionally result in prosecution serves to create a presumption in the mind of the decision-maker that present cases of the same sort are to be decided in the same way. These may be regarded as 'normal' prosecution cases (Sudnow, 1965). A number of examples of this practice came to light. Perhaps the most memorable instance, given its singular character, was given by an AD (86–31) who explained: 'We always used to take a prosecution if someone was struck by an overhead travelling crane.' 'Why?' 'Because it was an absolute requirement and we always did it.' Another AD reminisced on the same theme:

'In the past perhaps there was the extent of a knee-jerk reaction—certain types of machines . . . would almost inevitably lead to prosecution.'

Q: 'Overhead cranes, I remember.'

A: 'Overhead travelling cranes, radial-arm drilling machines, unguarded circular saws, you know.' (97–04)

This decision-making practice reveals a notable irony, for it indicates how, within an organization, actors who are accorded wide discretion by the law can behave as if in fact they have little or no discretion (Lempert, 1992). Organizational custom suggests that when forces are sufficiently powerful, they can lead to a ritualized form of decision-making in which the presence of a compelling condition is enough to produce a specific decision outcome.

5. CASELOAD EFFECTS

Prosecution can be an important indicator for the regulatory organization of desirable activity in the often lonely, isolated, and low-visibility world of the inspector, and it can be turned to advantage by the official who wants to be noticed in a way that so many other aspects of the inspector's job cannot be, by virtue of their lack of organizational visibility. Yet while prosecution may be a particularly important part of what most inspectors do, it is only a small part, since other tasks crowd in on them, compelling them to organize very carefully how they spend their time. In particular, they are acutely conscious of the tension between two organizational imperatives. One demands the careful deployment of personal resources, and this restrains them from engaging in excessive prosecution activity for the benefit of their organizational superiors. The other demands the appearance of activity in which the visible and positive use of the power to prosecute is especially valuable. Resolving this tension requires inspectors to ration the amount of time they can devote to prosecution, leading to decision-making which reflects the intrusion of what Robert Emerson (1983) describes as caseload effects. Carrying a caseload of different problems that have to be attended to influences decisions about the numbers and the kinds of cases prosecuted since decisions are made not so much on some conception of the self-evident merits in a case, but more in relation to other competing demands upon inspectors' time in the form of other actual or anticipated problems to be dealt with. Decisions made at one point are made with 'a sense of the implications that past decisions have for current ones and current ones for the future' (Emerson, 1983: 433). In other words, cases are dealt with 'in relation to, or as part of, some larger, organizationally determined whole', and are not disposed of as discrete units. Each case is not dealt with on its merits, 'independently of the properties and organizational implications of other cases'. Indeed, features in the individual case may not be the most important matter in assessing and disposing of cases (Emerson, 1983: 425).

Emerson's brilliant analysis is concerned with decision-makers who handle caseloads, that is, a set of problems that must be dealt with simultaneously. Such practices are also to be found where decision-makers decide matters serially. Indeed, even though prosecution is a rare event for most inspectors, the length of the process often means that they have more than one prosecution under way at the same time. HSE inspectors are probably not conscious of carrying a caseload in the way that other legal actors like probation officers or social workers are, but they are certainly conscious of the need to respond in a balanced way to conflicting organizational demands of activity and restraint upon them. And they certainly operate with a real or imagined set of cases which provides a field against which the decision-maker classifies cases in organizationally relevant ways (Emerson, 1983: 426). The result is that they act in effect as if they were managing a caseload, and make decisions about the appropriateness of prosecution in relation to the demands of other actual or potential cases to be handled (Lipsky, 1980).

A rate of prosecution is assessed by reference to a period of time, leading to a consciousness of a quota, real or virtual, for prosecution. Problems may arise for decision-makers as they approach the end of the quota period. Inspectors may be encouraged to look more actively for possible prosecutions if they feel they are running behind their quota, or may be more reluctant to contemplate prosecuting if some notional quota has already been fulfilled. Thus a PI said, 'If I've not had a good situation [for prosecution] I'll suddenly rush out and find one, if I'm getting to the end of the year... And if I haven't had a prosecution for quite a long time I suppose when I come to those grey area cases, I would tend to err on the side of taking the case' (86–01). Another commented: 'Every inspector wants to have a healthy little [number] of prosecutions. There's no numbers racket as such. But if at the end of the year [an inspector] has no prosecutions to his name, somebody will say. And the daft thing is, you can go through a year without coming up against anything which is a prosecution' (86–51). 'If you take half a dozen [prosecutions] a year,' said another, 'you're showing that you can and will do it but you're also showing that you've got sufficient judgment not to go crazy about it.' If, however, there are fewer immediate demands on the inspector's time, or if the inspector has prosecuted rather less frequently than might be organizationally expected, the approach in the next case where the inspector is in some doubt as to whether to recommend prosecution may harden into a decision clearly in favour of prosecution. Thus one inspector remarked, 'If there is not one [prosecution] in the offing, and there haven't been for a month or two, then I feel a bit uncomfortable and think maybe I'm missing things and maybe I'm not taking as tough a line as I should be' (86–27). The approach was described by another as 'You're weighing up all the time with respect to the cost effectiveness of the potential prosecution' (86–22).

This 'weighing up' is a variable process dependent upon the seriousness of the matter confronting the inspector assessed in the context of the other demands on the inspector's time: 'Cases on hand at any one time are assessed by reference to what is "normal" and expected' (Emerson, 1983: 429). The more serious the incident, the less the inspector will feel able to manoeuvre by using less punitive enforcement moves. Where there are differences in the character of the cases handled by different inspectorates, what is 'normal', 'serious', and the like, will be defined differently, as suggested by a construction inspector in the following comment with his reference to the 'reaction threshold':

> 'You don't want to have five or six cases lined up on your desk at the same time. And to focus in clearly... you can probably handle two or three simultaneously, bearing in mind the amount of work that's involved in collecting the evidence, producing the prosecution reports, and getting the thing into court. They certainly need to be staged at reasonable intervals of time. To have two or three complicated cases in the same month would be far too much. [So if another case comes up?] Your reaction threshold is inevitably going to be moved up.' (86–53)

Similarly, a chemicals group inspector emphasized his feeling that the norms of activity were also bound up with his superiors' recognition that prosecution is a virtually inevitable consequence of the application of normal working standards in some groups: 'I know that if I weren't taking any cases, someone would be asking me why, and that is perfectly reasonable because there are so many breaches around... That is a pressure that's in the background. But it's there' (86–61). While inspectors appeared to recognize that any tacit norms about a desirable minimum of activity reflected the opportunities and approaches characteristic of different groups, some were also conscious of the fact that opportunities to find organizationally 'good' cases for prosecution do not appear regularly (except, perhaps, in construction) and that barren periods of several months were quite normal; hence the remark of a construction inspector who had previously worked in a general manufacturing group that he 'looked for prosecutions there [in the general manufacturing group] because they didn't come readily at you' (86–53).

For the inspector, it is always a question of balance

> 'between how many prosecutions you want in the air at any given time. I have none in court now, but I have two on my desk for approval. I'd be prepared to have two more, but no more than that, simply because in the event of me having four "Not guilty" pleas, it can make two or three months absolute murder. So you're trying to balance that.'[7] (86–63)

Balance is necessary since an appearance of measured activity needs to be maintained. This leads to a working rule that it is essential to take the occasional prosecution, but not to prosecute too frequently, for that gives the wrong signal to one's seniors, suggesting an inability to handle difficulties in a more conciliatory or cost-effective way. Besides, to take too many cases devalues the currency of prosecution. An inspector in a general manufacturing group who regarded himself as more prosecution-minded than his colleagues was quite clear about this: 'If you're taking 15 or 20 a year you must be over-zealous, or lacking judgment. There's a happy mean somewhere' (86–56). The need to be near 'the happy mean' is mirrored in the ambition referred to by some inspectors to be in the middle of the league table, whether real or virtual. From the inspector's point of view, 'As long as you're in the middle of the pack for numbers of prosecutions, your area director won't pressurize you. If he finds you slipping down in . . . the league . . . he will say very gently "You haven't done many prosecutions this year, chaps." And I will pass it on . . . I think there's this inbuilt dynamic in us all to get about the right number of prosecutions' (86–51). This holds good both for individuals and for administrative areas when prosecution data are seen in the aggregated national picture.

Some inspectors were intuitively conscious of caseload effects and responded to the need to balance the demand for prosecution and the necessity of not being over-zealous by rationing their prosecution activities over time: 'I used to like to feel we did that number [one prosecution a month] and didn't fall much below . . . I can see there'd come a point

[7] The speaker was a construction inspector, and therefore someone more accustomed to taking larger numbers of prosecutions, and the occasional need to prosecute cases simultaneously.

where you wouldn't want to do many more than that because I used to reckon that was about the most I could handle realistically without losing track of other work' (86–23). Caseload effects are not simply a question of 'If you're prosecuting, you can't be doing something else' (86–22). Conducting a case well demands care and attention. Those inspectors most frequently involved in prosecution spend so much of their time preparing cases that a plethora of new cases detracts from the care which can be given to existing ones. This also demands rationing, which is managed by framing new cases with greater stringency.

Thus the existence of one or more prosecution cases currently being dealt with may well discourage an inspector from taking on one more. Whether the formal law is used in these circumstances depends, once more, not on the intrinsic merits of the case or the necessity of prosecuting for instrumental purposes, but on the organizational burden to which the legal decision-maker is subject. One PI complained, for instance,

> 'It has occurred from time to time that inspectors have been saturated, as it were, by cases, and have come to me and said, you know, "I would have liked to have prosecuted in this instance, but I just can't cope with another one at the time." And I've had to agree, sadly, that in this instance we've had to let that one go with a very severe and strong warning to the occupier.' (86–52)

6. CONCLUSION

The centrality of organizations to legal life has been rather neglected by socio-legal scholars. This neglect is unfortunate, for organizations have lives of their own and so much of legal life is also organizational life. Accordingly, it is important to understand better how law is fashioned by organizations and the actors within them. One helpful way of doing this is to analyse the behaviour of officials when they act in ways that are directly shaped by their organizational membership. Organizations are not static but dynamic, their activities changing in response to shifting public and political expectations and levels of resource. They are regarded as rational actors, but we should not necessarily expect them to act always as rational entities, as the instrumental view of law tends to, tempting though that may be. Sometimes they work in very human ways. Sometimes organizational norms supplant what may be regarded as rational decision-making objectives; sometimes they encourage individuals to place organizational goals over legal goals when the two conflict (Edelman *et al.*, 1991: 74). At the same time, law is ambiguous and constantly evolving, dependent on the social context in which it finds itself.

The interests of the regulatory organization require that those who work for it make decisions in organizationally desirable ways. Special pressures and constraints operate here on the behaviour of officials within the organization, given that various audiences exist within the organization itself. Sometimes decisions to prosecute may be based primarily on the gravity of the harm done or the hazard presented, but sometimes officials act on the basis of expectations believed to be held by the organization's managers. Prosecution is both a sign which offers a means of evaluating the public work of regulatory organizations, and a sign which serves as a tool for evaluating the performance of individual organizational actors. Organizations are subject to sometimes conflicting expectations from their publics, just as their members are subject to conflicting expectations within the organization, their discretion in enforcing the law being subject to, and moulded by, organizational concerns. For each inspector, prosecution is an act which is both visible and permanent, since its outcome creates a record, bringing into play the conditions in which the organization may make an evaluation of an individual's competence and success.

Organizational activity itself can be assessed quantitatively as well as qualitatively. Inspectors sense that tacit norms of prosecution activity exist in the form of annual 'quotas', real and imagined (an imaginary quota is still a quota for practical purposes, and though a formal and visible index of activity in the form of a 'league table' may no longer actually exist, inspectors nevertheless behaved as if it did). The quota is an important form of performance indicator, and is vulnerable to the usual problems associated with performance indicators, particularly their capacity to distort behaviour in ultimately undesired ways. Inspectors were, however, quick to deny there were any 'league tables' or 'numbers rackets', yet equally quick to acknowledge that they were conscious that they needed to be seen to be prosecuting. It would frequently be observed that in the past such 'league tables' did exist, and were employed by ADs to achieve some organizationally determined desirable level of prosecution. Inspectors often recalled how visible the practice was and how they were sometimes called to account: 'I was once actually criticized one year', said an inspector of his earlier experience in a different area, 'for having done eleven prosecutions that year, when the average was twelve' (86–43). A PI said that he had interpreted his superior officer's report on him as reflecting an expectation that he should be more willing to prosecute. The report had stated: 'Excellent qualities. Unfortunately has had little prosecution experience' (86–51).

While prosecution is a relatively rare phenomenon for most inspectors, it is both an intrusion and a burden. This leads to a certain degree of elasticity in its actual use. Indeed, given its importance and visibility, it is ironic that prosecution seems consistently to be regarded as one of the inspector's activities which can most readily be adjusted in light of other demands: 'If I was in a situation where, towards the end of the annual programme, I was behind with certain parts of my inspection and it was a fifty-fifty [prosecution] case, then I'm sure, being frank, that I would drop it' (86–25). This illustrates well how the need to allocate available resources among cases as a whole fundamentally affects how an individual case is treated (Emerson, 1983).

Resource constraints impinge on the inspector's discretion in such a way that they do not tend simply to regulate the level of prosecution activity, they also tend to deflect it into certain kinds of case. The egregiously big or bad case will almost always demand prosecution; otherwise overstretched inspection resources may lead to the quicker, less complicated cases which are less likely to be defended taking precedence over other kinds of case which, although possibly more deserving or appropriate for prosecution on public policy grounds, fall to be dealt with by other means, if at all.

11 The Symbolic Frame: The Social Construction of Blame

1. ON BLAMING

> 'When I'm looking at a potential prosecution, I don't consciously think to myself "Will my PI expect me to prosecute on this one, or will anybody else expect me to?" I will try and be objective about it and say "Is this a case which warrants prosecution?" ... I mean, you can never be truly objective. There's always a certain amount of subjectivity in there, and that subjectivity is going to be a mixture of things ...'

These remarks hint at the mixture of calculation ('Is this a case which warrants prosecution?') and personal feeling ('always a certain amount of subjectivity') which shapes inspectors' thinking as the prosecution process develops. The personal feeling which is most prominent and pervasive in legal decision-making is a desire to blame. This chapter explores the ways in which inspectors frame, that is, understand and ascribe meaning to, features in an incident or state of affairs. This process helps define what kind of a problem they are encountering, and therefore what would be an appropriate response to it. Those features come into play in the decision whether or not to prosecute, either by defining those that are to be treated as salient, by moulding the decision directly, or by justifying a decision to prosecute that has possibly been made on other grounds. These are not legal, but social, processes.

Blaming is not only central to the ultimate decision to prosecute; the desire to blame may well inform the original decision to create an organizational case in the first place. It is often responsible also for the problem surviving as an organizational matter. And it may dominate the disposal of offenders. The importance of blameworthiness was, for example, emphasized by Wheeler *et al.* (1988) in their study of the sentencing of white-collar offenders in the United States.

Whether or not a case is prosecutable is only understandable by reference to the various ways in which inspectors interpret features they define as relevant, since they do not make prosecution decisions in a vacuum. Prosecution is reserved generally for 'bad' cases, and occasionally for 'big' events. What makes a case 'bad' is the subject of this chapter. The present analysis is intended not to be exhaustive but rather to set out an argument and illustrate it by reference to some of the more persistent and pervasive features which emerged from discussions with staff of all ranks, and from close analysis of the prosecution and fatalities files. It stresses the dominance of common-sense, not legal, logic. The analysis of patterns presented is possible because decision-making about regulatory prosecution, like other forms of legal decision-making, is a socially organized process.

The interpretive work of framing is itself contingent upon the surround and fields within which inspectors operate. The inspector confronted with a problem is preoccupied with a number of questions: Why did this event take place? What does it mean? Is it a violation of the law? Does the behaviour deserve to be prosecuted? What might the impact of a prosecution be? Is there a matter of public interest, perhaps of the sort contemplated by the Code for Crown Prosecutors? Do I need to be seen to be taking action? Inspectors may not consciously separate the issues in this way (reality is usually much less simple and clear-cut), though they would almost certainly acknowledge that they address them in their decision-making. Even having considered these questions, and with answers pointing clearly in the direction of prosecution, there remain problems of evidence and proof that exist in the legal frame, to be applied to all otherwise worthy prosecution cases (see Chapter 12).

Legal processes bear the imprint of moral values. The decision-making of legal officials constantly reflects conceptions of right and wrong, and the desire to do justice and to be even-handed. Such values are often starkly exposed in the regulatory process when decisions have to be made about whether to prosecute, whom to prosecute, and for what sorts of acts and events. Decision-making here is not simply a dispassionate evaluation of an act or event, a detached instrumental assessment of the likely impact or effectiveness of a criminal prosecution in changing undesired behaviour or states of affairs. It is one in which the moral character of prosecution is never far from the surface, for inspectors have a robust view of fault and desert and their place in enforcement:

> 'we're not taking a bureaucratic view of things; we are looking at the raison d'être for the legislation, which is moral, at the end of the day. It's about people's health, safety and welfare. [Inspectors] are only prosecuting obviously where the evidence is there, and therefore where they feel there is genuine guilt, and they are conditioned to some extent by their experiences as to the outcomes—the pain

and suffering that accidents and ill-health cause, and they can't help to be affected by that.' (97–04)

Blame, culpability, or desert are in practice interpreted by inspectors to mean 'Some blatant and wilful disregard of the law' (86–04), or to occur 'When people are blatantly put at risk' (86–05). Blame here is a social, not a legal, conception. The inspector's freedom to characterize event, act, motive, and the like admits interpretive behaviour which relies heavily on lay rather than legal logic, and may address much wider matters than contemplated in the legislation.

The existence of blame is virtually a prerequisite to a decision to go to criminal trial, and often one that is so powerful it can smother any potentially mitigating features. Lack of blameworthiness in the offender is in most cases therefore likely to put an end to any further consideration of prosecution. Furthermore, a moral breach warrants a punitive response. Inspectors generally believe that 'where there's been an accident, somebody ought to be punished'. In their world the use of prosecution is so bound up with punishment that to prosecute itself is to punish.

Inspectors were asked if they had ever prosecuted a blameless company. Almost without exception they said they had never done so. Most responded to the effect that 'It would be rare to prosecute a defendant who was morally blameless' (86–37). Another said it was 'virtually impossible' (86–05). 'I wouldn't feel personally comfortable prosecuting people', said a third inspector, 'if I didn't think they were in some way culpable' (86–27). Senior officials take the same view. Asked what cases prosecuted in Mines and Quarries Inspectorate had in common, a former chief inspector replied, 'gross breaches, and deliberate breaches of legislation. Contraventions, gross and deliberate.' These sentiments are echoed in official policy, HSC's *Enforcement policy statement* (n.d.: 11) noting that: 'the gravity of the offence, taken together with the general record and approach of the offender warrants [prosecution], e.g. apparent reckless disregard for standards, repeated breaches, persistent poor standards.' This emphasis may be due to the fact that blaming is often aligned with public expectations, for officials observe that to blame is to reflect public attitudes.

It might be thought that it is hard for inspectors to attribute blame, given that the business organizations subject to occupational health and safety regulation are often complex. Yet even in such organizations, when untoward events happen people look for and assign blame. Perrow (1984) has shown that organizational failures are often attributed to individuals when they are in fact consequences of the ways in which elements of organizational systems are coupled in ways that make failure not only unpredictable but inevitable. 'What is interesting', writes Reiss (1985: 817) in this connection, 'is that men and their laws persist in holding someone—some person—accountable for those organizational coupling failures.'

To illustrate these issues generally, here are two cases in which prosecution was seriously considered. In each one, the precipitating event, a fall, was similar.[1] The first case, in which the employee was injured, was prosecuted, but prosecution was not deemed appropriate in the second, in which the employee was killed.

In the prosecuted case, an employee had fallen three metres from a slurry tank when a fellow employee had turned on a supply of air to an air lance which the injured person was using, knocking him off the tank. No measures had been taken by the company to prevent this kind of accident, and no instructions given to the workforce. Though the employer's safety measures had been lacking before the accident, the file recorded that desirable preventive efforts had been made since: there had been no fixed ladder, but since the accident, a hooped, fixed ladder had been installed, with walkway and handrails spanning the tanks from which the victim fell. The precise reasons for the inspector's recommendation to prosecute were listed as:

'1. The IP [injured person] sustained severe injury and could have been killed.' [That is, the matter was serious, indeed a potential tragedy.]

'2. This was a job that had been done very regularly over a long period of time without, apparently, any thought, instructions, information or training being given to the workers involved in how to go about it safely.' [The employer's failure to maintain health and safety at work was extensive and of long standing.]

'3. No provision had been made for safe access to these tanks.' [There was a dangerous omission by the employer.]

The inspector then explored any 'Possible mitigation', listing reasons which might weaken the argument for prosecuting:

'1. Good overall track record of co. and the effort they have put into health and safety, and appointment of full time health and safety officials.' [This is important in thinking about prosecution because it is essential to avoid the appearance of vindictiveness which can be created by prosecuting those who do not seem to deserve it.]

[1] Note that prosecution files (the main source of data for this analysis) typically cite an array of reasons for legal action. There will be some repetition therefore in some of the illustrations, since I have organized the material to illustrate the main features in the way that inspectors frame matters.

'2. They do unprompted seek advice from HSE, have kept up to date with legal obligations, have conducted risk assessments and implemented policies without intervention from HSE. There is clearly a financial and moral commitment at senior level within the company.' [There are various indicators of compliant behaviour and desirable attitudes towards regulatory demands. The company is prepared to recognize its obligations.]

'3. Co. policy of hard hats when working above 2 metres.' [The employer has complied with an important and relevant requirement.]

'4. Job done many times before without incident, and none of employees thought it unsafe.' [The hazard was a familiar one and there had been no previous accidents. The employees did not regard themselves as at risk.]

Having listed the pros and cons of prosecuting for her PI [principal inspector], the inspector opted for prosecution and suggested an information be laid under s. 29 HSW [Health and Safety at Work] Act, 1974. She concluded 'I feel that appropriate measures have been taken to prevent a further recurrence of such an incident.' Since there was no remedy to effect, this suggests that the inspector regarded the prosecution either as a means of punishing the company or as a means of deterring others. The PI, in approving the recommendation, summed the matter up as 'An accident waiting to happen.'[2] (P97–03)

In the second case, in which prosecution was not thought to be appropriate,

a 66 year-old man employed by a religious institution fell 3.5 metres from a vat while blending wine at a winery and was killed. He suffered a fractured skull, brain damage, and spinal injuries. There were no witnesses, leaving the inspector to speculate as to what might have happened. In her report to her PI, she wrote: 'On basis of information received to date, PR [prosecution] not proposed (pending coroner's inquest).' She subsequently confirmed her decision not to prosecute, although the local paper had reported her as saying that safer working methods could have been used. The inspector's description of the incident goes on to mention various apparent breaches: HSW Act, 1974 s. 2 (1); Workplace Regulations, Reg. 13 (1) and Management Regulations Reg. 3 (1). A Warning Letter was sent on the recommendation of the PI, requiring the employer to review risk assessments.

The inspector noted several mitigating features. Various preventive measures had been taken before the accident; the dead person was 'a highly experienced worker'; extra features had been added to the storage tank; the employer had hired a health and safety consultant for advice, and to conduct audits. The employers had acted on this advice, and were taking further steps to improve

[2] The company pleaded guilty to a charge under s. 2 (1) of the HSW Act and was fined £1,500 with £1,500 costs. This case was prosecuted for HSE by a firm of solicitors, perhaps because the company originally intended to plead not guilty.

safety, following the accident. The dead person had previously suffered a fall a few years earlier, which had been recorded by the victim himself in the employer's accident book, and further protective measures had been taken as a result. 'Whilst a previous fall from the tank may affect the decision re prosecution,' the inspector reported, 'in the absence of further evidence and given the testament of what must be considered to be a reliable source, this accident will not have a bearing on action taken.'

'Any contributory responsibility on the part of the D/P [deceased person] for his accident has not been included in the scope of this report, as the circumstances are supposition only. No previous advice has been given by HSE. The risk of falls was highlighted in advice given [by the company's] safety consultant [but he] was apparently not aware of the filling operation requiring access and assumed this was done as for incoming wine—from the ground level valve.'

On the first two of the breaches the inspector identified, she concluded: 'It would have been reasonably practicable to have provided a second handrail along the open edge of the walkway, to prevent anyone stepping off the walkway onto the curved tank top.' On the third breach, she wrote: 'A suitable and sufficient assessment of the risk of falling from these tanks had not been made, in that the assessment in relation to falls was not made with the work activities carried out on the top of the tank in mind. Application of an assessment to such activities would have significantly affected the control measures identified as necessary.

'Prosecution is not recommended. [The employers] have taken certain actions to deal with the risk of falling from the tanks; they had also employed professional help, as they recognised a deficit in their knowledge and according to the consultant's report...had made significant progress. In addition, the D/P's own actions may have contributed to the course of events which led to his accident. It seems highly unlikely that prosecution would serve any useful purpose and would probably result in a nominal fine.' In a letter to the employer, the inspector said that she did 'not propose to recommend any formal action...An important factor in reaching this decision was the evident commitment to health and safety within your organisation.'[3] (F97–11)

The remark about the nominal fine suggests that the inspector was in no doubt about the legal strength of the case; indeed, she seems confident she would secure a conviction if she were to prosecute. She seems, however, to have expected a sanction that would have hardly justified the trouble and expense of legal action. What leads up to this indicates

[3] The file carried a note reporting 'Enforcement action not taken due to overriding circumstances', but someone, presumably the PI, had later crossed this out and amended it to read 'Enforcement action taken: warning letter requiring review of risk assessment.' HSE's protocol on work-related deaths now requires the police to be more centrally involved; matters are now dealt with prima facie as potentially criminal.

that too much speculation is needed about the nature of the event to allow blame to be securely attached to the employer. On the other hand, there is reliable knowledge about what the employer had done both before and after the accident, and this probably helped to confirm in the inspector's mind an impression that the employer was not sufficiently blameworthy to deserve prosecution. The company 'have taken certain actions to deal with the risk of falling'; they had 'also employed professional help' in recognition of their own lack of knowledge, and 'had made significant progress'. Besides, the victim may have contributed to his own demise. It is hard to escape the conclusion that the employer was not regarded as sufficiently blameworthy.

Inspectors focus on various parameters in searching for blame, readily acknowledging their importance both to their own decision-making and to the expectations of others. HSE (1986: 36) has officially recognized a number of them: 'In weighing up what is the most appropriate [the inspector] takes into account factors including the seriousness of the risk, the nature of any breach of law, deliberate, flagrant or accidental, the ability and willingness of the organisation to remedy the problem and its previous history. There are no hard and fast rules.' While the rules may appear not to be 'hard and fast', working rules are nonetheless clearly discernible in inspectors' practical decision-making. When some precipitating event which is a cause for concern occurs, they in general apply a moral test to see if they can assign fault, unless the event is so big, dramatic, or otherwise newsworthy that it compels serious attention for those reasons alone: 'The first threshold you go over', said a PI, using a helpful metaphor, 'is the question "Is prosecution *deserved*?"' (86–52; my emphasis).

2. ON MITIGATING BLAME

Certain conditions serve to temper or even to eliminate blame. Sometimes the moral breach does not, upon closer analysis, seem so blameworthy: other matters casting doubt on the offender's blame may come to light and the employer may be redefined as fundamentally compliant with legal obligations. These may repair the moral breach before a prosecution takes place, such mitigating features diverting the handling of the case away from prosecution to a notice or an informal means of handling the matter. Sometimes there is a lesser type of mitigation which takes the form of a reduction in the number or severity of the charges laid.

Mitigating circumstances are routinely listed and discussed by inspectors in the prosecution files. Many of the reports reflect a balanced debate for and against prosecution, a considered view of the risk of losing being counterpoised against an assessment of blame. Certain sorts of case, such as fatalities, self-evidently require that they be treated as potential prosecutions.[4] Sometimes an event is defined as a pure accident ('accidental' rather than 'an accident'), and in such circumstances prosecution seems inappropriate because the conception of the accidental places an event outside the sphere of blame. The frame 'accidental' is too resilient to be replaced by another, as was the case in the example quoted at the beginning of this chapter (see F97–11).

The practice of mitigating blame involves very human, common-sense working rules that are easily recognized, not least by employers. Not surprisingly, the prosecution files frequently contain evidence of companies anticipating the inspector's reactions by making strenuous efforts to mitigate blame or shift it elsewhere.[5] Evidence of a company trying to avoid legal proceedings if at all possible is explicit in the remarks of a plant manager facing prosecution for a serious violation of occupational health regulations: 'we are having a meeting with our company doctor to establish a procedure for preventing any health problem to our employees. I hope you can see from this that we are putting more effort into health and safety concern to fulfil all requirements within a reasonable [*sic*] short time' (P97–13).

Deflecting blame onto the victim is sometimes tried:

In a case in which a woman had had her hands trapped in a machine, losing both her middle fingers, a regional newspaper quoted the employer's lawyer as trying to put some of the blame on the injured person: 'What was mysterious was that the front guard from the machine had gone missing without being reported at all, and strange that [the injured person], having worked on the machine for three years, did not see fit to report the fact that the front guard was missing.' Meanwhile, a local newspaper reported the lawyer as saying 'It was a mystery why the absence of the safety guard had not been reported, but immediate steps

[4] Indeed, the fatalities files, some of which I rely on in this part of the analysis, proved to be extremely useful in understanding the conditions of mitigation.

[5] Defendants frequently attempt to mitigate blame, even when in court on a strict liability charge (Croall, 1988). If legal decision-making is seen as the doings of officials, there is a danger that the important part played by those about whom the decisions are being made may be overlooked. They themselves often act to influence decisions made about them. Where appropriate, legal decision-making needs to be treated as an interactional phenomenon, and not simply as about the unilateral exercise of power by a state authority.

were taken to make sure an accident of that type could never be repeated. It occurred during a busy season following the closure of the company's [works] in [the south of England]. That put added pressure on the . . . site [at which the accident happened] to ensure that output was maximised.'[6] (P97–36)

A combination of circumstances in which the acts of the employer are capable of being construed in alignment with other benign features can make a persuasive argument for not pursuing a prosecution.

In one fatal case, the victim had been working with an electrician to remove redundant telecommunication aerials from the roof of a four-storey building when a mast struck him in the chest, piercing his heart and lungs. The company issued a 'method statement' ten days after the accident, couched in the language of risk management, which clearly deflected some of the possible momentum for a prosecution. It referred to the recovery being made 'by an experienced and competent . . . employee, we relied on his competence and experience to assess the level of risk, resource requirement and safe method of gaining access to, and recovery of the antennas.' Later the report refers to '. . . the benefit of hindsight to ensure we learn from this unfortunate incident and put in place preventive measures to prevent a reoccurrence.' The Process Papers noted that all riggers were equipped with head protection, safety harness, etc. but it was thought that these would not have prevented the accident nor reduced the severity of the victim's injuries. The dead person was very experienced and assisted with the company's training. After the accident all work of a similar nature was suspended nationally; riggers were consulted and a method of working agreed and circulated.

A prosecution under s. 2 HSW Act, 1974 was thought possible, but the inspector thought it very hard indeed to predict the danger of a falling mast, which was deemed a 'very unusual accident', given the positions of rigger and mast. The Personal Protective Equipment Regulations, 1992 were also considered. However, since the company responded so promptly and on a national basis, the inspector finally decided to recommend no action. The PI added: '. . . this was a serious accident (as are all fatalities), the factors which led to it were unusual and not obviously foreseeable. I agree with your identification of relevant legislation of which there do not appear to have been *serious* breaches. I have considered the public interest factors in the CPS Code for Crown Prosecutors and on balance agree that prosecution is not appropriate. The company took swift action to amend procedures following the incident so further follow up with them does not appear necessary. The Coroner's verdict was 'accidental death'. The PI stressed that what the dead person was doing was the normal procedure for that kind of job and that it was a combination of unforeseeable circumstances that

[6] The defendant was fined £11,000 for a breach of s. 2 (1) of the HSW Act, and £3,500 for a breach of PUWER, Reg. 11 (1), with nearly £1,500 in costs.

led to his death. The company's public statement of intent and remorse combined to rule out prosecution.[7] (F97–12: original emphasis)

The sort of reasoning employed exculpates. There are breaches of the law but they are not framed as serious, even though a fatality occurred. This case illustrates well that what people may regard as a serious breach, because there is a grave outcome, will not necessarily be viewed as such by the law.

In the workplace the concept of accident tends to emphasize the fortuitous, the chance event, and to deny ideas of system and organizational responsibility which are the law's guiding principles. This usage may assist in mitigating blame. Richard Johnstone (1994: 456) has explained how it may be exploited in court: 'Individual causation, coupled with the good corporate citizen plea, takes an already isolated event and argues that the incident is an aberration in an otherwise unblemished business career.' The idea of individual causation is congruent with the conception of 'accident', as is often appreciated by the defence in cases that are tried. The aim is to portray an act or event not as an inherent part of a workplace organized and structured so as to institutionalize risks to the health and safety of workers, 'but rather as a phenomenon that is aberrant, unpredictable, and unrelated to the way in which work is organised and carried out. [The] centrality of this ideology is epitomised by the use of the word "accident" to describe the event at the centre of the prosecution process.'

3. THE CONDITIONS OF BLAME

Breaches of the law are commonplace. Although regulatory inspectors can only think of prosecution following an alleged or apparent violation of the law, very few breaches are dealt with by formal action. 'Technical breaches occur all the time', said one inspector. 'You don't go onto a site or into a factory without spotting some aspect of the law which isn't being complied with.' Most rule-breaking is not, however, regarded as serious enough to warrant action: 'The fact that a notice isn't posted on a wall isn't prosecution material' (86–05). 'I would not expect an inspector to take a prosecution for lack of marking of controls on its own,' said an agricultural inspector, 'unless that had been the cause of an accident and could be demonstrated to be the cause of an accident.' ['Because it's not

[7] The conception operating here resembles Braithwaite's (2002) idea of 'reactive fault', which suggests that blame is not for the wrong but for the failure to remedy.

intrinsically serious enough in itself?'] 'Yes!' Detected regulatory violations generally do not warrant criminal enforcement unless they are wilful or pose a serious risk of harm. The vast majority of violations are screened by inspectors and handled—if they are handled at all—by informal compliance-seeking strategies. What inspectors need is some rational and acceptable way of satisfying themselves that the full rigours of the law are only visited upon those for whom they are most appropriate. The existence of moral fault creating the occasion for blame is an important way of applying a practical test, the degree of the employer's moral failure being central to the way in which the inspector understands and frames the particular event:

Q: 'So in a sense, it would be fair to see what [HSE] does as, as it were, exacting retribution for the moral failings of employers in failing to safeguard the safety of the employed?'

A: 'Absolutely. Spot on. Yes. And, of course, with any publicity, it's also a marker to others that this is, you know, unacceptable behaviour if you do this.' (97–03)

Administrative discretion allows play to the importance of wilfulness. In this process, legal rules, sometimes involving strict liability, are subverted by a social conception of blame (Hawkins, 1984). Law enforcers in practice need more than a breach of the law as grounds for legal action.

Blameworthiness is established by reference to a number of conditions which must be analysed in some detail. Reading the prosecution and fatalities files and the justifications for prosecuting employed by inspectors suggests that blame may be evoked by both key words and core ideas; thus a failure to be constantly active in the pursuit of good occupational health and safety practice may result in the neglect of obligations, and trigger a pejorative evaluation. Some of the process papers in other cases suggest, however, a rather general search for blame which sometimes has a speculative quality, especially where there seem to be contradictory conditions. Sometimes the moral construction is very impressionistic. In one case a landlady was prosecuted for failing to maintain gas appliances, leading to the death of a tenant. The inspector said to his PI that she was 'completely unaware of her duties as a landlady under the Gas Safety Regulations'. If the appliances had been inspected each year, the inspector thought it likely that the faulty appliances would have been remedied. 'Although [she] was upset at having been cautioned I formed the view that she did not appear particularly bothered about the death itself' (P97–37).

The seriousness of a hazard or an accident or the extent of the offender's legal breach seem only rarely to be sufficient in themselves to prompt a decision to prosecute. Instead, other properties give meaning to an act or event, since the interpretation of an event takes place in the perspective of other features in the decision-maker's field which serve to frame a matter as more or less 'serious' or blameworthy.

1. Deliberation

The social construction of intention is crucial. Choice or deliberation in an act of rule-breaking is regarded as highly blameworthy. The degree of harm done or hazarded is less significant than the degree of calculation employed in committing the offence. In cases where safety precautions are deliberately defeated, and an accident results, this is prima facie blameworthy behaviour:

A man received severe lacerations when his hand was drawn into an unguarded machine. Photoelectric guards had been turned off and no guard was in place over the chain and sprocket (none had been 'for some time'). The inspector reported that the guards had to be turned off to allow access to the machine, but if the guard had been in place, the injury would have been prevented. 'No-one knew when the guard had been taken off but the IP who had been working on this machine for 6 years did not remember the guard being in place. There was no need to gain access to the chain and the guard in no way interfered with the job of setting up that the IP was doing. The fact remains that there were guards stored on the premises and that these were not fitted, which resulted in an accident. ... As it is foreseeable that a setter would require access to this part of the machine and that guards were available but had not been fitted for some time I would recommend prosecution.' A special reason for prosecution was added:'... there has been a blatant disregard of the legislation.'[8] (P97–57)

If a direct causal line between a deliberate violation and the resultant accident or hazard can be traced, there will be a stronger sense of blame and greater willingness to prosecute, for the greater clarity leaves little room for doubt:

A safety switch had been defeated on an unguarded power press, resulting in a worker suffering serious injury to a hand when the power press stroked with her hand between the tool heads. 'An adequate guard mechanism was available on site at the time of the accident', reported the inspector, 'however, this had been deliberately defeated to allow for the machine to run unguarded.' The inspector

[8] The firm pleaded guilty to one charge under s. 13 (1) of the Factories Act, 1961, and was fined £3,000, with nearly £230 in costs.

concluded that 'the accident was the direct result of the dangerous machine being unguarded,' while at the same time 'it was clearly foreseeable that access would be required to the tool head . . .'. Elsewhere, the inspector observed that 'This accident would appear to be the direct result of the lack of management control combined with attempts to maximise production via cutting corners on safety.'[9] (P97–63)

In another case, the injured person had both hands trapped between the rams of a press machine, resulting in bad lacerations, with both wrists and one thumb broken, and damage to ligaments in both hands. A photoelectric guard had been defeated (described as 'custom and practice' in this workplace, and 'company policy'). A charge under s. 2 HSW Act 1974 was dropped, but the employer was convicted under s. 14 (1) Factories Act, 1961, for failing to fence securely.[10] (P97–10)

In these cases, the deliberate defeat of legally required safety precautions indicates a rational choice which is morally repugnant and deserves censure. If it is for material gain—improved productivity or reduced costs (as in P97–63, mentioned above)—it is even more blameworthy. Prosecution is almost irresistible when deliberation and culpable ignorance can be combined, as in the big asbestos case (described in Chapters 3 and 7):

The inspector justified prosecution with a claim that the employer's misconduct was consistent either with 'a total ignorance of the relevant legislation (unlikely given the nature and business [of the defendant]) or a deliberate cutting of costs at the potential expense of his employees' health.' The defendant had not previously been prosecuted 'by this office but he was convicted following proceedings for illegal disposal of classified waste.' Special reasons for prosecution were given as: 'Total disregard for the health and safety of both employees and the public.' There was said to be 'No mitigation.'[11] (P97–30)

The idea of deliberation is communicated in internal reports with a number of familiar terms. Adjectives such as 'flagrant' or 'blatant' are frequently used. 'Flagrant' rule-breaking suggests a very public form of wrongdoing, a conspicuous attempt to 'get away with it' that is especially morally reprehensible. It carries a clear implication that the behaviour is such that the perpetrator is sufficiently unconcerned about offending to think it worth concealing, and it also conveys a sense of indifference

[9] The company pleaded guilty, and was fined £250 under s. 14 (1) of the Factories Act, 1961, with £310 costs.

[10] The company was fined £5,000, with just over £900 costs.

[11] The defendant was convicted of five counts under the Asbestos Regulations and the Asbestos (Licensing) Regulations, and was imprisoned for three months and fined £4,000.

about the act or hazard and the harm it might do. 'Blatant' behaviour often implies that the firm was well aware of its legal and moral responsibilities. The moral offence to the inspector in one case is very evident in his justification for prosecution, in which he reported that the 'Employer [was] fully aware of circumstances and blatantly disregarded the Regulations.' As the 'Special reasons (if any) for recommending prosecution', it was said that the 'Defendant has displayed a blatant disregard for health and safety and he is also a deliberate liar' (P97–20). An employer who not only has knowledge of the law, but also has failed to honour an agreement about compliance negotiated with an inspector, may well invite a punitive response. 'Blatant' rule-breaking amounts to a symbolic assault upon the legislation and the values it embodies. In the big asbestos case the inspector wrote to his PI: 'I hope you will agree that this is a most serious incident where there has been a total disregard for the health and safety of both employees and members of the public.... [T]his is without doubt the worst disregard for health and safety legislation I have ever seen...'. The prosecution report and input form, as an internal office report and not a piece of legal evidence, is an opportunity for inspectors to speak freely, and these are the words of an official who is determined to see the defendant prosecuted. Gone is the appearance of a relatively dispassionate and even-handed assessment of the evidence apparent in other case reports; instead there is an uncompromising demand for legal proceedings against a blameworthy person. The inspector spoke of

> 'the nature of the danger he has imposed both upon his employees and members of the public which probably breaches every criteria [*sic*] for prosecution in the HSE Legal Proceedings Manual,[12] at a time when issues relating to demolition, health matters and particularly asbestos work are of increasing concern and profile, then you may agree that it is appropriate that this matter would be best dealt with in the Crown Court. The Crown Court would obviously have a more exemplary penalty at its disposal and referring such a serious disregard... carried out by a small but adequately resourced demolition contractor, would send a very clear message to the rest of the industry that this office views these matters with the utmost seriousness and is prepared to take the strongest action at its disposal against those who blatantly disregard the law.' (P97–30)

The offender's conduct is the more blameworthy because he is 'adequately resourced', and therefore has no economically rational

[12] The rare reference to this manual, and elsewhere to the Code for Crown Prosecutors, may be some indication of the extent to which policy guidance intrudes upon the discretion of inspectors (see Ch. 6).

excuse for breaking the law. A memo from the field inspector to his PI spoke of 'the scale of [the employer's] disregard for health and safety legislation . . . [and] his completely unco-operative attitude towards any legal duties he may hold'. It is as if the wrong demands to be punished for doing violence to the principle of occupational health and safety regulation. Not to act in such a flagrant case is to demean the worth of the legal values and rules that the officer enforces, and to which he or she has made an occupational commitment.

If the asbestos case exemplifies the abuse or denial of a moral responsibility, there is also a managerial responsibility to whose abuse inspectors are sensitive. In a report to the PI in a case in which a site manager was seen ascending to a factory roof on an unsecured pallet on the forks of a fork-lift truck, the inspector stated: 'This was classic dangerous behaviour of the kind we would normally bring forcefully to the attention of an employer—perhaps by prosecution. This was different in that [the employer] had taken this action unilaterally, despite better options being available to him. The strongest reason for prosecuting is that he was in charge of the factory—a large, well-organised unit with about 50 employees and various hazardous processes—at the time. He set an appalling example' (P97–31). In this case the employer is more culpable, because he is in charge. He is an exemplar and if he breaks the rules he deserves to be punished.[13]

On the other hand, blame can be lessened if an act or omission can be understood as 'normal', 'typical', or 'customary'. Practices sanctioned by time or routine tend not to be regarded as so reprehensible, even though they may be hazardous and sometimes cause illness or injury.

In a case in which a crane driver was found dead beside his crane with a wound to the side of his head, a note from the PI to his AD observed that the death was being treated as a fatality and not as due to natural causes. The inspector asked for specialist advice because he was 'attempting to establish if access routes on the crane were adequate and what standards if any we expect with regard to safe access on the crane.' The specialist inspector's report noted that 'Access arrangements on this crane are no different to many other similar machines, HGV vehicles and locomotives in common daily use. The means of demounting by climbing onto the track and jumping down is an accepted arrangement on this type of machine and the provision of steps and grab rails on the machine appear no worse to the other instances mentioned above.' Any form of remedy for the risks involved seemed to be unrealistic: 'The site is littered with debris over which one might trip or cause one to stumble if you were to jump down onto it.

[13] The employer was fined £500, with almost £320 in costs.

However this results from the nature of the work being carried on there . . .' The PI concluded: 'We consider the access on the crawler crane was satisfactory and do not propose to make any further enquiries.' The AD replied: 'Thankyou. Presumably no witnesses, so not much more we can do.' (F97–20)

Since access to and from the crane was achieved normally, the implication of the inspector's comments is a categorization of the matter as a 'normal' accident. Since what is normal is not the occasion for blame, the fatality is instead framed as 'accidental' (rather than 'an accident'), and that is the end of the matter. Legal rules inevitably focus attention on occasions where they are breached, but if an event can be framed as 'accidental', that is helpful to the decision-maker, because it may not imply blame, thereby helping move the matter out of the zone of indecision and lead to a decision not to prosecute. Similarly, where a company has displayed an apparent willingness to comply, it becomes correspondingly more difficult to prosecute because it makes it much harder to blame: 'They've put a lot of work in . . . It would have to be a very, very serious incident for me to prosecute them' (86–42).[14] This reluctance is also evident if there are other 'good' (that is, understandable) reasons for non-compliance: 'If you've got a company that has by bad luck or perhaps lack of resources [not complied] then . . . you have to consider whether morally a prosecution is the right thing to do,' said an inspector who quite explicitly recognized that the concern was an expressive matter, not an instrumental one (86–34).

The chance that mitigating conditions may be exploited by the defence and act to reduce the penalty imposed, if not actually persuading the court to find for the defendant, is something to which inspectors are alert in their pre-trial decision-making. 'Accepted practice' is important in tending to discourage prosecution of questionable activities, since some inspectors regard it as a practical defence that may be viewed with sympathy by the courts. In one case, the inspector said to his PI in a memo: 'The activity involved, whilst obviously not a safe system of work, is, however, regarded by many in the agricultural industry as acceptable practice and this may be used in mitigation. . . . Comments on previous visits indicate a reasonably positive attitude towards matters of health and safety' (P97–35). Mitigation may be a problem for the regulatory agency in this particular conflict between conventional work practices and legal

[14] In the Industrial Air Pollution Inspectorate the emphasis given to negotiation of standards and a compliance strategy of enforcement led to a continuing desire to settle all but the most egregious of cases by negotiation (Weait, 1989).

requirements, especially if magistrates are from rural areas and thought inherently sympathetic to agricultural interests and customs.

2. Evil Motive

The motive of the offender is often addressed in assessments of blame and, if pejoratively interpreted, it will amplify culpability. For inspectors, one of the most reprehensible of employers' motives in occupational health and safety regulation is to seek to cut production costs at the expense of employees' health or safety. This amounts to a particularly offensive form of deliberation, putting money before people: 'This accident would appear to be the direct result of the lack of management control combined with attempts to maximise production via cutting corners on safety' (P97–63). The behaviour is more blameworthy if the employer is thought to be prosperous, and therefore easily capable of compliance without financial embarrassment. The reasoning in some case files suggests that this can actually become a reason to prosecute in its own right. Inspectors routinely report on the financial status of a firm in the course of debating the merits of prosecution. The following remarks, from an inspector in a letter to her superior, are typical: 'the . . . Group as a whole are reported in the local press to be in a stable financial position, with good profit margins . . . They are certainly one of the more high profile companies [in this area of the county]. . . . [O]n the whole, conditions at their factory sites are quite good' (P97–03). The blame for the misfortune (a worker's fall and serious injury) is the greater because of the clear implication that the employer had apparently succumbed to the temptation to violate the law for financial gain.

Paradoxically, it seems even more blameworthy to violate the law for a financial motive where the costs of compliance involved are not substantial, but minimal, for this smacks of a deliberate neglect of legal obligations for which even any rational economic reason is lacking. In one case an inspector wrote: 'The cost of compliance with the Prohibition Notice was for perforated metal sheet which would only be a few pounds. In addition the time taken to fit this was only 40 minutes, again insignificant in comparison to the seriousness of the potential injury received on this type of machine. . . . It took only 40 minutes, at minimal cost, to upgrade the standard of guarding on the machine to the appropriate standard' (P97–15). It was not only cheap to comply, therefore, but doing so did not interrupt production to any extent, so the defendant had absolutely no reason not to guard a dangerous machine.

It is a moral affront also to appear to take unfair commercial advantage of those who do comply, for this suggests a reprehensible sort of ruthlessness. A former Chief Inspector of Agriculture explained the sentiment, noting that in his experience moral outrage was expressed by members of trade unions and compliant farmers. They often exerted a general pressure for prosecution because 'Those who comply and get to know that somebody else doesn't and has had an accident, tend to think "Well, he has got away with something. He has failed to comply with the regulations. Life has been cheaper for him . . . he's taken short-cuts. He is letting us down. And if no one does anything about it, why shouldn't we?" Therefore you ought to [prosecute].' It is hard to escape the conclusion that the fundamental objection here is a moral one because there is a violation of the principle that one person ought to be treated equally with another in a similar position. That this is a strong sentiment is evident in comments by a PI:

Q: 'So in a sense, they've been penalized because you see them as taking unfair advantage, unfair commercial advantage, over firms that have spent extra money to safeguard their employees' interests?'

A: 'Yes, I think so. I mean I don't think it's in a quantifiable amount it would actually add to anything significant; I think it would be farthings on the difference in the total bill, you know, it's a very small sum of money that would be lost. But it's just the moral part there, that they do have this moral duty, and they should do it, irrespective of what the law says.' (97–03)

3. Negligence

Negligent behaviour leading to a violation of the law with unfortunate consequences is treated as clearly blameworthy. Indeed, a negligent offender is almost as culpable and deserving of censure as one who breaks rules deliberately. Inspectors probably encounter more instances of negligent than of deliberate misconduct. In a study of the prosecution of occupational health and safety violations in the Crown Courts in the period 1975–90 F. Wright (1995: 10) concluded that, of those that appear in court, 'Most cases involve inadvertence or negligence rather than deliberate wrongdoing.' A typical case in which the employer's negligent behaviour was stressed involved a 17-year-old trainee who fell 2.9 metres through a roof light, breaking his wrist. No covers had been provided for the fragile roof light, and there were inadequate instructions on the precautions to be taken. The reasons for prosecuting were said to be the failure to take simple precautions; the reliance by the employer on verbal instruction; the absence of supervision; and it was high-risk activity common in that sector of industry (P97–22).[15]

Inspectors are especially concerned with acts or events that seem preventable; not to act in the face of an obvious hazard is culpable. Many types of omission suggest a neglect of the duty of care owed to employees. The fact that events might have taken a different turn, and it was knowable in advance that this was so, aligns the act with one in which a morally bad choice has been made. Inspectors will therefore regard omitting to fulfil a duty as blameworthy, for it indicates a lack of attention both to the legal requirements of using a safe system of work and a disdain for the common-sense sentiment that one is morally obliged to attend to the well-being of others. Also culpably negligent are those who fail to be informed, or fail to acquire appropriate training for the workforce. Thus in one case in which a worker lost two fingers while cleaning an unguarded machine, it was recorded that

> '[The company] have apparently been trying to heap all the blame on Mrs Morris saying that she was doing something that she shouldn't have been doing. However... [t]he company still has a duty to protect its employees so far as it is reasonably practicable which they have failed to do through a lack of instruction and training. Based on the company's apparent complacency and the fact that they have appeared to have learned little from the previous prosecution it is proposed to prosecute them...'[16] (P97–64)

Sometimes the legislation, which sits in the inspector's decision field, intrudes to encourage the application of a decision frame that attends to evidence of carelessness, indifference, or complacency:

> In a case in which the employer had failed to notify HSE of the undertaking (thereby avoiding inspection), and an employee had been injured on a poorly guarded moulding machine, the inspector noted that prosecution was '...particularly appropriate as the type of defects noted in the investigation were so obvious that they would have been picked up during a routine preventive visit to the premises and almost certainly enforcement action would have been taken. This would have prevented the accident.' That is, this 'technical' omission was regarded by the inspector as directly responsible for the injury to the victim, and therefore culpable.[17] (P97–15)

[15] The employer was given a conditional discharge for 12 months, with £400 in costs.

[16] The company pleaded guilty to a charge under s. 2 (2) of the HSW Act and was fined £5,000, with nearly £300 in costs. The recommendation for prosecution in another case reported the 'Very poor attitude of company. Do not accept any liability even though evidence is plain. Previous advice of competent person ignored. This has a direct bearing on the accident. Nothing by way of mitigation' (P97–04).

[17] No fine or costs were recorded.

If failing to be aware of legal obligations is blameworthy, knowing the law but failing to act on it is equally so. A number of instances of neglect symbolizes contempt for the law, as was suggested in a case in which a workman had been crushed and killed in machinery when a conveyor suddenly started up. The inspector reported that

> 'The accident resulted from a failure of management at [the company] to ensure the safety of [the dead person], this was a failure not only at the depot level, but also at national level. The company had had the experience of the serious accident . . . they were issuing new procedures, but had not effectively ensured that they were adopted, completed and understood. The company's own depot audit did not . . . identify the failings of the existing system. There were no safeguards in place to sound an alarm . . . Although the issue of access to the top of the silo had been brought to the company's attention by their insurance company, no-one had addressed it. . . . I hope that the court will view the string of management failings which led to [the victim's] death seriously because in my opinion this accident was wholly preventable.'[18] (P97–40)

Knowledge and ignorance make for a double bind for the employer, since common-sense reasoning dictates that if you knew, you should have known better. If risks are self-evident but ignored, then lay reasoning dictates that the employer 'should have known'. In a case in which an elderly woman in a mental hospital drowned in a bath, giving rise to suspicions of suicide, the main justifications for prosecution were 'Known risk disregarded. . . . [T]here is a need to take a firm position that patients are not allowed to harm themselves if sensible precautions can be taken. Fatality' (F97–24). However, if you do not know, this is itself culpable. In one case, for example, the PI noted: 'The defendant appears to have been complacent in that he recognised a risk but failed to deal with it despite having read "Farmwise" [an information brochure] which he seems to regard as mere common sense. The H & S [health and safety] checklist was not complied with as the "supervisor" does not seem to have the knowledge to be regarded as competent in roofwork. Case approved' (P97–22).

It is the existence of a known or knowable risk which can transform an event defined as 'accidental' into an accident in which blame can be attached to the employer. This is suggested in the comment in one case, in which the official reason for prosecuting was that there was an 'Obvious risk from working on a fragile asbestos roof—risk supported by the outcome—both men falling through it.' For this inspector, the risk

[18] The offence received a fine of £18,000, with nearly £2,000 in costs.

was clear, and the employer's culpability was endorsed by the familiar sentiment of 'should have known better' (P97–05). In inspectors' eyes, even if many risks are not self-evident, they are either known or knowable on any common-sense analysis. If they are known and not acted on, or if precautions are inadequate, that amounts to culpable neglect. In a case involving a fatality, the inspector concluded: 'We should focus on the particular circumstances of this case where there was clearly an identification of the risk which the DP [deceased person] faced. That was in the nature of the clinical judgment and yet the precautions taken were inadequate' (P97–24).

4. Guilty Knowledge

Foreseeability and notice are two key elements in blame because they give rise to ideas of guilty knowledge, actual or constructive, and the making of informed, but morally wrong, choices. Knowledge is an important general precondition for the application of blame: when an inspector was asked to explain the meaning of 'blatant', he replied: 'people know what's required... to safeguard people they're putting at risk' (86–05). On the other hand, 'If a firm generally had not been warned by the inspectorate before, or weren't as familiar with the law [as] they should've been, one tends to give them a second chance, if the situation's not too desperate' (86–17). While ignorance of the law may not be a defence to a charge once a case is brought, it can often serve to prevent the case from being considered for prosecution in the first place. Companies which have not previously been inspected are less to blame by virtue of their presumed lack of knowledge about their legal obligations. Inspectors often give a 'second chance' so that employers have an opportunity to apply the inspector's information or advice, in recognition of the feeling that 'In most situations I would wish to see people have an opportunity to comply.' There is, however, a limit to ignorance of the law as an excusing condition, especially where some regulations are very well known, where hazards are obvious, or where a company has had prior advice. In these circumstances the matter is shifted into the realm of constructive blame: 'They can't flout well-known safety regulations,' said one inspector. 'I've only taken cases where the hazard's well-known and the section's well-known' (86–02).

Notice, in the form of information, advice, or warnings, is usually very important in laying the groundwork for subsequent legal action: 'We will rarely out of the blue swoop on any company and prosecute. Nearly always they get some warning at some stage in the past, before you actually prosecute' (86–21). Knowledge of risks can be assumed if an inspector has made a point of advising on previous visits: 'For whatever reason Mr Venables has ignored previous advice, with the subsequent effect of putting the safety of his employees at risk by failing to ensure adequate edge protection was in place during extensive roofwork operations' (P97–61). 'Previous relevant advice' is sometimes recorded as an item in the Prosecution Report and Input Form compiled by inspectors. The first among several 'Reasons for Prosecution' in a case involving a fall was said to be that '[The employer] clearly knows the required standards, having been given adequate advice on a number of previous occasions . . .' (P97–50). In another case the inspector observed that serious advice had been given to the company on four previous occasions about fencing dangerous equipment. An improvement notice and a prohibition notice had been previously issued for guarding problems. In the legal conclusions it was said that 'management and employees were aware of the danger, therefore it *was foreseeable*' (P97–45: original emphasis).

In another case, the injured person, a 21 year-old man, fell off a working platform supported on, but not bolted onto, the forks of a fork-lift truck, receiving serious injuries, including two fractures in his skull. Four years earlier a similar incident on the premises had led to a notice being posted telling employees always to bolt platforms to forks. This was reported as 'indicating foreseeability'. Both improvement and prohibition notices were issued following this earlier accident. It was accepted that the company knew about, but did not condone the practice of using an unsecured cage on the forks of the fork-lift truck. The inspector concluded from this that the company had failed to provide and supervise a safe system of work, and this was the reason given for prosecuting.[19] (P97–23)

Guilty knowledge attributable to an offender has a number of dimensions. If there is a breach of a well-established, generally recognized rule, or there is great familiarity with a danger, an employer will be considered more blameworthy and is more likely to invite prosecution. In another case the inspector noted: 'The law is basic, simple, and has been around for a long time (30 years) in current form. It is there to prevent serious or fatal injury accidents. Roofing activities [are] the major cause of death and serious injury within the Construction Industry—itself having an accident rate some six times that of manufacturing and 15 times that of the service sector' (P97–05). The reasoning here suggests that since roofing is even riskier than other construction work, there is correspond-

[19] The employer was fined £3,500, with £500 in costs.

ingly a greater duty of care upon the employer, who is correspondingly even more blameworthy when an accident occurs. Besides, there is well-established, familiar law on the subject; the employer could reasonably be supposed to have known about it, and could have no objection to it. The inspector's Case Progress form in another case listed the informations to be laid, and the PI commented on them: 'Both cases approved. Well known risk and vulnerable client. Topic needs to be publicised, guidance available since 1993' (P97–68).[20] In other words, the defendants should have known, and it is this failure that justifies the prosecution. In contrast, an employer who violates a new rule, or commits a violation involving an unfamiliar hazard, is less blameworthy. These sentiments are clear in the following remarks by a former Chief Agricultural Inspector, discussing a policy which crystallized a common-sense approach. The fact that notice appears in what amounts to a statement of working rules for prosecution decision-making indicates its importance:

> '[W]hen we introduce a new regulation, it has to be a very blatant case to justify prosecution within the first six months of it coming into force... Where a power take-off was unguarded and in use, that was virtually a certainty for prosecution. Children riding on tractors were virtual certainties. The inspector almost had to justify why he didn't prosecute in these circumstances because they were known to be major sources of serious injury or fatality so that people who broke such a regulation and got away with it deserve prosecution because they were seriously putting people at risk... Equally, when advice has been given previously, this amounts to extra information and greater culpability.'

Notice is also treated as constructive knowledge because it amounts to the capacity to be informed and to do otherwise. If a legal rule is of long standing, inspectors normally assume that employers should know its requirements. If an injury then follows the breach of such a rule, the employer will be blamed: old, settled law gives less leeway to employers to plead ignorance or difficulties in complying. They can reasonably be expected to know of the law's requirements; their failure is therefore more blameworthy. To fail to comply in these circumstances indicates an indifference to the consequences which is highly reprehensible. In various cases there were observations that, for example, the need for personal protective equipment when using chainsaws had been publicized for several years (P97–21), or that it was a 'Well known requirement' that vehicles carrying liquid propane cylinders should also carry fire

[20] Similarly, the reasons for prosecuting in another case were said to be: 'Serious accident. Well known hazard. Well known protective measures not in use' (P97–46).

extinguishers (P97–27). Similarly, employers are also to blame if they tolerate known hazardous practices by employees. Ideas of guilty knowledge, neglect of advice, and lack of foreseeability are bound together here. Thus the special reason for prosecuting in one case was that the 'Defendants' site management had guilty knowledge of risks taken by subcontractors. The accident resulted in serious injury' (P97–09).

Notice is assisted by clarity and precision in legal rules. In inspectors' reasoning, the breach of a rule is more blameworthy if a plain and well-defined rule is violated. The inspector in one case concluded: 'A man died because a specific old legal requirement had not been complied with and therefore prosecution of [the company] must be pursued' (P97–11). The moral compulsion arising from the blameworthy breach is underlined by use of the words 'therefore' and 'must'.

5. Responsibility and Denial

Attempts by employers to deny or evade responsibility for an accident also disclose moral fault. Their unwillingness to recognize or accept their own failings are frequently remarked on in the prosecution files. A Process Paper justified prosecution in one case by observing, 'This man does not appear to accept that he has done wrong and needs to be brought to account. There was risk of fatality in this situation' (P97–16). Such behaviour suggests in common-sense logic an indifference to a tragic outcome and a lack of remorse, an inability to feel shame for what has happened. These sentiments were powerfully expressed by the inspector involved in the big asbestos case:

> 'Throughout . . . [the employer] has failed to accept his responsibility for what has happened and has always tried to deny the existence of a danger and the duties of control that go with it, or to blame others for the failings on the site . . . [The employer] has throughout seen our intervention as interfering with his own affairs which are his own private business, and although I am in no doubt he is aware that he is likely to be prosecuted both by ourselves and possibly the local authority, he has yet to show any signs that he accepts the errors of what he has done. To some extent, [the employer] attempts to put forward an image that he does not really understand the issues that are being put to him. However, this is somewhat difficult to believe as he has in the past held a licence to dispose of hazardous waste, although I believe that was taken away from him as a result of a prosecution by the Waste Regulatory Authority some years ago.' (P97–30)

The employer's wrongful act or omission becomes the worse if in the meantime there is no repair or any other symbolic indicator of a recognition that the employer has learned from past mistakes and realizes it is essential to prevent a recurrence. Repair or remedy as a goal of prosecution appears in the reference to the desirability of 'changed attitudes' which is reminiscent of the emphasis in rehabilitative penology which used to be given to 'change' or 'insight' in offenders, and, in a moral frame, to their display of remorse. Repair is as important for what it signifies about the rule-breaker as it is for representing some instrumental improvement in reducing hazards. 'Action by company following the accident' is also an item routinely reported on in the case files. In one case an inspector was prompted to cite among his reasons for prosecuting: 'Staff continue to be at risk; despite this defendant had not written plan of action for implementing measures to reduce risks.' He concluded that the employer had done the minimum to comply without really addressing risks to staff, despite previous advice and an extension to the date by which compliance was required with an improvement notice (P97–39).

Just as it is easy to condemn deliberate or flagrant rule-breaking, its opposite, a willingness to recognize responsibility, is often taken into account as a mitigating feature. An early sign that the defendant is willing to plead guilty suggests to inspectors an acceptance of responsibility, and this is symbolically significant of a readiness to accept blame (even though for defendants the incentive may be a reduction in penalty). Case files sometimes observe that credit was given for a 'timely guilty plea' (P97–05).[21] Similarly, signs of contrition or remorse in the defendant also contribute to a view of a diminished moral culpability. Contrition may be symbolized for the inspector in repair—the efforts that a defendant makes after an incident to reduce a risk: 'There's always an element in the decision whether or not to prosecute about the effort being made by a firm' (86–26). Thus it will be regarded as a matter of mitigation if employers take steps to remedy a problem that has caused an accident, and have also engaged the services of a safety consultant. When an employer makes conspicuous efforts to correct the matters causing concern, the moral props of the prosecution may be kicked away, prompting inspectors to think again about whether prosecution of a now compliant company would be desirable or would, in contrast, even appear vindictive. 'When I know they've remedied the situation, and things have been tidied up,' said one inspector, 'I start to think "Is it really worth proceeding further?"' (86–35).

[21] In this case, an appeal against sentence, there was a reduction in costs, quite possibly as a result of the 'timely guilty plea'.

In a case in which an employee had been injured in an accident with a chainsaw which he was using with a logging horse, the employer's contrition was symbolized for the inspector by his actions after the event. The saw was not designed for use on a logging horse. The injured person had been hurt when the saw jumped onto his hand when he was holding a log. After the accident protective equipment was provided, together with a new logging horse, and a new chainsaw. The inspector noted: '[Employer] asked for advice on the type that would be suitable.' These actions suggested remorse, and the appropriate attitude. The employer said in a letter to the inspector: 'I was more than worried when you said that an offence might have been committed because I have spent my working life trying to ensure that rules are complied with. . . . I wonder if you could please arrange for a set of all appropriate [safety] leaflets to be sent to me as soon as possible.' Although the contrition displayed by the defendant was not enough to prevent a prosecution, it was probably enough to have gained the sympathy of the court, for it granted the defendant a conditional discharge.[22] (P97–21)

If defendants in a case appear to be cooperative, blame may also be diminished, and continuing the action may need to be justified on instrumental grounds. In one case in which a woman had lost the tip of a finger in a machine, the Process Paper referred to 'preventive measures taken after accident', adding: 'The company have co-operated fully throughout the investigation and have been keen to find the cause and carry out modifications to HSE satisfaction.' The inspector explained she was considering prosecution 'because (1) high risk machine, (2) not adequately guarded, (3) potential for serious injury'. The company's directors were said to be concerned 'they might be prosecuted, even though they had responded positively following the accident' (P97–06). If, as in this case, an employer remedies the problem, any subsequent prosecution is more easily justified as a deterrent or as a means of symbolizing the power and position of the regulatory body.[23]

Cooperativeness is also symbolized in a willingness to forgo legal entitlements, which prompts an inclination to think better of those who do, since the act reflects an acceptance of responsibility. In the case of the big explosion and fire at an oil terminal the inspector observed: 'This firm have attempted to control health and safety issues and have taken steps to reduce risk on site. Unfortunately their control over the activities involving the death of [the victim] were insufficient.' Subsequently, the

[22] In another case the operations director was 'clearly concerned that the accident happened', and explained that the injured person would be kept in employment. 'Everyone at this small company, from the Directors downwards, were *fully co-operative and anxious to help* with the investigation' (P97–45; my emphasis).

[23] The company was fined £1,450, with more than £500 in costs.

inspector noted that the firm had spent £100,000 on replacing the equipment 'and they did not of course appeal against my Prohibition Notice' (P97–28). In such circumstances the firm is regarded as displaying the right attitudes, and is showing practical contrition, though the gravity of this particular case was such that it was extremely likely that prosecution would have been regarded as an imperative.

6. Persistence

Repeated rule-breaking is a familiar condition of blame. Persistence in offending, whether the result of an inability to make the right moral choice or to know better, incompetence or ignoring previous advice, or for some other reason, is a major moral shortcoming. If an inspector comes to the conclusion that the 'Company appears not to have learned lesson from last accident', this will be treated as strong grounds for prosecution (P97–64).[24] In one typical case an employee suffered the amputation of two fingers of his right hand following contact with an unguarded screw elevator while cleaning out powder in a food hopper. It was said 'PR [prosecution] proposed as company was prosecuted last year over similar incident' (P97–64).[25]

Evidence of persistent rule-breaking is sometimes put into the amplified perspective of a historical view of the nature of the regulatory agent's enforcement relationship with the rule-breaker, or on the employer's career of compliance or wrongdoing, and this often helps inspectors reason about the desirability of prosecution. An indicator of what is past is important to them because they hold it to be a means by which they can understand present conduct better and speculate more confidently about the future. Blame is easier to attribute if a sequence of unhappy events comprising a career of rule-breaking can be assembled for reasoning about prosecution because that can suggest persistence in offending, or a systematic disregard of the law (Hawkins, 1983*a*). Indeed, in criminal justice generally, previous convictions are a familiar marker of past misdeeds and an important device for attributing blame to a present act and predicting future misconduct.

[24] See also P97–10, mentioned in the text at n. 10 above, where the offending behaviour was described as 'custom and practice' in this workplace, and as 'company policy'.

[25] Previous convictions of a company at another site indicate pattern or repetitiveness. In the case of the explosion and fire at an oil terminal, it was recorded in the file that although there were 'no previous convictions of this firm', a 'serious fire' had occurred at another of the firm's terminals (P97–28).

A career of rule-breaking helps strip away doubt or ambiguity and simplify the task of decision-making. A particular incident can be located within a wider array of events allowing the present matter either to be portrayed and understood as 'isolated' or 'accidental',[26] or, if a pattern of rule-breaking can be discerned, as 'repetitive'. If repetitiveness in the events seems to suggest that the present incident is merely the latest in a long sequence of deliberate or negligent misconduct, blame is much easier to attribute. Inspectors have ready access to records going back several years of past visits, correspondence following visits, site inspections, and prosecutions. The regulated firm's past often exists in the personal knowledge of the inspector. These sources of data are assembled to build up a picture of the career of the employer, delinquent or otherwise.

In one case the inspector stated in a memo to his PI: 'The company have a poor health and safety record which has resulted in the company being prosecuted twice and a personal prosecution for the Works Manager. A number of other informations have been laid against the company recently' (P97–17). This history implies the existence of a general malaise in the company that makes its present act particularly blameworthy and therefore prosecutable. Sometimes, therefore, evidence of a similar accident in the past or a prior prosecution can be enough themselves to prompt prosecution.

In a case in which a fitter had fallen through a skylight, inspection reports going back over a period of nearly 35 years were in the file. They recorded unsatisfactory safety standards, a number of accidents, and at least one prosecution. Reports to employers following visits by inspectors identified various problems and suggested necessary remedial work. In a letter sent some years earlier following a dangerous occurrence when a liquified petroleum gas cylinder suddenly burst, releasing propane gas, the then PI reported that 'Serious consideration was given to the institution of legal proceedings in relation to this matter but it has been decided not so to proceed in this case.'[27] (P97–43)

If repetitiveness is blameworthy, it may be easier to define circumstances as potentially mitigating if it is possible to regard an event as isolated, and not as part of a pattern of non-compliance. Inspectors

[26] Thus an inspector noted that 'His Honour took into consideration the fact that the company had operated on this site for 23 years without such an accident and the great concern the company had shown both to the family of [the victim] and in respect of the action it had taken following the incident in replacing the [equipment]' (P97–28).

[27] The employer was not so lucky this time, and was convicted under s. 2 of the HSW Act, receiving a fine of £5,000 and more than £400 in costs.

sometimes acknowledge this: in one case involving two falls in the course of roofing work, the inspector, though opting formally to prosecute, did acknowledge that the failure to provide crawling boards which had led to the accident 'was an isolated matter from a company that did not regularly flout the law' (P97–62). In another case in which a worker had been killed in the collapse of a trench, the inspector spoke of the employer's 'first fatal despite lots of activity. They generally have high standards, and the project manager had been on holiday the week before. He never saw the drainage gang working under the embankment' (P97–34).[28] Nonetheless, though recognized as mitigating, in both cases these features were not enough to prevent the prosecution of the employers.

Common sense dictates to defendants that they should try to present evidence which prevents others from establishing a pattern or suggesting that wilful persistence or neglect has led to non-compliance. Such common-sense reasoning suggests to employers that they exploit the absence of a record of past regulatory difficulties in the hope of dissuading HSE from prosecuting. So much is suggested by the expectations of the PI in the big asbestos case: 'Do we have any record of [the employer] from the past—I assume not and envisage that he would attempt to use the fact that we have had no previous contact with him to his advantage and you [the inspector] also mention that he attempted to pass blame on to others including HSE' (P97–30). This is a strategy intuitively sensed, even by those who represent themselves in court. For example, the defendant 'said he was very sorry about what had happened. He said he was a competent foreman and this was an isolated incident' (P97–52). The tactic was unsuccessful in this case, in which a contractor had damaged a gas pipe and had tried to mend it himself, prompting the comment from the inspector that 'It could have resulted in the deaths of many people.' It is likely, however, that the court had some sympathy with the defendant since his costs were reduced.[29]

7. Outcome, Risk, and Breach

There is a tension for inspectors between evaluating an undesired outcome, the risk of such an outcome, and the degree to which the law has

[28] The employer pleaded guilty to a breach of Regulation 4 of the Management of Health and Safety at Work Regulations, 1992, and was fined £3,000, plus more than £1,800 costs.

[29] It fined him £1,000 with £200 costs, where the actual costs had amounted to £408.

been breached. Common-sense logic tends to blame for the outcome rather than the nature or degree of the legal breach. As Hutter and Lloyd-Bostock (1990: 418) have pointed out, prosecutions are frequently perceived as being 'for' the death or injury involved, rather than the breach of a rule that gave rise to the accident. The importance of the distinction between breach and consequence is important, not least because a routine violation can sometimes lead to appalling consequences, as Carson (1982: 6) found when studying oil and gas operations in the North Sea. Sometimes the need to blame where there is a grave outcome is very powerful, and the desire to prosecute becomes irresistible, even though the legal breach may not be as serious as in many other cases. 'If there's been a fatal accident, it's very difficult not to take action if the evidence is there and there's a breach there . . . although we are told it's the seriousness of the breach we should consider, rather than the accident resulting from it' (86–17). 'Initially you tend to react to the severity of what's happened,' said another inspector, 'especially if there's a vulnerable victim' (86–02). Lloyd-Bostock's (1987) research showed that nearly 40 per cent of prosecutions in the former Factory Inspectorate (FI) followed an accident.[30] This poses problems:

> '[O]ne of the difficulties we have, one of the areas we get the most difficult arguments relate to the seriousness of the accident versus the seriousness of the breach. A fatal accident . . . is always a very serious accident. But it doesn't necessarily arise because of a very serious breach. . . . The difficulty we have is that there can be a lot of pressure on to prosecute, say, this fatal accident when they are not necessarily the most serious offences.' (97–01)

The decision-maker faces particular difficulty when there is a breach of the law but no harm done. Inspectors are unwilling to consider prosecution of less serious cases (such as so-called 'paper violations'), simply because, however visible they may be, the harm done is insufficient to warrant such a weighty and official response. Harm suffered makes it easy to blame. It is much harder to blame in the absence of harm. The problem is acute when dealing with hazards, and inspectors have difficulty in deciding, partly because there are questions about how sympathetically the case will be received in court:

[30] She found that the largest single category of prosecutions was comprised of guarding offences, and the majority of them followed accidents. She also found that machinery accidents, especially those caused by failure to guard, comprised the largest category of accident investigations (Lloyd-Bostock, 1987).

'I mean one of the issues that we have . . . [is] prosecutions without accidents. A lot of HSE's prosecutions traditionally have revolved around accidents, because then there is often clear evidence of breach. But you can argue, of course, that an accident is a consequence of a set of circumstances. There are lots of other sets of circumstances where accidents don't arise. The problem we find practically is that the reception in courts for non-accident prosecutions is not always very favourable.' (97–01)

In common-sense reasoning, accidents are significant. First, they are more persuasive in demanding a legal response than risks that are posed. Second, it is the big and dramatic incident which has the greatest impact (Lloyd-Bostock, 1987: 2). The concern which inspectors display for accidents is not surprising. Accidents are vivid and concrete events and often serve as a spur to action. It is harder to apprehend risks. They are partly understood by means of accident statistics, but these, in contrast, seem to decision-makers to be abstract, bloodless, and disembodied, even though they may be a better and more rational basis for enforcement action. Risks are less compelling as practical influences upon an inspector's decision-making and do not create the same demand to act as those risks which have been realized (the 'body on the floor', as some inspectors put it). Prosecution is sometimes used following an accident not only because of its unique capacity to serve other relevant and important functions, especially to respond to the expectations of the public and the workforce (see Chapter 7), but also because it is a response to what Lloyd-Bostock (1987: 25–6) refers to as the 'knew it all along' effect. This serves to frame an accident, with hindsight, as more predictable than it really was, therefore making it, in an inspector's mind, less excusable.

Putting workers at risk is nonetheless treated as blameworthy, and in general the greater or the more familiar the hazard, the greater the blame. Thus it is culpable to allow a person to operate dangerous machinery without safety precautions because familiar and frequently encountered risks make them 'obvious'. Common sense dictates that a reasonable person should appreciate the risk. The matter is firmly lodged in the moral sphere: 'If anyone operates a power press without a guard and someone gets hurt, they *deserve* what's coming to them' (86–37; my emphasis). 'Power presses we still would do,' said a senior official. 'Someone injured with a power press we'd still prosecute . . . because it's a permanent, non-reversible injury. The remedies are known. There is a code of regulations to bolster up those [requirements]. And if you're running power presses and you run it without a guard, you're just asking for it.'

Where a familiar or obvious risk has been realized in the form of an accident, common sense dictates that it is much easier to blame and to think seriously about prosecution. Falls often prompt this sort of blaming behaviour. The reasons for prosecuting in a case in which there had been two separate incidents on two consecutive days involving two different people were given as: 'The hazards associated with work on fragile roofs are well documented. Falls from height are after all the biggest cause of death or major injury in the construction industry.' The defendants 'admitted that they were fully conversant with the necessary precautions in respect of fragile roof work. They also both admitted to knowing [the injured person] was a novice (an 'inexperienced school leaver') and their inactions [*sic*] had led to his safety being put at serious risk' (P97–62).[31] In another case in which a fitter fell 4 metres through a skylight, the inspector's rationale was that it was a 'Well established risk. Little thought had been given to safety in roof work by management' (P97–43). The inclination to blame is particularly strong where the risk should be plain.

The self-evident risk means a hazard that is foreseeable. If a risk is foreseeable and reasonably practicable measures to ensure the safety of employees could have been implemented, the common-sense desire to blame can be harnessed to the legal requirement in s. 2. of the HSW Act. Foreseeability is an important value because it suggests that an outcome was preventable, thereby creating a clear duty for the person responsible to take appropriate precautions. This accounts for the simplicity of the reasoning in one prosecution report in which the inspector observed: 'IP [injured person] suffered traumatic amputation of left ring finger when using inadequately guarded power press. Accident foreseeable and easily preventable.' The 'Special reason' for prosecuting was put simply as 'Easily preventable accident' (P97–54).

Where risks are foreseeable, inspectors go on to judge the adequacy of any precautions taken. Their existence is per se not enough, for employers have an obligation to ensure precautions are both appropriate and adequate.

In a case in which a 17-year-old trainee had fallen three metres through an uncovered roof light, breaking his wrist, the employer's solicitor wrote asking the PI to drop the matter and instead to caution his client. The PI refused, and reported that because of the degree of danger involved and the foreseeability of that danger he had instructed the inspector to institute proceedings under Reg.

[31] The employer was fined £1,500 with nearly £500 in costs for an offence under s. 2 (1) of the HSW Act.

36 of the Construction (Working Places) Regs. 1966 (SI No 94). The case went ahead despite the solicitor's letter which detailed the number of warnings that had been given to the injured person by the employer, the fact that the ladder had been tied, and so on. There was also a letter from a college where the trainee had done three days' induction, pleading for the defendant not to be prosecuted.[32] (P97–22)

There is sometimes a suggestion in inspectors' reasoning that big firms should take more extensive precautions than smaller ones. One possible explanation is that they are expected to have greater resources of knowledge and money to comply readily with legal requirements. This thinking is hinted at in one case where the 'Special reasons' for prosecuting were said to be: 'The company are a fairly large concern who should be managing H&S better, I feel that a prosecution would have a salutary effect' (P97–56).

8. The Speculative Tragedy

One sort of risk especially impresses inspectors, and is recruited as a powerful justification for a decision to prosecute. This is the accident which seems more culpable by virtue of what might have been. Some violations result in harm, and it is believed that it is only by chance that the harm was not much greater. Inspectors here assess the gravity of a breach by reasoning not about its actual but rather about its potential consequences. They are able to augment existing blame by reasoning about the 'speculative tragedy'. This is a persuasive reasoning tool (one also employed by other agents of social control, like the police), since it intensifies the nature of the harm done by the employer's act or omission, speculating about even graver consequences creating a sense of greater offence. In a memo to his PI in a case in which a worker had received serious head injuries, the inspector stated: 'At this early stage it must be emphasised that in my opinion this is not the most blatant of offences alleged against this company, but that although the injuries were severe, they could have been far worse, almost certainly fatal [the following had been added in handwriting:] and *it is the latter which is the reason for the [prosecution] to be proposed*' (P97–17; my emphasis). There are three instances of this form of reasoning in the following:

A complaint had been received that roof work was under way without the provision or use of adequate edge protection. The inspector reported that it

[32] The employer pleaded guilty, and received a conditional discharge for 12 months. HSE was awarded £400 in costs.

was 'incomprehensible' that the work should have started without protection: 'Should either a person or materials have fallen from the roof then serious injury to the roof worker concerned or a [member of the public] could have resulted. The carriage of hot tar up an untied ladder is also unacceptable. Had the ladder slipped then serious burn injuries could have resulted.' This reason to recommend prosecution was said by the inspector to be important because 'It was only fortuitous that a serious accident was prevented.'[33] (P97–58)

There are many other examples. In a case in which students were overcome by carbon monoxide from a faulty gas boiler installation, the inspector reported: 'This is a particularly bad example of poor workmanship. Three students suffered carbon monoxide poisoning. Had [the landlord] not returned to the premises when he did fatalities could have occurred' (P97–45).[34] In some prosecution reports the speculative language is aligned with the language of the HSW Act. For example, reporting a case in which five gas cylinders which had not been stored in a fire-resistant structure exploded in a fire, the inspector stated:

'If [the employer] considered it not reasonably practicable to store the cylinders outside because of the theft problem, he could have built a storeroom of fire resisting material inside which would house the gas cylinders. This he did not do, thus possibly endangering employees who had to work [there]. A leaking cylinder could have been a source of ignition and could have engulfed employees or trapped office workers in the first floor office—there being only one exit from the upstairs office' (P97–14).[35]

The breach becomes more blameworthy when the potential consequences extend beyond those in the employment relationship, to members of the public. In the case of a collapsed crane, the inspector observed: 'This was a serious collapse and it was fortunate that the jib fell where it did. Had it fallen 90 degrees in another direction it would have been the roof of a neighbour's house.' Special reasons for this prosecution were recorded as: 'Potential fatal event which could have had off-site consequences' (P97–02).

[33] The employer was fined £1,500 with £200 costs for an offence under the Construction (Working Places) Regulations, 1966, Reg. 33.

[34] Similarly: 'This accident could have been a fatality' (P97–66); 'Accident could have been fatal' (P97–03); 'The accident could easily have resulted in fatal injuries' (P97–25); 'Should someone have fallen from the rear roof edge or from the unfenced area at the front of the premises then serious injury or even death may have resulted' (P97–50).

[35] The employer was fined £1,500 and £3,000 under, respectively, the Highly Flammable Liquids and Liquefied Petroleum Gas Regulations, 1972, and s. 3 (1) of the HSW Act.

9. The Character of the Offender

Blame is frequently attributed or abandoned in response to the perceived personal character and attributes of those involved in the accident or hazard, whether as victim or offender, rather than by virtue of what they have done or failed to do. Personal characteristics give wide scope in general for moral evaluation by inspectors.[36] Various cues suggest to inspectors what sort of an offender, whether person or organization, is being dealt with. The idea of the offender here is a complex one. It may include an individual in a position of responsibility, immediate or more remote. It may refer generally to the management of a particular site or plant. Or it may be conceived broadly as the total organization. The crucial question for inspectors is whether they think they are dealing with a cooperative, basically compliant offender, or one whose attitudes towards the workforce and the running of the work site are open to criticism: 'Not only did he display a total disregard for health and safety, but he is an habitual liar and *therefore deserves* to be prosecuted' (P97–20; my emphasis). Reputations, however, are not always particularistic and derived solely from inspectors' own practical knowledge and experience of an individual firm or employer. Typification of sorts of work, site, or employer is a resilient tool in framing. As is evident in some of the files, inspectors rely on typifications of certain types of industry or occupation in deciding to prosecute: 'I consider the defendant, *like most small roof/repair firms* to be a non-complier and would I'm sure go back to his old ways, if we let him off the hook. The defendant has in effect shown complete lack of thought and we have no choice I consider, than to prosecute' (P97–67; my emphasis).

Character and reputation can be powerful framing devices both to enhance and to mitigate blame: 'A lot depends on your knowledge of a company... There are companies where you know they're a thoroughly bad organization and clearly in those situations I won't say you're looking for a prosecution, but situations will arise where you'll take a prosecution, but with another firm you might not' (86–02). One implication of disreputability is that evidence which in other circumstances might be regarded as mitigating is framed as less credible. The character of business, an inspector said, is interpreted by reference to 'their attitude, their co-operativeness' (86–34). The response of a company to

[36] And others, for this has been a persistent finding in the decision-making of police officers and other legal officials, from the very earliest studies (see e.g. D. Black, 1980; Piliavin & Briar, 1964).

inspectors' enforcement practices in general, and to accidents in particular, invites interpretation of its 'attitudes', 'cooperativeness', 'respect for the law', and so on. This conception is at once personal yet less concrete than one focused on the rule-breaker's behaviour, action, or inaction. This social construction of the company awards it a human character and personality, and contributes critically to the framing of a particular decision. A negative evaluation as a 'bad firm', or one with 'poor attitudes', frames the way in which other features in the case will be understood. The same accident can be seen in a 'bad' company as a symptom of poor management, indifference to health and safety issues, or a general malaise. In a 'good' company it may be regarded as an isolated and unfortunate event, or otherwise as a matter beyond its control, and in such circumstances a prosecution may seem unfair: 'I've often felt', said one inspector, 'that it would be wrong to prosecute the company as a whole for an individual act which has placed them in a position [of being prosecuted], where in general they're very safety conscious and very safety minded' (86–17).

The behaviour of the employer towards an unfortunate event is taken as a significant indicator of character in the social construction of blame. Acts and omissions can symbolize a deeper underlying 'attitude' which offers an important clue to the existence of moral fault. Companies may be characterized by inspectors as having a 'bad attitude', a convenient catch-all idea which suggests apathy, or even hostility to legal obligations. A 'bad attitude' is revealed in a number of indicators. Seeming indifference to an untoward act or event suggests a lack of concern for actual or potential victims, as well as fundamental disregard for the legislation. Thus inspectors often observe, for example: 'The management of the company did not appear concerned about the irregularities noted' (P97–58);[37] or 'Because of . . . nonchalant attitude prosecution warranted' (P97–61); or 'This company has an extremely negative attitude towards HSE whilst claiming to have a positive attitude to safety . . . Two directors cannot except [*sic*] blame, despite a wealth of evidence. They tend to regard events as pure accident' (P97–04).

When employed as a reasoning device, attitude serves as a composite concept embracing a variety of characteristics which are taken to exemplify the degree to which the rule-breaking is held to be typical of the

[37] Similarly, in another case a memo from inspector to PI observed the poor state of the industrial relations at the firm and reported that 'The directors at past visits have seemed to be particularly disinterested in health and safety and willing to let me conduct inspections alone' (P97–08).

offender, or the extent to which the offence seems to be out of keeping, or 'accidental', and not therefore truly blameworthy. Thus in a case in which the employer had been prosecuted on an earlier occasion, it was observed that 'No representative from the company attended court' (P97–64), the lack of interest, in the context of the case, seemingly indicating a bad attitude. The inspector in another case reported:

'A comprehensive letter addressing health and safety was sent to the company following [the inspector's] visit to which they had paid very little regard. *This gives some indication of the general approach to health and safety*. . . . The company appears to lack a cohesive and effective formalised health and safety management system. This I feel could be caused by lack of genuine and committed regard for health and safety from senior management and possibly from lack of financial funds.' (P97–69; my emphasis)

The centrality of the employer's attitude is conspicuous in the following case, in which an untrained driver had both his legs crushed when his fork-lift truck overturned:

The inspector's report indicated that no formal system for training fork-lift truck drivers was in place. The company director was not aware it was a legal requirement but 'believed it to be an optional luxury.' After the accident, the firm 'enlisted services of a professional FLT [fork-lift truck] driver training firm to train all personnel who need to operate fork-lift trucks at the premises.' Immediately after the accident, however, 'there were a number of phone calls from employees who said they worked for [the firm].' They said that they had refused to drive fork-lift trucks because they were not properly trained. 'The management, however, had told them to continue driving the trucks.' The inspector then observed: 'Although the above information cannot be proved it would appear to be indicative of the firm's attitude towards health and safety.'

That is, although this matter may not become the substance of a charge, because it would fail in court for want of suitable evidence, it is an indicator which may be taken into account by the inspector or PI as a reason for prosecuting on another more suitable charge. Furthermore, the inspector takes the company's view about the proposed prosecution as itself illustrative of its 'attitude' and may take this into account:

'. . . ATTITUDE OF MANAGEMENT
The firm have not prepared a safety policy and the MD [Managing Director] would appear to believe that health and safety is not a management issue. . . . The company's MD feels that because he was unaware of the requirement to train forklift drivers, the proposed prosecution is unjustified.'

Prosecution was recommended under s. 2 (1) HSW Act 1974, for failing to train forklift truck drivers, as required by the Code of Practice on forklift truck driver training. Recorded as reasons for prosecuting were: 'The MD . . . believes that managing health and safety is not his problem. The firm do not have a safety policy and have a poor attitude towards health and safety. The serious nature of the accident and the potential for a fatality.'[38] (P97–19)

In the big asbestos case the inspector recorded that workers were 'simply ripping down the building with the excavator without any thought for a safe system of work or the possible presence of asbestos'. When the employer returned to the site, he 'did so *reluctantly and was simply belligerent* when he attended' (P97–30; my emphasis). The implication of this is that 'The firms who show themselves to be receptive to your advice are treated more leniently than those where there's a bit of aggro' (86–01). The less favourable inspectors' images of firms are, as a general rule the more willing they become, when some cause for concern has arisen, to think about prosecution.

The employer's attitude is sometimes discernible from behaviour that takes place after an accident. In particular, evidence that risks have been repaired by the employer to prevent the recurrence of an accident, or steps taken to abate hazards, may indicate the right attitude and help to mitigate the degree of blame directed towards the firm, as is suggested by the decision-making in the fatality discussed at the beginning of this chapter (F97–11). Efforts to mitigate blame by remedying a breach can sometimes backfire, however, by creating suspicions that the employer is being manipulative and is cynically trying to get away with it, therefore actually displaying the wrong attitude. This serves to increase blame. 'I am sure the company will try to blame their failings on the Water Board,' reported one inspector in a welfare case. 'However, temporary arrangements could and should have been made . . . The company will claim they were quick to rectify the matter at the time of my visit. This is true as within 20 minutes of my arrival on a site a [boiler] had been delivered . . . This however strengthens my reasons for prosecuting, as why could such an arrangement not have been made before my visit rather than as a result of it . . . ?' (P97–61). And in another case, in which a worker manoeuvring a heavy panel had fractured his spine, the inspector reported:

[38] The MD was prosecuted and pleaded guilty, receiving a conditional discharge, with costs of a little more than £550 awarded to HSE. There was no fine, presumably because, as the field inspector recorded afterwards, 'firm produced new witness, FLT trainer who claimed had trained most employees except IP (due to illness)'.

'The company certainly initially appeared reluctant to bear any responsibility for this accident. The company were very surprised at the Health and Safety Executive's further investigations into this accident and evidently horror struck when statements were taken. It is my belief that they are of the opinion that as long as there is an investigation into accidents and an investigation report is produced, this will satisfy the enforcing authority. It is important in my opinion that they understand that it is not alright to breach health and safety legislation, simply because they will always investigate an accident/incident and write a thorough report after the event.'[39] (P97–55)

The implication that the company is trying to evade responsibility by producing what it regards as appropriate signs of remedial behaviour to symbolize its remorse only adds to the desire to blame.

Companies whose character is regarded unfavourably may find that their remedial efforts are more likely to be interpreted pejoratively by inspectors. In the following case apparently drastic action impressed the inspector not as real evidence of a changed attitude on the company's part, but as an attempt to shift the blame:

The victim had been crushed in machinery when doing maintenance work and killed. There was evidence of another accident involving an identical machine at another depot, in which a worker had been seriously injured. The depot production manager and maintenance team leader had been dismissed. The inspector asserted that she did 'not think that the company have fully learnt the lessons of the accident in its [other] depot. Whilst it has gone a long way in requiring depots to carry out risk assessments and in issuing procedures it has not taken steps to ensure that the improvements in the documentation are actually implemented in the form of action in the depots.' As to the dismissal of the two men, which might appear to be prompt action following the accident, the inspector said '... [T]he company internally seem to be placing the blame squarely on the Depot Production Manager and Maintenance Team Leader. The company are however aware of *Regina v British Steel plc* from issues brought out in the [earlier] prosecution and given the shortcomings in auditing and training I do not think that the company could successfully argue that they had done everything reasonable to ensure [the dead person's] safety.'[40] (P97–40)

Prosecuting in cases where the rule-breaker's response is lacking in a significant way symbolizes disapproval of both the original event and its aftermath. The case suggests that even if action seemingly to remedy a

[39] The employer was fined £1,500, with £775 in costs, for an offence under Reg. 4 (1) (a) of the Manual Handling Operations Regulations 1992.

[40] The employer was convicted under s. 2 of the HSW Act, and was fined £18,000, with costs of nearly £2,400.

problem has been taken, there is a precariousness about how such action will be framed by the inspector.

With large companies, the construction of the character of the particular site or employer is sometimes drawn from the general reputation of the company concerned, sometimes from the inspector's own personal experiences of past dealings with a particular individual. While disreputability may be readily imputed to individuals, the firm itself is also open to moral evaluation, often on several fronts, as the following example shows. A 'bad' and therefore blameworthy company was prosecuted following an isocyanate-induced form of occupational asthma which was suffered by two employees who had been spraying glues.

The PI described the matter in a letter to HSE in London as 'extraordinary... production pressures are colossal. Matters such as routine maintenance, housekeeping, training etc. and any others which are unrelated to the production process are largely neglected. The working conditions are most unpleasant, being hot, dusty, fumey and noisy. As a result they have an extremely high staff turnover rate, with a very high proportion of temporary agency workers. They are notorious in the town and have an extremely poor reputation. This reputation periodically attracts the attention of the media and the local MP.' Elsewhere it was recorded that in addition to three recent convictions of the company, one of their managers had also been convicted personally. Various enforcement notices had been issued. There was also a possibility of an unrelated prosecution following an accident in which employees had nearly been killed as a result of defective safeguarding systems. Eight civil actions, which the company was defending vigorously, were under way. The factory was also reported to account for 40 to 50 per cent of the call-outs for the local fire service.[41] (P97–13)

Mitigating features cluster around a conception of the 'good' company. Some offenders may be awarded socially approved attributes. It is often noteworthy that an employer may be adjudged to be 'cooperative', 'honest', or 'responsive'. Inspectors sometimes record as mitigating features statements such as '[the defendant] and his employees have cooperated in full with my investigation. Although not admissible (as I did not caution him) [the defendant] admitted at the first opportunity to having carried out the unauthorised repair' (P97–52). Several approved features may be noted in reports on the same case, each contributing to a more benign portrait. In one, for example, the following were recorded: 'Good prior record of Co. Previous good response of Co. to advice or other enforcement action. The fact that the Co. had already eliminated

[41] The company received three fines of £1,500, with £2,500 in costs, for three breaches of the Control of Substances Hazardous to Health Regulations 1994.

the risk' (P97–10). In another case it was observed that the defendant had a better than average standard of compliance, that he 'acted on advice given by HSE, was regarded by the placement officer and father of the IP as a safety conscious employer, IP acknowledges that he was warned of the risk and failed to exercise due diligence to prevent the accident' (P97–22).

The character of rule-breakers also speaks to the issue of the credibility of their accounts when interacting with inspectors, the social construction of credibility being based heavily on the personal relationships between inspectors and those they regulate (see Frohmann, 1991).

In a case in which the directors had been pejoratively framed as 'particularly disinterested', the inspector observed that it was 'all the more notable when you consider that the employees have taken full advantage of this to complain directly to me. Even more remarkable against this atmosphere is the fact that three employees' statements are totally consistent with one another despite there having been no opportunity for a story to be concocted. The Directors corroborate one another although I have to say that I have doubts about the veracity of some of their statements, especially since they have a particular stake in this matter.' (P97–08)

Inspectors are constantly concerned with the trustworthiness of evidence presented to them, and reports in the prosecution files often comment on the veracity of respondents. Evidence congruent with other accounts may be noted (in one case, the defendant was said to be 'Co-operative, information given is in line with that obtained from IP [injured person]').

10. The Character and Vulnerability of the Victim

Characteristics of victims also help inspectors understand how blameworthy a rule-breaker may be. A victim accorded socially valued attributes, thereby generating particular sympathy, often adds to an inspector's sense that the employer is to blame.[42] It may be worthy of note if a victim can be described, for example, as 'an intelligent and credible witness who had previously expressed great dissatisfaction with his employer's approach to health and safety' (P97–08).

Members of the public are treated as somehow more significant victims—actual or potential—than employees in assessing blame and judging the merits of a prosecution. In one case a fire caused the

[42] The importance of the character and identity of the victim in the social construction of sympathy and blame within the criminal justice system more generally is emphasized in Hoyle & Young (2002).

explosion of five gas cylinders, three of which endangered other people on the site, since the cylinders effectively became missiles and were found some distance from the fire. A prosecution was taken because of the potentially serious consequences for the public of failure to store properly (P97–14).[43] Vulnerability in the victim owing to youth, inexperience, or lack of training is also important. The vulnerable victim deserves special care from the employer, and if this is lacking, such people are regarded as more in need of the law's protection: 'Anyone who puts a sixteen year old at risk doesn't deserve a second chance' (86–17). In a case in which a 17-year-old had had his hand crushed and three fingers broken in an unguarded power press brake, the inspector noted that there was no evidence that the injured person had done 'anything perverse to cause his injury'. The victim was operating a dangerous machine, and although he was being supervised, 'it might be argued that no amount of training or supervision can adequately compensate for a complete lack of guarding at a press brake' (P97–45).[44]

The character and actions of the victim are also central to judgements about the extent to which the employer's blame can be mitigated. Sometimes victims are simply characterized as disreputable, leading to corresponding sympathy for employers.

In one fatal case, the victim fell between four and six metres from a large wooden potato crate on which he had been standing. The crate itself had been raised on a fork-lift truck. The driver of the fork-lift, who was a director of the company, was told to 'get me down'. He started to lower the victim who fell, and the large heavy crate fell on top of him. The victim was dead at the scene. He suffered from Parkinson's disease, arthritis, and high blood pressure, conditions, according to the pathologist, which would have made him unsteady. The company was prosecuted because there was a serious risk which could easily have been removed. There was, however, no prosecution of the director who had been driving the fork-lift, because 'due to personal circumstances' a prosecution 'may well be excessive . . . ' In mitigation it was pointed out that the dead person had a strong character (elsewhere he was described as 'strongwilled') and was in a position of authority. Furthermore, there was a 'General positive attitude to health and safety that the company had also raised.'[45] (P97–26)

[43] See n. 35.

[44] The employer received fines of £2,500 and £1,000 for offences under s. 14 of the Factories Act, 1961, and Reg. 3 of the Reporting of Injuries, Diseases and Dangerous Occurrences Regulations, 1985, plus costs of £440.

[45] The company was fined £7,000, with more than £500 in costs, for a conviction under s. 2 (1) of the HSW Act.

Similarly, a victim believed to have acted irresponsibly is regarded as sharing the blame for any accident. In one case, involving a worker who had had his hand crushed in a machine, it was noted in mitigation: 'Use of experienced employee with . . . experience indoctrination [on the particular machine]', and elsewhere: 'Guards were provided, and it was the IP who removed them. . . . Directors did not condone operation without guards.' The act of the injured person who had elsewhere been described as 'an intelligent and credible witness' was described as 'irresponsible' (P97–08).[46] Indeed, the facts as understood by inspectors can sometimes suggest that it was the victim who was largely at fault.

In a fatal case a self-employed, experienced tree surgeon was pollarding a willow nine metres from the ground with a chainsaw. He was sitting in full safety harness secured by a rope strop, wearing leg irons. He had cut part way through the tree trunk when the top of the tree fell away from him stretching his harness and strop so tightly that it crushed him against the trunk. He had prepared inadequately by failing to trim to lighten the top of the leaning tree which could have been expected to break and fall away before the cut was completed. In a Coroner's report the inspector said that the equipment was satisfactory, but the method of cutting was not. His view was that the accident was due either to 'inadequate training or recklessness on the part of the deceased and perhaps a combination of these factors which could have been mitigated by greater diligence and closer supervision of the contractors by [the landowners'] staff. At the Inquest a verdict of Accidental Death was returned. The inspector regarded the fatality as largely the victim's own doing, and no further action was taken. (F97–17)

Thus an injured but experienced worker may be blamed for having caused the accident. In a case in which an agricultural worker had been found dead inside the chamber of a round baler, the inspector thought the victim may either have failed to isolate the power source (by not disconnecting the power take-off or stopping the tractor engine) or have been pulled into the machine when trying to work on the twine-threading mechanism. No legal action was recorded as having taken place, presumably because the victim was regarded as the author of his own misfortune (F97–08).

[46] The employer pleaded guilty to a charge under s. 2 (1) of the HSW Act, and was fined £4,500 plus nearly £500 in costs.

4. CONCLUSION

Blame is a powerful sentiment. The durability and resilience of common-sense norms and their immunity at a fundamental level to far-reaching intervening legal and bureaucratic changes is evident from the fact that more than 30 years ago an inquiry for the Law Commission (1969: 30) found that 'the Inspectorate normally applies a broad conception of fault and blameworthiness in enforcing'. Similarly, it saw (1969: 27) 'lack of blameworthiness' on the part of employers as 'the principal consideration' in FI in decisions not to prosecute. Blame is pervasive in inspectors' everyday decision-making about regulatory prosecution and is shared by others caught up in the legal process[47] Analysis of the prosecution and fatalities files suggests that inspectors frequently decide about prosecution or justify decisions about prosecution by reference to institutionalized terms and categories such as 'accident', 'attitude', 'blatant disregard', and 'negligence'. These have a common currency in the organization and serve as a formal means of reasoning. Such language locates decisions made in a repertoire of moves, expectations, and rationales that is recognized throughout the organization. Acting against the 'blatant' or 'flagrant' violation of the law helps salve our consciences by making it clear that formal legal action is being taken against a blameworthy, and therefore deserving, wrongdoer. Blame is a major stabilizing feature in framing cases, an important matter in legal decision-making, because when decisions are made serially by different actors, there is always the possibility that different sets of values are brought to bear on the framing and handling of a case (Manning & Hawkins, 1989).

The cluster of familiar conditions of blame that inspectors attend to in framing is mobilized to provide reasons for and against prosecution, depending on whether they are framed pejoratively or benignly. Equally, since courts also seem to employ the same sorts of common-sense reasoning, the same features may well serve as reasons for them to punish more or less severely. Thus employers may be prosecuted (rather than dealt with in another way) because they are held to be to blame for what happened, and if convicted they may be sentenced by the court more severely because in the court's view also they are to blame.

[47] For example, the power of moral evaluations of conduct pervades Nelken's (1983) subtle analysis, and Benson and Cullen (1998: 99) encountered 'expressions of moral outrage' by prosecutors, especially when discussing health and safety violations.

In making prosecution decisions, the formal law is overlaid by inspectors' own blaming behaviour and their personal conceptions of justice and desert. The merits of the case at this point and throughout its processing are assessed in moral, not legal, terms.[48] 'Most of the statutes that we deal with', said a PI,

> 'are . . . absolute liability . . . And so intention doesn't really . . . matter a lot [in] deciding whether there's a strict breach of the law or not. But the . . . ethics behind it means that one tends to prosecute if there's been a deliberate, knowing, flagrant breach of the law. If someone has breached the law inadvertently in total . . . "innocence" [his conversational use of implied quotation marks], there isn't a lot normally to be gained by prosecuting . . . So one of the main elements is looking at the ethics of it.' (86–38)

The 'ethics of it'—common-sense conceptions of culpability—enter at the stage of screening potential defendants for access to the formal legal system; they enter also as a threshold test that has to be satisfied (except in big and dramatic cases which are more likely to be framed in political and organizational terms) before the inspector feels able to contemplate other issues which may assume importance in disposing of the case at hand.

However, it is again important that there is a close fit between an inspector's and an employer's sense of blameworthy behaviour because that informs them both about the desert of a prosecution, hence the remark of a PI: 'Where a firm has pleaded or been found guilty one hopes that one convinces them that they've deserved it' (86–52). An employer who cannot acknowledge the strength of the inspector's moral case will regard a prosecution not merely as unjust, but as vindictive. Where, however, a person has been killed or injured, some companies are said to cooperate fully in their own prosecution, which suggests a kind of corporate expiation of guilt. Where the employer's blame seems clear, the inspector will feel comfortable prosecuting the moral breach, for the interested public can recognize and understand the appropriateness of the official action, and the company may also acknowledge that such action is right and inevitable. This applies also to the courts and the way in which they are likely to evaluate a case.

[48] The important qualification to this statement, of course, is that cases always end up being assessed for their legal strengths and weaknesses, a process analysed in Ch. 12. The moral character of the matter, however, is what usually transforms it into a 'case' in the first place, and prompts serious thought of prosecution.

Part of an inspector's willingness to blame is shaped by past experience in regulating a particular firm, or in dealing with similar employers, events, or hazards, which has a sensitizing effect, increasing the tendency to blame. Sometimes the importance of the past is revealed in its capacity to create a general frame for understanding present problems, helping shape particular decisions made by individual inspectors. 'Whether you personally have investigated a very bad incident on that type of machine', said a PI, 'contributes a great deal to a decision to prosecute' (86–01). An AD elaborated on this:

> 'In terms of influences . . . I think it's probably true to say that if you have investigated a particularly unpleasant accident under certain circumstances, that tends to condition your view of that risk, over and above others that perhaps you've had no first-hand experience of. If you've investigated a child being killed on a construction site, or whatever it may be, then, you know, it affects you, because the inspectors . . . are involved in the whole process. They may arrive on site and see the body; they may have to go and speak to the grieving relatives; they've got to speak to the . . . the witnesses. And that has an effect on them.' (97–04)

In these circumstances reflection and calculation give way to perceptual shorthand and recipe knowledge shaped by experience and practice. The seeming simplicity of this process has the disadvantage, from a policy point of view, that it is inherently conservative and can 'lead to idiosyncrasy and a tendency to miss new trends or unusual occurrences' (Lloyd-Bostock, 1987: 30).

In terms of the theory on which this book is based, the decision field is altered by the framing practices adopted by decision-makers. This transformation arises as a result of the detailed scrutiny of the event which gave rise to the prosecution, an approach which is central to the legal method. To focus on the event, Johnstone (1994: 47) argues, is to decontextualize it, because it 'draws attention away from the fact that the event is part of a pattern of work practices leading to danger to workers'. From the point of view of regulatory policy, the practice of blaming when thinking about the causes of untoward events and hazards encourages the individualistic focus in the law, and tends to deflect attention from working systems and practices. Johnstone (1994: 266) refers to '"common sense" defences reliant on individualistic blame-shifting ideologies', and points out that in Victoria, Australia, defendants at one time were notably successful in persuading courts to adopt defences based on such conceptions of causation and workplace practices

(Johnstone, 1994: 323). The concept of 'accident' presupposes individualistic rather than systematic causes, and this impedes understanding of occupational health and safety regulation problems as systemic events. The implication of this argument is that in the trial and sentencing of offenders the formal law's view of occupational health and safety matters as embedded in systems of production and work sometimes struggles for recognition in the face of an individualistic conception encouraged by the practice of blaming.

12 The Legal Frame: Can a Case be Made?*

1. THE LEGAL FRAME

The formal law has so far hardly been addressed directly in this book.[1] This is not to imply that the rules of the law and the formalities of the legal process are unimportant. On the contrary, they assume particular significance when regulatory inspectors start considering the legal strengths and weaknesses in any case. This is when the legal frame comes into play.

Adjusting to the strictures of the formal legal system is the culmination of inspectors' decision-making about prosecution. Legal framing transforms a matter into something legally recognizable: a matter so far defined in lay or organizational terms is redefined as a legal case. The law compels attention by virtue of its demands, particularly in the stringency of its evidentiary requirements, and in the implications arising from the choice of legislation to enforce. Law reaches out to decision-makers through its use of words, whose interpretation shapes whether and how legal rules are acted on. As this chapter will show, variations in the words and form of the law are crucially important in these determinations; indeed, the form of a rule actually matters most when prosecution is contemplated. And, sometimes, the action taken and its results are not always those which may have been contemplated by the legislature.

Before any decision to prosecute can finally be confirmed, then, officials apply the legal frame to the case before them. It is not that all other forms of framing have to be deployed before the legal frame is, for decisions are not made in such an organized and systematic sequence. Indeed, the legal frame is employed throughout the pre-trial process. However, the burden of pre-trial decision-making is concerned with whether, in principle, prosecution of a particular matter is desirable. If it is, then the matter has to be subjected to scrutiny by the legal frame to

* Some of the ideas in this chapter appeared in my paper '"FATCATS" and prosecution decision-making in a regulatory agency' (Hawkins, 1989*a*, which is reprinted in Short & Clarke, 1992).

[1] Though Ch. 3, which should be read in conjunction with the present chapter, deals at length with pre-trial legal processes.

see if a prosecution is legally supportable. Unless it has already suppressed them, once concerns prompted by the use of other decision frames have been satisfied, the legal frame becomes dominant.

The significance of the legal frame is that it embodies its own distinctive and overpowering conception of reality. Its application demands that a decision-maker who has concluded that substantively a case is worth prosecuting assess whether evidence to be marshalled in support of the prosecution case can meet legal standards of proof in court. This decision is inseparable from a second question about precisely which legal rules are to be enforced. Inspectors usually have a choice in the matter, but it is one profoundly affected by the way in which a law or regulation is written. How public policy is formulated and crystallized into precise rules shapes the discretion of the legal actor in deciding whether to resort to the formalities of the courtroom.

The legal frame operates with a special decisiveness, acting to test the strength of a case whose existence and survival so far have been justified on other than legal grounds, whether instrumental or expressive. Such is the power of the legal frame that it almost always suppresses any others in play: any legal flaw in the case will usually be fatal to its further progress. The only possible exception arises with those egregious cases where the moral, political, or organizational demands upon the agency to be seen to be taking decisive action outweigh the risk that the case will actually be lost. If legally weak, however, the case must be expressively very strong for it to go to prosecution. The command of the legal frame otherwise is such that it imposes an imperative to prosecute only clearly winnable cases: '[I]f you can't prove it in court,' said a former Chief Agricultural Inspector, 'there's no point in going.'

Law carries with it its own distinctive form of reasoning, which intrudes upon regulatory officials' decision-making during their organizational processing of a case. It imposes its own view of the world by employing its own rules about what is to be recognized as real, and how that is to be accomplished. Law does not take things for granted in the way that lay people do. Accordingly, law ignores those conceptions of act, event, consequences, social context, and the like, that it does not deem to be relevant to its task, which is to answer a question (Aubert, 1984). In the case of prosecution for the alleged breach of a rule, the objective of legal formalities is to answer the question whether the defendant is guilty or not guilty of the offence charged, beyond reasonable doubt. The binary outcomes of formal legal proceedings compel a highly simplified view of social reality, so that law can produce its answer without difficulty. Thus matter which law regards as irrelevant to the answering of the question of legal guilt is stripped away in legal framing, a process which begins in the course of preparing the case for prosecution and is pursued subsequently during trial.

What begins life as a problem for organizational attention is converted in the process of legal framing into something to which legal rules and legal reasoning can be applied. Any forces which decision-makers are now conscious of in handling the matter are legal forces. Which rules should be employed? Is the evidence sufficient? Is it reliable? Are the witnesses persuasive? What is the legal strength of the other side's case? Will the defendant plead not guilty?[2]

2. CAN A LEGAL CASE BE MADE?

1. The Risks

To those who would use law, risk is inherent in the nature of law and its processes. Contemplating prosecution in regulatory work creates a risk for the legal decision-maker wrestling with the question whether a workplace problem should become subject to formal legal proceedings. Whether a case can be made involves an assessment of the chance of failing to convict. If this is calculated to be too great, it may lead to relinquishing the idea of using prosecution and a substitution (sometimes even an abandonment) of other means of control.

If the conception of risk organizing inspectors' routine enforcement decisions is one which emerges from their legal and occupational mandate to protect workers and others from the hazards of the workplace, the formal law poses a different sort of risk. When the prospect of prosecution becomes real, the legal actor's decision behaviour is redirected towards the convictability of the case, more precisely, minimizing the risk of failing to convict (Frohmann, 1996; Stanko, 1981). The accident or hazard, the precipitating concern, is now overtaken by the legal frame, which demands that reality is selectively reconstructed in the law's perspective. Implicated here are an inspector's place as a competent member of a regulatory agency, allied with the agency's interest in displaying certain sorts of activity, effectiveness, and 'success' to its interested publics. At this point inspectors behave rather like lawyers, and become more interested in what is likely to happen than in what has

[2] These questions are analogous, of course, to the evidential test in the Code for Crown Prosecutors. See also Ashworth (1987).

happened (Hosticka, 1979). In all of this, minimizing the risks of losing demands a careful assessment of the strength and credibility of the available evidence and some anticipation of the behaviour of the other side. Indeed, their reports show that inspectors often weigh up the legal considerations with great sophistication.

Preparing a case to meet the standards of evidence required can be extremely time-consuming for inspectors, especially if specialist expertise is involved. One inspector has observed that 'Collecting the evidence to bring a case to court is in itself a time consuming matter, but laying informations, arranging witnesses and conducting a case can far outweigh it' (Rothery, 1998: 5). They calculate the personal resources they can afford to devote to prosecution, a question crucially dependent on other demands on their time (see Chapter 10). The occupational and organizational concern for a substantively 'good' case gives way to a coldly pragmatic concern for what is legally prosecutable, and whether the inspector's workload can justify legal action. The shift is the consequence of features inherent in the character of law, legal standards, and legal procedures operating in an organizational setting. In practice, the legal frame almost always operates in one direction only: to facilitate the prosecution of legally strong cases while preventing the prosecution of legally weaker ones.

2. Debating the Strength of the Evidence

Prosecution is not something that HSE or its inspectors undertake lightly. Inspectors' preoccupation with winning cases leads them to amass the strongest possible evidence, and encourages them to debate the merits thoroughly with their principal inspectors (PIs), as was evident in the prosecution and fatalities files. Without sufficient legally relevant evidence, however, prosecution cannot normally be risked. And while a fatality always raises the question whether a prosecution should be taken, there will normally be no further action in the absence of compelling evidence to support it. 'It seems [the dead person] lost his footing and fell, resulting in his death,' reported the inspector in one such case. 'There is no evidence to suggest he was working incorrectly or did not know what he was doing' (F97–21). In another fatal case in which a lorry driver had caught his foot while securing the load and fallen head first onto the concrete yard, the PI mentioned two possible charges, then discounted them. One he had 'never seen' in 28 years of inspection. The other was dismissed as 'universally disliked'. He noted the absence of preventive provisions, and concluded: 'Until a workable and acceptable method of sheeting and roping without climbing onto the load is developed then very occasionally somebody will be hurt or, sadly, killed' (F97–10). The tone of resignation is unmistakable and the conclusion that prosecution was not possible entirely predictable.

Good evidence is credible, an attribute frequently the subject of comment by inspectors when pressing for a prosecution: 'There is considerable corroboration to the evidence. The facts are not likely to be disputed to any degree. The staff of this unit appear to be of an unusually high quality who have given firm clear statements and would perform well in the witness box' (P97–24).

In a case in which four students had been overcome by carbon monoxide poisoning from a faulty boiler installation, the inspector debated the difficulties in prosecuting. For example, on using the Gas Safety (Installation and Use) Regulations in connection with the need for a suitable flow of air to the appliance, he said 'Prosecution not proposed. Although lack of ventilation may have contributed to the incident, the main cause was the acute bend in the flue. It may be difficult to prove that the flyscreen was in place at the time of the installation in 1991.' [This statement was ticked in the margin.] Two other Regulations were not proposed for prosecution, one because of difficulty over when the Regulation came into force, the other because 'the interpretation of a gas fitting does not apply to a flue, therefore this Regulation cannot be used.' [Also ticked.] Action was proposed under one Regulation relating to installation: 'It is felt that a lack of competence and knowledge at the time of the installation was the installer's downfall.' In a section headed 'Credibility of evidence and quality of evidence', it was said: 'It is felt that all persons from whom statements were taken, would make good witnesses. I would be surprised, with the evidence available, if Mr Cooke pleaded not guilty, although he has not indicated what his plea will be.'[3] (P97–01)

Credibility and persuasiveness are assisted by the use of expert evidence, usually in the form of a specialist's report. HSE's specialist inspectors and its laboratory are frequently consulted as inspectors try to cover every contingency. While specialist mechanical, electrical, engineering, and other forms of knowledge are frequently required by inspectors in mounting a legal case, their problem is that guilt has to be established before lay magistrates. (This assumes, of course, that the employer will plead not guilty, which has always to be the inspector's starting point.) Reliance on specialist advice can, however, create problems for inspect-

[3] The fine of £5,000 upon a guilty plea was later reduced to £1,500. No costs were awarded.

ors if it points in the wrong direction. Field staff may already have spent valuable time collecting evidence for a case to whose prosecution they have become committed. Medical evidence in occupational health cases was regarded as the source of particular difficulty, sometimes serving, it was believed, to deter inspectors from contemplating prosecution:

'The medics are the last in the chain. And if they say "No", you've spent days—days!—on that case, to no avail because the final link in the chain says "No". So that's a deterrent. . . . We will not now be taking cases like that, even though we think they are gross breaches. We might chance our arm with a prohibition notice, but we might go down on appeal if the medics won't support us.' (86–63)

The difficulties faced when inspectors do not have clear, uncontentious, and readily comprehensible evidence to present to the court are apparent in the big case in which employees had received high doses of radiation. The substantial dossier indicated the huge amount of internal consultation that preceded the decision to prosecute. The inspector wrote a note of a 'Defended Case Scenario' by way of asking what evidence was needed. This two-page memo had been embellished with hand-written comments by another person (the PI?) adding further evidence and reasoning. In response to a specialist inspector's comments the inspector also prepared a four-page document detailing each of nine recommended grounds for prosecuting and offering his own comments on the desirability or feasibility of prosecuting. The PI asked his area director (AD) about the desirability of sending the file to a solicitors' firm for their advice because

'[the field inspector] and I have spent a long time discussing various aspects of the case over the past few months and I am finding it difficult to take a detached view of the evidence. I am under considerable pressure . . . to prosecute. Although many of the issues are very technical ones I think it would be beneficial to have the opinion of a lawyer, rather than an inspector, on whether we would have sufficient evidence to proceed and the likely response of a lay bench or jury. . . . I think prosecution of [the company] is justified and I am prepared to approve the case. However we have no evidence of actual bad practices that would cause the high exposures. There is evidence that supervision by management was perfunctory and that records were not kept but no explanation of what must have gone wrong on a number of occasions to give the exposure. Our case is largely based on our expert witness saying that the high exposures automatically mean that exposure was not kept ALARP [as low as reasonably practicable].' The AD replied: 'Like you I feel that this is a case which we will have to take but that the evidence as at present set out looks a bit weak.'

Here there is a clear sense of *force majeure* compelling a prosecution, owing to the gravity of the matter, given that a number of employees had received excessive doses of radiation. However, the PI's prediction was that the firm would plead not guilty 'if only because of the potential commercial damage that may result from a successful prosecution'. The specialist inspector involved did not share his colleagues' doubt about the likelihood that the case would be defended, arguing confidently:

> 'In your list of possible defences you raise the fact that none of the employees has admitted that they were exposed to any significant levels of radiation. Their dose records on the other hand clearly show that they have been exposed to significant levels so their denials must be untrue. Either they were unaware, and they shouldn't have been if proper monitoring had been carried out, or they were aware and they're lying.
>
> We have evidence in four forms. Firstly there are the personal dose records. Secondly the breaches that were committed by omission and which are detailed in the statements given by employees. Thirdly, the RPA reports, which whilst deficient in the ways described in my previous letter, describe contravention of the IRR (85) [Ionising Radiations Regulations, 1985] by the firm. Finally, expert evidence from myself. Personally, if the firm is presented with this evidence, I doubt that they would plead anything other than guilty.'

The frustrations caused by the difficulties of securing credible evidence in these more difficult areas of occupational health are clearly evident.

The inspector reported the view of another specialist who urged prosecution and noted the high levels of exposure to radiation, indicating 'an extraordinary sequence of events and indeed a very poor attention to radiation protection within the company.' The specialist concluded: 'I therefore urge you to encourage your colleagues to take enforcement action in the form of prosecution as this is clearly appropriate in these cases—if we don't act in these situations when will we act?'

The HSE's own solicitor thought serious consideration should be given to a trial on indictment, but both the PI and inspector were reluctant to pursue this. The inspector 'fundamentally' disagreed that the case should be tried in Crown Court: 'Although there is certainly evidence to pursue legal proceedings under IRR 85, there are not in my opinion either flagrant or reckless breaches, and there is no evidence to suggest gross neglect or a serious lack of concern by the employer for the wellbeing of his employees.' The solicitor then anticipated what moves the employer might make: 'The Defence may claim that [the company] had done all that was reasonably practicable to reduce exposure to ALARA [as low as reasonably achievable]. We can argue that the doses provide prima facie evidence that this is not the case. However, it becomes much more difficult to provide evidence of [the company's] guilt in this regard. The fact is that in terms of engineering controls [the company] has done all that we can reasonably ask. The work done by [a particular employee] was all done inside a radiation enclosure with concrete walls, radiation alarms, interlocked doors etc. In theory exposure should be zero.

We concluded therefore that our evidence needs to emphasise the weaknesses inherent in [the company's] systems of work. Here we found . . . that [the company] were not recording radiation levels at the enclosure, nor was the system of supervision up to the standard envisaged by regulation 11. It was these two planks that we considered the best to use to prove the absence of reasonable practicability. However, we still think this is relatively thin ice to be skating on. Perhaps this is because in general the average inspector usually has some "hardware" such as machinery or blood to work with. In this case I feel as though I am dealing to some extent with the esoteric. Nevertheless, we would argue that had supervision been adequate, and had monitoring records been available for management to analyze, [the employee] would never have received such a high dose.' The long detailed response from the HSE solicitor in London also instructed the PI how to conduct the case. Some of this advice is the stuff of more familiar legal proceedings: 'because the defence will, it seems, be trying to discredit [one particular individual], it would be helpful if we could avoid calling him as a witness.' (P97–53)

HSE finally decided to prosecute the matter. The inspector later wrote to HSE's solicitor that owing to 'the high profile being given to exposure to ionising radiation in the media, plus the public perception of the hazards associated with radiation, it was considered appropriate to institute legal proceedings. However, from the start we envisaged problems associated with the presentation of evidence and the most appropriate legislation to use.' The firm pleaded not guilty. The key witness (one of the workers suffering the overdose) changed his story of how the over-exposure reading had occurred, and the prosecution case collapsed. The case was withdrawn, the magistrates awarding costs to the defence.

3. LOSING

In regulatory agencies in which the power to prosecute is little used there is a marked concern among both field and senior staff that cases taken to court should not be lost.[4] Many of the factory inspectors interviewed had never lost a case; others had lost only one or two (and were usually able to

[4] In the former Regional Water Authorities, for example, where only a few water pollution cases used to find their way into court each year, inspectors would complain that senior officials had to be '110 per cent sure' that they would win before deciding to prosecute (Hawkins, 1984).

recall the number immediately and with apparent precision, suggesting the salience of the event). Yet despite the time and care taken by inspectors in assembling materials and considering the evidence and the merits of court action, the decision to prosecute always presents them with a risk of losing. This is not simply because the defendant may plead not guilty, or produce new evidence, or that the courts simply interpret a rule in an unexpected way. The vagaries of witnesses' memories and the drama of the proceedings often cause problems: 'Witnesses very rarely say what they said when you spoke to them six months before, which is hardly surprising. They are intimidated by court; they are intimidated by magistrates' clerks; [and by] me when I'm trying to cross-examine them, when they don't say what they said before' (86–13).

Losing a case was a major preoccupation among the inspectors interviewed. Some feared it damaged their credibility as law enforcers and encourged disrespect for the inspectorate as a credible enforcement agency,[5] encouraging not guilty pleas and making it correspondingly more difficult to persuade employers to comply. A lost case may also create an unfortunate precedent for the inspectorate: 'It tends to reduce the standing of [HSE] towards industry if they prosecute a bum case.'[6] Indeed, there is a view that the risks of legal action are such that even a successful prosecution may prove counter-productive if the resultant fine is so small that it trivializes the original offence. Inspectors' primary concern, however, was how failing to convict would appear to their superiors: 'I worry more about what people in headquarters think about lost cases than what industry thinks'[7] (86–61). 'When I was a lad,' said an AD, 'if you lost a case, [an] immediate six-page memo had to go up, and people questioned this, that, and the other' (97–05).

Losing was taken by inspectors to be a reflection of their competence: 'There was . . . quite a silly attitude, I think, over cases that were lost, and in the past I think some inspectors were very unfairly criticized, or made to feel that they'd failed as individuals for taking a case' (97–02). This seems to be less true these days:

[5] Yet some argued that prosecuting and losing could produce beneficial effects by serving to publicize official concern about a problem. One AD suggested that lost cases could sometimes still produce cooperation from employers, and that if a case was rightly taken, properly prepared, and lost, it should not be seen as a failure on the inspector's part.

[6] Hutter (1997: 223–4) found that a significant reason for not proceeding with a prosecution among her factory inspectors was a fear that failing to convict would set a precedent, forcing the inspectorate to change its working definitions of compliance, leading to a lower standard of protection.

[7] Senior staff are also concerned not to lose too many cases, though their concern is one that springs from a desire to portray the agency as powerful, credible, and decisive.

'I think we're becoming much less risk-averse than we were. Ten years ago, to lose a case was a pretty heinous sort of a crime. Nowadays, I think we recognize that with more complex legislation, you have to push the boundaries, that there are always potential technical get-outs, in terms of the rules of evidence, because of the complexities . . . with PACE [the Police and Criminal Evidence Act, 1984] and disclosure and everything else. There are people who lie; expert witnesses who have a particular view of the world—we've had one recently. And really, my view in assessing a case that we've lost is: did we apply the right criteria in assessing the evidence at the outset? Was it a case that was worth taking? Did we consider the reliability of witnesses and so on at the outset? Did we present the case to best effect—either ourselves or our solicitors? And if so, are there lessons to learn there about our forensic skills, our legal knowledge, our advocacy skills? But if we've applied ourselves correctly in all of those areas—we took the decision for the right reasons—then I see it as a learning experience, because . . . we're still continuing to define the boundaries of what the law does and does not require, and the only way you learn is by testing.' (97–04)

This is not to suggest, however, that senior staff are now indifferent about losing.[8] One AD who was asked if she was concerned about a failure to convict replied:

'Yes, yes. . . . I suppose because of the retribution element . . . you feel that somebody who has been cavalier over the welfare of his employees feels he's got away with something. I suppose there's an intellectual side of it as well. You don't like to feel you've been outsmarted by the opposition. And I think because of the wider messages that it might spread around that HSE—I mean, we do have a high success rate, and I think that a lot of defendants do think twice about entering not guilty pleas, because it is generally recognized that we sort of take cases only when they are justified, really justified. And, you know, I think it could perhaps weaken that position and perhaps encourage many more to defend, and then a bigger consequent knock-on resource implication from it.' (97–02)

Many inspectors acknowledged the salutary effect of losing on the care with which they prepared for subsequent prosecutions. Others recognized that the experience of losing had encouraged them to review their approach to prosecution, particularly in the use of the Health and Safety at Work Act, 1974 (HSW Act) and 'where there isn't wide-ranging case law to give you clear direction' (86–53). This had led to greater caution about prosecuting certain kinds of case, the guiding rule being 'If you don't take them, you don't lose them' (86–34).

[8] HSE expects an 85 per cent success rate in its prosecutions, to ensure cost-effectiveness (Eves, 1998).

Some believe that the general duties of the HSW Act may have encouraged a greater willingness by employers to defend cases.[9] If a not guilty plea seems likely, inspectors can respond by prosecuting for the breach of a specific rule instead to put the matter on safer ground, as one did in a case in which a worker had lost four fingers in a milling machine:

> 'It is clear that the company had disregarded the rubber industry guidance,' the inspector noted, 'although it is impossible to say whether this was a deliberate omission. Although the [safety bars] were tested regularly absolutely no thought had been given to regular preventative maintenance of safety devices. . . . Several of the . . . mills within the factory did not comply with rubber industry guidance in relation to the provision of switches on the [safety device]. Overall, the company does appear to make an effort to ensure effective health and safety management at the premises . . . There are no grounds to take proceedings against any particular individual for breaches of health and safety requirements. I would not be surprised if the company chose to defend this case on the grounds that in their opinion they had done everything reasonably practicable, i.e. their testing programme with regard to the [safety bars], and that they did not consider that they needed a maintenance programme in addition to this.'
>
> This concern was probably the reason for the recommendation of a prosecution under the specific provisions of s. 14 (1) Factories Act, 1961 only, even though s. 2 (1) HSW Act. 1974 was also noted as clearly relevant.[10] (P97–29)

4. APPLYING THE LEGAL FRAME

1. General Concerns

The legal frame demands that inspectors calculate their personal resources, and confront some specific, often difficult, questions about the rules to be enforced in any prosecution. One problem is that while general rules may ultimately lead to more efficient use of an inspectorate's resources because of their potentially broader impact, they can also impose new burdens on inspectors' personal resources of time and energy. These are prominent considerations, for it is not simply the sign of failure in a lost prosecution which inspectors wish to avoid. The need to make work go as smoothly as possible is encouraged by scarce resources at field level. A decision to lay an information usually involves an inspector in a commitment which demands many hours of effort, and

[9] Some inspectors noted that a potentially large civil claim gave the employer an added incentive to defend the criminal case, as a means of learning more about the matter as a whole and acquiring more evidence.

[10] The employer pleaded guilty and was fined £4,000, with more than £450 in costs.

care over the collection of evidence and the other preparatory work before trial. From the inspector's standpoint, the need for care is compelled by the uncertainty surrounding the prosecution process. This prompts a defensive strategy. An incident that could become a prosecution case has to be treated at the outset, for the purposes of taking statements and collecting other potential evidence, as if it will be prosecuted. Once it is decided that a matter should be prosecuted, the case has to be prepared on the assumption that it will be defended, even though few are. The risk of losing was seen as less of a risk from the resource point of view than 'the risk of landing yourself with a defended case. Because that can involve an awful lot of work' (86–43). Defended cases are both a burden and an anxiety, effects likely to be exaggerated while resources are constrained, yet demands on inspectors' time increase.[11] Furthermore, cases have to be prepared thoroughly in anticipation of the unlikely event of trial in the Crown Court. The more serious the case, the more carefully these contingencies must be guarded against.

The demands of producing legally acceptable evidence reduce the number of prosecutions. Complex legislative drafting is partly responsible. 'It's very understandable that inspectors will tend to shy away from the more complex ones,' said a former Chief Inspector of Factories, 'simply because they are under tremendous pressure of work all the time and you can get bogged down with prosecutions.' The more complex cases are also more likely to be defended. Where resources do not permit the proper preparation of a case, or if the legal requirements seem too severe, a notice or some other enforcement move may have to be substituted instead, the lack of reward for the preparation often creating the feeling of a 'total waste of everybody's time'. Thus one inspector said simply: 'I go to court when I think I can win, and when the situation deserves it' (86–63). 'I tend to go for certainties,' said another. 'It's foolish to put in too much time and effort if you're not too sure' (86–55).

Notices have their advantages:

'I think you'll also find that because of the resource required to prosecute some of these management cases, that where we find deficiencies in management . . . that haven't resulted in an accident, where our options may be a little bit more limited, that we may opt for an enforcement notice, as a better means of promoting our objectives. Because clearly to serve an enforcement notice, all

[11] Though note that HSE received significant extra resources for the financial year 1999/2000 (Health and Safety Commission, 1999).

you need is the inspector to be of the opinion that there's been a breach, rather than being able to prove it beyond reasonable doubt. And you can word a notice in a way that will achieve improvements which you would perhaps have difficulty proving.... And therefore not only are improvement notices highly effective and highly efficient as a means of regulation, but where they are breached, then it's much easier to prove the breach of the notice (because you've already set out the standard in advance, and you can check against that), than it is to perhaps prove the underlying offence.' (97–04)

In certain circumstances, however, another principle of substitutability may operate. Where an inspector wants to prosecute an occupational health problem but is unable to do so for want of evidence, it may be possible to substitute a safety violation as the cause of legal action: 'One might let go by... an alleged offence under health and wait for an easier prosecution under section 14 [Factories Act, 1961] to come along, where we can with less resources, less problems, have the same effect' (86–28). However, while they may be reluctant to make the initial investment of time and effort in initiating a potential prosecution case, once inspectors have decided on legal action they generally want vindication of their efforts and have the case pushed through to prosecution: 'If you're going to spend a number of inspector days on an investigation,' said one, 'there is an expectation at least that something will come of it'[12] (86–50).

To win cases, inspectors need to produce credible evidence and persuasive arguments. This has become more challenging owing to the developing skills of the legal profession in this area. The growth of occupational health and safety legislation is believed in HSE to have been accompanied by greater knowledge and expertise among practitioners, demanding better preparation of prosecution cases. This prompts a concern among inspectors that their expertise, which is perfectly sufficient when dealing with employers in the workplace, may be inadequate when faced with the extra demands of legal proof.

'[C]ases have got more complex over the years.... The law we're dealing with now very rarely is black and white. It demands higher, greater competence in evidence, far more corroboration... We're taking a far wider range of issues... we're tackling cases where, although it might not be section two [HSW Act]... there are still things where we're looking at what's reasonably practicable...' (97–02)

[12] Though only about 1 per cent of investigations lead to prosecution (Hutter & Lloyd-Bostock, 1990: 411).

A hint of this concern appears in one case, for example, when an inspector considered at length 'weaknesses in [prosecution] evidence and possible defences': 'The only difficulty I foresee lies in my second argument in which I give my opinion. I am not an expert in work at heights, or fork-lift trucks, and my opinion may not be considered authoritative. I rely on the actions being self-evidently dangerous' (P97–31). A handwritten note between colleagues in another case pointed to HSE's vulnerability to conflicting evidence: 'it lays us open to differences of opinion between experts. Could you . . . satisfy yourself that any inconsistencies can be explained?' There was also a reference to the possibility that another witness 'might confuse a jury'. An HSE solicitor's view was that 'Normally we would want to restrict the number of expert witnesses that we called so that they cannot contradict each other and weaken the case'[13] (P97–32).

2. Choosing the Rule

Breaches of occupational health and safety rules vary widely in their nature and the severity of their consequences. While a substantial proportion of offences in criminal law deal with acts or omissions, in health and safety regulation the concern is frequently with work practices and the organization of work systems. Some regulatory prosecutions may address discrete events or incidents, but others are concerned with processes or systems of work. These two sets of problems affect the decisions made by inspectors and the choices made by defendants.

Section 2 (1) of the HSW Act states:

> 'It shall be the duty of every employer to ensure, so far as is reasonably practicable, the health, safety and welfare at work of all his employees.'

Subsection (2) goes on to embellish the general principle:

> 'Without prejudice to the generality of an employer's duty under the preceding subsection, the matters to which that duty extends include in particular—(a) the provision and maintenance of plant and systems of work that are, so far as is reasonably practicable, safe and without risks to health . . .'

This clause is followed by four others, all requiring, 'so far as is reasonably practicable', attention to related matters. The burden of proof is important in this section: it is for the company to satisfy the

[13] Head office lawyers scrutinize problematic cases with great care to be sure they are watertight.

court that it has, on the balance of probabilities, discharged the duties placed on it. The practical meaning of the term 'reasonably practicable' was summarized in an inspector's Report to the Coroner in one case: it 'implies that a calculation needs to be made relating the risk to be controlled to the sacrifice (in money, time or trouble) needed to achieve that control. Where there is a gross disproportion between them—the risk being insignificant in relation to the sacrifice—then it is not "reasonably practicable" to control that risk'[14] (F97–09). If the general principle of reasonable practicability requires a balancing by the court of the risks and costs involved, for inspectors it implies a loss of control over the outcome, since in shifting from absolute to general duties matters are moved from questions of fact to questions of value.

The crucial question whether a case can be proved according to legal standards brings with it a secondary but also important choice about the precise legislation or regulation to be employed in the prosecution (see Chapter 3). Inspectors often have a choice when settling upon the information to be laid. They may either prosecute an employer for the violation of a general duty, as embodied in the HSW Act, or they may prefer to prosecute for the breach of a specific rule, usually found now in the various sets of regulations which HSE enforces. Since the 1980s greater reliance has been placed on prosecuting by regulations, which are drawn more strictly than the HSW Act. Both decisions are profoundly affected by the way in which a rule is formulated, leading to a marked preference among inspectors for the prosecution of breaches of specific rather than general rules, which carry with them absolute rather than general duties. Lloyd-Bostock (1992: 64) found, for instance, that accidents were selected for investigation on the basis of characteristics that indicated the probability of an opportunity to enforce a quite specific range of safety regulations. This leads in turn to the prosecution of events rather than hazards, encouraging the prosecution of violations of the rules of occupational safety, rather than health. There is a further tension for inspectors, who must balance the potential impact of the case, if successful, against the need to win. This causes problems, since it is generally easier for the prosecution to prove that a specific act or event was against the law than that a system of work was inherently risky. The

[14] This conception is borrowed from *Edwards v. National Coal Board* (1949) 1 All ER 743. A variant appeared in a speech to magistrates (typed out verbatim) by the inspector in another case: '"Reasonable practicability" is a balance between level of risk on one hand and the sacrifice, whether in money, time or trouble involved in the measures necessary to avert that risk on the other' (P97–40).

potentially broader impact has to be balanced by inspectors against greater difficulty in proving guilt. These dilemmas were exposed in a case in which an employee suffered severe injuries to an arm when he was dragged between the rollers of a machine. The inspector debated the merits of Regulation 6 (1) of the Provision and Use of Work Equipment Regulations, 1992 (PUWER) and HSW Act s. 2 (1), observing 'both deal with maintenance':

'Regulation 6 (1) states every employer shall ensure that work equipment is maintained in an efficient state, in efficient working order and in good repair. There is no qualification to this, it is an absolute obligation, a result to be achieved. Guidance on PUWER regulation 6 indicates the importance of maintaining equipment so that performance does not deteriorate to the extent that it puts people at risk. Equipment may need to be checked frequently to ensure safety-related features are functioning correctly. Frequency of checking is dependent on the equipment and the risk involved, it could be each day, every 3 months or even longer. Therefore it would seem that PUWER is the most appropriate legislation in this case as 1. There is no qualification and it should be easier to prove as a result. 2. HSE could be criticised for using the Act when there is a specific regulation. Training is a subsidiary issue in this case. [The injured person] has been given some training even if its quality is questionable. Proving it was inadequate would be difficult and anyway does not seem to go to the heart of the issue.'[15] (P97–44)

One way in which inspectors can mitigate their anxieties about losing is to employ the HSW Act in conjunction with a charge under a regulation. The latter has the advantage of easier proof, the former a more substantial penalty. Thus in one case in which a worker fell to his death through a roof, there was said by the inspector to be a clear breach of the Construction (Working Places) Regulations 1966, Reg. 36 (2),

'in that a fragile thin perspex roof light was neither covered nor surrounded by a guardrail etc. Failed to follow safe system of work. HSW 1974 s. 2 (1) or s. 3 (1). These breaches resulted in a fatal accident.' Given as a 'Special reason' was that it was a 'Serious breach of specific legal requirement . . . resulting in a fatal accident.' Thus it was a matter that was therefore easy and quick to prove. In a section in the PI's memo to the AD called 'Company attitude', the PI reported that he told one of the company's directors that it would be prosecuted because "there was a clear specific breach" of the Regs.' 'I told him prosecution was automatic in these circumstances.' HSE prosecuted on two counts, the breach of the Regulation receiving a £3,000 fine and the breach of s. 2 HSW Act, 1974 a

[15] The employer was fined £2,500, with just over £450 in costs.

fine of £10,000 with more than £500 in costs. The charge under s. 3 was not proceeded with, as it was an alternative. (P97–11)

Despite the claims of some who argued that a successful prosecution under s. 2 may produce a broader and more lasting impact upon employers, some inspectors appear to use this piece of legislation, for want of something easier and quicker to prepare, as was wistfully suggested by a PI: 'You might sometimes wish there was a sharper bit of law' (86–59). However, one AD quite clearly saw the indeterminacy of the 1974 legislation as a resource to be exploited rather than a risk to be avoided: 'The more general the law is, the more scope it gives us, the more freedom, as it were, in the way we use our evidence' (86–04). Indeed, the figures suggest that inspectors' worries about s. 2 of the 1974 Act are overdone, since about 85 per cent of prosecutions under s. 2 of the HSW Act are currently successful.[16]

The HSW Act changed the conception of enforcement in occupational health and safety regulation. Earlier legislation, which relied heavily on absolute requirements, suggested a view of enforcement as a straightforward matter of punishing the breach of a clear rule. The introduction of general duties broadened the emphasis to a conception of enforcement whose objective was to remedy general problems. A trial using s. 2 of the HSW Act, an HSE lawyer explained, 'is a somewhat unusual animal, because it looks to the court much more like a civil case, with experts arguing on either side, rather than an ordinary criminal trial'. 'What is reasonably practicable is an especially acute problem in air pollution control,' said one inspector. 'You get into an argument in court about what is practicable and how much you spend in terms of real tangible costs, for a benefit which is really unquantifiable.'

3. Implications of the Form of Rules

Catch-all sections of legislation, such as s. 2 of the HSW Act, are over-inclusive, and the legislature presumably relies on enforcers' discretion to make them less so. The purpose of such broad legislation is not necessarily clear, whereas the purpose of specific laws is usually self-evident: there is no need to enquire why a machine should have a guard. General rules and principles appeal to policy-makers by their very nature, however, since they tend to think in generic and abstract terms and wish to err on the side of broad inclusiveness, rather than risk under-inclusiveness. Rule

[16] From data provided by HSE for the period 1999–2001.

enforcers, on the other hand, are practical people who continually confront the risks and tragedies of the real world. The notion of reasonable practicability embodied in s. 2 of the HSW Act often seems to them less suited to the pragmatic approach compelled by the nature of inspection work, which much prefers the certitude of an absolute prohibition and the clarity of a specific rule.

The general legal statement may, however, be more far-reaching in its impact. The potential applicability of the 1974 Act is very wide. One inspector asserted that 'Nearly any offence could also be covered by section 2 of the Health and Safety at Work Act' (86–34). Though the section has wide applicability, there are sometimes events which even its broad formulation cannot reach:

A worker fell from the bed of a lorry, broke his hip, and died two weeks later from a blood clot. The inspector said briefly in her investigation: 'No history of problems with task. Conditions good. Severity of injury and outcome not foreseeable. Although job now eliminated, I do not think precautions were reasonably practicable before accident. NFA.' That is, she did not think it was reasonable for the employer to have taken precautions beforehand, therefore no action under s. 2 seemed possible. The PI noted in a memo: 'I agree with your assessment, I don't think we could show causation here.'

The inspector wrote to the Coroner: 'In considering whether there has been a breach of Health and Safety law, it is essential to determine the foreseeability of risk. Whilst it was foreseeable that someone might have fallen off such a lorry, the severity of injury and eventual consequences were not reasonably foreseeable. It is worth remembering that the term risk is a computation between the likelihood of a harmful event and the severity of the harm which might result. I would not have regarded the operation undertaken by [the dead person] as high risk.' (F97–01)

No further action was taken. Indeed, the matter would not have been investigated had it not been for the worker's death.

The problematic standard of the 'reasonably practicable' test is more contentious and more likely to invite a defence, thereby making real the possibility of losing. The indeterminacy of s. 2 becomes something of a deterrent to prosecution because of the extra work and risks involved (an effect also noted by S. Shapiro, 1985). Establishing what is 'reasonably practicable' is often difficult, and the test gives ultimate discretion to the court to decide the issue. 'You've got to weigh up the seriousness of risk against the costs of compliance, and so on . . . So you've got this doubt, and it's up to the court to decide' (86–10). A construction PI said simply: 'It's nice to be able to get a case where there's an absolute duty. There's no doubt about that... At one time the words "reasonably practicable" filled me with dread' (86–08). Inspectors complained, for example, that magistrates frequently failed to grasp the meaning of the concept of the 'reasonably practicable', and that courts were 'more likely to let them off than where there's an absolute breach'. Furthermore, some inspectors argued that general duties are less suited to the control of serious and specific problems, where the regulatory technique depends on analogic reasoning relying heavily on the judgement of the court rather than digital reasoning, where the task is proving the existence or non-existence of a state of affairs. This is because proof is easier with a digital test (was there a guard or not?) than an analogic one. It is not difficult to prosecute for a failure to have a licence or a medical examination. It is much easier to prove that a limit has been exceeded, for example, than to establish a long-term risk to workers' health. 'Since we've got licensing regulations, which are easy to enforce [asbestos is now no longer a problem. The regulations are] relatively easy to enforce, virtually absolute requirements' (86–07). What is regarded as 'reasonably practicable' is contingent upon the kind and degree of risk involved, and difficulties of proof (which are not excessive where the risk is clear and the remedy simple and cheap) mount as risks seem more remote or become harder for courts to grasp. Risk itself is not a one-dimensional concept but embraces notions of likelihood and gravity, as well as costs and benefits that may be very difficult to establish. General duties also make demands of magistrates' scientific and engineering sense, as they are the ones who have to make the ultimate judgement, for example, as to what is 'safe' behaviour. Indeed, the court's position as arbiter of what is 'reasonable' places the central issues in a case into the realm of value rather than fact and, from a prosecution point of view, adds to the contentiousness of the case. This again makes more demands upon an inspector than making a case, which requires essentially that the existence or non-existence of a particular state of affairs be established.

Where inspectors can choose whether they wish to proceed upon a breach of a specific requirement or for a failure to observe a general duty, they frequently prosecute for a breach of a specific rule. This is not only an easier task, it was also HSE policy in the mid-1980s that inspectors should go for the specific rather than the general.[17] 'If you've got the evidence to prove an absolute breach you're home and dry' (86–10).

[17] Inspectors have since been encouraged to use the HSW Act. However, as the data from prosecution files show, inspectors still prefer to use specific rules embodied in regulations, rather than the HSW Act.

Thus a clear preference is evident in the files to prosecute the breach of a specific rule.[18] A breach of an absolute requirement, or a specific rule, are themselves features which suggest to inspectors that the case may be one to prosecute. The law is thereby focused on particular sorts of event. Thus Lloyd-Bostock (1987) found that the largest single category of prosecution in FI comprised guarding offences, and that the majority of those prosecutions followed accidents, and Hutter (1997) that inspectors were more likely to prosecute in the event of an accident. In the big radiation case the HSE Solicitor's Office in London HQ opted only for a charge under Reg. 7 of IRR 'because it is easier to prove than section 2 (1) of the HSW etc. Act 1974 because this deals with the inadequacies in the system of work without appearing technical' (P97–53). In another case an inspector explained his thinking about the charge in a note to his PI. An employee had received severe injuries to a hand from an unguarded chain and sprocket:

'As the chain and sprocket classes as transmission machinery I opted for Section 13 [Factories Act, 1961] rather than Section 14 (other machinery) which is more general. PUWER does not apply as the machinery has been in place since 1964 and therefore classes as existing machinery. Did not use HSWA 1974, Section 2 as again Section 13 is more specific.'[19] (P97–57)

In the case of a collapsed crane the inspector recognized the potentially wider impact of a conviction under s. 2 of the HSW Act, but said in his report:

'The Factories Act case is essentially factual and therefore simpler. However, the Section 2 (1) case is a matter of degree, it is inherently more complicated but it does tell the better story. I favour the former on the basis that it is simple, factual and we are more certain of success, and on a political level, it will show local neighbours that HSE are taking action in respect of a crane.' A prosecution under s. 2 (1) HSW Act, 1974 was more difficult to prove, and therefore to be avoided: 'the time and trouble in [taking this section] may not add very much to what is already a certain breach with regard to crane examination. We can in the preamble to the failure to examine bring in wider issues to paint a fuller story

[18] There are several examples. Where an employee had fallen through a roof, the inspector opted for the Construction (Working Places) Regulations, 1966. In proposing a prosecution under Reg. 36 (1), he stated that 'Reasonably practicable is not within the sub-section,' a comment clearly implying that the matter should be easier to prosecute (P97–05). In another case the inspector reported: 'The evidence has not revealed any evidence which could be used as a defence. The requirements . . . [of the regulation concerned] are absolute requirements . . .' (P97–14).

[19] The firm was fined £3,000, with just over £200 in costs.

for the bench.' The inspector accordingly laid an information under the Factories Act 1961 s. 27 (1).[20] (P97–02)

The preference of inspectors to prosecute the breach of an absolute requirement, rather than a failure to observe a general duty, remains, despite the fact that conviction for the breach of a general duty may be more successful in achieving more far-reaching remedial measures. However, while in theory general duties, if successfully enforced, may be more effective because they may have this broader impact, the risks in prosecuting under a general duty make it a more difficult and cumbersome proposition.

Most inspectors find absolute requirements and specific rules more attractive for two important reasons. They are 'the easy option, the dead certainty' (86–24), making the case correspondingly quicker to prepare. 'And of course when you've got absolute offences you shouldn't lose a case. Because the evidence must be there or not there. The machine is fenced or not fenced. So if you've got nothing but absolute offences, inspectors who constantly lose cases can't be doing a very good job' (86–11). The specific provision is also useful as a fall-back, in the absence of a more appropriate charge.

In a case in which a worker fell from the roof of a house and was killed, the PI noted: 'I agree we prosecute under Reg. 35 Con (WP) Regs. [Construction (Working Places) Regulations, 1966] for lack of edge protection for both houses when extensive roofwork had been undertaken. It is a pity we haven't the evidence to support a prosecution specifically related to the fatal accident but the defendant and his friends have put up a barrier which we cannot overcome and prove to the court beyond reasonable doubt.'[21] (P97–67)

The comparative ease with which breaches of specific rules can be prosecuted contrast with the difficulties caused by the need for proof under s. 2. It was said by a former Chief Inspector of the Industrial Air Pollution Inspectorate (IAPI) that cases actually prosecuted in IAPI tended

[20] In this case the PI approved a charge under s. 27 of the Factories Act, 1961 ('failure to have examined') with a second case ('failure to have available') as an alternative. The specialist HSE group to whom the matter was referred for advice suggested a 'failure to maintain' case, but if insufficient evidence was available, suggested prosecuting for a failure to have the crane statutorily examined, 'which is easier to prove'. But 'the former case allows the "bigger story" to be told'. The defendant was fined £500, with more than £130 in costs.

[21] The employer was fined £325, with £200 in costs.

'to be simpler. They are usually the case where the firm has got the equipment in and its maintenance is sloppy . . . and you can produce hard evidence to say "The filter was switched off or the pump was not working," or whatever. And the inspector can produce this very hard evidence because it is much more difficult to produce hard evidence when you are wanting to justify that firm must spend so many hundreds or thousands or millions on some new plant and it's failing to do so because we and the firm disagree on what is practicable. You are in a very difficult area. Very difficult indeed.'

One of the commonest choices that used to confront inspectors was whether to prosecute with s. 2 of the HSW Act or s. 14 (1) of the Factories Act, 1961.[22] An analysis of their practices in Phase I showed that they preferred to work with the absolute requirements of the latter, rather than the general requirements of the former (Hawkins, 1989*a*). The Factories Act, 1961, s. 14 (1) was taken by inspectors as imposing for all practical purposes an absolute duty on an employer to guard a dangerous machine. 'You go for section 14 of the Factories Act,' said a PI in a general manufacturing group, 'because it's absolute and there are hundreds of decided cases. You can't lose' (86–51).[23] The clarity of absolute requirements is also believed valuable for the way in which the law is broadcast. Absolute requirements convey an easily understood message, representing the law to both employers and workforce in a straightforward fashion: 'They're clear, cast-iron cases, which the company can see, or their lawyers can see.' The simplicity of the absolute breach makes it harder for an employer to deny the failure to comply, but easier to recognize the justice of the prosecution. Where there is a breach of a general duty, an employer may genuinely feel he or she was doing all that was reasonably practicable. Here a prosecution may provoke resentment.

Certain circumstances, however, do favour the use of s. 2 HSW Act, despite its difficulties. For instance, choice of charge is a matter of conveying messages to the court and the use of a regulation which is precise and specific may not carry the same weight as a s. 2 charge. Inspectors occasionally complain of the difficulties of drafting a charge

[22] Section 14 of the Factories Act, 1961, was replaced on 1 Jan. 1998 by PUWER, but this does not affect the general point of the analysis that the form in which legal rules are drafted can profoundly affect whether and how those rules will be acted on.

[23] The success with which it was used is evident in statistics supplied by HSE for 1987–9, though HSW Act prosecutions also achieve a high rate of convictions. The success rate of informations laid under s. 14 (1) of the Factories Act, 1961, was 98 per cent, while that for s. 2 of the HSW Act cases was 90 per cent. Lloyd-Bostock (1992: 66) found that breach of s. 14 of the Factories Act, 1961, was the commonest ground for prosecution.

under regulations which can indicate to the court that matters were more serious than 'a paper breach'. A single charge under s. 2 may be enough:

'Ten, fifteen years ago it was quite common to prosecute a firm and lay multiple charges against them, you know, maybe ten, fifteen charges. That wouldn't tend to happen now except in very, very rare circumstances and we do rather often bring a single case... a single section 2 charge to show the management failings. The results of those management failings could be individual machines which weren't guarded properly, rather than bring fifteen charges...' (97–02)

Many inspectors believe there is a broad educative effect in this piece of general legislation. In arguing for a prosecution under s. 2 (1) of the HSW Act, the inspector in one case claimed that 'A prosecution for this breach [that the employer failed to take reasonably practicable precautions to protect the safety of his employees] would allow the full complexity of the shortcomings of the situation to be explored' (P97–46). Besides, using s. 2 is simpler where the risks are clear and easy to quantify, and the remedy cheap and straightforward. The riskier strategy may also yield more far-reaching results, the law's general requirements conveying to the employer a broad statement of what is wrong and what is required by way of remedy. Its flexibility and adaptability may also be valuable if technological change has rendered long-established—but ostensibly simpler—regulations obsolescent. Though difficulties begin where the risk is harder to apprehend and requires expert evidence to help make the case, the HSW Act can sometimes avoid the appearance of being unnecessarily fussy and technical. In the radiation case it was observed that 'it is often helpful to lay such a [general duty] charge and not restrict the prosecution solely to charges under regulations'. Whilst it may involve an added burden of proof of risk, and an explanation of reasonably practicable precautions, these are issues which it is as well to lay before the court if we are to avoid being perceived as laying technical charges (with the defendant fined accordingly)' (P97–53).

The potentially far-reaching impact of the 1974 Act sometimes appeals to inspectors, as is evident in the justification for prosecution advanced in a case involving an employee who had had his hand trapped in a machine, losing parts of three fingers:

The inspector actually recommended a prosecution under the Management of Health and Safety at Work Regulations Reg. 3 for not carrying out a risk assessment, but later changed the charge (possibly at the behest of his PI) to HSW Act, 1974, s. 2 (1), which was 'more appropriate'. 'The obvious breach here is for Section 14 of the Factories Act, however to prosecute under Section 14 would be to treat the symptom and not the cause of the accident. The root cause is a poor safety culture, under which such an unsafe system of work could develop, this will be difficult to address and needs commitment from management. A prosecution... may have a salutary effect on the company and cause them to question their commitment to health and safety.' (P97–56)

4. Effects

From a policy point of view, the form in which the written law is actually drafted may drive decision outcomes in a particular direction. The nature of legislation and the extent of its indeterminacy exert a strong influence over routine enforcement decisions. One effect may be to encourage compliance-based approaches to routine enforcement in the field. Under a regime of precise rules inspectors had to know the particulars of a rule in order to forbid an employer from a course of action, but the enforcement task was simpler and bargaining made easier. 'If there are clear standards written in law,' said a former Chief Inspector of Factories, 'then inspectors can enforce without a lot of argument' (R. Baldwin, 1987: 35). If inspectors want to rely on the HSW Act, there is an irony in that the generality of the rule in s. 2, which might make it easier for an inspector to negotiate, might actually make some more reluctant to prosecute.

A second effect acts directly on decision-making about prosecution, and arises from the demands of proof in the criminal law, which alert inspectors to the dangers in prosecuting certain kinds of offence written in the statutes in certain ways. The risks of losing encourage them to search for and act on violations which are less problematic in legal terms: they look for cases that are easier to prosecute, can be prepared quickly, and are unlikely to be defended. Lloyd-Bostock (1992: 64) found that inspectors appeared to select accidents for investigation on the basis of characteristics that indicated the probability of an opportunity to enforce a quite specific range of safety regulations. Furthermore, she found that inspectors not only repeatedly investigated certain types of accident, but in doing so repeatedly enforced certain regulations which met 'enforceability' criteria (Lloyd-Bostock 1992: 65). She describes s. 14 of the Factories Act, 1961, as 'widely recognized as a favorite amongst inspectors because it is so readily enforceable' and 'the commonest grounds for prosecution', concluding that this behaviour can lead to certain events being subject to enforcement action, while others are perhaps under-enforced (Lloyd-Bostock (1992: 66)). Their preoccupation with the risks posed by the legal process to a successful prosecution leads in turn to legal control being more readily applied to certain kinds of case: to those in which the alleged breach is of an absolute rather than a general duty, and to accidents (in which the damage has been done), rather than risks (in which damage is only a future possibility).

This can produce perverse effects. One is to skew the distribution of prosecuted cases towards straightforward matters at the expense of those which may be more complicated or may be defended. Perhaps the most notable effect is that safety cases tend to be prosecuted more frequently than cases involving threats to health.[24] Safety cases are generally regarded by inspectors as easier. They can usually be handled as breaches of absolute requirements and there is considerable case law to assist in establishing what the courts regard as 'safe' or 'unsafe'. There is, in contrast, 'much less about what's healthy and not healthy', an AD said (86–19), which itself results from the legal difficulties confronting inspectors when contemplating occupational health problems. If the latter are sometimes dealt with by improvement notices, safety problems are seen in simpler terms as breaches deserving punishment since 'It takes five minutes to put a guard on a machine, and everyone knows it should be guarded' (86–25). The extra risk faced by the inspector who wishes to prosecute for a violation involving occupational ill health is inherent in the evidentiary demands of the law,[25] whose effect is to thrust enforcement in a direction which might not accord with the broader objectives of social policy. Some problems may be dealt with not as seems most appropriate, while others receive the attentions of the formal law because they are more easily brought to it.

The effects of legislative wording suggest that the broad purposes of law may be subverted by the law's own frailties of language as a result of the relationship between the form of words and legal actors' strategic decisions about law enforcement. Patterns of enforcement develop. Because inspectors enforce specific rules more readily than general duties, finite and discrete forms of rule-breaking are more frequently prosecuted than a general and vague malaise in a company. A further

[24] It is impossible to support this statement with empirical evidence, given the problems in identifying cases of occupational ill health. It is notable, however, that only two of the 68 cases in the sample of prosecution files involved damage to workers' health.

[25] In the United States the attractiveness of civil penalties is connected with their lower standard of proof. Such sanctions are more popular than criminal penalties: there are about four civil cases for every one criminal (Kagan, 1993).

implication is that the ease with which evidence can be obtained and presented in support of a prosecution case will also concentrate formal enforcement action on certain industries. It is usually simpler to obtain viable evidence in construction, general manufacturing, and engineering industries than, for instance, in the chemicals industry. Construction cases are relatively straightforward compared with the difficulties which often face inspectors who are dissatisfied with working conditions, practices, or hazards in chemicals works with their complex and often invisible processes (see Chapter 4). When faced with a possible prosecution case, the preoccupation of the chemicals inspector, who may be involved in no more than one or two prosecutions a year (if that), is whether he or she can afford the time. This is ironic in light of the fact that the typical construction inspector is involved in many more prosecutions annually. Where evidence is harder to find, or potentially less persuasive to a court, inspectors are more circumspect in thinking about prosecuting.

The less imposing legal impediments to the prosecution of safety cases combine with the inherent character of safety problems. Safety is a simpler matter to regulate since cases have properties which facilitate legal action. The clarity with which most present themselves, their unproblematic quality, and the vividness of accidents bring violations to light more readily: 'The hazards we are dealing with vary considerably both in kind and degree. Accidents resulting in injury or death are obvious enough' (Health and Safety Commission, 1983: 10–11). Safety violations tend to involve clearer risks and more dramatic consequences than problems of occupational health. 'There's something, to my mind, more immediate about a man having his fingers chopped off than in 20 or 30 years' time getting asbestosis, or whatever' (86–63). These more vivid problems of control tend to become the focus of inspectors' attention. 'What confronts us as inspectors', said a PI (86–01), 'are people maimed, injured, and killed.' Remedy is often more straightforward and immediately effected. Nearly all factories have machines of some sort, and machines usually pose visible and readily identifiable threats to worker safety. Appropriate precautions in the form of guarding or changes in working practices are relatively easy to take and to enforce, and failures therefore prompt more complaints. A study of trade unions' safety representatives found that factory inspectors were believed to lay too much emphasis on accident work, at the expense of problems of occupational ill health (Freedman, 1989). In discussing the enforcement of health standards a former Chief Inspector of Factories referred to the 'much more shadowy potential risks: health hazards where you haven't got blood on the floor or bodies to count. You've got the prospect of things going wrong in twenty or thirty years time and you won't find, when you look at our records, anywhere near as many cases for occupational health matters, as you will for safety matters. Simply because they are far more difficult to prove.'[26]

Certain kinds of work activity are more easily regulated than others, then, and certain laws are more easily enforced than others. The form and demands of the law make it easier to act in the cases that are routinely encountered: the much greater preponderance of prosecutions for safety violations not only reflects enforcers' impressions of the prevalence of safety rather than health problems and the greater readiness with which accidents present themselves, but also the greater chance of winning. Compared with safety cases, occupational health problems, are 'less clear-cut always. You're trying to achieve an improvement which will have a long-term benefit. With a safety situation you're trying to achieve an improvement that will have an immediate benefit' (86–01). This tends to reinforce the difficulties acknowledged by inspectors that they (and others) find it difficult to apprehend danger to health in contrast with risk to safety: 'You more often get in a situation where you know it's absolutely wrong that moment. Whereas with a health problem I know it's creating a long-term problem every moment. *But it's hard to see it in that context*' (86–01; my emphasis).

Also helping to depress the level of prosecutions in occupational health cases are the limits of knowledge about risks to health, and the difficulties of establishing cause and effect to acceptable legal standards. A major difficulty in prosecuting an occupational ill-health case is that of establishing a clear link between working conditions and the onset of some later illness. Latency is a problem: 'In some cases the effects may take a long time to show up and may not be entirely attributable to occupational causes' (Health and Safety Commission, 1983: 12). While some threats to health are familiar, such as those associated with lead or asbestos, aetiological knowledge in other areas of occupational ill health is much less secure. Problems arise where toxicity is disputed and people are correspondingly more careless about complying, adding to the difficulties in proving a case beyond reasonable doubt. It is often difficult to

[26] Johnstone (1994: 35) has shown that in the period 1960 to 1982 most prosecutions under the occupational health and safety legislation in the state of Victoria were brought in relation to machinery safety. Just under 5 per cent of the prosecutions about guarding of machinery were dismissed, but about 15 per cent of prosecutions for other offences were dismissed, indicating the convictability of guarding offences.

find medical evidence to support a prosecution. 'It's very difficult', said an AD, 'to convince a court that the activity that's gone on has actually been sufficient to cause ill-health unless you can produce a person whose health has been affected and a doctor who will say so' (86–19). When it is presented, the defence is often able to oppose it by submitting its own evidence to the contrary. A safety case, on the other hand, can usually be prosecuted by an inspector without having to rely on medical experts, occupational hygienists, and others. This keeps the matter under control: 'You're reliant on so many people in a health case. There are doctors, there are scientists, there are [others]. With a safety case I can do it myself' (86–63). At the same time magistrates find the issues involved more comprehensible. After all, an unguarded machine is self-evidently dangerous.

The significance of this for public policy is that an estimated 2 million people each year believe they suffer ill health caused by their work. Recent figures show the total costs to society of work related ill health to amount to some £11 billion (Health and Safety Commission, 1999, p. x). Even more striking is the fact that a substantial number of inspectors believed that more people (possibly 10 times as many) die as a result of occupationally induced disease than as a result of accidents at work (though there are huge measurement problems here: Wikeley, 1993). One estimate has put the number of deaths from occupational disease at between 8,000 and 20,000 a year (Meacher, 1988), while Benson and Cullen (1998) similarly report in the United States a much higher proportion of deaths from occupationally induced disease than from accidents. It is not known how many instances occur where inspectors wish to prosecute where there seems to be a threat to workers' health but feel they cannot because legally provable scientific evidence is lacking.

5. BREAKING FRAME

There is not necessarily a good fit between a public policy conception of a 'good case' and a legal conception of a good case. An important consequence of this is that in applying the legal frame, the decision-maker becomes concerned with the demands of proof rather than of policy. There is a further irony here, given that the interests of public policy are embodied in the broad legal mandate which is overtaken by the precise technical concerns involved in the inspector's legal frame. The potential of the legal method as expressed in the legal process to frustrate the interests of public policy has been observed by others. After a detailed legal analysis of prosecution and sentencing practices, Frank Wright (1995: 149) concluded: 'a strong impression has evolved to the effect that the courts are more likely to convict and impose penalties where a serious accident has occurred leading to loss of life or serious personal injury rather than where the system of health and safety is at fault such that loss of life or serious personal injury could result'. Similarly, Weaver (1977: 30) said of US anti-trust lawyers that they were 'too exclusively concerned with the actual, current behavior of business firms and with winning the case at hand, not enough with the economic impact of their work'.

It is only in exceptional cases that the grip of the legal frame can be broken. Where an event is grave, the legal frame can be thrust into the background, as an AD explained:

> 'I think there are plenty of cases where, you know, even if it wasn't absolutely cast iron on evidence . . . it's still *preferable for us to be seen to be having a go* trying to bring a particular defendant to book, rather than saying "Well, you know, we haven't quite . . . got every little bit of evidence corroborated, there's a vague chance we could go down, we're not venturing anything." Now, that's a circumstance that not infrequently happens where fatal accidents are concerned, because your one key witness can't give you any evidence. But I would . . . I think there are plenty of cases where I would rather, you know, live a little dangerously, and be seen to have a go, and do our best, and . . . it's sort of honour satisfied then.' (97–02; my emphasis)

In the radiation case, which HSE lost, the inspector anticipated a not guilty plea in the Prosecution Report to his PI:

> 'on the basis that they have done all that is reasonably practicable to ensure the safety of their employees and that the Informations are based on merely technical offences. They may argue that working in the enclosure is intrinsically safer than working on site and that employees have all the necessary equipment, qualifications and knowledge to avoid receiving any significant doses. In addition some witnesses may not perform well in court. However I believe *the issues are too serious to avoid prosecution despite the relative weakness of the evidence.*' (P97–53; my emphasis)

Where other decision frames compel a prosecution, the threshold of evidential sufficiency is lowered, and the legal frame gives way.

6. CONCLUSION

While the formal law and its demands are never far away in the handling of potential prosecution cases, the legal frame creates an almost overpowering focus in the final stages of prosecution decision-making since it determines whether and how the law will be used, encouraging the prosecution of that which seems legally precise. Central to this is the culpability of the violator and the prospects for successfully negotiating the vagaries of evidence, proof, and trial. The legal frame reflects the law's concern for clarity and credibility in its demands for evidence and proof. Its effect is to produce a form of decision-making that is typical of the method of the Anglo-American common law: ad hoc, worked on case by case, and court-focused. The application of the legal frame brings case-handling to a critical point where an inspector moves from using information to deal with a problem as effectively as possible to a position where information is assessed primarily for its utility in prosecution.

When applying the legal frame inspectors think like lawyers, for the structure of the adversarial process imprints itself upon their behaviour in significant ways. They apply to a potential prosecution case the criteria and tests that operate in the courtroom. The nature of the legal method is to create its own reality by particularizing, to allow the ready application of legal rules to produce an outcome, an answer to a question posed in legal terms. Indeed, one implication of the imposition of legal reality, according to Johnstone (1994), is that the form of the criminal law involved in the prosecution of occupational health and safety offences encourages a particularistic view of the incident prompting the prosecution, at the expense of a broader sense of the context of health and safety in the workplace. Johnstone concludes that the form of the criminal trial tears selected facts about events in the workplace from their complex social reality, transforming them into individualistic criminal law conceptions of responsibility and sanctioning, thereby depoliticizing the issues before the court. He observed that this effect was especially noticeable in sentencing, where defence counsel were able to isolate the event from issues connected with the general organization of the workplace and instead to shift the blame for the incident onto workers. By transforming matters connected with systems of work into an individualistic concern for an incident and an individual's responsibility, Johnstone argues, the culpability of the defendant can be reduced for sentencing purposes.

Adversarialism is not necessarily conducive to systematic law enforcement in the public interest. The legal frame's concern for the specific and the concrete, although rational in legal terms, may work contrary to public policy by defeating the broad instrumentalist mandate. This is a feature that may operate more widely in the legal process, since the goal of adversarial legal action is to win the case at hand. Inspectors are encouraged to gather evidence for legal purposes, rather than to find facts for regulatory purposes, leading to a systematic tendency for certain events or acts to be repeatedly subject to enforcement, to the neglect of others. If a case seems to be one worth prosecuting, the inspector's decision-making is shaped by an assessment of the prospects of conviction rather than by some broader strategic policy interests to be advanced, preserved, or protected. Winning the present case takes priority. In this part of the regulatory process lawyers and legal thinking do not sit comfortably with the aim of public policy.[27]

People are uncomfortable with risks to health, perhaps in part because they are less readily apparent. Increased public concern has been mainly associated with those hazards that are uncertain in scope, and can have effects beyond the workplace whether locally or, as is the case with some radiation hazards, more generally.[28] This is a view that HSC (1985: 5) adopted several years ago:

> 'The traditional and immediate risks to life and limb in particular industries, though still very important, are no longer paramount. By contrast, increasing importance has to be attached to health risks associated with toxic, carcinogenic, etc. substances; to such general hazards as noise; and to those risks, principally of explosion or radiation, for which the term 'major hazards' has been coined. Finding a proper balance between the attention to be devoted to these two orders of hazard is one of the most difficult tasks facing any national authority on safety and health; the more so that the assessment of the new kinds of risk has to be made against a background of increasing public concern...'

Some find it difficult to grasp and to convey the extent and importance of risks that are often invisible and exceedingly remote, or to balance the importance of a grave but remote risk against the day-to-day predictability and measurability of death and injury in the workplace. Moreover, in the case of risks to health, for example from substances in use in industry, the effects can be so long delayed and their attribution so uncertain that the presence or the size of the hazard may not be fully ascertainable.

[27] For example, in Australia 'Accident investigation was seen as a highly detailed and technical exercise, a process which had the potential to allow the event itself to be decontextualized, and reconstructed or explained in terms of its own unique details, rather than as part of a broader process of production. The technical nature of the investigation was continually emphasised...' (Johnstone, 1994: 177).

[28] This concern was evident in the case of discharges from Sellafield, emissions of gases to the atmosphere, the implications of nuclear power generation manifested at the Sizewell Inquiry, asbestos, and, in a different way, by the explosion at Abbeystead.

Paradoxically, however, people are often prepared to live with serious risks. Familiar, clearly toxic substances are less of a problem for regulatory control since people will comply in accordance with the received wisdom about their dangers. This is true of the behaviour of employers, employees, and regulatory inspectors. But people respond to the clarity and immediacy with which risks present themselves, not to the gravity of the threat a risk poses. It is a feature of the hazards generated by modern industry that the nature and extent of any risk is often not immediately apparent to the uninformed observer, so that personal precautions can be taken. The effects of hazards may be very sudden or long delayed, and their assessment and control is often dependent on technology which few understand. Indeed, the people who are themselves likely to become victims are often less likely to take health matters seriously: 'People out there don't react as well to health issues: the "My father's been doing that for years and its hasn't affected his health yet" view' (86–09).

The prosecution process in regulatory agencies reveals the legal frame and the method of law at work. The difficulty of grafting the regulation of occupational health and safety offences onto the criminal law was a matter recognized in the Robens Report, which suggested that a fundamental weakness in prosecuting violations was that the

> 'criminal courts are inevitably concerned more with events that have happened than with curing the underlying weaknesses that caused them... Traditional concepts of criminal law are not readily comparable to the majority of infringements... Relatively few defences are clear cut, few arise from reckless indifference to the possibility of causing injury, few can be laid without qualification at the door of a particular individual.... The lengthy process of investigation, warning, institution of criminal proceedings, conviction and ultimate fine is not a very effective way of producing an early remedy for known unsatisfactory conditions.' (Robens, 1972, para. 60)

The characteristic approach of the legal system is to strip away the complexity of everyday life so that it may do its work most efficiently by applying rules to what it has defined as legally relevant reality established in court in adversarial debate. (There is a nice irony in the fact that although the law likes to create its own conceptions in the interests of certainty, legal practitioners like to create uncertainty.) The risk of failing to do this encourages enforcers to emphasize accidents rather than working practices, general hazards, or longer-term problems. When it engages the formalities of legal action in this way, the regulatory process tends to focus on individual acts and events, and turns away from broader concerns of public policy.[29] 'The legal form, deeply rooted in individualistic notions of responsibility, is preoccupied with events and details, and with scrutinising individual actions' (Johnstone, 1994: 530). Law is uncomfortable dealing with generalities, with the social, political, and economic contexts of untoward events, and with the uncertainties and vagaries of causation. In the occupational health and safety arena law is unhappy contemplating broader social, organizational, and industrial relations processes and cultures that create or contribute to risks and lead to accidents and occupational ill health.[30] This leads to problems in using law proactively, pre-emptively, and preventively, a feature observable throughout the legal process, from writing rules to the exercise of field-level discretion. The operation of the legal method in particular cases may run counter to the thrust of the law as a whole.

What is a 'good case' in regulatory terms is not necessarily a 'good case' in legal terms. Much of the discourse employed by regulatory officials in debating the substantive merits of a prosecution is of a moral, not a legal (or instrumental), character. Prosecution reports are frequently framed in moral terms with conceptions of blame and desert dominant (see Chapter 11). The character of legal framing, in contrast, is a discourse organized around legal categories, conceptions, rules, and preoccupations. These become prominent in prosecution reports once the substantive merits seem satisfied, because the legal system itself creates risks for the legal actor. The risks to the regulatory inspector and to the regulatory organization posed by a potential prosecution case—the risks inherent in using the law—shape the ultimate decision about prosecution. One important implication for public policy may be that the control of occupational health problems might be more readily attained by altering the techniques and forms of regulation to make them more easily enforceable, rather than by seeking to alter enforcement agents' decision-making practices within an existing set of regulatory forms.

[29] This may also be true of legal processes more generally. See e.g. the criticisms of the tort system of compensation for personal injuries in Harris *et al.* (1984).

[30] Indeed, the same impediments act in civil cases to make it difficult to sustain a claim for compensation for ill health, probably reducing the incentive for employers to cut exposure to potentially harmful substances (R. Baldwin, 1987).

Part V

Reflection

13 On Prosecution, Legal Decision-Making, and Law

In this final chapter I summarize and reflect further upon a number of issues which surfaced during the analysis, considering more generally the character of legal control and the role of prosecution. The first point to make is that this book reports fieldwork which was conducted over an extended period. The value of generating a large data set comprising different forms of qualitative material should be clear in the various ways in which different facets of the process of prosecution decision-making have been exposed. It is also hard to discern any change of a fundamental kind in the way prosecution decisions were made over the period from the mid-1980s to the late 1990s. This is because it is not usually the substance of the law, or changes in legal procedure, or other explanations of a primarily instrumentalist kind that are the primary determinants of a decision to prosecute. Clearly, the structure of the law is significant in its allocation of authority, while a violation is the legally recognized occasion that permits the law to comprehend and act on the breach or the hazard created. But decision-making by legal officials is a human process which sometimes follows legal rules, sometimes transcends them, sometimes distorts them, and sometimes, indeed, operates independently of them.

The underlying logic of the Health and Safety at Work Act, 1974 (HSW Act) and the many sets of regulations reflects an instrumental concern to reduce the prevalence of workplace illnesses and accidents, and it is to be expected that their operation would be regarded and evaluated instrumentally. The analysis, however, has emphasized the power of expressive forces in decision-making. Instrumental and expressive concerns are not exclusive approaches, but mutually reinforce each other. Audiences have different interests and expectations. In serving instrumental purposes for some audiences by prosecution, the regulatory agency can at the same time serve expressive ends for others. An instrumental view of law provides the means by which a bureaucracy can claim legitimacy for what it does in its efforts to change the world for the better.

Yet prosecution is the formal and public way of allocating blame, and as such might ironically be regarded as representing the failure of regulatory control.

1. ABOUT PROSECUTION

1. Prosecution as Symbolic Act

The act of prosecution carries with it meanings beyond any instrumental purpose to be served in reducing rule-breaking. The significance of the symbolic approach is its concern to achieve and express a conception of moral order which may outweigh any instrumental objectives, for which prosecution may in some cases be intended. Though the purpose of prosecution may sometimes be to alter behaviour (and may indeed sometimes achieve such an impact), its various expressive features frequently dominate decision-making. In practice the decision to prosecute in HSE is primarily one taken for expressive purposes, making a moral statement while seeking to advance organizational interests. Moral ordering is salient in shaping how people interpret events and act in response to them. The selective use of prosecution, in conjunction with the infrequency of its use, enhances the force with which the act conveys messages. Indeed, on one view, the value of symbolic ordering 'is usually enhanced by its selectivity. By choosing the strongest cases and the symbolically most important "targets", prosecutors maximize the impact and effectiveness of this strategy. Far from being a sign of weakness, therefore, the relative rarity of prosecutions may be a sign of strength' (Stenning *et al.*, 1990: 114).

Prosecution is a ceremonial restatement of the norms by which people and individuals order social life. Its use sustains the moral world which the regulatory organization inhabits. One way it does this is through the satisfaction given by the prosecution of a blameworthy defendant that moral boundaries are being maintained and reinforced. This is a pervasive function of legal processes, one most apparent in their formal proceedings. For those deemed not to be in some sense 'good' or not to have acted rightly, prosecution becomes a means of marking the exceptional, and signalling disapproval of moral frailty. Thus, for those whose moral status indicates that they deserve it, the law is recruited as a means of punishing. It serves as a formal way of allocating blame, for criminal law reflects, shapes, and cements current conceptions of right and wrong. Prosecution provides an authoritative and legitimate means of making statements about good and bad, right and wrong, and singles out for the condemnation of the criminal law those who have failed to meet desirable standards. It affirms to those who comply that those who do not will neither escape censure nor gain undeserved advantage. Prosecution is thus a means of endorsing, underlining, cementing, and in some cases changing the symbolic constitution of social and business life.

Prosecution is the formal means of announcing the enforcement of the law and the defence of public interests, serving at once as a dramatic affirmation of the right of the state to regulate and the regulatory agency's willingness and capacity to do so. Prosecution, when viewed as right, proper, and appropriate, is legitimate (Gusfield, 1963), and can therefore make both an expressive claim founded in moral legitimacy and an instrumental claim derived from action in the public interest. It is 'the ultimate expression of the state's power... an expression of large symbolic significance' (Yeager, 1991: 251). At the same time the act of prosecution endorses the standing of the agency, its legitimacy as a regulatory organization, and these in turn underscore the essential rightness of the regulatory agency's actions. In the context of occupational health and safety regulation, it is a partisan declaration, clarifying what is intolerable, condemning the hazardous, and endorsing our conceptions of the worth of those in the workplace. Here prosecution is a ritualistic encounter which formally identifies and encapsulates the existence of a problem between the agency and a regulated firm, in which the agency publicly aligns itself with the sick and injured who are the victims of an employer's failure to comply with the law. In making public those standards of conduct deemed proper, decent, and desirable, prosecution can be cathartic, since it can sometimes satisfy a demand, whether from the victim, the victim's family, the media, or people generally, for a public statement of the worth of the victim and the culpability of the defendant.

One important function of prosecution is its ability to resolve ambiguity in the rules of the legal system. Inspectors in regulatory organizations, like many other types of law enforcers, inhabit a fuzzy and uncertain world. They are accorded, or assume for themselves, a high level of administrative discretion which is both caused by, and further contributes to, indeterminacy. In everyday enforcement, inspectors exploit ambiguity and take advantage of their discretion to work towards compliance by enforcing the law by bargaining. Negotiations about compliance are conducted in largely technical, engineering, and scientific terms, with an ostensible focus on the management and reduction of risk. The negotiation facilitated by extensive administrative discretion and low visibility can lead to practices that appear controversial, such as sometimes turning a blind eye to a problem, or not reporting it to superiors. In all of this, the formal law hovers in the background, clarifying uncertainty only when summoned up. But when the formal law comes into play in a prosecution, it produces a sharp focus.

Since the act of prosecution expresses deeply held values of right and wrong, of blame, or personal worth, it can provide the occasion for conflict and tension where those who are being prosecuted do not share, or at least fail to accept in a particular instance, the legitimacy of the prosecution's position. Such conflicts can occur when both sides frame the matter giving rise to the prosecution, and the enforcement response, in expressive but contrasting terms. Conflict may also arise when a prosecution pursued to satisfy instrumentalist purposes is framed symbolically by the defendant employer. Such differences might arise, for example, where an employer who is being prosecuted for general deterrent purposes repairs the harm done by the breach before the case comes to court. The rationale for the prosecution in this sort of case holds good, regardless of any remedial action taken by the individual employer, and despite the employer's belief that the prosecution is unjust because it is now undeserved.

In these circumstances the instrumental and symbolic positions need to be reconciled and conflicting interests made to fit together better if an inspector wants a clearly deserved prosecution to have a beneficial impact on a defendant's future behaviour. The search for a good fit acknowledges the importance of shared framing and the readily recognizable principle of commensurability. The result should be that 'you should be able to convince the company that the action you're taking is reasonable. And in 99 per cent of the cases you can do that, if you choose the right circumstances and the right case. I say that because there are some offences that get people bristling, and some that don't' (97–05). The matter hinges on the credibility of the rationale, as a principal inspector (PI) pointed out: 'We can justify, credibly justify our actions, whether it's a prosecution or not . . . that action can be justified. . . . If you've got a good argument, a good reason, then put it out, and they will see that good argument. . . . You will find yourself not in the minority of one' (97–03).

2. Prosecution as Organizational Work

Prosecution decision-making is heavily imprinted with its organizational provenance. In the regulatory arena there is both dependence on organizations to enforce the law and law enforcement which is conducted (for the most part) against other organizations. Whatever else it may be, prosecution has to be understood as a product of organizational structures and behaviour. One implication of this is that prosecution takes place because inspectors conceive it to be in the interests of the organization that it does so. Equally, organizations impose demands of their own upon their actors, who respond in turn by making prosecution decisions for their own organizationally motivated reasons.

Dependence on legal bureaucracies for the furtherance of public policy creates a number of problems. Inspectorates substantially influence how regulatory policy is practised, yet decision-making power varies according to organizational structure and the location of the actor within it. The structure of an inspectorate is one in which relatively few senior officials monitor and direct the activities of a relatively large number of others, those 'street-level bureaucrats' (Lipsky, 1980) and their immediate superiors who are in direct contact with the practical problems of the world. This results in a heavily decentralized organization whose street-level decisions risk fragmenting, distorting, or even subverting broad policy. This poses problems in controlling the discretion of inspectors. The autonomy of those at the periphery of the regulatory organization is a powerful force: inspectors make decisions in essentially private settings, and are subjected to constraints and pressures to act (or not) in particular ways peculiar to their position in the organizational hierarchy. This is especially important in the context of prosecution, which is decision-making of a public and consequential kind.

From the point of view of developing a theory of legal decision-making it is important to understand the formation of policy as a decision-making exercise involving processes of interpretation and translation in an organizational setting. Regulatory bureaucracies have profound choices to make about the meaning of legislative intent. This broad organizational mandate has to be crystallized in the form of a particular set of bureaucratic policies and rules so that they may guide action at the periphery. Chapter 6 showed that the structure of legal bureaucracies is an important influence on how policy works, and on the extent to which it can work as expected by its authors. It is the inspector, after all, who serves as the organization's primary decision-maker and its public face, but who usually operates in private settings of low visibility. It is one thing to think about the decision-making that goes into the formulation of policy, but quite another to contemplate how that policy is transformed or distorted within the organization in the decision behaviour of lower-level officials, as it is shifted from centre to periphery to be translated into practical activity.

3. Prosecution as Public Act

Various contrasting implications arise from the fact that regulatory bureaucracies are bodies that operate on the public stage when they prosecute. The practice of enforcement in its most public aspect helps shape perceptions of the nature of regulatory violators and violations. At the same time, prosecution may confer a wider legitimacy on the enforcement work of the agency pursuing it, as long as the cause of the prosecution is itself regarded by the public as legitimate and justifiable. For many employers, however, prosecution is a declaration of hostilities. The act moves any personal relationship that exists between regulator and employer into the impersonal glare of the courtroom, exposing the defendant as an alleged wrongdoer.

Its public position puts competing pressures on the regulatory organization. Compared with routine enforcement practices, prosecution consumes disproportionate resources. Limited resources shape the decision field for inspectorates, compelling enforcement strategies which select targets or priorities to make what is in reality a rather constrained effort go as far as possible, exploiting whatever multiplier effects can be achieved, through extensive and varied publicity, well-chosen prosecutions, and so on. Meanwhile, inspectors continue to work in the curiously equivocal way that many other street-level bureaucrats must work, acting at once as educator, counsellor, and police officer.

A regulatory agency may have to answer to other audiences which have contrasting expectations, requiring it to justify prosecution in instrumental terms to some, and in symbolic terms to others. Sometimes it has to justify its action to the same audiences (for example, to political masters who want to see that the organization is not only taking action to make the world a better place in some way, but is also taking action in those cases of which they particularly approve). So there is a sense in which different messages go out to different audiences and different expectations come back from audiences to the regulators. Moreover, different parts of the regulatory organization may be receptive to different kinds of message, those in senior positions being more sensitive to larger forces of politics and economics and probably more concerned with instrumental objectives than those in the field.

The public meaning and role of prosecution changes in light of different conceptions of enforcement. This is especially the case with sanctioning and compliance strategies. In sanctioning strategy, a form of public and punitive enforcement demanding prosecution and punishment for the breach of a legal rule, prosecution is a logical consequence of a desire to punish for retributive or deterrent reasons. Here, prosecution is an important part of a regulatory agency's sense of itself and the values it represents. From the perspective of those committed to compliance strategy, a form of private negotiated enforcement, involving advice and education for the rule-breaker in the pursuance of the regulatory agency's broad legal mandate to improve standards of occupational health and safety, there is, in contrast, a sense in which prosecution represents the failure of regulatory control. To have to prosecute, having employed a strategy of compliance-seeking, is practical recognition that bargaining and negotiations have not worked. Compliance strategy is associated with preventive control, whereas sanctioning strategy responds reflectively after the fact of a violation. Prosecution is used less in an anticipatory or pre-emptive way for dealing with the existence of a hazard, but is more frequently employed reactively in responding to damage done. And because harms accumulate over time and the victims of hazards are not knowable, it is more difficult to see the benefits of compliance strategy, whereas sanctioning strategy is visibly put into action. In enforcement by compliance strategy, much depends on informality, personal relationships, and the trust between inspector and regulated firm that makes negotiated compliance possible. Yet enforcers believe prosecution can destroy trust. Trust itself is founded on experience and the mutual reciprocity which is an integral part of enforcement by compliance strategy, for these grant a sense by which the participants are able to know and to expect how each other will act. This provides a strong push for continuity in relationships. Prosecution is more likely to be employed where trust has broken down, or where an act or event is so serious that trust is trumped by other demands to act to which the regulatory agency feels vulnerable.

The practical importance of prosecution in compliance strategy, however, is as the ultimate threat of the law's public intrusion which underpins relationships between enforcers and regulated business and makes them workable. Negotiation usually forecloses use of the formal law and ensures its adoption as a sanction of last resort. Where negotiation fails, law enters explicitly, even though it has constantly cast a shadow over the conduct of negotiations and the behaviour of the parties. Prosecution stands in the background, its presence clearly registered, even if little used.

4. Prosecution as Transformation

Prosecution means transformation in the fate of a case. Important boundaries are crossed with the decision to prosecute. Private troubles become public affairs. The process of enforcement in routine regulatory work has a private character and is primarily directed towards the idea of ordering and problem-solving, rather than enforcing rules and delivering an unproblematic, all-or-nothing conception of legal justice following trial and adjudication in the courts (Rees, 1988: 12; M. M. Shapiro, 1981). But with prosecution, private ordering by negotiation gives way to public law enforcement and adjudication. At the same time the character of the legal response, one concerned with the repair of a problem, submits ostensibly to a form of retributive or deterrent justice (Rock, 1995: 24). The mode of law enforcement switches abruptly from private bargaining, in which compromise outcomes are not only possible but regarded by enforcers as desirable, to public adversarial debate, in which legal justice is delivered in a binary verdict of guilty or not guilty. Negotiated problem-solving gives way to the imposed and uncompromising rigours of adjudicated justice, the decision-maker abandoning the possibility of commitment to a solution by both parties. Another form of transformation occurs, as prosecution is likely to be regarded by regulated firms as a hostile act, and, like other areas of legal activity, the nature of relationships is changed when there is a move to formal proceedings. The nature of the contact between the parties is depersonalized. In court the law pulls away what it deems to be unnecessary material so that which is legally relevant can be laid bare, problem-solving giving way to a legal and moral declaration about the legal guilt (or otherwise) of the accused. Previously amicable relationships may be destroyed in the process.

Prosecution decision-making can be seen as a progressive loss of control by enforcers.[1] Control of case outcomes is important to inspect-

[1] This is a matter for inspectors: control of case-handling and outcomes is hard for senior organizational officials to achieve in a decentralized organization like the Field Operations Directorate (FOD) since they are so dependent upon their field staff; see Ch. 3.

ors, and rests with them, until they feel constrained to resort to prosecution. But a transformation occurs in the control of the case when a problem is defined as worthy of the attention of the courts. At this point reliance on regulation by the threat or application of legal penalties places the regulatory body in a position of curious vulnerability, which it has to manage in terms of the kinds and numbers of cases that it chooses to prosecute. While negotiating for compliance, inspectors maintain control of a case and its handling. But as soon as a serious decision to prosecute is made, and the inspector has to apply the legal frame to fulfil the evidentiary and procedural demands of the law, control over the handling and disposal of the matter begins to be lost. And in contested cases the inspector surrenders substantial control over the ultimate disposal of the case to a third party—the magistrate or judge and jury. One source of control remaining open to the inspector is to drop the case. Another rests with the various bargains that might be struck pre-trial, for this allows inspectors to try to align a guilty plea with their conception of the needs or deserts of the particular case. A final source of control might rest with the inspector's persuasiveness in court, for their opportunity for advocacy confers some residual sense of control upon them. That some inspectors do not seem to feel that they have lost all control during trial is evident in the remarks of a PI who, speaking of the symbolic importance of a decision to convict, said, 'that's the important one, *that's the one you can influence*. You can't influence the penalty. That's in the lap of the gods, that's in the courts' (97–03; my emphasis). The ultimate decision about the outcome of the defended case nevertheless rests outside inspectors' hands, making prosecution a risky strategy for them to embark on.

While in resorting to the courts the agency substantially loses control over the case, it is at the same time able to pass troublesome cases to the courts for final disposal. In selecting out certain numbers and kinds of case for prosecution, the agency is also defining the 'troublesome' cases for the courts and for the wider public, as well as the kinds of case that demand formal legal action. The type of cases actually prosecuted is important where resources are limited, which encourages regulatory staff to think about the quality of prosecutions, as well as about their quantity. The quality of a prosecution is shaped partly by the agency's public position and its sensitivity to its special environment. Its willingness to chance its arm in prosecution is contingent upon the perceived balance of conflicting interests in an environment of ambivalence, and upon the degree of victimization or threat: actual harm done to the person, or an immediate threat of it, raise more concern, hence HSE's probable greater willingness to prosecute than some other regulatory agencies.

Another type of transformation in the control of a case is to be found in the opportunities created in a centralized system of serial decision-making for senior officials, who review proposals for prosecution, to visit their own conception of the aims of prosecution upon a case whose career may have been initiated by an inspector to serve quite other purposes. The forces that make a case worth acting on to begin with are not necessarily those that see the matter pursued to prosecution (Lempert, 1992). Weaver (1977: 112) observed one aspect of this effect in her research in Washington, DC, noting that a 'case moves up the hierarchy as far as the director of operation's office facing an ever increasing tension between the imperatives of prosecution and the demands of what superiors see as both the division's reputation for winning its cases and its reputation for legal craftsmanship in general'. In organizations where arrangements for prosecution decisions are centralized in this way the opportunity to review cases that reach the higher levels of the organization is a means of regulating the number and kinds of case prosecuted. Such review presumably has some value for inspectors in acquainting them with the expectations of senior colleagues. This is true to a more limited extent in the decentralized FOD, where only inspectors and their principals normally make prosecution decisions. The effect of the shift of decision-making control in an organizational context is to permit the play of overlapping and sometimes inconsistent decision frames.

2. ABOUT LEGAL DECISION-MAKING

1. The Pervasiveness of Discretion

Discretion arising from a number of sources suffuses the processes of law enforcement and regulation. Discretion is plastic, shaped and given form to some extent by the institutions of law and legal arrangements and more substantially by decision-makers' framing behaviour. Systems of formal rules, for all their appearance of precision and specificity, work in only imprecise ways. Indeed, precision and consistent practice are not necessarily assisted by the drafting of ever more elaborate schemes of rules. The legal system is not neatly carved up by smoothly functioning institutional arrangements, but in reality, as a loosely coupled set of subsystems, is much more messy, with internal inefficiencies and conflicts. Those enforcing rules may seek to attain the broad aim of a legal mandate in general terms, but the specific question of whether and how a particular rule applies in a particular circumstance will inevitably be reserved for, or assumed within, the discretion of the legal actor concerned. Structural features in inspectorates lead to the concentration of discretion in the hands of those in the field who first encounter problems. Enforcement practices are marked by a high degree of informality and invisibility, fostering the play of discretion. This is true of all stages in the cycle of regulatory activities, and most explicitly so at the point of implementation and enforcement. Field-level inspectors, in particular, have a wide range of choices to make: whether to take action at all, what kind of action to take; whether to prosecute, and with what charge or charges, and so on. The inspector acts as a sensor, detecting signals and controlling their input to the organization. As an experienced PI said: 'My inspectors have always got one freedom, and that's not to tell me about something' (86–11). 'If I go out this afternoon', said a field inspector, 'and find a sixteen year-old on an unguarded circular saw and decide not to prosecute, then it's highly unlikely my PI would pick it up.' ['He wouldn't get to hear about it?'] 'That's right, even though notionally he oversees my work' (86–43). Needless to say, the decision to do nothing may be profoundly consequential.

Inspectors are well aware of the autonomy accorded by the discretion that is allocated to or assumed by them, as well as the corresponding dependence of the organization upon them: 'If an inspector doesn't report what he sees, nobody else ever knows. If he doesn't write his report and if he doesn't submit a prosecution report, his PI doesn't know. If he doesn't record the facts that he has seen properly, nobody will know. And he can cover up what he's seen, if he wants to' (86–07). The presence of the inspector at the incident or investigation as the representative of the regulatory organization is crucial: 'Almost totally, we are the ones who make the decision because we are there . . . The only time we don't is where there's a major incident [causing publicity]. In 99 per cent we probably take the decision as to what action to take' (86–34). Direct contact with the event or incident causing concern gives inspectors considerable power over the official handling of any problem, since they regulate how more remote staff will assess the matter by framing the version of reality that senior colleagues will receive. This occurs as a result of the structural position which the inspector occupies in the legal organization. 'The further down the chain one passes the responsibility', one said,

> 'the more perhaps out of direct touch that person [receiving a recommendation for prosecution] is with what happened. It's sometimes difficult to convey in a written report why it is you think a case should go ahead. But there is a certain feeling, if you like, which comes across during the investigation which will tend to push you in one direction or another. And that is extremely difficult to capture and put down in words and convey to somebody else who wasn't actually present.' (86–24)

Though the regulatory organization has an obvious interest in the control of inspectors' discretion, especially where decisions about prosecution are concerned, in the nature of things such control tends to operate more effectively in one particular direction only, namely, in constraining possible action to those events or problems which are brought by the inspector within the agency. Those matters which inspectors handle differently, or decide not to handle at all, are much less likely to come to organizational attention by another route.

The play of discretion is facilitated since these junior officials frequently act in settings of substantial privacy in which their decisions may remain wholly or substantially invisible to others. In occupational health and safety work, furthermore, the variability of harms threatened leads to a tendency on the part of rule-makers, whose concern is to address all conceivable contingencies, to write over-inclusive rules. This demands adaptive behaviour by inspectors to achieve a closer fit between rules, their enforcement, and the risks and conduct that are subject to control. Regulatory inspectors routinely encounter cases where rules do not fit the problem at hand well, or where a violation does not pose a serious risk of harm. There can also be a substantial degree of variation in the cost of preventive measures: remedial costs are sometimes very high in some cases where the risks of harm are very remote. The responses of employers to regulatory demands may also vary substantially in these circumstances. Sometimes firms are well informed about their regulatory obligations and are willing to cooperate in taking remedial or preventive measures. Sometimes, however, they are ignorant and totally unwilling to cooperate. Often, of course, there may be cooperation up to a point.

In practice, compliance is itself a matter of human judgement. It is not simply a statement of whether an act or state of affairs accords with a particular standard of conformity, but depends entirely upon the interpretive behaviour of inspectors. Their discretion is significant, not simply because it amounts to an official designation of employers as compliant or not, but because full compliance or complete non-compliance are unlikely to be encountered. Instead, inspectors will find varying degrees of compliant or non-compliant behaviour on each visit, and each time they must exercise their discretion over whether and how to respond. But inspectors, of course, see and make sense of the world in different ways, and differences in framing behaviour raise the question of the consistency or inconsistency with which decisions are made. The irony is that discretionary outcomes are, in the aggregate, highly patterned (Baumgartner, 1992), being guided by shared systems of meaning, tacit understandings, organizational routines, and mutually recognized ways of deciding matters and acting upon them.

In such a highly discretionary system the formal law usually serves as a series of markers towards desirable standards around which are zones of tolerance, and beyond which are areas where some measure of control or enforcement is deemed necessary. Far beyond these zones, prosecution may be an imperative. When employed as a marker, the law may serve as a statement of aspiration, as a referent, a shaper of practice, or as a realistic target for actual practice. Which of these possibilities it is depends on an administrative discretion moulded to some extent by bureaucratic policy, but formed much more substantially by the framing practices of individual decision-makers. Formal systems of rules can never be closed and complete, speaking to all conceivable circumstances.

2. Reflective and Axiomatic Decision-Making

Handling a potential prosecution case involves a variety of forms of deciding which reflect different social settings and different degrees of demand to prosecute. For some problems or events prosecution may be seen as a virtual imperative. Two conditions likely to warrant less discretion are the existence of great blameworthiness, and a potential for a high level of public concern. For other matters, prosecution may be seen as a possibility, but as undesirable for yet others.

When the time comes for a decision to be made about prosecution, it is usually made routinely. Except in egregious cases inspectors tend to follow the same sorts of framing procedures in producing decisions. The process of deciding the initial question 'Is this a prosecution case?' is a two-stage matter. First, has the moral threshold been crossed? If so, and prosecution can be regarded as a deserved response, what other features would support a decision to prosecute? Many inspectors do not seem to regard this part of their decision-making as particularly difficult or complicated. While they recognize that there is a good deal of interpretive leeway which gives rise to different views of the law, or results in colleagues making different decisions from those they themselves would have made in the same circumstances, they also tend to see 'facts' as objective conditions. While discretion is pervasive in legal systems, some sorts of legal decision-making are almost non-discretionary, axiomatic. This leads some inspectors to operate with a simple binary classification of a case as 'prosecutable' or 'not prosecutable', leading to decisions about action being made almost immediately, hence their fondness for describing some cases as 'open and shut', as 'clear-cut', or as 'staring you in the face':[2]

> 'You can make your mind up within minutes of getting to the site, and... [you think] "That's a breach and I'm going to have a go." It's almost a gut reaction... I have this belief about cases: if you go there you'll *know*. If you're having to *work* to find a case, it'll be a useless case. You *know* that it's going to be a case and you get the evidence accordingly.' (86–63: original emphasis)

This approach to decision-making is also found among those who have much more time for reflection. Writing of sentencing judges, Ashworth *et al.* (1984: 50) reported: 'Only a minority... regarded sentencing as a matter of principles and reasoned conclusions. Most judges described it as an intuitive process, using such terms as "instinct", "hunch" and "feeling".'

Regulatory inspectors work particularistically, like other enforcers, handling situations as they arise. They may act in rule-governed ways, but in observance of the rules of routine, of how things are normally managed, rather than in ways imposed by legal or bureaucratic stipulations. Typification is an efficient means by which an organizational actor can respond to recurrent problems, and it leads to the patterned outcomes that make much legal decision-making quite predictable. The issues in decision-making, which, if Rubinstein (1973) is correct, probably become more distinct as inspectors gain experience, allow straightforward and swift categorization of a problem as prosecutable, or not (Lloyd-Bostock, 1992). This decision is not a matter of calculation and

[2] Decisions about conducting an accident investigation are made in a very similar way. They are taken very quickly and seemingly without reflection: discretion is often used 'in much simpler ways than might appear from people's accounts of what factors they consider' (Lloyd-Bostock, 1987: 33).

reflection, but almost of intuition, as the following comments suggest: 'I never look for a case. Normally a case hits you in the eye'[3] (86–55); 'When I go to an incident and see something, I can tell almost straightaway "This is prosecution stuff"' (86–02); 'You get a feeling, an instinct, in this job, when things are not right, similarly an instinct when you ought to be prosecuting' (86–10). Similarly, Lloyd-Bostock (1992: 50) found that 'Accidents were scanned and sorted very rapidly during observations made of accident screening: as many as thirty accident reports might be scanned in fifteen minutes or less, and some were rejected in less than twenty seconds.' Typification makes for considerable economy of decision-making effort: 'Some are just so blatant, there's not a lot of thought process goes into it' (86–09). Parts of the process of arriving at a decision may be more automatic than others, so that inspectors may reach a certain point very quickly, and then ponder over further details. Lloyd-Bostock (1992: 52) discovered that when accident reports were scanned for accidents to be selected for investigation, the majority were rejected very quickly, but possible candidates for investigation were considered at greater length before being finally selected or rejected for investigation.

One of the characteristic features of the exercise of discretion by legal actors is that the extent of their experience is such that they are readily able to categorize most events according to some existing framing scheme derived from past events and organizational precedents in order to decide what they ought to do in any particular case. The allocation of a certain event, person, or problem to a particular type or category itself tends to determine the action to be taken, since specific consequences often flow from the type or category settled upon. Thus, for example, different expectations about the ability and willingness of employers to comply, leading in turn to a particular decision about enforcement, are often associated in the inspector's mind with a simple categorization of a firm as 'large' or 'small'. It is partly for this reason that the notion of compliance is in practice not only flexible, but also reflexive, since most employers seek to create a particular impression of themselves as willing to comply, essentially law-abiding, and so on. Similarly, inspectors appreciate the strategies adopted by employers while doing their best to learn 'what actually happened', leading to enforcement behaviour becoming a kind of game played between two

[3] This remark could be partly a function of the scarcity of inspection resources, the seriousness of many events, and the categorical way in which many regulations are cast.

sides, each of which is dependent upon the other to a significant degree in matters such as the provision of information.

Where prosecution is regarded as an imperative, decision-making is relatively straightforward. The decision to allocate a matter to the category 'prosecutable' becomes a major determinant of the sequence of actions which follow. The 'intuition' that inspectors claim may reflect what may be thought of as axiomatic decision-making. This occurs when a problem is immediately framed in a particular way by a decision-maker. Many accidents, for example, tend to be identified by inspectors as belonging to, or as typical of, a class of accident. An area director (AD) gave a number of examples where he had encountered axiomatic decision-making by inspectors:

> 'Overhead travelling cranes, radial-arm drilling machines, unguarded circular saws, you know, whatever. And of course, to an extent, they will still feature, because they fall into that category where it's an obvious risk, there's a clear accident history, and standards in the industry are generally good, and therefore poor performers have got no excuse for not knowing what the standard is.'[4] (97–04)

Some events or offences seem to inspectors so self-evidently worthy of prosecution that they do not feel that for practical purposes they have any discretion to exercise, but a decision to prosecute is the 'obvious' or 'expected' outcome. Here, the decision to prosecute is a last resort in the sense that no other course of action is realistically possible:

> Q: 'What is a cut and dried case?'
> A: 'Lack of protection for a scaffold—no guard rails, no edge protection. Clear violation, clear breach of regulations. Obvious breach, even to the layman. No excuses, really, for that. You know, examples have been untrained people using dangerous equipment. You know, 16 year-olds on dumper trucks getting injured. I would be quite happy to . . . unless there were major extraneous factors, take a case on that. . . . People operating unguarded machinery are injured. I mean, perhaps "cut and dried" is the wrong word because you've still got to get the evidence.' (P97–01)

This type of decision-making is an example of what Richard Lempert (1992) has called the phenomenology of discretion, a term describing the

[4] Sally Lloyd-Bostock's (1987: 10) study of accident investigation decision-making suggested that an apparently simple process was at work in categorizing matters, if only because the decision, one based on accident reports, tended to be made in 'a second or two'. Those cases in which it was judged that investigation was necessary took a little longer but were still decided quickly.

extent to which people sense that their choices are constrained or not. Ironically, legal decision-makers possessed of high discretion often do not regard themselves as having much choice to handle certain problems: as a matter of routine practice cases are handled according to settled non-legal rules. The conventional conception of discretion as the freedom to choose from a range of legally permissible options is often, then, routinely constrained in practice by legal decision-makers themselves into a narrow range of options. 'Prosecution is time-consuming, so there is a number of occasions where it's debatable . . . [but] other occasions it's so obvious—every fatal accident,[5] it's automatic' (86–22). The extent of a decision-maker's discretion may not be especially significant in the production of actual outcomes, that is, precisely where it is imagined to be important and possibly a problem. The process of categorization is the crucial decision, since it essentially determines the outcome, for once a matter is allocated to a particular category, its fate is settled, since all cases so categorized are routinely disposed of in the particular way reserved for such cases. If inspectors normally prosecute in this type of violation, the key decision is not the prosecution, but the earlier categorization of the violation as of this kind rather than that. Since this is hardly an overt or conscious process, decision-makers often find it difficult to suggest what decision rules they are using.

In the case of inspectors in FOD the evidence suggests that the initial characterization of a problem as a potential prosecution is largely intuitive, in the sense that it is a decision usually made swiftly, on the spot, and with little reflection. Lloyd-Bostock (1987: 5), for example, discovered that certain types of accidents were repeatedly chosen for investigation, and that inspectors claimed that the process of selecting accidents for further investigation was also a matter of 'intuition' or 'gut feeling'. The following remarks by one suggest the powerfully intuitive character of the decision-making at the beginning of the process where the existence of something untoward can be defined as a potentially prosecutable matter: 'Usually I feel I can recognize a situation when I first arrive at the factory, that it's going to be prosecutable, or it isn't going to be worth it. And if I feel it's likely, I treat it as if it's going to happen, and I get the evidence and I do the work as if it's a dead cert' (86–40). This kind of axiomatic decision-making does not always lead to prosecution, because legal flaws may appear when the legal frame is applied, but the words suggest that

[5] Presumably the inspector is defining 'fatal accident' in a particular way here, to exclude assumed accidental deaths where there were no witnesses, and other instances in which a fatality is not followed by prosecution.

the matter begins as such in the inspector's mind. Most inspectors seem not to ask for guidance at this stage, but simply keep their PI informed. This may reflect the development of some commitment to a case by inspectors as 'their property'; certainly it is an encouragement to it. After all, they have done the work and they would prefer to see something come of it.

Decision-makers simplify the complexities involved in the decision to prosecute, even though the matter may be officially portrayed as one of great complexity. Inspectors do not confront for practical purposes a unique world of distinctive events, problems, and people. Matters are simplified and made sense of by seeking pattern, by using past experience and aligning the present with the past. Decisions are likely to be made 'intuitively' when existing simple decision rules can be employed to allow the matter to be categorized readily, and made reflectively when a new problem arises, or when the possible implications of a course of action seem serious. It seems also to be the case that decisions not to take action are made more quickly than decisions in which prosecution is a possibility (see Lloyd-Bostock, 1992: 52–3), though it is clear that some cases present features which are so egregious that inspectors treat them as virtually 'automatic' prosecutions.

What informs enforcers' 'intuition' deserves further enquiry. In some cases inspectors may use a form of decision-making by analogy. That is, action is settled upon immediately because the nature of the problem closely resembles one in which the inspector may previously have been involved, and in which an initial decision to prosecute was made. Aligning present events, rationales, or principles with corresponding ones encountered in the past is a familiar way of deciding, and decisions about prosecution are easier where settings, harms, problems, risks, rationales, or principles recall others. A lack of such experience or knowledge makes decision-making more difficult, giving rise to what a former Deputy Chief Inspector of Factories called the 'blue sky' problem, where a serious accident occurs at a site where a new process or plant has been introduced since the inspector last visited.

Sometimes, however, matters do not prompt such a spontaneous or intuitive approach, but demand careful consideration by the inspector about whether and how to act. These are the marginal cases which fall into the discretionary zone since they are not necessarily egregious or potentially newsworthy matters. When prosecution is not seen as inevitable, but merely as desirable or possible, a decision outcome often emerges, rather than being 'made' in a categorical way. When events or offences lack a 'taken for granted' quality, the decision-maker feels a substantial latitude in deciding. These cases place problems in a zone of uncertainty and indecision about whether prosecution is the best course of action in all the circumstances. They give inspectors more trouble. Uncertainties are usually resolved by the organizational pressures and resource and other constraints to which inspectors are subject, and the existence of any technical difficulties with evidence when they apply the legal frame (see Chapter 12).

When a matter has been defined organizationally as a real prospect for prosecution (when, that is, the legal frame comes into play, and the PI is involved) more studied decision processes are employed. In the case of centralized inspectorates, reflection is inevitable as the matter moves up for final decision through the organizational hierarchy, to be considered by decision-makers not involved in the day-to-day demands of inspection and enforcement. When decisions are made after a substantial period of reflection on the issues, certain stages in the decision-making may be marked by the predominance of one type of framing or another.

3. Surround, Field, and Frame Revisited

Surround, field, and frame are concepts which help organize thinking about decision-making (see Chapter 2). They direct attention in understanding legal decision-making away from the atomistic approach characteristic of most existing research[6] and show how the making of decisions about individual cases can only be understood in a much wider context. The features in an individual case gain their special meanings in framing from the surround and fields in which they are set. The concepts link micro-level features seemingly relevant in deciding about discrete cases with a wide variety of broader forces, such as caseloads, resources, organizational priorities, and the like. All of these need in turn to be set in the organization's and the decision-maker's surround so as to bring the macro-level forces of politics, economics, and so on into play. The links between surround, field, and frame can then be made explicit.

The concepts allow the researcher to distinguish the forces, internal and external, large and small, which act on decision-making. They assist in appreciating the interaction between micro-level features inherent in a particular case and those broader forces that help to mould how an individual case may be created and framed, or how classes of case are

[6] Robert Emerson's (1983) work is the most notable exception.

dealt with. The behaviour of a legal bureaucracy is shaped not simply by imperatives arising from its legal mandate, but by forces arising from the political, economic, and social environment in which it is set. Politics and economic forces can intrude from the surround to affect very directly the way in which individual decisions may be framed, quite apart from whatever influence they may exert on the decision field, with matters of a more general character connected with matters of law, policy, and the like. An inspector's social construction of a case may ultimately shape some of the reasons why a particular matter may be prosecuted. Other forces acting on the decision-maker have their origins in features not necessarily related to an individual case, such as the current political setting, the state of the economy, governmental ideology about regulation, or the attitudes, values, and policy of the agency or the AD. How a case is framed is determined by a number of matters, including inspectors' personal values, their training, and the influence of colleagues, especially the PI. It is possible, for example, to discern the influence of background and experience in the remarks of an inspector in a construction group who was regarded by himself and his colleagues as erring on the side of leniency in his approach to enforcement in a sector of occupational health and safety regulation widely regarded as demanding more stringency and punitiveness: 'Coming from industry itself, I do have a certain sympathy with industry and its problems. Having been in charge of a very large group of construction workers, I appreciate the problems firms have' (86–17). What the inspector is asserting here is his ability and willingness to adopt a 'business', rather than a 'law enforcement', decision frame. This framing may, however, be overtaken by others, since there is a hierarchy of frames potentially in operation.

Framing, however, produces variable outcomes which shift towards higher and lower levels of prosecution, or towards a more or less punitive approach to certain kinds of case. The search for cause is crucial in the frame that is applied. If the cause of the event or the nature of the act was a bad choice, then the instinct is to punish. If it was some antecedent condition, the propensity is to treat or repair. Yet this decision is not taken independently of external forces in the surround or field which may serve to alter the way an inspector frames the features in a particular case. The forces may act either to encourage or to discourage prosecution, for inspectors are subject to conflicting and shifting forces in their surrounds and decision fields, which alter framing behaviour, leading them to increase or depress the numbers and kinds of case prosecuted.

Frames link features thought of as criteria or factors deemed relevant in a case with a legally mandated outcome. A criterion varies in meaning, depending on what view is taken of the character and task of the decision-making to be done. On the instrumental view prevalent in positivist analyses of legal decision-making, a criterion is an item of information taken into account in arriving at and contributing to the production of a particular outcome. Since, however, it is only after the fact that one can make systematic sense of decisions taken (Manning, 1986), an alternative view from a naturalist perspective is that a criterion should be regarded as an item of evidence which, when framed, self-evidently renders a decision already made as rational and therefore as defensible. The important thing about framing in a naturalistic perspective is that it moves beyond the usual approach of exposing 'factors' or 'criteria' that seem somehow to be associated—in some unspecified way and with some unspecified set of priorities—with decision outcome (Hawkins, 1986).

Analysis of surround, field, and frame shows how what may be described by decision-makers as 'factors' or 'criteria' are given meaning, order, and primacy. The frame will be more readily apparent, for it determines what features in a case are selected, what each one means, and how and to what extent they are relevant. Once settled upon, one or more features can be presented as criteria in ostensible explanation of or in justification for a decision outcome.

3. ABOUT LAW

1. Law and Risk

Prosecution decision-making involves different systems of understanding which act as decision frames comprising different forms of rationality. Their contrasting approaches to risk, the central preoccupation of legal regulation, throw their differences into bold relief. There are at least three different systems of understanding or decision frames about risk operating in the occupational health and safety field (Hawkins, 1989*a*; Nobles & Schiff, 2000). These conceptions of risk operate in all sites for occupational health and safety decision-making, whether at the level of policy-making, enforcement in the field, or in the form of decisions by workers themselves. Those at the centre of the regulatory organization formulate policy using natural scientific rationality, allied with a sensitivity to political values. Enforcers in the field employ a mixture of lay or common-sense reasoning, and, where appropriate, legal reasoning. Workers, victims, the media, and members of the public rely on lay reasoning. Scientific, legal, and lay forms of decision-making are all forms by which a problem or case may be reconstructed (Reiss, 1989).

The *natural scientific* conception calculates risk in a quantitative fashion, transforming risks of the real world into bloodless, dispassionate probabilities which are sometimes so remote as to defy lay comprehension. Those who think in terms of the logic of natural scientific rationality do not find risks difficult to apprehend precisely because they are reducible to numbers which present a calculation of how likely or unlikely it is that something untoward may happen. Natural scientific rationality is comfortably aligned with a bureaucratic rationality which stresses the formal mandate, aims, and tasks, of the regulatory agency.

The *legal* conception of risk, in contrast, regards acts, events, working practices, rules, and standards of proof as central. Criminal law demands that a claim that a causal relationship exists between an act or omission or a state of affairs and an undesired outcome be established by proof beyond reasonable doubt. The officials who must fulfil the demands of the legal system are concerned as a result with certain forms of information whose validity rests in the extent to which they comprise evidence a court will accept. The legal conception consequently introduces its own patterns of decision behaviour that serve to shape the numbers and kinds of cases handled by formal legal means (see Chapter 12). Another consequence is that the formal legal process individualizes the approach taken in the handling of problems, and frequently deflects attention from broader conceptions of systems and patterns of work and hazard (Johnstone, 1994).

Finally, the *lay* conception of risk is notable for a preoccupation with what may happen if something untoward occurs, rather than how likely it is that something untoward will occur. This conception has real difficulty in apprehending risk when cause and effect are attenuated by the passage of time (Schrager & Short, 1978). In the context of occupational health and safety regulation, the risk of immediate injury seems to be much easier for people to grasp commonsensically than a risk to health which may only manifest itself many years later. This poses the practical enforcement problem of how to persuade employers and employees that certain activities or states of affairs are actually hazardous and demand immediate remedy. This can be particularly acute if workers' familiarity with occupational hazards is such as to encourage indifference or complacency.[7] Indeed, this lay conception may operate in complete contradiction to the tenets of scientific rationality. It was for this reason that a very senior regulatory official (not in HSE) expressed impatience with the strong public sentiment in Britain which is opposed to the permanent deep burial of radioactive waste. Public opinion instead prefers that it be kept on the surface, where it can be seen and if necessary moved, but where it is, in his view, much more at risk, whether from terrorist activity, natural calamity, or accident.[8] Nevertheless, even scientists (not to mention lawyers, members of the public, and regulatory officials) may find it hard to appreciate certain sorts of risks, since it is much easier to know a risk from past experience. Increasingly, technological developments threaten to outstrip the legal capacity for the control of risks.

These forms of rationality come into play at different decision-making sites, and regulatory decisions are variably informed by them. The lay conception is crucial in being the form of rationality that usually prompts the enforcement process into action, whereas scientific rationality tends to be employed in policy-making as a formal means of apprehending the nature and extent of any problem. Furthermore, the lay conception, with its sensitivity to palpable harm and existing damage, coexists with a belief in retribution or deterrence as an appropriate response to an untoward event. A hazard is much more difficult to act on by formal means, especially where it is one not readily apparent to those at risk. That is why inspectors find that pre-emptive prosecutions, brought in response to what seems to them to be an intolerable risk, sometimes cause them great difficulty in justifying to an employer and are less frequently used. Regulatory inspectors feel more secure in prosecuting when there is already 'a body on the floor', and people are sufficiently chastened by the experience that they do not demur, and respond readily to demands for remedial measures. In such circumstances, prosecution often comes as no surprise to employers or the workforce. It is partly for these reasons that inspectors often prosecute after an accident, in spite of the existence of a formal policy which encourages them to implement a preventive approach and act on risks. An inspector expressed a typical view: 'If there's been a fatal accident, it's very difficult not to take action if the evidence is there and there's a breach there . . . although we are told

[7] What one inspector described as the 'My father did that for forty years and he's alright' problem.

[8] From a private conversation with the author; these views are echoed in Ginniff (1988).

it's the seriousness of the breach we should consider, rather than the accident resulting from it.' Compared with accidents, most hazards are much less visible or public, create fewer concerns, and are not accompanied by the same expectations.

Applying its own standards and tests to a problem, especially its concern for proof, encourages law's preference to focus on the particular, the concrete, and the legally unproblematic. Law finds it difficult to address certain kinds of social problems, such as long-term risks to health arising from occupational exposure, because of the demands it makes for its own kind of certainty. Inspectors sometimes spoke as if there were many instances where they had wished to act when faced with a threat to workers' health, but could not, because legally provable scientific knowledge about cause and effect was lacking. Instead, legal rationality encourages enforcers towards reactive rather than pre-emptive behaviour. The result is that legal forms of understanding introduce their own patterns and distortions in the numbers and kinds of cases handled by formal legal means.

Where a risk has been realized and someone hurt, a decision that prosecution is appropriate brings a different set of considerations into play. The nature of the demands imposed by the legal system and legal rules operating upon organizations and organizational actors create their own kind of risks, as Chapter 12 showed. The HSE inspector has to handle occupational risks to workers on the terms laid down by the law's construction of risk, which serves in turn to create a different set of risks to the inspector. These legal risks operate to deflect handling and investigation resources away from troublesome cases and into those which can readily be prosecuted, in much the same way that doctors, we are told, sometimes prescribe treatments which they know for diseases about which they may be uncertain.

2. Law's Pragmatism

Law operates more comfortably in retrospect, when a risk has been realized, where it can react to the certitudes of things past rather than seek to anticipate what might happen in future. To the extent that regulatory control is concerned to act pre-emptively—in response to risks—difficulties arise where knowledge and the ability to predict are problematic. Such difficulties are often expressed in differences of opinion among those who claim medical and scientific expertise. While some risks are familiar, such as those associated with lead or asbestos, aetiological knowledge elsewhere is less secure. This makes medical evidence in support of a prosecution more difficult to find, and encourages opposition from other expert evidence in a defended case. In a safety case, in contrast, an inspector can usually expect a guilty plea, while magistrates find the issues in a contested case simpler and more comprehensible: a guard missing from a dangerous machine is a visible and self-evidently risky matter.

The ambivalence with which many inspectors regard prosecution as an enforcement move means that its use is rather elastic. Though it is both drastic and public, it seems, ironically, to be regarded as that method of enforcement whose use can most readily be adapted in light of other demands upon an inspector's time. This adjustment takes two forms. One is a reduction in prosecution activity if inspectors have too much other work (see Chapter 10). The second is to divert its use into certain kinds of case. The very big or very bad case (a relatively rare phenomenon) usually demands prosecution whatever the risk of losing, but otherwise the risks to the inspector and the agency of pursuing cases which are not secure in law—whatever their substantive merits—lead to a preference for cases which are straightforward to prove, quick to prepare, and unlikely to be defended. These take precedence over other kinds of case which, although regarded as more deserving or appropriate, are dealt with by other means, if at all.

Law's pragmatism is reflected also in the lay rationality that is reluctant to punish hazard. Allied with its preference for responding to past events rather than future possibilities, law seems better able to react to the particular rather than the general. Inspectors not only find it easier to deal with actual accidents rather than risks of accidents in general; they also prefer to enforce the law formally when they can charge a defendant with the breach of an absolute rather than a general duty (see Chapter 12). To require that something is done 'so far as is reasonably practicable', or to require (as in the air pollution legislation in force at the time of Phase I of the research) that an industrialist use the 'best practicable means' of controlling emissions, opens up an array of interpretive problems which can discourage inspectors from attempting enforcement in court. Instead, they opt, where possible, for an absolute standard which will be easier to prove, at least as an alternative charge. Sometimes they issue a notice and, in some cases, drop the idea of formal legal action altogether. Absolute standards are less likely to be defended and they demand less of the magistrates: the case is essentially 'open and shut' (as inspectors are fond of putting it), and magistrates simply have to decide, for example, whether a guard was or was not present on a dangerous machine, not whether something was or was not reasonably practicable. The result is that enforcement is channelled into particular types of case. The complex, the costly, and the legally defensible are less likely to be prosecuted. The enforcement behaviour is patterned; the biases are systematic.

Concern for the particular is not limited to enforcers of occupational health and safety legislation. In the 1980s inspectors were sometimes criticized by trade union officials for being too preoccupied with individual fault and not concerned enough with general systems of working, general hazards, or the business organization as a whole (Freedman, 1989). Yet some inspectors retorted that trade union officials were also guilty of the same narrow focus and too concerned with winning compensation for injuries suffered, at the expense of a generally activist stance which would encourage more broadly based preventive work. Furthermore, inspectors sometimes find that employers may cooperate more readily in the remedy of a particular difficulty, rather than a general problem, since risks which result in accidents tend to be cheaper and easier to correct, compared with those that threaten ill health (Genn, 1987).

Why are so few violations treated as warranting even the beginnings of the formal process of prosecution? Reluctance to prosecute is institutionalized in the formal legal structure provided by the HSW Act, which presumably envisages prosecution as a last resort, given the central position accorded by the qualifying phrase 'so far as is reasonably practicable'. This phrase reflects in turn the views of the Robens Committee. The evidentiary demands of law which come into play in preparing for the courtroom compound this piece of institutional design. In fact, occupational health and safety regulation is typical of other forms of law implementation. Law is a last resort in both criminal and civil law in general, not simply in prosecution decision-making in regulation. One important reason for this is that the formal legal system is a scarce resource, whose actual use demands severe rationing. The formal apparatus of law is effectively rationed through the choices made by actors controlling access to the system through the practices of case creation, case-handling, and pre-trial bargaining. The impact of resource constraints is significant in a regulatory agency where there is a strong commitment to enforcement in general by reliance on compliance strategy. To prosecute seems to regulatory officials in all but the most egregious of circumstances to be an unwelcome intrusion and burden, a distraction from the essential tasks of achieving improved standards of occupational health and safety through inspection and negotiation. While resources certainly impose a direct constraint on the number of cases that end up in court, they do not form the only, or even the dominant, constraint, but rather a combination of forces acts on the regulatory organization and the actors within it. The relevance of resources is in the judgement by staff that organizational capacity is limited, and a balance needs to be struck between the competing demands on their time. Regulatory agencies could, as a matter of policy, double or treble the number of cases prosecuted, but to do so would be at the cost of other regulatory activities deemed essential.

The reluctance to prosecute also arises from features inherent in the character of occupational health and safety regulation itself. The willingness of a regulatory agency to chance its arm in prosecution is contingent upon a balance being attained between the conflicting interests in its surround, and upon the degree and kind of harm or hazard suffered by victims, actual or potential. Since prosecution is the most drastic action an inspector can take, it is a matter reserved for the most dramatic cases, either where something appalling has happened (a worker badly injured or killed at work), where an egregious hazard threatens the workforce or public, or where an employer persistently fails to comply. Some cases almost always demand prosecution, even in the face of legally weak evidence: very serious incidents; newsworthy cases prompting a great deal of public concern, multiple fatalities, an especially vulnerable victim, and so on. Note that these are all examples of accidents or other untoward events, where a risk has been realized.

Harms that are immediate and palpable are more likely to invite prosecution. The environment in which most inspectors operate is rich in violations of the law, but does not yield very large numbers of viable prosecution cases from which they can select those to take to court. Accidents may seem to be events that are out of the ordinary, but for many inspectors even accidents are routine matters. Inspectors frequently encounter violations of the law; what is rare is to frame such matters as potential prosecutions. In the nature of things, PIs encounter potentially more cases, simply because they have to approve all cases proposed by their field inspectors, as well as having the occasional case themselves. Yet there may be a greater readiness to prosecute in HSE than in many other regulatory agencies, because people are killed and injured at work.[9] In environmental offences, in contrast, there is generally less specific, less direct, and usually less serious victimization.

The use of prosecution depends on the capacity of an enforcement system to discover offences, detect offenders, and gather legally relevant evidence linking offence and offender in such a way as to satisfy the demands of the criminal law. The invisibility with which decisions about these matters are made allows individual actors substantial power to impose their own preferences in the handling of cases. Decision-making about prosecution embraces a much wider set of issues than is apparent in or implied by the law and is expressed in a variety of decision frames. The relative rarity of serious events limits the extent to which cases may be decided about and processed according to routine or normal practices, though the more frequently inspectors happen upon a potential prosecution, the more likely it is that they will develop a sense of the typical attributes of 'a prosecution case'.

Inspectors are likely to be preoccupied with a variety of questions prompted by the application of different frames. Is it a bad case? (Does it involve deliberate wrongdoing, repetitive rule-breaking, or wilful persistence in wrongdoing?) Is it a big case? (Is it a matter in which the media and the public are likely to take a particular interest, or is it a matter which is likely to affect large numbers of people?) Is it something that poses either a serious risk of harm or a risk of serious harm? Priority between competing frames may be accorded by the character of the surround and field.

3. Law's Morality

The underlying reality about the decision whether or not to use law is normally framed in moral terms. Enforcing regulation, like many other kinds of legal activity, is at its core a moral enterprise. Law is what Gusfield (1981: 18–19) calls a 'cultural performance'. In both its formal and its routine activity, 'law embodies and reinforces meanings. It creates a day-to-day authority and legitimates control through building the image of a social and natural order based on moral consensus.' This is borne out in a closer focus upon the use of prosecution. We employ culturally approved signs of contrition and repair, and we expect to see

[9] It is impossible to create any prosecution rates, quite apart from any comparative rates, since the total number of actual offences is unknowable.

both of these things in the behaviour of those who break the rules of the criminal law. Their presence and display helps encourage a lifting of the criminal sanction, but only up to a point. Where a breach of the law has occurred, and where serious harm to another has been done, human beings blame. Where the law is at their disposal, blame is sometimes expressed in legal action.

Law work is very much like many other kinds of work. It is not about the application of self-evidently clear rules to self-evidently obvious problems and situations, but an ad hoc, pragmatic, interpretive exercise. Legal officials respond to the events that confront them in particular ways, and where those problems are recurrent and persistent, actors tend to respond in patterned and predictable ways, leading to the emergence of typification practices. In this way, legal work and activity reflect and reproduce the familiar features of everyday activity, including its blemishes and its prejudices. This is not to claim that the formal law has little place in shaping the nature of law in the real world. The rules and procedures of the formal law are closely implicated in the everyday activities of legal actors. Their influence can be seen in the pages of this book to be all-pervasive, if mediated by other forces.

The idea of 'law' has multiple meanings, many of which may be carried simultaneously in people's heads. It can be conceived, among other things, as a structure of rules, a set of values, a mandate, or a statement of aspiration. More than one of these meanings may be employed by a regulatory official when making decisions about enforcement. The ideals of law are important expressions of values, even though some of these ideals may be articulated in formal legal action relatively rarely. They are part of the rhetorics that are themselves part of legal cultures. Ideas of fairness, justice, desert, consistency, and the like are familiar to everyone. Where the ideals of the law are concerned, there seems to be a high degree of moral cohesion in the social world, in which people share a common moral vision which embodies ideas about the appropriate response to offenders and to rule-breaking. The ideals of law are carried through into the everyday practices of law enforcement, and are to be found both in the day-to-day enforcement practices of regulatory officials, and in their pre-trial decision-making about possible prosecution as the formalities of the courtroom loom closer. Law enforcers respond not simply to the tangible threat, however, but to the symbolic threat posed by any apparent lack of consensus about what is right and wrong.

The law in action is a system of meanings, a fluid normative system, not an abstract structure of rules mechanically applied. The formal law is brought into use as the product of a web of understandings held by regulatory officials about what is or is not 'a prosecution case'. Bringing order and stability to an uncertain world is the ultimate purpose of formal legal proceedings. Prosecution helps to stabilize meanings and understanding. In enforcing regulation as they do, and especially in choosing to use the formal law as they do, regulatory officials are reaffirming, in a life of uncertainty and conflict, their moral connection with shared social values. They are ultimately engaged in their corner of the legal world in cementing the moral and social cohesion of the society in which they live. In the creation and re-creation of reality in formal legal processes fundamental models of human character and motive are central. The legal process is a morality play.

Appendix: Research Methods and Data Sources

1. RESEARCH AS A SOCIAL PROCESS

When reporting the results of research, socio-legal scholars often neglect to give a sufficiently full explanation of how their findings came into existence. But how the research was designed, how access was gained to individuals and organizations, how the data actually came to be collected, and what problems were encountered in the course of fieldwork are questions that cannot be ignored. If discussing these issues may seem tedious, to neglect them is unfortunate. The generation of data is critical to the analysis of a problem and what are treated as findings. The actual conduct of a social science research project, contrary to the impression given in many methods textbooks (which often present a spurious picture of social research as an orderly and rather straightforward process[1]), is usually a complicated and rather messy business. Several important decisions have to be made early on, involving crucial matters of concept, design, logistics, resources, and implementation. These have to be sorted out before precise questions of method, sampling, and instrument design can be properly thought through.

An equally serious neglect, however, is a frequent failure to recognize that social research is itself a social process. Thus it is important to acknowledge that the data which comprise the raw material for analysis are themselves the product of interaction with the research subjects, and that we recognize that the social science researcher is also given to substantial interpretive work as analyst and writer. Data in social research—quantitative as well as qualitative—inevitably reflect the researcher's own distinctive ways of thinking about a problem and interacting with the materials. This is especially true of those sorts of data that arise from personal interaction with the research subjects. The nature and presence of the self is crucial in social research. It is essential to appreciate how one related to the subjects, both in gaining access and in collecting data. Equally, it is important to remember that the researcher determines what are to be treated as data, as well as how they are to be treated. In short, it is essential, in the interests of transparency in the conduct and dissemination of social research, to disclose as fully as possible how the research was designed, how access to research subjects was gained, and how data were generated, collected, and recorded.

[1] Though see Arksey & Wright (1999) and King & Wincup (2000) for two recent exceptions.

2. THE HISTORY OF THE STUDY

This book reports a research project that has been conducted over a period of nearly twenty years. Data were collected in two stages, the period 1986–8, then in 1997 and 1998. The first phase of the research was itself part of a larger programme of research, involving other researchers, into policy and practice in the various occupational health and safety inspectorates presided over by the HSE. This programme consisted of nine interrelated socio-legal research projects on the regulation of occupational health and safety conducted by staff of the Oxford Centre for Socio-Legal Studies between 1983 and 1987 (Centre for Socio-Legal Studies, 1983). A report on prosecution decision-making arising from this first phase of the work was presented to the HSE at the end of the grant period (Hawkins, 1987), followed by an overview of the entire programme (Hawkins, 1992*a*) and a number of papers (Hawkins, 1989*a*, *b*; 1990; 1991). However, though the plan was to publish a monograph after the completion of the first phase, it proved impossible to complete at the time for important, if rather banal, reasons.

Events by then had taken a different course. First, I had been invited by the then Director-General of HSE, John Rimington, to write a synthesis and overview of all nine projects in the Centre's research programme, and also to add a certain amount of new data on regulatory work at the centre of the HSE organization (Hawkins, 1992*a*). This was too good an opportunity to miss, partly for the additional insights into policy-making the work promised to yield, and partly because the budget of the Centre for Socio-Legal Studies was under even more severe strain than was usual, and the prospect of extra income was very welcome. The second reason for not writing the book immediately illustrates the predicament in which many academics have found themselves in recent years. In 1985 I had been appointed Deputy Director of the Oxford Centre, and by the late 1980s was becoming increasingly involved in administrative and—especially—transatlantic fund-raising activities at substantial cost to my research and writing opportunities. The discontinuities in organizing research and the disruption to writing caused by this administrative work made it impossible to continue with the project at the time. Indeed, I was not in a position to resume work on the research until the mid-1990s.

To return to the work after a period of some years raised new problems. One, of course, was the age of the original data. I was also concerned about the organizational changes that had been under way in HSE. I therefore decided that it would be desirable to collect further data to see whether the changes had had any impact, or whether decisions about prosecution continued to be made in a recognizable way. I approached John Rimington for further access to HSE, and he again proved to be very willing to allow more research. However, constraints of time and money meant that it was not possible to replicate the original interview methodology which had been the primary data-collecting method used in the 1980s. Instead, I designed a systematic content analysis of prosecution and fatalities case files in the same four area offices in which I had conducted the original interviews. The lack of symmetry in data-collecting methods, which was originally a source of concern, in fact proved a considerable advantage, since the case files yielded data and insights about decision practices that could not have been gained from interviews of inspectors (see Arksey & Wright, 1999, ch. 2). The enforced intermission has also proved valuable in a more important respect, as it has allowed me to refine the theoretical perspective quite considerably, as well as to set impressions gained from analysing one set of data against those from another. Essentially, this book now reports research that has been conducted in two phases in which several sets of data have been collected and analysed in pursuit of a common question and their findings integrated into the present analysis.

Given the complexity of decision-making behaviour, and the difficulties in studying it empirically, it seemed essential to employ a variety of data-collecting methods. Thus, in conducting the first phase of the work in the mid-1980s, my intention was to maximize possible contrasts in decision-making behaviour about prosecution. Accordingly, I planned a project which deliberately avoided looking only at decision-making within a specific inspectorate. Instead I selected agencies with both centralized and decentralized decision-making structures, and designed an enquiry that looked as much as possible across the board at prosecution processes in HSE. This meant exploring prosecution decisions made about individual cases, but equally importantly, decisions made by senior officials about the handling and disposal of classes of case; in other words, investigating how policy about prosecution was formulated. This required, in effect, conducting a number of studies, the analysis of which has been woven together in the present book. The use of a combination of methods outlined below was helpful in suggesting pervasive features in prosecution decision-making. But before questions of design could be taken very far, it was necessary to sort out precise questions of access to the HSE organization.

3. GAINING ACCESS

Negotiations for access were conducted with HSE for the large research programme, rather than for my own study, which was merely a rather small part of a set of enquiries. Obviously, it was essential with such an undertaking to approach the most senior officials in HSE for their consent. Access to senior levels of the agency for this work was swiftly achieved via a local factory inspector and his area director. These meetings led to an introduction to the then Chief Inspector of Factories, and a subsequent meeting with all the then Chief Inspectors of HSE, after which research access was formally granted. At this meeting the objectives of the research were explained, and an indication given of the methods to be used, the level of cooperation required, and so on. Any fears there might have been that HSE would be uncooperative and reluctant to proceed turned out to be misplaced. Indeed, perhaps HSE appreciated the value of independent research into its practices because it was still a relatively new organization, one created less than a decade earlier out of an amalgamation of existing inspectorates, each with its own culture and practices. The agency seemed keen to learn about itself from an exterior vantage point. HSE proved in fact to be very committed to the research, to the extent that it agreed to contribute more than £120,000 over a four-year period towards the costs of the entire research programme.

A protocol was agreed between the Oxford Centre for Socio-Legal Studies and HSE about the conduct of the research and the dissemination of findings. This required the Centre's researchers to respect the need for anonymity and confidentiality throughout, and to show HSE all pre-publication drafts arising from the research. The researchers agreed that they would correct any errors of fact pointed out by HSE staff, who were given eight weeks in which to respond. The researchers also agreed that they would note any differences of view or interpretation, but that ultimately they remained free to publish as they thought fit. This protocol worked well, and I continued to observe its terms in the second phase of my own research, and in preparing this book for publication. Note, therefore, that any names that do appear in the data are fictitious.

4. PROBLEMS IN DESIGN

Researching legal decision-making behaviour is challenging. First, the topic is elusive, and all research methods are flawed in some way. While it is easier to study the behaviour of people whose job involves continuous action, such as inspection work and negotiation, it is much more difficult, from a methodological point of view, to use ethnographic techniques such as participant observation when the research subjects are essentially involved in tasks of management and administration where work tends to be less visible, less explicit, and (in a sense) discontinuous. And, of course, the presence of a researcher can be a serious intrusion into the time of senior staff. A major problem is that there is often little or no action immediately associated with the making of a decision about prosecution, in contrast with some other kinds of negotiated enforcement decisions. We only know a decision has been made after the event (Manning, 1986). Accordingly, it is difficult to distinguish the making of a decision from the ratification of an earlier decision (Hawkins, 1986). It is also difficult to distinguish a feature that has prompted a particular decision outcome from one that is employed after the event as a justification for a decision.

Second, the world of decision-making and administration in large organizations at senior levels is extremely difficult for the outsider to penetrate. The HSE appears to an outsider to be an organization of prodigious complexity, and its sheer size and dynamism make it very daunting to the observer who needs to understand the tasks and roles of the various parts of the organization and how they fit together. Hence this research has relied on primary sources wherever possible, so as to maintain a high level of contact with the data.

Prosecution decisions are an organizational as well as an individual matter, and are usually the culmination of a series of relevant decisions often made by different actors. The number and kind of decisions made vary according to organizational structure and procedures. The Factory Inspectorate (FI), one of the major research sites in this work, had a particularly truncated and decentralized prosecution decision-making structure, as does its successor, the Field Operations Directorate, while the other inspectorates involved employ more complex systems of referral to senior officials in the organizational centre. Where such a complex practice as legal decision-making in an organizational setting is concerned, no single research method commends itself as the obvious way of generating valid and reliable data and a good understanding of what is going on. This project was therefore designed deliberately to employ a variety of methods and a number of sources to be used in conjunction with each other to build up as complete a picture of practice as possible.

Study of documentary evidence may provide only a partial picture of the decision-making process (that committed to paper, and in that sense in a fixed form, not open to interrogation) and one possibly coloured by organizational requirements (Garfinkel & Bittner, 1967). Though such evidence is often of a presentational kind, it is nonetheless helpful in providing indications of patterns of decision behaviour and ways of reasoning within (and sometimes beyond) an official, institutional frame. Interview methods, on the other hand, allow interaction between researcher and subject, the exploration of issues and clarification of obscurities, that documentary analysis cannot permit. Study of interview data, however, needs to guard against the problem of drawing unreasonable or inaccurate inferences about what people do from what they say. Decision-making is difficult to research, partly because people are not necessarily able to describe how they decide what to do; and when they do provide such descriptions, their accounts depend to a greater or lesser extent on their own theories about the processes of decision-making concerned, or their conceptions of how decisions ought to be made, rather than direct experience of them. 'As a result, when people are asked to explain how they make decisions and diagnoses it seems their answers often, quite unintentionally, exaggerate the extent to which decisions are consciously reasoned over in elaborate detail' (Lloyd-Bostock, 1992: 57). In the present research this difficulty is reduced since the emphasis is less upon inspectors' reported behaviour, more upon their ideas: their theories of business compliance, their theories of punishment, their conceptions of blameworthy behaviour, and so on. Nevertheless, it is not enough to try to understand decision-making behaviour from reliance upon interview data alone. There is a tendency for officials to serve as carriers for the organization's public ideologies and present an official view of the world and their place in it, and it is sometimes difficult to know when the 'real' as opposed to the 'official' line is being put forward. But it is possible to avoid some of these problems, for example, by making the occasion informal—a conversation rather than a formal interview—thereby allowing dialogue to develop. The informality of the setting also makes it easier to test the data by questioning proffered views. Sometimes, of course, officials wish to present their own, rather than their organization's, views. The analysis of prosecution and fatalities files also proved to be a valuable corrective.

5. SOURCES OF DATA

By employing different methods, and drawing from a variety of sources of data, problems arising from the elusiveness of decision-making can be mitigated to an extent. The analysis is based therefore on six sources of data generated in different ways. Some of the data collection was concerned with decision-making about prosecution in HSE generally, while some was focused on particular inspectorates. Some was centred on decision-making about policy, though most dealt with decision-making about cases. There were no limits to my research imposed by HSE in terms of what I saw, asked, or read. In drawing on a wide variety of data, collected over a substantial period of time, I try to combine their various strands to produce as complete a picture as possible.

1. Socio-Legal Research on Decision-Making

First, the theoretical perspective on decision-making (presented in Chapter 2) was developed in the course of more general research on legal decision-making conducted in collaboration with Peter Manning (Hawkins, 1986; 1992*b*; Hawkins & Manning, forthcoming; Manning, 1986; 1992; Manning & Hawkins, 1989; 1990). This work involved library research of the literature on the sociology of legal processes, and studies of legal decision-making and regulation in particular. These sources served to clarify theoretical issues about the nature of decisions made by legal actors, and substantially informed the data-gathering and analysis in the various empirical studies.

2. Official Materials

Second, for insights into the organization of HSE and its internal operations, I studied a large quantity of materials produced by HSE itself, in the form of official reports and internal documents. This was to gain a sense of the various changes in organizational policies and practices that have taken place in HSE over the last 15 years or so (HSE is an organization that seems to be constantly reinventing itself), but it was also to understand how HSE officially views itself and what it does, and how those views have changed. In an effort to familiarize myself as thoroughly as possible with HSE policy and practice on prosecution and law enforcement as inspectors would understand it, I also participated in a week-long residential training course on law enforcement organized by HSE for field inspectors. This was in the company of a large number of factory and agricultural inspectors. In the course of the week I spoke to several inspectors, and in the text I occasionally draw from these conversations. I do not, however, refer to them as a data source, as with the factory inspectors interviewed, or the prosecution or fatalities files analysed.

3. Interviews with Senior Staff

Third, it was necessary for the research to attend to the tasks, problems, and dilemmas of health and safety regulation as seen by senior staff at the centre of the organization, where policy is formulated and far-reaching decisions made. This reflected the view of prosecution adopted in the research as a complicated decision, shaped by a variety of forces, in contrast with a simplistic view of prosecution as a discrete choice exercised by inspectors in conjunction with a superior officer. Thus, to learn at first hand about enforcement policy and practice from their vantage point, I conducted a number of lengthy interviews with senior HSE officials. These included all three members of the then Executive of HSE, two agency lawyers, and the then chief inspectors of the main HSE inspectorates, as well as two retired former chief inspectors. These interviews, like all others, were tape-recorded, and were conducted informally in an effort to make conversation as natural as possible. Topics were organized in advance so that standard themes were dealt with; there was, however, a degree of improvisation whenever the conversation took an interesting turn. In total 16 individuals were involved in this part of the research. I have referred to office-holders no longer in post by their office, simply to convey a sense of the authority of the source.

4. A Study of 'Infraction' Letters

The fourth part of the research involved a small documentary analysis of correspondence and memoranda surrounding the issuing of 'infraction letters' in the Industrial Air Pollution Inspectorate (IAPI). This inspectorate was removed from HSE in the course of the fieldwork in 1986 and became part of the newly created HM Inspectorate of Pollution, which in turn became in 1996 part of the new Environment Agency. I was given access to material relating to all infraction letters issued in the years 1983, 1984, and 1985. This study was conducted primarily to see whether there were any discernible differences in decision-making in a centralized organization, where the decision to prosecute is ultimately made at the deputy chief or chief inspector level, with a referral system of information supply and evaluation being transmitted from the field up through the organization for final determination.[2]

[2] I am grateful to Matthew Weait for his research assistance in this part of the project (some of which was published in Weait, 1989).

5. Interviews with Factory Inspectors

Fifth, it was essential to learn about the activities and decision-making of regulatory inspectors working at field level in the front line of enforcement, and the role of prosecution in such activities. There were a number of good reasons for this emphasis. What inspectors and others in contact with employers and the workforce actually do represents, after all, the everyday reality of occupational health and safety law. Such people make decisions about practical action or inaction, and represent their inspectorate and the HSE to the public. Accordingly, I collected data in the mid-1980s about prosecution decision-making in FI, the largest of the various inspectorates then within HSE, and one making relatively frequent use of prosecution, yet with variations depending on the type of regulatory work involved. In a decentralized inspectorate, like FI, a decision about whether or not to prosecute is not something that routinely involves senior staff (the exception being the newsworthy or otherwise difficult case). Since prosecution is a more familiar event for factory inspectors, compared with many other HSE inspectors, greater emphasis was given to data collection by means of interview in this part of the enquiry, as it could reasonably be expected that most inspectors would have had experience of prosecuting. I also researched the decision-making of their area supervisors and managers.

Four administrative areas of FI with stable prosecution rates were sampled, with apparent inconsistencies in approach to prosecution as the basis for the selection of areas in this part of the project. These areas were chosen for their inspectors' apparent propensity to use, or to avoid using, the ultimate sanction of prosecution. In the absence of data on rates of prosecution, the selection of areas was based partly on statistics of prosecution by area, partly on the reputation within the inspectorate of the supposed willingness among staff in certain areas to prosecute (on advice from HSE headquarters), and partly to align the choice of areas with other colleagues working in the research programme who were conducting field research on related matters. To ensure coverage of a wide spectrum of opinion and experience, two areas which appeared to make above average use of prosecution, and two below average use were selected. Within each area, subsamples of inspectors were drawn according to the nature of their regulatory work. Members of the same four industry groups were selected in an effort to standardize the nature of the problems encountered by inspectors. The particular industry groups selected were intended to present contrasting types of enforcement problem: construction (a high-risk activity, with relatively frequent use of prosecution), chemicals (where problems were often of a long-term character), general manufacturing (the traditional core of FI work), and the National Interest Group (NIG) (to see if there was any characteristic approach).[3] Within

[3] It turned out that the symmetry of this scheme was upset a little. In the course of fieldwork it emerged that two of the NIGs in the areas selected did no enforcement work, and they were accordingly substituted with two further general manufacturing groups. One of the selected areas had no chemicals group, and a general group was added instead.

each group the principal inspector (PI) was interviewed together with two trained field inspectors (i.e. 1B rank). There were usually only two 1Bs in each group; where there were more, and a choice had to be made, I selected the most and the least experienced inspectors.[4] Each area director (AD) was also interviewed. In total, 52 individuals were interviewed.

It proved, however, to be difficult to draw conclusions about the punitiveness or otherwise of different areas owing to variations in the industries located there. Furthermore, in FI the practice of moving field inspectors around different industry groups tended to obscure some of what might otherwise have been distinctive responses from groups. The result was that although four contrasting FI areas were selected, it was impossible to discern in three areas any distinctive prosecution 'policy' or practice, other than by reference to numbers of prosecution cases.[5] Analysis of the four areas suggested little difference in decision-making approaches, even though outcomes may have varied. This supports the argument that the features in reaching a decision about prosecution are the same, but the tolerances in the way the matters are framed are different (that is, the emphases accorded them by individual decision-makers differ), and it is this which produces different outcomes.

The data were collected by means of lengthy, loosely structured interviews, which, like the interviews with senior staff, were made to seem as much like natural conversations as possible. They were organized around general themes connected with the practice of prosecution decision-making, and centred upon the respondents' ideas, experiences, and attitudes. Though there were standard themes, inspectors were not slavishly queried about every single topic, and there was plenty of opportunity to follow up particular points. Interviews were not rigidly structured, and ideas which emerged as important matters in the course of early interviews were routinely incorporated into subsequent conversations. Almost all the interviews were tape-recorded, allowing me to monitor a conversation and at the same time formulate follow-up questions. Unfortunately, despite my assurances of anonymity and confidentiality, four inspectors declined to have their conversations recorded. I took written notes of these four conversations as best I could, but much valuable information was inevitably lost. A tape-recording error also led to the loss of a substantial part of one other interview.

Where possible, counts were made where responses coalesced around particular findings of attitude or value, and this helped in the analysis, though I have deliberately refrained from quoting figures or percentages, since doing so would confer a spurious sense of precision and confidence upon the findings. Instead, I have used the data in a qualitative way, to indicate broad patterns and associations. Quotations that appear in the text are verbatim remarks by staff

[4] A chemicals inspector from one area was substituted by an inspector from another group owing to illness.

[5] There were some exceptions to this, however, and they have been discussed in the analysis, where appropriate.

sampled as part of this study, unless otherwise stated. Where quoted material is given, respondents are identified by a number, to mark its source and to give an indication of the variety of respondents and the breadth of opinion, while maintaining anonymity. Thus codes preceded by the number 86 refer to interviews conducted in 1986, and 97 to interviews conducted in 1997 (see below).

6. Analysis of Prosecution and Fatalities Files

The sixth set of data was collected in the second phase of the research. A preliminary, unpublished, analysis of the materials from the first four phases of the research had been carried out and written up in the late 1980s. However, to explore further the issues raised in this preliminary analysis, to update the research, and to expand the database, I collected more data in 1997–8. There were two components to this fieldwork. First, I carried out a content analysis of the files of all cases prosecuted in a six-month period (1 January to 30 June 1996) in the same four regional offices of the HSE in which I had conducted the interviews of factory inspectors in the first phase of the work. However, study of prosecution files only assists in understanding the decision-making that leads to a case being prosecuted; it cannot uncover those properties in a case that lead to a decision not to prosecute. Prosecution is the visible part of regulatory enforcement, and we have to be alert to the instances where law is not enforced in a formal sense—where a case is not created, or where a case, once created, is not proceeded with (sometimes the most interesting and important decision that an inspector makes about prosecution is to choose not to prosecute). The fatality at work seemed to be the obvious case to analyse for this purpose. For this reason a second component was added in the form of a representative sample of fatalities files. This was analysed in an effort to pick up some of the cases that prima facie might have been expected to have proceeded to prosecution. Thus records relating to all workplace fatalities occurring within the period 1 January to 30 June 1996 were studied. There were, in total, 93 files, of varying degrees of completeness; of these, 68 related to prosecutions and 25 (of which three were prosecuted) to fatalities.

While collecting these data in 1997 and 1998, I also held several further conversations, many of them lengthy tape-recorded sessions, with three of the current ADs of the four areas, plus two particularly experienced PIs in the fourth. This was to learn accurately about current practices in HSE, and how (if at all) they may have changed since the 1980s.[6] I employ these later conversations quite extensively as illustrative devices, to illuminate ideas and findings derived from other, sometimes older, sources, rather than as sources of data in their own right.[7]

[6] These later interviews are clearly identified with a number beginning with 97.

[7] Each case in the prosecution or fatalities files is numbered consecutively: P97–1 up to P97–68 (for prosecution), and F97–1 to F97–25 (for fatalities).

It should also be noted that some of the prosecution files contained details of earlier incidents or accidents (some of which may have been prosecuted, but some of which were not prosecuted, even though the inspector concerned was clear that a breach of the law had taken place). Where records of earlier prosecutions were stored in the later prosecution files, I had the benefit of reading them as well. There were sometimes details of further prosecutions in some of the fatalities files since some had resulted in legal action (even though they may not have been tried during the sample period for prosecution).

6. A REFLECTION ON CONTENT ANALYSIS OF CASE FILES

The use of a combination of different sources and methods proved helpful both in suggesting pervasive features as well as in revealing differences in prosecution decision-making. Observation is valuable in social research, usually because people do not find it easy to dissimulate (even if they wish to), but if research subjects are not engaged in continuing activity which the researcher can monitor, it becomes much less useful. The work of senior officials and the formulation of policy matters are examples of activity in which decision-making behaviour is largely tacit. This was a particular benefit in analysing prosecution and fatalities files, since although case files reflect directly upon decision-making matters relating to a particular case, they sometimes cast light also on questions of policy. On the other hand, interviews as an interactive form of data collection can address matters of policy, and reveal strategic issues as well as matters which are (for whatever reason) unlikely to appear in the written record as a 'proper' or 'desirable' reason or justification for a decision made.

The prosecution and fatalities files proved to be particularly valuable data sources. Analysis of prosecution files allowed tracking of decisions from the time an inspector was first involved in suggesting legal action. Collecting the data was easy. In each area headquarters I was given the relevant dossiers, and was able to work uninterrupted in an empty office. I took notes in considerable detail, and verbatim wherever possible, using a laptop computer (which certainly beats the old days of notepads, ballpoint pens, and hastily scribbling notes on the spot, or (even worse) writing up notes in a cheap bed and breakfast place in the evening). Some files were relatively straightforward and could be read carefully in half to three-quarters of an hour. Some, however, were very much more complex and needed half a day, or more, of careful study. Some of the material appeared in several copies; some of it was repetitious. With practice, however, it was possible to learn how to read the files relatively quickly.

The dossiers were kept in varying degrees of internal order. They varied also in the amount of information they contained. Most seemed to be complete, but a few seemed to lack important details. A degree of disorganization in one area office meant that a few files were incomplete, while a small number of others were described as 'out' or 'being used for training purposes'.[8] It was therefore impossible to tell whether I was given deliberately incomplete or otherwise sanitized files. In most of the files, however, there was a plethora of information, a substantial part of which was duplicated. The bundles of documents contained all sorts of odd scraps of paper, jottings, and personal notes. Most important information was present, so far as I could tell (if it was not, I was usually able to fill in any gaps with further enquiries in the office). There were many formal documents in the files—copies of informations laid, witness statements, memos between field inspector and PI or PI and AD, correspondence between various parties, including solicitors. There were sometimes several copies of the same letter, or faxed copies, together with the originals. Police and Criminal Evidence Act, 1984, interview transcripts were included, often in both handwritten and typed form. The files would sometimes include details of earlier prosecutions, and of informations laid and later withdrawn. Some files held reports on inspections going back nearly 20 years. Prior records of visits and incidents involving a defendant company were sometimes included. A number of incidents might be listed, which presumably serves to build up a profile of an employer who may appear to be insufficiently attentive to occupational health and safety matters. Complaints about an employer received by HSE from employees or others are also recorded, thus giving inspectors further suggestions about the character of the company with which they are dealing.

Files often contained a number of photographs, often in duplicate. Many of the letters and memos bore interpolations by one or more hands, in light of changing circumstances or views on a particular matter. Some prosecution files contained information about defendant company profits and turnover and similar sorts of financial data. It was explained that such information was available for inspectors to pass on to magistrates when they needed to think about an appropriate penalty for a convicted defendant. HSE information sheets would also sometimes be enclosed. These give the 'correct' or approved view of how to deal with an occupational health and safety problem. Statistical data are regularly supplied as a decision-making aid by the Statistical Services Unit of HSE and are intended to give inspectors some idea of the prevalence of a particular problem they may be dealing with.[9] Statistics of falls in the construction industry, for example, may well appear in the file of a case involving a fall. These are normally classified according to consequences ('death', 'major', 'over 3 days' in hospital). Files would also frequently contain technical data relating to engineering or technological matters. Or it may be noted that 'employers currently report just over 40% of reportable accidents . . . Self-employed people are poor reporters of work-related injury. They consistently report less than one in ten reportable injuries.'[10] The

[8] In these cases I was given somewhat sketchy details of each prosecution.

[9] A typical example would be the number of injuries caused by a fall from a height, as reported to HSE over a recent five-year period.

[10] This is from *Levels of reporting of workplace injuries*, an HSE publication.

contents of the files are a good indicator of the qualities of knowledge and versatility required of the health and safety inspector. HSE staff not only have to be expert in mechanical and electrical engineering and in other technical matters relating to factory production, methods of working, and so on, they also have to know the relevant law and legal ways of thinking and reasoning.

Documentary records are, of course, made for official organizational purposes, but they also contain data that are more private—handwritten notes and comments intended for limited circulation, often to one other colleague only. Many files included personal notes and informal jottings made by inspectors—idle musings by individuals on issues to think about or to explore with others, notes made during or after phone conversations, and the like. Often the most useful comments for research purposes were informal, scribbled remarks in the margin of a report, or handwritten notes accompanying the papers. Memos (usually communications between field and supervisory staff) were often very informative, and sometimes revealing because they were not written to be read by anyone other than a specific colleague. Encouragement from senior officials would occasionally be recorded following a successful prosecution. A typical example, a note on the outside of one file, read: 'Ed, Thank you for sight of these papers. A well worthwhile case and a good fine for an individual.' The files also give detailed access to field inspectors' working methods. For example, one file contained a speech to the magistrates written out by the inspector, who went so far as to write out 'Thank yous' and instructions to himself to 'Hand up photographs' in large capital letters.

While files may not always convey the ideas of the decision-makers concerned, they can give very clear indications of their practices (matters relating to plea-bargaining often emerge clearly from the files) and reveal how inspectors interpret events, acts, and characters. Yet at the same time such records take on an objective quality, in the sense that they, like other written records, may be discussed, argued over, transmitted to others, stored, retrieved, and employed for multiple purposes (and not necessarily the purposes for which they were originally compiled). There seems to be in these files a routine and ritual quality in some of the explanations or justifications for recommendations proposed or decisions made. A frequent feature is that decisions or recommendations are often announced with no rationales, or only very brief ones, when they are recorded in formal documents (letters, reports, and the like). A particular form of words is often employed, perhaps because it is usual for it to be used in such cases, or perhaps because it represents an organizationally acceptable form of justification, or perhaps because it may artfully be expected to produce the desired response from a senior colleague. In official documents like the Statements of Witnesses the rationale for prosecution, if it is articulated at all, tends to be bland and uninformative along the lines of: 'I concluded as a result of my investigations that serious breaches of health and safety law had occurred, and that in this case prosecution of [the company] was appropriate.' Informal notes and intra-office communications, however, yielded more. It is often in the internal memos, notes, and similar documents that the researcher gains the sharpest insights into the underlying rationales for or against prosecution.

7. ARE 'OLD' DATA A PROBLEM?

Some academics are exercised by analysis based on data that seem not to be fresh. The age of the data on which part of the analysis in this book has been based (those data from the mid-to late 1980s) has not proved to be a problem in this study, for a number of reasons. First, after close study of prosecution and fatalities files from 1996, nothing emerged in the patterns of reasoning to suggest that there was any fundamental (or even superficial) change in the approach of inspectors in their decision-making. Second, the analysis is concerned with generic processes. Experience shows that in institutional practices the routine activities of legal officials are largely unaffected in any material way by attempts to constrain or guide their discretion. While inspectors and their supervisors continue to have the same mandate and tasks, and continue to enjoy wide discretion coupled with low visibility in which to exercise it, I would expect to see no change in the fundamental patterns of decision-making behaviour. While the institutional setting in which field agents and their superiors make decisions has changed to the extent described in Chapters 4 and 5, the organization's mandate, the fundamental issues involved, and the structural features analysed have not changed. Thus there is again no reason to assume prima facie that 'old' data from the mid-to late 1980s have lost their validity as raw material. Finally, the data analysed arise from close contact with the research subjects. There was excellent cooperation and access in both phases of the research project, and the project was one willingly undertaken (and, indeed, partially funded by) the subject regulatory agency. I did not encounter regulatory behaviour that could reasonably be regarded as unrepresentative, misleading, or an attempt to dissemble.

8. POSTSCRIPT

The last words belong to Antoine de Saint-Exupéry, who captured well the essence of the naturalist approach to decision-making adopted in this study:

Les grandes personnes aiment les chiffres. Quand vous leur parlez d'un nouvel ami, elles ne vous questionnent jamais sur l'essentiel. Elles ne vous disent jamais: «Quel est le son de sa voix? Quels sont les jeux qu'il préfère? Est-ce qu'il collectionne les papillons?» Elles vous demandent: «Quel âge a-t-il? Combien a-t-il de frères? Combien pèse-t-il? Combien gagne son père?» Alors seulement elles croient le connaître.[11]

[11] 'Grown-ups love numbers. When they talk to you about a new friend, they never ask you essential questions. They never say, "What does his voice sound like? What games does he like? Does he collect butterflies?" They ask you "How old is he? How many brothers does he have? What does he weigh? How much does his father make?" Only then do they think they know him': *Le Petit Prince.*

References

Alschuler, A. (1968), 'The prosecutor's role in plea-bargaining', *University of Chicago Law Review*, 36: 50–112.

——(1975), 'The defense attorney's role in plea-bargaining', *Yale Law Journal*, 84/6: 1179–1314.

Arksey, H., & Wright, P. (1999), *Interviewing for social scientists* (London: Sage).

Ashworth, A. (1987), 'The "public interest" element in prosecutions', *Criminal Law Review*, 595–607.

——Genders, E., Mansfield, G., Peay, J., & Player, E. (1984), *Sentencing in the Crown Court*, Occasional Paper no. 10 (Oxford: Centre for Criminological Research).

Asquith, S. (1982), *Children and justice: decision-making in children's hearings and juvenile courts* (Edinburgh: Edinburgh University Press).

Aubert, V. (1984), *In search of law* (Oxford: Blackwell).

Ayres, I., & Braithwaite, J. (1992), *Responsive regulation—transcending the deregulation debate* (New York: Oxford University Press).

Baldwin, J., & McConville, M. (1977), *Negotiated justice* (Oxford: Martin Robertson).

——Wikeley, N., & Young, R. (1992), *Judging social security* (Oxford: Clarendon Press).

Baldwin, R. (1987), 'Rules at work', Paper presented to HSE, Centre for Socio-Legal Studies, Oxford University.

——(1995), *Rules and government* (Oxford: Clarendon Press).

——(1997), 'Regulation after "Command and control"', in K. Hawkins (ed.), *The human face of law: essays in honour of Donald Harris* (Oxford: Clarendon Press).

Bardach, E., & Kagan, R. A. (1982), *Going by the book: the problem of regulatory unreasonableness* (Philadelphia: Temple University Press).

Barrett, S., & Fudge, C. (eds.) (1981), *Policy and action: essays on the implementation of public policy* (London: Methuen).

Bartrip, P. W. J. (1987), 'The regulation of lead poisoning in the white lead and pottery industries in the nineteenth and early twentieth centuries', Paper presented to HSE, Centre for Socio-Legal Studies, Oxford University.

——& Burman, S. (1983), *The wounded soldiers of industry: industrial compensation policy 1833–1897* (Oxford: Clarendon Press).

Bartrip, P. W. J., & Fenn, P. (1980*a*), 'The conventionalization of factory crime—a re-assessment', *International Journal of the Sociology of Law*, 8: 175–86.

——— (1980*b*), 'The administration of safety: the enforcement policy of the early Factory Inspectorate 1844–1864', *Public Administration*, 58 (Spring), 87–102.

Baumgartner, M. P. (1992), 'The myth of discretion', in K. Hawkins (ed.), *The uses of discretion* (Oxford: Clarendon Press).

Benson, M. L. & Cullen, F. T. (1998), *Combating corporate crime: local prosecutors at work* (Boston: Northeastern University Press).

Bernstein, M. (1955), *Regulating business by independent commission* (Princeton: Princeton University Press).

Black, D. (1980), *The manners and customs of the police* (New York: Academic Press).

Black, J. (1997), 'New institutionalism and naturalism in socio-legal analysis: institutionalist approaches to regulatory decision-making', *Law and Policy*, 19/1: 51–93.

Braithwaite, J. (1985), *To punish or persuade: enforcement of coal mine safety* (Albany, NY: State University of New York Press).

—— (2002), *Restorative justice and responsive regulation* (Oxford: Oxford University Press).

—— & Makkai, T. (1991), 'Testing an expected utility model of corporate deterrence', *Law and Society Review*, 25/1: 7–39.

—— Walker, J., & Grabosky, P. (1987), 'An enforcement taxonomy of regulatory agencies', *Law and Policy*, 9/3: 323–51.

Breyer, S. (1982), *Regulation and its reform* (Cambridge, Mass.: Harvard University Press).

Calavita, K. (1983), 'The demise of the Occupational Safety and Health Administration: a case study in symbolic action', *Social Problems*, 30/4: 437–48.

Carson, W. G. (1970*a*), 'Some sociological aspects of strict liability and the enforcement of factory legislation', *Modern Law Review*, 33/4: 396–412.

—— (1970*b*), 'White-collar crime and the enforcement of factory legislation', *British Journal of Criminology*, 10/4: 383–98.

—— (1974), 'Symbolic and instrumental dimensions of early factory legislation', in R. G. Hood (ed.), *Crime, criminology and public policy: essays in honour of Sir Leon Radzinowicz* (London: Heinemann).

—— (1979), 'The conventionalization of early factory crime', *International Journal of the Sociology of Law*, 7: 41–60.

—— (1980), 'The institutionalization of ambiguity: early British Factory Acts', in G. Geis & E. Stotland (eds.), *White-collar crime: theory and research* (Beverly Hills, Calif.: Sage).

—— (1982), *The other price of Britain's oil* (Oxford: Martin Robertson).

Centre for Socio-Legal Studies (1983), *An agenda for socio-legal research into the regulation of occupational health and safety* (Oxford: Centre for Socio-Legal Studies).

Cicourel, A. (1968), *The social organization of juvenile justice* (New York: Wiley).

Clement, B. (2001), 'Alarm at huge rise in deaths at work', *The Independent*, 31 July.

Cranston, R. (1979), *Regulating business: law and consumer agencies* (London: Macmillan).

Croall, H. (1988), 'Mistakes, accidents, and someone's else's fault: the trading offender in court', *Journal of Law and Society*, 15/3: 293–315.

Daly, K. (1994), *Gender, crime, and punishment* (New Haven: Yale University Press).

Darbyshire, P. (2000), 'The mischief of plea-bargaining and sentencing rewards', *Criminal Law Review*, 895–910.

Davis, K. C. (1969), *Discretionary justice: a preliminary inquiry* (Baton Rouge: Louisiana State University Press).

Dawson, S., Willman, P., Clinton, A., & Bamford, M. (1988), *Safety at work: the limits of self-regulation* (Cambridge: Cambridge University Press).

DiMento, J. F. (1986), *Environmental law and American business: dilemmas of compliance* (New York: Plenum Press).

Dingwall, R., Eekelaar, J., & Murray, T. (1983), *The protection of children: state intervention and family life* (Oxford: Blackwell).

Diver, C. (1983), 'The optimal precision of administrative rules', *Yale Law Journal*, 93/1: 65–109.

Duff, P. (1997), 'Diversion from prosecution into psychiatric care', *British Journal of Criminology*, 37/1: 15–34.

Edelman, L. B., Petterson, S., Chambliss, E., & Erlanger, H. S. (1991), 'Legal ambiguity and the politics of compliance: affirmative action officers' dilemma', *Law and Policy*, 13/1: 73–97.

Edelman, M. (1964), *The symbolic uses of politics* (Urbana: University of Illinois Press).

Emerson, R. M. (1969), *Judging delinquents: context and process in the juvenile court* (Chicago: Aldine).

——(1981), 'On last resorts', *American Journal of Sociology*, 87/1: 1–22.

——(1983), 'Holistic effects in social control decision-making', *Law and Society Review*, 17/3: 425–55.

——(1991), 'Case processing and interorganizational knowledge: detecting the "real reasons" for referrals', *Social Problems*, 38/2: 1101–15.

——& Paley, B. (1992), 'Organizational horizons and complaint-filing', in K. Hawkins (ed.), *The uses of discretion* (Oxford: Clarendon Press).

Erez, E., & Rogers, L. (1999), 'Victim impact statements and sentencing outcomes and processes', *British Journal of Criminology*, 39/2: 216–39.

Ericson, R. V., & Baranek, P. M. (1982), *The ordering of justice* (Toronto: University of Toronto Press).

Eves, D. (1998), 'Prosecution—the ultimate sanction?', Paper presented to the Conference on Prosecution by Regulatory Authorities, Oriel College, Oxford.

Feldman, M. (1992), 'Social limits to discretion: an organizational perspective', in K. Hawkins (ed.), *The uses of discretion* (Oxford: Clarendon Press).

Freedman, D. (1989), 'Health and safety at work: perceptions of trade union officials' (Oxford: Trade Union Research Unit).

Friendly, H. J. (1962), *The Federal administrative agencies* (Cambridge, Mass.: Harvard University Press).

Frohmann, L. (1991), 'Discrediting victims' allegations of sexual assault: prosecutorial accounts of case rejections', *Social Problems*, 38/2: 213–26.

——(1996), 'Prosecutorial accounts for filing unconvictable sexual assault complaints', *Current Research on Occupations and Professions*, 9: 189–209.

——(1997), 'Convictability and discordant locales: reproducing race, class, and gender ideologies in prosecutorial decisionmaking', *Law and Society Review*, 31/3: 531–55.

Galanter, M. (1974), 'Why the "Haves" come out ahead: speculations on the limits of legal change', *Law and Society Review*, 9/1: 95–160.

——(1986), 'Adjudication, litigation, and related phenomena', in L. Lipson & S. Wheeler (eds.), *Law and the social sciences* (New York: Russell Sage Foundation).

Garfinkel, H., & Bittner, E. (1967), ' "Good" organizational reasons for "bad" clinic records', *Studies in ethnomethodology* (Englewood Cliffs, NJ: Prentice-Hall).

Geis, G., & DiMento, J. F. (1995), 'Should we prosecute corporations and/or individuals?' in F. Pearce & L. Snider (eds.), *Corporate crime: contemporary debates* (Toronto: University of Toronto Press).

Genn, H. (1987), 'Great expectations: the Robens' legacy and employer self-regulation', Paper presented to HSE, Centre for Socio-Legal Studies, Oxford University.

——(1993), 'Business responses to the regulation of health and safety in England', *Law and Policy*, 15/3: 219–34.

Gilboy, J. A. (1991), 'Deciding who gets in: decisionmaking by immigration inspectors', *Law and Society Review*, 25/3: 571–99.

Ginniff, M. (1988), 'The case for deep storage', *The Observer*, 15 May.

Goffman, E. (1974), *Frame analysis: an essay on the organization of experience* (Harmondsworth: Penguin Books).

Grabosky, P. (1989), *Wayward governance: illegality and its control in the public sector* (Canberra: Australian Institute of Criminology).

——& Braithwaite, J. (1986), *Of manners gentle: enforcement strategies of Australian business regulatory agencies* (Melbourne: Oxford University Press).

Grady, A. (2002), 'Female on male domestic abuse: uncommon or ignored?' in C. Hoyle & R. Young (eds.), *New visions of crime victims* (Oxford: Hart).

Gray, W. B., & Scholz, J. T. (1991), 'Analyzing the equity and efficiency of OSHA enforcement', *Law and Policy*, 13/3: 185–214.

————(1993), 'Does regulatory enforcement work? A panel analysis of OSHA enforcement', *Law and Society Review*, 27/1: 177–213.

Gunningham, N., & Grabosky, P. (1998), *Smart regulation: designing environmental policy* (Oxford: Clarendon Press).

——& Johnstone, R. (1999), *Regulating workplace safety: systems and sanctions* (Oxford: Clarendon Press).

——& Rees, J. (1997), 'Industry self-regulation: an institutional perspective', *Law and Policy*, 19/4: 363–414.

Gusfield, J. R. (1963), *Symbolic crusade: status politics and the American temperance movement* (Urbana: University of Illinois Press).

——(1970), 'Moral passage: the symbolic process in public designations of deviance', in C. Bersani (ed.), *Crime and delinquency* (London: Macmillan).

——(1981), *The culture of public problems: drinking-driving and the symbolic order* (Chicago: University of Chicago Press).

Haines, F. (1997), *Corporate regulation: beyond 'punish or persuade'* (Oxford: Clarendon Press).

Ham, C., & Hill, M. (1993), *The policy process in the modern capitalist state* (London: Harvester Wheatsheaf).

Harris, D. R., Maclean, M., Genn, H., Lloyd-Bostock, S., Fenn, P., Corfield, P., & Brittan, Y. (1984), *Compensation and support for illness and injury* (Oxford: Clarendon Press).

Hawkins, K. (1971), 'Parole selection: the American experience', Ph.D. diss., Cambridge University.

——(1983*a*), 'Assessing evil: decision behaviour and parole board justice', *British Journal of Criminology*, 23/2: 101–27.

——(1983*b*), 'Bargain and bluff: compliance strategy and deterrence in the enforcement of regulation', *Law and Policy Quarterly*, 5/1: 35–73.

——(1984), *Environment and enforcement: regulation and the social definition of pollution* (Oxford: Clarendon Press).

——(1986), 'On legal decision-making', *Washington and Lee Law Review*, 43/4: 1161–1242.

——(1987), 'Prosecution process', Report presented to HSE, Centre for Socio-Legal Studies, Oxford University.

——(1989*a*), '"FATCATS" and prosecution in a regulatory agency: a footnote on the social construction of risk', *Law and Policy*, 11/3: 370–91.

——(1989*b*), 'Rule and discretion in comparative perspective: the case of social regulation', *Ohio State Law Journal*, 50/3: 263–80.

——(1990), 'Compliance strategy, prosecution policy, and Aunt Sally: a comment on Pearce and Tombs', *British Journal of Criminology*, 30/4: 444–66.

——(1991), 'Enforcing regulation: more of the same from Pearce and Tombs', *British Journal of Criminology*, 31/4: 427–30.

——(1992*a*), *The regulation of occupational health and safety: a socio-legal perspective* (London: Health and Safety Executive).

——(ed.) (1992*b*), *The uses of discretion* (Oxford: Clarendon Press).

——(1997), 'Law and discretion: exploring collective aspects of administrative decision-making', *Education and Law Journal*, 8: 139–60.

Hawkins, K., & Thomas, J. M. (eds.) (1984), *Enforcing regulation* (Boston: Kluwer-Nijhoff).

—— & Manning, P. K. (forthcoming), *Legal decision-making.*

Health and Safety Commission (HSC) (1978), *Report 1977–78* (London: HMSO).

—— (1979), *The Act outlined* (London: HMSO).

—— (1983), *Plan of work 1983–84 and onwards* (London: HMSO).

—— (1985), *Plan of work 1985–86 and onwards* (London: HMSO).

—— (1988), *Annual report 1987/88* (London: HMSO).

—— (1990*a*), *Annual report 1988/89* (London: HMSO).

—— (1990*b*), *Annual report 1989/90* (London: HMSO).

—— (1993), *Annual report 1992/93* (Sudbury: HSE Books).

—— (1994), *Annual report 1993/94* (Norwich: HSE Books).

—— (1997), *Annual report and accounts 1996/97* (Norwich: HSE Books).

—— (1998*a*), *Annual report and accounts 1997/98* (Norwich: HSE Books).

—— (1998*b*), *Health and safety statistics 1998/99* (Sudbury: HSE Books).

—— (1998*c*), *What to expect when a health and safety inspector calls* (Sudbury: HSE Books).

—— (1999), *Annual report and the Health and Safety Commission/Executive accounts 1998/99* (London: HMSO).

—— (2002), *Highlights from the HSC annual report and the HSC/E accounts 2000/01* (Sudbury: HSE Books).

—— (n.d.), *Enforcement policy statement* (London: Health and Safety Commission).

—— /Executive (1987), *Annual report 1986/87* (London: HMSO).

Health and Safety Executive (HSE) (1977), *Industry and services 1975* (London: HMSO).

—— (1978*a*), *Manufacturing and service industries 1977* (London: HMSO).

—— (1978*b*), *One hundred fatal accidents in construction* (London: HMSO).

—— (1979), *Construction: health and safety 1977–78* (London: HMSO).

—— (1980), *Manufacturing and service industries 1978* (London: HMSO).

—— (1981), *Fatal accidents in construction, 1978* (London: HMSO).

—— (1982*a*), *HM Factory Inspectorate* (London: HMSO).

—— (1982*b*), *Industrial air pollution: health and safety 1981* (London: HMSO).

—— (1982*c*), *Manufacturing and service industries 1980* (London: HMSO).

—— (1983), *Construction: health and safety 1981–82* (London: HMSO).

—— (1984), *Manufacturing and service industries 1983 report* (London: HMSO).

—— (1985*a*), *Manufacturing and service industries 1984 report* (London: HMSO).

—— (1985*b*), *Measuring the effectiveness of HSE's field activities* (London: HMSO).

—— (1986), *Report by HM Chief Inspector of Factories 1985* (London: HMSO).

—— (1987*a*), 'Zerobase for HSE functions. I: Introduction', unpublished report (London: HSE).

—— (1987*b*), 'Zerobase for HSE functions. II: Functions', unpublished report (London: HSE).

Heumann, M. (1978), *Plea bargaining: the experiences of prosecutors, judges, and defense attorneys* (Chicago: University of Chicago Press).

Hopkins, A., & Parnell, N. (1984), 'Why coal mine safety regulations in Australia are not enforced', *International Journal of the Sociology of Law*, 12: 179–94.

Hosticka, C. J. (1979), ' "We don't care what happened. We only care about what is going to happen": lawyer–client negotiations of reality', *Social Problems*, 26/5: 599–610.

Hoyano, A., Hoyano, L., Davis, G., & Goldie, S. (1997), 'A study of the impact of the Revised Code for Crown Prosecutors', *Criminal Law Review*, 556–64.

Hoyle, C., & Young, R. (eds.) (2002), *New visions of crime victims* (Oxford: Hart).

Huntington, S. P. (1952), 'The marasmus of the ICC: the Commission, the railroads, and the public interest', *Yale Law Journal*, 61/4: 467–509.

Hutter, B. M. (1988), *The reasonable arm of the law? The law enforcement procedures of environmental health officers* (Oxford: Clarendon Press).

——(1989), 'Variations in regulatory enforcement styles', *Law and Policy*, 11/2: 153–74.

——(1997), *Compliance: regulation and environment* (Oxford: Clarendon Press).

——(2001), *Regulation and risk: occupational health and safety on the railways* (Oxford: Oxford University Press).

——& Lloyd-Bostock, S. (1990), 'The power of accidents: the social and psychological impact of accidents and the enforcement of safety regulations', *Briitish Journal of Criminology*, 30/4: 409–22.

——& Manning, P. K. (1990), 'The contexts of regulation: the impact upon health and safety inspectorates in Britain', *Law and Policy*, 12/2: 103–36.

James, P. (1992), 'Reforming British health and safety law: a framework for discussion', *Industrial Law Journal*, 21/2: 83–105.

Jamieson, M. (1985), 'Persuasion or punishment: the enforcement of health and safety at work legislation by the Factory Inspectorate in Britain', M.Litt. diss., Oxford University.

Jesilow, P., Pontell, H. N., & Geis, G. (1993), *Prescription for profit: how doctors defraud Medicaid* (Berkeley: University of California Press).

Johnstone, R. (1994), 'The court and the factory: the legal construction of occupational health and safety offences in Victoria', Ph.D. diss., University of Melbourne.

Kagan, R. A. (1978), *Regulatory justice: implementing a wage–price freeze* (New York: Russell Sage Foundation).

——(1984), 'On regulatory inspectorates and police', in K. Hawkins & J. M. Thomas (eds.), *Enforcing regulation* (Boston: Kluwer-Nijhoff).

——(1989), 'Editor's introduction: understanding regulatory enforcement', *Law and Policy*, 11(2): 89–119.

——(1993), 'Criminal prosecution for regulatory offenses: trends and questions based on published data from EPA, FDA, and OSHA', Paper presented to the Workshop on Regulatory Law Enforcement, Ohio State University.

——(1994), 'Regulatory enforcement', in D. H. Rosenbloom & R. D. Schwartz (eds.), *Handbook of regulation and administrative law* (New York: Marcel Dekker).

Kagan, R. A., & Lochner, T. (1998), 'Criminal prosecution for regulatory offenses in the United States: trends and patterns in the Federal system', Paper presented to the Conference on Prosecution by Regulatory Authorities, Oriel College, Oxford.

—— & Scholz, J. T. (1984), 'The "criminology of the corporation" and regulatory enforcement strategies', in K. Hawkins & J. M. Thomas (eds.), *Enforcing regulation* (Boston: Kluwer-Nijhoff).

Kaufman, H. (1960), *The forest ranger* (Baltimore: Johns Hopkins University Press).

Kelman, S. (1981), *Regulating America, regulating Sweden: a comparative study of occupational safety and health policy* (Cambridge, Mass.: MIT Press).

King, R. D., & Wincup, E. (eds.) (2000), *Doing research on crime and justice* (Oxford: Oxford University Press).

Kolko, G. (1963), *The triumph of conservatism: a re-interpretation of American history, 1900–1916* (New York: Free Press).

——(1965), *Railroads and regulations, 1877–1916* (Princeton: Princeton University Press).

Law and Society Review (1979), Special Issue, *Plea Bargaining, Law and Society Review*, 13/2.

Law Commission (1969), *Strict liability and the enforcement of the Factories Act 1961*, London, Working Paper no. 30.

Lempert, R. (1992), 'Discretion in a behavioral perspective: the case of a public housing eviction board', in K. Hawkins (ed.), *The uses of discretion* (Oxford: Clarendon Press).

Lipsky, M. (1980), *Street-level bureaucracy: dilemmas of the individual in public services* (New York: Russell Sage Foundation).

Lloyd-Bostock, S. (1987), 'A psychological study of responses to accidents', Paper presented to HSE, Centre for Socio-Legal Studies, Oxford University.

——(1992), 'The psychology of routine discretion: accident screening by British factory inspectors', *Law and Policy*, 14/1: 45–76.

Lovegrove, A. (1984), 'The listing of criminal cases in the Crown Court as an administrative discretion', *Criminal Law Review*, 738–49.

Lynxwiler, J., Shover, N., & Clelland, D. (1983), 'The organization and impact of inspector discretion in a regulatory bureaucracy', *Social Problems*, 30/4: 425–36.

McBarnet, D. (1981), *Conviction: law, the state and the construction of justice* (London: Macmillan).

McConville, M., Sanders, A., & Leng, R. (1991), *The case for the prosecution* (London: Routledge).

McCoy, C. (1993), *Politics and plea-bargaining* (Philadelphia: University of Pennsylvania Press).

Makkai, T., & Braithwaite, J. (1995), 'In and out of the revolving door: making sense of regulatory capture', *Journal of Public Policy*, 15: 61–78.

Manning, P. K. (1977), *Police work: the social organization of policing* (Cambridge, Mass.: MIT Press).

——(1980), *The narcs' game: organizational and informational limits on drug law enforcement* (Cambridge, Mass.: MIT Press).

——(1986), 'The social reality and social organization of natural decision-making', *Washington and Lee Law Review*, 43/4: 1291–1311.

——(1987*a*), 'Ironies of compliance', in C. Shearing & P. Stenning (eds.), *Private policing* (Newbury Park, Calif.: Sage).

——(1987*b*), 'The policy process in the NII', Paper presented to HSE, Centre for Socio-Legal Studies, Oxford University.

——(1992), '"Big bang" decisions: notes on a naturalistic approach', in K. Hawkins (ed.), *The uses of discretion* (Oxford: Clarendon Press).

——& Hawkins, K. (1989), 'Police decision-making', in M. Weatheritt (ed.), *Police research: some future prospects* (Aldershot: Avebury).

————(1990), 'Legal decisions: a frame analytic perspective', in S. Riggins (ed.), *Beyond Goffman* (Berlin: Aldine DeGruyter).

Mather, L. (1979), *Plea bargaining or trial? The process of criminal case disposition* (Lexington, Mass.: D C Heath).

Mayhew, L., & Reiss, A. J. (1969), 'The social organization of legal contacts', *American Sociological Review*, 34/3: 309–18.

Maynard, D. (1984), *Inside plea-bargaining: the language of negotiation* (New York: Plenum).

Meacher, M. (1988), 'The shameful rise and rise of preventable deaths at work', *The Independent*, 12 Oct.

Merry, S. E. (1990), *Getting justice and getting even: legal consciousness among working class Americans* (Chicago: University of Chicago Press).

Mitnick, B. (1980), *The political economy of regulation* (New York: Columbia University Press).

Moody, S. R., & Tombs, J. (1982), *Prosecution in the public interest* (Edinburgh: Scottish Academic Press).

Nelken, D. (1983), *The limits of the legal process: a study of landlords, law and crime* (London: Academic Press).

Noble, C. (1986), *Liberalism at work: the rise and fall of OSHA* (Philadelphia: Temple University Press).

Nobles, R., & Schiff, D. (2000), *Understanding miscarriages of justice* (Oxford: Oxford University Press).

Ogus, A. (1994), *Regulation: legal form and economic theory* (Oxford: Clarendon Press).

Packer, H. (1969), *The limits of the criminal sanction* (Stanford, Calif.: Stanford University Press).

Pearce, F., & Tombs, S. (1990), 'Ideology, hegemony and empiricism: compliance theories of regulation', *British Journal of Criminology*, 30/4: 423–43.

Pearce, F., & Tombs, S. (1991), 'Policing corporate "skid rows": a reply to Keith Hawkins', *British Journal of Criminology*, 31/4: 415–26.

Perrow, C. (1984), *Normal accidents* (New York: Basic Books).

Piliavin, I., & Briar, S. (1964), 'Police encounters with juveniles', *American Journal of Sociology*, 70/2: 206–14.

Posner, R. (1974), 'Theories of economic regulation', *Bell Journal of Economics*, 5: 335–58.

Powell, W. W. (1985), *Getting into print* (Chicago: University of Chicago Press).

Prottas, J. (1979), *People-processing: the street-level bureaucrat in public service bureaucracies* (Lexington, Mass.: Lexington Books).

Rees, J. (1988), *Reforming the workplace: a study of self-regulation in occupational safety* (Philadelphia: University of Pennsylvania Press).

——(1997), 'Development of communitarian regulation in the chemical industry', *Law and Policy*, 19/4: 477–528.

Reimer, J. W. (1976), '"Mistakes at work." The social organization of error in building construction work', *Social Problems*, 23/3: 255–67.

Reiss, A. J. (1983), 'The policing of organizational life', in M. Punch (ed.), *Control in the police organization* (Cambridge, Mass.: MIT Press).

——(1984), 'Selecting strategies of control over organizational life', in K. Hawkins & J. M. Thomas (eds.), *Enforcing regulation* (Boston: Kluwer-Nijhoff).

——(1985), 'Compliance without coercion', *Michigan Law Review*, 83/4: 813–19.

——(1989), 'The institutionalization of risk', *Law and Policy*, 11/3: 392–402.

Richardson, G., Ogus, A., & Burrows, P. (1982), *Policing pollution: a study of regulation and enforcement* (Oxford: Clarendon Press).

Robens, Lord (1972), *Report of the Committee on Safety at Work 1970–1972*, Cmnd. 5034 (London: HMSO).

Rock, P. (1973), *Making people pay* (London: Routledge & Kegan Paul).

——(1986), *A view from the shadows: the Ministry of the Solicitor General of Canada and the making of the Justice for Victims of Crime Initiative* (Oxford: Clarendon Press).

——(1995), 'Sociology and the stereotype of the police', *Journal of Law and Society*, 22/1: 17–25.

Rosett, A., & Cressey, D. R. (1976), *Justice by consent: plea bargains in the American courthouse* (Philadelphia: J. B. Lippincott).

Ross, H. L. (1970), *Settled out of court: the social process of insurance claims adjustment* (Chicago: Aldine).

Rothery, D. (1998), 'Prosecution policy making: a field inspector's perspective', Paper presented to the Conference on Prosecution by Regulatory Authorities, Oriel College, Oxford.

Rubinstein, J. (1973), *City police* (New York: Ballantine Books).

Sanders, A. (1987), 'Constructing the case for the prosecution', *Journal of Law and Society*, 14: 229–43.

——& Young, R. (2000), *Criminal justice*, 2nd edn. (London: Butterworths).

Scholz, J. T. (1984), 'Cooperation, deterrence, and the ecology of regulatory enforcement', *Law and Society Review*, 18/2: 179–224.

Schrager, L. S. & Short, J. F. (1978), 'Toward a sociology of organizational crime', *Social Problems*, 25/4: 407–19.

Schuck, P. (1972), 'The curious case of the indicted meat inspectors', *Harper's* (Sept.), 81–2.

Schulhofer, S. J. (1984), 'Is plea-bargaining inevitable?' *Harvard Law Review*, 97/5: 1037–1107.

Selznick, P. (1992), *The moral commonwealth: social theory and the promise of community* (Berkeley: University of California Press).

Shapiro, M. M. (1981), *Courts: a comparative and political analysis* (Chicago: University of Chicago Press).

Shapiro, S. (1985), 'The road not taken: the elusive path to criminal prosecution for white-collar offenders', *Law and Society Review*, 19/2: 179–217.

Short, J. F., & Clarke, L. (eds.) (1992), *Organizations, uncertainty and risk* (Boulder, Colo.: Westview Press).

Shover, N., Lynxwiler, J., Groce, S., & Clelland, D. (1984), 'Regional variation in regulatory law enforcement: the Surface Mining Control and Reclamation Act of 1977', in K. Hawkins & J. M. Thomas (eds.), *Enforcing regulation* (Boston: Kluwer-Nijhoff).

—— Clelland, D. A., & Lynxwiler, J. (1986), *Enforcement or negotiation: constructing a regulatory bureaucracy* (Albany: State University of New York Press).

Simon, H. A. (1957), *Administrative behavior* (New York: Free Press).

Simpson, R. C. (1973), 'Safety and health at work: report of the Robens Committee 1970–72', *Modern Law Review*, 36/2: 192–8.

Simpson, S. S. (1990), 'Corporate crime deterrence and corporate control policies: views from the inside', Paper presented to the Edwin Sutherland Conference on White-Collar Crime, Indiana University, Bloomington.

Sinclair, D. (1997), 'Self-regulation versus command and control? Beyond false dichotomies', *Law and Policy*, 19/4: 529–59.

Skolnick, J. (1966), *Justice without trial: law enforcement in democratic society* (New York: Wiley).

Slapper, G., & Tombs, S. (2000), *Corporate crime* (Harlow: Longman).

Smith, D. J., & Gray, J. (1983), *Police and people in London: the police in action* (London: Policy Studies Institute).

Snashall, D. (1990), 'Safety and health in the construction industry', *British Medical Journal*, 301: 563–4.

Snider, L. (1987), 'Towards a political economy of reform, regulation and corporate crime', *Law and Policy*, 9/1: 37–68.

Stanko, E. A. (1981), 'The arrest versus the case: some observations on police/district attorney interaction', *Urban Life*, 9/4: 395–414.

Staw, B. M., & Szwajkowski, E. (1975), 'The scarcity–munificence component of organizational environments and the commission of illegal acts', *Administrative Science Quarterly*, 20/3: 345–54.

Stenning, P. C., Shearing, C. D., Addario, S. M., & Condon, M. G. (1990), 'Controlling interests: two conceptions of order in regulating a financial market', in M. L. Friedland (ed.), *Securing compliance: seven case studies* (Toronto: University of Toronto Press).

Stewart, R. B. (1988), 'Regulation and the crisis of legalism in the United States', in T. Daintith (ed.), *Law as an instrument of economic policy* (Berlin: Walter de Gruyter).

Stigler, G. (1971), 'The theory of economic regulation', *Bell Journal of Economics*, 2: 3–21.

Streets, S. (1998), 'Prosecuting directors and managers in Australia: a brave new response to an old problem?' *Melbourne University Law Review*, 22/5: 693–718.

Suchman, M. C., & Edelman, L. B. (1997), 'Legal rational myths: the new institutionalism and the law and society tradition', *Law and Social Inquiry*, 25/4: 903–41.

Sudnow, D. (1965), 'Normal crimes: sociological features of the penal code in a public defender office', *Social Problems*, 12/3: 255–76.

Szasz, A. (1984), 'Industrial resistance to occupational safety and health legislation: 1971–1981', *Social Problems*, 32/2: 103–16.

Utz, P. J. (1978), *Settling the facts: discretion and negotiation in criminal court* (Lexington, Mass.: Lexington Books).

Vaughan, D. (1983), *Controlling unlawful organizational behavior: social structure and corporate misconduct* (Chicago: University of Chicago Press).

——(1996), *The Challenger launch decision* (Chicago: University of Chicago Press).

——(1998), 'Rational choice, situated action, and the social control of organizations', *Law and Society Review*, 32(1): 23–61.

Viscusi, W. K. (1979), *Employment hazards: an investigation of market performance* (Cambridge, Mass.: Harvard University Press).

——(1986), 'The impact of occupational health and safety regulation 1973–1983', *Bell Journal of Economics*, 17: 117–40.

Veljanovski, C. (1980), 'Regulating industrial accidents—an economic analysis of market and legal responses' Ph. D. dissertation, University of York.

——(1987), 'The impact, enforcement and economic assessment of industrial safety regulation', Paper presented to HSE, Centre for Socio-Legal Studies, Oxford University.

Vogel, D. (1986), *National styles of regulation* (Ithaca, NY: Cornell University Press).

von Hirsch, A., Bottoms, A. E., Burney, E., & Wikstrom, P.-O. (1999), *Criminal deterrence and sentence severity* (Oxford: Hart).

Waegel, W. (1981), 'Case routinization in investigative police work', *Social Problems*, 28/3: 263–75.

Weait, M. (1989), 'The letter of the law? An enquiry into reasoning and formal enforcement in the Industrial Air Pollution Inspectorate', *British Journal of Criminology*, 29/1: 57–70.

Weaver, S. (1977), *Decision to prosecute: organization and public policy in the Antitrust Division* (Cambridge, Mass.: MIT Press).

Weick, K. (1979), *The social psychology of organizing* (Reading, Mass.: Addison-Wesley).

Wells, C. (2001), *Corporations and criminal responsibility* (Oxford: Oxford University Press).

Wheeler, S., Mann, K., & Sarat, A. (1988), *Sitting in judgement: the sentencing of white-collar criminals* (New Haven: Yale University Press).

Wikeley, N. (1993), *Compensation for industrial disease* (Aldershot: Dartmouth).

Wilson, G. K. (1985), *The politics of safety and health: occupational safety and health in the United States and Britain* (Oxford: Clarendon Press).

Wilson, J. Q. (1968), *Varieties of police behavior* (Cambridge, Mass.: Harvard University Press).

—— (ed.) (1980), *The politics of regulation* (New York: Basic Books).

—— (1989), *Bureaucracy* (New York: Basic Books).

Winter, G. (1985), 'Bartering rationality in regulation', *Law and Society Review*, 19/2: 219–50.

Woolf, A. D. (1973), 'Robens Report—the wrong approach?' *Industrial Law Journal*, 2: 88–95.

Wright, C. (1986), 'Routine deaths: fatal accidents in the oil industry', *Sociological Review*, 34/2: 265–89.

Wright, F. B. (1995), 'The enforcement policy and practice of the Health and Safety Executive 1974–1990', Ph.D. diss., University of Leicester.

Yeager, P. C. (1986), 'Analyzing corporate offenses: progress and prospects', *Research in Corporate Social Performance and Policy*, 8: 93–120.

—— (1991), *The limits of the law: the public regulation of private pollution* (Cambridge: Cambridge University Press).

Young, R. (1996), 'Will Widgery do? Court clerks, discretion, and the determinants of legal aid applications', in R. Young & D. Wall (eds.), *Access to criminal justice* (London: Blackstone Press).

Zimmerman, D. H. (1971), 'The practicalities of rule use', in J. D. Douglas (ed.), *Understanding everyday life* (London: Routledge & Kegan Paul).

Zimring, F., & Hawkins, G. (1973), *Deterrence: the legal threat in crime control* (Chicago: University of Chicago Press).

Author Index

Subject Index